NINTH EDITION

TEXTBOOK OF

SALES-

MANSHIP

FREDERIC A. RUSSELL, Ph.D., LL.D.
Emeritus Professor of Marketing
University of Illinois

FRANK H. BEACH
Deceased

RICHARD H. BUSKIRK, Ph.D.
The Herman W. Lay Chair
of Business & Management
Southern Methodist University

McGRAW-HILL BOOK COMPANY

New York   St. Louis   San Francisco   Düsseldorf   Johannesburg
Kuala Lumpur   London   Mexico   Montreal   New Delhi
Panama   Rio de Janeiro   Singapore   Sydney   Toronto

TEXTBOOK OF SALESMANSHIP

456789   KPKP   798765

Library of Congress Cataloging in Publication Data

Russell, Frederic Arthur, date
　　Textbook of salesmanship.

　　Includes bibliographical references.
　　1. Salesmen and salesmanship.　　I. Beach, Frank
Herman, 1895–1967, joint author.　　II. Buskirk,
Richard Hobart, 1927-　　joint author.　　III. Title.
HF5438.R954   1974　　　　　658.85　　　　　73-12216
ISBN 0-07-054334-8

This edition is dedicated to the memory of a great marketing pioneer, Dr. Frederic A. Russell, who passed away on July 22, 1973. It is with great sadness that I join the thousands of his former students at the University of Illinois and his innumerable friends and colleagues in mourning our loss, for he was a man of great merit and inspiration. We owe him much. The results of his pioneering efforts will be with us for a long while. In our personal conversations, I know that he was quite proud of the fact that the system he developed for teaching salesmanship in the early 1920s—the selling process used in this, his book—had stood the test of time so well. Perhaps it is the best of monuments to the memory of a man to have his work endure and be of use to other men. He will be missed.

CONTENTS

Preface   vii

PART ONE   **INTRODUCTION**

Chapter 1   Selling—Basic Social and Economic
             Behavior   3
Chapter 2   Careers in Selling   21

PART TWO   **PREPARATION FOR SELLING**

Chapter 3   You   53
Chapter 4   Product Knowledge   69
Chapter 5   Why People Buy   93

PART THREE   **THE SELLING PROCESS**

Chapter 6   Prospecting   133
Chapter 7   The Preapproach   164
Chapter 8   The Approach   186
Chapter 9   The Art of Persuasion   225
Chapter 10   The Presentation: I   246

Chapter 11   The Presentation: II   274
Chapter 12   The Presentation: III   299
Chapter 13   Handling Objections: I   322
Chapter 14   Handling Objections: II   350
Chapter 15   The Close   382
Chapter 16   Servicing Accounts   405
Chapter 17   Retail Salesmanship   415

PART FOUR   THE SALESMAN AS A PERSON

Chapter 18   Ethical Problems in Selling   447
Chapter 19   Attitudes, Philosophies,
             and Work Habits   467
Chapter 20   The Managerial Environment   498
Chapter 21   The Legal Aspects of Selling   527

Name Index   543

Subject Index   547

PREFACE

One of the keynote speakers from industry at the August, 1971, meeting of the American Marketing Association severely criticized marketing educators for not providing students with the skills most needed for their business careers—selling skills. Yes, the marketing theorists were being told to start teaching more selling. We hope this is the harbinger of things to come, for we certainly agree that selling is far more important to a businessman's career than is currently reflected in how we are training him.

In this edition we have continued switching the emphasis toward industrial selling and away from consumer-specialty selling. Moreover, we have added to the behavioral material previously included.

A new chapter on the Legal Aspects of Selling has been added because recent changes in business curricula have frequently eliminated such material from the core and such knowledge is important to the salesman.

As usual some old cases were eliminated and replaced with new ones which we think will prove to be superior.

The key aspect of the past eight editions—teachability—has been retained. The material is still presented in the same basic selling system that has been proven to be the most effective method for teaching people how to sell.

We wish to thank Sylvia Arnot for her usual excellent processing of the manuscript.

Frederic A. Russell
Richard H. Buskirk

INTRODUCTION

SELLING—BASIC SOCIAL AND ECONOMIC BEHAVIOR

Failure is man's inability to reach his goals in
life, whatever they may be.
Og Mandino

You are a salesman. You've been one since the day you were born. Remember when you wheedled that bicycle from your old man? Salesmanship. How about that time you talked the teacher into giving you a higher grade? Salesmanship. Or your first date—salesmanship! You sell something several times each day, like it or not. The question is whether you are a good salesman or a poor one, because your success in business, and life, will depend in large part upon your ability to sell yourself, your firm, your services, your ideas, and your products to others. The American Marketing Association defines selling as "The personal or impersonal process of assisting and/or persuading a prospective customer to buy a commodity or a service or to act favorably upon an idea that has commercial significance to the seller."[1] But the application of the principles of salesmanship has a much broader scope.

We prefer to define salesmanship as the art of persuading another person to do something you want him to do when you do not have, or do not care to exert, the direct power to force him to do it.

[1] *Definitions of Terms* (American Marketing Association, Chicago, 1961).

PERSUASION—UNIVERSAL BEHAVIOR

While the role of persuasion in everyday life will be discussed in the next chapter, we wish to stress here how it is needed throughout all economic endeavors.

Leadership requires persuasion

The ability to handle people is the basis of leadership in all fields of endeavor. Men and women in managerial positions in government, education, labor, the armed services, medicine, and business are constantly confronted with the necessity for getting along with others—"handling people."

And here's the point: This "ability to handle people" is little more than salesmanship under another name.

It is this universal application of the principles of selling which justifies its study by young people, even by those who never expect to be professional salesmen. But you probably aspire to leadership in some area—whether social, professional, political, or business—and this leadership will be attained by those individuals who master the art of handling people—selling ideas to them. A leader is a leader because he has followers and his main task is to persuade his followers, by one means or another, to strive to do what he wants done.

The uses for salesmanship

You may ask, "Why should I study salesmanship? I'm never going to be a salesman." Perhaps not, but who knows? Millions of people have been unexpectedly thrust into jobs demanding the ability to sell. Even though a person may not engage directly in any kind of selling work, the hard fact still exists that one can find virtually no occupation or profession that does not demand selling skills if he is to perform his job satisfactorily.

Many talented physicians, architects, engineers, scientists, musicians, and lawyers have not advanced professionally because they have failed to recognize the selling aspects of their work. A brilliant electronics engineer, a man who developed numerous valuable patents for his employer, not only was unable to advance into management but was eventually fired. After hours of venting his frustrations to a confidant, he concluded, "I've never been able to sell myself or my ideas to other people."

To learn what errors youngsters starting on their first jobs should be warned about, a group of vocational teachers wrote to several thousand employers asking them to look up the last three persons dismissed and tell why they had been let go. The teachers had expected a long catalogue of reasons. They were amazed that more than two-thirds of the persons losing jobs had been fired for one reason. It was the same in every sort of business, for workers of all ages and both sexes. "They couldn't get along with other people."

Frequently a young man who has no intention of becoming a salesman enters some other department of a business only to discover that he is expected to sell. "Every Employee a Salesman" is a slogan of a great number of businesses and it can work wonders. The modern marketing concept now embodied in the management philosophies of most leading corporations dictates that *all business is selling*.

The Irving Trust Company, one of New York's leading commercial banks, staged a drive for new accounts and in 10 weeks gained 11,763 new customers, this selling job being handled by bank employees from every department.

Many men begin their careers in some nonselling position only to discover sales to be their forte. Little did James M. Roche, former president of General Motors, dream in 1927, when he went to work for GM as a statistician, that he would rise through the sales department to become sales manager of Cadillac in 1957 and 10 years later be placed in charge of all aspects of GM car marketing.

Recently two young engineers employed by Beech Aircraft approached one of the authors with a problem for which they found themselves unprepared: "How can we persuade our top management to expand our efforts in manufacturing cryogenic hardware?" They continued, "We are convinced that the market for cryogenic hardware will grow rapidly in the next decade. If we don't expand our facilities now in advance of the market's needs, we will be left behind by our competitors. Presently, oceanography is the prime market we would like to develop. But how can we convince our top management to make the necessary financial commitments to go after this market?" A problem of salesmanship!

It is only through the sale of a commodity or service to the ultimate consumer that any job is created or maintained for anyone within the entire organization. Unless sales are the goal of everyone in an organization it will finally fail in a struggle with a competitor whose people have a sales point of view.

A young electrical engineer working full time for a small electronics company while studying for his master's degree was dismayed when given the full responsibility, the product managership, for a small line of analytical instruments that the company made for analytical-chemistry teachers. On returning from a short trip during which he visited several colleges in the hope of selling some sets, he confessed, "I couldn't sell a one! I just didn't know what to say or do. It was awful! I thought they would just order the sets, but all they did was ask questions." This man was quickly taken aside by his boss, who suggested that even engineers often had to know how to sell something.

This same firm had to dismiss a purchasing agent who was an inept salesman. That's right, even purchasing agents must sell! Prompt deliveries of critical items are crucial to a project's profitability. This man had so alienated suppliers that he was unable to persuade them to do him any favors when the need arose.

Top management and selling

It would be difficult, if not impossible, to locate a chief executive who has not spent some significant amount of time in the sales field and who does not even now spend a good portion of his time selling something. Arthur E. Larkin, Jr., who rose to the presidency of General Foods through "an unswerving devotion to sales," says, "I would like my epitaph to say that I was a good peddler."[2]

Vincent C. Ziegler, of the Gillette Safety Razor Co., still spends 25 percent of his time on the road and further insists that every department head, every year, "spend some time in the field with our sales people." And for major promotions in *all* departments, actual sales experience is required.[3]

He claimed that during his entire business career he has been trying to persuade someone to buy something.[4]

Every employee should be vitally interested in boosting the sales of the firm employing him. Moreover, when he catches the spirit of the real salesman he will find that his life is pleasanter, more fun.

Indeed, in this age of large-scale manufacturers selling to equally large mass distributors, the importance of *top-level selling* has greatly increased. *Sales Management* reports: "There are a variety of reasons why the top man is spending more of his time on the road. ... Consolidation of accounts into more and bigger chains or group buying offices makes the individual transaction far more substantial and meaningful than ever before. The sale is bigger and means more to the company. . . . The buying influences cannot be reached by anything less than a top-level 'salesman'. . . . Industrial buyers have been showing an increasing tendency to 'marry' suppliers of regularly purchased commodities. The size and long-term nature of such arrangements may mean transactions at the highest marketing level."[5] The article also reports that the increased use of large buying committees that prefer to remain anonymous and secluded many times requires a big title to penetrate the barriers against personal contact.

[2] *Forbes Magazine*, Dec. 1, 1966, p. 125.
[3] *Sales Management*, July 21, 1961, p. 77.
[4] *The New York Times*, July 24, 1966.
[5] "Pace Picks Up in Top-level Selling," *Sales Management*, Mar. 20, 1964, pp. 121–122.

All of which simply means that in a great many situations a firm's most important and effective salesmen are its top executives—and you are not apt to become one sans selling skills.

THE SALESMAN'S FUNCTION IN SOCIETY

Competition is keen in any free market, but in economies in which the government controls the means of production and distribution, competition among sellers is feeble or nonexistent. For example, there is little competition in the sale of postage stamps. There may be some justification for the government's operating the postal system, but our economy was built largely on the basis of private enterprise and free competition. It may be granted that this system has been modified in recent years and that a condition of imperfect competition now exists in most areas, but we must also recognize that most business concerns are in competition—a competition often brutal and fierce—with many firms striving to sell a similar product to the same buyers.

It is the persistence of this competition which makes salesmen necessary. An economic society in which much of the business is done in a free market is a marvelously complex network of individuals and institutions whose relationships with each other are maintained in such a way that the order functions as desired with a minimum of friction. Each cog in this concept we call society performs definite functions that the culture deems necessary. When certain cogs no longer perform functions that society values, they are discarded. Witness the near demise of rail travel in favor of driving or flying, the rise of television and the decline of motion pictures, the advent of synthetic fibers and the fading away of natural ones—all victims of society's relentless drive for efficiency and functionality.

Salesmen are an economic institution in our society; selling is a service our society has found must be performed if our order is to continue on its present course. Society is both ruthless and benevolent; ruthless in eliminating unwanted firms, activities, or people; benevolent in rewarding those who give it what it wants. Thus the salesman must be performing functions which society values or he would have been eliminated.

However, the duties of salesmen are forever changing and some commentators on modern marketing suggest that unless salesmen change with the times they may find themselves nonessential. What factors are operating to bring about this change?

First, there is the massive advertising of manufacturers' brands which establishes a preference for these brands among millions of consumers. When this is accomplished, dealers are virtually forced to carry such brands and little salesmanship is required to persuade them to do so.

Second, the gigantic retail organizations are buying more and more through committees instead of through departmental buyers. The manufacturer's salesman finds it extremely difficult to get through to these committees. The decisions of these committees are being governed more and more by the answers given by a computer which has been fed data concerning sales of each item, profit margins, turnover, shelf space needed, etc. It is difficult to do much creative selling to an electronic computer.

Third, in the largest chains the buying decision may rest with the very top executives, and these men may prefer to deal with their counterparts in the manufacturer's organization rather than with some salesman. Even the purchasing agents of some big manufacturers may not possess final buying authority on important items. This authority may reside higher up where it is hard for the salesman to climb.

The net result of these and other changes is to emphasize even more strongly the *service function* which salesmen must perform. Also, the role of the salesman must be upgraded to meet the new challenge; and this cries loudly for better-trained salesmen. The modern salesman should know how to get to a buying committee, man by man, and to win a chance to present his proposition to the whole committee; and he should not be awed at the prospect of talking to the top men in a big organization. But he must be prepared to present a *plan* which will persuade his prospect that he will profit by buying what the salesman is selling. This demands imagination, research, thought, and time—which add up to constructive and creative *work*.

The salesman today is a part of a marketing team or organization; he is not carrying the entire load, nor as much of it as he formerly may have carried. But he is far from being nonessential, and he never need be if he will recognize the changes that are taking place and adapt his philosophy and activities to these changes.

One rather widely quoted book, *The Vanishing Salesman*,[6] has a somewhat misleading title; its author writes not of a vanishing salesman but, instead, of a changed one.

Mr. Dudley Dowell, president of New York Life Insurance Company, recently told a marketing seminar of The National Industrial Conference Board: "The salesman still is the center of the selling process. Selling is still preeminently a matter of human persuasion; that's why, with all our new tools for the elimination of human effort in various areas of business, the man continues to hold the center of the marketing stage."[7]

Despite the varying demands placed upon the salesman by the changing times, several definite functions will always remain to be performed by

6 E. B. Weiss, *The Vanishing Salesman* (McGraw-Hill Book Company, New York, 1962).
7 *Chicago Tribune*, May 11, 1966.

him. He must dispense innovation, possess knowledge, facilitate consumption, act as a channel of communication with the market, and service his trade.

Dispenser of innovation

In our society we welcome the new rather than venerating and clinging to the old. Compared with the past or with many other countries today, our rate of innovation is staggering.

The Certified Grocers of California review each week 250 new products. Of these, an average of 57 will be accepted; 50 old ones will be dropped to make room. The life cycle of products is growing shorter. As fast as one new item reaches the market, two things to do the job better are coming out of the laboratory.

But innovation is of little value to society until it is brought out of the laboratory and the warehouse. New products and services can be of value to society only when knowledge of them is dispersed to the people who can use them.

How can a shipping room foreman keep up with all the new techniques and products designed to assist him in his job? How can the accountant know about all the innovations in data processing? How can the marketing manager know about the latest developments in packaging materials? How can the electronics engineer keep abreast of the availability of the latest developments in various components? How can the physician keep up with the latest drugs? The answer to all these questions is the same. These people cannot, *by themselves,* possibly keep informed concerning all the innovations affecting their fields.

One recent study of physicians and their sources of information concerning the drugs they prescribe clearly proves the importance of the manufacturer's detail men in the process.[8] In reviewing several independent studies on the subject of drug distribution and the physician the evidence is quite clear that doctors rely on the detail men calling upon them for important information concerning new drugs more than on any other single source. In each study the detail men were given a strong vote of confidence.

The detail man for the pharmaceutical manufacturer calls on physicians to inform them of new developments and products. The busy M.D. depends upon this salesman to keep him abreast of new drugs, their characteristics, and side effects. The salesmen for packaging concerns call regularly upon marketing managers and other executives connected with the

[8] Raymond A. Bauer and Lawrence H. Wortzel, "Doctor's Choice: The Physician and His Sources of Information about Drugs," *Journal of Marketing Research*, February, 1966, pp. 40–48.

packaging of products so that they can consider the latest packaging ideas for use in their business. IBM and other salesmen call upon accountants to inform them of recent developments in data processing.

Without salesmen the process of introducing innovations would be greatly impeded because people have neither the time nor the inclination to be continually seeking out the newest developments in their fields. Emerson was removed from the realities of life when he said, "Build a better mouse trap and the world will beat a path to your door." Without salesmen the world will not know of your latest mouse trap, let alone the location of your door.

Innovations, no matter how meritorious, do not sell themselves. Eli Whitney could find no buyers for his cotton gin and was so impoverished at one time that he was compelled to borrow a suit of clothes to make a public speech. Jacquard, the French inventor of the loom that promised to revolutionize the production of lace, was beaten and mobbed by his fellow townspeople because they thought that he was robbing them of their opportunity to earn a living. Edison was compelled to install his incandescent lights in an office building free of charge to persuade anyone to give them a trial.

Charles Newbold invented an iron plow in 1797, expecting that it would quickly supplant the clumsy and short-lived wooden plows then in use. These wooden plows only scratched the surface of the soil and were so dull that it required a small herd of oxen to pull one, whereas the new iron plow not only penetrated the ground more deeply but could be pulled by one team of oxen. But Mr. Newbold struggled for years to convince the farmers that the iron plow would not poison the soil and kill the seeds planted in it.

It took King Gillette five years to sell his first seven safety razors.

Few businessmen would undertake to produce any new product if they did not have available the means to sell it. Without aggressive selling our economy would bog down, and new and improved products and services would not be brought forward for the betterment of our lives. No manufacturer would take such a chance, and no investors would risk their capital in such a hopeless venture. Aggressive selling has been an important factor in making available a wider range of constantly improved products.

Some skeptics may say that this innovation-dispensing function of salesmen is greatly magnified here. However, any businessman who has had contact with salesmen will quickly recall that the salesmen who call upon him spend much of their time selling something that is new to him. The wholesale drug salesman talks little about the old standby items in his line, but spends his time on the new products.

We should also remember that even well-established products may still require selling. Millions of new buyers enter the market each year—

buyers who have not heard the salesman's story. Every product is new and unfamiliar to many potential buyers. And even the old, familiar products are constantly being improved, and each improvement must be sold. Moreover, many products are bought so seldom that even present users have not kept abreast of developments and are surprised to discover what great changes have taken place since they last bought a camera, typewriter, corn planter, lawn mower, or office machine.

Possessor of knowledge

The salesman is an expert in his line. He should know more than any other person about his products and the problems they will solve. This knowledge function of the salesman is so important that Chapter 4 is entirely devoted to it. But knowledge of the product is only part of the story. The salesman must also know how his products will solve the customers' problems; he must know their applications. An IBM salesman might know his computer inside out, but how many sales would he be able to make if he were unable to show the prospective customer how the computer would fit into his system?

Catalytic agent in the consumption process

Considerable friction exists in the marketplace thus stifling consumption. People want all sorts of goods and services. But many times natural inertia keeps them from satisfying these desires, and this slows down and disrupts our economy. If goods and services are not bought in sufficient volume (and today that necessary volume is extremely large), people producing them lose their jobs. Consumption is necessary for employment. The salesman lubricates and stimulates consumption by reducing the inertia inherent in people. Not only do his persuasive powers attempt to overcome such inertia and encourage people to go ahead and buy what they want, but in many cases he makes it easier for them to buy.

Intelligence agent

One of the growing problems involved in operating our huge, complex society is that of communications between the market (society) and the maker. In olden days the shoemaker knew his market personally; his customers told him exactly what to make for them. Today, middlemen, advertising, retail salesmen, etc., have been inserted between the shoe manufacturer and the shoe consumer. Yet, the basic problem still exists of communicating the consumer's desires back to the maker. This essential function is performed largely by salesmen. One manufacturer of men's slacks for the collegiate market was caught napping one year when styles changed slightly. College men were wanting a slack with a distinctly tapered look; he was producing a slack with the leg fuller than that desired. His salesmen quickly detected the problem when retailers told them of it; the retailers had learned of it from their clerks who were continually in contact with the ultimate consumer. Many of the product advances on Mack trucks come from suggestions by salesmen. The ideas flow from field salesmen to sales management to engineering.

Firms without salesmen in the field may not know what is really going on in the market. One firm selling supplies to floral wholesalers was being run out of the market by the competitor who was giving an additional 10 per cent free-goods deal under the table to key wholesale accounts who agreed to handle his products exclusively. The management knew its sales were dropping but did not know why. They were fortunate that a friend of the company eventually told them of the competitor's practice and they were able to counter it before they were bankrupt. However, this delay seriously injured the firm. A salesman would have uncovered this practice quickly when he called upon a friendly wholesaler.

Service function

The salesman's job does not end once the prospect has given an order, as will be examined in detail in Chapter 19. Any great salesman knows that when he gets an order he has just started to work for the customer. And a salesman may perform many services for a prospect *before* he makes the first sale to him. As is stressed throughout this book, people do not buy *products,* but rather they buy *benefits,* and if they do not get them, they will cease dealing with that source. The IBM salesman, after he sells an electronic computer, must make certain that it is operating properly, that the customer's personnel know how to operate it, and that the programming satisfactorily solves the customer's problems. Furthermore, he will try to learn or devise new ways in which the buyer can use his machine.

A Remington Rand salesman whose only account is a large bank in New York has spent many nights at the bank helping out with some urgent work load. He constantly asks himself, "How can I be of the most assistance to my customer?"

A sportswear salesman called upon a small apparel dealer who had a serious overstock of outerwear, thereby reducing his open-to-buy budget. The salesman spent no time trying to sell his line, but rather spent hours planning a promotion that reduced the dealer's outerwear inventory and created a loyal customer.

A salesman for a pencil manufacturer asked to see the orders sent in by a prospect's salesmen. He found them hard to read, because soft pencils had smudged the originals and made poor carbons. Hard pencils made good carbons but faint originals. The salesman recommended a certain grade, demonstrated it, and sold thousands to that manufacturer, who insisted that every one of his salesmen use them.

THE SERVICE ATTITUDE

The attitude toward life which emphasizes service to society characterizes many young people. They join the Peace Corps, work with underprivileged children, etc. This outgoing attitude also characterizes many salesmen. To these it is not only a fine ethical standard, it is thoroughly practical as well. When the seller is interested in obtaining repeat business from his customer, this idea of mutual profit and satisfaction assumes more importance than it does when the salesman expects that he will never see the buyer again. But even here the salesman knows that the buyer will talk, so the smart salesman makes certain that the buyer will say nice things about him.

This idea of a permanent, continuous relationship between salesman and customer was what John Wanamaker, famed retailer of Philadelphia and New York, insisted upon in his concept of real salesmanship. It is related that Wanamaker, determined to improve the quality of salesmanship in his stores, sent for a certain teacher of salesmanship. After listening to him Wanamaker said, "Now I have your story. Your statements have been general, but I want to ask you one question. What is the center of your proposition, your *type* of salesmanship training?" The man replied, "The center is my definition of salesmanship, which is: the art of persuading men to buy what you have to sell." The great merchant prince sat silent for a moment and then said, "That will be all. I do not think I am interested in your proposition." He then sent for another expert in sales-training work and propounded to him the same question, to which the reply was, "My definition of salesmanship is this: the art of so successfully demonstrating the merits of the goods and the service of a house that a permanent customer is made." Wanamaker immediately exclaimed, "Fine! That's exactly what I have been looking for."

The salesman who holds to this ideal of service in all his dealings really serves three people—his customer, his employer, and himself. He serves the customer by aiding him in the wise selection of goods. He serves his employer by building up a clientele of satisfied users who were sold upon the basis of their own needs rather than the needs of the seller. He serves himself by establishing a reputation for fair dealing, which results in consumer confidence, goodwill, and future business.

A sale has been defined as "a solution of a problem." The buyer is not looking for a product or a service; he is seeking a solution to a problem—

his problem. The salesman who carries in to the prospect a helpful idea is likely to carry *out* an order for his product.

The Chicago based department store chain, Carson Pirie Scott & Co., tells its new salespeople, *"Serve when you sell.* Put yourself in your customer's place and give the service that you would expect . . . the most important rule of superior salesmanship . . . . Always advise a customer for her own best interests . . . that's service-selling . . . that's Carson's selling."

Of an outstanding salesman who sold to repeat customers it was said: "He didn't have any customers—he had only friends." To this man's customers he was never a salesman—just an always helpful friend.

Service to the buyer may be big. "Here are the plans and specifications for that blasting job you have to do," said the industrial salesman to the contractor working on the new state toll road through the hills, as he laid out the complete picture of the placements of the blasts, with full details of needed supplies and with all costs estimated.

Or service to the buyer may be small. "You told me this morning that you were having trouble with that spring on your big machine," phoned the salesman to a customer. "As soon as I got back to the plant I asked one of our men about it, and he says it can be fixed with only a slight adjustment. If you'll have one of your men call him in the morning, he will be very glad to tell him over the phone exactly what to do."

Big or small, the spirit of service was at work, making friends and making sales.

A word of caution: when a salesman is offering help or advice to a prospect, he must avoid assuming a patronizing air. He must listen to his prospect's problem and avoid the attitude of a superior. He and his prospect must tackle the problem *together* and reach its solution *together.*

THE MODERN CONCEPT OF REAL SALESMANSHIP

When one grasps the true role of salesmanship in society, he no longer places much emphasis upon overpowering personality, a blatant line of sales talk, and a liberal use of high-pressure tactics to get the order. Businessmen have seen so many salesmen of this sort that they recognize the type, regard them as nuisances, and give them but a short hearing, if any.

With this elevation in the standards of salesmanship has come an improved position of the salesman and saleswoman socially. Now they are regarded as a necessary and highly respectable part of our social and economic structure.

The very term "salesman" is being redefined. The medicine man of the movies has given way to the pharmaceutical expert equipped to brief the doctor and the pharmacist on the virtues of the latest wonder drug. The life insurance agent has been replaced by the Chartered Life Underwriter and the estate planner, while the furniture salesman has become an interior designer. The former paper bag salesman is now a packaging consultant.

The salesman is now regarded as an expert, a man professionally trained and competent to render a highly valuable service.

Even the ethical attitude of salesmen is changing. In fact, it is not uncommon for a salesman to advise the prospect against buying, even though a sale might easily be made. A shoe salesman will frequently tell a customer that he should not buy a certain shoe, even though an immediate sale may be lost thereby. There is no better way to win the confidence of the customer than by proving that his interests are supreme. A truck salesman told a prospect that he did not need a truck yet but that when his business reached a certain figure he would be wise to invest in one. The prospect waited until his business had grown to the volume specified, sent for the salesman, and told him to "prescribe" the type of truck needed. No competition was invited by the buyer, for he had confidence in the salesman.

IS SALESMANSHIP AN ART? A SCIENCE? A PROFESSION?

Science is systematized knowledge, while art is knowledge made efficient by skill. A salesman may first absorb the "systematized knowledge" concerning selling and, armed with this information, go out into the field and learn to apply it, thereby mastering the *art* of selling. There is a growing body of knowledge dealing with selling methods. This has been accumulated by study, experiment, and testing, so that today it is no exaggeration to claim that there exists a science of salesmanship. Even more obvious is the fact that there is an art of selling. The *art* of performing in any field consists in the *act* of doing the required things. It may be poor art or excellent art, depending on the results. This is as true of selling as of golf or playing the piano.

In claiming that salesmanship has accumulated a sufficient body of systematized knowledge to entitle it to be classed as a science, the authors are keenly aware that it is by no means an exact science (if indeed there be *any* such). The conditions under which experiments must be conducted are not easily controlled, a number of variables usually being present—a condition not conducive to accurate findings. But great progress has been registered, and more may reasonably be expected.

Whether selling has attained the rank of a profession is a question likely to provoke sharp differences of opinion. In former times only three professions were recognized: the triumvirate of the church, law, and medicine. Today half a dozen others have been recognized by the census: actors, artists, educators, engineers, musicians, and writers. Just where can the salesman squeeze his way into this growing but still select group?

Louis F. Weyand, under whose direction the Minnesota Mining & Manufacturing Company's annual sales pushed past the half billion mark, tells his salesmen: "Realize that selling is a profession. Study for your job just as hard as the chemist or the lawyer. Be well grounded in all phases of the marketing function."

The professionalizing of salesmanship will come about gradually, with various branches of business setting up high standards and recognizing those who are deemed worthy. The American College of Life Underwriters has taken a long step in this direction with its certificate of Chartered Life Underwriter, granted only after the successful completion of a rigorous course of study.[9] Colleges and universities are offering students the chance to major in marketing, thereby giving them a start toward obtaining the book knowledge needed for success in selling.

The knowledge of three fundamentals—personality, product, and prospect—together with a complete mastery of the strategy and tactics of salesmanship in the sales interview, characterizes a professional salesman. He is an artist, getting in touch with those who need his service; presenting it to them tactfully, sympathetically, and convincingly; and educating them, both as to their real need for it and as to how he can help them satisfy that need. Anything less, anything that emphasizes the good of the salesman rather than the benefit to the buyer, is not professional salesmanship in the true sense of the term.

CAN SALESMANSHIP BE LEARNED?

This is a logical question at this point. The best answer is found in the experience of hundreds of well-managed corporations which have for many years trained or taught their salesmen by every device known to educators. They have demonstrated over and over again that the trained salesman can far outsell the untrained one.

Would such firms as IBM, Xerox, National Cash Register, Armstrong Cork, and Remington Rand maintain expensive sales training schools for their men if they were not convinced that people can be taught how to sell? Many of these concerns prefer to hire bright young men who have had no selling experience in the belief that they can more easily be taught to sell properly if they have not had their minds confused by some misguided "salesman" of the old school.

The Xerox Corporation advertises that its Educational Division is prepared to offer a sales training course, especially designed for any client willing to pay $50,000 for it, which has enjoyed great success when used by

[9] The CPCU (Chartered Property and Casualty Underwriter) is receiving similar emphasis today in the field of general insurance.

various clients, among them Massachusetts Mutual, Southern Railway, W. R. Grace, Diamond Alkali, and Commercial Credit. Gains in sales are said to reach from 5 to 10 percent, a figure which would delight any sales manager.

Johnson & Johnson increased the sales of their products in chain and independent drug stores by as much as 300 percent through training courses for retail salesmen.

The "get-rich-quick" ads for salesmen have given people the wrong idea about selling. Many men who would have otherwise made excellent salesmen have been shunted into other fields of endeavor because of unfortunate experience on their first sales jobs. Without proper training they were thrust into the field only to experience humiliating failure for which they were not prepared.

The old adage that salesmen are born and not made has caused untold damage because it leads the uninformed to believe that all he has to do is grab some firm's sample kit and go into the field. If he was born a salesman, then he will succeed, and if he was not so endowed, he will quickly find it out. This is utter nonsense. Such people are usually doomed to failure before they make their first call. Selling is a complicated art, which takes several years to master. It is incredible to observe the ego of many would-be salesmen. The doctor, lawyer, CPA, and the plumber all realize that they must spend years studying and practicing their trades before they can be considered proficient. Not the "born" salesman; he is a superman who can give the product a quick once-over and sell it right away. Of course, this attitude gets the neophyte into trouble quickly. He learns the hard way that he must study and practice his art just as any other professional must before he gains proficiency.

The *principles* of salesmanship can be taught and learned just as surely as those of agriculture, engineering, law, or medicine. As in these other occupations, the student is not a skilled practitioner until he has enjoyed a wholesome amount of practical experience. But he will become a skilled doctor or salesman much more quickly if he first absorbs the principles and does not attempt to learn entirely by the method of trial and error, a method likely to be rather rough on both parties.

Modern psychologists tell us that we are molded more by our environment than by our heredity. They insist that it is possible even to alter personality by training; some assert that proper environment and training can materially raise one's IQ. The young person aspiring to a career as a salesman should be heartened by the news that nearly everything essential to selling success can be acquired, assuming that he possesses normal physical and mental assets. The old saying that "salesmen are born and not made" is no more true of salesmen than of singers or artists or writers or athletes—perhaps not nearly so true. A man of average natural endowments can make himself a good salesman if he is willing to put forth the required effort, even though he could never hope to become a great athlete or singer.

Vincent Riggio, formerly president of the American Tobacco Company and known as one of the country's finest salesmen, bluntly asserts, "Salesmen are made, rarely are they born; and generally when the so-called 'born salesman' gets into rough going, he fails."

DISCUSSION QUESTIONS
1. What do you expect of the salesmen with whom you do business?
2. You have decided to make accounting your career. In what ways would you have need for selling talents? What common situations would you be facing that would require such abilities?
3. What makes you the maddest in your dealings with salesmen?
4. What is a "born salesman"?
5. "If I never see another life insurance salesman, it'll be too soon. I don't understand how they serve any function at all!" A freshman student uttered these words. How would you answer him?
6. Why are top managers called upon to sell?
7. Why does the widely criticized door-to-door salesman still exist if it is true that society eliminates those it no longer needs?
8. Why is "handling people" or "getting along with people" essentially a task of salesmanship?
9. Why do many people dislike salesmen?
10. Think of some professional person such as a doctor, lawyer, or professor, and itemize the situations in which he has need for salesmanship.

CASE 1-1   ELECTRONETICS, INC.:
Sales Representation in the
Defense Electronics Industry

"Gentlemen, the next item on our agenda is the matter of our representation in Washington, D.C.," said Mr. Arthur, president of Electronetics, Inc. of Palo Alto, California, to his Board of Directors at its annual meeting in 1967.

Electronetics, Inc. had been formed in 1942 to manufacture highly classified electronic devices for the use of the Allied armed forces. After World War II the firm introduced several commercial products, such as an automatic garage-door opener, an FM deviation meter, instruments for analyzing chemical compounds, and electric filters, but defense contracts remained the backbone of its sales volume. The marketing of all commercial products was separate from the procurement of defense contracts.

The company's defense contracts were obtained either by bidding on IFBs (Invitation for Bids) issued by the Department of Defense or by negotiation with some branch of the services for some special item the company was particularly well-equipped to develop or manufacture. The firm obtained most of its defense volume from nearby defense contractors and installations simply because it maintained excellent facilities that happened to be most convenient to use because of the firm's location. Such business was obtained through the efforts of Mr. Arthur or one of his vice-presidents: no sales representatives were employed in the western region. However, the company retained NADCO, a sales agency for Marconi, a Canadian electronics manufacturer, as its sales representative on the east coast. NADCO was located in Washington, D.C., but had men traveling to key military bases such as Cape Kennedy, Huntsville, Fort Monmouth, and Norfolk. On Mr. Arthur's trips to Washington, NADCO had been quite helpful in lining up interviews for him and escorting him into the proper offices. Mr. Arthur had remarked many times, "It is quite easy to get lost in Washington."

NADCO received for its efforts a 5 percent commission on all contracts obtained through its efforts with a minimum fee of $50,000 per year; the minimum fee was justified by the number of small detail contacts that had to be made continually in the execution of defense contracts. On other contracts coming out of NADCO's region, but not obtained through its efforts, its fee was negotiated. For example, Electronetics had just received a 5-million-dollar IFB contract from Fort Monmouth (Signal Corps) in which NADCO played no part; it was an open-bid situation. However, its services were required in handling the multitude of paperwork and details that go along with such contracts, so a fee of 1 percent was agreed upon as being a fair payment for services rendered on this one contract.

Mr. Arthur continued, "As you know, we have at many times in the past questioned the effectiveness of NADCO in representing our interests in Washington. After all, its principal, Marconi, is interested in many of the same contracts that we are. It is difficult to single out any one contract that we have obtained solely because of their efforts. It always seems as if we have to go out and get the business ourselves and then they are willing to backstop us on it in Washington. The question I now wish to put before you is, should we now hire a full-time man to represent us in the Eastern markets? He would live in Washington and would have a good working knowledge of the defense electronics business."

Mr. Anderson, an outside director who was also on the boards of several other companies in the defense industry, asked, "I have been wondering if we shouldn't include in this discussion the question, do we really need any representation in Washington at all? It has always seemed to me that these guys just hang around waiting for us to do all the work in getting a big contract and then they wine and dine us while we're in D.C. winding up the details. For all the dough that we pay them we can well afford to buy our own booze. Just how realistic is it to expect us to be able to hire the calibre of man who could really do us some good in Washington?"

1. What functions would a Washington representative perform for Elec-tronetics? Be specific!
2. About how much would it cost to maintain a Washington representa-tive?
3. What are the pros and cons of keeping NADCO versus hiring the company man versus having no representative?

CAREERS IN SELLING

No man who is enthusiastic about his work has
anything to fear from life.
Samuel Goldwyn

Few topics are of more importance to an individual than the selection of his career—his path to glory. Indeed, your happiness in life depends in large part upon how well your job meets your needs: money, type of environment, tasks performed, people encountered, and accomplishments. While selling careers have a great many things to offer, there seems to be a great deal of ignorance and misinformation about them. While it no doubt will seem that we are trying to influence you to go into selling, for after all we are advocates of the calling, keep in mind that there are many people who should look elsewhere for their fame, for they will not find it in selling.

The purpose of this chapter is to help you make a wise choice of a career by providing information on how various types of salesmen earn a living.

We also recognize that the choice of a career is only the initial step toward success and satisfaction in one's work. *Managing* that career follows and this includes one's entire life, both during and outside of working hours. It is tempting to digress at this point and to contrast the weak person who lets himself be pushed around all through life with the "take charge guy" who plans ahead and then carries out those plans, but this chapter is concerned chiefly with *choosing* a career, one of the most important decisions any individual is called upon to make. In making a wise choice he will try to match, as nearly as possible, his aptitudes and liking for various types of activity with the demands of any job he is considering, for he knows that when these most nearly coincide he is most likely to succeed and be happy. Success and happiness seem to possess an affinity for each other; the successful man is usually happy in his work.

From his work he extracts generous amounts of psychic satisfaction—a feeling of accomplishment, the obvious respect of colleagues, a calm certainty of security, the pleasure of mingling with other successful people. And overriding all these is the satisfaction found only in doing what one *likes* to do. The singer would rather sing than anything else; the artist simply goes along with an inner urge to draw or paint. The best salesmen feel the same way about their work; to them it is fun.

In these days of aptitude tests and vocational guidance many young people have formed a general idea of what they would like to do for a life work, but their knowledge of various possible occupations may still be incomplete; they need more detailed information.

It is to provide this detailed information that this chapter is written. It is one of life's saddest tragedies for a person to spend one-third of every day, tomorrow and tomorrow and tomorrow, doing something which he dislikes.

So now let's see what kinds of lives various types of salesmen lead.

CHARACTERISTICS OF SALES CAREERS

Sales careers possess some distinctive characteristics which set them off from most other vocations. And yet, *selling is not a homogeneous activity.* There are tremendous differences between sales jobs which make it almost impossible to generalize concerning them. Thus it is difficult to assume a "sales type" of individual who will succeed in any line of selling. The salesman who is an outstanding success in one field of selling may fail miserably and be extremely unhappy in another field. These things being true, we must keep in mind that to nearly every broad statement some exception may be found.

Relatively high earnings

Most studies of businessmen's incomes indicate that selling is one of the more remunerative vocations. Not only is the average income of salesmen higher than that of other personnel at the same organizational level, but the salesman can aspire to a much larger income than can most other workers. It is not at all uncommon to find salesmen earning more than their managers; many salesmen have refused promotions into management because they could not afford the decreased earnings. Some IBM salesmen earn between $30,000 and $40,000 a year; a man who covered one large cus-

TABLE 2-1 COMPENSATION OF THE FIELD SALESMAN, BY PRODUCT GROUP, 1971

PRODUCT GROUP	1971 TOTAL EARNINGS				1971 BASE SALARY				INCENTIVE AS A PER CENT OF SALARY			
			MID 50%				MID 50%				MID 50%	
	NO.	MEDIAN	LOW	HIGH	NO.	MEDIAN	LOW	HIGH	NO.	MEDIAN	LOW	HIGH
Textiles and apparel	28	$16,750	$14,000	$19,825	15	$13,506	$10,500	$16,000	11	15%	13%	25%
Machinery (except electrical)	36	16,500	14,780	18,000	33	13,000	11,200	14,750	29	20	15	30
Instruments and controls	22	16,350	14,092	18,000	21	12,689	10,850	14,743	14	22	17	36
Electrical machinery	38	16,250	14,000	18,528	34	13,000	9,750	15,000	29	23	14	40
Transportation equipment	25	16,000	14,111	17,063	24	12,108	10,000	15,600	19	20	10	38
Fabricated metal products	21	15,200	14,300	16,250	20	13,500	12,531	14,500	16	11	9	13
All sales forces	341	15,000	13,000	17,076	307	12,300	10,100	14,486	230	17	9	29
Paper and kindred products	32	15,000	13,593	17,585	28	13,416	10,103	14,587	19	14	8	45
Building products	19	14,937	13,542	16,642	17	11,216	10,000	14,206	15	20	17	29
Rubber and plastics	17	14,800	12,681	16,825	17	12,300	11,466	14,863	13	14	8	29
Primary metals	24	14,750	12,650	16,842	24	14,000	11,450	15,800	11	18	8	21
Industrial chemicals	16	13,678	12,598	14,762	14	12,217	10,492	14,700	10	13	6	26
Stone, clay, and glass	20	13,350	12,238	17,100	20	12,113	11,000	14,700	14	10	8	21
Consumer chemicals	13	11,312	10,550	13,658	13	9,950	9,273	11,401	11	12	10	17
Food and tobacco	30	11,260	9,270	13,000	27	10,000	8,620	11,000	19	10	8	17

Source: Compensating Salesmen and Sales Executives, The Conference Board, Conference Board Study No. 579, p. 34.

tomer earned $75,000 one year. Several salesmen for Florsheim shoes earn in the neighborhood of $50,000 a year. Even the truck salesmen for one small, regional coffee company, Cain's, earn an average of $14,000 a year with the top men earning about $20,000. A representative for Lanz dresses in a sparsely settled Western territory makes about $40,000 a year.

One more point concerning salesmen's incomes. The college senior who goes into engineering or accounting work will perhaps start at a slightly higher salary than those who choose sales work, but figures show that, in most cases, the salesmen are earning more than the others after a few years. It requires actual training in the field to become a profitable producer of sales.

However, a better overall view of salesmen's earnings is provided by a National Industrial Conference Board study of over 341 large national companies conducted in 1971. The pay of the average salesman with these firms ranged from $11,260 to more than $16,750 a year; the median 1971 salesman earned $15,000 with the middle 50 percent of the averages falling between $13,000 and $17,076.[1] These figures are shown in Table 2-1 broken down by product groups. It should be noted how a salesman's earnings are strongly influenced by the industry in which he works.

One of the explanations for the large differences in the pay between industries is disclosed by the data in Table 2-1. It can be seen that the larger earnings are mostly accounted for by compensation plans with strong incentives. The apparel and furniture industries rank at the top of the earnings scale largely because straight commission plans dominate in those industries. These figures merely support what experienced salesmen have declared for many years; good salesmen who want to make a lot of money work on a commission. These data also suggest that the materialistic college graduate would be wise to give a second look at many of the firms soliciting his services on his campus because many of them are in the product groups not paying at all well. Seldom do apparel, furniture, leather products, or textile firms recruit on college campuses. The significance of this is rather clear; if you want these top-paying jobs, you will have to hustle them yourself because they will not come begging for your services.

Ability quickly recognized
In many fields of endeavor it requires considerable time to prove one's worth, and promotions tend to be based on seniority. Not so in selling! If a man can sell, he can prove it quickly and clearly. If he is working on a commission basis, his pay is directly proportional to his sales. The salesman

[1] "Compensating Salesmen and Sales Executives," The Conference Board, Conference Board Report No. 579, p.34.

TABLE 2-2 COMPENSATION OF THE FIELD SALESMAN, BY SALES FORCE VOLUME, 1971

GROSS SALES	1971 TOTAL EARNINGS				1971 BASE SALARY				INCENTIVE AS A PER CENT OF SALARY			
			MID 50%				MID 50%				MID 50%	
	NO.	MEDIAN	LOW	HIGH	NO.	MEDIAN	LOW	HIGH	NO.	MEDIAN	LOW	HIGH
$250 million or more	29	$13,000	$10,645	$16,150	29	$11,600	$ 9,523	$14,436	20	13%	8%	18%
$100 - $249 million	47	13,900	12,000	16,000	43	11,216	9,300	13,958	34	15	9	24
$ 50 - $ 99 million	55	15,000	12,500	17,350	51	12,216	9,970	15,000	38	22	12	37
$ 25 - $ 49 million	74	15,480	13,570	17,502	68	12,781	11,076	14,837	48	19	10	30
$ 10 - $ 24 million	89	15,370	13,450	18,000	81	13,000	11,100	15,000	64	15	10	25
Less than $10 million	47	16,000	13,000	17,200	35	12,000	10,000	14,000	26	18	10	38
All sales forces	341	15,000	13,000	17,076	307	12,300	10,100	14,486	230	17	9	29

Note that small firms tend to pay better than large ones. Whether or not that is caused by their size or is a result of the tendency of smaller concerns to use compensation plans containing large portions of incentive pay cannot be determined. There is some logic leading one to believe that smaller firms must pay a bit better to attract their men for they may not be able to offer as much in the way of nonmonetary rewards.

need not wait until he is an old man to earn recognition and a larger income. One eighteen-year-old man was earning $1,500 a month selling kitchenware before he decided to go to college; while in school, his pay varied between $300 and $500 a month selling only part time. On the other hand, if a man lacks talent or is lazy, there is no place for him to hide. His sales tell the story.

Do not jump to the conclusion that success in selling automatically comes quickly to the trainee. Most beginning salesmen must learn the trade just as a doctor or lawyer must learn his—by hard work. The companies included in the National Conference Board study reported a median salesman's age of forty; 55 percent of the firms reported no salesmen under the age of twenty-five.[2] Many sales situations are so critical to a firm's success that it simply cannot let inexperienced men deal with its customers—a company's most valuable asset.

Freedom of action

While most business personnel spend most of their time in the office, salesmen should spend most of their time in the field. They are seldom subject to direct supervision over their every move, but are relatively free to get their job done in their own way, as long as they show satisfactory results. A salesman can usually arrange his time to be where he wants to be. Should he want to see a ball game, he may locate some prospect who would enjoy sharing the experience.

This aspect of selling appeals to men who value their freedom and like to operate in their own manner. However, this freedom carries with it tremendous responsibilities for the man to manage his own time wisely; he must be able to manage himself. This many men cannot do.

As an example of this aspect of the sales job, the junior author was invited to play in a Pro-Am golf tournament at Oklahoma City by a former student who is a salesman for a Caterpillar distributor there. While the salesman was able to arrange his time so that he could participate in the tournament, he still had to get up at 5:30 two mornings and travel 100 miles to see some good prospects who would not wait. (He got the orders.) He also went to the office on two nights to catch up on some paper work. But that is just the point! A good salesman will get the work done, but he does have some control over when he does it.

Mobility

The salesman enjoys almost unparalleled mobility. This high degree of job mobility is one of the factors underlying the relatively high earnings of

2 *Ibid.*, p. 15.

salesmen. If a man can sell, he has a job. If his present employer goes out of business or for some reason cannot keep him on the payroll, he can make a connection with another firm more readily than many types of workers can; and he can accomplish a change without a long period of retraining unless his new job is too technical and different. The salesman is less at the mercy of managerial whim than most workers whose value to the firm is not so clear and who can be more easily replaced. The .350 hitter stays in the line-up, even though the manager does not love him.

During the aerospace layoffs in 1970–1971 few salesmen were fired while a great many engineers and other support personnel found themselves without work. Those few salesmen who were displaced quickly found new positions elsewhere while the others faced tragic career problems created by the unsalability of their extremely limited talents.

Salesmen are seldom locked into one company. They can take their talents elsewhere when they feel it best to do so.

Promotional opportunities

Through the years there have been many studies conducted on the route corporate presidents have taken through the ranks to reach the top. All of them have reached the same conclusion: the sales department has furnished the president's basic experience in more cases than any other functional area. This is particularly so in firms whose major task is marketing.

Challenge

Intelligent men are easily bored with routine jobs; if sufficient challenge is not provided by their work, they soon tire of it. Most selling jobs are anything but boring, and this is especially true of the better-paying jobs. Each customer or prospect presents different problems. Conditions in the market are continually changing, and the salesman must make adjustments to allow for such changes. The thrill of matching wits with a clever prospect adds zest to a salesman's work. He often views his work somewhat as a mountain climber expressed his reason for attempting to climb a difficult peak: "It's there, isn't it?" To a salesman the challenge is always there, and he accepts it eagerly.

Writers and politicians have extolled the charms of "security" as opposed to jobs offering the challenge of greater opportunity until it is not strange that some of our young people think of their future as being devoid of opportunity, a future in which they will perform routine tasks for what they hope will be a steady income, even though it may not be as large as they could wish. To such timid souls the life of a salesman seems hazardous and uncertain; they have no wish to confront unknown situations with which they have never coped. This pioneer stuff may have been fine in Daniel Boone's time, but not for them today! They prefer to play it safe.

But this very reluctance of many people to tackle a job like selling is playing right into the hands of the chap who aspires to be a salesman. He will encounter weaker competition and will earn a larger income and garner for himself more personal satisfaction because of this timidity on the part of his contemporaries.

Frequently salesmen are called upon to solve some significant problems for the prospect. An IBM salesman, thus called upon to make a survey for a company to determine its data processing needs, is faced with a sizable problem presenting many technical aspects.

The *Reader's Digest* recently related a tale of a six-man IBM selling team that spent four years in a hospital studying patient care and handling to determine how their firm could improve procedures. Another salesman spent many hours in St. Louis police stations studying crime reports and records. He now has programmed them in such a way that St. Louis police can call upon a computer to help them solve crimes.[3] No one should avoid a sales career on grounds that it presents no challenge and offers no outlet for one's creative talents.

Working conditions

Certain misconceptions exist concerning the nature of the work done by salesmen. Many people think of the salesman as a man who travels extensively, has an unlimited expense account on which he can live an exciting life, is seldom home, tells off-color jokes, and ends up a broken man. Such is the way with myths; they seldom touch reality.

TRAVELING   It is true that there are sales jobs which require the man to be away from home for several days at a time. However, these jobs are far from being in the majority. The typical salesman is home nearly every night in the week. Salesmen for retail outlets, wholesale houses, and industrial firms selling to a wide assortment of customers usually have small territories which allow them to get home every night. A drug detail man for a pharmaceutical house will have a relatively small territory to cover because of the density of potential prospects—doctors, drug stores, and hospitals. It is this *customer density* factor that determines the size of a salesman's territory. Those salesmen who have only one or a few customers in each city are the ones who must travel the most. But the number of potential customers for most firms has increased significantly. Also firms are

---

[3] Lester Velie, "The New Look in Selling," *Reader's Digest*, May, 1965, pp. 251–257.

attempting to get a more thorough coverage of each sales area. Result: smaller territories. For example, in 1957 one publisher's representative had the states of Colorado and Wyoming for his territory. In 1967 there were three men covering the same area.

In addition, even in those firms which require a substantial amount of traveling, management is aware of the problem created for both the firm and the man. Some firms fly the man home every weekend regardless of the distance. Others are so devising and revising their sales territories that the man regularly reaches his hometown every few days. And there are many excellent jobs in sales which require little or no traveling.

EXPENSE ACCOUNTS   Again this aspect of selling is overemphasized. Many salesmen have no expense accounts at all, but must pay their own expenses. Intelligent men who are paying their own expenses do not spend excessively. Those salesmen who are on expense accounts are usually under careful instructions as to how the company's money shall be spent. And their expense accounts are strictly audited at headquarters. Moreover, the men quickly tire of too much entertaining of prospects and customers.

In this matter of entertainment, selling jobs differ widely. It is true that some salesmen are expected to do considerable entertaining; but some actually do none at all. If a man is a nondrinker, he can find good selling jobs—in fact, some employers much prefer such a man. The Internal Revenue Service is scanning expense accounts with a highly critical eye directed at this item of business entertainment. Many claims are being rejected that would have passed a few years ago.

CUSTOMER CONTACT   Mythology has it that it is always open season on salesmen, that they are fair game to bait. True, some customers do browbeat salesmen, but they are a small minority. Friction with buyers is a minor problem with most *good* salesmen. Warm and enduring friendships with his customers can be among the most rewarding aspects of his work for the professional salesman.

ON THE OTHER HAND   It would not be honest to oversell the pleasant features of selling as a career. The salesman's life is not idyllic; some salesmen are not completely happy in their work, and they register their complaints or "gripes" with their managers. Many of these complaints concern personnel and policies of the particular company for which the salesman works, such as: too much supervision, too little supervision, too much paper work, territory too large or too small, quota too high, lack of adequate training, not enough advertising support, too much traveling, too much after-hours selling, too low income, slow delivery of goods he has sold, too strict credit policy, too heavy sample cases, and so on. Most of these can be dismissed as applying only to certain situations.

The reason for mentioning them here, aside from a desire to be fair, is to suggest that a young salesman should investigate these matters before he takes a new job. Any of the listed "gripes," if well founded, could render a sales job unpleasant, sometimes extremely so.

We should also bear in mind that there are complainers in every sort of activity; even college students and some professors are critical of certain aspects of their work.

Company representative

To many customers the salesman *is* the company for which he works. The grocer in Green River, Wyoming, probably has never met any representative from Procter and Gamble other than the salesman who calls upon him. He forms his ideas of the company from his contacts with the salesman. Hence, the salesman is in a vital position to influence, for better or for worse, the public relations of his employer.

TYPES OF SELLING JOBS

It is almost impossible to say just how many salespeople there are in this country, but most estimates are around six or seven million. This number is not subject to much erosion by automation, although self-service stores, advertising, vending machines, and other selling methods have perhaps slowed somewhat the growth in the demand for salesmen. However, we encounter items in business journals warning that our expanding economy will demand more and more salesmen and that an acute shortage always seems to exist.

The reader is again reminded that in the ranks of these millions of salesmen there are places for people of widely varied talents, intelligence, age, experience, and personality. The duties performed by different salesmen cover a wide range. The difficulties encountered differ tremendously in number and formidability. Financial rewards run the gamut from the legal minimum wage for women in retail stores up to annual incomes in six figures.

The following suggest some of the ways in which selling jobs vary:

- Some salesmen work for manufacturers, some for wholesalers, and others for retailers.

- Some salesmen sell tangible products like shoes and automobiles; others sell intangibles like insurance and securities or advertising space in magazines.
- Some selling jobs can best be performed by men, others by women.
- Sales jobs differ in their complexity. Some are extremely simple, while others involve the performance of a score or more distinct duties.
- In some selling jobs the salesman spends most of his time in actual selling; in others he sells during only a small fraction of his working time.
- Some types of selling work call for extreme aggressiveness on the part of the salesmen; others prefer what the psychologists call the "submissive" type who can employ the low-pressure or "soft sell" technique.
- Some jobs demand that the salesman be moving about a good deal, perhaps being away from headquarters weeks or months at a time; others require him to be in the same section of a store six days a week, week after week.
- Some jobs demand that the salesman meet the same customers at frequent intervals; other jobs find the salesman calling on prospects who are nearly always strangers to him.
- Some jobs find the prospect coming to the salesman, while in others the salesman must spend much of his time seeking out prospects.
- Some kinds of selling work make strenuous demands on the salesman's physical strength and stamina; other kinds may be carried on by a bedridden cripple over the phone.
- Some jobs may best be filled by salesmen who have attained a certain degree of maturity; others demand younger men or women.
- Some sales are commonly consummated in a few seconds; others may require months or even years to bring them to fruition.
- Some types of selling require a very considerable preparation and education before the salesman can hope to make good in them; others can be stepped into with virtually no training and scant formal education.
- In some jobs the salesman sells to manufacturers; in others to middlemen such as wholesalers or retailers; while in still others he sells to ultimate consumers.
- Some selling jobs demand salesmen with high intelligence; in others salesmen with a much lower IQ are preferred.
- Some jobs offer a steady salary and scant opportunity for advancement; others offer greater opportunity, usually coupled with a less steady income, although it may go much higher.
- Some salesmen sell staples; others sell specialties.

This list could be lengthened indefinitely, but the conclusion is already clear; there are many kinds of selling jobs, calling for a wide variety of talents and training. Nearly anyone can find some position in selling that is suitable and satisfactory.

Different types of salesmen on the same sales force

Even on the same sales force there are often openings for men of different talents. Albert Pick Co., Inc., manufacturer, importer, and jobber of equipment, furniture, and supplies for hotels, restaurants, institutions, hospitals, etc., employs five different types of salesmen. The *house salesmen* are always in the salesroom at headquarters to wait on visiting buyers and to look after stock. The *road salesmen* visit dealers, hotel owners, and other prospects, collecting information about construction projects, following up leads furnished by the general office, and taking orders for small amounts. The *technical experts* talk with the architects about buildings, make surveys of physical conditions, plan the location and uses of equipment, and get the orders. The *servicemen* are available for use by the purchasers of equipment, giving them advice and instructions in the most efficient utilization of equipment sold by the company. The *field operators* are not salesmen at all but merely good-will builders, traveling throughout the field, studying conditions, listening to complaints, and supervising the work of the salesmen.

Even some concerns selling over and over to regular customers have found places on their sales forces for the one-call type of salesman. Such representatives are used to open new areas, to revive ailing territories, and to supplement the work of the regular routine salesmen. These men have in their make-ups something of the pioneer; they chafe at the settled routine of ordinary selling; they are exhilarated by the challenge of the new. Such men will go into a territory where sales have been poor and will revive it, but they do not like to be left there after the campaign is over; they long for new worlds to conquer. A plodder may take over the territory that such a man has opened up and may hold the business in line nicely, but he will never expand it greatly. There is a place for each type of salesman.

In this connection it is interesting to note that several hundred firms are now prepared to *rent* salesmen to companies who wish to use them to open up new territories or to introduce new products.

The Ballantine Breweries, whose product may be familiar to some readers, employ two types of salesmen. For their draught salesmen, who sell to taverns, they choose amiable, middle-aged men who can swap jokes with the proprietors and bear up under the ritual drinking. For the grocery routes they employ sturdy youngsters who can cover a large number of stores each day.

Another interesting basis for employing different types of salesmen for jobs in the same firm is found in the setup in Beckman Instruments, Inc., makers of a wide line of scientific instruments. To sell to the *dealers* handling their simpler instruments, they hire men without much scientific background; but to sell their more complicated and highly specialized instruments to *users* of those instruments, they employ men with rich scientific training and experience.

TYPES OF SALESMEN

Now we are ready to proceed to a more detailed description of the work which salesmen do. This may be broken down into five categories: (1) the manufacturer's salesman, (2) the wholesaler's salesman, (3) the retail salesman, (4) the specialty salesman, and (5) the sales engineer.[4]

The manufacturer's salesman

There are three major types of manufacturer's salesmen—those who sell to wholesalers, distributors and dealers, those who sell to ultimate consumers, and those who sell to industrial concerns. *The work of the salesman who sells to wholesalers, distributors, and dealers is discussed here.* Later sections will discuss the other types of manufacturer's salesmen.

Men who work for manufacturers and who sell to the distributive trades can be grouped into three major types: (a) the pioneer who gets distribution for a new product, (b) the man who resells and services the dealer, and (c) the merchandising man who seldom takes an order but who helps dealers and jobbers to sell more of his firm's merchandise.

PIONEER FOR NEW PRODUCTS   The "distribution-getting" salesman convinces wholesalers, distributors, and dealers that they should take a chance on a brand-new product. Sometimes it is a product which has never been on the market. For example, recently there has been a tremendous development of electronic devices. Many companies are competing in this new market. Salesmen for these companies must either wean some of the established distributors away from their former connections or help other individuals set up new distributing organizations.

A salesman to be successful in this field must be self-reliant and self-generating. He must be aggressive. He must be imaginative. He must be able to locate prospects who never existed before. He must be able to make quick decisions and to paint a convincing picture of how the dealer is going to benefit by taking on his franchise or dealership. He must be well versed in the knowledge of how such businesses should be operated successfully, because he will be asked for advice and counsel. Although he is selling a

---

[4] There are other ways of classifying salesmen. Derek A. Newton in "Get the Most Out of Your Sales Force," *Harvard Business Review*, September–October, 1969, pp. 130–143, saw four kinds of selling: trade, missionary, technical, and new business.

tangible product, the work that he does is quite similar to selling an intangible, since he is also selling an idea and must persuade his prospects to accept a goal of future volume and profit.

The rewards are very high for this type of salesman. There has never been—and never will be—a surplus of men in this field.

DEALER-SERVICING SALESMAN   This type of salesman need not be as aggressive or imaginative as the first type. He "calls on the established trade" at regular intervals, and his chief task is to assure his employer of a never-ending flow of reorders for the firm's merchandise. He needs a great deal of energy because he must make many calls during a day. He needs persistence and enthusiasm, and he should have a warm, friendly personality.

If a salesman in their field represents a well-known manufacturer, especially one who is a consistent advertiser, much preselling work has already been done. There is an established outlet for the goods. The salesman's job is to enlarge this outlet. To secure the constant increase in sales which the salesman's manager may insist upon, certain factors must be well developed. Some of them are within the immediate control of the salesman; others are controlled by the factory but the salesman must use and interpret them.

If the product is a mass-selling item—such as a packaged food or drug item—there must be wide distribution of the line. Customers cannot be expected to walk miles to get a particular brand of tooth paste or cigarette. The salesman will follow the policy set down by his superiors in selecting the number of distributors most likely to get the largest volume out of a given community. If there are too few outlets, sales will be lost because the would-be purchaser will accept a competitive product rather than go far out of his way; if there are too many outlets, the potential sales are split into so many parts that no dealer has enough volume to make the line interesting to him, and some will drop it.

The line should be well and favorably known   This is largely beyond the control of the salesman. The advertising which the company has done and is doing, plus the reputation it has built up for making a good product and selling it at a fair price, will determine this factor. The salesman must be able to interpret what has been done by his company, however, so as to convince the dealer that he can make easy sales at a good profit to a large number of customers.

The store must be identified as a retail outlet for the salesman's product   Very few people succumb to the command of the television commercial announcer who says, "go out right now and buy yourself a tube of this mouth-filling, breath-taking new tooth paste." They hear it, and maybe the idea is lodged in the back of their minds as a result of constant repetition. But they don't start out deliberately to buy the tooth paste. What happens—with a sufficient number of them to make the advertising successful—is that they are walking along the street and they see the product in a drugstore window or on a supermarket shelf, or see a sign about it pasted on the window, or a metal fixture attached to the store front, or a decalcomania sign on the door, and they say to themselves, "Why, this is that new tooth paste I've been intending to buy." And they get a tube. It is up to the salesman to utilize the display materials furnished by his employer, the manufacturer, and to set up identifying signs in the largest possible number of retail outlets.

The goods must be well displayed inside the store   Surveys in many types of retail stores show that almost half the purchases made are "impulse" purchases—people buy things that they did not intend to buy. The sales made in the variety store or supermarket are a good example. People may go in to buy two or three things and come out with a dozen. They *see* things which they like but which they hadn't thought of buying. They *feel* the articles temptingly displayed. They *hear* what the salesgirls say about them. They *smell* them, and some they can even *taste*. The reselling salesman has the task of convincing the dealer that his goods should be well displayed inside the store.

The dealer and his clerks must know how to sell the merchandise   It is distinctly to the advantage of the manufacturer and his salesmen that all the people who come into contact with the public know all the talking points about the firm's merchandise. They must be able to give intelligent answers to questions raised by customers, and they should use tested methods designed to make the consumer want a particular product. The salesman will use the sales help given to him by his employer for this purpose and he will also use his own ingenuity. He must be a teacher as well as a salesman.

The dealer and his clerks must want to sell the merchandise   They may want to sell it because the profit is very attractive, or because the company does a remarkably effective advertising job, which makes the goods easy to sell and, consequently, extremely profitable. They may like the high quality of the product, the policies of the credit and collection department, or the promptness with which exchanges and repairs are handled. Maybe they just like Salesman Joe Doakes, who represents the manufacturer. Dealers and clerks are human; they like to do business with certain people much better than with others. It is up to Joe Doakes to make himself and his firm popular with the dealer and his salespeople. If they like him they can switch many a sale to his product which might otherwise go to a competitor.

The reselling type of salesman may not lead such a glamorous life as his brother who pioneers in new fields but he has greater security, a steadier income, and less wear and tear on his nervous system. If his company is an established success, he too can be an established success if he is willing to work hard and follow orders.

MERCHANDISING MAN   The third type of manufacturer's salesman gathers information and gives advice but is seldom compensated on the basis of the orders he turns in. In this group we place *merchandising* salesmen, *detail* men, and *missionary* men.

Merchandising salesmen are more promoters of sales for their companies than they are creators of direct orders. When a merchandising salesman goes into a city he is likely to perform some or all of the following tasks: He calls on the jobbers handling his product. He tries to arrange a meeting of the jobber salesmen and attempts to win their cooperation in giving an extra push to his product. If his company is advertising in local newspapers or on local radio stations, he sees the advertising directors of those organizations and tries to talk them into giving his product special promotion, such as publicity mentions.

He will call on the local dealers and check the stock of his company's merchandise. If fill-ins are needed he will possibly take an order and pass it over to the jobber from whom the dealer buys most of his merchandise. He will try to obtain the consent of the dealer for bigger and better displays of his product.

The best merchandising men are merchandising *counselors.* They are prepared to offer sound and unselfish advice on a variety of wholesaler and retailer problems, such as store layouts, displays, special events, store advertising, pricing practices, credit policies, service facilities and policies. Merchandising men are used widely in grocery, drug, and tobacco fields. They build added sales for their employers by giving helpful counsel rather than by direct sales efforts. They show other people how to sell more of their products and make them want to sell more of them.

The *detail* man, especially as used by the drug industry, is even more indirect than the merchandising counselor in building business for his employer. He may perform most of the functions of the merchandising counselor in dealing with jobbers and retailers. But he goes a step further, especially when his company brings out a new product. These drug organizations know that much business can be created by the recommendation of doctors, dentists, and nurses. If the product, such as Metrecal, for example, is nationally advertised, the manufacturer wants professional people to be aware of its merits, to recommend it to their patients, and to give favorable answers about it when patients ask for their opinions.

The detail man must be fully informed about the product and its claims. He must be able to talk intelligently with professional people, visit doctors and dentists—especially after office hours—give them literature and a convincing talk, and leave samples of the product which the professional men can give to patients.

In the case of drug products sold only under doctor's prescription, the detail man is entrusted with the task of introducing any new product and distributing samples widely among professional people. He usually represents a house which has a wide line of ethical products, and his job is to sell the general reputation of the house and the quality of its products. Just as in the case of the merchandising counselor, one of his main tasks is to make the doctor or dentist want to specify his products instead of those of a competitor.

The *missionary salesman* is defined by the American Marketing Association as "A salesman employed by a manufacturer to call on customers of his distributors, usually to develop good will and stimulate demand, to help or induce them to promote the sale of his employer's goods, to help them train their salesmen to do so, and, often, to take orders for delivery by such distributors." The missionary man is used by firms desiring to gain aggressive promotion behind a product which must, because of marketing considerations, be sold through wholesalers. Unfortunately, most wholesalers provide minimal selling for any one product in their line; hence, the manufacturer desiring aggressive promotion for his goods must do the job himself by using missionary salesmen.

The wholesaler's salesman

The wholesaler (sometimes called jobber or distributor) is the middleman between the manufacturer and the retail merchant or industrial consumer. He serves an exceedingly useful function by carrying thousands of items in his warehouse which are available on short notice to his customers.

The average druggist, for example, carries several thousand items, made by several hundred manufacturers, in his stock. The retail druggist would have no time left for serving his customers if he had to deal direct with each of these manufacturers. His favorite drug wholesaler, however, carries most of these several thousand items in stock, and the druggist will probably do some 80 to 90 percent of all his purchasing from one house.

The salesman for this drug wholesaler—or hardware, or grocery, or electrical supplies, or any other type of wholesale business—calls on his customers at regular intervals. He usually cannot do very much selling on any particular item because his catalogue may contain anywhere from 1,000 to 10,000 items. Usually he is so well and favorably known to the store proprietor that he walks in and makes up his own order from the "want book."

In other words, the first sale was made to that druggist years ago. It is an open account on the books, with the size limited by the credit rating of that particular druggist with his house. It is the salesman's job to keep the business coming. He is the company so far as the retailer is concerned. It is his responsibility to see that his company is prompt and accurate in filling orders, and that his customers get fair and equitable treatment in all other respects. He may act as a collection agent for his company or he may merely keep the company accurately informed about the credit rating and responsibility of his customers.

He is not entirely a "pickup" order salesman but often pushes specific items, either following orders from his superiors or his own dictates as to what he wants to push. His mind is often made up for him by manufacturers and their representatives who seek him out to teach him how to sell their specialties and make him want to concentrate on their lines. He has to be a sufficiently good salesman so that he can sell a specialty item, but because his catalogue contains thousands of items he does not have the time to do as much creative selling as the specialty man.

The salesmen for some wholesalers call upon business firms to sell such items as office supplies, maintenance materials, and various factory supplies such as abrasives, hand tools, and hardware.

Seldom would a wholesaler's salesman be accused of using high-pressure tactics. They get and hold their business by being reliable, friendly, and punctual, always available. The aggressive or creative type of man might not be contented as a wholesaler's salesman.

One study of wholesale salesmen for appliances and electrical equipment indicated that they averaged about $300,000 in sales per year; were paid between $8,100 and $13,500 a year if on a straight salary, but earned between $9,250 and $23,600 if paid by salary and commission; they had expenses per week of about $90.[5]

The retail salesman

There are two types of retail store salesmen, the *in-the-store* man and the *outside* salesman who comes to your home or your office and tries to sell you an item. *Only in-the-store selling is discussed here.* The other type of retail selling is considered under specialty selling.

[5] Sales Manpower Foundation Division of Sales Executives Club of New York.

The chief characteristic of retail store selling is that the customer usually comes to the salesman instead of the salesman's seeking out the customer. As pointed out by Burton Bigelow in a speech:

In this type of selling, the customer has discovered his own need and has converted it into a want. Nevertheless, the retail salesperson has numerous opportunities to sell items related to the item which the customer comes in to buy. He can also exercise insight, imagination, and ingenuity in an effort to unearth additional customer needs and to persuade the customer to buy the right product to meet them. Knowledge of stock, prices, and materials is especially important in inside selling.

Almost anyone who can wrap merchandise, write out a sales slip, and make change can generally qualify as a retail store salesman, but the rewards for that type of selling are not interesting to the average college graduate. However, retail selling can be a desirable experience, a stepping-stone to more lucrative, more interesting work.

Most owners of retail establishments started as clerks for others. They used their opportunity behind the counter to study human nature, to learn all phases of store management, to meet men who could give them a helping hand. With the knowledge and experience thus gained, money saved by being prudent and frugal, and contacts made with wholesalers and manufacturers, they then started out on their own.

In a large organization, such as a department or chain store, successful in-the-store selling often leads to steady advances within the organization—first to a better and more profitable department where earnings are greater, next to an assistant buyer's job, and eventually, perhaps, to the top post.

Another opportunity open to the ambitious, hard-working retail salesman is in the sales organizations of wholesalers and manufacturers. These companies often given preference to men who have had behind-the-counter experience. They know that successful retail salesmen have learned how to handle customers, and they assume that a man with experience in the retail business is likely to be well equipped for dealing with other retailers; he will understand their problems and talk their language. Furthermore, if a man has been selling Omega watches over the counter for several years, he has picked up knowledge which the makers of Omega would find it difficult to impart to a salesman who had never been in the watch business. Retail selling experience is a desirable asset, no matter what a man may do in later years.

While it is all too true that most retail salespeople are paid so little that to expect anything resembling salesmanship from them is unreasonable, nevertheless there are numerous situations, largely in high-class specialty stores, where excellent salesmanship can be found and those practicing it are commensurately paid for it. There are men's clothing salesmen who make upward of $20,000 a year. Good appliance salesmen can make in excess of $15,000 a year. Unfortunately, such good salesmen are rare.

It was for this reason that the author loved to sit for hours in a men's apparel store, the Wardrobe Shop, to watch Jack Moser work. He is truly a great salesman. One example: He was alone in the store waiting on a suit customer when a student walked in to pay his bill. As he laid his bill and check down on the desk a light golf jacket on display caught his eye. He paused to look at it; his hand reached out to feel the fabric. Jack had been keeping his eye on these developments while giving full attention to his customer. He directed an invitation to the student, "Go ahead, slip it on! There's a mirror over there." The man took the suggestion and stood in front of the mirror for some time admiring either the jacket, himself, or, more probably, both. It was obvious that he wanted that jacket but that the price was bothering him somewhat; he kept looking at the price tag rather forlornly.

Jack waited for the proper moment and said, "Note how full the shoulders are cut! That's to make sure it won't bind your swing. We looked for three years to find a jacket cut like that and couldn't so we had that one made up to our specifications."

The student took a few swings at an imaginary ball to confirm this bit of information. He still said nothing, but he went back to the mirror. After a few moments, during a pause in his suit sale, Jack said, "You really look good in that." As an added sales point, he mentioned, "You know that is one of the most practical garments you can get for this Colorado climate. You'll get more use from that than anything else in your closet."

The student surrendered, "OK, OK, you got me. Add it to my bill." He turned to the author to say, "How do you like that? I come in to pay off my bill and end up with a bigger one."

The key thing to note was how Jack handled the sale without ever waiting on the man and without disrupting his suit sale in any way. It was all so natural, just a few remarks at the right time.

But more importantly, Jack has also trained many other men to be excellent retail salesmen; far more than one outstanding businessman has marveled, "How do you do it? How do you find such salesmen? We'd give our eye teeth to have such men working for us." Retail selling can be just as interesting and challenging as any other type of selling if given the proper management.

The specialty salesman

The work of the highly creative salesmen discussed here is of two types: (a) specialty selling of consumer goods, and (b) specialty selling of factory-office goods.

A specialty good has been defined as any article of relatively high price, of fairly durable nature, nonconsumable in use, irregular in time of purchase, and in practically every case calling for the exercise of personal selection upon the part of the buyer, that is, the one paying for it and planning to use it.

SELLING CONSUMER GOODS The specialty salesman of consumer goods usually seeks the prospective customer in the latter's home, although sometimes the sale is consummated in a showroom or store. Products sold in this way are automobiles, washing machines, refrigerators, electric sweepers, radios, aluminumware, air-conditioning units, and many other items where maximum sales effectiveness calls for house-to-house selling.

Salesmen for such articles as brushes, cosmetics, books, hosiery, and greeting cards operate directly from their homes, have no store or display room, and try to make a sale in one call.

Salesmen of such specialties as automobiles, electric sweepers, washing machines, and refrigerators are usually attached to a retail establishment. It is difficult, if not impossible, for them to bring a line of samples into the home, but through their persuasive sales talk and a display of literature and demonstration models they attempt to interest the housewife and her husband sufficiently so that demonstrations can be given at the showroom. It is at the store or showroom that the sale is most often closed.

In selling established products a salesman must make numerous calls each day. He must get in to see the prospect, make a convincing and interesting demonstration, and be prepared to answer many questions and objections; and he must learn the knack of persuading his customers to recommend him and his products to friends.

Sales managers in this field of selling used to prefer the pushing, aggressive, high-pressure type of salesman. But the trend has changed. Manufacturers and retail merchants have found that the man who is too aggressive makes as many enemies as friends. Responsible heads have learned that the goodwill of the organization is too precious to risk with a man who is interested solely in the immediate commission he can make. There are opportunities in this field for both the high-pressure and the low-pressure type of individual.

Speaking generally, *the more difficult a product is to sell the higher are the rewards for selling it.* The most difficult product to sell is the new and unknown one. Very few people have to be convinced that mechanical refrigeration is superior to no refrigeration at all or to the old-fashioned icebox, but it is more difficult to sell refrigerators of manufacturers whose names are unknown to the general public than well-known, well-advertised refrigerators.

Still more difficult—and still more rewarding—is the selling of products or services that are in the educational or pioneering stage. The home video tape recording systems that are now being introduced to the market will require the efforts of salesmen with special abilities. They will first have to convince the consumer that he needs such a system, needs it now, and that the salesman's brand is the best one to buy. He must create a want which his prospects do not know exists. Consequently, he must show a great deal of initiative in locating prospects and a high degree of persuasiveness in getting a prospect to buy.

SELLING FACTORY-OFFICE GOODS   Another type of specialty salesman sells industrial products, materials, or services to business executives, purchasing agents, and professional people. A Xerox salesman would fall into this category, but his is an easy job compared with that of a representative of some new, unheard-of product whose need is not recognized by the prospect.

Wherever an industrial salesman sees a smokestack there is a prospect for him. Smokestacks mean producing businesses and they are prospects for his machinery, office equipment, and business machines. This is a tremendous field with sales running into billions each year.

To be successful in industrial selling a man must be technically minded. He must be able to advise manufacturers and help them buy intelligently. He must be able to discuss technical specifications with engineers or chemists and to justify his price list to a tough purchasing agent. Some employers insist upon graduate engineers for this work, but just as frequently the salesman gains his education in the business itself. Usually these men are trained to render service as well as to make sales. Their ability as troubleshooters is as important as their ability to obtain direct orders. There aren't many "born" salesmen in the industrial selling field. Most of them become good salesmen through coaching, study, and experience. This is especially true for a new product.

An industrial salesman does not make a large number of sales compared to the number made by a jobber or a manufacturer-to-dealer salesman, but the size of the order usually amounts to thousands of dollars. He may call upon an industrial customer for years before getting an order. What has the buyer been waiting for? He wants to be shown ways to cut his costs, increase his sales, improve his products, or solve some problem that has been plaguing his operations. He buys from those salesmen who bring him helpful suggestions. Such salesmen must take the trouble to study the problems of their customers. They may know a thousand facts about their products, but they *must* also know how it can be used to the best advantage in the particular prospect's business—in solving his problems.

The sales engineer

The so-called "sales engineer" almost always has a technical background. He must be an expert at finding problems and using his product to solve them. Perhaps he must create a product to meet some customer's needs. He may design some special-purpose machine or arrangement of machines to solve the problem at hand.

A sales engineer for a small electronics manufacturer called regularly upon the engineers and purchasing agents of all manufacturers using electronic components—largely defense and aerospace concerns—to examine with them what problems they were having with the electronic packages they needed. Problems were never in short supply; when he gave the firms the best answer he usually got an order.

Sales engineers serve as counselors, troubleshooters, and "improvement engineers" for industry. They follow up old customers to keep them informed about new products or processes and new applications for old ones. They contact new industries and new companies to learn what they need so that their own company may supply the basic materials or have the laboratories develop them. Their job is to assist industrialists in gearing their facilities for more advanced production.

There are many types of sales engineers, but the following quotation will suffice to give the reader some conception of the complexity and difficulty which may characterize the job:[6]

A project to build a superhighway to include several tunnels is financed and authorized. When the project originates, an engineering firm is retained to prepare the plans and specifications. Bids are prepared and contracts let for the highway, and subcontracts for the drilling of the tunnels.

A manufacturer of air compressors and drilling machinery assigned a sales engineer to the job at the time the project was first considered. It became his responsibility to follow the entire project, do the necessary groundwork, reach every individual who would in any way influence the placing of business, and concentrate sales effort in the right way at the proper time with the greatest intensity possible.

This sales engineer's first step was to become thoroughly familiar with the original plans and follow every change made. He obtained a general picture of what apparatus might be required and was on the job when the first test drillings were made. The engineering firm selected to prepare final plans was located in a sales territory other than his own and served by fellow sales engineers within his company located at a distant point. He worked closely with them, making sure that they were actively cultivating the customer's engineers and supplying them with technical information on his product, its application, and the success gained through its use by others. The contracting engineers on the project, therefore, knew what this supplier recommended,

6 Bernard Lester, *Sales Engineering* (John Wiley & Sons, Inc., New York, 1950), 2d ed., pp. 114–116.

when it could be obtained, what it would do, and what would be its initial cost and the expense of maintenance.

As the time came for obtaining bids, this sales engineer for the supplier saw that those contractors who prepared to bid understood fully the part that he might play in providing means of performing drilling operations in the best and most inexpensive way. With the over-all contract placed and the subcontract for the tunnels awarded, the work narrowed down to concentrated effort on the subcontractor. With technical assistants within his own company, the sales engineer set up a demonstration of sample equipment recommended for use on the job and proved its suitability to the contractor requiring it. Since the project was a large one he prepared to provide local service facilities on the job to rectify promptly any troubles that might develop, and he stood ready to recommend experts to be employed by the contractor for supervising the use of his equipment and operators who were experienced and efficient. Terms of payment on his apparatus were adjusted so that the contractor could pay for it in accordance with a schedule of payments received by him on his entire contract.

The movements of this sales engineer were quick and carefully timed. Through the developing of acquaintance and an understanding of their respective problems, he gained favorable consideration from every individual who in one way or another influenced the purchase of equipment, and after he was successful in obtaining orders for compressors and drilling equipment he made repeated visits to the ground where this equipment was used to see that it met the requirements of the contractors.

Perhaps the following job description for a chemical salesman will provide additional insight into the job of a sales engineer.

MONSANTO CHEMICAL COMPANY: POSITION GUIDE—SALESMAN
I. Function
   He is responsible in his territory for making the maximum sales of the products assigned to him in accordance with the sales policies and budgets of the division and for gathering and reporting any and all information and ideas of possible significance to Monsanto. He is responsible for showing the broad interest expected of all members of management in the progress of the company beyond his specific responsibilities. He is to ably represent Monsanto in appearance, activities, and deportment.
II. Major Responsibilities
   A. Sales
      1. Analyze the sales potentials of all customers and prospects in his territory, and keep records to focus attention on major accounts.
      2. Develop and carry out a well-planned weekly schedule of sales calls.
      3. Determine specific problems of each customer and potential cus-

tomer. Develop a definite sales strategy for each account which will promote the better and increased utilization of our products bringing to bear any applicable service, such as technical or promotional.

4. Solicit orders and contracts, planning the strategy for each call in advance to dramatize benefits.
5. Take initiative in investigating new sales areas:
   a. With present customers
   b. By always searching for new accounts
6. Have a full knowledge of all the division's products and sufficient knowledge of products of other divisions to enable him to alert the proper division to sales opportunities or competitive developments.
7. Keep on top of complaints, giving full report to district manager, and keep in close touch with customer until completely resolved.
8. Seek and report promptly to the district manager field intelligence of possible consequence to the company.
9. Take active part in trade associations of which he is a member.

B. Operational
1. Make regular and special reports:
   a. Write sales reports on a current basis on all essential calls.
   b. Submit daily call reports listing *all* calls made.
   c. Prepare annually an account and prospect evaluation showing information requested on standard form.
   d. Submit itineraries to district office well in advance of trips.
   e. Prepare annual sales budget for his territory.
2. Maintain efficient communications and carry out promptly instructions from district manager.
3. Maintain adequate records, and keep such files and records of customer purchases as are necessary for intelligently planned calls.
4. Keep adequate records of expenses.
5. Be responsible for safeguarding confidential information so as to avoid its release to outsiders or Monsanto personnel not authorized to receive it. Respect customer confidences.
6. Pursue a course of self-development which will result in benefit to himself and Monsanto.
7. Carry out promptly instructions from district manager, and cooperate with all individuals within the company.
8. Conduct himself as a gentleman at all times, bearing in mind that in public contact Monsanto will often be judged as a company by his actions as an individual.

III. Organizational Relationships
He is responsible to the district manager and will look to him for guidance and instructions. He has no supervisory responsibility except as given in special assignments.

A salute to the unseen salesmen

The retail salesman and the house-to-house canvasser are familiar to every-one. The traveling salesman who calls on retailers at regular intervals is known to most. But there exists an army of salesmen who do not come in contact with most of us, but whose work is nonetheless important. The sales engineer is one of these.

On the same plane is the salesman who installs a new accounting system in a department store or sells a more fruitful advertising campaign to a manufacturer. The life insurance salesman who has specialized in the field of estates and can show his prospect how to avoid the loss of too large a share of his estate in taxes is rendering a service greatly appreciated by those who avail themselves of it.

We usually think of salesmen as selling manufactured goods; but there are many stages of such goods. Someone must sell the clothing manufac-turer the cloth, thread, buttons, sewing machines, office equipment, etc. Someone must sell the wholesaler the thousands of items he carries in stock and sells to the retailer. The manufacturer buys many items not included in his finished product, such as coal, insurance, office supplies, trucks, machinery, oil, brooms, a public-address system, cafeteria equip-ment and food for his employees, medical supplies for his first-aid room, rest-room equipment, and scores of other things.

Thus, these behind-the-scenes salesmen carry on their work, helping to distribute thousands of products and services to people who need them. In one sense they are the people who keep our economic system operating smoothly. They do much to equate supply and demand, to prevent short-ages of certain items and surpluses of others. Taken as a group, we can almost consider them as among our foremost "economic planners."

DISCUSSION QUESTIONS

1. In recent years there has been much comment about equal employment opportunities for women. What types of selling jobs can best be filled by women? Can women be industrial salesmen?
2. In what type of selling would an older man probably be more effective than a younger man, other factors being equal?
3. Would the type of customer upon whom you would call be of importance to you? Should it?
4. As you study the jobs of different kinds of salesmen, what factors other than purely economic ones might influence you toward some of them, assuming that you had the ability to make good in any of them?
5. In what kinds of sales work would a high IQ be an asset? Would it ever be a liability to any salesman?

6. What would be the differences between selling for a large corporation and a small company? Might there be any differences in the nature of the sales jobs between large firms in the same industry?
7. If you had your choice between selling only one product line to all classes of customers or selling several product lines to one class of trade, which would you prefer?
8. If you are interested in high earnings in selling, tell exactly how you would go about getting them. What type of selling would you enter? How would you go about getting into that field?
9. What are some of the advantages and disadvantages of being a sales person in a quality furniture store?
10. Would the geographical location of your sales territory make any difference in the nature of your sales job?

CASE 2-1   MARK CALDWELL:
Where to Now?

"I decided to let them fire me rather than resign so I could get a good hunk of separation pay plus unemployment compensation," said Mark Caldwell to one of his old professors. He continued, "I had told them that I had to be transferred out of building materials and out of South Dakota but the boss didn't seem to offer much hope for relief. I just couldn't take calling on all those small-town lumber dealers out in the boondocks, so here I am a year older, back home, out of a job, and getting married next month. Got any suggestions, prof?"

The professor recalled that Mark had returned to State University after serving a hitch in the navy. While Mark had started out to be an engineer, he had second thoughts about it and began a program which a kind person might describe as a random sampling of the university's curricula; he was trying to find something in which he could get interested. The field of marketing caught his interest when he took the basic course in it. Upon graduating with a fair record overall, and an excellent one in marketing, he accepted employment as a sales trainee with a well-regarded national manufacturer of building materials and flooring products.

The professor had a close relationship with Mark's employer and had been told that Mark had been the outstanding trainee in the six-month training program held at the company's home office in the East. He was immediately assigned to the building materials division and given a sales territory in South Dakota. Many trainees had to be assigned to various office jobs around the home office while waiting for territories to open up: they were not always so fortunate in being assigned to a major division. Management had high hopes for Mark.

Being at a loss to know what to tell Mark, the professor asked him, "Well, what do you really want to do with yourself?"

"That's just it, I don't know. I think I want a job in management somewhere. I am tired of pushing a car over the roads," Mark replied.

"Well, if I hear of anything that might be for you, I'll give you a ring," the professor said in parting.

1.   What did the professor feel like telling Mark?
2.   What actions should Mark take in locating a job?

CASE 2-2   DICK STARR:
A Change of Jobs

"I've just been offered a job with Ben Hogan to cover a territory in upstate New York. Not sure yet what I should do! How about talking it over?" said Dick Starr to Mack Nelson, one of his close friends.

Dick, a former football star at a Southwestern university, upon completion of his eligibility had accepted a job with a newly established wholesaler of golf and tennis equipment in Denver. While the two partners in the business handled all the inside sales work, Dick covered all the pro shops in Colorado, Wyoming, New Mexico, and Montana. His major lines were Dunlop and PGA equipment, Etonic shoes, Burton bags, and several lesser known brands of clothing. His selling efforts, considered relatively successful, resulted in his being offered an opportunity to buy into the business. He declined the offer because he did not have the money and would not have had much influence in the management of the business.

Dick gained a small amount of fame in the area among the pros because of his rather unusual golfing talents. There are numerous pros with whom he had played who would swear that he could hit a ball farther than anyone in the world; unfortunately, some of his putts almost matched his drives for distance. However, he was a good golfer overall, but would not have been able to go on tour without considerable work which he was unwilling to undertake.

Dick was presently being paid a 6 percent straight commission. While this presented him with opportunities to make good money, there were some complications. One month he took orders for $40,000 worth of goods, but the company was only able to ship $10,000 because of limited inventories. His earnings seemed to be more a function of the firm's inventory than of his efforts, but this had somewhat abated in recent months as the firm became stronger financially. Dick paid his own expenses.

The Ben Hogan offer was for $600 per month plus expenses plus a commission that would allow him to make about $12,000 a year if he sold as much as the previous representative in the territory had sold the previous year. He would have about a four-month vacation each year during the time the courses in his territory were closed for the winter. Presently, Dick was working 12 months a year; most courses in the Southwest were open throughout the year.

1.   What are the advantages and disadvantages of each position?
2.   What would you have done? Why? What do you think Dick did? Why?

CASE 2-3   GEORGE ROPE:
Getting Started

"I want to become a manufacturer's rep for several women's wear lines," George Rope, a senior marketing major at a Southeastern university, explained to his advisor. He continued, "What I want to know is how should I get started? My father says that I should get some experience in retail women's wear merchandising by going to work at a leading department store, but I don't know about that. What do you think?"

George's advisor commented, "Without doubt you would learn a lot about the rag business that would be useful to you as a rep."

"Yes, but enough to warrant the time put in?" George countered. Since the advisor's silent shrug answered his question, George went on, "It seems to me that I should just start right out by lining up several manufacturers and have at it."

"A rep just like that!" smiled the advisor.

"Why not?"

The advisor did not answer. Instead, he asked, "How about getting a job selling for one manufacturer first? Or there are some manufacturer's representatives who hire salesmen to work for them. How about working for one to start with?"

George thought a moment, then asked, "But what pays the most to start?"

"That's important to you?" asked the advisor.

"Money's always important!"

1.   What advice would you give George about how he should go about becoming a manufacturer's agent for several manufacturers?
2.   Is money always important?

TWO

PREPARATION FOR SELLING

YOU

Experience is a good teacher; she doesn't
allow dropouts!
Anon.

An outstanding sales manager was asked, "What do you think is the most important factor leading to success in selling?" He answered, "The salesman's character." When one studies successful selling careers he cannot help being strongly impressed by the importance of personal character traits as a major factor supporting success. Indeed, many men with severe handicaps have overcome such barriers by great determination or by other strengths of character. Unfortunately, far more frequently a man with great natural ability fails because of deficiencies in his personality or character. So it seems proper to spend some time studying ourselves.

IMPORTANCE OF YOUR PERSONALITY

"All I am looking for is an honest man who is not afraid of hard work." "I am mainly interested in a man who can sit down with me and carry on an intelligent conversation." "Our firm simply wants men with good workable intelligence who can get along with people." "We want people who make a good impression on those whom they meet." "I keep asking myself, can our people live with this guy for the next twenty years?" These were the replies given by sales managers visiting a college campus when asked what they were looking for in the people they interviewed.

In general, when choosing young men for sales work, sales managers usually look for personality rather than for specialized training. IBM's policy for hiring salesmen is to seek a man with certain fundamental characteristics and then furnish him with the necessary sales training. In fact, they strongly prefer that the man not have had any previous selling experience. A district manager for Gardner-Denver said, "Show me some men with workable personalities and we'll give them all the technical training they'll need." They regard these young people as raw material rather than as finished products. No candidate whose personality fails to measure up is accorded further opportunity with most firms.

The earlier in life a person realizes the importance of this selling fundamental the easier it is for him to develop in himself the desired traits. Whether or not that person contemplates a career in selling, these same traits are invaluable, because they contribute to one's ability to make and hold friends, to gain social prestige, to adjust to one's environment, and to influence others in any field of activity.

WHAT PERSONAL CHARACTERISTICS
DO GOOD SALESMEN POSSESS?

What traits, qualities, characteristics, aptitudes, attitudes, and abilities make up the effective salesman? As a chef would put it: What ingredients must be used and how much of each?

One fact should be made clear at the outset: *there is no such thing as one ideal sales personality.* As we have pointed out in Chapter 2, there are many kinds of selling jobs and these require different types of salesmen. But experience has indicated clearly that the possession of certain traits greatly enhances a man's chances for success in selling. Some of the more significant success traits are discussed below.

Before we launch into this sermon, a word of warning—or apology, if you prefer—about the obvious nature of the following material. Frequently students complain that they do not need to be told these simple truths— "Any idiot knows that stuff!" We only wish it were so. Happily, most people do know these things, but observation clearly indicates that a sufficient number of salesmen evidently do not know it and consequently some mention of it here seems advisable.

Appearance

Fortunately for most of us, perfection of figure or features is not essential to an effective sales personality, nor, for that matter, to a winning personality quite outside the selling field.[1] However, a conscientious salesman makes an effort to present himself favorably to the prospect.

He does this not only for its good effect on the prospect but also because of its psychological effect on himself. A man who knows his appearance is above criticism radiates a self-confidence which he cannot feel when he sees the buyer's eyes focused on some neglected imperfection in dress or grooming. One salesman relates the harrowing details of how he lost a sale when he disclosed an unsightly tear in the lining of his coat while he was searching his pockets for an important paper. He was keenly aware that the prospect had noted it, and this knowledge upset him completely and ruined his presentation. A salesman must present a good appearance, not because he is eager to *flaunt* it, but because he wishes to be able to *forget* about it and *sell*.

Let us observe the salesman through the prospect's eyes. These first impressions are important, especially in sales situations where the salesman calls only once on each prospect. They are likewise important in those cases where the results of the first call determine whether the prospect is willing to let the salesman return later to present his proposition in more detail. If this first call fails, there will be no follow-up calls.

CLOTHING   Appropriateness is the keynote—appropriateness for the occasion and perhaps for the type of selling work the salesman will be expected to do if he is employed. Clothing that is too conspicuous attracts attention to itself and away from the message the salesman is trying to put across. Thomas J. Watson, long-time International Business Machines Corporation president, insisted that his salesmen wear dark suits, black ties and shoes, and white shirts. On the contrary, many salesmen make a practice of wearing unusual clothes in the belief that people will remember them for this. This may be good tactics when a salesman is calling regularly on customers who learn to know him well, but it may not be so smart when he is trying to make a favorable first impression.

Detailed suggestions are superfluous, as most salesmen learn how to dress. These suggestions are designed to be helpful if a salesman wears a business suit, but should not be interpreted as dictating that every salesman must *always* be so attired. One Southern Purina feed salesman claimed that it was the kiss of death for him to wear a suit while calling on

---

[1] It should be noted that since the advent of television, the candidates for political office are chosen with more thought for their photogenic assets than was formerly the case. And the "salespeople" who deliver the commercials are usually not too hard to look at. These situations involve brief exposures, however. First impressions are often the only ones. A salesman usually has more time to put across his personality and to overcome an unfavorable first impression.

a farmer. He maintained that a salesman should be dressed much in the same manner as the people upon whom he is calling lest he make them feel inferior or self-conscious.

At this point we used to delve into a long list of personal cleanliness habits which can interfere with the persuasion process. However, reading about these matters evidently bothers students as much as the reality bothers customers, so let us just say that many sales are lost when some aspect of the salesman's personal cleanliness or grooming so disturbs the prospect that his mind is blocked from considering the salesman's proposition. All he can think about is the salesman's offensive characteristic.

One college graduate found it impossible to get the selling job he wanted (selling men's wear for a manufacturer) because he was grossly overweight—250 pounds and only six feet tall. During college he had successfully sold men's clothing in a retail store, but even with the contacts made during that time and the strong recommendations supporting him no manufacturer would hire him because of his appearance.

Unquestionably the sharp-looking, well-dressed, physically fit all-American-boy type finds the total impression created by his appearance to be of great assistance in making a sale, particularly in selling to customers for the first time. The old adage about first impressions was not idle prattle.

Voice and conversational habits

While appearance, or how one looks to others, partly determines the first impression created, one's voice and conversational habits are also important in gaining acceptance. Although movies, radio, and television have done much to improve our speaking voices, many people still suffer from speech defects of some kind.

Speech clinics have made tremendous strides in correcting many of these defects, so that even rather serious faults may be eliminated by a person willing to work at the problem. Improvement can be attained in enunciation, tone placement, timbre, unpleasant mannerisms, stuttering, stammering, pitch, and other characteristics of faulty speech. Stage-struck youngsters in their teens learn to speak beautifully; the aspiring salesman can do it, too. Speech is more important in business than it used to be, for we conduct more of business through spoken words and less through letters. The telephone, especially long distance, has made it possible to talk with almost anyone at will, and soon we may be able to *see* the person at the other end of the line. Air travel can bring people together so easily and quickly that business which formerly required perhaps weeks of correspondence is now done face to face. Facility in using the spoken word is spreading; so it behooves the salesman to keep abreast of the times.

Many salesmen utilize a tape recorder to learn just how their voices sound. A common reaction is one of almost incredulous perplexity, not only at the tonal quality but also at other unrealized defects as well. With the weaknesses thus revealed, the determined salesman can attack them.

Some voices lack friendliness, warmth, personality. The lower tones sound warmer than higher tones; they have a richer timbre. A salesman is likely to let his voice rise in pitch when he tries to emphasize a point. His voice, as it rises, grows thinner, more shrill, less impressive, and less masculine. It indicates that he is under considerable tension. When the salesman is obviously tense, his prospect will usually grow more tense also; this is bad, for the prospect should be relaxed and receptive.

Certain speech characteristics seriously detract from the salesman's effectiveness. Among the more common problems are mumbling, talking in a monotone or too fast, mispronunciation, overuse of slang, and unenthusiastic delivery. The professional salesman carefully develops his speaking techniques because he fully realizes that a clear, enthusiastic voice which he can vary as the need arises conveys meanings and thoughts to the prospect apart from the words spoken. It is difficult for the prospect to believe that the salesman's product is the best one made if the salesman's voice lacks the enthusiasm and earnestness that should be associated with such claims.

Manners and mannerisms

Edmund Spenser wrote, back in the sixteenth century, "a man by nothing is so well betrayed as by his manners." In a very real sense a man's manners reveal his inner personality. Good manners are founded on consideration for others; the utterly selfish person cannot have truly fine manners.

Shall we check up on our salesman's manners and mannerisms through the prospect's eyes? Some of these relate directly to his *speaking* habits and manners while others consist of his *actions.*

Is he a good listener, or does he interrupt me constantly?

Does he speak disrespectfully of his employers, his company, or of friends and acquaintances? If so, he will probably ridicule me when I am not present.

Is he vulgar?

Is he natural, or is he putting on an act?

Does he appear relaxed, poised, at ease, and confident, or does he seem nervous, ill at ease, and tense?

How about his handshake? While the way a person shakes hands should not be given undue emphasis, still it is one way to create that initial good impression, or if improperly done, that undesirable poor impression. Just consider your own personal reaction to a stranger who gives you the wishy-washy dish-rag handshake, or the finger-tip grip. Just as bad is the bone-crusher hand-shake of the muscleman.

Does he have any nervous little gestures, habits, or mannerisms betraying his lack of experience, poise, and social maturity? Such things as rubbing hair, forehead, face or chin, pulling at tie or collarband, drumming with finger tips, and tapping floor with toes, which may irritate other persons, should be noted and corrected. These habits divert attention to the salesman himself, away from what he says.

Common courtesy is an increasingly rare commodity. And as com-modities become rarer they become more valuable. Dick Sewell comes to mind as a case in point. Dick is a young man but two years out of college whose sales record rapidly advanced him from a part-time clerk in a college men's shop to manager of a large Denver men's store. In the beginning there was real doubt among the owners of the chain that Dick would make it. He missed too many sales and did not seem to have the natural flair for clothing sales demonstrated by some young men. But he dug in! He applied himself and quickly mastered the task. But the foundation that supported him through his difficulties was his manners. Many customers, particularly women, voluntarily commented favorably on Dick's unfailing courtesy. As a general rule it is particularly important when dealing with women to show the courtesies so often absent in most mass-distributing institutions today. But do not be misled; men also notice good manners. The rudeness that seems to be so much the order of the day only makes courtesy more effective. Simple things like thanking the customer for his business or say-ing "good morning" can set an entirely different tone to the relationship between the salesman and his customer. One of the more pleasant discov-eries the author made upon his move to southern California was the retail sales clerks' widespread habit of saying, "Have a nice day," as the customer departs. It is a friendly gesture, makes one feel good, and it costs the giver nothing. The art of selling is the art of pleasing people and this starts with the way you treat them.

SMOKING   Salesmen who smoke should remember that smoking in the presence of prospects should be indulged in only when the prospect invites the salesman to light up. Such an eminent authority on salesmanship as Arthur "Red" Motley advises every salesman to stop smoking when he starts to sell, even though his prospect may continue to smoke. His reasons:

1. Smoking distracts attention from what he is saying. This is especially true if the salesman prides himself on his ability to inhale strongly.
2. There is always the concern of a prospect for rug, desk top, or papers when a lighted cigarette or cigar is handled carelessly or laid down.
3. Some prospects just don't like smoke.

The salesman loses no sales by refraining from smoking, but he may lose quite a few if he does smoke while trying to sell. One real estate salesman had the dubious pleasure of smoking a $750 cigar, for that was the commission he lost on a $25,000 sale when he lit up his stogie inside a car on a cold winter day. It took the wife of the couple (prospects) only two minutes to remember an appointment she had "forgotten" which had to be kept immediately. They bought one of the houses the salesman had intended to show them that afternoon, but from *another* salesman that evening. Make no mistake about it, nonsmokers strongly resent the lack of consideration of salesmen who smoke in their presence. Have you ever heard of anyone buying something *because* the salesman smoked?

The problem is aggravated in retail stores since personnel, because of their continual exposure, become insensitive to how the store smells to people entering it. The smell can cling to the merchandise. Few people like to shop in a store that reeks of stale tobacco smoke.

Some helpful personality elements

Without trying to be too scientific in our analysis, let us examine a few of the personality elements that seem to be important in selling. The list is not complete.

INTELLIGENCE   Speaking broadly, the better selling jobs demand intelligent men. If one is to deal with prospects who have reached a position of prominence or must make complicated computations, he will do better if his IQ is high.

On the other hand, selling in retail stores, or house-to-house, or to dealers who buy the product frequently, as a grocer buys bread, will not hold much interest for men whose IQ is high. In fact, men may do better in such jobs, or at least remain more contented, if they are not too bright. Not that all men engaged in these types of selling are dumb—far from it. But we are forced to deal in generalities.

Perhaps it would be more accurate to say that the salesman needs to be quick-witted. He has to think fast on his feet. It doesn't do much good to think of what you should have said to the prospect an hour after the presentation.

SOCIAL INTELLIGENCE AND TACT   Social intelligence is the ability to say or do the right thing in a social situation that facilitates the social intercourse between the parties present. Almost needless to say this trait is essential in selling. The person low in social intelligence should seek other fields for earning his living if he cannot develop it.

Charles Schwab was passing through one of his steel mills one day at noon when he chanced upon some of his workmen smoking. Immediately above their heads was a sign that said, "No Smoking." Did Schwab point to the sign and say, "Can't you read?" Not Schwab. He walked over to the men, gave each one a cigar, and said, "I'll appreciate it, boys, if you will smoke these on the outside." Every man there knew that Schwab realized that a rule had been broken—and they respected him for the tactful way in which he handled the matter. They could understand how he had climbed to his place as one of the big men in the steel industry.

The tactful man has the knack of putting others at their ease. He never says or does anything to wound the sensibilities of another. We have all heard someone say, "I think you're a swell guy; you're aces with *me*. But I heard *Tom* say that he thought you had gone about as far as you could ever go in business. *He* seems to think that you aren't too sharp." The person saying this may think that he has protected himself, but he hasn't. The friend he is addressing is hurt; his ego is badly bruised—by the speaker and not by Tom. Any time you put a man in the wrong or deflate his precious ego, he will seize the first chance to do the same to you, no matter how you try to place the responsibility on someone else.

Many stores instruct their clerks to refrain, even by implication, from pointing out a customer's mistake. Clerks selling Pall Mall cigarettes have been told that if a buyer asks for "Pawl Mawl" cigarettes, they are to reply, "Pawl Mawls? Yes, sir." The temptation to correct him by saying "Pell Mells" is strong, but to do this would not be tactful for it would make the customer feel inferior.

Tact is called for in dealing with those who feel inferior on account of a different background. For example, foreign-born Americans may suffer from this feeling of inadequacy. A university graduate was working in a meat-packing plant and was being shifted from department to department while he learned the business. At one stage he found himself working between a couple of semiliterates. One of them asked him where he had gone to school and he replied that he had attended a certain high school for a while. That was tact and good sense, that young man became a very successful salesman and the president of a corporation. This aspect of tact is closely related to what is often referred to as "sales sense."

Tact may be displayed as emphatically by what a person *refrains* from saying as by what he *does* say. Often a prospect may drop some remark that "lays him wide open" for a crushing rejoinder; but the tactful salesman bites his tongue and bottles up the blasting retort that is struggling for utterance. It sometimes takes a big man to do this, but the very act of doing it strengthens and develops his personality.

While we are discussing "golden silence," one of the important elements of a good personality is the ability to listen courteously. It is a tragedy of life that a baby takes approximately a year to learn to talk and then requires the remaining sixty-five or seventy years to learn the importance of keeping still. Although this remark may appear facetious, its point is serious. How many times have we conversed with people who gave us the impression that they were paying no attention whatever to what *we* were saying because they were so intent upon what *they* were going to say the moment they could interrupt us! To the salesman this is especially important, because the prospect or the customer invariably likes the person who is not only a good talker but also a good listener. Being a *good* listener involves listening with attention, with evident understanding, and without interruption, especially by putting words in the speaker's mouth. He may be a slow talker, and maybe you could say it better than he can—but don't do it!

If we cultivate the knack of letting the other fellow have *his* say, then he is much more inclined to let us have *our* say. Furthermore, the more the other fellow talks about himself, the more the salesman learns things that he may use effectively later in the interview. It has been truly said that few people learn much while their mouths are open.

Tact is founded not upon hypocrisy, but rather upon a genuine liking for others. It is a notable fact that most top-flight salesmen are inclined to see the good points in others and to overlook their weaknesses. They are charitable and tolerant because they *like* people; we do not seek out and stress the flaws in those whom we like. And this liking for others can be cultivated and developed by anyone who really wishes to do it.

We devote quite a bit of space to this matter of social intelligence for two reasons. First, it is essential for success in the higher levels of selling; and second, it is a trait which can be developed more easily than can most of the other qualities usually possessed by good salesmen.

Social intelligence comes pretty close to being the heart of sound salesmanship. When a man possesses it, people say that he is a "natural-born salesman." But nothing could be farther from the truth; we repeat—social intelligence is almost wholly acquired. Small children possess little or none of it and their parents, teachers, and doting relatives expend much energy, time, and thought in teaching the elements of social intelligence to their small charges. Some children have better teachers than others—that is about the only difference.

DEPENDABILITY   This is basic, especially in salesmen. If a salesman says "I'll have that in your hands before noon on Friday," he must make good on his promise if he has to deliver it himself and drive all night to do it. If he says his machine will turn out 450 units an hour, his machine had better turn out 450 and not 449. This theme might profitably be elaborated because it is so fundamental to a sound sales personality. It is related to honesty, integrity, care to avoid exaggeration; it is the foundation upon which long-run relationships with customers are built. When a customer can say of a salesman, "He delivers," he is saying that the salesman is dependable—a high compliment.

A retailer who had bought from a traveling salesman for 32 years recently stated, "In all the years I never went wrong on any goods Bill sold me. If he didn't think they would sell to my trade, he wouldn't let me buy them. I depended on his judgment and he never let me down."

When a buyer knows that he can depend on what a salesman tells him, it is hard for any competing salesman to crack that account.

HELPFULNESS CHEERFULLY GIVEN   No need to discuss this, except to underline the word "cheerfully." Help rendered grudgingly is futile in building popularity and friendship.

LAUGHING AT THE RIGHT TIME   Laughing at the mistakes or misfortunes of others makes no friends. But laughing *with* others, when they want you to laugh, feeds their ego, and they like you for it. Greet their attempts at humor with a "dead pan," and they dislike you because you have wounded their ego. A good salesman can also laugh *at* himself.

DOMINANCE   A good salesman is in control of the sales situation. Though he may allow the prospect to do most of the talking, still they are speaking of what the salesman desires and he has matters well in hand. Many people confuse dominance with an aggressive, perhaps overbearing, forceful personality, but the two are not the same. In many sales situations the highly aggressive salesman loses control of the interview when he antagonizes the prospect.

In selling, dominance is not achieved by force but rather by behavior that clearly establishes in the prospect's mind that the salesman is master of his area of competence—he knows what he is talking about. The salesman can assert his authority, his dominance, if he does so tactfully, with finesse.

Master salesmen are able to dominate their relationships with customers without seeming to do so. Indeed, in dealing with prospects possessing strong personalities themselves, the adept salesman allows them to think that they are controlling the interview.

SELF-CONFIDENCE Self-confidence is developed as you gain experience and learn that you are able to do what has to be done—get the job done. Few young people have much confidence in themselves; they haven't had the experiences yet on which to base it. As you learn your trade and acquire experience, confidence will develop. You will know it when it happens; you'll have the feeling that you can handle whatever problem is cast in your path. You can cope! You can get the job done. It is a most satisfying feeling, one that will develop, but not without time and effort.

One women's apparel salesman, in discussing confidence, said, "I'd been working my territory for about three years. As I was returning home after a particularly successful trip, I began thinking about the success I had and remembering the failures I had experienced on earlier trips. Suddenly it came over me that I was now good, able to win, that the world was now mine. It made a new man of me."

Buyers are likely to take a salesman at his own estimate. They earnestly hope that he can help them solve their problems. The salesman who is confident awakens this hope and, for that reason, obtains an interview. Throughout the interview the confident salesman puts his statements across.

And yet, while he radiates confidence and force, the salesman must cultivate patience and tolerance. Out of regard for the feelings of others, the successful sales personality will naturally avoid dogmatic utterances, especially on controversial subjects. It is true that the good salesman serves and counsels, but the recipient is conscious of the *manner* in which the counsel is given. Flatly positive statements repel rather than convince. One can have definite opinions without stating them in a dogmatic fashion. An opinion offered modestly and as a personal judgment can be defended on the grounds that it is a conviction, without insistence that it is always and unalterably right or that the listener must concur in it. This does not apply to statements concerning the merits of his product, for here the salesman is expected to hold strong convictions.

Someone may object that the person without strong opinions will not be considered as of much force, yet few men have been more highly esteemed in their own time than Benjamin Franklin, and few men's opinions have been more respected. He seldom made positive statements, preferring to say, "It seems to me . . ." or "Under the circumstances it appears . . . ."

The man who is interested in getting along with people will take care to say, "This is my opinion under these circumstances." His words will carry as much weight as those of the man who is dead sure he is, always was, and always will be right.

VOCABULARY   It has been remarked by many authorities that intelligent people rate high in vocabulary tests. So do executives. Apparently there is a close connection between the possession of a good working vocabulary and getting on in the world. Certainly salesmen should be able to express themselves clearly and effectively; and the higher the level of selling, the more needful this becomes. The painting of word pictures, the conveying of ideas, addressing a board of directors or a committee of executives, or merely carrying on a conversation intelligently—these are done with words. Words are tools. We do our thinking in words and sentences. And salesmen must think!

IMAGINATION   Imagination is needed to enable the salesman to see problems through the eyes of the prospect and to devise means for solving them. This ability to *originate* ideas of value to their prospects is a trait of most successful salesmen. For example, a salesman for a paper products manufacturer sold a huge order of containers to a manufacturer solely on the strength of an imaginative approach. The prospect was of European origin, so the salesman wrote to a European genealogist to obtain a copy of the coat of arms of the manufacturer's family. This was incorporated in a package design which the prospect immediately favored; he gave this salesman all his business.

The imaginative real estate salesman reaps large rewards for his ideas on taking an idle property or one that is not being employed for its highest use and devising ways to increase its value. The client of one real estate salesman was stuck with an empty, unsalable 25,000-square-foot industrial building. The salesman devised a means by which the space was divided into smaller parcels that were most rentable at attractive prices and he arranged to finance the remodeling from the leases.

DETERMINATION   The sportswriters, in referring to a rookie trying to make a major league team, often comment favorably on his "desire." Every coach values this trait in a player and every sales manager values it just as highly in a salesman. It refers to his determination to succeed, to make good. The determined individual will study the fine points of the game; he will practice long and hard; he will accept coaching eagerly and not sullenly. In short, he will do everything he can to become a top-flight player. This attitude is noticeable in those who excel in any line of activity and certainly in selling.

SELF-MANAGEMENT   The salesman usually works without close supervision and must be able to manage himself. This aspect of his work is treated more fully in a later chapter, so it will be only mentioned here. Many salesmen fail because they cannot manage their time. They yield to the temptation to drop into a bar to watch television or to start their working day late and end it early. Work habits are critical to success in any endeavor.

The salesman tries to overcome these

CRITICISM OF OTHERS   Everyone knows that the person who criticizes others when talking to us will likewise criticize us when talking to others. Such people make us feel uncomfortable, and we do not like them. Sarcasm is closely related to this tendency. So is gossiping. It has been shrewdly said that we can tell more about a man by what he says about others than by what others say about him. The smart salesman refrains from criticizing others, either to their faces or behind their backs.

ARGUMENT   No sale was ever made by arguing with the buyer. Theodore Roosevelt was opposed to college or high school debating teams because he felt that they developed the argumentative attitude unduly.

CLUMSY ATTEMPTS AT HUMOR   The smart salesman never deflates a person's ego; rather, he builds it up. He knows that no man ever made a friend by making that person feel small—by puncturing his ego. Jack Benny has made millions by offering himself as the butt of all manner of jokes, and the salesman will do well to remember this and never make the prospect the object of clumsy humor. When the prospect inquires, "Do you keep Blank washing machines?" a salesman might reply, "No, madam, we don't keep them, we sell them." He may rate this as clever, but he has not advanced the sale, and perhaps he has killed it. The normal reaction would be, "OK, brother, you're going to *keep* the one we planned to buy." The lady who asked the meat-counter clerk if he had any dog bones that day did not smile when he replied, "Nope. We ain't killed any dogs today."

Some people seem to think that wisecracks at others' expense are all right among friends, even though they would not try them with strangers. But this is a poor way to *keep* friends, and no salesman can have too many friends. Anything that hurts the feelings of another should be avoided and will be avoided by the person who really likes others.

It all boils down to the fine art of making and keeping friends; nothing in the art of selling is more important than this. When possible, everyone buys from his friends. Saunders Norvell, one of the country's greatest sales-men and managers of salesmen, said, "If I were a salesman again, I would plan to get close to my customers, to make them stronger and better friends. Where a real tie of friendship exists, the rest is easy."

LAZINESS   Plain, unadulterated laziness is the downfall of more sales-men than any other personality trait. Selling is not a haven for those people seeking an easy berth in life. No purpose would be served in flogging this point, so we just mention it.

IMPATIENCE   Too many promising salesmen have jeopardized or even ruined their careers because they let impatience overrule good judgment.

Many things take some time to mature—selling abilities, large earn-ings, promotions. One young real estate salesman was doing quite well working for a leading realtor who specialized in industrial properties but he was getting only 35 percent of the total commissions on the sales he made. He listened to the offer of a small realtor who promised to give him 60 percent of his commissions. He changed to the smaller firm and found out rather quickly that 35 percent of something is more than 60 percent of nothing. He understood why he had to give his first employer 65 percent—for all the business that walked in the doors because of the realtor's repu-tation.

Many promising corporate careers are aborted when the individual becomes impatient with his progress, money, or rank and leaves for a posi-tion in some smaller organization. Sometimes the move works out, some-times not.

We conclude this discussion with the reminder that self-examination and self-improvement may turn out to be quite a project; but also that it can prove amazingly rewarding throughout life, whether we earn our living as salesmen or not.

DISCUSSION QUESTIONS
1. Can imagination be developed?
2. Why do so many salesmen use humor in their general approach to the prospect?
3. Can social intelligence be developed? If so, how?
4. Can an introverted person be a successful salesman?
5. To what extent can a person alter his personality?

6. How would you go about altering the biggest weakness you perceive in your personality?
7. Why is dominance important to a salesman?
8. Determination is highly praised as a character trait but how does one go about acquiring it if one does not already possess it?
9. What, in your opinion, would be the most serious personality defect a salesman could have?
10. Select a salesman who is quite successful and analyze his personality. Which of his personality traits contributes most to his success? What bad traits does he have?

CASE 3-1 TOM HUFF

"I need some help. Let's face it, I don't know how to sell cars. You know my situation; I've got to be number one salesman in the place or Dad will . . . well, let's not get too far into that. Will you teach me how to sell cars?" asked Tom Huff of an acquaintance, Ed Carnes, who was a noted sales trainer.

Tom was the older of the two sons of a Ford dealer in a prosperous growing town of 70,000 in the Midwest. He was twenty-five years old, married, and had a young son. He had dropped out of college for scholastic reasons, much to the consternation of his parents. Upon his marriage he took a job with a local bank but left that after a year to work in the dealership. While he also sold cars, his father placed him in charge of the distributorship for Cushman golf carts for the region. This job consisted of arranging for rental contracts with the golf clubs in the area; few personal sales were involved.

Tom made a good personal appearance; he was clean looking and dressed quite nicely. His voice and mannerisms were generally favorable. Unfortunately, Tom had gained some small reputation locally while in high school for being a bit wild. He had played basketball and football and was an excellent golfer.

Ed Carnes knew Tom through frequent contacts at the golf course and by seeing him several times a week at a local sporting goods store where they both loafed while looking for a bull session with the local sports.

Tom and Ed spent some time exchanging views. Tom admitted that his father had wanted him to return to college, but he did not want to. They recalled the previous summer when Tom had tried to sell Ed a new car; Ed ended up buying another brand. Ed said, "Well, for one thing you were selling the wrong car. I just don't want a Ford and I doubt if many of your friends want one either. They drive Caddys. So you see you've one strike on you right away; most of your natural prospects, the circle of people you know, are not good prospects for your product." Tom rallied around that point for some time, then admitted that there was little he could do about it. He had Fords to sell.

Ed asked, "Why do you feel that you must be the best salesman in the place? You don't need to be best to be a good sales manager."

"I know that, but Dad doesn't," was Tom's reply. "How about it? Will you spend some time with me? I need a prospecting system in the worst way."

"Well, I'm not sure I can really be of much help to you, but we'll see. I've got to run now. Oh! By the way, have you ever done anything about the enclosure for my golf cart that we talked about last fall? Sure would like to have it on the cart next winter. We froze several times this past winter," Ed terminated the conversation.

1. What do you suppose Ed thought about Tom's plea? What would you do? What do you suppose Ed did?
2. What is your hypothesis about Tom's difficulties?
3. What should Tom do? What will he do?

PRODUCT KNOWLEDGE

The essence of knowledge is, having it, to
apply it.
Confucius

"I lost my first account today, and it was a big one, too," moaned big Jim Perkins, a rookie salesman for a large adhesive manufacturer.

"How'd it happen?" asked a friend who sensed that Jim wanted to talk about it.

"I got too big for my britches; thought I knew everything. I recommended the wrong epoxy to them for a certain application and the result really messed up their production line. They booted me out and gave the business to a guy who knew what he was talking about. I found out that I've got a lot more to learn than I realized. I came out of training thinking that I really knew everything about adhesives."

While Jim had been given excellent introductory training, he was still not prepared to cope with the more complex problems that only experience and much additional study could solve. He found out the hard way how vital product knowledge is to successful selling—particularly industrial selling. Customers demand correct answers to their frequently complex problems; they do not continue to patronize those salesmen incapable of solving their problems.

That last clause contains the keynote of this chapter. It is not so much what or how much a salesman knows about his proposition as it is whether he can apply this product knowledge to the solution of the prospect's prob-

lems. *Every sale is, essentially, the solution of a problem.* Unless the salesman can put his product knowledge to use, he is like a chemist who knows
exactly what a drug contains, but has no notion as to what it will cure. The
physician knows this and prescribes accordingly. The salesman resembles
the physician more than he does the chemist. The doctor has studied chemistry, of course, and is familiar with the ingredients of the drugs he prescribes; but he knows them chiefly for their remedial results.

So it is with the salesman. His product knowledge has been acquired
for but one reason and with but one purpose—to enable him to prescribe
intelligently for his prospect—to *apply* it.

In this connection it is interesting to note that some companies, in
referring to product knowledge, call it "benefit facts," thus stressing the
viewpoint of the buyer instead of the seller.

APPLICATIONS

Not only must the salesman know his own business, but he is most effective when he also knows the business of his customers. Experts in the
management of salesmen claim that for maximum effectiveness a sales
force should be organized by class of customer; that is, each salesman calls
on but one type of customer. For example, Gardner-Denver Company
maintains separate sales forces to call upon contractors, mine operators,
and oil well drilling contractors; the applications of its equipment in mines
bears little similarity to the applications in an oil field. The oil field salesman must know oil field technology and the problems of the drilling contractor; he is a petroleum engineer.

There are other advantages to concentrating on but one type of customer. It is easier to become identified with that industry, to be looked
upon as being a member of the industry. When he specializes the salesman
gains an image of an expert and in this age the buyer likes to do business
with experts, not generalists. And the salesman often gets more job satisfaction when he is identified with one group of customers; his interpersonal
relationships become more rewarding.

Mastering applications takes a great deal of study and experience. The
insurance salesman who wants to do a real job of applying his product
knowledge to the needs (applications) of his customers may have to learn
about income and estate taxes, wills, trusts, corporation buy-out agreements, and other aspects of the law.

It is insufficient for a computer salesman to know how to operate his
hardware. He must also know how to apply it to the problems of his customers. He should be able to show the buyer how his inventory control can
be set up on it and how it will take care of his accounting difficulties. This
requires a great deal of knowledge of business systems and control techniques.

The salesman for Aero Commander airplanes has to know about the tax aspects of airplane ownership, means of financing them, the transportation economics of private flying versus public carriers, and the legal problems entailed in ownership of an airplane.

Many times application knowledge can seem to be rather remote from the actual product being sold. The oil company salesman calling upon dealers is required to know a great deal about the successful operation of an oil station; he is not selling gasoline but rather profits to the operator. This is true of a great many men calling upon retailers. The Weyerhaeuser salesman must know how to merchandise a lumberyard successfully; many of his dealers need help in selling wood products.

The representative of Norman Hilton, an expensive line of men's suits, taught the salesmen of his dealers how to sell expensive suits to selected customers. Not only does he know his own merchandise, but he knows what the dealer must do to sell them.

Wayne Curtis, owner of Curtis Equipment Company of Oklahoma City, sells restaurant equipment. He knows his goods but that is not all; he also knows how to set up and operate restaurants. His people plan the entire operation for the buyer and render many services not connected directly with the equipment. They view their product as being the establishment of a profitable restaurant, not merely selling the equipment that comprises it. This typifies the attitude of most successful salesmen today. They sell the end result—profits.

While a great deal of application knowledge can be taught in sales training, still there are many things that can be learned only through experience. This is one of the advantages the experienced salesman has over the rookie. The only advice that can be tendered to the "rook" is to dig into the customer's business and learn everything he can about his problems. And he should keep right on digging as long as he is a salesman.

DOES THE RETAIL SALESMAN NEED PRODUCT KNOWLEDGE?

In these days when product knowledge is disseminated by advertising, when more stores are converting to self-service, when so many goods are sold in containers bearing product information, it may appear unnecessary for retail salesmen to know much about the products they sell. Yet there are several cogent reasons why the retail salesman should strive to expand his knowledge of the products he handles.

Perhaps as important as any is the fact that such study will make his work infinitely more enjoyable. Psychologists lay great stress on the point that satisfaction in one's work is the basis of personal happiness. Those persons who dislike their jobs are maladjusted, they tend to become mental cases, they compensate for their frustrations during working hours by kicking the family spaniel, slapping the children, and growling at the wife.

Hobbies sometimes relieve the pressure for such persons and render them fairly fit to live with, but they would be happier and pleasanter if they could make a hobby of their work, too.

There are many salesmen who study the thing they are selling until it does become a hobby. They love the goods they handle because they know their history and their devious routes in reaching the ultimate buyer. They know what the goods will do; they delight in telling the story to others, partly because this affords them an opportunity to assume the role of an expert authority.

One seldom becomes enthusiastic about something concerning which he is ignorant; but almost anyone generates enthusiasm for a subject about which he knows a great deal. Therefore, if a man is destined to spend his working hours selling shoes, he could make his labors much less wearisome if he would set himself to learn as much as he possibly could about shoes and how to fit them properly. This latter involves foot health and comfort, as well as the fashion factor.

There is always the chance that a more thorough knowledge of the products he is selling may result in his promotion, whether within the store where he is working or to a better post with some manufacturer or wholesaler.

Even though this fails to occur, he may build up a more enjoyable type of job right where he is. Take, for example, a salesman in a men's haberdashery. He may spend his life doling out shirts, ties, and socks; or he may devote most of his time to filling phone and mail orders from customers who depend on him to choose the right articles for them. In this way he is able to function as an expert stylist, to employ his talents to the full. He becomes, in effect, the manager of his own business, looked up to by his clientele and by his colleagues.

A thorough knowledge of merchandise enables a salesman to sell much more and thus earn more. This is due to several factors.

First, he can justify the higher prices for products bearing these prices. The ignorant clerk, when asked why a certain watch cost more than another, replied, "It's better. It must be, because it costs more." Quality goods require expert selling, because the buyer must have reasons for spending the additional amount involved. Also, the buyer of such products is usually accustomed to expert service and is inclined to be intolerant of slipshod selling.

Second, a knowledge of his proposition inspires the salesman with confidence in himself. Authorities on selling have written a great deal on this theme, pointing out that when a salesperson radiates confidence he kindles the same emotion in his prospect.

As to the desirability of obtaining the customer's confidence, it should be pointed out that one unanswered query is sufficient to destroy this confidence in the mind of the buyer. The salesman may answer two of every three questions asked, or nine out of every ten, and yet the one *unanswered* query will awaken doubt as to his ability to speak with authority. This is true in *every* type of selling—not only in retail selling.

Sometimes the benefits of complete product knowledge have a sort of delayed action, as shown by the experience of a woman who went shopping for a sewing machine. She wanted a portable, priced at under $50, and planned to look at several makes. She started at the Singer store and was given a thorough demonstration, during which the salesman dwelt at length on the superiority of the rotary bobbin. He answered all questions fully and cheerfully. But the shopper announced, "I want to look around some more before I buy."

She shopped several other stores, but in an hour she was back at the Singer store and bought the $179 machine she had looked at. What had changed her mind? Product knowledge! This the other salesmen lacked. "Why did you go to all that trouble to demonstrate your machine when I was here an hour ago?" she asked the Singer salesman. "You knew I was not going to buy then." He replied, "I knew that I might not sell you, of course, but I also knew that if I gave you a thorough demonstration I'd be making it mighty hard for other salesmen to sell you because you would know more about sewing machines than most of them would."

Third, the salesman who knows his merchandise is better able to provide the goods that will suit the customer. After all, the function of the salesman is just that, and he can scarcely perform this function efficiently unless he is completely familiar with every item in stock.

A knowledge of buying motives is vital, but the salesman cannot make an effective appeal to the right buying motives unless he knows a great deal about the uses and the performance of his product. In other words, *he cannot fit the product to the prospect's needs unless he knows his product thoroughly.*

For example, a good life insurance salesman knows that there are 25 or 30 different ways in which life insurance can be utilized; the salesman who knows only 10 ways will lose many sales because he is often unable to present the proposals which will best meet the prospects' needs.

Fourth, the salesman who knows his product thoroughly is never at a loss for strong talking points, especially for those last, clinching points that must be found to close the sale. And he can answer every question and meet every objection raised by the customer.

A final reason why the salesman should know his proposition is that most people would never discover the values in many products unless these were pointed out. This is true for two reasons.

In the first place, many values are hidden from sight, or at least are not obvious. The salesman who sold a spring-tooth lawn rake made a sale

because he pointed out that the rake was made by a manufacturer of quality saws who used the same grade of finely tempered steel in these rakes.
To demonstrate this claim the salesman bent the teeth far back and let
them spring into place again. This was a telling point to the customer who
was buying the rake because six teeth in his old rake had broken off.

In the second place, many of us don't fully appreciate what we do see.
From a mail-order catalogue we reprint a partial description of a boudoir
chair:

. . . hot-glued corner blocks lock frame securely; solid oak frame throughout;
glued grooved dowel pins hold all joints rigid, add strength at points of strain;
fabric sewn around strong cord on all outside seams gives tailored appearance; painstaking hand-finished edges and corners for neat appearance; seat
has no-sag steel springs that give you much better and longer lasting comfort;
amply padded throughout; button-tufted seat.

Here is a description of a shovel:

Blades are forged from high-carbon steel, heat-treated and tempered. Thick
center frog or ridge assures greatest strength. Blade and front strap formed as
one unit; back strap electrically welded to blade. Pre-formed front strap for
correct balance and "hang." Straps are heat-treated, high-carbon steel. Factory tests prove that these shovels can withstand extreme weight without frac-
ture. Handles are of select, straight-grained ash; sanded, waxed and polished
for comfortable grip. Handles are driven into blade to point of frog. Steel
armor completely surrounds the "D" handles, protecting them against
weather.

How many salesmen in a retail store could offer as convincing descrip-
tions? But it would be good salesmanship, because few customers would
ever discover all these features without having them pointed out.

If the reader will pause for a moment at this point and think of the two
or three best retail salespeople he knows and reflect on this particular aspect of their efficiency, he will discover that every one of them measures up
fully to an exacting standard in his knowledge of merchandise. Various
surveys have been conducted in which students "shopped" certain salespeople chosen because of their excellent selling records, and *in every case*
these superior salespeople were found to be genuine experts in the
products they were handling.

The importance of product knowledge on the part of retail salesmen in
hardware stores is stressed continually by the editors of *Hardware Age*. For
example, from one issue we quote:

Ask your star salesgirl: "Which kind of skillet is best for use on an electric
range?" or how many minutes it takes to cook vegetables in a pressure
cooker, or what size roaster is needed for a 22-pound turkey?

If a blank stare instead of an informed reply is your answer, you need to do one of three things:

First, sell cookware at cost to your salesmen to take home and use, so that they will really know what they are selling.

Second, call in wholesaler or manufacturer salesmen to conduct training clinics on the uses of their lines.

Or, have your staff spend every possible moment reading labels, fact-tags, and guarantees.

How many pieces of glass ovenware have you taken back and thrown away because your salespersons did not know enough to warn customers that the item wasn't for use on an open flame?

How many of your staff can set up and operate a pressure cooker?

The reason for big sales in small wares (cutlery, flatware, gadgets) is informed selling. How does a roast slicer differ from a ham slicer? How do I change blades in this can opener?

Learn comparative values of carbon steel, stainless steel, vanadium steel, chrome steel, serration, and hollow grinding.

How are you fixed for product knowledge on cleaning aids? Do you know a bathtub brush from a bowl brush? Could you tell a customer how to use a liquid or powdered rug shampoo? Do you know why some floor waxes won't work on asphalt tile?

You might get up a quiz about products, as: "Most rolling pins are made of: ash, maple, tulip, pine."

Can your salespeople explain how many pounds of grass seed, lime, or clover seed are needed for a 10 × 10 foot plot, or for a half acre? Do they know how big a half acre is?

Helping the retail clerk to know products

Because of the multiplicity of articles that the average retail clerk has to handle, it is extremely difficult to know the exact details of materials and methods of manufacture of each.

Some manufacturers help by printing factual selling points on the package or on a tag attached to the merchandise. Others, whose products are displayed on counter cards or racks, print selling helps on the backs of these cards where the salesperson can read them.

Capitalizing on the quiz-program idea, Carson Pirie Scott & Co. of Chicago inaugurated the plan of stimulating as well as amusing their retail and wholesale sales forces by pitting one section of a department against another in contests to determine the product knowledge of the employees. Salespeople submit questions from which those used in the program are selected. A typical question: "Is it true or false that white rayon will launder without turning yellow?" Another question stumped a store executive: "Name a department other than the regular playclothes section where women's slacks can be found." The executives of the company report that the plan has proved valuable for two reasons—it increases product knowledge generally, and it forces the clerks to take a greater interest in their merchandise. It has definitely increased the customers' confidence in the clerks.

The urgent need for retail salespeople who know the merchandise they are selling is recognized by manufacturers, and many of them are striving by every possible means to educate these salespeople in product knowledge.

The Radiant Manufacturing Corporation of Chicago issued a 16-page booklet entitled, "Know Your Stuff" which told about the projection screens made by the company. They followed this up with a contest among retail salespeople based on their ability to answer promptly and properly any one question propounded to them by long-distance phone from the manufacturer. Prizes were generous and several thousand salespeople entered the contest.

The Mohawk Carpet Mills, Inc. stages educational clinics for retail floor covering salesmen, these clinics being held at the factory and lasting for three and one-half days. Thousands of retail salesmen have availed themselves of this educational opportunity, which includes escorted tours through the company's woolen yarn mill, spinning mill, dye house, chenille mill, Wilton carpet mill, tapestry and velvet mill, and Axminster mill, in addition to the various lectures and conferences. A textbook is furnished each "student" and the lectures are all taken down and reproduced for him, the net result being that he returns to his job with a greatly expanded ability to help his customers in their selection of floor coverings.

Among the devices employed by enterprising manufacturers to teach retail salespeople more about their products are the following:

Training manuals.

Periodical bulletins.

House magazine aimed at retailers and clerks.

Tags on the merchandise, each tag containing brief, vital information about the product.

Meeting of retailers' salespeople addressed by manufacturer's traveling salesman.

Portfolio containing diagrams, pictures, coming national advertisements, and other material, for use by the salesman who is to do this educational job.

Motion pictures showing the way the product is made or used. Such a movie may serve almost as well as a trip to the factory or to inspect some installation of the product.

Talking slides. These are not so expensive as movies and may sometimes serve the purpose almost as well.

Correspondence courses, to enable the salesman to study at home.

Some firms have devised questions to be answered by the salesman, those salesmen turning in the best answers being awarded cash prizes. The questions deal with the product's selling features.

The traveling demonstrator is used by some firms, this individual going from store to store and demonstrating the product. When Toni was first brought out, many retailers doubted that a home permanent could be satisfactory and they would not stock the item. So the Toni salesmen were instructed to give permanents to salesgirls in the stores. Their enthusiasm was so great that the stores agreed to handle Toni and the girls sold it with authority sponsored by their own knowledge of what the product would do.

Many advertisements in business papers are quite frankly addressed to retail salespeople, the purpose being to provide them with more product information.

SALESMEN CALLING ON EXPERT BUYERS

If retail salespeople need product knowledge, salesmen calling on professional buyers and selling complicated products need it even more. Purchasing agents are expert buyers, and it is a truism that "it takes an expert to sell an expert."

An electrical engineer for a steel company was discussing a 2,000-horse power induction motor which the salesman recommended for a rolling mill drive. "What's your air gap between rotor and stator?" asked the engineer. The salesman didn't know. "Well, I have several other questions to ask, but it looks as if that wouldn't get us anywhere. Good-by."

Many professional buyers assert that the greatest weakness of the salesmen calling on them is their lack of product knowledge.

A purchasing agent for a chain of hotels asserts:

The word "selling" is a misnomer as far as the job of calling on institutions goes. Salesmen who cover institutions should put *service* first, and their products should help us to perform our own functions better within our hotel. This selling involves knowledge of product technicalities. You'll find that most of these salesmen haven't the first inkling of their own product's technical aspects. Interrupt their canned speech to ask a technical question, and they're lost.

As an example he cited the case of the wastebasket salesman who called on him recently. A wastebasket in a hotel room takes a terrific walloping. It must withstand the shock of broken bottles tossed into it and resist burning cigarette butts. It must be waterproof to keep liquids from oozing onto expensive carpeting.

The salesman extolled the attractiveness and reasonable price of the basket.

"But what gauge is the metal? What adhesive is used to stick the leatherette to the metal?" he was asked. "Would a good squirt of seltzer soak it off?"

Salesman's reply: "Huh?"

"It's hard to believe in this modern age of sales training," this p.a. says, "but most salesmen seem to have been told if they call on enough people every day, they are bound to make a couple of sales. Yet the *successful* salesman knows his product, knows his home plant and its manufacturing processes. He can quote prices. He can answer questions. He's a walking encyclopedia on his product. And why not? His living depends on selling it."

Much of the friction between salesmen and professional buyers is due to the salesman's lack of knowledge of both his prospect and his own products. The mention of purchasing agent, department store buyer, or chain store buyer to many salesmen is a signal for a wry face. They consider the professional buyer as a petty clerk, skilled in the art of haggling and "chiseling," a man whose digestion never was right and who would not want it right if it could be right. He plays favorites and expects graft. But the man who is really worthy of the name salesman usually has a different point of view. Professional buyers spend millions of dollars every year; they must know what they are buying or their firms lose money. This knowledge, furthermore, must be more than superficial. Consequently, they lack patience with the salesman who is too lazy to study what he should know most about.

Harry Erlicher, general purchasing agent for General Electric, sees over 10,000 salesmen every year and has formed definite ideas about their strong and weak points. He says:

In my opinion, the Number One qualification for a salesman is "Know your product"; the Number Two qualification is "Help the buyer." If you have these qualifications, you cannot fail to impress the buyer and the men in the factory who have so much to say about what equipment shall be used. . . . A salesman must keep posted and up to date on what is constantly being done by his engineering and research departments. We like to see the salesman who can present new ideas, keep us honestly informed as to market conditions, and, last, but not least, help out on special or unusual problems. . . . In what respect is your apparatus superior to your competitor's for the particular job? Why did your engineers decide upon the best material regardless of cost, such as stainless steel; or where a stamping might have proved satisfactory but a forging was decided upon to obtain a higher safety factor? Are you familiar with the safeguards taken by your engineers to make certain that materials used in your apparatus best serve a given purpose? Do you know of the test methods followed to be certain that all shipments from suppliers are up to the required quality standard? Are you familiar with the precision standards which are established for all moving parts and with the test methods and costly instruments which are employed for checking the accuracy of these parts? . . . I wish to stress particularly that it is most important for the salesman to learn everything he can about products he is selling *and their application*, so as to be able not only to answer questions but to advance valuable and pertinent information that will sell his products to the buyer.

There are indications that, in the past few years, salesmen calling on purchasing agents are receiving better grounding in product knowledge. *Purchasing* magazine queried a good-sized sample of its readers on this point and learned that 77 percent of them report that the salesmen calling on them are better trained technically. But about half of them assert that the salesmen are not yet trained to make intelligent, helpful contributions to their cost-reduction programs. That is, the salesmen cannot *apply* their knowledge to the solution of their prospects' problems.

Specific vs. vague statements

The accurate knowledge of his proposition enables a salesman to make specific statements in place of vague, general ones.

Many statements sound specific when as a matter of fact they are not. The salesman for a small car might say, "This car will run 20 miles on every gallon of gas." (This sounds specific but it could be more so.) "Compared with a car that delivers 15 miles per gallon you save 50 cents every 100 miles. If you drive 10,000 miles a year that's $50. You can buy quite a bit with $50 even these days."

Incidentally, two oft-used words in a salesman's vocabulary are "for instance." He uses them because they promise something *specific*. He *avoids* the use of such general words as economical, automatic, efficient, modern, attractive. He tries to define each of such words in *specific* terms. "Economical" becomes "$3.20 per month saved."

The sales manual put out by a meat packer has this to say to the company's salesmen:

If a buyer asks how many pounds of corned beef he should order to serve 200 people, the salesman should be able to tell him. He should be able to tell him how many portions he will get out of a 20-pound turkey, how many 10-ounce steaks from a 20-pound strip; what an 85-cent rib will cost him for an 8-ounce portion.

The need for being specific in dealing with industrial purchasing agents has prompted some salesmen to concentrate on one *industry* at a time, studying the problems of that industry intensively and, armed with this specific information, to direct a selling campaign at prospects in that industry. For example, a salesman for conveyor belts used in factories might study iron foundries until he had a firm grasp of their problems; then he could call for a time principally on iron foundries. While he was working on this list of prospects, he could be preparing himself to make calls on the buyers in plants assembling radio receiving sets.

As has previously been pointed out, some salesmen are assigned only to certain industries, but the foregoing is presented as a sort of compromise plan to be employed by companies which cannot specialize so minutely.

WHAT SHOULD YOU KNOW?

The answer that readily suggests itself is "everything." But it is impossible for any man to know everything about anything. The problem is one of degree. The wholesale hardware or drug salesman, with 50,000 items in his catalogue, can scarcely be expected to keep in mind their prices, to say nothing of detailed facts concerning their production. The retail clerk in a drug, grocery, furniture, jewelry, or general store is in much the same predicament. The specialty salesman, however, should aim to become a real authority in his more limited field, as he will be expected to know every detail about it.

Consider the case of the salesman selling one specialty. What facts ought he to know in order to be a good salesman?

History of the firm

The salesman should know something of the firm's history, for these reasons: (1) It enables him to converse intelligently with older buyers who have had dealings with the firm for many years and like to reminisce. If the salesman cannot show some knowledge of these earlier years, he has lost a valuable point of contact with many prospects. (2) It gives him a feeling of "belonging" to the organization if he has in mind the background of its inception and growth. It makes for greater loyalty and interest on his part; unless he knows the "old man" and the other executives, at least by reputation gained through reading and inquiring about them, he cannot feel himself a part of the organization or appear to his prospects as an integral part of it. It can build an image in the mind of the prospect that the company is the type of organization with which he wants to do business.

The firm's policies

Every article is a product of three factors: raw materials, labor, and capital in the form of buildings and machinery. The salesman should know the *policies* behind the product because it will reflect them. As to the raw materials, he should know whether they are the best obtainable or merely the best for the price paid. The processes of inspection should be known to him.

As to labor, he should know whether the employees are well paid and efficient or poorly paid and probably inefficient. The quality of the product may be dependent in large measure on the skill and care of the workmen producing it, as no amount of inspection can detect the results of indifferent work. The working conditions may affect the product materially. Good light may improve the accuracy of machine work; adequate ventilation results in cleaner food products; and clothing produced in factories where the health of workers is guarded should be of better grade and more sanitary than that produced in tenement homes.

A knowledge of the firm's policy as to financing enables the salesman to answer questions about it to prove that it is sound, solvent, likely to continue in business. Many buyers hesitate to deal with a concern that is unknown or of doubtful stability, as they fear that deliveries cannot be made according to contract. Besides, retailers or wholesalers do not wish to go to the expense of developing a demand for a product only to have it withdrawn from the market by the failure of the producing concern.

Production methods

Obviously, every salesman should know something of the processes through which the product passes in the factory. A salesman, when the buyer objects that the price is too great for such a small article, may save the situation by his thorough knowledge of the manufacturing process. When he finishes his detailed account of the way the article is made, the buyer has been enlightened and is ready to concede that the price is reasonable, after all.

A knowledge of the raw materials used should be exhaustive. The sources of these materials must be studied, the salesman's aim being to make himself an authority on their supply, the demand for them, and their probable price trend in the future. In cooperation with the purchasing agent of his firm, he can do this and make himself of real service to his customers.

We are not keenly interested in the process of manufacture involved in turning out a magazine, a package of dog food, or a pair of socks; but when we buy a technical product, as many purchasing agents do, we insist on knowing a great many details about how it is made and tested.

A writer in the magazine *Industrial Marketing* broadcasts a plaint that he often cannot tell which one of numerous competing products is the best. He cannot afford to test them all and is forced to "depend on the selling abilities of the company and of the salesman. This opens up a wide approach to selling—but it must be selling of the highest type. It must be selling based on helpful ideas, on service, on integrity, on straight-shoot-ing."

This frank confession of a purchasing agent reveals the dependence of even expert buyers on salesmen whom they can trust. And such trust is based on the salesman's *knowledge* and on his *integrity*. But first, he must possess the knowledge of what he is selling and how it can benefit the buyer.

Service
Of critical importance in many sales is the availability of excellent servicing facilities. The customer wants to know what service the company stands prepared to render him should something go wrong with the product. Many times the salesman himself should be able to correct minor difficul-ties so that the customer is not bothered with calling for service. The indus-trial salesman in particular will find that the servicing facilities behind his sales are critical to his success; hence, he had better be well versed concern-ing them.

Distribution
The salesman should understand the distribution policies for his product. Through what channels is it distributed? Why? What is the company's policy on exclusive dealerships? Selective distribution? Can he sell to dis-counters and chains? How much protection will the company give its deal-ers?

He should know the firm's pricing policies. Is resale price maintenance attempted? What discounts are available to the buyer? What are the terms of sale? Are proposals for special deals entertained? Is preticketing avail-able?

The company's promotional program can be of special interest. What advertising efforts support the product's sale? Are advertising allowances available? What promotional assistance is given?

What is the firm's brand policy? Will the company make private brands? For whom? Are there multiple brands available?

The sales representative should understand the basic strategy of the product's marketing program. To what markets is the item aimed? What are the basic motives underlying the demand for it? Who is apt to be its best customer? When will it be purchased? Where is it bought? How do people go about buying it? What image is the company trying to project?

Competition
Almost inevitably the salesman will encounter competition. The wise buyer looks at all the leading brands before making a decision. Many times he

asks, "What makes your product better than that one?" An intelligent, honest answer had better be forthcoming. The salesman must know what his product has to offer that is not available in competitive products. Conversely, he should know what the competitor offers that he cannot. This will enable him to know what the buyer has been told and what he will have to overcome if he is to make the sale.

Obviously, prices of competitive items should be known. Just what price is the salesman selling against? If he does not have such information, it is all too easy to bluff him in negotiations. The author was neatly handled by an alert car salesman from whom he was trying to buy a car. "I can get a new Olds for $4,200" was the claim.

The tactful reply was, "You'd better take the deal quick before that salesman finds the error in his figures. That car cost them $4,430 by their own price lists! And I would carefully examine *exactly* what equipment is on the car that they are quoting you. You know that old trick."

Without such knowledge of competitive products, policies, and prices, the salesman is at the mercy of the buyer who tries to exaggerate the merits of another product or the deal being offered him by competition. Knowing that the buyer is either lying or in error gives the salesman the strength to stay in the negotiations and stick tight to his proposition.

Delivery

Promptness is an important consideration with many buyers. The salesmen for Johnson & Johnson, manufacturers of over 500 products in the surgical and drug supply field, are instructed to promise the customer: "Every order you send us will be filled, checked, and loaded within four hours after it enters our plant."

The salesman may often help his prospect by offering suggestions as to whether the goods should be shipped by rail, truck, or air. He should also be familiar with rates, classifications, routes, packing, etc. The prospect may apply such knowledge to the shipment of items other than those sold by this particular salesman.

The uses of the product

Some firms have conducted contests, offering prizes to customers who sent in the longest or most original list of uses, these ideas being utilized by the salesmen and in the firm's advertising. The salesman should, where practicable, picture his prospect as using the article, and a wide knowledge of its various uses provides talking points for selling to prospects with varied tastes, interests, and problems. Many concerns maintain research departments whose function it is to discover or devise new ways in which their products can be used.

Technical details of the product

We cannot itemize all the details a salesman must know about his product or product line, for such a list would naturally vary with the type of goods he is selling. However, the beginnings of a generalized list can be attempted here.

MATERIALS   The salesman should know exactly what materials the products are made of and what characteristics they possess. An aluminum salesman was able to sell his material to a manufacturer of fence hardware by proving that a certain special alloy would have the necessary strength, yet be lighter and rustproof. Prior to that time certain parts had been made out of steel because the manufacturer believed that aluminum was too soft for the job. A furniture salesman lost a sizable sale when his customers discovered he did not know his woods; he tried to convince them that a certain wood was cherry when it was walnut, as inspection of the tag later indicated.

In these days of synthetic fabrics, a salesman who knows the advantages and disadvantages of each is in a position to earn the respect and loyal patronage of customers who are unable to keep up to date on the frequent changes in the field.

A printing salesman lost a large sale of letterheads when he said that he did not know what the customer wanted when he specified a "laid finish." Later he found out, but it was too late; another, better-informed salesman had beaten him to the order.

PERFORMANCE DATA   Just what will the various products do? How fast will they run? How much weight or stress will they stand? How long will they last? How much fuel is required? How much maintenance do they require? How easy is it to repair the products? What is their output per dollar input or per hour or per anything else that is relevant? What is their efficiency or ratio of output to input? These are just some of the questions to which the salesman must have ready answers. The performance factor is especially critical in the sale of industrial products for, after all, that is exactly what the industrial firm is buying—a certain performance. One salesman for an electronics firm persuaded a large aircraft company to use a certain item in one of its missiles when he stressed the low amperage his unit used. He knew, from talking with the company's engineers, that the current demands by all the various electronic devices in the missile were already straining the power source's capacity. Had he not been aware of this performance advantage of his unit, he would have lost the sale because his unit cost was $400 more than that of the closest competing product.

PHYSICAL SIZE AND SHAPE CHARACTERISTICS   The same electronics salesman sold another electronic product to another aircraft company for its drone missile for a price $600 higher than the nearest competitor when he stressed the smaller physical size of his unit. As in most missiles, space was at a premium, and his product knowledge paid off.

HOW IT OPERATES   The salesman should be an expert in operating his products. One salesman for a reproducing machine lost a customer when he failed to operate the machine properly during a demonstration. The customer felt that if the salesman had trouble operating it, he would doubtless have even more. He bought a competing machine from a salesman who made its operation seem simple.

UNIQUE MECHANICAL FEATURES   Usually a machine possesses some unique features which set it off from the competition. These exclusive features are usually stressed in the presentation. Hence, it is necessary that the salesman know with complete thoroughness the exact nature of these unique features, their operation, and why they are important to the customer. Also he should know what unique features are possessed and stressed by his competition and should be prepared to show the prospect why these other features are not so important to him or how his product meets these problems satisfactorily.

Can a salesman know too much about his proposition?

Some managers believe that it is possible for a salesman to know too much about his proposition.

A sales manager for a firm selling mining machinery and other highly technical products told the authors that he was through hiring engineers to sell his products. He had proceeded on the assumption that the chief requisite for successful selling was to know all about the product; but he had come to the conclusion that this was not the most important, after all. He stated that his engineer-salesmen put the emphasis in the wrong place, that they insisted on *arguing* technical principles of construction with their prospects instead of finding out what the prospects wanted and then selling them machinery embodying those features. In other words, these men did not have the selling viewpoint. All they saw was the machine.

All this should not be interpreted to mean that engineers cannot be good salesmen or that highly technical products should not be sold by salesmen with technical training. Thousands of engineers are excellent salesmen—indeed, this type of selling is considered just about the highest to which any salesman can aspire. The foregoing discussion is intended merely to stress the point that the wise salesman utilizes his product knowledge *to help the prospect buy wisely* and not for the purpose of showing off his own technical erudition.

One veteran salesman, to whom was put the query, "Is it possible to know too much about what you are selling?" offered a reply that seems to meet the situation precisely. "No," he said, "but it is possible to talk too much about it." This distinction is at the root of the entire discussion. It is not possible to know too much about one's proposition, but it is easily possible to talk so much about it that one becomes a bore. The same is true of anything—music, art, the drama, literature, golf, travel, or one's precocious children. The *selling viewpoint* consists in considering first the prospect and trying to find out what he hopes your product can do for him. If this selling viewpoint is maintained, there is little danger of knowing too much about what one has to sell.

One sales manager put the idea neatly when he said, "The typical prospect is interested in just one thing—what the item you are selling *will do for him.*" If this idea or viewpoint seems to be overemphasized in this book, it is because too many salesmen *under*emphasize it. Most of us are pretty self-centered.

Sources of salesman's product knowledge

An interesting anecdote is related about Daniel Webster. He had just completed his famous reply to Hayne, which in essence was a defense of the United States Constitution. An enthusiastic listener said to him, "Mr. Webster, that was a marvelous speech. How long did it take you to prepare it?" "All my life," was the brief but pointed reply. What did he mean? As a matter of fact he had spoken almost extemporaneously with little or no preparation for that particular talk. However, he had become so familiar with the subject through a lifetime of study that he could talk fluently about it at any time. So it is with the salesman who really knows his product.

Therefore it seems that the first and most important source of product information must be actual experience. Still, this often takes so long to acquire that it is out of the question for many new salesmen. Obviously, also, it is necessary to give most beginning salesmen some product knowledge before actual selling work starts. What, then, are the best sources of product knowledge in addition to the facts gained from actual experience? The best ones appear to be (1) libraries and general reading; (2) educational institutions such as high schools, colleges and universities, commercial schools, and correspondence schools; (3) the company sales manual and sales portfolio; (4) the company training course; (5) miscellaneous follow-up instruction from the company; and (6) trade journals.

THE LIBRARY   Here is a much neglected source of product knowledge. There are books written on every conceivable topic and product; these can provide a wealth of background and technical information about the product, its industry, and the customer's industries. A regular reading of the trade journals relevant to the products and industries involved will pay handsome dividends.

EDUCATIONAL INSTITUTIONS   This source of product knowledge is the one that, next to the library, is least utilized by salesmen as a group. However, such educational institutions as business schools, commercial colleges, correspondence schools, and some colleges and universities offering night work and extension courses provide valuable educational material in practically any desired field. The extension courses of the "correspondence" type in particular adapt themselves most satisfactorily to the needs of the salesman living in the smaller cities and towns, since the work may be done in spare time with a minimum of inconvenience and cost.

A new space salesman for a newspaper took some night courses in advertising to learn more about his business. A real estate salesman took a course on income tax to become expert on the tax aspects of real estate investments.

THE SALES MANUAL   The sales manual, often referred to as the "salesman's Bible," is a company publication planned to give the salesmen helpful information about their product or line and the proper procedure to follow in all relationships with the firm, such as making out orders, keeping expense accounts, the daily work reports, handling of credits, adjustments, and similar matters. These manuals run the gamut from brief, simple little mimeographed presentations all the way to elaborately printed, illustrated, and bound volumes. But all of them contain product information. Some are veritable treatises in engineering, replete with complicated graphs and tables. A few are tossed together by someone in the head office, while others are produced by firms that specialize in compiling sales manuals. In passing, it may be remarked that any salesman can profit by examining the sales manuals of several concerns, especially those in lines related to the one he is selling.

The sales *portfolio* is distinguished from the manual in that it is planned to be *shown to the customer,* whereas the manual is usually designed only for the education of the salesman and not as a visual aid in the interview.

THE COMPANY TRAINING COURSE   This may be taken either by correspondence or in person. All such training seems to come under one or more of three types: telling, showing, or discussing. The chief weakness of the correspondence type of training course is that it must confine itself largely to telling. In spite of this handicap, many such courses are made highly interesting and instructive by the liberal use of illustrations that go far toward introducing the second phase—showing. If the instructor is smart, he will carry on a lively personal correspondence with his better pupils, thus injecting into the course the third element—discussion.

If the course is administered by correspondence the lessons are usually brief and the questions to be answered are easy. The problem in administering such a course is not to prepare the course but to persuade the salesmen to take it. As one veteran salesman puts it, "In no other profession save that of salesmanship do the men who engage in it put up such a determined fight against instruction." One of the reasons why so many firms prefer college men as salesmen is that these men have formed the habit of studying.

The Ralston Purina Co. maintains a huge farm with 26,000 animals on it that is used in part as a training school for salesmen. A salesman after a period of training here is better qualified to go out and talk with intelligence about the problems of feeding livestock—has he not fed them himself and watched the results? He knows that the claims made by the company are true because he has weighed many animals and recorded the gains in weight.

Here is a true story about a graduate of the University of Illinois. This young man specialized in animal husbandry in the College of Agriculture, taking many courses in veterinary science, and when he was graduated he took a job selling livestock feeds to farmers for the Ralston Purina Co. One day he called on a hog raiser—one of the biggest buyers of hog feeds in that part of the state. The farmer was not interested in Purina products. While our young salesman was talking with him, one of his hogs lay down and died in the mud right in front of them. "Worms," said the salesman. "No such thing!" said the farmer. "I've had my hogs tested for worms and they don't have any." "Give me a sharp knife and let's see," suggested the newly graduated youngster. So he performed an autopsy on that porker and revealed that it was full of worms.

His next step was an offer of *service.* He said, "Now lets de-worm the rest of your hogs before you lose any more of them. I'll hang around and help you do it." He spent the best part of three days helping with this rather unpleasant chore, then made bold to suggest that the farmer would be wise to put a solid floor on his pens so that the hogs could live under cleaner conditions. By this time, the hog raiser was somewhat humbled and genuinely grateful; so he promised to make this improvement. Then, without being asked, he came across with this startling proposition: "Young fellow, you know hogs. You know things that I had never learned. I'd like your advice on how I should feed my hogs."

Of course, he became one of the biggest buyers of Purina hog feed and, through his influence, almost an assistant salesman to our young friend. Two factors built this and the resulting sales: product knowledge and service to the prospect—a solid foundation for almost any successful career in selling.

The Burroughs Corporation, maker of office machines, puts its sales-men through a correspondence course requiring from four to six months to complete, all of which is devoted to instructions concerning the products to be sold. Then the salesmen are brought into the factory for another course dealing with the same subject.

The National Cash Register Company offers its trainees a fine corre-spondence course on knowing the product, this course being taken while the student is learning other phases of the business as an employee of a branch office. If he does well on his preliminary work, he is brought in to the factory for more intensive schooling.

The United States Steel Corporation has its trainees spend weeks in the plants, observing the processes of manufacture. Teaching manuals are also used.

The International Business Machines Corporation alternates between on-the-job and formal training for a year and a half before trainees are classified as junior salesmen. A new trainee works in a branch office for two months, getting acquainted with the line. He is then brought in to head-quarters for a three-month course in product and product application. Classroom instruction is supplemented with factory visits.

Xerox maintains excellent sales training facilities at several locations in the country that not only provide the initial six weeks' training given to new salesmen, but also furnish continual training for experienced sales-men.

Belknap, Inc., a hardware wholesaler in Louisville, Kentucky, puts new salesmen to work in the warehouse until they learn the product line.

Many new salesmen begin their careers in the plant to learn about the product. The South Wind division of Stewart Warner sent all its new men to the service department from which they could not leave until they could take apart and reassemble the company's products.

Frequently it is not convenient or feasible for all salesmen to visit or work in the factory, but the factory may be brought to them by movies and other visual aids.

The training of salesmen in product knowledge is a never-ending proj-ect. No matter how thoroughly a salesman may have been trained when he was first employed, he must continually be retrained in new methods that have been adopted or new products that are being brought out. The real salesman is forever a learner.

We keep returning to the theme with which this chapter began: "The essence of knowledge is, having it, to apply it."

A duplicating machine salesman labored through a long, technical pitch about careful machining, case-hardened gears, precise feeding mechanism, guaranteed-perfect register, ability to print on heavy stock or onionskin paper—proving beyond doubt that his product was as good as the factory could make it. The prospect said, "It looks like a fine machine, but I don't think we need one." The salesman had made no attempt to ascertain the number of forms, letters, price lists, or bulletins which had to be duplicated regularly by his prospect's firm. He failed to apply his product knowledge.

The salesmen for a quality motor truck could talk for hours about the engineering and construction features of their product, but they did not really begin to sell until they were taught to show the prospect he could save 1½ cents a mile by using their truck. "The essence of knowledge is to apply it."

An interesting example of product knowledge and the fitting of this knowledge to the needs of the prospect is the following:

A man wanted to buy a home for his family but was not obtaining from the real estate salesmen the information he felt he needed. Finally, he fell into the hands of a real salesman, who showed him a house and then surprised his prospect with this approach. "This is a fine house, but I'll have to know more about you and your family before we can decide whether you'll be happy here." He asked the ages of the children, then checked his notebook. He pointed out that in a similar age group there were six youngsters, four boys and two girls, in fourteen of the houses of the development that had already been sold. Since the prospect had one child, a toddler, he told him the name and address of the nearest nursery school. Then he tackled other problems, showing the prospect on a city map the most efficient route for getting to and from the office. Other helpful information was added until the prospect felt that he could clearly picture just what it would be like living in that home. So he bought.

A carpeting salesman, selling to dealers, decided to take the factory course in carpet laying. He was amazed at how much there was to learn about what certain carpets would and would not do under various conditions. He could now measure a church or other potential area and prescribe the best type of carpet. Besides, he could compute costs and make a definite bid right there. His sales soared as he became known as an expert advisor—all because he took a course in how to lay carpet.

DISCUSSION QUESTIONS

1. The lack of product knowledge exposes the salesman to what risks during the sale?
2. How do retailers give their salespeople product information?

3. What should a men's shoe salesman know about shoes?
4. Can you think of any type of selling in which product knowledge is more important than personality?
5. Why is product knowledge more important today than it was several years ago?
6. Why do many customers become antagonistic toward salesmen lacking product knowledge?
7. Under what circumstances would the salesman play down the technical aspects of the product?
8. What is the difference between product and application knowledge?
9. How does a salesman learn about application problems?
10. Of what value would knowing the history of an industry be to the salesman?

CASE 4-1 THE WARDROBE SHOP

Jerry Rutledge pondered his new assignment: to develop the product knowledge section of a sales training manual being prepared for the opening of two new stores.

The Wardrobe Shop, a relatively large traditional men's apparel store near the campus of the University of Colorado, was opening a new store in Colorado Springs in August, 1967, to be followed in March by a large store in a huge new shopping center being built in south Denver. The Wardrobe's management had always maintained a policy of giving its sales personnel excellent training. Thus it was no accident that its people were recognized throughout the industry as being quite talented. However, in the past training had been given face to face in a relatively informal continual program by the chain's owners. With the advent of the new stores under the management of former trainees, management recognized that it would have to provide a great deal of training in a short time to more men than ever before. And the training would have to be done by the new managers. In order that the new training program be complete, standardized, and facilitated, it was decided that a complete training manual should be prepared. A basic outline was developed and each section was then delegated to a man for execution. Jerry was assigned the responsibility for developing the section on product knowledge.

First, he planned to write each of the firm's suppliers asking for information on its wares plus any sales training material it might have developed on them. In that manner, the trainees could become familiar with the technical aspects of each item carried in stock.

Second, he thought that the inclusion of a booklet published by the British woolen industry on clothing terminology would be helpful. The beginning salesman seldom knew a worsted from a hopsack fabric.

Finally, he thought that the trainee should know the location of all back-up stocks in the store. He planned to draw a diagram indicating their location.

He took his plans to Mr. Davis, his boss, for review. Mr. Davis looked over Jerry's work and said, "I think you need to give some more thought to what the new man needs to know about the products we sell. I fail to see some critical areas covered and I question some of your present plans."

1.   What areas has Jerry missed?
2.   What is wrong with Jerry's present plans?

WHY PEOPLE BUY

Men can not be forced to trust.
Daniel Webster

The past decade has seen a tremendous increase in the study of human behavior as it affects marketing. We now realize that the behavioral sciences have much to contribute to the study of marketing and to its practice and one of the areas of greatest importance is that of motivation.

The essence of selling is motivation; the motivation of someone to do what you want him to do—obey you, hire you, promote you, or buy from you. While you no doubt have learned much about motivating human behavior from your daily dealings with people, still you can sharpen your motivational skills by carefully honing them on some of the material recently provided by the behavioral sciences. Much of this chapter is based on such research.

Most sane behavior is motivated. Though the actual motives behind human activity may not be readily apparent to an observer, people do have reasons for their actions. When a prospect buys something, his action is motivated behavior; people do not just buy things without reasons. Typically, a good salesman attempts to ascertain the major or most forceful reason which will motivate the behavior he desires in the prospect, and then he concentrates his presentation around it to keep the prospect's attention on the things which are evidently most important to him. It is a serious mistake for a salesman selling tires to keep stressing their low price if the prospect is most interested in safety. Such emphasis on price may actually lose the sale, because the prospect may believe he would be giving up what is most dear to him—safety—for the low price.

NO SELLING WITHOUT BUYING

In any study of salesmanship the words that should be emphasized are "buyer," "buy," "buying." The modern viewpoint approaches the subject by regarding the selling process as a buying process. Strictly speaking, the salesman does not *sell* anything; he merely helps to condition the mind of the prospect so that the latter *buys.* There is no change in the mind of the salesman regarding the merits of his proposition. But, if the sale is to be made, the *prospect's* mind must undergo a change.

A sale is made, not in the mind of the salesman, not over the counter or desk, but in the mind of the buyer. Therefore our attention is rightly centered first on this factor of the sale. The salesman's every word, every gesture should have only one objective—the making of the right impression on the mind of the prospect.

This is merely another way of saying that every salesman, whether he sells in person or through the written word, must cultivate the knack of penetrating his prospect's mind and trying to fathom what goes on there. This habit of giving consideration to the other person's reactions benefits the salesman also by making him a more agreeable person, more popular, more highly regarded as a friend. And it assuredly does help to make him a better salesman.

First, guess a man's ruling passion, appeal to it by word. Find out each man's thumbscrew. You must know where to get at anyone. All men are idolators; some of fame, others of self interest, most of pleasure. Skill consists in knowing these idols in order to bring them into play. Knowing a man's mainspring of motive, you have as it were, the key to his will.
—Baltasar Gracian (1601–1658)

PEOPLE ARE DIFFERENT

The salesman is interested in human behavior and how to induce the desired behavior in the particular prospect whom he is trying to sell. He is, however, keenly aware that all prospects are not alike and will not react in the same way to the same stimulus. He knows that their *backgrounds* are different so that they have differing sets of values. One person has been taught to be thrifty, while another thinks of money as something to be spent as quickly as possible. One has a burning urge to study, to learn, to acquire knowledge; another has never entered the world of ideas and lives for the satisfactions of his senses.

These basic differences may be fundamental, rather permanent aspects of the buyer's personality; they influence his behavior in about everything he does; they merge with his personality traits and habit systems. These have been termed by some psychologists as a "frame of reference" and include such behavior tendencies as conservatism or radicalism, optimism or pessimism; they are deeply rooted and general in guiding his actions.

The salesman can tell a good deal about a prospect's frames of reference by closely observing his previous purchases, because the factors which influence a person to buy or not to buy a particular article are basically similar to the factors which have influenced his previous purchases. We may go even further and say that they are similar to the factors which influence his *general* behavior. For example, a man has owned a succession of medium-priced black cars, although he could afford a dashing model of a more expensive make. This puzzled his friends until he chanced to drop a remark that his mother drilled into him, the attitude that he should always "stay humble." And he stayed humble in *everything* he did. His cars matched this personality trait, as did his garb, his office, his home. A man's desk will usually reveal similar inner attitudes.

Figure 5-1 illustrates the forces which forge one's frame of reference. They are a complex combination of his total experiences in life which the salesman at best can only partially comprehend. But it is not necessary to understand a prospect's complete frame of reference in order to sell him something; many times it is necessary to know only one small aspect of his motivational structure. Just knowing that a businessman considers himself to be modern and progressive may be enough to sell him some new equipment.

Not only does our smart salesman realize that people are different from each other; he also knows that the same person is different under different conditions. For example, he knows that conditions such as these may cause a person to react differently at various times:

1. Physical environmental factors such as temperature, humidity, altitude, ventilation, illumination, distraction of other stimuli
2. General organic states such as fatigue, hunger, sleepiness, moodiness, comfort or discomfort, anger, anxiety, frustration or triumph
3. Specific conditions induced by chemicals such as alcohol, tobacco, caffeine, morphine, medicine taken for pain or hay fever
4. Previous events that have conditioned his mind such as loss of his job, a traffic ticket, or a fight with his wife
5. Incentives and motives such as praise, reproof, rivalry, reward, punishment

The man who has just returned from a vacation is in no frame of mind to talk vacation tours with the representative of a travel agency. The flop-

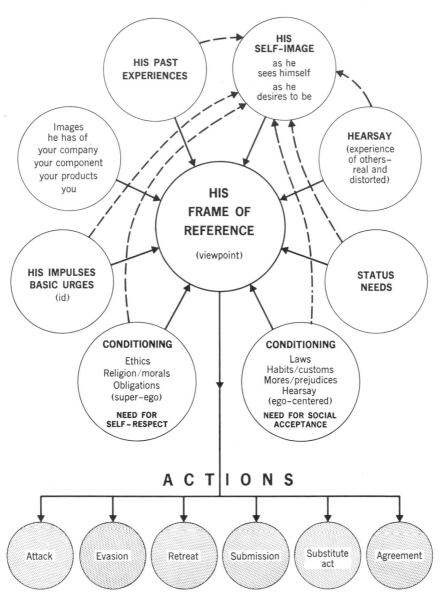

Figure 5-1   Frame-of-reference chart: A man will usually act from his own frame of reference, a way of seeing things that is conditioned by many things: status needs, past experiences, and so on. Most important of these, however, is his self-image, which changes as he matures and grows. (*Sales Management,* June 1, 1967, p. 49.)

house derelict who has just inherited $10,000 is a very different person from the one he was a week before. The girl who has recently married and set up a home of her own reacts very differently to certain sales stimuli from the way she reacted previously. After a poor night's sleep or after having partaken of indigestible food a person will find his reactions changed.

If the purchasing agent for a factory has suffered from breakdowns in machines, he will respond to appeals that the salesman represents a firm that can give him quick service on repair parts. If the buyer has had an accident of some sort, he will be in the mood to listen sympathetically to an offer of a product guaranteed against such accidents. An element of "timing" exists in many sales situations.

One young man selling auto insurance called only on people who had just had an accident—the event had prepared their minds to accept an appeal to buy better coverage. He was most successful.

The salesman must analyze the prospect to determine just how he is likely to react to certain stimuli at the particular moment. Although a knowledge of his former behavior may serve as a valuable guide, the salesman is not safe in assuming that his prospect will invariably react in the same manner to the same stimuli. Indeed, the prospect is never entirely normal when in the presence of a salesman. He is likely to throw up defenses, be hypercritical, and be more sensitive to imagined insults.

There are also the inhibiting factors to consider. We sometimes refer to an individual as "uninhibited," but everyone is restrained by a variety of constraints. For example, one man is restrained by his reluctance to do anything that is dishonest, while another might feel no such compunction.

The salesman schools himself to observe and "size up" his prospect so that he may discover what causes him to act favorably on a suggestion and what holds him back. The salesman's approach to this problem may be strictly common sense and not couched in scientific terms, but this is his objective.

Please glance back at those five sets of conditions which may influence the prospect's reaction. It will be seen that the salesman has little control over the first four. To be sure, he may be able to interview the prospect in a salesroom where lighting and temperature are favorable and where distractions are absent. He may buy the prospect a dinner and a couple of drinks and give him a fine cigar. He may time his call on an important prospect so that as many of these factors are in his favor as possible. But generally speaking, he is forced to take these things as they come, recognizing them and handling his presentation accordingly.

The fifth group is different. This area involves motivation and it is in this field that the salesman usually becomes something of an expert. He *can* control his appeals to various human motives that prompt action. He *can* utilize various incentives to action. In other words, he *can* control the stimuli which act on the prospect to induce the desired reactions.

These reactions to stimuli are of two main kinds: (1) inborn or innate reactions or reflexes and (2) conditioned reflexes which are acquired during one's life.

INSTINCTS AS MOTIVATIONS

Among earlier psychologists the instincts were thought to explain nearly everything that people did; we behaved as we did because we were born that way. Various lists of instincts were compiled, but no two of them were alike. Some mentioned only one instinct—self-love. Others suggested two—egoism and altruism. Some distinguished 50 or 60 instincts. Actually, more than 14,000 "instincts" have been listed by one psychologist or another. Certain writers refer to "neural predispositions" as covering the scope of the older instincts.

Psychologists have engaged in fierce debates concerning whether certain human reactions were prompted by instinct or habit; whether they were inborn or acquired. Admittedly, it is sometimes difficult to distinguish between them.

In an effort to find a term sufficiently general to gain wide acceptance, psychologists have adopted the word "drive." "In the strictly psychological sense, drive is a motivating factor of personality—such as wish, purpose, ideal—which regulates and directs one's conduct. Human and animal activity contains countless goals and hence innumerable drives."

Some of these drives are clearly physiological: hunger, thirst, sex, need for rest, and the desire for the most comfortable bodily temperature. Food and drink satisfy a fundamental demand. Stoves and refrigerators are sold because they appeal to man's desire for good food and drink. But by no means are all the efforts of salesmen directed at appealing to these primary desires. Enough food and water to sustain life, a rude shelter from the elements, and clothing sufficient to keep him warm are not too hard to obtain—the Indians had these, as have the inmates of properly managed prisons and insane asylums.

Clearly, the salesman is mainly concerned with the learned wants of man. And these wants may be powerful driving forces, sometimes more powerful than instinctive urges, especially when instinctive wants are pretty well satisfied. The well-to-do society woman who must have a luxurious home in the right part of town is not simply providing shelter for her family, yet the strength of her drive for that home may far exceed the drive of another woman who is merely seeking a functional house in which to live.

DIFFICULTY ENCOUNTERED IN DETERMINING MOTIVES

As important as the determination of buying motives is to all marketing men and to salesmen in particular, it is also a most difficult undertaking. The current interest in motivational research has been largely generated because marketing men have continued to experience failures unexplainable with existent knowledge. They have come to realize that many prevailing theories of consumer behavior were not being validated by experience and that they had much to learn about why the consumer behaves as he does.

Motivation research and the salesman

Over the past decade or two we have witnessed a mushroom growth of motivation research. Specialized organizations have sprung up to conduct such research for clients interested in learning the reasons why people buy or reject their products and services. Advertising agencies have installed new departments, manned by scholarly psychologists and sociologists, to help them plan advertising campaigns and to impress clients and prospective clients. The literature on the subject has now overflowed the scientific journals and is appearing in marketing publications. Whether it is a fad or a valuable new tool of marketing only time will tell, but indications are that motivation research will win for itself a permanent position as it grows more practical and devotes less attention to debating pet theories of the psychologists and sociologists, largely couched in terms unintelligible to the lay reader.

Admittedly, motivation research seeks to solve extremely difficult problems. For example it is not enough merely to ask people why they bought certain items. Such naïve techniques elicit little of value because (1) most people do not know why they bought and (2) they tend to rationalize. When an individual is asked why he bought something, he searches his mind for a rational explanation, to appear rational not only to the investigator asking the question, but also to himself. J. P. Morgan once cynically observed, "A man always has two reasons for doing anything—a good reason and the real reason." This tendency distorts the results of such a survey.

It was just stated that the buyer does not himself know *why* he bought. This is true chiefly because his purchase was prompted by a vast complex of inner personal forces and external social forces. These forces are not only numerous, they are also of varying strengths, thus complicating the problem to the point of rendering it virtually insoluble even to the trained investigator, and certainly to the average individual trying to define his own reasons for buying.

Motivation research, as the seller views it, therefore deals with the *totality* of factors influencing buying behavior. Relationship between cause and effect (stimulus and response) cannot be attributed to a single, simple motivational factor. It is, indeed, bafflingly complex, but fascinatingly intriguing.[1]

Human nature is too complex and too many other factors enter into the buying process to make it feasible to offer a complete list of these buying motives. Nor can we distinguish and discuss every motive that might cause a person to buy any one of a variety of products under any one set of environmental factors. But it is hoped that the following discussion will serve to emphasize the importance of approaching every sale from the angle of "what motives are most likely, right now, to influence this prospect to want what I have to sell?"

Barriers to studying motives

As has been pointed out, the problem of ascertaining just which motives are most likely to prompt a prospect to buy permits no simple solution. But every salesman must make an effort to solve it. Even a partial solution is better than none.

However, he must recognize and often allow for certain significant barriers to the attainment of a complete solution. Some of these are suggested in the next few paragraphs.

PROSPECT UNAWARE OF MOTIVES As has been mentioned, the prospect is frequently unaware of his real reasons for buying or not buying any given product. How many executives realize the influence of styling on their machine buying decisions? How many people realize that they purchase automobiles for reasons of status? Instead, they like to talk in such terms as mileage, safety, dependability, low repair costs, and riding comfort.

Why does a housewife buy a new evening gown? Because she has none? From the standpoint of clothing alone, she no doubt has many garments that will adequately cover (or reveal) her for the occasion. Indeed, her behavior can be explained only in terms of a multitude of social motivations of which she is probably only vaguely aware. The salesman, for these reasons, must clearly understand that he cannot determine buying motives by directly asking buyers.

[1] The reader is referred to *Motivation Research*, Hans A. Wolf (ed.), published in 1955 by Motivation Research Associates, Boston, and to *Consumer Behavior and Motivation*, Robert H. Cole (ed.), published in 1955 by the University of Illinois. Both of these contain further references on the subject.

UNWILLING TO DISCLOSE   If the prospect is in the position of knowing exactly what will motivate him to buy a certain product, frequently he is unwilling to disclose the reason. How many men would admit that they bought that new suit to impress the new secretary? How many buyers of new cars would admit that there is nothing wrong with their old cars except that they are becoming burdens on their egos? How many purchasing agents would admit that they buy from the boss's nephew largely for reasons of job security? Thus the salesman must not assume that the buyer will disclose his motives, even when he knows them.

COMPLEXITY OF MOTIVES   The actual motives behind a purchase are frequently so complex and interwoven that ferreting all of them out and recomposing the picture of just what will motivate a given purchase may be practically impossible. Therefore, we find a decided tendency in selling to oversimplify the buying process. For example, to say that an executive has purchased a new computer in order to solve a problem in controlling the operation of his firm may be only a half-truth. There are no doubt other ways the executive could solve the same control problem at perhaps less cost. However, in modern business the possession of a computer has become somewhat of a status symbol to many executives. They like to be following the current fashions in business, and the installation of computers has some faddish overtones. Also involved in the purchase may be some rather vague idea that with the new computer he may be able to enter new fields and do new things. In addition, he may believe that the computer may solve some particular personnel problem with the current paper work staff. In any event this administrator's decision to buy a computer was probably a complex process involving several reasons, both rational and emotional.

The adroit salesman must ferret out this complex set of motives, stress in his presentation the positive reasons and attempts to minimize the negative ones. Many times the real function of the presentation is to provide rational reasons to a prospect so that he can rationalize what his emotions urge him to do. The salesman of the Learjet frequently encounters this problem. Many businessmen wish to own the Learjet largely for reasons of status, prestige, and other personal, emotional satisfactions it would provide. However, the salesman must frequently furnish them with such rational reasons as low cost per mile and the alleged savings the plane will give the company, considering the tax angle and other financial aspects of the transaction. Once the executive is able to rationalize his behavior in terms of accepted reasons for buying business assets, he feels free to do what he emotionally wanted to do all along.

THEORIES OF MOTIVATION

No one overall theory of motivation has been universally accepted. Various authorities have taken slightly different approaches to the problem. As a result, it is necessary for us to approach this discussion of buying motives from several directions in the hope that the reader can thereby obtain a more comprehensive view of the problem.

Semantics becomes a barrier to the study of motivation when the reader compares the writings of one authority with those of another. Frequently two writers are talking about the same basic forces but they use different words to describe their concepts. This will be particularly evident when the topic of self-concept is introduced. One writer builds his theory of motivation around an individual's perceptions. "They behave according to how they *perceive* and *interpret* these outside forces and the possible consequences to themselves."[2] We will see how this fits nicely into the self-concept theory. Such additional viewpoints of essentially the same thing are good for they give the reader an opportunity for a deeper understanding of the extremely difficult subject of motivation.

The three approaches to understanding buying motives which seem to be most fruitful for salesmen are: (1) the traditional emotional-rational approach, (2) the problem-solving approach, and (3) the self-concept theory. Each of these is discussed below.

TRADITIONAL APPROACH

The traditional approach to understanding buying motives divides them into two major groups: (1) rational and (2) emotional. The terms "rational" and "emotional" permeate practically all discussions of buying behavior; therefore, it is necessary to understand them before going into the more modern, more complex theories of motivation.

Rational buying motives

Rational buying motives concern such matters as price, cost-in-use, durability, servicing, reliability, length of useful usage, and, in general, *any consideration affecting the full long-run cost of the article to the purchaser.* The classical economist predicated much of his theory on the basis of the so-called "economic man," who was a sort of ambulatory computer able to feed into his brain a multiplicity of cost and performance data and produce an answer, that is, the most economical behavior pattern he could follow.

[2] Richard M. Baker, Jr., and Gregg Phifer, *Salesmanship: Communication, Persuasion, Perception* (Allyn and Bacon, Inc., Boston, 1966), p. 116.

Obviously, this is too much to expect where the factors are numerous and complex, the human brain being unequal to such a formidable calculation. The rational motive, however, does play a role in practically all buying. As was noted previously, many times a salesman's problem is to select the appeals that will most effectively stimulate this motive, even though the prospect may already desire to buy to satisfy emotional drives.

This definition of the rational buying motive may appear narrow, but if we are to attempt a clear-cut distinction between rational and emotional motivation, it seems that we must make it on this basis.

We should bear in mind, however, that this factor of long-run cost is not limited to dollars-and-cents cost. It may involve cost in time or in degree of labor, in surrender of security. But the fact remains that a rational decision even in such matters is made on the basis of long-run cost compared with the long-run benefits.

In general, businessmen attempt to buy as rationally as possible, but they, too, frequently fail to be completely rational. Personal friendships, prestige names, reciprocity, and status symbols may influence their buying decisions. The industrial salesman must never delude himself that he is dealing with a completely rational individual across the desk from him, for that business executive or purchasing agent is moved by emotions the same as anyone else, and many times these emotions take precedence over rational pressures. Many industrial transactions can be explained only in terms of personal friendships or other emotional buying motives which are more fully discussed in the next section.

Emotional buying motives

Long lists of emotional motives like security, comfort, ego, emulation, pride, sex, recreation, and many others, have been compiled by various authorities. Although it is helpful to study such lists and discussions, one must realize that a complete classification of *all* emotional buying motives is impossible. One's emotions are so complex that it is difficult to isolate each motive and classify it. Two executives may purchase exactly the same luxurious office furniture for ostensibly the same emotional motive of ego gratification. However, the "motive mixes" underlying these two purchases could be quite different. The first executive may have purchased his furniture in order to prove to his fellow employees that he possesses certain status *within* the organization. The other executive may have purchased his office furnishings in order to impress such *outsiders* as competitors, other businessmen, and customers—to convey an image of success, largely for business reasons. The salesman must be able to detect these differences in buying motives, because he will be making a serious mistake in appealing to the first executive in terms of external prestige when internal status is desired. Similarly, the second executive would not respond to appeals dealing with internal prestige alone.

Some of the more common emotional buying motives follow.

PHYSICAL PLEASURE; COMFORT; AVOIDANCE OF EFFORT   Man is an animal and naturally lives much of his life on a physical level. He requires food, drink, sleep, and a temperature that is not too hot or too cold. Many humans spend most of their effort in acquiring these basic necessities; others are able to satisfy these with a portion of their efforts and go on from there to acquire other desirable things. This urge is basic and accounts for the purchase of food, an easy-riding car, a soft mattress, a comfortable lounge chair, shelter, clothes, conveniences about the home or place of work. Washing machines, vacuum cleaners, automatic dishwashers, elevators and escalators, beverages, ranchtype houses, precooked foods, gas furnaces, inside toilets, and cars with automatic transmission, power brakes, air conditioning, and power steering are all examples of things which we value because they satisfy this urge.

The absence of anything that gives us pleasure will cause us discomfort or pain. Perhaps this discomfort or pain is merely the necessity of putting forth physical or mental effort—but to most of us effort is akin to pain. This is a generalization that has exceptions. Some people enjoy physical effort; their muscles seem to demand it.

PLAY AND RELAXATION   A form of physical and sometimes esthetic pleasure may be found in play. Leisure for play has expanded with the use of power-driven machinery to replace human labor. It is not uncommon to hear a couple of mechanics or truck drivers discussing their golf scores. The vacation with pay is today accepted as a routine fringe benefit of nearly every job. Parks and playgrounds offer facilities; the automobile and airplane afford means of reaching these and other facilities; movies, radio, television, and athletic events cater to this urge for play. Books and magazines satisfy this urge too. Clothing manufacturers are turning out an increasing proportion of sport styles. Even frugal families include in their budgets an item for the satisfaction of this desire. Winter and summer resorts have mushroomed in the past decade, and one can now find dude ranches in Michigan and North Carolina and even within 50 miles of New York City.

This drive for play is quite basic in all animals. Psychologists have developed a limited body of thought concerning play; they believe it to be mentally therapeutic. Problem children are encouraged to play out their troubles in what is called "play therapy." On an older level there is much evidence that adults seek play as relief from their frustrations, aggressive pressures, and inhibitions. This desire for play seems quite strong and is manifested in many ways in our society. Note the success of stores decorated in some make-believe decor; erect a playhouse and customers will come play with you. Witness the success of many nonsense advertising campaigns; Mother Nature reacts adversely to being fooled by some margarine, while the Jolly Green Giant goes "Ho Ho Ho," and Charlie the Tuna bemoans his lack of breeding. Say "Come with me to Fantasyland!" and step aside lest you be trampled by the horde. Disneyland does not make its money on children; they are simply the excuse or rationalization of millions of men and women who want to escape the realities of their boring or harried lives by "taking the kids" to Disneyland.

Play theory leads to some rather useful thoughts for the salesman. Obviously, if someone wants to play he needs playmates. Many successful salesmen owe their fortunes to their abilities as playmates. A successful executive has a limited number of people with whom he can play. His own people in the organization are usually precluded because of managerial considerations. He may prefer not to let his hair down with his peers in the business community for image reasons. He often has few friends from whom to choose his playmates. The adroit salesman may be able to play just the right role for such a man. If the executive wants to escape to the golf course, a short vacation to Greenbriar, Pinehurst, Palm Springs, or Pebble Beach may develop a lasting relationship for the salesman that would never be achieved in any other manner. But the key fact to remember is that people must play; the salesman's problem is to discover just what form that play takes in his customer's behavior pattern.

ESTHETIC PLEASURE   We derive a strong satisfaction or feeling of pleasure from the impact of the beautiful on our senses and emotions. This may be beauty of form or color or sound. It may be found in art, in music, in literature, in nature, in the home or the place where we work. We have only to look about us to realize how strongly this motive has influenced the design of thousands of items, such as automobiles, washing machines, kitchen sinks, stoves, furniture, architecture and landscaping, clothing, interior decorating of home, factory, office, and store. The purely utilitarian and functional approach has been modified by this determination to produce things that will also appeal to the esthetic motive.

The ascendance of these three motives is a result of discarding the harsh ethics inherited from our pioneer-Puritan ancestors. For them life was hard, work was arduous, conveniences were few, leisure was almost nonexistent. Idleness was a sin; pleasure was achieved only by ceasing work; so pleasure was almost sinful, too. Traces of this older thinking persist, but in diminishing amounts.

The smart salesman capitalizes on this drive by selling particularly well-designed products and by displaying them in such a way that these virtues are brought out. And it does no harm to point out to the prospect, "Isn't it beautiful? It's the best looking Widget made!"

SELF-ESTEEM; PRIDE; URGE TO FEEL IMPORTANT; EGO STRIVING; URGE TO ACHIEVE; STATUS; PERSONAL ADEQUACY; WILL TO POWER Whatever we call it, all of us have it. We want to be appreciated, to be complimented, to be made to feel important. No salesman can afford to forget this motive; indeed, many authorities on salesmanship assert that this is the most powerful of all buying motives.[3]

It is nothing of which we need to be ashamed. It is the basis of democracy—the belief that every citizen has a right to share in governing the political unit of which he is a part and that the government is his servant and not his master. The conviction that the human soul is too important to die is the foundation of belief in immortality. Without this trait mankind would languish in mediocrity, unwilling to make the effort to climb above the level of the lower animals.

Not only must a man feel that he is of some importance, but he craves recognition of this from his fellows. Robinson Crusoe may have felt a satisfying sense of personal adequacy before his man Friday appeared, but it obviously was tremendously enhanced by the gratitude and veneration displayed by his faithful servant. This desire for the approval of others leads us to do things merely because society has laid down certain behavior patterns as correct. We strive to climb in society, to earn election to exclusive clubs or college organizations; we labor diligently to become proficient in athletics or music; we seek the spotlight by becoming entertainers; we cultivate acceptable social manners.

Why do rich people leave thousands of dollars to elevator operators, taxi drivers, or waiters? Simply because these latter have been kind, have shown respect or affection, thus helping the benefactor to feel that he or she was appreciated and liked.

We crave attention and a position from which we can issue orders to others. Some people find it is far preferable to be a martyr, persecuted by the majority, than to live unnoticed. This is illustrated in every large university, where various minority groups stage demonstrations, write letters to the student paper, and otherwise seek to attract attention. They often are

[3] Baker and Phifer, op. cit., p. 123. Baker says, "Man strives to make himself as adequate a personality as possible." He goes on to build most of his behavioral theory around this drive for adequacy.

sustained by the hope that disciplinary action may be taken against them, as this would focus even more attention on them.

Surveys indicate that people who stop trading at certain stores do so because the salespeople have shown indifference, which is simply another way of saying they acted as if the customer was unimportant. Perhaps their offense was merely a lack of promptness in coming to greet the customer, but this wounded the latter's self-esteem.

An appreciation of this very human trait makes it natural for the salesman to use indirect methods in place of the often offensive direct methods. It is more tactful to use indirection because this recognizes the right of the other person to feel important. We therefore merely *suggest* instead of *dictating.* In the long run people in this country like to make their own decisions, at least in matters that concern them intimately and on which they feel competent to decide. We all resent back-seat drivers. So the salesman tries always to present his views so that the prospect can buy without feeling that he has been forced into it. He must be made to feel that he did the buying, that he made a wise decision of his own free will.

The smart salesman, willing to cater to the prospect's desire to feel important, will not do all the talking. He will learn to listen, acknowledging with courteous deference the opinions of the prospect. He is even careful of the manner in which he tells his story, avoiding the appearance of showing off or of being the final authority on the subject or of telling the prospect something which the latter did not know. Thus he shuns such introductory clauses as, "Maybe you never thought of this angle, but—" or "You probably didn't know this before, but—." Rather, he is quick to impute his own ideas to the prospect or to someone else. If he can say, "As you remarked a few minutes ago" (or "the last time I was here") he knows the prospect will more readily accept the idea.

The common clause, "See what I mean?" irritates many listeners, who mentally react, "Of course I do. You think I'm a moron?"

The wise salesman utilizes praise judiciously. It has been said that praise is one of the salesman's least developed resources. It costs so little and pays such huge dividends. In passing, it might be observed that usually it pleases a person to be complimented on some skill or trait for which he is not frequently complimented, as when a beautiful girl is told that she has a wonderful mind.

Someone said, "Make a man like himself a little bit better and he will henceforth like you very much."

IMITATION OR EMULATION   Pure imitation, such as that displayed by monkeys and small children, is found to a certain extent in adult human beings, but most people imitate others in the purchase of certain things with the idea that by so doing they are showing themselves superior to those who do not thus follow the fashion. To this extent, then, this motive is akin to the urge for self-importance, because we imitate those who are, in our opinion, more important in this respect than we are. The youth wears sport clothes like those the male movie stars wear; his sister has her hair done like some prominent woman; her mother labors to master the system of the currently accepted bridge authority; Dad buys a more expensive car than he can afford because many men whom he admires drive that make. This is emulation.

The salesman can utilize this buying motive in the sale of many things, but he must always be certain that the person or persons whom he is suggesting that the prospect imitate are among those to whom the prospect looks up. Only then will being like them satisfactorily inflate the buyer's ego.

Usually this motive is automatically working for the salesman in the mind of the prospect and little may have to be said about it during the sale. If the salesman chooses to bring this motive into the open, he must do so with care because people do not like to talk about it.

In selling style goods appeal to this motive is important. It can be utilized best, also, in selling to prospects who are not entirely sure of their own judgment. Skilled purchasing agents and experienced buyers for retail stores may resent the salesman's use of this appeal, feeling that it implies a lack of knowledge on their part; they prefer to use their own judgment. In selling to any opinionated person the salesman will be well advised to soft-pedal this appeal.

MONEY GAIN   This is probably the motive to which most salesmen appeal, especially those selling to manufacturers or to merchants who resell the product. It is not important in the sale of fashion and luxury goods at retail.

It may be argued, and with some logic, that this is not a genuine *emotional* motive. And sometimes it is not, as in the case of the purchasing agent for a manufacturer or the buyer for a chain of retail stores. Their objective is simply to make more profit for the corporation which employs them, and they have no knowledge of or interest in what is done with the money they thus help to make. It is not theirs to spend, and it does not satisfy any emotional yearning except to make them feel they have done a good job.

But many persons have formed a *habit* of trying to make or save money, without giving much thought to what they will do with that money after they have it. Through years of grooved thinking and action, the gain of money has become an end in itself. This is not rational behavior.

But when the buyer's attention is focused on what he plans to buy with the money saved or made, his emotions may play an important part in his decision, if he hopes to satisfy some emotional urge by the purchase.

But admitting all this, it is still smart salesmanship to point out, when practicable, the wants which can be satisfied with the money gained by accepting the salesman's proposition.

This motive of money gain has two phases. The one prompts the buyer to *make* money; the other emphasizes more strongly the *saving* of money. Buyers of the first class are willing to *spend* money to make *more* money. They are large-visioned men to whom *saving* of money is not their aim—there is nothing of the penurious or the miser in them. The making of money is more of a game, a competitive sport, than a mere accumulation of wealth. Money is the symbol of power, of success, which is their real aim. Such men are more willing to take a chance with their money than are men of the "saver" type.

Statements such as "Nothing ventured, nothing gained!" or "It takes money to make money!" may strike pay dirt with such prospects. Many door-to-door sales propositions appeal to this desire to make money when they promise to pay the buyer money for every prospect name furnished the salesman if that person later buys the deal. The success of such propositions indicates the effectiveness of the money-gain appeal. The illusion of something for nothing is still strong.

To the buyer of the second class—the saver—the salesman appeals differently. This man *saves* rather than *makes* money. His outlook is narrower—he is more cautious. To him a bird in the hand is likely to be more desirable than two in the bush. Business is not a sport to be pursued for the thrill of winning but merely because it may add something to the wealth already accumulated.

Statements such as "A penny saved is a penny earned!" or "Why pay more? This will do the same work for less money!" or "Why should you have to pay for their advertising?" will hit home to the buyer. It is a mistake to believe this desire to save money cannot be effective in many sales in which the circumstances might indicate otherwise. One man of means purchased an Imperial rather than a Cadillac simply because he could save $1,000 for an equivalent model; he would have preferred the Cadillac but just could not see paying the $1,000 extra—he did not like it that much better. Many people with money still do not like to feel "taken." With people of little means, the saving appeal can be explosive; just the illusion of a saving can bring forth a sale. Witness the success of many so-called discount houses whose prices are frequently little if any lower. The word "discount" can work wonders, as can the word "wholesale."

ACQUISITIVENESS The acquisitive or possessive urge may manifest itself in many ways. A few of us hoard things, more of us collect things, most of us like to own things. We seem to have an urge to possess, to call things "mine." Experiments in socialism or true communism have all failed because of this desire. Even in a college fraternity house some members are so imbued with these drives that they prefer to wear their own clothes instead of having the brothers wear them!

Much of the underlying motivation toward home ownership is the basic desire of many men to own land and property; to be a renter makes them feel rootless, homeless, insecure. The ownership of property is one avenue men travel in their search for security.

The retailer who refuses to stock a new line of goods until the salesman threatens to give the exclusive agency to his competitor is allowing his action to be governed by this trait.

Another manifestation is seen when the prospect who has had an adding machine or an electric iron on trial for 30 days confronts the painful prospect of surrendering it. The instinct of possession comes to the front and insists upon the article's being kept. The automobile salesman plays upon this motive when he allows his prospect to drive the car. Once behind the steering wheel, the average man imagines himself the owner of the car and rebels at the idea of giving it up.

ROMANTIC AND SEXUAL DRIVES; RELATED DESIRE TO BE WITH PEOPLE   The old books on psychology termed this simple "gregariousness." Today we are more frank and recognize that much of this drive is the desire to be with, to appeal to, members of the opposite sex.

Interpreting the term in the most general sense, it is clear that sex accounts for the purchase of many things other than the obvious ones such as cosmetics, clothes, tours, hair styling, and tickets to dances or movies. The young of both sexes are usually interested in romance, of course, but the middle-aged are not to be overlooked. Especially when they have reached the age when romance is apparently about to pass out of their lives, it is natural that people cling to it whenever the opportunity occurs. The circulations boasted by certain magazines purveying pure (or not so pure) romance testify to the unquenchable interest in this phase of existence. Most novels or plays or movies are based upon a romantic plot, so that the public may revel in vicarious romance.

We struggle to retain our hair, our complexion, our figure, in the hope that romance will remain or will come to us. We add a bit to Arthur Murray's fortune by signing up for dancing lessons. We take vacations in the hope of meeting an eligible girl or man; coeducational institutions of learning are attractive to many because they *are* coeducational.

The venerable man who remembers his wedding anniversary with a gift to his silver-haired partner of eighty is indulging his romantic propensities as truly as he was when he asked her to go buggy riding with him 60 years before. Conjugal love and loyalty are based on romance in the finer sense.

Fortunately, this motive is usually working automatically for the salesman in the mind of the prospect. Little needs to be said of it overtly in the presentation; it may even offend many bashful prospects if the salesman alludes to it. But at times the clever salesman will make certain he lets the prospect know that his proposition will satisfy this yearning for companionship. Many times illustrations showing the presence of the opposite sex in some relationship to the product being sold will do the job better than words. "There's something about an Aqua Velva man!" A man surrounded by lovely girls in a supersonic eight convertible will communicate the desired thoughts better than words.

PHYSICAL AND MENTAL HEALTH; PHYSICAL FITNESS Man has an inborn urge to live as long as he can; suicides are so rare as to be genuine news. It may be as truly said today as in olden times, ". . . all that a man hath will he give for his life."

Young people do not worry much about dying or being ill. There are many years ahead for them, so each year is of scant value. They may eat unwisely, sleep too little, and generally abuse their bodies, because the consequences are not yet evident to them. But after forty, it is different. Then people begin to watch their diet, cut down a bit on liquor and perhaps tobacco, visit the doctor oftener, take vacations as a means to health instead of purely for fun. The bacterial enemy is feared and fought with every weapon available, and the bottle of vitamins sits on the dining table.

We tend to rationalize, to explain our purchases on the grounds that they will promote health. We join a golf club for the exercise; we go to Florida or buy a sun lamp; we eat various unpalatable foods; we force ourselves to take loathsome exercises; we buy reducing pills; we consult psychiatrists to retain our mental health.

The fewer our probable remaining years on earth, the more jealous we are of each one and the harder we struggle to prolong our stay. The shrewd salesman never overlooks this urge, because he knows that it is powerful. Without it, mankind would have vanished from the earth.

This desire for health may not be an end in itself; that is, health may be sought as a means to an end. In fact, it usually is; but this does not lessen its force as a buying motive.

It should be pointed out that in discussing health we include not only the negative aspect of avoiding illness but the *positive* aspect of physical fitness, of a condition in which we possess energy and zest for living. Life yields far more pleasure to persons who enjoy abounding health than to those who are merely well enough to be "up and around."

A statement such as "You know, you really ought to get out and take more exercise" may just sell an expensive set of golf clubs after which, of course, the man just may buy a golf cart so "he won't overexert himself."

CURIOSITY OR THE DESIRE FOR NEW EXPERIENCE   We like to go places and do things, to travel and visit new scenes, to extract new thrills from life. This urge is found more strongly in the young than in the old.

The salesman appeals to raw curiosity frequently in gaining initial attention and interest but does not utilize this appeal so often in closing the sale, as it is rarely the motive that finally prompts the purchase.

An illustration of the use of curiosity in the narrower sense is found in the technique of a costume jewelry salesman who carries a small paper bag with samples he plans to show the next buyer he calls on. The buyer usually declares that she is not interested in looking at his line, whereupon he sets the bag on the counter and chats a few minutes. When the buyer asks him what is in the bag, he tells her that it contains some samples he is going to show another customer—some stuff she probably couldn't sell. At this stage he dashes out to check the parking meter. When he returns, the samples in the sack are out on the counter and the buyer is demanding just why he thinks she could not sell them.

THE URGE TO CREATE   Boys build rockets and model airplanes; girls design dresses and decorate their rooms; people write poems, paint pictures, invent gadgets, grow flowers, and make home movies. Football coaches devise new plays and systems of defense; men build businesses and women raise children (with some help from their husbands perhaps). All these activities and scores of others are creative. Many men who spend their working hours at some uncreative task find an outlet for their creative bent in hobbies. One of the rewards of farming or gardening is the satisfaction of this urge in assisting nature in her continuous creation of growing things.

One of the biggest obstacles that confronted the manufacturers of cake "ready-mixes" was the reluctance of many housewives to abandon the pleasure of exercising their creative skill in baking a cake. They wanted to *create*.

DESIRE FOR JUSTICE AND RIGHT; SENSE OF DUTY; LOVE OF OTH-ERS   These are doubtless acquired motives, but we cannot deny their power. Men have died for what they thought was right; they fight to obtain justice for themselves or for others; they forego pleasures for the higher satisfaction of feeling that they have done their duty. In the average man a sense of duty and the desire to be of service are intermingled with the wish to play a conspicuous role in public affairs, and the salesman can utilize both appeals with success.

The appeal to such a motive yields better results when used on a conscientious prospect. Parental or romantic love, a selfless devotion to others, is a motive prompting millions of purchases daily.

The salesman for a room air conditioner calls on a family that already has one in the master bedroom. He says: "Like yourselves, my wife and I slept better after we bought our first conditioner." He then pauses and looks his prospects straight in the eye before continuing, "But, you know— a funny thing—since we got a second conditioner for the little ones' room, well, . . . now my wife and I can *really* sleep."

FEAR OR CAUTION   This motive is listed last because it is the antithesis of all the previously listed motives. All these motives are based on the search or desire for pleasurable results. Fear is simply being afraid that we cannot attain these results or that we may lose these pleasures after we have enjoyed them for a while.

We fear the loss of life, of health, of friends, of reputation, of security, of job, of money, of freedom, of comfort, of everything which we value.

To fail to gain the things we crave or to lose them causes pain. Thus we conclude that we chiefly fear pain. It may be physical or mental, but it is pain and we strive to avoid it.

The feeling of fear is natural; it is nature's device for preserving us from pain and even from destruction. Animals (including members of the human species) who are devoid of fear usually die an early and often a violent death.

The fear motive is closely allied to caution and the desire for security. People buy insurance, homes, bonds and stocks, or put money in the bank because they are trying to gain security for their old age or for a "rainy day." Fire extinguishers and sprinkler systems, locks for doors and windows, railroad signal devices, air conditioners, and a thousand items are bought because the buyer fears the consequences of not buying them and prefers the security he hopes to gain by having them.

As people grow older, the fear or caution motive becomes stronger. The twenty-year-old youth would choose a motorboat for its speed, while his father wishes rather to be assured that it will not easily capsize. Some salesmen believe that this motive of caution is stronger in older sections of the country than it is in those more recently settled.

Of late we have heard much about the yearning for security. We find pension plans being put in operation by business concerns for their employees. Social security measures have been adopted by Congress to help millions feel more secure in event of illness or old age. We all would like to feel reasonably sure that we shall not go hungry in our old age, that we shall have a decent place to live. We want our children to have an education. We demand hospital care when we are ill. We are beset by doubts and fears for the future, and if the salesman can dissolve these and reassure us that they are taken care of by his proposition, he has a good chance to sell us, because he is satisfying a real need.

THE PROBLEM-SOLVING APPROACH

Possibly the best way for the salesman to look at the basis for buying behavior is that all purchases are made to solve some problem. The housewife has a problem of preparing an attractive, palatable meal for her family approximately twenty times each week. She buys diverse food products and kitchen equipment in the hope that they will solve that problem. An executive has a multitude of problems such as controlling the operations of the firm, increasing sales volume, lowering costs, decreasing personnel turnover, bringing out new products, and increasing the effectiveness of his men. He may buy a new computer in the hope that he can obtain better control over operations to increase consumer satisfaction. He may buy new plant equipment in the hope of lowering production costs. He may buy better office equipment and furniture in the hope of improving morale and lowering turnover. He may even buy a new plant location in the hope that all his problems will be solved.

One corporation president was persuaded to move his research and development laboratory from Chicago to a small Western town largely on the basis that it would solve many of the personnel problems in his Chicago plant. He felt that he had considerable deadwood in his Chicago organization and that by moving west he could select only the key men he wished to keep, thereby pruning the deadwood from his corporate tree. While this was the basic motive behind his decision, he sold the idea to his board of directors on the basis of lowering overhead costs and other rational aspects of the move. He pretended that the major motive was merely incidental.

The salesman should never forget that the main things he has to sell to any prospects are solutions to their problems. This is actually only a slight variation of the consumer benefit theory of marketing. It is axiomatic in all marketing that *one does not sell products but instead sells consumer benefits.* The housewife isn't buying a vacuum cleaner for the metal, bolts, and motor that it contains. Instead, she is buying it because it delivers certain benefits to her, such as a cleaner house with less work. Since the benefits to the businessman are usually solutions to his problems, the industrial salesman should be a seeker of problems to solve.

When he first obtains the name of a prospect, he should immediately start looking for various problems which his product can best solve for that prospect. The salesman walks in and asks an executive if he has a such-and-such problem which is troubling him. When the executive admits that he does indeed have such a problem, the salesman then asks for permission to make an intensive study of it to see if his product offers a good solution. After such a study has been made, the salesman presents his recommendations showing how his product will solve that problem.

This is one reason industrial selling is attractive for the college graduate. If one is selling a product which solves certain problems, the sales presentation will be more effective and pleasant than if the product is somewhat questionable. Most of the time in industrial selling the salesman is making money for his customers.

Many products and services solve more than one problem. The installation of a dictating system in a company may solve a serious shortage of adequate secretarial help, but it can also solve a problem of the expenditure of excessive executive time in getting out correspondence. It may also solve a problem of communicating with various people operating in the field. In general, the *more* problems a product solves, the stronger appeal it will have to potential customers. Also the *seriousness* of the problem solved directly affects its attractiveness. The prospect seldom buys items which solve only minor problems; he must use his limited funds to solve his most pressing ones.

THE SELF-CONCEPT THEORY

The self-concept theory of buying behavior is closely tied to the emotional buying motive of ego gratification. However, it furnishes a much more definitive explanation of the consumer's behavior than just the simple assertion that one buys a given product in order to gratify his ego. This last statement is subject to the additional question, "Just how does it gratify his ego?" *The theory of the self-concept is probably the best integrated thought on buying behavior to date* because it nicely combines the rational-emotional approach, the pleasure-pain theory, and the problem-solving approach into one unified concept. In addition, it is equally applicable to nonbuying behavior.

This theory of behavior is a recent contribution of the behavioral scientists and is consequently being continually refined and supplemented. There also arises the problem of semantics. When dealing with anything as complicated as a person's behavior many new concepts must be tagged; unfortunately different scientists have assigned slightly different tags to essentially the same concept. The term "self-image" and "self-concept" are two examples. Others talk in terms of one's perceptions of himself. Clearly, the student of behavior must be well up on his terminology if he is to comprehend what he reads.

THE DIFFERENT SELVES THAT DETERMINE BUYING
The term "self-concept" is a bit misleading, for it implies that a person has but one self-concept. Actually buying is strongly influenced by several different selves which each individual conceptualizes in his mind.

REAL SELF   The Real Self is what one really thinks he is. It is the man's concept of his abilities, personality, character, and other factors which go to make up his total existence.

THE IDEAL SELF   The Ideal Self is how one would like to think of himself. It is one of his personal goals. Much of his behavior is directed toward making his Real Self coincide with his Ideal Self. One small portion of a man's Ideal Self might be that he is a great football player. Through the help of his coach his Real Self screams that he is only an average player. His Ideal Self would drive him to perfect his football skills and participate in the game with extreme vigor. Another player whose Ideal Self claims only average talents would behave differently.

THE REAL OTHER   The Real Other is how one perceives other people really see him, what other people think of him, his abilities, and his personality. Notice that this has nothing to do with how other people actually do see the individual; one's Real Other may be far out of tune with reality. He may believe that other people think him to be a social lion while in reality they see him as an utter bore. The entire self-concept theory is based on what the individual perceives of himself and what he thinks others think of him. He can only translate, to the best of his ability, what others actually think of him by their actions around him. Unfortunately, many people have faulty translating devices. In protecting their Real Other from damage, they will either refuse to acknowledge many messages from other people or will mistranslate them into whatever they wish to hear. Never underestimate the power of the mind to screen out or distort messages it does not want to perceive.

THE IDEAL OTHER   The Ideal Other is how one wants other people to think of him. A woman may want others to think that she is a good wife, a kind mother, and wise homemaker; she will buy and do many things to create this impression among the members of her reference groups.

The Ideal Other and the Ideal Self do not coincide completely; they can differ significantly. An executive may wish others to think him a generous employer while secretly he wants to be as tightfisted as possible. Another man may wish others to believe him to be religious but nowhere in his Real Self is there religion: this is hypocrisy. Most people want others to think them honest, but experience indicates that many harbor no such restrictions on their behavior in their Real Self.

In theory an individual has many different Other concepts, as many as he has reference groups. That is, he wants different groups to see him in different ways. Let's take a successful executive as an example. On the job he wants his work group to see him as an enlightened, intelligent, responsible executive. This Other will vary between subordinate and superior groups; he will want his subordinates to see him differently than his superior groups do. He will want his peers to see him in a different light. At the country club he wants his buddies to see him as a certain sort of person, while at home his family will have even different ideas about him.

Behavioralists have assigned the term "Generalized Others" to denote a rather total overall Ideal Other when discussing an individual without connection to a reference group. In strict theory it is difficult to consider the behavior of an individual outside of a reference group.

Impact upon behavior

People express themselves to others and to themselves with the goods and services they buy as well as through nonconsumptive activities. However, it should be pointed out that there are extremely few activities in this society that do not require the consumption of something. The individual is constantly trying to bring his Real Self and Ideal Self closer together and to make the Real Others and the Ideal Others coincide.

Think of the impact of driving a new Corvette upon one's self-concepts. What is the man trying to say to himself and others? Wouldn't he receive much satisfaction from it even if others did not perceive of his ownership—frequently the situation in very large cities? Think of the effect upon a woman's self-concepts as she strolls around a luxurious home among her fine furnishings even though few people may be aware of her fortunate situation. All of these tangible symbols reinforce her self-concepts. Of course, when a purchase affects the Real Other also, then far more satisfaction is obtained. But the point is that many seemingly ostentatious purchases are made partly for purposes other than impressing other people. A wealthy man may buy expensive silk undergarments solely for the effect it will have on his Real Self. They will serve to remind him constantly that he is a highly successful man.

The key point is that the mind continually requires evidence of who and what it is. It is insufficient that one is in fact highly successful if there is little or no evidence of it which can be perceived by oneself and others. Some readers may be bothered by the constant reference to the desire for success. Remember that the mind seeks the knowledge that it is adequate; this drive for personal adequacy is basic. A man is successful when he achieves this adequacy. Success can be obtained at any level; it is a reference word denoting how close one is to *his* goals.

People constantly tell the world who and what they are by the various things they do, say, and *buy*. The college student shouts to all his status through his clothes, speech, and other less subtle forms of behavior. He wants to make certain that no one confuses him with a high school student or with a workman of his own age. Similarly, a member of the motorcycle set clearly proclaims his allegiances. This symbolic communication is not in the least foolish; it serves as a silent, but speedy, means of communication. Walk into most offices and the boss can usually be identified by the symbols surrounding him. This saves embarrassment to all.

The role of reference groups

Reference-group theory is extremely important to motivational analysis because of its effect on the individual's self-concepts.

Every person is a member of several sociological groups. He may be a member of a neighborhood, work, musical, church, square dancing, or golfing group. His role in each of these groups may differ considerably. In some he may be a leader while in others he may be a follower with little stature. In addition, there are usually groups which the person wishes to join—he is not now a member but wishes he were. The price of admittance and dues to a group is conformance to its standards. One must behave within certain limits to be a member of a group. Groups vary in their pressures for conformity. Some are quite strict and maintain narrow limits for behavior while others are relatively permissive in the behavior they will tolerate, but all of them do have some standards and those standards must be observed if the individual wishes to stay in the group's good graces.

These reference groups interact with the individual's self-concepts. He selects his reference groups largely on the basis of his self-concepts and the reference groups give many additional dimensions to those concepts. A man may visualize himself as a sportsman and join several athletic groups such as a country club, a rod and gun club, and a football booster organization. Once he is in those organizations their membership will sharpen his ideas about himself; his golfing buddies will let him know exactly how much of a hacker he is.

Study a man's key reference groups and you will know a great deal about him. With whom does he spend the most time? Whose company does he seek?

Four levels of abstractions

The self-concept is such a complex phenomenon that it is almost impossible to chart it completely. Actually one can observe about four levels of abstraction in the self-concepts of most people, as indicated in Figure 5-2.

First, at the top, people have broad general feelings about themselves such as, "I am a good husband and father. I am honest and law-abiding. I am rather shrewd, and no one puts anything over on me. I am athletically talented, etc." These are the broad, overall generalities which guide most of the individual's behavior. One should not jump to the conclusion that all people hold these same general concepts. Many men, judging from newspaper accounts, do not see themselves as good husbands and fathers or as particularly law-abiding. Evidently too many people believe that they are criminals, capable of outwitting society. Some men see themselves as anything but athletically inclined; such people frequently go to the other extreme and decry anything resembling exercise as an utter waste of time.

The second level becomes a little more specific under each of these general categories. The man who visualizes himself overall as being an athlete might see himself more particularly as being a good golfer, a poor bowler, an inept baseball player, an excellent swimmer, etc. The man holding the general opinion that he is a good businessman might qualify that thought with the idea that he is good at selling but poor with paper work.

The third level becomes considerably more detailed. The athlete who believed he was a golfer might have as a Real Self that he was a high-70s shooter and have as an Ideal Self that he is a par golfer. These specific concepts will strongly influence his buying behavior. It would be unthinkable for a par golfer to tee up a cheap ball; instead he will be hitting the best he can buy. How could he possibly push his Real Other Self and his Ideal Other Self up to where he wants them if he were to tee up a cheap ball in front of his immediate reference group, the other members of the foursome? He will also have to buy different clubs and other equipment to match this self-concept.

The fourth level becomes quite specific. The golfer now has certain qualifications to his game. He may see himself as a long-ball hitter who is rather inaccurate with the long irons. In addition, he knows that he is strong around the greens but that his putter is erratic. These ideas will all cause certain buying behavior. Certain golf balls are sold on the appeal that they are for the "long-ball hitter." Certain putters appeal to the individual who is uncertain of that portion of his game.

While we have devoted our illustration to developing some of the

ramifications of the self-concept of a golfer, this same exercise can be repeated for each of the other segments of one's self-concept. Naturally, one
can become aware of his self-concept only with experience; experiences tell
us what we can and cannot do successfully. Hence, it is only natural that
the older one becomes, the clearer his various selves become to him. A

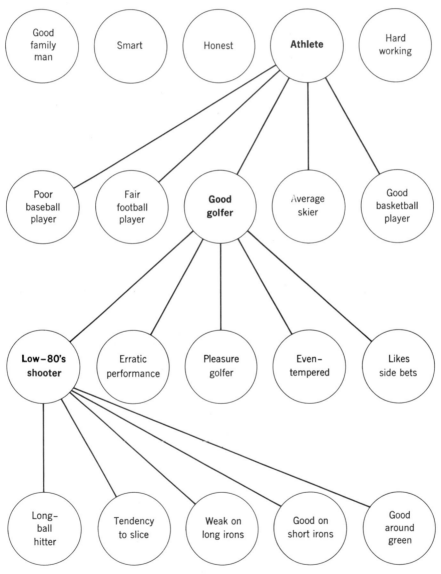

Figure 5-2   Levels of abstraction in one's self-concept.

young person has difficulty with the self-concept theory because his concepts are not yet clearly formed. Interestingly, one bit of research on this theory indicated that young college women have a far more definite idea of who and what they are than do their male counterparts.

Perhaps the foregoing appears forbiddingly theoretical and complex—too much so to be practical. Most salesmen are likely to view with scorn the theories of the academician. They avoid the use of the word "psychology" and prefer to use the term "human nature."

But this self-concept thing *is* human nature. And it is not so complex. It merely puts this question to the salesman: What sort of a person does this man think he is, and what would he like to be? What kind of a man does he believe other people think he is? What would he like to have others think about him? (This paragraph is extremely important.)

Every salesman tries to "size up" his prospect along these lines. He knows that it is important to find out what his prospect wants; then the smart salesman can show how his proposition will help the prospect to get what he wants. It's as simple as that.

Of course, no salesman expects to obtain a complete self-concept of any prospect. But this is not necessary, because he needs only a segment of the whole—the segment which affects the prospect's attitude toward buying what the salesman is selling.

Naturally, the self-concepts of every individual are constantly changing, but this is not too difficult to detect. The small boy abandons his dream of being an astronaut and settles for playing forward on his school basketball team. Later he erases this picture and sketches one of himself at a drawing board designing buildings or at a 7-foot desk with an intercom, three telephones, and a framed picture of his family.

Too, some people formulate these self-concepts earlier in life and in more detail than do others. They are more introspective and imaginative. Frequently the salesman finds it necessary to *help the prospect to formulate a self-concept* which has been vague or even unformed, as when the salesman for a correspondence course awakens some youthful prospect to the possibilities of climbing out of his humble environment and becoming a person of consequence.

But, even with all these qualifications, this theory will be found practical and helpful because it forces the salesman to *focus his attention on the prospect* and his hopes, needs, and aims in life. Only when a salesman does this can he present his proposition most effectively.

Merchandise as an aid to focusing self-concepts

People use merchandise and other purchases as a means of superimposing their Real and Ideal Selves over one another while at the same time strongly affecting the Other Selves. The golfer, by using a Titleist ball, is not only convincing himself that he is a good golfer, but he is also trying to shape the ideas of the others as to his golfing talents. The woman who buys a mink coat is using it to help move her Real Self closer to her Ideal Self and at the same time moving the Real Other Self closer to the Ideal Other Self. The businessman who feels that he is an important executive will frequently surround himself with many symbols of his status, such as luxurious office equipment and furniture, so that other people will recognize his high place in the hierarchy, while at the same time he is continually reminding himself that his Real and Ideal Selves are now quite close. This executive for the same reasons may prefer to drive a Cadillac, live in the most desirable section of town, and regard with satisfaction the swimming pool in his yard. All this consumptive behavior is designed to serve the same end—to help him superimpose more of his Real Self on his Ideal Self. These goods serve as a constant reminder to him and to others of what role he is playing in life and what goals he has attained.

Using the self-concept

Quaker Oats has capitalized upon the self-concept theory in advertisements portraying a housewife as saying that when she feeds her child Quaker Oats for breakfast, she "knows she has done her best for him."

If a woman is playing the role of a socialite, the social aspects of the purchase should be presented with emphasis on the fact that women whom she recognizes as social leaders have bought the product, proving that it is the smart thing to do. On the other hand, if the woman sees herself as being essentially a housewife, such appeals could be disastrous. Instead, the salesman should emphasize how she is fulfilling her housewifely role by buying the product. "You owe it to your family!"

An electric typewriter salesman can tell much about the concepts of the businessmen upon whom he calls by observing the environment in which they work. One executive may have surrounded himself with modern equipment and a fine working environment while the next works in some dingy hole with outdated equipment. The salesman now must vary his presentation to take into consideration these obviously different self-concepts. The first man probably sees himself as a progressive and successful professional businessman. He can best be sold by implying that an electric typewriter is the mark of a truly efficient modern office, that manual typewriters are passé. The second executive seems to be of the old school—those who pinch pennies and discard machines only when they wear out; he probably believes that he runs an efficient operation and prides himself on his low overhead. He can best be sold by stressing the actual out-of-pocket costs which can be *saved* by operating with a smaller office payroll.

Barriers to buying

To continue with the self-concept theory of buying behavior, it becomes logical that barriers can exist which will prevent a prospect who has the authority to buy from buying a given product. There are three such barriers: (1) incompatibility of product with self-concept, (2) risk of moving away from Ideal Self, and (3) guilt.

INCOMPATIBILITY WITH SELF-CONCEPT A person may refuse to purchase a product because its purchase is simply incompatible with his self-concept, or, to put it another way, it does not fit into the rôle which the person is playing in life. A successful businessman seldom will wear shoddy clothing or allow his personal appearance to deteriorate because such behavior is incompatible with his rôle as a successful businessman. A par-shooting golfer would be unable to bring himself to use certain branded balls. An intellectual would be incapable of reading trashy magazines. A landmark motivation study on the purchase of instant coffee discovered that one of the barriers to women's use of that product was the fact that they considered it incompatible with their concept of themselves as diligent housewives and good cooks.

In selling cake mixes to housewives, manufacturers have found that they must leave something for the woman to do or she will not buy the mix. She must feel that her rôle in making the cake is sufficient to enable her to claim that it is her own and not a baker's cake. The small part she plays helps her fulfill her rôle as a housewife. One may ask why she buys cake mixes at all; if she made the cake from raw materials, she would be playing a more important rôle. The answer is that with the cake mix, not only can she usually make better cakes, but make them oftener, thereby giving her family more pleasure with her culinary activities and maximizing her satisfactions. In conclusion, the salesman must make certain that his product is compatible with his prospect's self-concept; if it is not, his chances for a sale are slim.

RISK OF MOVING AWAY FROM IDEAL SELF OR IDEAL OTHER A person is constantly striving to bring his Real Self closer to his Ideal Self and his Real Other closer to his Ideal Other and he will want to buy any goods which he believes will facilitate this movement. However, if the purchase of an item involves some risk that it may move the buyer away from his ideals, he usually will not buy it even if ultimately the purchase might prove to be a wise one. The prospect prefers the status quo rather than risk moving away from his ideals or jeopardizing his self-concept.

The preference for the status quo may explain in part why the Edsel did not enjoy more success. The Edsel presented a tremendous risk to the prospective buyer that he might be buying an eventual orphan, thereby making himself appear rather foolish. In addition, the buyer was uncertain of exactly where the Edsel fitted into the status hierarchy of automobiles. In line with this reasoning, it would be anticipated that most of the purchasers of the Edsel would be people for whom it would be an improvement over the car they had been driving; for them there was no risk of moving away from their Ideal Selves. The Edsel salesman probably found a Buick or Oldsmobile driver a poor prospect.

GUILT   All aspects of one's self-concept are not completely harmonious with one another. The man who visualizes himself as an excellent golfer may have difficulty reconciling this concept with another—that he is a good husband and spends considerable time with his family. Similarly, a businessman may believe himself to be exceedingly shrewd, able to extract the largest profit out of a given level of sales, while at the same time he may consider himself a good man for whom to work. There are many areas of business operation where these two concepts would come into conflict. His union, for example, might propose a substantial pension plan which he feels would unduly lower profits but definitely provide his employees an attractive retirement system. The final choice between conflicting concepts, if the person is free to choose, usually is in favor of the one which ultimately is more important to *him*.

Although a person might like to own a sports car, the desire is not fulfilled because it creates guilt feelings. It is in conflict with more dominant concepts. A sports car is a selfish purchase for a family man because there is room for only one passenger other than the driver; the family cannot enjoy the purchase. Hence, a man who values his relations with his family finds it difficult to buy one. Along comes the four-seat Thunderbird to allow this man to satisfy his sporting urge and yet rationalize that the car can be enjoyed by his family. Similarly, a man who desires to buy a Cadillac may refrain from doing so because he knows that if he spends his money for it, he will have to penalize his family in other areas.

On the other hand, if a person can rationalize his buying behavior in terms of a socially accepted concept, buying becomes quite easy. It is easy for men to rationalize the purchase of sporting equipment and other recreational goods on the grounds that they are trying to maintain their health and want to have fun with the family at the same time. A man may desire an expensive camera and may rationalize the purchase on the basis that he wants to keep a pictorial record of his beloved family. Though an inexpensive camera would probably do the job, he might nevertheless spend several hundred dollars for elaborate equipment.

In conclusion, the salesman must do everything in his power to remove guilt-causing appeals from his presentation. He must frame his appeals around rationalizing reasons for purchase. In selling photographic equipment to a family man of limited income, the wise salesman would play *down* the hobby aspects since they tend to be selfish ones, and he would play *up* the love-of-family appeals. A salesman for appliances, instead of telling the housewife that she will have more time for loafing, playing bridge, and gossiping if she buys a dishwasher, should tell her that she now will have more time to spend with her family.

Motivational analysis of the prospect

As pointed out at the start of this chapter, this study of buying motives is a part of the "preapproach" or preparation for the meeting of prospect and salesman. But this is only the beginning of the salesman's effort to understand a *particular* prospect. After he has determined that a certain individual may be a good prospect (discussed in the next chapter), the salesman then tries to learn all he can about *this one prospect*. (Chapter 7 covers this.) This process resembles the work of the football scout who studies a particular opponent's use of formations and plays, as well as strength and weakness of individual players. But even this does not end the task of studying the opponent; the process continues throughout the game. So with the salesman, who should observe quickly any facts which might throw light on the self-concept of his prospect. He can note the environment of office or home; the purchases that the prospect *has* made may provide a clue to his tastes or reasons for buying. Too, the salesman may learn much by discreetly encouraging the prospect to talk about himself. Shrewd questions may elicit opinions concerning firms or products with which the prospect has had experience.

Distinction between buying motive and talking point

It is very important to distinguish between a buying motive and a talking point. A buying motive is an inner urge that makes us desire the proposition that the salesman presents. It is a psychological concept, not a material one. *It is in our minds, not in the product.*

For example, the automobile salesman says, "This car is air-conditioned." This is a talking point, not a buying motive. To sharpen this talking point and drive it deep into the prospect's mind, the same salesman says, "This means that the car will have a higher trade-in value, because in a few years nearly all cars will be air-conditioned and most buyers will demand it even in used cars." Here he appeals to the buying motive of gain of money. Or he may say, "Remember when cars did not have heaters? Well, air conditioning is as important in hot weather as a heater is in cold weather. The comfort of riding in 72-degree temperature when it's 95 outside is really something. There is no noise of wind or tires or 'swoosh' of passing cars to interfer. with conversation or listening to the radio. The lady's hair-do is not ruined. And will it impress your friends!" Several buying motives are here stimulated, including comfort, pride, and the love of conversation or music (which *might* be appealing to the esthetic appreciation of the prospect).

In these various appeals the talking point is the same—air conditioning. But quite different buying motives are stimulated.

Some writers have failed to distinguish between buying motives and talking points, sometimes listing such qualities of the product as *dependability* or *performance* or *style* under the head of buying motives. Clearly they are no such thing. They are talking points which may be presented in such ways as to appeal to different buying motives. Why does a buyer desire good performance in the article that he buys? Because it will give him less trouble (comfort or ease or security), or because it will be economical to operate (thrift or gain), or because it satisfies his desire to feel important, as in the case of a fast car. *Performance* is such a vague quality that it ought never to be listed even among talking points. In an automobile, for example, what do we mean by performance? Power or gasoline economy? We cannot have both. Ease of riding or ease of parking? We usually must sacrifice one to obtain the other.

Style is no more a buying motive than *red* or *big* or *sweet*.

No quality of a product is a buying motive. The buying motive, it is repeated, is in the mind of the buyer and not inherent in the product. The failure to distinguish between these has been evident in many poor sales manuals and training courses.

It may be a good idea to mention again that any talking point is likely to appeal to more than one buying motive. For example, an air conditioner to be installed in a window may be sold with the talking point that it filters the air as it enters the room. This talking point may be presented by a clever salesman so that it will appeal to several buying motives. He can point out that it keeps the room cleaner and saves frequent dusting; that it is a boon to sufferers from hay fever or asthma caused by inhalant allergens; that it filters out smoke and dust which are unpleasant and yet bound to come in when the window is open for ventilation; that walls and curtains will stay clean longer. Read that last sentence over again and list the buying motives appealed to by this one talking point.

Organization of selling presentation

These various motives should be studied carefully, and every talking point at the salesman's command should be classified under one or more of the buying motives. One way to go about this is to use a small card-index system or a loose-leaf pocket notebook with guides. Each guide should be labeled with one of the buying motives, and the talking points should be jotted down on the cards or leaves of the notebook and filed under the proper buying motive.

This classification of talking points enables the salesman to choose his talking points intelligently instead of bringing them up indiscriminately, as they chance to occur to him. Many salesmen who have not studied the science of selling string their talking points together as a small child strings beads—with no regard to their relationships or sequence. The result is a presentation that leaves the prospect confused and undecided. The scientific salesman should have each talking point or argument for his proposition filed away *mentally* under the particular buying motive to which it is designed to appeal. *Only in this way can he work out a presentation that will fit the particular prospect on whom he happens to be working.*

For example, the automobile salesman would file under the buying motive of *money* or *saving* or *thrift* such talking points as low gasoline consumption, low initial cost, ease on tires, long life, high resale value. Under *pride* or a similar motive he might list the appearance of the car, its prestige, the names of very prominent owners, etc. Under the motive of *health* he could classify talking points that aim to show the prospect that he could reach the golf course or the beach oftener with a car than without and thereby conserve his health. He could show how riding to and from his work in an automobile would be better than depending on germ-infested busses and how Sunday outings would improve the health of the entire family.

Thus he could continue throughout the list of buying motives. It will be observed that the *same talking point may be included under more than one buying motive at times.* For instance, the possibility of Sunday outings would appeal to the prospect's desire to build up his health; to the instinct that impels most men to get near to nature, to "rough it," to hunt or fish; to his love of family; to his pride in being able to visit friends in other localities, driving up in a fine car; or to his desire to save money, if it was his custom to take the family on frequent trips over the weekend in an old car that was a "gas hog" or an "oil pumper."

The chief reason for thus organizing the talking points under buying motives is to enable the salesman to use those which he believes *will appeal most strongly to the particular prospect* whom he is trying to sell.

Concentrate on the strongest buying motive

Some salesmen study the motive most likely to move each prospect to buy and then concentrate on that particular motive, much as a boxer concentrates his attack on his adversary's sore nose or cut eye. But it is not necessary to consider the sales interview as a battle. The salesman should look at it in this way: "Here is a prospect who is eager to make money; he wants money above all else. By showing him how my proposition can make money for him I will be doing him a real service—I will be bringing into his life great happiness. The satisfaction of this want will mean more to him than anything else I could do for him."

When the salesman discovers that no progress is being made by his appeal to a certain motive, he can often shift the appeal to another motive without any change in the talking points he is using. For example, the salesman for a medium-priced automobile was attempting to sell a car to a family consisting of a man, his wife, and eighteen-year-old daughter. He felt the sale slipping away from him and knew from the conversation that his prospects were probably going to purchase another car costing $500 more. He had learned that neither the man nor his wife knew much about the mechanical construction of a car, and he rightly reasoned that they were buying the more expensive car to satisfy their pride. He therefore casually inquired, "Have you joined the new country club, Mr. Andrews?" "No," was the reply, "we should like to but feel we can't afford it." This gave the salesman the opening for which he had been sparring, and he proceeded to emphasize the improved social standing that membership in the club would confer on Mrs. Andrews and their daughter, the opportunities to mingle freely with the elite of the community, and the business prestige that would come to Mr. Andrews. He so stimulated this same buying motive—pride—although with different talking points from those used by his competitor, that he persuaded his prospects to buy his car in order that they might invest the amount saved in a country-club membership.

This is only one illustration of a big principle in selling. *The salesman can frequently transfer his appeal to new talking points while he still plays upon the very buying motive that seems to be operating in favor of his competitor.* Wherever the salesman is offering a proposition that will save time or money for his prospect, he should bear this in mind. The desire to make or save money may not dominate this particular prospect, but perhaps he can be shown what he might *do* with the money saved through its purchase. He should be shown how this money can be used to satisfy some other buying motive or desire.

The appeal to saving used by the salesman selling bonds, for example, is weak unless at the same time he conjures up in the mind of his prospect the use that he would make of the money thus saved or made. This offers unlimited play to the salesman's powers of description, as he calls up the pleasures of a winter in California, an automobile trip through New England, the delights of books long desired, the possibilities of sending the children to college, the desirability of employing additional help to relieve the wife of some of her household labors, the added prestige that financial success would bring in the eyes of business associates, the satisfaction of gaining on a business rival. He is moving that prospect's self-concept much nearer his ideal.

This line of reasoning also applies to the saving of *time*. Time may be ". . . the stuff life is made of," but it is of no value if merely *saved;* in fact, it is impossible to save it in the sense of hoarding it. Time can merely be *spent* in another way, and it is the task of the salesman to show the prospect, in as alluring a way as possible, just how this saved time may be spent to bring him the greatest satisfaction. When one considers what a multitude of things are sold on this basis—the saving of money or time—it will at once be seen that unlimited opportunities are opened up to the salesman who is sufficiently alert to seize them.

That this discussion of buying motives is not wholly theoretical and academic is proved by the experiences of many concerns. The general sales manager for a company selling fire extinguishers says in the company house organ:

From many years' experience in this business, meeting hundreds of successful fire extinguisher salesmen, I am convinced that our most successful men use the "fear of fire" appeal. . . . After you have sold him on the "fear of fire" and the value of fire protection, the order will come easy. In fact he will do the buying.

It is good strategy to cover about all the possible buying motives early in the canvass, not dwelling too long on any one of them, until you can determine which of them are most likely to interest the prospect. After you have thus touched on all of them and made up your mind as to the ones that you wish to stress, you can spend the balance of your time on those.

DISCUSSION QUESTIONS

1. The term "perceived risk" is used in marketing to describe the mental evaluation a person makes of a proposition that is made to him. If the perceived risk is sufficiently low for him, he buys. How does perceived risk fit into the self-concept theory?
2. How may the salesman make his prospect think he is buying instead of being sold?
3. Is the salesman ever justified in appealing to fear as a buying motive? Give an instance!
4. Sometimes a person is prompted by one buying motive to make a purchase while a different motive restrains him. A housewife might like to buy an automatic dishwasher for its convenience. What motives might restrain her from doing so?

5. What are some of the more common self-concepts American men have about themselves?
6. How can a salesman appraise a prospect's self-concept?
7. Carefully diagram your Real Self, Ideal Self, Real Other, and Ideal Other in every category you feel is appropriate to you. List various purchases you have made and describe their impact on these selves.
8. You are a salesman for Norman Hilton, a manufacturer of expensive ($150 to $250) suits. What buying motives would you use in getting a fine men's wear store to carry your line?
9. You are the retail salesman selling Norman Hilton suits. What buying motives would you use in selling the suit to a customer who has been buying in the $125 price line? Why might you buy one as a customer? What might restrain you besides lack of money?
10. Frequently, the salesman encounters a prospect who has been premotivated (conditioned) by previous experiences to do certain things. Perhaps he has previously owned a television set that required frequent repair and he is now motivated to buy a trouble-free set. How should the salesman handle such instances?

THREE

THE SELLING PROCESS

THE SELLING PROCESS

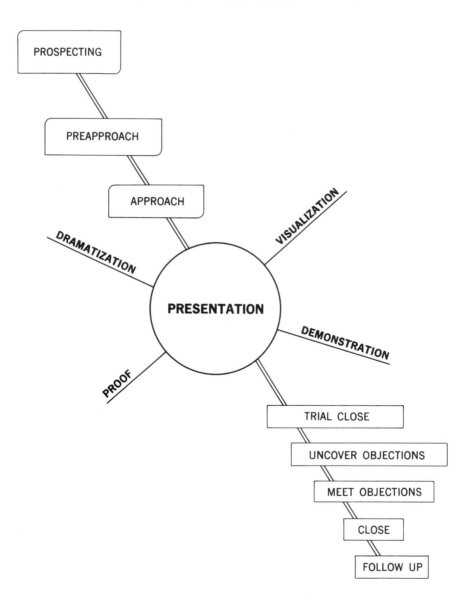

PROSPECTING

Small opportunities are often the
beginnings of great enterprise.
Demosthenes

The importance of prospecting, the first step of the selling process, is often overlooked by the uninitiated. There are many good salesmen who would maintain that the key to successful selling is successful prospecting. It is *that* important. Unquestionably, the route to an order begins with prospecting; for that reason, this discussion of the selling process must begin with a thorough analysis of prospecting methods.

Good prospecting means more sales because it allows the salesman to spend his scarce selling time in contact with people whose probability of buying is high. One of the realities of selling is that the salesman spends a relatively small portion of his working day in actual contact with potential customers. A great amount of his time is spent traveling, waiting, and servicing accounts.

Many salesmen make only one or two calls a day. If those few calls are not made on good prospects, the day is wasted. The salesman's performance will be seriously impaired if he continues to waste his time trying to sell to people who are poor prospects. Let's examine the mathematics involved.

Suppose two salesmen of equal persuasive abilities each make 500 calls on potential customers. Sam is a better prospector than Gus; he has selected 500 prospects who, on the average, have a 50 percent chance of buying while Gus, on the average, will only be able to get orders from one-third of his prospects. Moreover, Sam's calls were made on potential accounts who were larger than Gus's accounts. Sam's average order was $700 compared to $500 for Gus. Now let's see what this would mean in sales volume.

	SAM	GUS
Calls	500	500
times		
Probability of order	× .50	× .33
Orders	250	167
times		
Average order	× $700	× $500
Sales volume	$175,000	$83,500

Certainly these figures are hypothetical and there may be no such thing as two men of equal ability, but actual sales experience proves that the differences in the potential payoff of various prospects is much greater than that assumed above.

Remember for a moment the great disparity in size among business concerns. You can call on hundreds of small concerns all year and still not bring in the volume that would be available from one large corporation.

Some people believe that a good salesman is someone who could sell ice to an Eskimo—get an order from someone who neither needs the product nor can afford to pay for it—but that is a mistaken idea. Such a man is not a salesman; he is little more than an extortionist. The great salesman calls on good prospects, not caring to waste his time on poor ones.

Frequent use has been made of the word "prospect" in referring to the potential buyer for a product or service. It is now time to define this and some other terms.

Prospect

A *prospect* is a person or institution who can both benefit from buying the product and can afford to buy it. Notice, there are two conditions about which the salesman must satisfy himself before he can classify a lead (pronounced *lēēd*) as being a prospect. First, the person or organization must be able to benefit from buying the product; someone who has no use for it is not a prospect. Second, no matter how badly the party may want the product or how much he can benefit from it, if he cannot pay for it, he is not a prospect.

The word "benefit" is used instead of "need" to avoid difficulties in attempting to determine exactly what anyone truly needs. The important thing is whether or not the product or service will furnish sufficient utilities to the individual to warrant his buying it.

Lead
A *lead* is the name of a person or organization who might possibly be a prospect. A lead must first be "qualified" before it can be considered a prospect. Sometimes the term "suspect" has been applied to a lead to indicate that the name is suspected of being a prospect.

Qualifying
This is the act of determining whether or not a lead or suspect is really a prospect. To qualify a lead means to evaluate it in terms of ability to benefit from the product and to pay for it. If the lead meets these qualifications, he ceases to be a suspect and becomes a prospect. The qualifications which a suspect must meet in order to be classed as a prospect differ for different selling situations. In varying and separate situations the prospect should be young, or male, or a physician, or a parent, or wealthy, or married. Each salesman must draw up a set of specifications or qualifications which a real prospect must meet. For some propositions nearly everyone is a prospect, while for others the qualifications are so rigid as to exclude all but a select few. But the salesman must qualify his prospects, or he will waste his time on suspects who will never buy.

China eggs[1]
These are persons who appear to be good prospects but who fail to "hatch" or to materialize into buyers after the salesman has tried to change them into wanters and customers.

Cold-turkey canvassing or cold canvassing
These are calls made by a salesman with no advance knowledge about the person called upon. Calls upon all the dentists or lawyers in the community or upon each resident in a certain section of the city would be cold-canvass work.

Some salesmen dislike the term "cold turkey" and prefer to use "cold canvassing" or "new account" in referring to such calls. The latter has a

[1] When hens are not laying or are hiding their nests in haymows and under corncribs, farmers sometimes place a china egg in a regular nest as a suggestion to the hen that she should deposit her eggs there. She often follows this suggestion but meets with frustration when she tries to hatch this egg along with the others.

positive connotation, a hint of probable success, is more dignified, and
carries no unpleasant association.

One firm attributes its success to a policy of making cold calls. "We
went around the city looking for smokestacks. When we found a smokestack we knew there was a manufacturer and, therefore, a prospect," said
Mr. Norman Stone, president of Stone Container Corporation.[2]

While most industrial salesmen consider the random calling upon all
business firms to be cold canvassing, in strict theory this prospecting
method still contains considerable selectivity. Any sizable manufacturer
would have need for containers and could probably pay for them, so he
would qualify by sight as a prospect.

QUALIFYING PROSPECTS

Once the salesman has a name of a possible prospect—a lead—he must
qualify it. Is that person or firm a good prospect or not? Does he have a
need? Does he have the money? The answers to these questions may be
quite apparent or they may require considerable investigation. It would not
take much imagination on the part of a drapery salesman to realize that the
people who have just purchased a new home will probably be needing
draperies and will probably be able to pay for them; they are good prospects.

On the other hand, someone selling swimming pools is not as fortunate; good prospects are not as obvious. He will have to dig a bit, for there
are no observable facts to indicate if someone in the family is interested in
swimming. Perhaps some observable factors would indicate if they could
afford a pool—cars, furniture, price of house, etc.

The same situation exists in industrial selling. A 3-M salesman selling
sandpaper knows that a furniture factory is a top-quality prospect, but he
would have to qualify a firm called the Acme Manufacturing Company.
What do they make? Do they sand or polish anything? Fortunately, all he
has to do is ask the company's purchasing agent for the answers.

Observe what a life insurance company tells its new agents about
selection of prospects:[3]

Select the names of persons who qualify on all five points of a good prospect:
(1) has need for life insurance, (2) can pay for it, (3) can qualify physically, (4)
can qualify morally and is in an acceptable occupation, (5) is accessible and
of the right type for you (age, race, etc.). Read down the list, name by name,
giving each a numerical value. If the first name qualifies on all five points, write
in the number five; if the second qualifies on three points, write in the number

2 "'Cold' Calls Make Hot Prospects," *Chicago Tribune*, Nov. 1, 1966.
3 From the Penn Mutual Life Insurance Company's course for new agents, "Organized Life Insurance Selling," Book II, Prospecting.

three, so that when you finish, the highest ranking names will be easily seen. Leave the low-rated names until you can clear up doubts or you have called on all your best prospects.

There is a financial reason for carefully selecting your prospects. The shopkeeper cannot succeed in business if it costs him too much money to get people into his store. You cannot succeed in the life insurance business if your sales cost you too much time to locate, for your time is money. Careful as you can be, there always will be a large percentage of "no sales" in the prospect pack, and calling upon these is an experience that will wear you out and undermine your courage. On the other hand, those that you do sell will give you confidence and renew your courage.

Reverting briefly to the analogy between the salesman and the prospector for valuable ore, we may observe that some mineral deposits may be five or ten times as rich as others. It is the same with a prospect list—one list may contain 10 percent of really good prospects, while another will contain 25 percent or even more. The difference is in the care and intelligence with which the salesman qualifies each name on his list. Prospects are not merely *names*—they are *people*. Some are more likely to buy than others are. What is being stressed here is that a smart salesman qualifies or tests each name before placing it on *any* list of prospects. Quality of prospects is fully as important as mere numbers or quantity.

SOME COMMON PROSPECTING SYSTEMS

Several so-called "systems" have been worked out to make the salesman more efficient as a prospector. It should be emphasized, however, that no system is a guarantee of successful prospecting unless it is followed intelligently and consistently so that it becomes an integral part of the salesman's work schedule. Every successful salesman has developed his own method of getting prospects, which is probably a combination of the plans here suggested. The important thing is to follow a plan that proves effective in supplying a constantly fresh list of live prospects; any system that does this is a good one. If a system fails to yield this result, it should be abandoned for one that does.

No effort has been made to discuss different systems in the order of their effectiveness. Some may be better adapted to certain types of salesmen and kinds of products than are others. Six prospecting systems are used widely enough to justify some explanation and comment. These are (1) endless chain; (2) center of influence; (3) personal observation; (4) junior salesman (sometimes called the "spotter" plan); (5) cold canvass; and (6) direct mail and telephone.

No matter which system is used, the salesman must ever remind himself that *friends* furnish him with more names than he can usually pick up from any other source. The first four systems are based on the help given by *people;* if these people are also *friends,* they will provide the salesman with more and better names than mere acquaintances would.

The endless chain

This system is based upon the idea that from each interview the salesman should secure the names of additional prospects for future interviews. Most salesmen who employ this method attempt to get from each person *interviewed* (not just called upon) the names of two or three of his friends who possess the same needs for the product or service. Naturally, the plan is more effective when the salesman has been successful in selling the prospect just interviewed, as the new buyer is probably enthusiastic about his purchase and may believe that some of his friends might like to consider the same proposition. However, even when the sale has not been made, the plan can work. The prospect was probably interested in the sales offer or he would not have consented to listen to the salesman's story. Even though he was unable to act immediately, he should still be able to suggest two or three acquaintances who would have the same need for the product and might be able to act at once.

The salesman may say to such a person, "I understand why you feel you cannot buy just now, but I'm sure you can think of three or four of your acquaintances who could use my product to advantage."

Occasionally the prospect will object, "I wouldn't want to inflict you on any of my friends." A reply is, "All right (with a broad smile), how about giving me the name of a few guys you don't like very well?"

An encyclopedia salesman uses a flattering technique in getting referrals. He says: "The recommendations I'd like to get from you are not recommendations of just anyone, but of those who *share* your appreciation for an educational program of this caliber." He says that more than one-third of his sales are from referrals.

Many companies have trained their salesmen to use parts of the endless-chain plan for securing prospects, but only a few companies have applied the plan in its fullest extent. One company conducts a Good-will Club, with special privileges and gifts for those who cooperate by turning in names of others who might be interested in the product. Other companies provide salesmen with introduction cards to be filled out by individuals willing to introduce the salesman to other prospects. One of the more complete plans employing many ramifications of endless-chain prospecting is that of the International Correspondence Schools. In the sales manual of the ICS, this prospecting system is discussed completely.

The division director who gives the details of this plan explains that he used it for years when he was in charge of a route and that most of the men under his direction are now using it with great success.

On the assumption that an enrollment constitutes the first link in this "chain," the following request is made of the newly enrolled student, and a record taken in a notebook of the information furnished:

"Please give me the name of one person who works at the same place you do. Give me the name of another." Continue until you have the names of all the people working with him. Then ask for the name of one person with whom the student is intimately acquainted, and continue to ask for the names of other acquaintances, until all the names possible are obtained.

Then take each name in turn, and ask if that person will make a good student. If the answer is "No," ask "Why?" for often the answer will lead you to believe the person is worth interviewing. But, when the answer is "Yes," inquire further so as to learn where the prospect works, hours he works, approximate salary, where he lives, marital state, etc. Ask your informant when he will see this particular person again; and, if possible, get the student to promise that he will show his lessons to the prospect and explain what he thinks of the schools and his courses, and what he expects to accomplish through his studies. If the student agrees to do this, make a definite appointment to get a report of the interview. When you have obtained this report, you will know what to do.

If you cannot induce your "endless chainer" to interview the prospect, interview him yourself. Whether or not the interview results in an enrollment, you can use the endless-chain process on him also, obtaining the names and the other information about several of his friends. For example, starting with one person, these data are obtained about two more. When these two persons are interviewed, two more are obtained from each, or a total of four. These four will yield eight; these eight, sixteen—therefore, the name endless chain.

Analyzing this plan, you have: first, the name and address and working hours of a prospect, as well as the name of his employer. This information will guide you as to the most suitable time and place for an interview. Second, you have learned the approximate earnings of the prospect, which will indicate whether or not he can afford a course. Third, you know in advance whether the prospect is married or single and whether he is thrifty and ambitious.

The endless-chain method is especially effective in the development of prospects for intangibles like investments and insurance. In the sale of such services, it is necessary for the salesman to establish a feeling of confidence and goodwill between his prospect and himself early in the sales interview. If this is not done, the prospect will frequently prove unwilling to enter into a discussion of his private financial problems with a comparative stranger. However, if the salesman can come bearing a short note or card of introduction from a friend of the prospect, it is much more likely that he will be accepted upon essentially a basis of friendship and confidence. Although the salesman has not actually been *recommended* to the prospect, still the introduction carries with it an element of recommendation because the prospect reasons that unless his friend had felt confidence in the salesman he would not have given him the introduction.

This constitutes what is called a *referred lead*. It is the best kind of prospect, because a basis of friendliness and mutuality of interests has been established between salesman and prospect. However, it is not any guarantee of success in the sale; that will depend upon the skill of the salesman in discovering the real problems of the prospect and solving them.

An executive for the Singer Sewing Machine Co. said: "A year ago we relied to a great extent on the cold canvass method. We now put a great deal of emphasis on referrals, especially in the more populated areas. . . . These referrals come mainly from satisfied customers, and we go a long way in trying to satisfy a customer."

Salesmen for mutual funds use the referral method almost exclusively, as do house-to-house salesmen for cooking utensils.

In industrial selling the endless-chain prospecting system, also known as referral selling, is widely used. Who is in a better position to know other businessmen who might be prospects than the businessman with whom the salesman is talking? One salesman of popular-priced men's slacks called upon a small dealer handling men's apparel, one who carried only quality lines. While he quickly turned the salesman down once the price line of the slacks was discovered, he did refer the salesman to the stores in town which would be the most likely to take on the line. A salesman for Inland Container was referred by a customer to a new firm that was opening its doors and would be needing some packaging for its products.

Center of influence

In this system the salesman develops in his community or territory a number of persons who serve as his "centers of influence." These people may be customers of the salesman or they may be influential friends who are willing to cooperate.

As an illustration of how this system might function, let us assume that a salesman of stocks and bonds returns to build up a business in the town where he attended college, and was a prominent athlete and a member of a fraternity as well as other college organizations. He starts to develop several centers of influence to aid him in obtaining good prospects. He gets in touch with his old professor of finance, his former coach, his fraternity adviser, and two or three well-known businessmen who remember him. To these centers of influence he explains what kind of persons he hopes to do business with, what his investment service offers, and to what extent his knowledge and experience could benefit his clients. He persuades these centers of influence to assist him in meeting good prospects. Probably he will try to make clients out of as many of these centers of influence as possible, although that is not necessary to the success of the system.

Referring to the Penn Mutual Life Insurance Company's training course for agents, this is the company's suggestion for the use of this prospecting plan:

Call on the most important man you know and say as follows:

"George, you know I'm in the life insurance business. I haven't come around to talk to you about that or to try to sell you anything. But there is something you can do that will help me a lot. Who is the most promising young businessman you know? I'm going to tell you exactly what I expect to say to him. You can punch it full of holes if you don't like it and I would consider it a favor."

Give him your sales presentation. (He *may* buy. This is known as a by-product sale.)

Ask for card of introduction.

Here is another method of approach for new agents:

"Mr. Brown, I have made what I believe to be a mighty fine connection with a real future for me. I am at present taking the training course of the Penn Mutual Life Insurance Company, but I am doing no selling as yet. As I expect this to become my lifework, I am anxious to build a permanent and substantial clientele.

"You can help me to this extent, if you will. My job is to get before people in a favorable light. Who is the most promising young married man you know?"

In the event that a man says that he cannot think of anyone, it will be necessary for you to stimulate his recollection by pointing out such men as his office associates, his doctor, his dentist, neighbors, fellow members of his church, etc. The important thing to remember in prospecting through centers of influence is that they should be *favorably impressed* with you. Do everything you can to enhance this feeling.

A life insurance salesman aided the minister of his church in solving a critical financial problem in connection with a new church building. The minister was not able to buy life insurance, but he did prove an invaluable center of influence. By putting the agent in touch with members of the congregation who had need for the services of the insurance expert he supplied qualified prospects and provided an approach to them upon a basis of friendship and confidence. Although the minister received no direct reward for his cooperation, he was a good enough salesman himself to realize that he received in return the support and financial assistance of the salesman. This recognition of the value of such cooperation is what enables the salesman to build up centers of influence. A businessman will help because he knows that the salesman in turn may be in a position to assist him. The banker helps because he values the goodwill and the patronage of the salesman.

Industrial salesmen frequently use other salesmen as sources of prospect information. Representatives for noncompeting products are usually more than willing to talk about developments in the territory—new firms opening up, personnel changes, troubles being encountered by various concerns, new activities being initiated by existing firms, and other gossip. They are willing to help you, for they expect you to return the favor—you scratch my back, I'll scratch yours.

For many salesmen, bankers prove most helpful. They have more contacts than most people and know just about everything that is going on in the business community. The larger banks have officers who are highly specialized in their training, one being an expert on the steel industry, and others who have spent years learning about oil or textiles or paper. It is a wise salesman who cultivates a close friendship with a knowledgeable banker. Similarly, many stockbrokers are especially well informed about what is going on in the area.

Businessmen in an industry usually are the best source of information as to what is going on in that industry, for they must keep abreast of current developments. They have lunch with other executives and pick up many bits of information that may be of value to salesmen. Who is thinking of remodeling his office, who is looking at computers, who is having packaging problems, who is unhappy with his trucking connections, who needs a new conveyor system, etc. Naturally, some executives are more in the know than others. Many salesmen make it a point to become good friends with executives who seem to know what is going on and who like to talk about it. Those who wonder why men will give such information to salesmen should realize that in doing so they make themselves feel more important, and they hope to enhance their prestige with the salesmen; they like to give the impression that they are industry big shots.

Salesmen employing the center-of-influence method usually make an effort to repay the services of their contact group by periodic expressions of appreciation such as gifts at Christmas time, cards on anniversaries, and fairly frequent calls to thank them personally for a recent courtesy, to explain a new service or feature of the salesman's line which might reawaken their interest in it and in him, and to direct their thought so that names of new possible prospects might come to them. These calls take little of a salesman's time if planned for regularly, and they are essential to the success of the plan. No one is going to give much thought to helping a salesman unless that salesman proves himself grateful and a helpful friend in return. In addition, many businessmen expect information in return. They expect the salesman to give them some prospects which he encounters in his calls. Walter Schreibweiss, sales promotion manager for Lily-Tulip Cup

Co., claims,[4] "I teamed up once with three other salesmen in noncompetitive lines to furnish information to each other. We called on the same market. I had tie-ins with a salesman who sold ice cream cabinets, for example, and another tie-in with a man calling on the restaurant trade. Anyway, I'd come home at night and there'd always be three or four leads. And I'd have three or four for the other fellows."

Just one further thought: *every* individual is a center of influence. He is the center of his own little world, and he can exert *some* influence on certain persons. The more friends a salesman has, the more centers of influence he can utilize in finding prospects.

Personal observation

The personal-observation system is used many times by the great majority of salesmen. Some salesmen call it the "intuitive" or "eyes-and-ears" system. It consists of being constantly alert to recognize prospect leads no matter where the salesman is or with whom he may be talking. This ability to discover prospects in the routine of daily existence is much more highly developed in some salesmen than in others.

A life insurance salesman was sitting at a service club luncheon with seven friends. One of the men seated at this table was a competitor; the others were business and professional men. During the luncheon various members of the little group dropped remarks which our salesman noted particularly, because each remark appeared to him to contain a valuable prospect lead. As a consequence of those chance remarks this salesman gathered information that enabled him subsequently to make two sizable sales. His competitor, sitting at the same table, evidently failed to appreciate that the remarks had "prospecting" significance.

In the use of this method a salesman should develop a "nose for prospects" as keen as the good reporter's nose for news. Indeed, a tip concerning a hot prospect *is* news of the best kind to such a salesman.

The local newspaper is filled with news items which are leads. Some of these items are useful to certain salesmen and of scant value to others; hence it is necessary to evaluate each one in terms of the individual salesman's prospecting problem.

For example, the insurance salesman notes news of promotions, engagements, weddings, births, deaths, and stories dealing with business and finance. The salesman of machinery and factory equipment watches for news of awarding of contracts for roads or buildings, for building permits,

4 "Roundtable Report on Finding and Following Up Leads to More Sales," *The American Salesman*, June, 1960, p. 74.

for classified ads seeking additional workers, for fires or other catastrophes
involving factories, for news concerning new products. The society page
contains many items of interest to salesmen for home furnishings, wearing
apparel, jewelry, etc. The route man driving a milk delivery truck notes
births and marriages in the paper. The real estate broker is keenly interested in approaching weddings, transfers of executives to or from the community, expansion plans of local business concerns, and promotions of
personnel to better paying jobs. A change in a zoning ordinance or a legal
inquiry concerning eviction of tenants is grist for his mill.

Just about every salesman can find items of real value to him in his
local newspaper and he should learn to read it with a seeing eye.

The industrial salesman and the sales engineer will find that trade
publications in their industry and the industries of their potential customers are filled with news that will provide good leads. Certain firms are
expanding their operations into new fields. A company is building a new
plant in West Overshoe, Montana. An advertisement of a firm announcing
a new product may suggest additional needs this item will create for its
buyers, as many products complement each other. A merger may free a
customer from his reciprocity buying arrangement with a competitor. Every
action in the business world creates markets for many different firms. Every
business start-up, expansion, or demise brings forth demand for certain
products. Think of all the goods and services required by a new company
just getting its operations under way.

Many rather ingenious prospecting methods based on using one's eyes
in coordination with the brain have been developed by resourceful salesmen. Some of these involve leg work, too.

Charles M. Stern, field manager for Toch Bros., Inc. (waterproofing
chemicals), relates:[5] "I take walks just to look for problems which our
products can solve. Not long ago I was walking near New York's Central
Park. I noted that the casement windows in a new apartment development
had started to warp, a condition our product can correct. I've sold the management 150,000 linear feet of our stripping since that day."

Salesmen for printing paper scan magazines for poor half-tones, un-
even opacity, or lint buildup on printers' presses. They find in these and
other signs evidence that the publication is using the wrong kind of paper
and is, therefore, a prospect for a paper that will give better results.

An Indiana office furniture salesman does some of his prospecting by
prowling the streets at night. He scouts for office lights burning long after
the end of the work day and approaches the burners of the midnight oil the
following day with the idea that they set up a second office at home. He

[5] *The American Salesman,* February, 1962, p. 17.

also cites tax deductions the Internal Revenue Service allows for home offices as a strong second inducement.

In Los Angeles there's a highly successful Cadillac salesman who has a telephone in his demonstrator. Out prospecting, he cruises down residential streets looking for old Caddies. When he spots one, he turns right into the driveway behind it. Then he looks up the homeowner's name in a criss-cross telephone directory which he carries. Picking up his radio-telephone, he calls up.

"Good afternoon, Mrs. Jones, this is John Smith of Super Motors. Have you seen the new Cadillac?"

"No, I haven't."

"Would you like to ride in one? I'm sitting in your driveway right now, Mrs. Jones, in a brand-new Cadillac and would like you to feel how it drives."

One insurance salesman uses this system to locate male prospects he can call on at home during the day: He stops at factory parking lots in the evenings and jots down license plate numbers of cars. Then he checks them with car dealers for the names of the owners. Since they're working on the swing shift, he can see them late in the morning or early in the afternoon.

Real estate salesmen cruise the streets looking for clues to prospects: houses with "For Sale by Owner" signs on them, empty buildings, new "For Lease" signs, new construction, etc. One enterprising Los Angeles real estate salesman who specialized in industrial properties developed a particularly effective way of discovering manufacturers who were thinking of moving to a larger building. He would walk around industrial areas looking for plants whose parking lots were overflowing. He reasoned that if the company had outgrown its parking facilities it might also have outgrown its plant. He was usually right.

If this method of personal observation is followed to its logical conclusion, the salesman will be on the lookout for bits of information while on the way to work, in the office, on the street, waiting to interview prospects or actually talking with them, at lunch, or at home listening to the conversation or reading the newspaper. Prospects are everywhere; all you have to do is keep your eyes and ears open and learn to recognize the signs.

Junior salesmen (spotters) and bird dogs

Some concerns use junior salesmen—sometimes called "spotters"—to locate prospects, thus relieving more experienced salesmen of prospecting so that they can spend more time actually selling.

The "spotters" usually cold canvass a likely area under some guise— making a survey or making a free service call. When they encounter a person who seems to have a need and the money, they may make arrangements for the senior salesman to call or they may just pass the name on to the boss.

A variation of this method is found in the use of "bird dogs." These helpers are not employed by the company but by the salesman himself. For example, the meter reader enters the basements of homes on his route and can furnish information to salesmen of several types of product. The elevator boy in an office building knows a good deal about the tenants. The policeman on a regular beat learns much that might prove helpful to salesmen. In sales situations where prospects are located only after a search, such bird dogs may be valuable.

A more dignified and tactful name for these "bird dogs" is "sales associates." These persons usually operate on a paid-on-delivery basis, provided the sale is made within a stipulated time. It is essential that the salesman maintain close contact with them, telephoning them or meeting them personally at frequent intervals to keep them on their toes. He must *expect* some good leads from them and let them know that he is depending on them to come through. When they have helped to bring about a sale, the salesman should not only pay them promptly, but praise and thank them as well. The understanding as to payment must be clear. When the salesman is given a name by a sales associate, he should tell the latter whether the name is already listed, especially if another salesman has that prospect's name. Sales associates are found in many places.

Normally the salesman tries to hire "bird dogs" who are in positions in which they naturally intercept people who have a need for the salesman's wares. A Chrysler salesman developed a system of bird dogs among service station personnel who repaired cars. People talk to their repairmen. If they are looking for a car, or even thinking about a new one, they will frequently mention it to the repairman.

A milkman used moving van truck drivers as bird dogs for locating new residents in his territory.

Cold canvass

A story is related of a typewriter salesman in Chicago who had experienced little success. At the close of a week's work showing no sales, his manager said to him: "Next week I want you to work exactly as I tell you. I want you to walk into every office or place of business in every building you go by, place your business card in the hands of someone there, ask them if they want to buy a typewriter; and if they say they are not interested, get out. For every call you make in this manner, you will be paid 25 cents." At the end of a week, during which the salesman had followed these instructions implicitly, he had earned approximately $100 by averaging 80 calls each day. In addition he had sold three machines to people who kept his card and called up to invite him back. Five other machines were sold later as a result of this week's work.

This is generally called cold canvass, or cold-turkey canvass, or new account canvass. The salesman knows little or nothing about each person called upon except perhaps his name. The law of averages is supposed to result in a satisfactory number of good prospects and sales.

Many salesmen contend that such a prospecting plan is no system at all and that it indicates a lack of professional attitude. Here again the nature of the product being sold has a great deal to do with the prospecting methods employed. Cold canvass appears to be a sound system in the sale of *tangible* products in *general* use; it is more debatable in the case of intangible services which are sold largely upon the basis of confidence and familiarity with the individual needs of each particular prospect.

The Avon lady calls on a prospect for the first time. She is apt to get an audience, for the prospect knows that she will be buying cosmetics in the future and, "Who knows, perhaps Avon has something that I will like!" But a securities salesman or a life underwriter calling cold would probably encounter little more than rejection.

Because of this obvious difference in the reactions of prospects, the cold canvass seems best adapted to selling those articles and services which are almost essentials, such as cars, home appliances, fire insurance, automobile insurance, and similar necessities.

A leading manufacturer of washing machines lists 21 methods for salesmen to obtain leads and adds this conclusion:

Of all the different ways and means of securing prospects the most productive method is, unquestionably, straight canvassing. . . . Every doorbell rung is money in your pocket. . . . In some localities, where tests have been made, it was found that with certain salesmen each doorbell rung averaged for him approximately $1 in commissions earned. Others averaged slightly lower, but in every case the amount was surprisingly high.

The National Cash Register Company exhorts its salesmen to "go to the end of the street" when canvassing a new territory, for this company knows that prospects are discovered in proportion to the number of calls made. Sometimes a splendid prospect may be located in an out-of-the-way place where competing salesmen have overlooked him.

While the cold canvass is often thought of as being most applicable to the selling of consumer goods, it is employed in other types of selling also. Practically every industrial salesman or sales engineer has made his share of cold calls. The general sales manager of Chase Bag Company said, "I'm

(a)

You Get Big Valuable "Coupon Book" Awards!

SEARS will give you a $5.00 Merchandise Coupon Book for the name of any person who purchases from us one of the appliances listed. You simply send us the names of the prospects on the enclosed self-addressed cards (no stamp needed). We will do the selling.

This offer is subject to the following:

(1) The prospect card must be in our files prior to the actual sale of the product.
(2) The sale must be made within 60 days of the filing of the card.
(3) The prospect must buy from Sears Catalog Sales Office.
(4) For each prospect sent in you will receive a $5.00 Merchandise Coupon Book—provided a sale results within the prescribed time limit.
(5) Merchandise coupons may be used for purchases at Sears Catalog Sales Office only.

DON'T WAIT! GET YOUR POST CARDS IN THE MAIL EARLY!

(We reserve the right to discontinue this plan without notice)

(b)

SEARS, ROEBUCK and CO.   Date ....

I believe that· NAME ....

STREET ....

TOWN ....ZONE ....STATE ....

Is a prospect for

☐ Kenmore Automatic Washer   ☐ Kenmore Sewing Machine   ☐ Kenmore Electric Range
☐ Kenmore Automatic Dryer   ☐ Kenmore Vacuum Cleaner   ☐ Coldspot Freezer
☐ Air Conditioner   ☐ Automatic Water Heater   ☐ Coldspot Refrigerator
☐ Chain Link Fence (Orders of $100 or More)   ☐ Kenmore Gas Range   ☐ Silvertone Television

May We Use Your Name? Yes ☐   No ☐

NAME ....

STREET ....

TOWN ....ZONE ....STATE ....

-NOTE: If prospect is interested in more than one appliance, use a separate post card for each appliance. Tear off this post card and mail it postage-free to your Sears Catalog Sales Office.

Figure 6-1   Sears, Roebuck and Co. conducted a prospecting program for its appliances by distributing to its customers booklets of postcards as shown above. *(a)* inside cover of coupon booklet; *(b)* a self-addressed postage-free postcard.

very skeptical of a man who doesn't have a natural curiosity about what's going on in his territory. If he'll pass right by a factory and never find out what they make, I'm afraid for him.''

Direct mail and the telephone

It seems logical to ask, "Why does any salesman content himself with a direct-mail effort in the hope of securing a prospect when a personal call would be so much more effective?" One answer is that the salesman has so many potential prospects of widely varying quality that he wants to spend his time only with the best ones. So he sends the mail announcement to everybody and calls first upon those who invite him to come. The second answer is that direct mail uncovers new prospects. One real estate broker regularly sends a letter to each resident living in a certain highly desirable area inquiring if he is planning to sell his house. New, unknown prospects are discovered with each mailing.

Several door-to-door book companies maintain large direct-mail advertising campaigns from which they receive return postcards asking for information concerning their products. These leads are then usually sold to the salesmen; one firm gets $6 apiece for them.

Many firms generate the names of prospects from their advertising programs. Sometimes the magazine reader is provided a coupon which he can return if he is interested in receiving more information about the product. Most industrial trade journals provide product information cards on which each reader is able to check a number which corresponds to products in which he is interested. The magazine then forwards the list of prospects to the manufacturers who, in turn, send each name to the salesman in the prospect's territory who is supposed to call upon him immediately. At least that is the way the theory goes. Reality is a bit different.

For years salesmen and dealers have been sharply criticized for not following up the leads sent to them by manufacturers. A part of this laxity may be attributed to inertia or lack of time, but some of it is because many of these leads have been found worthless. A good many people, including thousands of youngsters, are addicted to clipping coupons which promise something (a free sample, for instance) for merely sending in the coupon. It is impossible for the manufacturer to sift these inquiries; he must leave this to the dealer or salesman on the scene. Perhaps it would pay to phone more of these prospects than is commonly done and thus determine whether they are good prospects. A personal follow-up could be made on the better ones.

The telephone can be a great time-saver. Phone calls to regular customers between personal visits may uncover something they need urgently at that time. One lumberyard salesman phones all the sizable contractors in town early each morning before the work crews go out in order to find out what they will be needing that day. The man on the spot gets the business. It pays to keep in contact with potential customers.

Some consumer salesmen do their prospecting by telephone. One vacuum cleaner salesman's wife systematically calls everyone listed in the telephone book to find out if he would be interested in seeing a vacuum cleaner demonstrated. Although many salesmen use the telephone deceptively, this man made a straightforward approach to the subject. His reasoning was: "I know from sales statistics that each day in this city a certain number of people are thinking about buying a vacuum cleaner. If they are, they will voluntarily ask for a demonstration of mine because they will recognize my brand name and want to get my deal before buying. My task is to locate such people. How do I do it? I just have my wife ask them. She keeps me supplied with so many goods leads that I don't have time for additional prospecting. Also these people I call on have asked me to show my machine, which puts a completely different light on my reception and the atmosphere surrounding the presentation than if I had used some of these trick ways of getting people to watch my demo."

Other sources of prospects

Different kinds of salesmen find prospects in different ways or from different sources. To every kind of salesman certain prospect sources are available; usually the firm has ample instructional material guiding its own salesmen to prospects for its products.

For example, the Maytag Company teaches its salesmen to dig up prospects from 30 different sources, as follows:

Regular customers who come back
Personal solicitation of Maytag owners
Field solicitation and house-to-house canvassing
Letter and return card to present users
Telephone solicitation
Circular letter with return card
Newspaper advertising
Exhibits at automobile shows, fairs, carnivals, etc.
Cooking schools and home shows
Demonstrations at church and society activities
Guessing contests
Drawing and registration schemes
Bonus for Maytag owners giving names of prospects
Home survey by calling at every fifth house
Demonstrations to high school domestic science classes
Classified ads of second-hand washers in papers
Store and window demonstrations
Newspaper coupons
Ask your prospects for other prospects
Newlyweds
Birth announcements
Washerwoman ads in papers
Situation- or laundress-wanted ads in papers
Newly wired houses or contracts for service
Radio, insurance, automobile, and vacuum cleaner salesmen
Regular charge-account customers
Bookkeepers, repairmen, linemen, clerks, etc.
News leads in daily newspapers
Special invitation cards to the store
Gas inspectors, meter readers, etc.

The list of prospect sources is planned primarily for the salesmen representing the retail dealer who handles the machine in his line of merchandise. Each one of these different sources is explained so that a beginner would understand exactly how it might be developed. For example, the first source is explained as follows:[6]

Regular customers who come into the store One of the most common sources of prospects for Maytag washers is from the regular customers who come into the dealer's store. In this, we are speaking of general merchandise establishments and hardware stores rather than specialty stores, because the general establishment has larger floor traffic than the appliance shop, which sells only a specialized type of merchandise. A greater percentage of the store's regular trade than one might suspect are actually washer prospects. Believe it or not, many people are not aware of their need for a new washer until the proposition is put up to them in the proper way. Many who know they are in need of a washer postpone buying from month to month because there are so many other things they want.

Some of these sources of prospects in the Maytag training manual are sufficiently important to merit a separate discussion at this point.

OLD CUSTOMERS As is clearly indicated in the Maytag material, old customers are frequently the best source of new business. This is particularly true of industrial selling. After all, these people have been using your product; *ergo,* they must like it. Such people are more than willing to tell others of their happy experience. Your old customers know *you,* and you have had a good chance to build up their confidence in you; hence, there should be no barrier between you and them that would make them reluctant to cooperate. Finally, old customers are frequently in the market themselves. The salesman who is so devoted to seeking new business that he fails to get all the volume available from old accounts is making his job unnecessarily difficult. It is commonly easier to get an order from an old customer than from a new one, and that order will often be larger if the salesman has won the buyer's confidence and his product has given satisfaction.

SERVICE PERSONNEL Companies maintaining departments to service the product they sell often find that the servicemen are in a position to furnish excellent leads. Stewart Gooding of Remington Rand claimed that leads obtained from their mechanical service department, the fellows who go around and repair machines, are the best they have. "Eighty percent of the time there is a return on the leads they give us."[7]

6 From the sales manual of the Maytag Company.
7 *The American Salesman,* June, 1960, p. 74.

A serviceman is one of the first to know when someone is needing replacement equipment. One TV repair shop sells such leads to an appliance store that sells a high percentage of them. One Oldsmobile dealer in Miami, Florida, has a salesman stationed at the drive-up islands at which patrons stop to have their sick machines diagnosed. He says, "While you are waiting, why don't we go for a drive in a new Oldsmobile?"

Naturally, servicemen should be given an adequate incentive to keep their eyes open for such opportunities. Some firms give their servicemen sales training to maximize their effectiveness as prospectors.

CLASSIFIED LISTS AND DIRECTORIES   Among the more important sources of leads to prospective buyers are various classified lists and directories which are available in great quantity. Starting with the largest prospect list of all, the telephone directory, the parade of such lists goes down to such specific ones as the membership rosters of various small organizations and lists of club members. One sales manager, Warren Runkle of American Chain and Cable, said, "I'd be tempted to discharge a man if he didn't have some yellow pages from the telephone book in his bag."[8] Naturally, the telephone company is not too happy with this practice.

Practically every industry has one or more trade or professional associations connected with it. Such an organization usually has available a roster of its membership. Salesmen find these rosters indispensable prospecting and preapproaching aids.

EXPOSURE   A basic tenet of selling could be stated as, "The productivity of a salesman varies directly with his exposure in the market." A salesman cannot sell hiding in the office, at home, or in a bar. He must get out and meet people. Most highly productive salesmen obtain maximum exposure of their personality and products by joining a number of clubs and participating in a variety of civic activities on the general thesis that they simply cannot know too many people. Rare is the salesman who cannot honestly say that he has come across some of his best leads during an idle conversation at some party, luncheon, golf match, etc. Leads can come from anywhere at any time, and one is never certain when any given individual is going to be in need of his product or service.

This factor of exposure is one of the reasons why it takes time for a salesman to become a top producer. One does not obtain widespread exposure and establish the necessary number of contacts in a few months or even a few years. It follows that the more experienced salesman generally

8 Ibid.

has higher productivity; he simply has more contacts. This is also one strong reason why a good salesman should not be hasty in changing his employer or product line; he may lose many of his contacts and be forced to spend considerable time in establishing new ones. One salesman for the Gardner-Denver Company selling oil field equipment devoted a full two years just making contacts with various executives connected with oil companies and drilling contractors. He spent some time around the Petroleum Club building in Denver playing gin rummy, a peculiarity of the industry, and getting to know all the influential people in the Rocky Mountain oil industry. He sold absolutely nothing for two years, but during the third year the orders rolled in, and he quickly established himself as one of the firm's best men. However, he would lose all those contacts should he change jobs to another industry.

Throughout the foregoing discussion of prospecting, many specific illustrations have been presented. The reader should not regard these as a comprehensive treatment of the subject, but rather as only a few suggestions to show that this business of finding prospects is not a dull, routine chore, but a phase of selling which frequently offers a stiff challenge to a salesman's ingenuity, intelligence, and industry.

DETERMINATION OF PROSPECTING SYSTEMS

We have seen that there are many sources from which prospects may be obtained. From these, how can a salesman go about determining the best prospecting system for him to use?

First, the salesman should realize that his system should be tailor-made for him. Because one salesman for his firm largely uses centers of influence for leads, it does not follow that this will be the best source for him. What is one man's food may be another's poison; there is no one best way for all men to operate. It is not unusual to find successful salesmen with the same firm using a wide variety of prospecting methods. Hence, in the early stages of his development the salesman should try all systems and keep records on every name he obtains, where it was obtained, and the outcome of his contact with that prospect. He will thus be able to determine what *his* best source of leads is, measured by sales performance. Thereafter, he will weed out the poorer sources of leads and concentrate on those that pay off best for him. Thus, he develops his own tailor-made system for obtaining leads to good prospects.

Second, with new products it is wise to do some experimenting to learn where the best prospects are. One Rich Plan salesman selling food freezers and food to families went against the advice of his boss and reaped large rewards. Normally, the presentation was built around the alleged savings which the family would realize should they buy a home freezer. The boss recommended concentrating on blue-collar workers to whom the freezer would represent a sort of safety deposit box of food upon which they could fall back when not working. Also he thought the savings appeal was most effective with this group. After working in this market for a short while, the new salesman had sold nothing. He began thinking. The people upon whom he was calling simply did not have the $800 which the program required; they could not really afford the product. Besides, he doubted that they really appreciated the quality of frozen food; they were not used to it. He reasoned that wealthy suburban areas might be the best territories to work because the two advantages of a freezer were (1) convenience and (2) quality of food. His analysis was that the people in the suburban areas need the convenience of the freezer because of their distance from supermarkets. Next, the higher-income families would not only be able to afford the freezer, but would appreciate quality food. He shifted his operation to a wealthy suburb with outstanding success. He said that every buyer just wrote a check for the amount; there was no struggling with credit reports and collections.

Another illustration of the value of thinking through on any prospecting problem comes from the Glidden Co., manufacturers of paint and varnish products. When they brought out a new satin-sheen varnish, they might have simply marketed it through paint stores, but they took time to think. They learned that from 60 to 75 percent of a lumberyard's customers buy lumber to build or remodel homes, and Glidden's new product was designed to finish off new lumber. So they decided (correctly, as it was proved) that lumberyards were the best prospects.

Third, a salesman usually does better selling to prospects with whom he is compatible. This compatibility is concocted of numerous ingredients such as age, educational level, hobbies, religion, race, occupational background, geographical location, income, tastes, and interests in a variety of fields. The more these overlap, the more common ground exists between buyer and seller, and the better they speak each other's language. Many employers assign their salesmen to certain sections of the country or to buyers in a certain industry because of this compatibility factor.

But a salesman should always strive to adapt himself to his prospect and never rule out the possibility of selling a man merely because they have different backgrounds. To confine one's efforts to one type of prospect may be a mistake, unless there are plenty of them.

For instance, an industrial salesman must often be able to communicate his product's benefits to workers, foremen, superintendents, engineers, and top executives. If he sells to business he must be on comfortable terms with office managers, secretaries, and executives. If he sells to retailers, he must deal with merchandising men, clerks, warehousemen, advertising managers, and so on. The salesman *must be adaptable.*

However, it is safe to generalize that a salesman will do better when calling on prospects whom he understands and likes.

Most salesmen maintain a prospect file, using 3- by 5-inch cards for that purpose. On these cards notations are made as to the various items of information gained in the preapproach and from any calls made on the prospect. Often, a general prospect list is maintained for the entire sales force, as in offices selling real estate, securities, or insurance. Here it is important to keep careful records of just which prospects belong to each salesman. As a rule, if prospects are not distributed geographically, the salesman who calls first has the first claim on the prospect, but it is customary to insist that he call at stated intervals, or the prospect will be considered "open territory" to be claimed by any other salesman on the staff who calls on him.

If the sales force is not too large, prospect cards may be filed alphabetically. In the case of a large sales organization they may be filed geographically, by neighborhoods, to facilitate making calls.

Colored tabs or guides may be used to indicate that the prospect should be called on again at a certain date. Other salesmen use a tickler file for this purpose, filing their "call-back" cards so that they will automatically turn up on the desired day.

As fast as prospects buy, the cards are removed from the *prospect* file and placed in the *customer* file. It should be the aim of every salesman to keep a fair proportion of *new* prospect cards in his prospect file. A file of old, dirty, thumbed prospect cards is an indication that the salesman is shirking the task of digging up fresh prospects.

The importance of maintaining a fat prospect file is strikingly proved by the experience of John Williams, an automobile salesman in Chicago, who sold in one year more General Motors cars than any other salesman in Illinois. He maintains a file of more than 2,000 prospective buyers, makes 50 telephone calls a day, and has a group of "bird dogs" who keep him informed about possible prospects. His file is further fattened by his record of his customers' children, and as each comes of age, his name is placed in the prospect file. It is evident that Mr. Williams owes much of his success to vigorous and intelligent prospecting.

"Hit from where your hand is"

Finally, no salesman can depend entirely on his "systems" to find prospects. A prospect may appear suddenly and unexpectedly. The salesman must be mentally prepared to deal with such a situation instantly. As a famous boxing champion put it, "You gotta learn to hit from where your hand is." A woman selling shares in a mutual fund tells this story:[9]

[9] *The American Salesman*, September, 1956.

I was waiting for my car to be brought from a garage where I leave it frequently. It was driven up by an older man. As he stepped out beside me, I
sensed that he wanted to say something to me, so I hesitated before getting
into the car. Almost mumbling with embarrassment he said: "Mrs. Kennedy,
may I ask you something?" "Certainly," I answered. "Well," he said, "I have a
son who is a priest, and he would like to invest some money. Could he come
to talk to you about it?" Naturally I said Yes, and the young priest arrived with
his mother at my house on a scorching August night. I sized them up, and
explained as solicitously as I knew how that they would have to be prepared to
invest at least $50 to start with, and continue with $50 a month. The priest
translated what I said to his mother, and I realized that the parents, not the
priest, were to make the investment. Following his talk with his mother, he
turned to me to say: "We want to invest Five." Patiently, I said that $5 would
not be enough. He immediately said: "Not five dollars—$5,000—to be fol-
lowed by $100 a month." They have kept up their payments regularly, falling
below $100 in only one month. You never know where a good sale is waiting
for you.

DISCUSSION QUESTIONS

1. You have just completed sales training for a large manufacturer of a wide
   line of adhesives (glues, cements, epoxies). Your assigned territory is in
   the Los Angeles area. With it you have inherited a few good accounts
   from the former salesman; however, you are expected to start building
   new accounts immediately. How would you go about discovering prospects? Be as specific as possible! Make a list of the types of firms you feel
   would be your best prospects.
2. Your mother has decided to become an Avon saleslady. She asks you for
   advice on prospecting. What would you tell her?
3. As a salesman for asphalt shingles, whom would you consider to be prime
   prospects? Make a specfic list of excellent prospects in the order of their
   quality.
4. Describe the best prospects for buying an industrial building for investment.
5. Who would be the best prospects for a Xerox copier/duplicator? What
   factors would the Xerox salesman look for in qualifying leads?
6. You are the regional salesman for a quality line of garden tractors and
   riding lawn mowers. You do not have representation in the town you are
   now in. Survey all possible outlets and qualify them as prospects. Which
   outlet would you most want to get your line into? Why? Justify the placement of each name on your prospect list.
7. If you are a salesman for an oil well drilling fund tax shelter, who would be
   your best prospects? How would you reach them?

8. If you were selling automatic garage door openers, who would be your best prospects? Be specific!
9. What constitutes a good list of prospects? What percentage of the names should develop into sales?
10. How can the want ads be used to discover prospects?

CASE 6-1 SOUTHSIDE CHRYSLER:
Training Salesmen to Prospect

Bob Ryan had just assumed the position of sales manager of the new Southside Chrysler automobile dealership in South Denver when his boss, Bill Crouch, asked to meet with him about the sales training program. His boss opened the meeting by saying, "We both know that we have a huge job ahead of us training an effective sales force. Many of our 16 salesmen will no doubt quit and we will have to be constantly replacing them so training will be a continual problem for us. As you well know, training a salesman takes time; we can't give them an injection of something and declare them salesmen. And the type of man we are able to hire is not the experienced, old professional that all of us might like him to be. So training will be critical to our success. Consequently, we will begin on it immediately. Every morning at 8:30 the entire sales force will meet in the training room for one-half hour. As you know, Chrysler provides a very complete sales training program for us to use. But I feel that it needs supplementing in one critical area—prospecting. And that is one of the most important activities new salesmen should learn. It seems to me that the one thing a car salesman needs, to get him going right away, is a good prospecting system that fits this dealership and that salesman. So my direction to you is: Design a series of half-hour programs for giving our men a sound prospecting system."

Bob replied, "I certainly agree that prospecting is that important, but don't you think that we must first give them product information before getting into prospecting?"

"No, I don't. They already know a great deal about cars, enough to get by most sales. And what they don't know they can quickly pick up while on the floor. But many of these men have no idea how to go about getting enough prospects each day so they can earn a living. I say let's give them the prospecting system and let product knowledge take care of itself. We'll get to it rather quickly in the program anyway."

"Well, how about doing a bit of each? Devote part of each day to product knowledge and then give them some prospecting?" asked Bob.

"You work up the program you feel is right for the next month and bring it in. Then I'll pass judgment on it. OK?" replied the boss.

Bob retreated to the safe confines of his office to mull over his assignment. He was eager to please the boss because this was his first job as sales manager and he had little desire to go back to selling cars full time.

Prospecting had always come easy to Bob. He had a lot of friends locally from his high school days and he had made many new ones through his numerous civic activities. It seemed to him that he always knew of somebody that was ready for a new car. But he knew that many salesmen did not have that flow of prospects. Some men were new in town. Others simply did not seem to have a wide range of friends to bird dog for them.

That evening Bob wandered down to the public library to get some books on selling in the hopes that they might be of some help to him in formalizing a prospecting training course. While they gave him some new thoughts, they still did not provide him exactly what he wanted.

That night Bill decided that he would set aside 10 minutes of each training period for the next month for giving prospecting tips: 30 tips on how to find a good prospect. At least he hoped he could come up with 30 tips. These would be offered just before the end of the meeting.

1. Evaluate Bob's plan. What, if any, changes would you make in it?
2. Work up prospecting tips for Bob to use.

CASE 6-2 AETNA INSURANCE:
Prospecting to Reach Selected Markets

"I made up my mind in my senior year that I wanted to be a life insurance salesman and eventually become a CLU. Naturally, I've been giving the field considerable thought since accepting your offer to work for you. I've come to the conclusion that one must specialize in the market to which he devotes his attention. You can't be all things to all people. You've got to specialize! Some men work the home mortgage insurance market while others go after new parents. There's currently a lot of interest in selling insurance to businessmen for buy-out agreements and other such business applications. So it goes with each man picking a market and going after it. I'd hate to have to list all the different segments of the life insurance market," related Scott Wood, a new recruit, to his boss, Harry Post.

While Harry was absorbing the lecture, he recalled Scott's background: age, twenty-three; good college record; local boy from middle-class family; good dresser; pleasant personality; married, one child; no selling experience; worked way through college as manager of tavern; and quite ambitious.

He replied, "I know that many men have been highly successful concentrating on one segment of the market. And you are certainly correct in your observations about the number of segments which comprise the life insurance market. But I think you are going a bit overboard on it. Keep in mind that there are also many more members of the Million Dollar Round Table who sell insurance to a wide range of prospects. True, many of them do write most of their volume in one segment or another, but it has usually just developed that way from the man's contacts. I think you would be making a big mistake if you focused all of your efforts on just one market. You'd miss a lot of business."

To which Scott declared, "I know that most underwriters cover many markets but that still doesn't make it the best way to operate. I've heard of a highly successful CLU in Lawrence, Kansas, who works only with doctors. He makes contact with them while they are in medical school. He finances some of their early insurance policies and sets some of them up in practice if they need it. He has their business all locked up."

He continued, "I am thinking of doing the same thing here in Indianapolis. We have a big medical school right here where I can meet them. Doctors are perfect prospects. They have a great need for insurance as few of them have any pension plans available to them, and they have the ability to buy it in large amounts. Look at the advantages of this strategy. I have to move in only a few selected circles. I can concentrate on the insurance problems of just one field and become an expert in it. Once I get a foothold in the medical field, the referred leads I can get from happy policyholders will pave the way for easy access to other good prospects."

"You make a good case for your plans," retorted Harry, "but I am afraid that you are only looking at one side of the coin. I urge you to consider the disadvantages of your plan as well."

"Disadvantages! Can you name me a better class of prospects than doctors?" argued Scott.

"As a matter of fact I think I could name several, but that is beside the point. There are bound to be disadvantages to almost any plan of action. At least that has been my experience. I still suggest that you think it over and then we can talk some more about it next week. How about coming in Monday morning at 9? In the meantime, you talk your plans over with some of the other men around the office and get their reactions. OK?" asked Harry.

"Fine! See you Monday. By the way, how much insurance has our company doctor got?"

1. What disadvantages or problems may Scott encounter if he carries out his plan?

2.   If you were Scott and wanted to persuade Harry to give you the green
     light on your plans, what would you have to present to him Monday
     morning?

CASE 6-3   NORMAN HILTON:
Prospects for an Expensive Suit Line

For the fall of 1967, Max Sourland, buyer for The Wardrobe Shop had
taken on the Norman Hilton line of high-quality men's suits and sport
coats by bringing into stock 53 pieces. Additional suits sometimes could be
obtained from the relatively narrow line of fabrics Norman Hilton carried
in stock. Unfortunately, the unique fabrics had to be ordered in advance
(February for the August delivery). These suits were priced to retail from
$150 to $200.

Previously, The Wardrobe's top suit line had been $125 and that had
only been taken on in 1965; prior to that the top price line had been $100.
In 1966, the $125 had been the store's best seller; this encouraged Max to
buy an even better clothing line.

The Wardrobe's salesmen had enjoyed selling the $125 suit because it
had so many talking points over less costly products. They would lay an
$80 suit alongside the $125 one and proceed to show the customer, point by
point, what he was getting for his money. It was an effective technique.

While the Norman Hilton had many talking points over the $125 suit,
still the difference was not as impressive as had been the previous comparison. One of the outstanding differences was in the fabrics used. Norman
Hilton procured exclusive patterns woven to his exact specifications; no
other suit manufacturer would have the same fabrics. And Hilton's fabrics
were unique; customers could easily perceive their superior quality and
"feel."

The Norman Hilton suit had many small tailoring advantages, such as
hand-sewn buttonholes, almost invisible stitching, perfectly matched patterns on seams, deeper hip pockets for larger billfolds, horn buttons, and
other such details. However, one significant difference between the Hilton
line and the others was its generous cut. Where one man might feel a bit
snug in a 42 regular in most suits, in the Hilton he would be comfortable;
sometimes a 41 might even give him a better fit.

The salesmen had been wondering how they would be able to sell this
higher-priced suit when the Hilton salesman called to train them how to do
it. According to him, experience clearly indicated that prime prospects for
the Hilton should be telephoned and invited for a private showing when-

ever some new Hiltons arrived in stock that were their size. The salesman was to get the prospect's permission to telephone him under those circumstances by asking him, "Will it be all right if I phone you when we get some new Hiltons in that are your size?" Cold telephone calls were discouraged except if the salesman knew the man personally. The salesmen were surprised and delighted with the ease of getting a prospect's permission to call him.

Now the men faced the question: Who are Norman Hilton prospects? Obviously, only a small percentage of the store's customers were prospects, but who were they? What characteristics do they possess that allow them to be identified?

1. Describe the Norman Hilton customer.
2. What key factors would you look for in locating a prospect for a Norman Hilton suit?

CASE 6-4 NATIONAL ADHESIVES COMPANY:
Prospecting for New Accounts

Bud Rogers, the new representative for National Adhesives in the Richmond, Virginia, territory, had been told by his manager that he faced a Herculean task in rebuilding his territory from its present low production up to its true potential. Many of the large potential accounts were firmly held by competitors and would take much time and solicitation before any volume would be obtained from them. In the meantime, Bud had to eat, so that meant that he had to get some quick volume from someone. He thought this could be accomplished by working among the smaller prospects where competition was not as vigorous.

National produced a complete line of adhesives; it had a product for every application. This was one of the factors that caused Bud to apply to the company for employment; he liked the idea of being able to sell to anyone needing adhesives, not just to those who needed what he happened to be selling. Bud was being compensated by a complex commission system which disproportionately rewarded him for producing new sales volume. Sales made to existing accounts were not overly profitable to Bud.

Bud had been given several different prospecting systems while he was in sales training school. One of the best systems, he had been told, was to take the list of present accounts and then locate every one of their competitors in the area. If a brewery was a good customer, then contact all other breweries. If a cigarette manufacturer was a good customer, then contact all other cigarette manufacturers. Bud saw one difficulty with this system in his instance: he had so few (11) existing accounts that he was sure that significant potential accounts would be missed by following it.

And then there was the telephone book system. Many men claimed that they sat down with the phone book and patiently went through the Yellow Pages firm by firm asking themselves of each, "Would this firm have use for adhesives?"

Some men reported success by privately contacting representatives of mill supply houses to learn about the industrial activity in the area and the identity of any large adhesive users.

Other men worked the new-firm listings in the newspaper almost exclusively for their new accounts. Bud did notice that there was a difference between the new-account prospecting systems of men whose territories were well developed and those whose territories were not.

Bud had to plan his activities for the next week, but he was at a loss to know precisely what he should do during the coming five days.

1.   What should Bud do on each day of the coming week? Plan each day specifically.

CASE 6-5   LANZ:
Opening a New Territory

Bob Gutzmer, newly hired representative for Lanz dresses, a line of unique high-quality women's apparel, was planning his first trip through his new territory of Nebraska, Kansas, Colorado, New Mexico, Arizona, Utah, Wyoming, and Montana. Inasmuch as Lanz was a relatively new line, it did not have any distribution in the area: Bob had to build distribution from scratch.

He was paid a straight 6 percent commission but had to pay all his own expenses. He had no previous experience selling, as he had just graduated with a master's degree in music from his state university. He had come to the realization that he would be unable to support his wife and family on what he was being offered to teach music in the high schools. Since his father had been an apparel salesman, he did know something about its nature and was able to persuade Lanz to hire him.

He now had some decisions to make. What towns and cities should he now visit and in what stores should he try to place his line? He was quite aware that the reputation of the Lanz line would suffer should he place it in the wrong hands. He had promised the president of Lanz that he would have the line in every town of 25,000 population or more within the year.

It was the policy of Lanz to give exclusive dealerships in all but large cities such as Denver, Phoenix, Kansas City, and Salt Lake City. In the larger cities the line was usually carried by the leading quality department store plus a few outlying quality women's specialty shops. However, to keep this exclusive the retailer had to increase the size of his order 25 percent each season. Surprisingly, this had not proved a problem as yet in the organization.

In pondering his coming two-month trip around the territory, Bob was somewhat in doubt about how he could best identify his best prospect in each town.

1. How can Bob identify the store in each town in which he should place the Lanz line?
2. In the city you are now in, what store or stores should carry the line? Do they?
3. How many calls a day can Bob make?

THE PREAPPROACH

Nothing is so difficult but that it may be found
by seeking.
Terrence

A young book salesman whose future career seemed in jeopardy began his presentation with the author by asking, "Now, what's your name?" After the author replied, the salesman continued, "Now what do you teach?" With patience greatly overtaxed and with a keen curiosity to see what was going to happen next, the answer was given: salesmanship.

The young salesman then began extolling the alleged virtues of the salesmanship book published by his employer. Finally he got around to asking what text was being used. Upon being quietly informed of the situation, the lad came unglued, quickly retreating in confusion, forgetting all about the other books he had to sell.

Had the fellow taken the trouble to read a bit about the importance of the preapproach, he could easily have avoided his embarrassment.

The professional book man has learned his prospect's name prior to calling on him and has looked at the schedule to see what he is teaching. Moreover, he will know what book is being used by checking at the bookstore. The real pro will also know a great deal about the prospect's background. Preapproach the prospect properly and such incidents will not happen.

In this chapter we take up the preapproach *to a specific prospect,* the facts about that individual which the salesman would like to learn in order to bring to bear on him the most effective appeals.

The question arises: When is the task of prospecting completed and at what point does the preapproach begin? The only way to answer this is to point out that the selling process is a continuous one with no sharp lines of demarcation between the stages. Speaking broadly, the prospecting job is finished when the salesman feels that he knows enough about a person to believe that there is a chance of selling him. For example, an automobile salesman learns in talking with a friend that Ray Smith has just received a promotion carrying with it a raise in salary. "Ah, a possible prospect!" thinks the salesman; so he inquires of a friend what kind of car Smith is driving. The friend is not sure but does know that it is not a new one. Mr. Salesman scribbles the name "Ray Smith" in his little book. That completes his prospecting work, since a raise in salary and an old car spell "prospect."

Now he begins his preapproach work. He does a bit of simple sleuthing and learns what make and model car Smith is now driving, how he uses it, how many are in the family, their ages, the kind of job Smith has, where he lives, his approximate economic status, and other helpful facts which he may be able to dig up. His objective is to enable him to *plan his campaign intelligently.* Especially, he will use this information in planning his approach. He is eager to avoid getting off on the wrong foot and to start the actual interview as favorably as possible.

When he meets Smith, the salesman will continue his preapproach by shrewd observation and the dropping of questions into the early phases of the interview. Thus the preapproach merges into the approach, the two actually overlapping somewhat. No matter how much the salesman may know about the prospect in advance of the first call, it is always wise to utilize the first few minutes of the approach to check the accuracy of the preapproach and to enlarge upon it. He may find that he must revise his ideas concerning the prospect and alter the sales plan he had mapped out.

What is meant by "the sales plan he had mapped out"? In brief, we can point out that any *good* salesman plans his interview in advance, just as a football coach formulates his game plan. He wants to focus the presentation on the benefits that seem most likely to appeal to this particular prospect. He wants to appeal to motives that seem most likely to move the prospect to buy. He avoids discussing matters which may irritate the prospect; he adjusts the speed of the interview to the prospect's mental tempo; he plans answers to the objections which he has reason to believe the prospect may raise. In short, he tailors and adapts his entire presentation to that particular prospect. This he could not do without a careful preapproach.

OBJECTIVES OF THE PREAPPROACH

There are five objectives of the preapproach: (1) to provide additional qualifying information, (2) to gain insights into how best to approach the prospect, (3) to obtain information around which the presentation can be better planned, (4) to keep the salesman from making serious errors, and (5) to give the salesman more confidence.

Additional qualifying information

Although the salesman may believe that a certain person or organization is a prospect, closer examination of the circumstances may disclose that he is not. He may already have the product. He may be financially unable to buy. He may have a relative or close friend who sells the same thing. All sorts of conditions can exist which would *disqualify* the lead. Therefore, the first thing the salesman tries to learn is whether or not the lead really *is* a good prospect.

A subscription salesman for the *American Lumberman,* a trade journal going to the mill operators, tells this one on himself. "One day things were going bad so I made up my mind that I was going to sell the next guy no matter what. 'No' would not be a word that I would hear. So I get in this guy's office and start pitching. He happens to stutter, so all the better. He would keep trying to interrupt by saying, 'But, but, but.' However, I was not letting him get into the act. I went on and on until finally I ran out of gas. So I let him say something. 'BBBBut I already take the dddddamn thing.'"

A simple qualifying question early in the interview would have provided the preapproach information that would have stopped the presentation short.

The approach strategy

Not all prospects can be approached in the same manner. Some are easy to meet, while others are quite difficult to contact. Some like a direct businesslike approach while others are best approached indirectly. Timing is important in some cases and not in others. Many other factors also vary. A sound preapproach should reveal many of these variable factors.

Another unfortunate book salesman approached one of the authors with the statement, "You should give serious consideration to [a new book his publisher had just introduced] because it has the most advanced quantitative treatment yet given the subject." Now a good salesman with some simple preapproach work would have discovered that this prospect had no interest in the latest quantitative treatment because he was a behaviorist. No doubt the youthful representative is still wondering just where he went wrong.

On the other hand, another book representative was spectacularly successful in the same region by his adept approaches to various professors. He would discover each one's particular interests and approach him through that avenue. A chairman of one English department was seriously involved with the campus international club. The representative attended several evening meetings of the group and met the prospect on a social basis. Small wonder he cracked the English adoption on that campus for the first time. This man is now high up in the management of his firm.

Planning information

A sales presentation can take many forms and go in many directions. Some are built around cost saving, others around certain unique product features. Obviously if the prospect is most interested in low cost, it would be a mistake to dwell on quality features with scant attention to the economic aspects. Similarly, if the prospect is most interested in acquiring status, appeals to economy may fall on deaf ears. A good preapproach should furnish the salesman some insights into which motives are most likely to move the prospect to action and what appeals would prove most effective. A good sales presentation should be tailor-made for the prospect in hand on the basis of the information uncovered in the preapproach.

Avoiding serious errors

People have many idiosyncrasies which must be humored if a presentation is to be most successful. Some people dislike overly aggressive individuals and react unfavorably to any salesman who tries to overpower them. Some people will react negatively to a salesman who smokes during the interview. One hat company executive, quite understandably, would throw out of his office any salesman who called on him bareheaded. Many times great rapport can be established with the prospect if the salesman is able to play up to some of his pet ideas. Perhaps a purchasing agent with a large firm is known to become quite perturbed with salesmen who contact directly anyone in his company without first going through his department. The salesman who explains, "I always believe in first contacting a firm's purchasing agent before seeing anyone else in the company" may be hitting a responsive chord with the p.a.

Confidence

The unknown breeds fear and uncertainty. The salesman who walks into the presentation completely ignorant of the prospect's nature and situation is likely to become uncertain, hesitant, and fearful of making mistakes. He seldom knows what he should be talking about. He is afraid to bring up certain subjects lest they offend the prospect or antagonize him. However, the salesman who has done a complete preapproach on the prospect is confident that what he says is right and that he has the key to selling this man. Experienced salesmen know that this factor of confidence is extremely important. They reason: "How can a prospect buy from me, if he has no confidence in me, and how can he have confidence in me if I show no confidence in myself?"

THE EXTENT OF THE PREAPPROACH

By this time it is clear to the reader that the amount of time and thought which a salesman devotes to a given sale is governed by the importance to him of making that sale. Nowhere is this principle more clearly evident than in the preapproach. A sales engineer may spend months preparing data to use in presenting his proposition. The representative of an advertising agency may, together with his colleagues, work out a complete advertising campaign for a prospective client, making the presentation of the proposed campaign purely "on speculation" or in the hope that it will be accepted. If it is not adopted, the work of this very elaborate preapproach, perhaps involving extensive and expensive research into the prospect's marketing problems, has failed of its purpose. On the other hand, the house-to-house salesman for vanilla extract cannot afford to make more than the scantiest preapproach, perhaps merely inquiring at each house the name of the family next door.

The point receiving emphasis here is this: most salesmen fail to make an adequate preapproach. They neglect to learn vital facts which might have helped them make the sale. They are like the life insurance salesman (?) who tried to sell a man a policy by appealing to the buying motive of affection—pulling out all the stops on the "Mary and the baby" appeal. His prospect remained coldly unmoved, a fact which puzzled the salesman until he made a too-late preapproach and learned that the man was at the time living apart from his wife and suing for divorce. Their only child had died three years previously.

Another factor bearing on the extent of the preapproach is the difficulty encountered in obtaining an interview with the prospect. Where this is a serious problem, the salesman will be well advised to make a careful preapproach and utilize the information gained thereby in the planning of an unusually effective approach.

Propositions demanding careful preapproach and strong approach are:

Unfamiliar ones. The less the prospect knows about the proposition the less likely he is to feel the need for it.

Expensive ones. Generally speaking, the more something costs the harder it is to sell; thus the salesman needs all the advantages possible in his favor.

Intangible ones   It is easy to drive a good-looking new car up to a man's home and persuade him to take a ride in it. He can see it and hear it and feel it; he immediately realizes the benefits of owning it. But the intangible proposition cannot be seen or heard or felt; the realization of its benefits is unawakened. The need is not keenly felt at the moment. To avoid an immediate turndown the salesman must develop a strong approach based on facts unearthed by a painstaking preapproach.

Complex or big ones   Such propositions present more "angles," each of which must be figured. They are likely to demand decisions by more than one person before the sale is consummated. Selling a heating plant for a new school building might come under this head—architects, contractors, school board members, school officials, and others must all be sold.

The emphasis being laid on the preapproach is in line with similar activities in other fields. Football and basketball coaches are guided by the reports of their scouts concerning opponents. The physician makes a careful diagnosis before prescribing. The criminal lawyer studies the judge and jurors and plays to their prejudices, if any. The architect may spend months studying the activities to take place in a building, so that he may design a functionally efficient structure. This attitude of practitioners of other professions is assumed by the salesman who approaches his work professionally.

What the preapproach may include

The information gathered in the preapproach will differ from the selling problem facing the salesman. If he is selling to an individual for the latter's own use, the salesman will confine his investigations to the prospect as a person. On the other hand, if the prospect is buying for a business, the preapproach should be broadened to embrace many facts about that business also.

TO THE PROSPECT AS AN INDIVIDUAL   Many of these items should also be checked when the prospect is buying for a business, as most buying is done by individuals.

His name   Learn to spell it and pronounce it correctly. People are sensitive on this point, and a mistake can be costly.

His age   Older men respond to the respect they feel is due them. Younger men in high positions appreciate a recognition of the fact that they have climbed fast.

His education   This may provide a topic of conversation. A college man usually likes to have this fact recognized. The self-made man is proud to have won his position without so much formal schooling.

Where he lives   This may reveal something of his social position, his friends, perhaps his ancestry.

His need for what you are selling   If he needs it, you should learn how he can best use it. If he doesn't need it, he is not a good prospect.

His ability to buy   Many a youthful salesman has taken orders from poor credit risks only to have them turned down by the credit department. It is not good sense to try to sell a man a Cadillac when you know he can afford nothing more costly than a Vega.

His authority to buy   Does he have to ask his wife or partner? Is he only a front man for the real buyer?

Facts about his family   Many a purchase is made by a man because he hopes it will make wife or children happy. The latter often exercise a strong influence in many purchases for a home. You may also find that he likes to talk about his son or daughter; most parents do.

Groups to which he belongs   Rotary, Masons, church, country club, trade association, etc. Very helpful information to have.

The best time to see him   Every man has a routine and probably dislikes to have it disturbed. He will give you a far better reception if you call when he is not accustomed and eager to be doing something else.

Personal peculiarities   Every one of us has them. The salesman caters to these—if he knows what they are.

Occupation   What does he do for a living? Is he self-employed? What is the nature of his business? For whom does he work? In what capacity? How long has he been with the firm? These are critical questions in many sales.

Recreations, interests, and hobbies   This point merits elaboration. Some salesmen feel that the most effective way to get by the so-called "cold spot" in the first minute or two of a sales interview—that moment when the prospect first learns that you are selling insurance, bonds, or cars and tries to get rid of you—is to discover his particular hobby or interest and utilize it to promote the interview upon a friendly basis. Although this seems to be something to consider in the approach rather than here, it will be discussed briefly at this time because the salesman must learn about the hobby in the preapproach if he is to use it later. The importance of this phase of the preapproach is brought out by a long-time salesman of magazine advertising.

My old professor of psychology told me that every man has two minds, so that in my first job I asked for the hundred men in New York City whom nobody had been able to sell on the magazine which paid me the handsome remuneration of $40 a week "to start." I was looking for the "yes" mind—the mind that could say "I will take it," not the mind which sat back all ready to say "No."

The question naturally arises as to how to find out the customer's "yes" mind, the things that he will shut down his desk for and talk about to the exclusion of all business.

There was a man I remember well, who at the words "There is open water this week up in Maine and I'll bet the trout will take a fly," would close his roll-top desk, turn around in his swivel chair, and send out word that he couldn't see Mr. Anybody from Anywhere, as he was very busy for the next half hour.

I never will forget the way old John Scullin's eyes flashed when I dropped in one morning with a chisel that I had picked up at a pawnshop. It had a fine, broad blade, a fluted wooden handle, and the initials of some carpenter or cabinetmaker who had used it. Scullin was advertising manager for a food product house, and a classmate of his at Purdue had told me of the workshop down in his cellar and the furniture which he spent all day Sunday working on.

A little inside information about Charles the XII of Sweden would sell almost anything to one of the hardest men to sell in the agency field. Any talk of a walking trip through the Berkshires could secure the favorable attention, interest, desire, and sometimes action of the vice-president of a motor-truck company in Newark. No matter how unpromising a prospect looked on the first five visits, a little work would always result in finding his particular hobby and the things he liked to talk about. This information once secured, the sale was easy if it was in any way possible to link up his hobby with what you had to sell.

My sources of information were all kinds of people in all kinds of places. I would first list the college and class of the man, if he had such a thing; his golf, tennis, fishing, or hunting club; his church; the school his children attended; whether he had ever lived on a farm or any facts of a similar nature about his past; the names of his neighbors; where he kept his automobile and the kind of car he drove; where he spent his vacations. From these sources, somehow or other it was always possible to find out the story of his hobby.

But let's not go overboard on this hobby matter! It is well to hold in mind that such preapproaches are abnormal, suitable for prospects who are hard to see or hard to sell and who can place large orders. They should be used mainly as a last resort unless the preapproach has revealed that the prospect likes to discuss his hobby with callers. Most businessmen would rather discuss their business than their hobbies—at least during business hours. The salesman who can offer a way to make that business more successful may be accorded a more cordial hearing than the chap who tries to talk hobbies. Besides, most salesmen are not well enough versed in the prospect's hobby to discuss it intelligently. A clumsy attempt to drag it into the opening conversation is so transparent that it is likely to defeat its purpose.

It is safe to say that the *obvious* hobby should be approached with extreme caution by the salesman. The bag of golf clubs in the corner will be spotted by most salesmen, and all too many of them will waste time trying to talk golf before getting down to business. The salesman who does get down to business at the outset may be mighty welcome. One prospect had a huge sailfish mounted and hanging above his desk. He was inordinately proud of it, for it represented the high spot of many years' fishing. But he was finally forced to take it down, because too many salesmen wasted valuable time talking about it. One businessman solved a similar problem by posting a sign just under a mammoth muskellunge on his office wall. It read: YES, I CAUGHT THIS. BUT PLEASE DON'T MENTION IT UNLESS I DO!

One other observation on this hobby question: the more salesmen a prospect sees in the course of business, the less he is likely to respond to the hobby approach. The man who sees few salesmen, on the other hand, may be glad to talk about his hobby.

TO THE PROSPECT AS A BUSINESSMAN In addition to the facts about him as an individual, certain facts about him as a businessman are pertinent. These chiefly concern the business with which he is associated and cover matters such as those revealed by the following questions.

The personnel of his company

(assuming he is employed and not in business for himself)

- Who owns the company?
- If a corporation, who is on the board of directors?
- What are the business affiliations of these directors?
- Do I know any of them personally?
- Who has the final word on purchases?
- Who else has an influence on purchases? Many salesmen insist that it is a waste of time to talk to subordinates; they prefer to go straight to the top. Others find it is helpful to enlist the cooperation of personnel in the lower echelons. Whichever policy is followed, the salesman should know definitely who has the final buying authority.
- Who is in charge of the department that will use my product or services?

The company in operation

- What does it make or have to sell?
- What market does it logically reach?

- Is the product top grade, medium, or cheap?
- What is the capacity of the plant?
- What parts of the finished product do they make and what do they buy?
- What processes of manufacture does the company employ?
- What type and make of machines are used in production?
- How about raw materials? Kind and amounts? Sources?
- What schedule of maintenance does it operate on?
- Do seasonal factors affect its operations?
- Where does the company rate in its industry—in volume of output?

Buying practices of the company

- What systems and procedures are followed by the purchasing department?
- Does the company buy from a few sources or diversify more?
- How about its credit rating?
- When does the firm buy my product?
- How much do they buy at a time?
- From whom are they now buying and why?
- Is the firm happy with its present sources of supply?
- What problems has the firm encountered with its present supplier?
- Does the firm practice reciprocity?
- Finally, but basically, will the company benefit from buying and using what I am selling?

The following useful quiz, which appeared in an issue of *The American Salesman,* illustrates some of the detailed information that the top-notch salesman wants to possess about his accounts.[1]

How well do you know this account?

Take one good customer, add a dash of detail knowledge, and maybe a little stirring will result in extra business. Most salesmen do know all kinds of things about their best accounts—from the first names of the receptionists to the tastiest dishes served in the company dining room—but sometimes there are also surprising gaps in their information. If you're curious about your own customer knowledge, try this quiz for a couple of accounts. Since you'll be both test administrator and subject you can keep the grades secret.

1. Just how many v.p.s does the company have?
2. What are their responsibilities?
3. What time does the p.a. arrive at work?
4. What's his secretary's first name and favorite flower?
5. Who's the brightest comer in the purchasing department?

[1] *The American Salesman,* October, 1967, p. 25.

6. What does the chief designer or engineer think of the p.a.?
7. Of what business deal is the p.a. proudest?
8. What does its principal competitor have that the account wishes it had?
9. How many executives at the account know important men in your company?
10. What are the account's worst-kept secrets?
11. On what days of the month does your chief competitor call there?
12. What departments are under particular pressure to cut costs?
13. Through what department did the company president come up?
14. How many of the account's customers can you name?
15. What grandiose plans is the company holding for an appropriate time?
16. How big a dividend did the stock pay last year?
17. Can you remember the company's slogan?
18. Who in the purchasing department thinks the account should buy from your competitor?

You should now appreciate the intimacy between the industrial salesman and his accounts.

The preapproach for regular customers

In the foregoing discussion prospects and customers have been treated alike since the careful salesman takes as many pains to keep informed on regular customers as on prospects. It is as important to keep present customers as it is to secure new ones, so the salesman should exercise every precaution in the care and feeding of existing accounts.

Many professional salesmen keep data books on the people with whom they do business. On each page they jot down the man's name; his religion or church connection, if any; his hobbies; his family; the service club and fraternal order membership; the amount of the last order; personal interests; political tendencies; other miscellaneous items; and the subject discussed on the occasion of the previous call. Few things are more pleasing to a customer than the subtle flattery implied by the saleman's casual remark, "As you said when I was last here, Mr. Smith," or "I've been thinking over what you said last May about . . ." The thought that this chance utterance of his has remained in the salesman's mind is deeply gratifying to the customer.

A knowledge of a customer's political and religious convictions will prevent the salesman from becoming embroiled in an argument.

Thus a page in this little memorandum book might look like this (all names in the following are purely fictitious, of course):

Brown, Horace W., Dayton, Ohio. Politics: Republican but rather progressive. Hobbies: oriental rugs—is real authority. Favorite sport: golf. Not baseball fan.

Hates football. Religion: Baptist—regular in church attendance. Personal interests: likes to discuss work of Rotary Club, of which he is active member. Is a Mason. Son on high school track team.

Graduated from Ohio State University in 1946. Majored in Marketing. No social fraternity. Member of golf squad.

Married Dorothy Miller 1948. Her father is prominent lawyer in Dayton. His father founded business in 1920.

Drives latest model Olds; trades in each year.

Member Mayfair Country Club.

Hard to get acquainted with at first but thaws later. Likes to argue, but does not lose temper. Responds to mild flattery.

Records of previous contacts:

March 21. Called and chatted briefly. Did not make sale.

May 15. Showed samples and got in good sales talk. Discussed son whose picture was on desk. Only child. Name is Donald.

July 10. Sold him order: $3,000.

After this, entries might include references to topics discussed or to unusual incidents or pieces of personal information on Brown. Such a job is never ended, and it supplements a salesman's memory, which may betray him at embarrassing moments.

Many salesmen, for items like automobiles or insurance, keep an "interview record" of prospects and customers which will include a date for next contact.

SOURCES OF INFORMATION

After one has decided just what information he wishes to obtain, the next problem is to find it. While one might be tempted to conclude that it would be quite difficult to gather the type and amount of information about a prospect that has been recommended, actually such is not the case. People, being people, like to talk about people. Even the prospect himself many times is willing to disclose many critical facts. Information is there for the seeker to find.

Fellow salesmen

It pays to cultivate friendly relations with other salesmen. Every buyer has peculiarities that are known to the salesmen who call on him, and such facts may profitably be exchanged. These hints will come mostly from noncompeting salesmen, who can be mutually helpful without injuring their own chances. A salesman selling fuel oil to a factory p.a. could safely give a suggestion to a salesman for office machines. Even competitors may occasionally divulge valuable information, especially if they have failed to sell the prospect. They are likely to feel that they have already lost and have nothing more to lose. Or perhaps the competing salesman, when led to talk freely about a prospect, may *inadvertently* drop hints that can be utilized. Conversations overheard in hotel lobbies and dining rooms, on planes, or in prospects' waiting rooms may yield suggestions of value.

When a salesman receives information of a confidential nature, he should never divulge it. If he betrays a confidence, he will receive no more information from that source. If he earns the reputation of being discreet and close-mouthed, he will be told a lot more than if he is loose-tongued.

Customers

Much can be learned from customers about prospects yet to be seen. The man who has just purchased usually wishes to vindicate his judgment by having others buy, too. He is likely to feel he is doing them a favor, so he suggests that the salesman call on some of his friends. The wise salesman strives to learn helpful facts from him about these friends.

Bird dogs and centers of influence

The person providing the lead should also be pumped for all the preapproach information at his disposal. Frequently, he can provide almost everything the salesman wants to know. Hence, salesmen develop the habit of questioning the source of any lead right at the time the lead is given.

The local newspaper

A source not sufficiently utilized is the *local* newspaper. The traveling salesman can often find considerable information from the files at the newspaper office, noting the advertisements of his prospects, and getting a general idea of the community interests. It should be emphasized that the salesman's preapproach consists not merely in gathering personal facts about his prospects but also in building up a background for each of them. It may help to know something of the town's activities and interests when calling for the first time on a prospect. Such knowledge furnishes just so many more points of contact upon which to establish friendly relations.

The industrial salesman can establish common interests with his prospect by reading articles and advertisements in technical and business journals, especially those containing stories about or advertisements by the firm he is trying to sell. It is not merely a coincidence that most good salesmen are prolific readers of the trade press.

Directories

Many directories exist which provide personal data on people of some position in practically all fields of endeavor. There is a *Who's Who* in each of many areas such as business and industry, education, science, various states, in America, etc. If the prospect is of sufficient stature to be listed in one of these directories, much personal information on him can be easily obtained by going to any good library. Various industries frequently publish rosters and biographical data of the executives or personnel of various companies.

Observation

As the salesman enters his prospect's place of business, he can learn many things. A salesman calling upon a retailer carefully notes the brands carried in stock, for they indicate a great deal about the policies and philosophies of the dealer. He can tell whether the prospect is enterprising or conservative by noticing stock display, fixtures, and the general atmosphere of the premises. He can observe the attitude of subordinates toward their employer and thus learn his real disposition. A man may appear to be a bully and a tyrant to the salesman; but if his employees treat him without fear, it is safe to assume that the attitude of gruffness is merely a pose.

The industrial salesman can determine many things about his prospect by simply observing the man's immediate environment. Is he playing the role of the big business executive? The appearance and formality of his office should give some indication of this trait. Is he a hard worker? Again, the condition of the man's desk and office may provide insights into his working habits. How modern or up-to-date is he? Look at his present equipment for the answer. What do the pictures on the wall tell about the man? Is he sports-oriented? Does he smoke? His ashtrays may tell a large story of his smoking habits. Is he prosperous? What school did he attend? Any class rings, diplomas on wall, or fraternal insignia visible? What clubs does he belong to? Look at his lapel or on his wall or desk. And so it goes; every bit of material around a man can tell the astute salesman something about the nature of its owner. A salesman must be a good detective to put together the clues and come up with a composite image of what the prospect is really like.

The prospect

Last, but certainly not least, is the prospect himself. Much critical information is known only by the prospect; so only he can provide it. While some skeptics may question the practicality of obtaining information from the prospect, actually it is quite common to do so. It must be remembered that in most sales the salesman is there to solve the prospect's problems. The prospect wants these problems solved most efficiently and effectively and is therefore highly motivated to give the salesman complete cooperation.

Sometimes the salesman can get some needed information over the telephone from the prospect or one of his agents, but more frequently the first part of the sales interview, or even all of it, is devoted to extracting it. Indeed, there are frequent instances in which men spend a considerable amount of time gathering information in preparation for the ultimate sales presentation. Such would be the case of a computer salesman who would study the various systems of a firm to determine if it could profitably use his hardware.

The salesman should never be bashful about asking the prospect for helpful information, even though it may be personal or confidential. If the prospect chooses not to talk he will say so, but more frequently the man enjoys talking about himself and his feats. The salesman who commands confidence and maintains confidence will find himself privy to a great many useful secrets.

"SIZING UP" THE PROSPECT

One of the most debated practices of salesmanship is "sizing up" the prospect. The salesman should be cautioned against allowing himself to make up his mind early in the interview that the prospect is *not* going to buy.

A farm equipment dealer in Oregon sadly relates:

We'll be pretty careful in the future to see that everyone who comes in here gets attention. The other day a guy came in, looked around, peeked under one of the machines. He was an odd-looking character, so we figured he was just curious. Finally he wandered out. We learned later that he went across the street to another dealer and, when a salesman asked him what he wanted, said he was interested in log haulers. After the sales pitch and a few questions, he placed an order for four. These haulers cost around $8,000 each, but the salesman merely inquired, "How would you like to arrange payment for them?" The "character" muttered, "I'll pay for them now." Whereupon he dug into his various pockets and came up with the full amount in cold currency.

Every veteran salesman can recount cases like these. One Atlanta furniture salesman learned the hard way when he avoided a customer who looked like a poor prospect—work-torn clothes, calloused hands with fingernails none too well manicured. But an old-timer in the store waited on the man and soon discovered that he had walked out of a competitor's store because the salesman there had tried to high-pressure him into making quick decisions on a few items. So the veteran salesman remarked, "Take your time and I'll just sort of trail along to answer questions. The boss says that my job is to help our customers find exactly what they want and I'll try to do that." That customer was furnishing a new motel which he had built with his own hands. When he had finished shopping he wrote the salesman a check for $3,450.

A not-too-well-dressed middle-aged woman was waited on in the shoe department of a well-known Texas store; the clerk was new and eager to close the sale so he could wait on some oil millionaire's wife. Shortly his customer put on her shoe and went in search of the floorwalker. She explained that she would like to have someone else wait on her; so he called one of the store's roving receptionists and asked her to look after the customer. After an hour and a half, the woman had purchased more than $750 worth of shoes, stockings, clothing, etc. She was the widow of an oil worker who had been killed in an accident and she was investing some of his savings and insurance in a trip back to her native Germany. The assortment of clothing was destined for relatives there.

A large wholesale dry goods house in St. Louis has had difficulty in impressing upon its house salesmen the desirability of *trying* to sell every prospect who comes in. Some time ago a rather unpromising-appearing individual strayed in, and all the salesmen promptly busied themselves at something to avoid waiting on him. That is, all but one. This young chap tackled the apparently hopeless prospect and eventually sold him $18,000 worth of hosiery. He turned out to be a buyer for a foreign government, but he dressed in such a manner as to deceive the average salesman. Indeed, this was his purpose, for he feared that if his identity were known it would cause the sellers to quote him a higher price.

These observations apply to traveling salesmen as well as to retail clerks. The salesman who relies too strongly on the hasty "size-up" is likely to allow himself to be whipped without putting up a strong fight. Often the prospect's exterior belies his ability to buy. Clothes do not make the man, as the experienced salesman has discovered.

Some salesmen feel that by acting as though they consider the prospect unlikely or unable to make the purchase they may shame him into buying just to prove that he can. Undoubtedly this needling of a customer's pride is instrumental in closing some sales with weak-willed buyers, but it may be doubted whether such tactics create lasting goodwill for the salesman or his house. A customer treated thus might buy at the time, but it is highly probable that, after considering the affair, he would register a vow never to be similarly duped in the future, certainly not by the same salesman.

A rare exception to this principle may occasionally be found. A wealthy dowager asked the salesman for exotic foods to quote her a price on a case of imported Danish shrimp. The salesman replied, "Madam, if prices concern you, may I suggest the A & P?" Even though she is alleged to have bought the shrimp, this practice is not recommended—simply reported.

Still other important indications
During the first moments of the interview the salesman should be alert to obtain answers to the following questions concerning his prospect.

IS HE MENTALLY FAST OR SLOW?   The fast man usually talks fast, moves quickly, is obviously "in high gear." He shows signs of impatience when the interview lags. His whole attitude shrieks, "Come, come! Let's get going!" He is likely to interrupt the salesman.

Such a person can easily be humored; if he wants a fast ride, give him one. Talk fast; hit the high spots; spare the details; keep in mental step with him. This person can often be rushed into a decision.

The slower type is even easier to please. He usually talks more slowly; moves more slowly; asks questions showing that he wants to go into details; is generally more relaxed in his attitude. To sell this prospect the salesman must throttle his own mind down; he must relax; he must not rush the prospect; he must be willing to go into details; he must often repeat a point he has previously made; he must speak deliberately.

The important fact here is that the salesman should look for the signs indicating the prospect's mental rpm right at the start, just as soon as he sees him. If he can learn about this feature in advance of the approach, so much the better.

CAN HE MAKE UP HIS MIND?   The vacillating person is not the same as the slow-thinking person. His mind may operate at high speed, yet he finds it hard to reach a decision; he procrastinates; he worries about the problem under consideration; he is not decisive in thinking or action. His voice betrays his uncertainty—he makes statements that are really half-questions. His gestures are vague; his gaze shifts from point to point.

Inasmuch as this chap hates to make decisions, the salesman should help him make them. It is not wise to confuse him with too many details as his mind may not organize them easily; they merely offer him more questions to decide, and he shrinks from deciding. The salesman should be decisive in his statements; he should not *ask* questions demanding decisions but *answer* the questions that are in the prospect's mind, perhaps unspoken.

Do not present alternatives; show him *one* course of action; tell him clearly *why* he will benefit from following this course; then proceed as if he had made up his mind to do what you have suggested. In retail selling, do not show this type of customer too much merchandise; narrow his choice so that it will be easier for him to decide.

The positive type of prospect must be treated in just the opposite manner. He is not hard to identify—his actions are positive, his speech is affirmative instead of questioning, he is poised and self-confident. He may have earned success in business and probably is an executive. He wants to make up his own mind and resents any effort to crowd him into a decision. He may be a bit cocky; he may be proud of his success.

It does not pay to put pressure on this man; he should be permitted to dominate the interview (or at least seem to). If the salesman is also a dominant character, he should adopt a meeker attitude and avoid a clash with this prospect. Don't offer criticism; dwell on his strong points. Feed his ego; don't deflate it. Let him *sell himself* on your proposition.

IS HE TALKATIVE OR SILENT?   Experienced salesmen differ as to which of these two types of prospects is the more difficult to sell. The friendly, chatty chap is easy to approach but sometimes hard to pin down. He may try to steer the conversation into channels having nothing to do with the proposition that the salesman wants to discuss with him—to use his talkativeness as a defense. The salesman's task is to guide the conversation gently but surely into the desired groove, never relaxing his friendly attitude. If he is adept at this, he may maneuver the prospect into a position where he talks himself into buying.

The "clam" is difficult: he uses his silence as a defense. It is not wise to try to thaw this prospect out and force him to smile and talk. It is usually better to meet him on his own level; to treat him with respect and dignity. Keep on offering value to him; don't show irritation or frustration at his cold silence. Hold the interview to a quiet tone, but gradually try asking simple questions requiring simple answers. In this way, if he is not frightened by the salesman's aggressiveness, he may loosen up. When he feels that the salesman is merely trying to serve his interests, he will relax. Low-pressure methods of selling are indicated here.

IS HE YOUNG OR OLD?   Generally the salesman will treat the older person without the lightness or flippancy which he might use with a younger one. The older person, if it is necessary to give him information about the product, must be treated with more respect and deference. He does not like to be treated like a school kid. The older customer will be harder to fool; he has learned from experience. He is likely to buy more carefully, to buy more on quality than on flash; and he is price conscious. Younger customers are easier to sell, as a rule. They like color; they are style conscious; they make up their minds quickly.

Prospect's state of decision

There is still another evaluation of prospects, this one based on how far the prospect has traveled mentally toward the decision to buy. That is, some prospects are already partially, or even completely, sold, while others have not even the slightest intention of buying. The preapproach should tell the salesman about how far the prospect has progressed and, therefore, what sales tactics should be employed.

There are three separate prospect decisions that should be appraised. First, to what extent does the prospect recognize his need for the product in general? A Xerox salesman should first determine if his prospect feels any need for a copying machine before he can begin worrying about selling him a Xerox. In marketing terminology, the primary demand for a product must exist before selective demand (brand) can be stimulated. The prospect's perception of his need varies from being totally unaware of any need for it to an outright confession that he not only needs it badly but fully intends to buy something to satisfy that need.

Second, how does the prospect perceive the salesman's brand of the product? This, too, can vary from "I want nothing to do with your machine!" through "I've never heard of it," to "I will only buy from you."

Third, how much is the prospect planning to pay to satisfy this need? The prospect who feels a *powerful* urge to buy will probably be willing to pay more than one nearer the other extreme who feels only a *mild* urge to satisfy his need. Some prospects are limited by the money they have available, while others feel more flexible as to how much they can pay. Again, we find variations or gradations here.

The salesman's task is to learn, so far as he is able in his preapproach, about where the prospect is likely to stand in each of these three scales. Even after he has come face to face with the prospect, this effort continues.

There is not much point in trying to sell a prospect at the negative extreme of all three scales. But the "in-between" prospect may be worth working on. However, the salesman wants to know whether to spend time trying to awaken a desire for the product in general or to stress the particular product he is selling. Perhaps he will find it necessary to justify the price if the purchase involves more money than the prospect had planned to spend. It comes down to putting the selling emphasis in the right place for the given prospect, thereby saving time and making it more likely that a sale will be made.

The order in which these three factors are presented here indicates the order in which the salesman will check on them with a prospect. If the prospect feels no need for *any* car, there is no point in demonstrating that your car is the best and that the price is right. The first task is to make the prospect want *a* car.

Similarly, if the car you are selling does not fit his idea of what he needs, there is little nourishment in trying to justify the price. So the salesman checks the points in the logical sequence.

CONCLUSION

The importance of the preapproach is widely underestimated by the average salesman. It is a lot of work, work most of us would prefer to avoid. Yet the diligent professional knows the advantages it gives him and does his "homework," thus preparing himself to sell the prospect.

The key to preapproaching is alert resourcefulness in using the sources of information that are readily available to all.

DISCUSSION QUESTIONS

1. Is the concept of the preapproach applicable to any other human activities besides selling?
2. If you were selling mutual funds, what prospect information would you want to obtain prior to making a sales presentation?
3. Under what conditions will a prospect willingly provide considerable preapproach information about himself in the early part of the sale?
4. If a salesman has been unable to obtain certain critical preapproach information about a given prospect prior to the presentation, how should he go about getting it from him in the interview? Exactly what should he say to the prospect?
5. You are a manufacturer's agent representing several lines of quality men's apparel. A store that has heretofore refused to buy from you has just been sold. What information might you want about the new owner?
6. If you were a Xerox salesman, from what source would you obtain most of your preapproach information on a prospective client?
7. You are a book representative for McGraw-Hill. You have heard that the psychology department at Big State U. is not happy with its present adoption for the beginning course. What preapproach information would you want before you attempted any interviews?
8. From what sources would you seek such information about the psychology situation above?
9. You are a manufacturer's representative handling a line of ice cream equipment and flavorings. One of your customers for flavorings looks

sufficiently large that he could profitably make his own ice cream by buying a machine from you that costs about $5,000. What additional informa-
tion would you want about the prospect before attempting a presentation?

10. You are a salesman for a leading manufacturer of componentized homes.
Your firm does not have a dealer in a certain significant metropolitan
area. You have been assigned to obtain one. Outline exactly what you
would do upon arriving in that city and what information you would want
to obtain. Where would you go to get it? Once you obtained a lead to a
probable dealer, what information about him would you want to get?

CASE 7-1 THE HIGH POINT FURNITURE COMPANY:
Preapproaching a New Outlet

Brian Rugg, representative for the High Point Furniture Company in the
Pacific Northwest was making his calls in the Willamette Valley of Oregon
when he learned from an existing customer that a large new furniture store
was being built in a nearby city. The customer knew little about the new
enterprise although Brian discreetly questioned him about it.

Brian had made all of his planned calls by noon, so he decided to grab
a quick bite to eat, then drive over to see the new furniture store. He
wanted to call upon its owner as soon as possible to determine if the new
store would be carrying lines such as those made by the High Point Furniture Company.

As he was driving toward the nearby town he began to think about
what he wanted to know and how he could find it out.

1. Precisely what should Brian try to find out?
2. Where should he go to find such information?

CASE 7-2 HORTON AND COMPANY:
Preapproaching an Individual

Mr. Tom Horton, president of Thomas Horton and Company, a publisher
of college textbooks, wanted an internationally noted psychologist to write
a textbook for the beginning psychology course for his company. While the
expert had written many highly esteemed works on various topics in his
field, he had never put all his thoughts together for the beginning student.

Mr. Horton thought it was time for such a book to be written, so he set
out to persuade the man to do the job, knowing full well that the psycholo-

gist had adamantly refused to do it for every publishing house in the nation. He had stated time and again that he just did not want to do a basic book.

Mr. Horton realized he needed to know a great deal about the man if he was to develop a presentation that would do the job.

1. What information should Mr. Horton seek about the psychologist?
2. Where could he get such information?

THE APPROACH

Always start at the beginning.
Anon.

Now the curtain rises. You meet your prospect face to face. It's time for your approach to him. And make no mistake about it, your approach is mighty important. Numerous studies over the years have indicated that sales are won or lost in the first few minutes of the interview—in the approach. Thus this will be a long chapter, for there is much to discuss about how to get the sale started off on the right foot.

OBJECTIVES OF THE APPROACH
The approach has three goals: to gain the prospect's attention, to stimulate his interest in learning more about the salesman's proposition, and to provide a smooth transition into the presentation.

Attention
The sale will go nowhere until the prospect focuses his undivided attention upon what the salesman is saying. This is a larger problem than one might suspect, for the prospect is frequently positioned in the midst of a great many demands upon his time. His mind may be dwelling upon any number of other problems with which he is plagued. Under no circumstances

should the salesman be lured into proceeding with the sale while the prospect's attention is diverted by something or other. Many times a businessman who is busy with work on his desk will say, "Go ahead and talk! I can listen while I finish signing these papers." Don't do it! A person can only attend to one thing at a time. If he is doing something else, he is not listening to you; you must first seize the prospect's *undivided attention.*

Interest

You may gain a prospect's attention for an instant but quickly lose it if he decides that he is not interested in hearing more from you. People's interest in your proposition can be most fleeting if you do not quickly give them a reason for listening further. Secretly, the prospect asks, "What's in it for me? Why should I give you more of my valuable time?"

A good approach provides the prospect with a reason for listening. Tell him how he will benefit, what problems you can solve for him, why he will be in a better position for having met you, or how much money you are going to make for him.

Transition

The third, and often unrecognized, objective of the approach is to lead easily and smoothly into the sales presentation. It should provide a transition so smooth that the prospect scarcely feels it, much as the passenger in a fine automobile can barely detect the automatic shift from one gear to the next.

A salesman could win attention and interest by pulling a gun on the prospect but he would find it rather rough to swing from there into his presentation (to make the transition).

As we discuss various approaches in this chapter let's try to watch for this transition or final phase. It is often the weakest part of the approach, especially when it appears strained, forced, and irrelevant to what has just preceded it.

IMPORTANCE OF THE APPROACH

Naturally the importance of the approach varies with the type of selling. It is most critical when the salesman is calling on the prospect for the first time to sell him a fairly big proposition. It is least important where the salesman calls upon regular customers with a relatively minor product or service. In the former situation, a careful approach should be worked out because, if the approach fails to do its job, the salesman may be ushered out of the prospect's presence without getting the chance to tell his story at all.

A sale may be likened to a chain; break one link and it falls apart.

GAINING THE INTERVIEW

In many lines of selling the salesman has little difficulty seeing his prospects or customers. Either they have invited him to call or his call is a routine matter. Sometimes the status of the salesman's company is such that prospects find it difficult not to give the representative a reasonable hearing. Should a busy executive be called upon by an IBM computer salesman, usually he will give the man an interview. However, in certain situations the salesman's first problem is that of obtaining an interview *with the right man.* This is most frequently encountered when the salesman is selling something the firm is not now buying or buys only on occasions. Salesmen for services and intangibles may encounter problems with seeing the right man. On a busy day the last man in the world a corporate controller might want to see is some insurance salesman or representative of a tax service. Such men have problems seeing the right people, the ones who have the power to buy.

Many young salesmen have returned to headquarters from their first trips discouraged with the job, chiefly because they were not able to see many of their prospects. "I knew what to do all the way through after I had said 'good morning,' but I couldn't get a chance to say 'good morning,'" one youthful salesman complained when his manager took him to task for his lack of success on his initial trip.

One sales manager claimed that his salesmen spent more time in reception rooms than with prospects and that more than one-half of their calls failed to become interviews. One prospect had been called on 26 times in two years, yet was never seen.

Really important business executives are compelled to conserve their time for important things; they properly expect protection from many useless interruptions, including salesmen. They surround themselves with secretaries and subordinates whose duty it is to keep out those callers who have nothing of value to offer their bosses.

Gaining the interview is actually a selling process

The salesman should regard gaining the interview in the same light as making a sale. His task is to *sell an idea* to the person who has the power to grant the interview.

Unquestionably the salesman's *attitude* is of prime importance in selling the secretary the idea that she should admit him. If he *looks* important, his chances of being admitted are improved. Poise, dignity, a direct glance rather than a furtive one—these help. The way he occupies his time in the waiting room is a factor. If he merely loafs or reads *Playboy* he does not make the impression that he does if he pulls from his brief case a copy of a leading business journal or studies an important-looking report. If he *acts* as though his time were valuable, the secretary will probably *think* it is.

There is another reason why the salesman should keep himself occupied while he is waiting to see the prospect. It helps to keep him calm and to prevent him from developing high blood pressure as he broods about being kept waiting while he could be earning money elsewhere. A sales-man who has been sitting in a waiting room for an hour or so will probably find it hard to conceal his irritation when he finally goes in to see the prospect, even though he knows that this feeling will communicate itself to the prospect and probably result in a thoroughly unsatisfactory interview. Hence, it is better to keep busy at something, even if it is only filling out a report to headquarters. Even a pleasant conversation with another salesman is far preferable to seething with mounting anger.

Some salesmen ask the receptionist for reading matter about the com-pany she works for, which often makes a good impression and may provide the salesman with valuable information.

Some salesmen feel so strongly about not wanting to wait to see pros-pects that they place a limit on the time they will wait, especially if they have appointments in advance. Even some salesmen calling cold advise against waiting if it appears as if a long wait is likely. One industrial equip-ment salesman claims, "I never wait more than 20 or 30 minutes to see a prospect. If he is tied up, I simply ask for another appointment later and go out and make some cold calls on nearby smokestacks. I think it is a mistake to wait too long to see a prospect. First, it puts me in a frame of mind that prevents me from making my best presentation. I get mad, and I can't hide it. Next, it gives the prospect the idea that I have nothing else to do. I want him to know that my time is valuable too. Finally, it keeps me from wasting time sitting in a chair. While I may spend two or three hours waiting to see some clown who is playing hard-to-get, I can be out taking orders from someone who is more accessible. Another thing, I have detected that when I do call back on a prospect who could not keep his original appointment, he is sort of apologetic about his behavior and willing to give me a fair hearing."

Selling the receptionist
Some salesmen treat the receptionist with scant respect, which is a serious tactical blunder. The wise salesman treats her as a person of importance and endeavors to enlist her cooperation. Then, when she goes in to tell the

boss the salesman is calling, and the boss asks, "What does he look like?" she can give the salesman a break. *The knack is to make her feel that she is showing her importance and authority by getting him in instead of by keeping him out.* Incidentally, when he leaves after obtaining an interview, the salesman should thank the secretary for her cooperation.

As a rule, the bigger the prospect, the smarter the secretary. Tricks do not work with these smarter, more experienced buffers. They will usually insist on learning what the salesman's business is. And yet, they are always haunted by the fear that they may exclude and offend some person whom the boss wanted to see.

Numerous techniques are used by salesmen to avoid coming right out and telling what they are selling. Some say, "Personal matter"; others just state, "Courtesy call." A common answer is, "Just tell him that Mr. Herbert James Warren of New York is calling." But such evasions frequently result in making the prospect wary.

If the salesman has made a real preapproach and has a concrete proposal to present, he may merely tap the neatly bound report and say, "I want to talk over these plans with him."

Some salesmen are forever about to catch a plane and would be terribly disappointed if Mr. Prospect could not see them for just a minute after they have come so far. Perhaps they can put on an act that is sufficiently convincing to win the interview.

But no trick or bit of acting will ever serve the purpose better than a confident attitude based on the conviction that he has something of value to offer the prospect and has every right in the world to present it. Every buyer is seen by *some* salesmen; there is some point of contact at which he is vulnerable. The real salesman finds it.

One way is to figure out *why* the buyer won't let him in. There are honest, legitimate reasons such as other engagements of importance. Then there are the excuses, which should be ignored. A careful preapproach will often enable the salesman to distinguish between valid reasons and excuses.

The following excellent treatment of this problem of gaining the secretary's cooperation was written by the late A. R. Hahn.[1]

At the January sales management conference in Boston "Red" Motley told a story about a hundred-thousand-dollar advertising contract that came through because he used good manners and common sense in talking with a prospect's secretary.

This matter of reception room behavior on the part of salesmen is something that could stand some discussion in the very next sales meeting of every

---

[1] *Sales Management* magazine. Miss Hahn was managing editor for many years.

sales organization in the country. We take entirely too much for granted an understanding of its importance on the part of the salesman.

George was a typewriter salesman in Chicago. One day he called on the president of a company with the object of selling a battery of typewriters for the company office. The president was out of town. George asked the president's secretary if she'd mind talking to him for a few minutes about typewriters. He drew her into a discussion of what she liked and disliked about the machine she was then using. One of the points she brought out led George to ask her to look at—and try—the new model machine he had in his car. He ended up (oh, wise salesman!) by giving her a complete demonstration. When he went off, he didn't forget to thank her for her time.

Several weeks later when George called for an appointment, Sarah arranged for him to see the boss.

George presented his story. Somewhere along the line the president expressed the opinion that any typewriter business the company had to place should go to a competitive firm because that firm was a customer—the old reciprocity argument. At that point George pulled an ace out of his sleeve.

"Your secretary, Mr. X., tells me the machine she is now using is good enough mechanically, but the action on it is unduly heavy. By two o'clock she is fatigued from pounding it. She says she makes more mistakes in the last three hours of the day than she does in all the rest of the day put together. The machine, then, is affecting her efficiency. I'm sure this means a great deal to you. . . . The action on our machine is definitely easier. . . ." And so on.

Mr. X. pushed the buzzer. The secretary appeared. "Sarah," said the boss, indicating the demonstrator George had brought in, "is this machine any good? Is it any easier to work on than the one you now have?"

"Oh, yes, definitely!" Sarah replied. And while George stood by, the secretary repeated the demonstration George had made to her three weeks before. George got the order. George, you see, was intelligent enough not to "underestimate the power of a woman."

For years I've known a Mr. B., here in New York City, whose work demands frequent audiences with very busy executives—usually presidents or general managers. Mr. B. is not selling a commodity; he's selling an idea. The nature of it doesn't matter at the moment. Some years ago he was working on a project which, by happenstance, took me on a number of calls with him. I've never forgotten my admiration for the way he handled himself in reception rooms.

In his case, I'm sure his pleasing manners were purely habitual, because he was raised in an English background where parents set very high standards for social conduct, and where some degree of formality is the rule rather than the exception. Yet anyone with common sense, a knowledge of the basic rules of courtesy, and a feeling of respect for all of his contemporaries, no matter what their station, could duplicate his behavior without any false note of insincerity or stuffiness.

Mr. B. entered a reception room quietly, without rush. He never carried a lighted cigarette or cigar or pipe. He took off his hat. He never charged up to a reception girl and began to speak while she was busy at some task. He waited quietly. When the girl gave him her attention, he first said, "How do you do?" to *her.* He introduced himself to *her.* Then he explained that he was calling on Mr. So-and-So, and he said, "Would you be good enough to ask him *if it would be convenient* for him to see me for a few minutes?"

Time after time I saw girls who were tired, or hurried, or harassed, or just plainly bored after a succession of pushy visitors, warm up and smile back and reply, "Of course!" Here was a gentleman. Here was a man who recognized her as an individual. He was a man who somehow gave her a sense of importance. Very seldom indeed did she ask, "Have you an appointment?" Very seldom did she ask, "What do you want to see him about?"

What she did do (and I know, because I made it my business to find out) was this: She went in to Mr. So-and-So and said, "Mr. B. is outside. *I think you'd better see him.*"

I've always felt that the short sequence of words, ". . . if it would be convenient," is one of the most skillful choices of language I've ever heard employed by a salesman. Mr. B. used them over and over again in his calls. Their charm rests on the connotation they carry of courtesy, of graciousness, of realization that the user is asking for a busy man's time and will appreciate it when he gets it. Even more important, they reflect an abiding confidence on the part of the caller that the proposition he is sponsoring is important enough to justify the attention of a key man.

What I've related here about Mr. B.'s approach is, like the techniques of experts in many another field, deceptively simple. Yet it embodies great skill and it pays off in results. I'd like to stress particularly the ease, confidence, and apparent leisureliness of this approach, its lack of *pushiness.* Never a sign of impatience, no matter what circumstances develop.

If we could only etch into the minds of salesmen the fact that a show of belligerence or irritation only results in lost sales! And that never, never is haste or pressure advisable when it's employed at the expense of courtesy and good manners!

Let no one be confused about one point: A salesman can observe all the canons of good taste and courtesy and still project warmth and friendliness. We tend to confuse informality in behavior and over-breeziness in language and attitude, with friendliness. If a secretary or receptionist has been on her job any length of time, she's heard everything, and she is likely to look with a jaundiced eye on any version of the "Am-I-a-killer!" approach. She is likely to resent (whether she shows it or not) any salesman who assumes that on his second call he is entitled to perch on the corner of her desk and bawl, "Hi, Beautiful! Have you missed me? Tell G.S. I'm here, will yuh?"

This sort of thing sounds particularly crude when it's put down, as it is here, in black and white. Yet it goes on every day. The line between what is an expression of natural friendliness and what is over-informality and bad taste is very finely drawn. The wise salesman is careful never to overstep.

Let every salesman take a candid look at his reception room manners.

The little lady behind the desk may be holding his next commission check in her pretty pink fingers. And the option on whether he gets a chance to cash it or not, may rest with her.

Many secretaries have offered helpful hints to salesmen, such as:

Let me have your business card.

Speak clearly and audibly; help me to get the right pronunciation of your name.

Act happy while you are waiting. At least, don't act bored or grouchy.

Be patient. Unavoidable delays may force you to wait, but fuming won't get you in any sooner or on any better footing.

Be friendly, but not fresh. Our waiting room is not a stag smoker.

Don't try to pump me for confidential information.

If you have a gripe against my company, I will refer you to the right person to take it up with. I'm not that person.

Thank me for my cooperation; don't ignore me.

Don't try romancing me as a way to gain my help in getting in to see my boss. Your type doesn't make me swoon.

Give me a piece of literature about what you are selling when you hand me your card. At the very least, it helps me to remember you the next time you call.

When I come into the room where you are waiting, stand up! I may have to work for a living, but I can still be a lady.

You are the guest; act like one.

If you are in doubt about how to act, it's smart to *under*play your role.

The difficulty of gaining an interview is greater for specialty salesmen who have the task of persuading the prospect to buy something that he had not contemplated purchasing—for which he felt no need at the time. However, the staple salesman meets the same difficulty frequently in his effort to introduce his line to new buyers and to establish new connections. It is fairly easy for any salesman to see the small retailer; but as he ascends the scale to the chief executive of larger concerns, he finds that the barriers between him and his prospect increase in number, strength, and height. Hence no salesman of these two types can consider his preparation complete until he has prepared for this first step in the actual sales process.

Other ways to gain the interview

There are three ways to gain the interview other than directly calling on the prospect and asking for it. Naturally, each of these must eventually be supplemented by a direct personal contact, but in some instances they do help to open the door to a prospect who is particularly difficult to see.

THE INTRODUCTION   One of the most effective methods for winning an interview is by means of an introduction. Perhaps its chief benefit is that it brings the salesman before the prospect as an acquaintance rather than as a stranger. Instead of having to introduce himself, the salesman simply hands the prospect the letter, note, or card of introduction, with a very brief comment: "Your friend, Mr. Smith, was kind enough to give this to me." This introduction may be obtained either from a mutual friend or from an executive of the salesman's firm who might be known to the prospect. Obviously, the more intimate the bond is between prospect and writer of the introduction, the more influential the introduction will be.

In asking for an introduction, the salesman does not request a letter of *recommendation*. This point is important, as it makes it far more likely that his request will be granted. It is not difficult to get a note of introduction from most men to a friend who might be a good prospect. If the salesman has made a good impression, it is easy to say, "Just give me one of your cards, please, and a word or two to Mr. Blank. I'd appreciate it greatly as I'm calling on him tomorrow morning." If such a request is made frankly and with a confident air, it will usually be granted. The words, "Introducing Mr. Salesman," penciled on a business card by an acquaintance of the prospect, will help wonderfully in obtaining an interview.

The *letter* of introduction is of still greater value, but it is harder to obtain. If such a letter cannot be obtained from a friend of the prospect, the salesman's own firm may supply it, giving him a letter personally addressed to each big buyer in his territory. This letter need not be long and should make no effort to sell the goods. It is sufficient to say, "This will introduce Mr. John Smith, who represents us. Yours very truly, William Jones & Company." Such a letter can have only a good effect upon the buyer who reads it, as it is practically certain to be taken to him by the guardian in the outer office. The very possession of such a letter has a beneficial reaction upon the salesman, as it enables him to conduct himself as one who has a right to a hearing. The office boy or receptionist will be far less likely to snub him than a salesman without credentials of any kind or with only the ordinary business card.

In New York there is a salesman who enjoys a reputation for getting in to see big men. He says:

The most inaccessible man in New York or Chicago is easy for someone to see. Someone has at all times the freedom of his office. It may be his secretary, a personal friend, or some other salesman who walks right past the various functionaries who guard his office. Find that person, and you've found a point of contact that will often lead to an interview if you really have a legitimate reason for seeing him.

It may be well to point out also that the name of a mutual friend should not be used in this way without his consent. A buyer makes this point forcefully:

Some time ago my phone rang, and I found a party on the other end of the wire who said he was a friend of a very dear friend of mine. He stated he would like to see me right away if it would be convenient. I was busy as the dickens; but my friend's name was the magic password, and I told him to come right over. And then I thought it would be a good idea to phone my friend. It cost a quarter, but it was worth it.

"Why, he is no friend of mine," my friend told me. "The other day when you called me up he happened to be here and heard me talk to you; and after I had hung up, he asked me about you, particularly about the amount of printing you bought, and in a general way I told him what he wanted to know. However, if he abuses a casual business acquaintanceship by suggesting that he is a personal friend of mine I think he will get the gate instead of an order the next time he calls on me."

When Mr. Tricky arrived I cross-examined him as to his friendship with my friend, and I can tell you that the last thing he thought of was trying to sell me any printing. His only thought was to get out of my office. I buy printing, lots of it, and on regular days he could have called on me and submitted his proposition. But my door is barred to him from now on.

It is obvious that the note of introduction or the name of a friend will get the salesman in to a certain prospect only *once.* If he wishes to see the same man again, he must do so on his own merit. The introduction merely gives him a chance to make such a favorable impression that he will be welcomed the next time he calls. Also be warned that there are people who resent being approached in this manner. They have a strong aversion to people who attempt to trade on friendships.

THE TELEPHONE   If a salesman uses the telephone in the approach, the assumption is that he will try to make a favorable impression and gain sufficient prospect interest to be invited to "come over and tell me more about it." At first thought, this way of gaining these two important prospect decisions appears to be rather hazardous; it is too easy for the prospect to say "No." However, many situations are ideally adapted to the use of the phone.

For example, the Farmers Mutual Hail Insurance Company of Des Moines, Iowa, encourages its 21 sales representatives to telephone ahead for appointments and claims that this saves about 9,000 miles of travel each month as compared to the former alternative of calling without phoning to make an appointment. The salesmen can see more prospects, give better service, and prepare themselves to discuss with their prospects the matters touched on in the phone conversation.

The salesman must have his opening remarks carefully worked out in advance to avoid having the prospect insist, "Just give me the gist of your proposition now and I'll tell you whether it will be worth your while to see me personally." If the proposition does not lend itself to telephone selling, this pitfall must be by-passed. [2]

Mr. Morgan offers these added suggestions:

Instead of saying, "This is John Smith of the Acme Company, may I speak to Mr. Jones, please?" Mr. Morgan suggests this: "May I speak to Mr. Jones, please? This is John Smith of the Acme Company." The latter is superior because: If you give your name first, the girl may not get it, particularly if it is unfamiliar or unusual. She asks you to repeat it, which gives her an opening to quiz you about why you want to talk to her boss, etc. If you tell her first that you wish to speak to Mr. Jones, she will be alerted and will get your name, knowing why you are calling. This approach does not offend the secretary, as many do.

Despite precautions, she may insist on asking, "What do you want to speak to Mr. Jones about?" One reply might be, "I just want to speak to him directly. Is he there?" This is not highly recommended for use with experienced secretaries, as they ask the question either to enable them to decide whether to put the call through or because the boss has ordered them to get this information. She would rather offend you than her boss. So she may report, "A Mr. X wants to talk to you, but he refuses to say why." This does not open the way for a pleasant conversation, even though the prospect may decide to talk with the salesman.

Generally speaking, it is smart to enlist the cooperation of the secretary rather than to try to push past her, even on the phone. Secretaries are people and they respond to courteous and complimentary treatment.

Sometimes the salesman is confronted with the problem of not know-

---

[2] This matter of making appointments and even sales by telephone is now so highly specialized that Boyce Morgan is operating a service devoted to this one aspect of getting business by phone. He calls it *Better Business by Telephone*, his service consisting of regular letters or memoranda to subscribers informing them of the latest and most effective ways to utilize the telephone in getting business. And the American Telephone and Telegraph Company has collected a huge amount of data on the subject of how salesmen can use the telephone in various ways to increase sales.

ing the name of the person he ought to talk to. It is sound practice to frankly ask the first person who answers the phone about this, stating your business and reasons for wishing to talk to him. In nearly every case, you will get the name, after which you will be connected with that person.

It will help in getting an appointment by phone if you make it clear that you have something to *show* the prospect and discuss with him. This might take the form of a report, a series of pictures of interest to him, the results of a survey of some sort that you had made of his problem, a magazine article, even a model of your product.

Another aid to getting appointments by phone is to send a letter in advance of the phone call. In this letter allusion may be made to the impending phone call, thus giving the caller a chance to ask: "I believe that Henry Brown, our sales manager, wrote you a week or so ago about our new No. 18 Flipodozer. Do you recall his letter?" Here the salesman pauses and then proceeds, no matter what the reply is, "Well, I'm in Hartford just for today, but I brought with me complete data and specifications for our large-sized model which I am convinced will save you money on at least three and perhaps four of your finishing operations. Would you have 12 or 15 minutes to look over the data this afternoon?"

This approach is not a high-powered monologue; it is a conversation between two businessmen. The prospect has had a chance to speak, but his reply is almost certain to be affirmative. The salesman also subtly suggests prompt action on the prospect's part. However, he does not name a time, as the prospect can too easily reply, "I'm tied up then." He offers a benefit and thus appeals to the prospect's self-interest.

Some specialty salesmen who depend upon the law of averages in making a large number of calls with little or no advance preparation use the telephone effectively. A good example of this is supplied by the working methods of a very successful life insurance salesman in a college town. Each school year this salesman has about two thousand seniors who are good prospects. Obviously it would be impossible for him to make a personal call upon each one. Much of his time would be wasted owing to students' being away or busy. Hence he uses the lunch hour and the dinner hour, when students are usually to be found at their houses, to telephone for definite appointments. In this way he eliminates immediately those who are not prospects at all, and he calls personally on those who are prepared to talk with him. It is true that many who might become good prospects are lost in this rather haphazard method; yet with so many to see, it is a question of meeting the best ones as quickly as possible.

The following points taken from "The Technique of the Interview"[3] are worth keeping in mind if this approach method is used.

[3] Published by the R & R Service, Indianapolis.

1. The telephone approach must move rapidly. The introduction of the subject must come quickly. The opening should be only a short sentence and
   should end in a leading question which invites the reply "Yes."
2. Get to the objective of the telephone call quickly. Brevity is permissible
   over the telephone which might not be permissible in the personal interview.
3. By all means avoid a telephone argument. No matter what the prospect
   may reply, drive through to your objective.
4. The telephone approach must be aggressive without seeming to be so. It
   is very easy for the prospect to say, "Thank you for calling but I am not
   interested." The short questions which invite a "Yes" answer are the best
   method of driving through without giving the prospect the opportunity to
   cut off the conversation.
5. Speed the conversation after the agent has announced his name and
   business. If the prospect is going to cut off, it likely will be just after the
   introduction. Hurry to reach your point on which a "Yes" answer is forthcoming. One life insurance man states his name and company and then
   says, "I would like to get your opinion on a new type of insurance service." Before the prospect can reply "No," the agent asks, "You were
   born in Minneapolis, weren't you?"

In passing it may be noted that, under certain conditions, some *selling*
can be accomplished over the telephone. Classified newspaper advertisements, groceries to housewives, standardized or graded staples like wheat
and cotton to brokers, or perhaps a bill of goods to a retailer may be sold.
Other illustrations could be given of the use of the telephone to obtain
orders, but the majority of these instances would be found to come under
the head of repeat orders from regular customers. A sales manager for a
New York house made a trip into the West during a holiday season when
business was dull and a blizzard had interfered greatly with transportation
in the mountain states. Making his headquarters at Denver, he called by
long distance as many of the firm's customers as he could reach and sold
many thousands of dollars' worth of goods in this way.

Most regular users of the telephone to make sales follow one or more
of three plans.

The *call collect* plan is used, for example, by the Moline Body Company, of Moline, Illinois, makers of truck bodies and equipment. On every
letter going out of town is affixed a sticker exhorting the recipient to call the
company collect any time he needs anything. This device is responsible for
one-half of the company's sales.

The *key-town* plan finds salesman selecting the key town in a section
of his territory, where he makes personal calls on larger-volume customers,
then covers the surrounding area by long-distance telephone. This cuts
time and costs, while maintaining customer contact and service.

The *skip-stop* plan has the salesman calling on *some* of his customers and telephoning others from nearby towns. On his next trip he reverses the process, stopping at towns he skipped before. Again, this cuts costs and takes good care of his customers.

A salesman for textiles in New York sends out swatches or samples of his wares and calls his prospects over long distance within half a day after the samples have arrived. The prospect can make inquiries about the goods, deliveries, terms, quantities available, etc., with the samples before him, and the salesman can take the order without making an expensive trip.

However, even the retailer who is sold by his regular salesman via the telephone twice in succession begins to feel neglected and is more open to the approaches of rival salesmen than if the first man had cared enough for the business to come after it in person.

When the sale is likely to prove difficult and the result is decidedly in doubt, it is unwise to trust too much to an ability to deliver a selling talk over the telephone.

But there are always exceptions to every rule and this is no exception. Mr. Bruce Gordon, president of Todd Chemical Company, manufacturers of floor cleaners and waxes, reports, "We're opening over 700 new accounts every month—with a telephone."[4] He has nine telephone salesmen who make between 18 and 24 calls a day to prospective industrial and institutional accounts. "One out of three calls results in a sale," says Gordon. The program was developed by the New York Telephone Company under its "Phone Power System." It employs *Wide Area Telephone Service* (WATS), which provides an unlimited number of long-distance calls at a fixed monthly rate.

Seeing the right man

One problem frequently encountered in industrial selling is that of trying to sell the wrong man. Sometimes the salesman has simply failed to pinpoint the person in the organization who makes the actual buying decision—the man who signs the order. Other times the real decision maker hides behind some subordinate; the salesman gives the presentation to the subordinate only to discover upon completion that the man has no power to buy. This problem was discussed in *The American Salesman.*[5]

In some large organizations, after you have started your interview in his office, Mr. Rightman will stop you with the statement that you should not talk to him

---

[4] "This Is Not a Recording," *Sales Management*, June 5, 1964, p. 85.
[5] William Wood, "How to Avoid Being 'Kissed Onto' a Subordinate," *The American Salesman*, January, 1965, p. 37.

but to his general manager, sales manager, office manager, or some other official of the concern.

When such a situation arises, say to Mr. Rightman: "Mr. President, as the head of this organization, you are responsible for all losses in this business. Isn't that true?" Then, continue with your regular openers.

After you see, from insistent statements on his part, that your story must be told to another, be sure to qualify, as follows: "Do I understand you to say, Mr. Rightman, that your under executive or sales manager is the man to sign my order?"

If Mr. Rightman says his subordinate has full authority and you cannot induce him to investigate further, go to the other man and sell him thoroughly. Remember, in a case of this kind, the new man becomes Mr. Rightman and is to be approached as though he were a brand-new prospect.

METHODS FOR APPROACHING PROSPECTS

There are eleven major methods by which the prospect may be approached: (1) the introductory approach, (2) the product approach, (3) the consumer-benefit approach, (4) the curiosity approach, (5) the shock approach, (6) the showmanship approach, (7) the question approach, (8) the statement approach, (9) the premium approach, (10) the survey approach, or (11) the compliment approach. Many times a salesman will use a combination of these eleven methods. He may start with an introductory approach but swing into a consumer-benefit one to facilitate easy transition into the presentation. Or he may open with a product or curiosity approach and then shift into a statement. Hence, the salesman should have all eleven of these techniques mastered and instantly available.

The introductory approach

The introductory approach is by far the most frequently used technique. Unfortunately, by itself it is also the weakest, for it does very little for the salesman. He walks into the prospect's office and says, "Hello, I am Bill Buffalo representing the Black Ball Express Company."

This approach will gain only nominal attention unless the prospect is already expecting the man. His interest will be minimal unless he has a previously recognized problem which this company may help him to solve. Finally, transition is sometimes awkward if the prospect's mental reaction is, "OK, so what do you want?" Therefore, most salesmen find it necessary to use one of the other approaches immediately after introducing themselves.

One purchasing agent reacted to this type of approach by saying, "I don't care who you are or who you represent. I only care about who I am and what you are prepared to do for me."

The brutal truth is that most introductions at the beginning of a sale are worthless as the prospect misses the name and has to ask again or look at a card *after* he has decided that he is interested in hearing what the proposition contains for him. Frank Bettger relates how he sold a $250,000 life insurance policy to an executive who did not know the name of the insurance company until the sale had been made. In the early stages of the interview the prospect had asked Frank whom he represented. His answer was "You."[6]

In many sales situations it is best to leave the introductions until after a successful approach has been made. Once the prospect has decided that he would like to hear the presentation, then a proper introduction can be made. How many times has a salesman introduced himself only to hear, "Go away, I don't want any"?

The product approach

The product approach consists simply of thrusting the product into the hands of the prospect. One costume jewelry salesman would merely hand the buyer one of his most attractive and salable items without saying a word. The buyer would naturally look at the merchandise, and if it interested her, she would ask, "Where's the rest of your line?"

One baby-furniture salesman also used the product approach very effectively in selling a new lightweight aluminum baby walker by simply handing the walker to the buyer without saying a word. He relates the story of one sale to Macy's buyer in New York City. "I walked into his department and saw that it was the largest operation I had seen in a department store. He carried a full line of baby walkers. I had his name from a directory but I verified it with a clerk when I asked where the buyer was. She said he was back in his office so I went back and walked right into his little cubicle. He said, 'Well, what do you want?' I handed the walker to him without a word. He said, 'How much?' I laid before him our full price list giving all the details. He said, 'Send me six dozen, all blue.' I asked, 'Don't you want to hear the story?' He replied, 'This product and the price list is all the story I need. This is the way I really like to buy. Come back any time; it's a pleasure to do business with you.'"

The product approach is best used when the salesman is selling a product that is obviously unique, possesses considerable eye appeal, and tends to tell its own sales story. It works because the unique merchandise attracts the prospect's attention, and interest, and it provides the best possible transition into the presentation.

[6] Frank Bettger, *How I raised Myself from Failure to Success in Selling* (Prentice-Hall, Inc., Englewood Cliffs, N.J., 1949), pp. 54–62.

One sales representative for a manufacturer of military electronic equipment carries with him a variety of exotic hardware that his firm has made for various branches of the armed forces. This hardware does three things for him. First, it gets him by the purchasing agent to see the man in the firm who makes decisions on such items because the p.a. quickly realizes that he cannot deal with the man technically and so promptly refers the salesman to the proper engineer. Next, he has found that engineers love to fondle such items; they are greatly interested in complex electronic devices. This gives him the entree he needs to gain the engineer's confidence, for many engineers are antagonistic to salesmen who lack the proper technical credentials. Finally, they give the engineer in the clearest possible way some idea of the firm's capabilities.

In general, people like to handle and examine products; they like to operate them and take them apart. The product approach capitalizes on this urge.

Consumer-benefit approach

The consumer-benefit approach consists of opening the interview with a statement or question which directs the prospect's thoughts to the benefits you propose to furnish him. Sometimes the statement is one designed to whet the prospect's curiosity. Other times it is a declaration designed to shock him, thus getting his attention and interest. However, often it is simply a question or statement designed to make the prospect think about the problem which the salesman proposes to solve for him.

An ice cream salesman addressed the manager of an ice cream parlor with the question, "How would you like to save 40 cents a gallon on all the ice cream you sell?" Needless to say, the manager wanted to hear more about it, so he was told about the virtues of making his own ice cream from a mix that the salesman sold.

An insurance salesman handed the prospect a facsimile check made out to him for $600 and asked, "How would you like to receive that check each month upon retirement?" The prospect admitted that he would like it very much, and asked to hear more.

A Volkswagen salesman opened, "Tired of paying gas bills?" Who isn't?

An offset press salesman began, "Your letterheads will cost you about $5 a thousand with this press. What did you pay last? $20?"

Curiosity

Frequently this quick offer of a benefit is coupled with an appeal to the prospect's curiosity.

A life insurance salesman called upon a prospect and asked him what he would give the salesman for 10 pounds of cork. When the prospect replied that he did not want the cork, the salesman asked him what he would give for it if he were in the middle of Lake Erie in a sinking boat. From this curiosity appeal, the salesman developed the idea that the prospect had to buy life insurance before the actual need for it arose.

When the salesman has to get past a minor employee of the prospect, such as a receptionist, the secretary, or the office boy, the curiosity appeal may be used by sending in a note on the back of a business card or scribbling it on a letterhead or memorandum sheet. An illustration of this is furnished by a salesman of men's neckwear who had tried repeatedly to gain an interview with the buyer of a large department store. This buyer had refused to see him because his store had handled the merchandise of another concern for years and he saw no reason to change. Upon one call, therefore, this salesman sent in a note to the buyer that read, "Will you give me 10 minutes to get your advice upon a business problem?" The note aroused the curiosity of the buyer, and the salesman was invited in. He showed the buyer a new line of ties and asked the buyer what he thought would be a fair price for the different ties in the new line. The buyer examined each one carefully and gave a thoughtful reply. The salesman noted his remarks; and when the 10 minutes were up, he prepared to go. However, the buyer asked to see some of the ties again and placed an order for a considerable number at the prices that the salesman quoted him, which were slightly lower than the prices that he himself had suggested.

Salesmen for one firm are taught to walk into the prospect's office with an envelope in their hands, remarking, "I have a little memo here about the 250 customers you lost last month."

Frequently the appeal to curiosity borders closely upon trickery, a means of obtaining an interview that is seldom profitable. In some cases where the prospect has already felt a real need for the product or service but refuses to see the salesman, a trick might be used as a final stratagem to win the interview. Usually, however, when smart-aleck tactics are used the salesman is at a distinct disadvantage as soon as the ruse is discovered by the prospect.

Shock

An insurance salesman obtained a picture of his prospect and had a photographer retouch it to make him look much older. He walked into the prospect's office, handed him the picture, and asked, "What are you doing for that old man today?" Variations of this have been employed using pictures of the prospect's wife or family. The idea is to shock some stubborn prospect into thinking about reality, thinking about things he prefers not to think about.

Such an approach is valuable in getting the attention and interest of a prospect who is not inclined to treat the salesman's proposition seriously, someone who refuses to become emotionally involved with the problem at hand. Amazingly, some people refuse to come to grips with critical problems; psychologically, they seem to feel that if they don't think about them, they will go away. The shock treatment may get through this defense mechanism thereby allowing the salesman to get on with his presentation.

The showmanship approach

Certain situations call for unusual efforts if a prospect's attention and interest are to be obtained. The following account from *The American Salesman* is illustrative of the use of showmanship in selling.[7]

Maybe you heard about the spectacular sales call Phil Patterson of *Sales Management* made on Pete Callaway, advertising director of *Sports Illustrated.* . . .

First, as background, . . . Patterson was trying to sell Callaway on advertising in *Sales Management* to persuade *Sales Management's* readers to advertise in *Sports Illustrated.* . . .

First scene is the lawn of Pete Callaway's Westport, Conn., home. A cable arrives from London . . . from *Sales Management* confirming Phil Patterson's appointment for the next morning.

Scene two is in Rockefeller Center, New York. Phil Patterson arrives at Callaway's offices bearing a dispatch case in one hand and a banded wad of simulated greenbacks in the other. This bundle, a note explains, totals $10,835 (the median income of *Sports Illustrated's* readers), a sum which mightily interests Phil's magazine's sales manager subscribers.

During the call, as the subject of *Sales Management's* audience came up, Phil asked if he might go to the door of the office for a moment. There he motioned to someone and into Callaway's office marched three Brinks guards. On Callaway's desk, they proceeded to dump bags full of money—not simulated money, but honest-to-Betsy $10 Federal Reserve notes to the tune of $320,000. This, Patterson explained, was the amount his magazine's readers had paid to subscribe—32,000 of them at $10 each.

Did Callaway examine the money? No, he didn't touch it but he actually pulled back as if afraid of so much green.

When the Brinks men had rebagged their bundles and departed, Patterson pulled out a copy of *Sales Management* into which had been bound an insert—set in type and printed just for this call—giving an example of the type of ad Patterson thought would work well for Callaway.

Wait! That's not all. As he left, Patterson handed Callaway a lucite block containing another honest-to-Betsy $10 bill with an engraved message about *Sales Management* on the outside.

[7] Rowe Pend, "That's Selling," *The American Salesman*, October, 1961, p. 57.

There have been numerous shows put on for the benefit of some important prospect who appreciates imagination and showmanship. One young man seeking employment with an advertising agency was having great difficulty obtaining an interview with the top man; so he had himself boxed up and delivered into the inner sanctum by an express company. Another salesman took space on a large billboard on the route his prospect took to and from home. It declared, "Mr. E. Duncan: You are losing $150 every day you fail to see me! Signed: R. Huff, Acme Tool Company." There is no limit to what an enterprising man can do to dramatize his approach when the situation warrants it. But that is the important thing to realize: showmanship can backfire if used in the wrong situations or on the wrong people.

The question

The use of the question to open an interview is an art in itself. It can be used in conjunction with other approaches, particularly the consumer-benefit approach, or it can stand on its own. "What will you be doing in 1999?" just might grab a young man in such a way that he would talk about retirement planning. "Are you big enough to use automated production equipment profitably?" might cause the president of a growing manufacturing company to answer, "I don't know. How big have I got to be?" And then the two can get right to the heart of the matter.

Psychological questioning immediately gets the prospect's attention, interest, and participation in the affair. It focuses his mind on an essential element in the proposition which gets the presentation off to a good start.

The salesmen for one firm are taught to say, "If you will just answer a couple of questions I'll know whether my product can help you with the packaging of your goods." This is really a question and usually elicits the reply, "What are your questions?"

A suggestive example of the use of the question in opening an interview is a plan employed by a salesman for a "personal efficiency" course. Instead of going in with a machine-gun selling talk he went in quietly and asked:

If I sent you a little set of books on personal efficiency and you opened them and found them interesting, would you read them?

After you had read them, would you buy them if you liked them well enough?

If you did not find them interesting, would you slip them back in the package and mail them back to me?

These questions were so simple, so direct, that the prospect could scarcely find reasons for saying no to any of them. The three little questions were adopted as the standard approach for all the salesmen of that company.

Another proposition, which usually is presented to executives but which sometimes has to be presented to individual office workers—either as a means of getting past them to the boss or as a means of persuading them to use the proposition after the boss has approved it—offers a simple way of using the question: "How would you like to have your pay raised?"

This question invariably arouses interest. It is followed by another.

"Would you be willing to study a simple *Service Bulletin* which tells you how to get your pay raised—if it didn't cost you anything?"

The third question is: "After you study this bulletin, would you be willing to *try* what it recommends, if I make it easy and it doesn't cost you anything and the big boss approves of it?"

When his prospect refuses to listen to his proposition, one salesman selling chewing gum to retailers asks this question, "Did you ever hear of the Westinghouse Company?" The dealer replies, "Of course. Everybody has." The salesman snaps back, "Do you know that they have a fixed rule that every salesman calling on their buyers must be accorded a hearing and within one hour? They are afraid of overlooking something good. Have you a better purchasing system than they, or are you afraid to look at things?"

A salesman selling a collection service used an approach consisting of the simple question: "I'm not sure if you're the man I'm looking for. Have you 20 accounts on your books that you have given up as dead?"

A vending machine company instructs its salesmen to carry a piece of heavy paper about 2 by 3 feet in size, which they unfold and spread out on the floor or counter, saying, "If I could show you how to make that space worth $250 a year to you, you'd be interested, wouldn't you?"

A salesman for an investment service inquires, "If you save as much in the next five years as you did in the last five, will you be satisfied?"

Of course, the questions must be well framed. Too many salesmen fall into the slack habit of greeting their prospects with, "How's business?" The space buyer for a large advertising agency kept a record of what salesmen said to him when they first approached. Out of the 14 so-called salesmen who called in one day, 12 opened the interview with "How's business?" "How do things look?" "Things picking up much yet?" The sales manager of a large furniture company says that four out of five salesmen open their talks with "How's tricks?" or "How's business?"

Such an approach may suffice in prosperous times, but it is loaded with dynamite when business is not so good. And when did any salesman ever find his prospects enthusiastic about business? It is a part of the buyer's defense to pull a long face, to insist that he cannot afford to buy, to swear that the salemen's product has been given a thorough trial and did not move or perform. To ask a buyer how business is invites only trouble.

Other approaches are equally ineffective. "Well, anything new since I saw you last?" "No, I guess not, Jim." And that's that.

"According to my dope, you haven't given me an order for four months. Isn't it about time you slipped me one?" Did this salesman get the order?

"I was just passing by and dropped in to see if you needed anything in our line today. Anything doing?" This approach is so weak and yet so widely used that it merits discussion. It is poor psychology to make the buyer think that the call is so casual; it makes it too easy to turn the salesman down. It is much better to give the impression that the buyer's problem has been given the most thorough consideration by the salesman and that this call is a very special one made for the purpose of presenting a very special recommendation.

"Mr. Prospect, I was thinking about you all last evening." Is Mr. Prospect likely to yell, "I'm not interested!"?

One industrial salesman selling fork-lift trucks would open an interview with the question, "Would you like to save $6,300 on your warehouse handling costs this next year?" What executive could say no to that question? The salesman had, of course, determined the figure from a preapproach survey.

A representative for a manufacturer in the electronics field catches a purchasing agent's attention and interest by asking, "What one electronic item that you are now buying is giving you the biggest headaches?" He had found that most p.a.'s have many headaches for which they are seeking the right "aspirin." This opening allows the salesman to dwell on the problems the prospect feels are most serious and about which he is most apt to do something. Sometimes he asks, "What electronic equipment you are now buying do you feel is most overpriced?" The point of this additional question is to find in what areas he would meet the least pressure on prices and could be most competitive.

This art of asking the right questions serves several purposes. It forces the prospect to talk in the areas chosen by the salesman. It elicits information of tremendous value, thereby pushing the preapproach to satisfying depth. It focuses the prospect's attention on the problems he is most eager to solve, thus guiding the salesman into the shortest path to a sale.

The salesman will find that the hours he spends formulating these "right" questions will be time well spent. Notice that the word is "hours" not "minutes," for it takes considerable time to develop properly worded questions.

There are some basic principles one should observe in phrasing these questions. First, the more specific the question, the better. Compare these questions: "Would you like to save several thousands of dollars in labor costs?" and "Would you like to save $15,500 next year on your costs of handling goods in process?" Which is most likely to whet the interest of the prospect and move smoothly into the sale of conveyor systems?

Second, whenever possible the question should be tailored for the prospect's situation, based on data obtained through a good preapproach.

Third, the question should be aimed at the major consumer benefit in which the prospect will be interested. Aim at the major buying motives rather than the minor ones. If you are convinced that the prospect is most interested in saving money, then your question should be directed to that motive. If you feel that status is the most important motive, then your question should suggest that your product will help the prospect to gain status.

Fourth, there are some areas in which the salesman should be extremely cautious about asking questions. There are some things which people will not talk about even when asked. Generally, men are hesitant to talk of their financial condition to strangers. Before a salesman can elicit such information he must establish his need to know the data for the good of the prospect as well as his ability to respect confidences. Rapport must be established between them, and this may take some time. Sometimes the salesman can probe these areas by using hypothetical data which he believes approximate the prospect's situation, yet allowing him to keep his own exact data confidential.

Statements

The interview can be opened easily by a statement of the benefits which the salesman wishes to bestow upon the prospect. Sometimes the statement concerns something which the salesman has done for someone else; other times it may simply be some declaration of fact about the product or what it can do. Frequently these statements are concluded with a question which asks for the prospect's reactions.

One container salesman opens an interview with a statement such as, "I was able to save the Martin Company $450 a month on their shipping boxes by showing them a new item we have added to our line. Would you be interested in finding out if I can save you some money too?"

A mailing equipment salesman opens by saying, "Joe Anderson over at the Rockmont Company says that our new equipment has saved him more than $300 a month and has upped his output by at least 500 percent." Of course, all these statements must be supported by proofs.

The representative for the electronics firm sometimes opens certain sales of printed circuit boards by saying, "We are one of the few firms officially approved by the Air Force for printed circuits." This factor is quite important, for most defense contractors cannot subcontract their printed circuitry to a firm that lacks this approval.

Notice that all these statements are aimed at one thing: to drive home to the prospect quickly some major point that is strongly in favor of the product, and it may include the consumer-benefit factor.

The premium approach

In some situations, salesmen virtually bribe the prospect to give his attention for a few moments in exchange for something of nominal value. The Marchant Calculator Company recently used this technique with great effectiveness. They advertised widely that they would give a silver dollar encased in a clear plastic paperweight to any executive who would watch a demonstration of their equipment. Those businessmen who sent in a coupon or contacted a Marchant office were called upon by a salesman who opened the sale by giving the prospect his promised silver dollar paperweight. The firm believes that if they can get businessmen to watch a demonstration of their equipment it is worth the cost.

The Fuller Brush salesman always has some little item which he leaves with the people on his route. One refrigerator salesman bought several thousand small thermometers to give to prospects on the first call asking them to place them inside their present refrigerators. On the next call, he would ask the woman to look at the thermometer to see if it was keeping her food at the proper temperature. This provided a natural opening for talking about a new refrigerator if she needed one; if she did not, then he moved on quickly to someone who did.

The electronics salesman sometimes uses a small printed circuit board on which he has had his prospect's name etched in copper. This is so unusual that the prospect always listens attentively to what the salesman has to say.

Frequently, salesmen use advertising specialties such as pencils, cigarette lighters, memo books, ash trays, etc., for premiums. The success of this approach rests in the human urge to get something for nothing; it puts people in a good frame of mind and creates a more permissive atmosphere in which the salesman can operate.

The survey approach

Unfortunately, this approach has been badly misused by unscrupulous door-to-door salesmen posing as researchers. Such operators claim that they are making a survey of furnaces or appliances or some other product related to whatever they are selling. Once inside the door, these men attempt to qualify the suspects through the use of the questions in the "survey." If the people are prospects, the "researcher" either slyly drops his disguise and goes into his presentation or turns over his qualified lead to another salesman.

However, this survey approach has its legitimate uses. In many industrial sales situations the salesman must obtain the permission of the suspect to do some type of research before he can tell whether he can be of assistance. One salesman for The American Automatic Typewriter Company opens by saying, "Sir, I would like your permission to make a study of your outgoing correspondence to see if you could profit by the installation of an automatic typewriter. It has been our experience that only certain types of operations can profitably use our equipment and that the only way we can find out whether someone like yourself can benefit is by making a careful study of their outgoing correspondence over a suitable length of time. Would you like to see such a study made of your situation?"

Actually, all the salesman is doing in such circumstances is asking to be permitted to collect preapproach information within the organization before actually making a sales presentation. Hence, the survey approach is not a full-fledged opening into the main presentation; however, when completed, it does provide an easy access to the executive and a smooth approach such as:

"Mr. Executive, as you know, you gave me permission a month ago to make a survey of your outgoing correspondence for the purpose of determining whether or not your firm could profitably use an automatic typewriter. I now have that study completed and ready for your inspection."

The survey approach works in industrial situations because the executive recognizes that no salesman can know the firm's specific problems without considerable study. Every businessman is sure that his business is different, and he likes the idea of the salesman tailoring his presentation to the company's specific needs. Also many executives are glad to get expert help on some technical problem they have not fully solved.

The compliment

If it can be accomplished sincerely, some expression of appreciation may be used to get the interview started. This may be called the "compliment approach."

"Wonderful lighting you have in here. No glare, no shadows. How do you do it?"

"That's one of the most beautiful desks I ever saw. How many varieties of wood are in that inlaid section?"

"Good morning, Mrs. Peters," the house-to-house salesman greets the housewife. "I was admiring your flowers. How did you ever find time to plant and tend, not to mention plan, such a lovely garden?"

The salesman should not push this approach too far over the line into flattery, although some people can absorb generous doses of the insincere compliment. Jonathan Swift wrote:

'Tis an old maxim in the schools,
That flattery's the food of fools;
Yet now and then your man of wit
Will condescend to take a bit.

If the prospect is honestly proud of something in his office or has labored hard to make her garden a thing of beauty, that person is likely to feel hurt if it is not noticed at all. A reaction of resentment is perfectly natural. Why should a salesman thus handicap himself needlessly?

Henry Clay put it neatly: "In all the affairs of human life, social as well as political, courtesies of a small and trivial character are the ones that strike deepest to the grateful and appreciating heart."

The salesman who finds it hard to pay a sincere compliment should probe for the reason. He will often find it in a feeling of inferiority and jealousy. This feeling should be conquered, not pampered.

All the approaches discussed have one factor in common—they contain something of *interest* to the prospect. Put yourself in the prospect's place when planning your approach in person and ask yourself: "Would this interest *me* and cause me to like this salesman?"

OTHER ESSENTIALS OF A GOOD APPROACH

The choice of the most effective method of approach is an important factor in this initial contact with the prospect. The type of buyer to be met and the kind of product or service to be presented will largely determine whether the personal call or the telephone, fortified by either a sales letter or some sort of introduction, should be employed.

After the method of approach has been selected, there are other important details that should be observed. Summarized, they are

- Making appointments
- Timing the approach
- Use of the business card
- Proper attention to appearance of salesman
- Avoiding the early dismissal
- Never apologizing for taking prospect's time
- Winning prospect's undivided attention
- Centering the prospect's attention
- Relieving or removing sales tension quickly
- The call-back approach

Making appointments

There is difference of opinion regarding the advisability of making definite appointments. Some salesmen deem it a disadvantage to commit themselves to a definite time, such as 10:30, for if they chanced to be 10 minutes late, they would perhaps lose the coveted interview entirely or at best would face the prospect's displeasure at the salesman's lack of appreciation of the value of time to a busy man. Frequently a salesman may be engaged in closing a big sale at 10:25, and he cannot terminate his interview too abruptly without offering offense to his customer. Or he may conclude a canvass at 10:00 and be afraid to begin another for fear that it would make him late to his 10:30 appointment. Thus half an hour is virtually lost. Therefore it is sometimes felt that a little leeway is desirable. This may be obtained by making elastic appointments, as for "between 10:30 and 11:00," leaving a half hour or so for unexpected delays. The prospect can usually keep busy while waiting.

On the other hand, it may be difficult to make an indefinite appointment with the busy executive whose day is completely filled. In obtaining an interview with such a man, it may work out more satisfactorily to ask for some odd times, as 10:20, 2:50, or 3:05. He may be flattered at this recognition of the fact that his time is very precious.

Most purchasing agents strongly favor having salesmen call at some specific time by appointment or during certain hours set aside for interviewing salesmen.

One IBM salesman starts each morning and afternoon with a definite appointment with an important, high-quality prospect. Not knowing how long his call will take, he schedules no more definite appointments for the day but fills in any time left with cold calls on likely prospects.

Above all, the salesman should not keep a prospect waiting, for when he arrives late he will encounter a definitely hostile individual.

Timing the approach

In the case of unusually important calls, it may pay the salesman to plan his call at the most opportune time. For instance, the salesman for home insulation may call shortly after a heavy snowfall, waiting just long enough for the snow on uninsulated roofs to melt from the heat inside the house. Then he can hit the prospect hard with something like: "Paying to melt snow and help heat all outdoors costs you at least 15 percent more for fuel than you would spend if you had your house insulated."

The life insurance salesman may time his call to catch the prospect soon after a friend has died. The salesman for mutual fund shares will call as soon as he learns of a salary increase or even of an impending one. In selling to industry many calls are timed to the awarding of contracts, model changes, seasonal factors, new inventions, strikes, and dozens of other factors.

The use of the business card

The use of the business card in the approach is a matter on which there is some difference of opinion. When the card *must* be sent in ahead of the salesman, there is nothing to do but send it in. Many salesmen feel, however, that they prefer to interview the prospect without allowing him to have a card in his hand. They insist that the buyer who is fingering a card, surreptitiously running his finger over it to discover whether it is engraved, folding or rolling it, is not able to concentrate upon the proposition in hand. As one salesman puts it, "My fingers have often fairly itched to reach over and snatch the card out of his hands and yell at him, 'Here! Quit playing with that card and listen to me!'"

On the other hand, when the salesman is representing a firm of considerable importance, whose name may carry weight with the buyer, it may be wise to use the card in opening the interview.

A salesman may attach a small article to his card. An automobile salesman buys tiny autos at the variety store and fastens them to his cards. Many salesmen devise unusual cards—oversize ones, odd-shaped ones, strikingly colored or illustrated ones. A salesman for the U.S. Plywood Company has his cards printed on a thin sheet of wood veneer. One steel salesman had his cards made of thin stainless steel upon which his name and address were engraved. True, these are not the cheapest cards available but where the stakes are high, one does not win the pot with penny-ante tactics.

It is a common practice to write something on a card, especially if it is to be sent in to the prospect's inner retreat. This may be a new price, curiosity appeal, or anything to arouse the prospect's interest.

Many salesmen prefer, when possible, to hand the buyer the card at the close of the interview rather than at the beginning. This serves to impress the names of firm and salesman upon the buyer, who may file the card for future reference. Thus the card does not distract the buyer's attention from the proposition.

It is appreciated that the card may be useful in *obtaining* an interview, but the question here is whether the salesman should hand the buyer his card at the *opening* of the interview.

Avoiding the early dismissal

Many a salesman with a good product and well informed about his line complains that prospects dismiss him soon after he has started to make his presentation. What accounts for this unwillingness to allow deserving salesmen an opportunity to explain worthy propositions?

The plain fact of the matter is this: the prospect is not refusing to *buy,* because he does not know enough about the offer to decide whether or not he wants it. What he is really refusing to do is to *give his own time and attention to something that he thinks he is not interested in at the present moment.* A man may refuse to see an automobile salesman because he does not consider himself in the market for a new car. Another prospect says "Not interested" to an investment bond salesman because he has no funds to invest. Another flatly refuses to talk to a life underwriter because he feels that he is "insurance poor" already. Yet these prospects might be sold if the salesman quickly pointed out a real need and explained how it could be satisfied.

Salesmen must anticipate and prepare for the prospect's effort to dismiss them prematurely by making a quick and potent appeal to an important buying motive so that the prospect will make the two important decisions—to see this salesman and to listen to his story.

One salesman for an automobile accessory house wrote as part of a very discouraging report: "Some of my folks would not even take the trouble to see me. Others cut me off before I got really started."

Another man was sent through the same territory. Not only did he see the majority of the accounts, but his trip was profitable.

He had simply gone about his task in a modern and thoroughly scientific manner. Extra personal inconvenience and labor? Yes. He was given a week, prior to leaving, to "ready up." This time was not wasted. He had nearly 300 accounts to see. First he had correspondence brought to him from the files, until he had briefed himself on the prospects.

He located the right man in each instance and made memos of complaints or compliments. And in that one busy week he wrote personal letters to the very men he wanted to see. They were not lengthy letters, but in every instance one idea was uppermost; he would bring information of interest and value. He had suggestions that deserved polite consideration. These suggestions and facts might not have anything to do with actual on-the-spot orders, but that did not detract from their significance. To back up this statement, the salesman conferred with the editors of four business publications, gathering gossip, news, facts about the latest developments, and business predictions.

He realized that he was addressing men who did not know him. He would come as a stranger. He had never been in that territory before. The approximate date of his arrival in each town was given.

The salesman was cordially received at offices where doors had been slammed in the face of his predecessor. And he kept his promise. He talked his own business only when he could lead up to it quietly and unassumingly. What he did do was to provide valuable and interesting information.

"Had you heard," he would open up, "that 63 patents have been taken out this month for automobile accessories? The market will soon see some genuine novelties." Whereupon he would proceed to run quickly over the cream of the patents. He retained financial figures and knew the trade gossip.

"My only trouble," he remarked, upon his return, "was to get away from those fellows. My experience has been that the glad hand is always extended to the salesman with a little something up his mental sleeve. The minute you leave the large commercial centers this accumulation of information becomes food and drink to the small-town prospect. He feels he can't get along without you. If he refuses to see you, he might be missing something.

"There is just one warning—and a point of honor—I never, under any circumstances, give away confidential information or tell secrets out of school. I do not take one man's personal confidences over to his competitor or to a prospect in another town. Just the straight, current trade news is good enough. The scandalmonger is soon found out, and then the door really is closed on him, for good and all."

Yes, a *planned* approach will not only help a salesman to *get in* to see his prospect; it will also help him to *avoid the quick dismissal.*

There are occasions where the prospect is obviously thinking of something else and is having a hard time transferring his attention to your proposition, even though he is willing to let you tell your story. Under such circumstances, it may be well to make a slower start and gain his attention gradually rather than to *force* him to shift his attention too suddenly.

Never apologize for taking the prospect's time

When the youthful salesman confronts a prospect who gives the impression of being busy, he feels an impulse to apologize for taking up valuable time. Such an apology would be unwise, as it places the salesman on the defensive at the start of the interview. Although an apology is not required, this does not mean that the salesman should force his way in where he is not wanted. If it is obvious that the prospect is occupied, the salesman might properly apologize for calling *at an inopportune time* and offer to call again when the prospect could receive him more conveniently; but if he expects to stay and try to sell his man, he should not offer an apology for so doing, as this weakens his case. A salesman who apologizes for his presence is admitting to the prospect that he feels guilty about making the call, thereby indicating that even he has reason to question the soundness of his proposition. He must believe that he is doing the prospect a favor by calling on him. With such an attitude there is obviously no need to apologize.

Winning the buyer's undivided attention

It is often a problem to obtain the buyer's undivided attention to the proposition. He goes on signing letters or looking over papers and suggests to the salesman, "Go right ahead and make your pitch; I can hear you perfectly." The young salesman is likely to be worried by these tactics. He fears to offend the buyer and often proceeds with his presentation in the face of this almost insurmountable obstacle. For it *is* an obstacle to the progress of the sale and one that should be removed at once, even though vigorous methods may be required. Few, if any, men can give adequate attention to two things at once, and the salesman who permits a prospect to attempt this is taking a needless chance of losing the sale. A number of methods have been devised to remove this obstacle.

A salesman who had made a number of attempts to see an executive of a company finally obtained an audience. When he was admitted to the prospect's office the latter barely looked up from the work he was doing on his desk—signing checks.

"Go ahead with your story," said the prospect. "I can listen while I sign these checks."

"All right," said the salesman, "I'll tell my story while you are signing those checks if you can make good on a simple little test."

The prospect stopped writing and looked up. "What little test?" he inquired.

"Write 'Mary had a little lamb' while repeating the first verse of 'My Country, 'tis of Thee.'"

Another salesman, who was ushered into the presence of a prospect of the aforementioned type, was coldly motioned to a chair, and the prospect continued reading some correspondence on his desk. For several minutes the salesman sat silent. Finally the prospect asked him what his business was. But he did not glance up from his reading.

"I know you are too good a businessman, Mr. Blank, to buy something without looking at it; and just as soon as you have finished with your correspondence, I am sure you will be interested in my proposition. Go ahead with your mail; I can wait a few minutes."

In a similar situation another salesman remarked smilingly, "I wish I had your power of concentration." The remark served to win the prospect's undivided attention.

The youthful salesman, new to his work, might be fearful of offending his prospect by these tactics, but he usually need not be. The pose is likely to be a bluff on the part of the prospect, the purpose being to place the salesman on the defensive. The average buyer admires the salesman with the nerve to call such a bluff.

Sometimes an innocent question will serve the desired end. For example, if the prospect is reading, the salesman may interrupt him with a question, such as: "How long has this firm been doing business?" The prospect will usually answer, as, "Fifteen years. Why?" To which the salesman can reply, "I was just wondering. You've been with them right from the start?" No matter what the reply, the salesman can comment, "That's plenty long enough to let you learn to tell a good buy from a poor one. Now this. . . ." Before the prospect can get back to his reading, the salesman is into his presentation.

In any event the salesman should seldom permit himself to be persuaded to continue his presentation while the prospect's attention is centered elsewhere. In the absence of some other means to compel attention he can simply say, "No, Mr. Prospect, I would much rather wait until you are through. Neither of us can do justice to this proposition if your attention is divided."

But no devices or tricks are any better than a quiet, dignified remark along these lines:

"Pardon me, Mr. Prospect, but I understood that you could see me at this time."

"Mr. Prospect, if you are too busy to go into this matter just now, would you tell me when I can come back and be sure of seeing you?"

There are rare individuals who are able to listen to a salesman while reading or pretending to read. If the buyer makes a regular practice of doing this, it may be wise to humor him, but the salesman should exercise unusual care to learn whether he actually has the prospect's attention, as by the use of test questions.

Many salesmen have borrowed a trick from the actor and speak softly at first. The prospect, although he does not actually have to strain to catch the words, is compelled to give the salesman his undivided attention. There is an art in knowing just how low to "tune the volume." The actor who comes on the stage with the audience still buzzing knows that if it is tuned too low the hearers will grow irritable; if not low enough, their entire attention will not be obtained.

Every buyer knows that he is more likely to follow the salesman's argument and be led to buy if he looks at the salesman while the latter is talking. The power of the human eye is great, and buyers know it well. They adopt a pose, as polishing their glasses, cleaning their fingernails, flicking specks from their clothing, arranging things on the desk, or simply refusing to meet the salesman's eye. This is disconcerting, and the salesman seeks to develop devices that will force his prospect to look at him. Perhaps he checks off certain points on his fingers; in which case he should hold his left hand up near his face. He may wag a forefinger under the prospect's nose. Some way must be devised to get his eye, for the salesman cannot well refuse to proceed merely because the prospect will not look him in the eye.

Another helpful idea for winning the prospect's undivided attention is to place something interesting in his hands or on the desk in front of him. The more intriguing this article is, the better. Sometimes a small model of the product is used. A salesman may use a portfolio of advertisements which his company is sponsoring. A flour salesman used to pour a handful of wheat into his prospect's hand and then explain that only such high-grade wheat was used in the manufacture of the flour he sold. An insurance salesman may use a clipping from the local paper, designed to remind the prospect of the uncertainty of things.

The big idea is to *capture the prospect's eye,* after which it is easier to get his ear.

Relieving or removing sales tension quickly

A sales manager in Philadelphia who employs a number of specialty sales-men made a study of more than five hundred actual interviews conducted by his salesmen in the general office, without either the salesman or the prospect being aware of any observation. He discovered that in the great majority of instances there was a noticeable *tension* on the part of the prospect. In other words, the buyer sensed that the salesman was trying to "sell something" and instinctively put up a barrier of resistance that inter-fered seriously with the satisfactory progress of the interview. How may this tension be removed or relieved?

(1) One effective plan is to talk about hypothetical situations rather than the prospect's own. By doing this he is led to think that *he* is not the object of the salesman's efforts. (2) Another plan is to state at the outset of the interview that there is no intention of making any sale *today* and that the only reason for the call is the salesman's desire to explain his proposi-tion so that, when the prospect is ready to consider buying, he will have the essential facts in mind. (3) Still a third possible means of banishing this instinctive tension is to tell the prospect that you have a plan upon which you would appreciate his candid personal opinion. You wish to tell him about it not to sell him but only to obtain his reaction to its features. (4) Some skilled salesmen state that they commonly tell prospects right at the start of the interview that there need be no fear of high-pressure tactics or of difficulty in getting rid of the salesman at any desired moment. The salesman must give an impression of absolute sincerity in this statement to make it effective. (5) Lastly, the approach is facilitated and tension is re-duced if the salesman can convince the prospect quickly that an interesting or profitable idea will be his reward for granting an interview.[8]

---

[8] A regular reading of trade papers provides a salesman with many such ideas.

The call-back approach

This is the approach that the salesman makes on the second or subsequent attempt to sell a prospect. In the salesman's vocabulary such a call is termed a "call-back."

A salesman for advertising space called a second time on a space buyer for an advertising agency who had turned him down previously. He opened his call-back canvass with, "Good afternoon, Mr. Agate. You remember I was here a couple of weeks ago to see you about an advertising contract and you said you couldn't see your way clear to use my publication at that time. I called today to see if, after thinking it over, you didn't want to try it." Such an opening, although fairly typical, invites only a second turn-down. It gives the buyer time to frame his reply, while it presents nothing new or interesting. The technique of a call-back opening is to *swing at once into a presentation from an entirely new angle* without giving the prospect a chance to think up another turndown. For instance, the advertising sales-man might open his second interview something like this: "Good after-noon, Mr. Agate. You folks handle the Star Tire account, don't you? Well, I got to thinking the other day that the Star firm must sell a lot of tires in the territory covered by my publication, so I wrote them. They have agen-cies in every town in which my paper circulates, and it is a sure thing that there would be no waste circulation there." In this way the salesman can start his canvass without being turned down before he can get going.

Or he might say, "Mr. Agate, since I saw you last I have been kicking myself because, for some unaccountable reason, I forgot to tell you the thing about my paper that you would be most interested to hear. The circulation by lines of business runs like this. . . ." And he is started again with a fair chance of completing his presentation.

Some salesmen utilize the device of leaving an article like gloves, book, or fountain pen, calling back later ostensibly to get this article "acciden-tally" left behind. But this tactic is fairly transparent and seldom provides a sound base on which to reopen the sale.

The whole problem is this: to get started. Best method: new informa-tion!

SUMMARY OF THE APPROACH

Success follows the salesman who possesses courage, courtesy, and confi-dence. The aspect of courage needed here is that which brings the salesman back time and again to the same prospect even after repeated repulses. Eventually this dogged persistence, if coupled with ideas and courtesy, will win the respect of superior and subordinate alike. They will gradually form the opinion that the man must have something to offer that he, at least, considers of value. Buyers often judge the mettle of a salesman chiefly by the way in which he comes back after frequent rebuffs. In the end, polite insistence will effect an entrance into almost any prospect's den, no matter how vigilantly guarded.

The salesman for a wholesale hardware house was asked how many times he called on a dealer before crossing him off his prospect list. "That depends on which of us dies first." This salesman then went on to relate how he called on a dealer 124 times without making a sale. On the next call that dealer placed an order for over $50,000. [9]

The courtesy required shows itself chiefly in the interest that the salesman feels in the welfare of his prospect. This viewpoint is what prompts the courteous salesman to offer ideas of value to his client, and to enlist the cooperation of the subordinate in obtaining the interview.

The confidence that helps get the salesman past the numerous barriers must be rooted deep in his belief that he can do his prospect a real service. Feeling this strongly, he can hold his head up and look guardian or buyer in the eye with the confidence that he *ought* to have a chance to present his proposition. Apprehension and fear arise from a lack of confidence in one's proposition. This lack of confidence is quickly conveyed to the prospect or his clerk, who at once concludes that if the salesman does not really *expect* to go in, it is not necessary to admit him.

Many salesmen, before making the approach to an important prospect, indulge in a "warm-up" session much as athletes do. They review what they are going to say and do; they build up their enthusiasm; they don't go to the pitcher's mound cold, but thoroughly steamed up.

DISCUSSION QUESTIONS

1. You are a salesman for Sony video cassettes. Devise a product approach, a consumer-benefit approach, and a question approach you could use. Which do you feel would be best?
2. Devise two consumer-benefit approaches for selling a Polaroid camera.
3. Under what circumstances is the product approach best used?
4. You are a salesman for McGraw-Hill Book Company calling upon a "trade" (noncollegiate) bookstore to get them to stock this book. Exactly how would you approach the buyer?
5. You sell expensive clothing for a retailer. What approach would you use on a man who had previously been buying $125 suits to trade him up to $175 Norman Hilton's?

[9] In *The American Salesman* for November, 1961, p. 70, appears a true, detailed account of how a salesman made 110 personal calls, about 150 telephone calls, and spent scores of hours on research in his persistent effort to sell 200 truck trailers for over $1,000,000. But he made the sale.

6. As a salesman for Dean Witter, a stock brokerage, devise some approaches that can be used on middle-management executives.
7. You are a salesman for a technical supply and equipment wholesaler calling upon a professor of analytical chemistry to sell him a line of electronic instruments for use in teaching analytical chemistry. Exactly how would you open the sale?
8. You sell air conditioning. You have learned that a well-to-do executive is thinking of air-conditioning his home. You plan to call on him cold in January. What approach would you use? Word it!
9. A hunter is fondly examining a Browning Automatic shotgun in your sporting goods store. You approach him saying . . . ? Another patron is carefully looking at the gold-plated Winchester 30-30 classic rifle made in limited numbers to commemorate the anniversary of its first production. How would you approach him?
10. You are selling typewriters. You learn that a close personal friend, Joe Blow, whom you see almost daily, is thinking about buying new typewriters for his secretaries, but he has not said anything about it to you. You call him up and tell him that you will be in to see him in an hour. Exactly what do you say upon entering his office?

CASE 8-1   TOT, INC.:
Approaching Chain Store Buyers

Bruce Johnson, salesman for the Tot line of juvenile equipment such as strollers, play pens, and high chairs, had just returned from a trip of two months during which he called on large chain and department store buyers for the purpose of pushing the new item in the line, the tip-proof lightweight aluminum baby walker. Now that his trip was completed, he had time to reflect on his successes and failures to see if he could learn something from them. Bruce always conducted a mental post-mortem on his sales presentations in an effort to improve his performance, as he had found that when he lost a sale he could usually trace back and locate the errors.

Overall this trip had been successful. However, two failures particularly bothered him, both of them with the central buying offices of large chain store organizations in New York City.

At the first he had no trouble seeing someone in the juvenile-furniture buying section. He was ushered into a showroom without an appointment one afternoon at about 1:30. Shortly, an ivy-league-type young man entered and introduced himself as the assistant buyer, explaining that the buyer was not in at the present time. He said that he had the power to buy and would look at the merchandise.

In selling the lightweight walker Bruce used a product approach which consisted of merely handing or tossing the unit to the buyer, depending on his personality. He handed the unit to the assistant and said nothing.

After a careful examination of the merchandise, Mr. Boyer asked, "What's the price structure?"

Bruce replied, "Retails for $7.95. Your cost is $4.75 laid on your dock 2/10 net 30."

"It's a $5.00 item if I ever saw one. Never would bring $7.95 no matter how hard it was pushed. I won't touch it for more than $3.00 on our dock and that's final," was Boyer's declaration.

Bruce had answered, "I can well understand why you would like to retail it for $5.00 because so would I. I would love to be able to get it to you for that price, but I can't because of costs. Those ball-bearing casters alone cost 90 cents in volume purchase. The aluminum tubing is not cheap. The lowest bid we have been able to get from outside experts in aluminum fabrication has been $3.95 unpackaged. When I first saw the unit, I had exactly the same reaction as you just had. It was a $5.00 item; no use trying to sell it for more. However, I have really been fooled. It is moving at $7.95 in both your own stores and in Sears. We have sold several of your own managers directly, and their experience has been very favorable. Mr. Gerry out in your Oklahoma City store moved 36 units last month, which is almost unbelievable to me, but it is a matter of record. Sears in the same city sold 480 units during the past eight months. So it has *proven* that it *will* move well at $7.95. I think it is the eye appeal that has done it. People are really attracted to it when it is displayed. It's unique."

The buyer repeated, "I don't care what it sells for, I'll only pay $3.00 and that's that."

"But it is a proven seller in your own stores at $7.95. How can I give you better proof than that of its sales appeal?" Bruce was now almost pleading in his frustration.

"Don't care about that at all. I've got to go now. Good-by," were the buyer's final words.

Bruce realized at the time that he had not gotten off on the right foot with Boyer, as their personalities seemed to clash. He sensed during the attempted sale that this buyer would not buy the walker regardless of price or other considerations. However, Bruce was at a loss to diagnose his trouble. Where had he erred? He formulated several hypotheses but found it hard to figure out anything that might help him in his efforts to sell similar buyers in the future.

Another interview was reviewed with anguish. It was 2 P.M. on a hot June day when he entered the main New York office of another department store chain. He was calling on Mr. Anthony, head buyer for juvenile furniture. Bruce had called on Halliburton's of Oklahoma City earlier in the year only to be told by the woman in charge of the juvenile-furniture depart-ment that she had no authority to buy; that Anthony in New York did all the buying.

On the elevator to the buying office a young woman commented fa-vorably on the walker which Bruce was carrying. She showed great interest in it and asked whom Bruce was calling on and, when told, said, "That's who I guessed. I am his secretary. I'll take you right in. I think he will be really interested. Follow me."

Bruce was now inwardly jubilant, as selling this large chain would be a significant accomplishment. He stood just outside a small glass-enclosed cubicle while he heard the young lady say, "There is a young man out here with a baby walker that looks real good. Can you see him now?"

"OK, send him in." As Bruce entered, he was greeted with, "When are you jerks going to learn that I only see salesmen on Tuesday?"

Bruce replied extra politely, "I am sorry. I did not know your days. I am just in from Chicago for today only. I have to go on to Boston tonight. I can come back next month on my return trip if you would prefer."

Mr. Anthony grunted, "Forget it, kid. Let's see your mousetrap."

As he handed him the walker Bruce said, "Miss Starr, the buyer in your Halliburton store in Oklahoma City, referred me to you because she was interested in getting this unit into her department."

Mr. Anthony countered, "Miss Starr is not a buyer. She is a depart-ment head. I am the buyer."

While the item was being inspected, Bruce noticed that Mr. A. was sloppily dressed, was reclining with feet on desk and cigar in mouth. He had been looking at a batch of little girls' dresses on display around the room. The entire room was in a state of chaos.

Anthony asked, "What's the story on this?" After hearing the presen-tation, he said, "Not interested. It's not for us."

Bruce started to ask some questions for the purpose of discovering Anthony's objections but was quickly interrupted, "Look, kid, there is no use arguing with me. When I make up my mind, it's final. Now get out of here, and let me work." Bruce fled the scene.

Bruce was really perplexed by this call, for it was the first time he had encountered such rudeness. Most buyers had been quite polite and consid-erate and generally were favorably disposed toward the walker. He just could not figure Anthony out.

1. Make some hypotheses about what went wrong in each of the above instances.
2. How could Bruce improve his approach to avoid such situations as developed in these interviews?
3. After he found himself in these predicaments, could Bruce have done anything to salvage either sale?

CASE 8-2   MR. GROOM:
Developing Approaches

Mr. Bruce MacNaughton, president of Mr. Groom, a multilevel distributive organization modeled after the Amway system, which sold a line of animal (dogs, cats, and horses) grooming aids and nutritional supplements, was busy revising the sales manual that was furnished to each of the firm's several thousand distributors.

Experience had indicated that the approach was especially critical for the new distributor, for if the sale did not get started off smoothly, the rest of the sale was usually in a shambles. Thus, Mr. MacNaughton was expanding the section in the sales manual on approaches.

The Mr. Groom line of products consisted of 159 different items, mostly bottled liquids, although the food supplements were solid, selling for less than $5 in most instances.

The salespeople—distributors—were mostly part-time workers, both male and female, who called on both the ultimate consumer—the pet owner—and the middlemen. The calls on the pet owner were usually made in the evening in the customer's home. The retail dealers were of two types: the pet store selling animals and supplies and the "beauty" shops catering to poodle owners. Some distributors also had been selling to some veterinarians.

1.   Develop several approaches to be used for each of the different types of prospects.

THE ART OF PERSUASION

Don't tell people how good you make your
goods. Tell people how good your goods will
make them.
Kenneth M. Goode

Selling is essentially a matter of persuasion, persuading others to buy the proposition. Persuasion involves *motivation* aimed at inducing *action*. When we persuade someone, we do not merely change his thinking on the subject; we cause him to *do* something. His *actions* are modified as well as his thoughts.

It is obvious that in selling the salesman's efforts to persuade are based on an understanding of buying motives (Chapter 5) and on the facts he has learned about the particular prospect in the preapproach (Chapter 7). The *action* which the salesman seeks to induce is that of *buying*.

In this chapter we shall consider a few of the fundamental principles which underlie all persuasion, whether utilized by salesman, lawyer, politician, preacher, advertising writer, labor negotiator, or public relations man. They may be applied daily by everyone. Properly applied, they may avoid misunderstandings, quarrels, hard feelings, and attempts to "get even" with someone who has forced us to take certain action without persuading us that it was the right thing to do. Perhaps these ideas could save some marriages and prove even more effective at times than the back of a hairbrush in training children!

PRINCIPLE OF INTEGRATING INTERESTS

Obviously, it is usually to the interest of the salesman to make a sale. But no sale will be made until the prospect is persuaded that it is to *his* interest to *buy*. The emphasis is placed on the interests of the prospects, of course, and the salesman avoids calling attention to any benefits he himself may receive. Nonetheless, the interests of buyer and seller are mutual and integrated. The task of the salesman is to make the prospect feel that it will benefit *him* to buy what the salesman is selling and that the salesman is chiefly interested in benefiting *him*. Thus the interests of the two are unified. They can never be unified by inducing the prospect to agree that it will help the *salesman* if he (the prospect) decides to buy. If the prospect feels that a conflict of interests exists between him and the salesman, he will not buy.

This brings us to the consideration of motives again. The smart salesman asks himself: What goals does this prospect wish to reach? What is his philosophy of life? Exactly how can he move closer to his goals by purchasing my proposition?

"What is meant by a philosophy of life? Does every individual have such a philosophy? It sounds terribly profound and rather abstract. I don't believe that *I* have one—never gave it much thought." Some reader may find such thoughts stirring in his mind.

Everyone does have a philosophy of life, and the concept is neither profound nor abstract. True, most of us have never sat down and put on paper a well-organized and comprehensive statement of our philosophy, but our actions and reactions reveal it clearly. A person's philosophy of life is constructed by assembling his attitudes as to aims or goals into a completed structure, as a mason assembles bricks. But let's be specific.

There is the goal of economic progress, financial success, climbing out of cramping poverty. Right here we encounter the element of force or drive. How *strongly* do we want to reach this goal? Are we willing to forego present pleasures, save the money they would cost, and then put that money to work for us? Will we spend much time thinking of ways to earn more? Will we study evenings to win promotion? Will we do things ourselves instead of hiring others to do them? Are we willing to gain this goal honestly, or will we cheat and steal if we think we can get away with it?

This enumeration of questions could be extended, but the point is clear. It boils down to this: what do I want, and what am I willing to pay to get it?

It would be easy to list many goals such as health, service to others, gaining prominence and publicity, climbing socially, indulging in our favorite hobbies, etc.

When we have listed all such goals, together with our attitude toward each, we have formulated a personal philosophy of life. It's that simple.

Now here is a most important point: a philosophy of life is not a psychological concept only; it is a pattern of *action*. Our actions reveal our *actual* philosophy of life.

The salesman, therefore, tries to learn all he can about how his prospect has *acted* in relation with various aims or goals. In this way he can determine which goals the prospect is most eager to reach.

In his effort to integrate the prospect's interests with his own, the salesman will also take into account numerous minor points on which a difference of opinion might arise. The prospect may be politically a strong conservative, a militant foe of alcohol or tobacco, a firm advocate of a protective tariff, in favor of abolishing the income tax, or a proponent of profit sharing plans for workers. If the salesman cannot agree with the prospect on such controversial issues, he should strive to sidestep them. If he can't integrate his interests with those of the prospect, he should at least try to avoid *disintegrating* them.

Putting the prospect into the sales picture

Still another angle to this integration of interests is to help the prospect to visualize the situation as it will exist *for him* after he has bought what the salesman is selling. In many college communities a photographer attends all football games and takes pictures of the crowded stands, section by section. Samples of the pictures are displayed in his window the next day, and the window is surrounded by a knot of students, each examining the photographs. For what is each seeking? The picture of the president of the university or the governor, who was a distinguished guest at the game? No. Each one is trying to find *his own picture* in that sea of faces. We each like to be "put into the picture," and the salesman must learn to put the prospect into the mental pictures that he is painting.

A house-to-house canvasser is selling a subscription to a woman's magazine, for example. He is not selling paper and ink. He is selling ideas— ideas in which the prospect is in the picture. He might paint many pictures of this sort. Here are the outlines of several: An evening about the 4th of the month. Housewife and husband in conference over the bills for the previous month. Sometimes a dreaded interview with husband frowning and disagreeable. This month it is different. Husband complimenting wife on keeping size of bills down. How did she do it? Through various suggestions on culinary economies and savings in making clothes that she found in salesman's magazine, of course!

Or the prospect may be pictured at a tea. Problem in etiquette arises. She meets situation confidently and correctly. Conversation turns to channels of recent books, plays, events of interest. Prospect takes leading part in discussion with knowledge gained from salesman's magazine.

Or an evening with the children about the mother as she guides their active minds to a discovery of wonderful truths. The development of these precious youngsters in their schoolwork, in leadership among their playmates.

Pictures—personal and potent!

A salesman for a trucking company tells this one:

I was assigned to see a family which was moving from Cleveland to Los Angeles, their expenses to be paid by their employer. They had already signed up with another company at a price lower than I could quote. I was never more astonished in my life than when the woman announced that she would switch the job to us and pay the difference out of her own pocket. I couldn't help asking her what I had said that caused her to change.

She answered: "When you told me how your truck would back up in front of our new home in Los Angeles, and how your men would carry those containers with my dresses in them up into my room, and when you pictured how nice and fresh my dresses would look when they came out of their special containers—well, that was when I decided to let you handle our goods."

Another effective word picture, with the prospect front center, is painted by the salesman for an electric kitchen range. He tells Mrs. Housewife: "You've had a hard day. You were downtown shopping all afternoon and you came home dead tired. The bus was crowded and you had to stand up all the way. Your feet hurt and your head aches, and you know that when you get home the children will be hollering for supper and in another half hour your husband will be back from work—hungry. You actually *dread* the prospect of getting home and tackling the job of getting up a meal. Has that ever happened to you, Mrs. Housewife?"

She will answer "Yes," whether it has or not. So the salesman unfolds a huge life-size color picture of a gorgeous electric range, with the oven door open and a mouth-watering, fully cooked, ready-to-serve meal just begging to be put on the table. "Wouldn't it be wonderful to come home to *this?* Dinner that cooked itself to perfection—piping hot and ready to serve—while you were downtown?"

The encyclopedia salesman inquires of the mother of children: "What do you do when Junior looks up from his homework and asks, 'Mom, what's the principal product of New Mexico?' Do you shunt him off to his father? And can his father answer? Wouldn't it be a lot easier for you, and wouldn't your children think more of you, if you just went to this beautiful encyclopedia and turned to the correct answer?" That's putting the prospect into the picture—with words only. But the picture is credible; it is in the circle of the prospect's experience. And it *is* dramatic.

Other things can be sold in similar fashion. The bond salesman sells not a piece of paper but an income and all the satisfaction this steady income will bring the purchaser. The automobile salesman does not sell steel, glass, fabrics, and rubber; he sells mental pictures of pleasures to be derived from the possession of this automobile—and in every picture the prospect is in the foreground. The salesman for a lot or cottage in a summer resort colony does not sell a strip of sand. He sells the pleasures of boating, bathing, golfing, tramping, camping—with the prospect ever in the fore-ground of the alluring picture.

Salesmen for the Hotpoint Electrasink are taught to talk in terms of buyer benefits with the housewife-prospect in every picture. After men-tioning the number of hours the average woman spends washing dishes, the salesman paints a picture of things which the prospect could do with the time saved by letting the Electrasink wash the dishes. He specifically mentions:

. . . more time after dinner in the evening with your husband and children . . . longer evenings for movies or other recreation . . . more time for enjoying golf, gardening, or other hobbies . . . more opportunities to see your friends . . . more time to make clothes or knit or crochet . . . more time to play with the children . . . more time for shopping . . . or an opportunity to get in a little extra resting or reading each day, while other women are standing at their sinks washing dishes.

He is offering benefits—not a piece of machinery.

People do not buy matches—they buy fires; they do not buy a new set of golf clubs—they buy a lower score; they don't buy ¼-inch bits—they buy ¼-inch holes; they don't buy a television set—they buy hours of en-tertainment.

The salesman integrates his prospect's interests with his own by show-ing what benefits the prospect can obtain if he buys. The prospect is per-suaded to buy because he has pictured himself enjoying the benefits of ownership.

Frequently, it is helpful to let the prospect get into the act—to take an active part in the sales presentation. Let him handle the product if it is a tangible item like a golf club, an automobile, or vacuum cleaner. Or per-haps he can help make computations in discussing investments or insur-ance. And, after he is partly sold, he can be encouraged to talk and thereby sell himself.

The participation of the prospect in the presentation promotes the integration of interests which the salesman is trying to achieve.

PRINCIPLES OF SUGGESTION

Psychologists are agreed that there are two methods of inducing action on the part of another human being.

The first is by suggestion. This is fully as important, and often even more important, to the salesman as the second method, that of logical reasoning. It is not very complimentary to the human race, but man is not essentially a reasoning creature. Some psychologists insist that many men reason scarcely at all—that practically all their acts are the result of imitation, habit, or suggestion. Most of their actions are only *reactions*. This being true, it behooves the salesman to understand and use this force called suggestion.

There are several principles of suggestion:

1. A person *accepts* as true every idea or conclusion that enters his mind unless a contradictory idea blocks its acceptance.
2. A person will act in accordance with a suggestion unless he is blocked by a physical obstacle or contrary idea. If he is merely indifferent, he will probably "go along" with the suggestion.
3. A person's acceptance of a suggestion depends upon the source of the suggestion.
4. A person's acceptance of a suggestion is influenced by the intensity with which it is made.
5. A person is more apt to accept a recent suggestion than one made previously.
6. A suggestion is more apt to be accepted if it is repeated.
7. People will believe a suggestion if they want to believe it, regardless of its merit.
8. A suggestion that appears to be natural, spontaneous, is more likely to be accepted than one which is apparently planned or contrived.

Blocking ideas

You must recognize that your prospect's mind is not a totally empty cupboard; it contains a great many ideas—some true, some not—that have been gleaned from a great many experiences. The car salesman suggests to a prospect that if a deal can be made immediately a higher price can be given for his trade-in because the dealership has an immediate customer for it. There seldom is much truth to such a suggestion, but it will be believed unless the prospect has had previous knowledge of this closing tactic. Also, the prospect may believe it because he wants to believe it—he wants to trade cars.

But if there are no blocking ideas, the salesman's suggestion has a good chance for acceptance. The salesman suggests that his company is a solid, reputable supplier by referring to its long relationship with other well-recognized customers. Unless the purchasing agent knows something to the contrary, a favorable image will likely result.

Source of suggestion

The authenticity of the source of a suggestion must be considered. If a nontechnical salesman suggests to an engineer that he can solve some sticky technical problem for him, he is not as likely to be believed as a salesman who possesses technical qualifications.

At times it is wise for the salesman to establish his expertise early in the sale so that his suggestions will be considered authentic by the prospect.

One young retail men's clothing salesman was having trouble selling suits to men older than himself until his boss spotted the problem: the older customers were not receptive to his suggestions because they had no reason to believe that he knew his trade and his age suggested that he didn't. Thereafter this young man would make a remark early in the sale regarding some problem the customer had in obtaining a good fit from his clothes, thus establishing his technical knowledge in the prospect's mind. It worked beyond all hopes.

In meeting with a prospect for the first time it may be wise for the salesman to establish his expertise in the field by some method.

Intensity

Yell "fire" at the top of your voice and you'll more likely be believed than if you say it calmly. The way the salesman delivers his lines affects their believability. This is not to suggest that he should shout his words. Words delivered in a firm, intense voice with feeling strongly suggest that the salesman not only knows what he is talking about but also believes it himself.

Recency and repetition

A salesman has little reason to expect that the prospect will act on a suggestion made much earlier in the sale. Key suggestions should be repeated for maximum effectiveness.

The clever salesman will disguise such repetitions by rewording them lest the more perceptive prospect detect them and not be impressed with a "broken record."

Desire to believe

People will believe whatever is told them if they are of a mind to do so; thus the basis of the "big lie" is disclosed. If a woman wants to believe that a dress is "just made for you," she will believe it no matter what physical evidence exists to the contrary. Tell a man that a Cadillac is his best buy and he'll believe it if he wants to do so.

If you are ever puzzled about how some people can believe some outrageous lies, just remember that they want to believe them.

Spontaneity

The strength of a suggestion varies directly with the degree to which it seems to be made on the individual's own initiative. People are more prone to act on autosuggestions than on suggestions from external sources. They tend to resent any attempt to dominate their thinking by others.

It is important for the salesman to realize that many prospects are already under suggestive influences stimulated perhaps by advertising, window displays, neighbors, or other influences. The salesman's main task in such instances is to reinforce such suggestions and proceed to guide them into the proper channels. It can be difficult to alter the prospect's train of thought. A man has seen a particular London Fog top coat that appeals to him; he walks into a store and specifically asks for that garment. In many instances, only a skilled salesman can switch him to the brand in stock even though the two may be practically identical. Such cases can be switched but only with skill. One salesman asked such a prospect, "I've heard a great deal about that coat. Have you seen it?" When the prospect replied that he had, he was asked, "Could you do me a favor? Come over here and show me how it differs from the coat that our buyer bought. I want to be able to tell him about it." When the prospect started comparing the coats, he discovered that the one carried by the store had more features and was a better value than the one he had in mind, so he bought it. But all the time he thought he was making up his own mind; that is *spontaneity*.

All of us see suggestion at work every day. The gas station attendant inquires, "Fill 'er up?" The waitress suggests the T Bone steak. A colleague stops by your desk and suggests, "Let's go get a cup of coffee." The wife innocently remarks, "The Smiths have a new color television set. They think it's wonderful."

A strong blockage to any suggestion may exist in the mind of the one at whom the suggestion is aimed. The motorist may have only $1.25 in his pocket, or the man may not like T Bone steak. Otherwise, the chances are that the suggestion will be followed.

The types of suggestion

There are three psychological types of suggestion: (1) ideomotor suggestion, (2) prestige suggestion, or (3) autosuggestion. When concerned with the *direction* of suggestion, one may classify them as being direct, indirect, positive, negative, or countersuggestion.

IDEOMOTOR SUGGESTION

Ideas entering the mind may result in some impulsive or dynamic action unless stopped by some competing idea. A salesman stops by an executive's office and says, "You look like a man who needs a cup of coffee; I'm buying." In most instances this would be enough to move a man to action unless some strong competing idea welded him to his desk.

A salesman's plea to a prospect, "Why don't you buy it now and save yourself all the trouble, fret, and worry of looking around?" may close a sale with a suggestible prospect.

You drive your old car into the garage for repairs, and a nearby salesman suggests, "Let's take a spin around the block in our new Supersonic Eight. I'd like to show you what we have done with our brake system this year."

Ideomotor suggestions are simply statements which suggest that the prospect *do* something.

PRESTIGE SUGGESTION

Persuaders from time immemorial have used the appeal of the great name. A breakfast cereal manufacturer may get a cowboy star or famous athlete to extol the virtues of his product. A salesman may state that a certain respected business executive has just purchased his product or that another large, highly efficient company has just installed his system.

This type of suggestion is widely used and, when based upon the truth, can be highly persuasive. However, it loses its power if it is based upon a rather dubious connection between the name and the product. If Johnny Bench were to endorse a baseball bat, no doubt the prestige name would carry some influence. However, should he endorse a set of medical instruments, one might doubt the effectiveness of this bit of suggestion.

AUTOSUGGESTION

Autosuggestion is a matter of selling ourselves something; the individual through his own thoughts and actions suggests things to himself. Sometimes autosuggestion starts in either of the other two forms of suggestion but proceeds on its own.

One of the first hot days of the summer may set you to thinking that perhaps it is time for you to purchase your summer wardrobe. Your stomach regularly suggests that you seek sustenance, thus steering you to various culinary institutions. You see a display of sporting equipment in a store window and it causes you to think about going to a ball game that evening.

SUGGESTION THROUGH ACTION   So far only the *spoken* or *written* suggestion has been considered, but there are other effective ways of suggesting purchase or at least of suggesting that the prospect follow the lead of the salesman.

The salesman's enthusiasm for his proposition, the manner in which he tries on the coat or manipulates the machine, all carry suggestions of his own evaluation of it and of his confidence that the prospect also appreciates it. Suggestion by *actions.*

The salesman can use action-based suggestion throughout his presentation. Suppose he wishes to convey to the prospect the idea that his machine is quite durable. He could treat it roughly, drop it, and pound on it. Suppose he wishes to suggest that it is time to sign the order. The simple act of handing the order blank and a pen to the prospect may suggest the proper action.

One salesman of plastic dishes selling to retailers would deliberately drop several dishes on the floor, ostensibly by accident, to convince the prospect of their unbreakability. Actions speak infinitely louder than mere words.

DIRECT SUGGESTION   A direct suggestion is one in which the immediate aim comes in an explicit straightforward manner. The salesman urges, "Will three shirts be sufficient, sir?" or "Would you care to take advantage of our financing plan, sir?" or "Feel this material, notice its high quality."

It is considered sound salesmanship to suggest directly such items as the type of product you feel is most appropriate for the prospect, the quantity you feel he should buy, the proper distribution of sizes or colors for his needs, and other factors on which he may be depending upon the seller for advice.

INDIRECT SUGGESTION   Indirect suggestion is used by salesmen who do not wish the prospect to realize that he is being made subject to a suggestion. Indirect suggestion must be subtle and not easily detectable.

Indirect suggestion should be used when the prospect is mentally alert, feels himself to be superior to the salesman, or when the salesman's prestige is comparatively low.

Suppose a salesman wishes to suggest to the prospect that the competitor's product, which he is about to buy, is inferior to the salesman's. In most instances, it is recommended that the salesman should not directly knock the competitor's product; however, most salesmen agree that there are times when one must take *some* positive action to counter a competitor's claims. He might ask, "Have you talked with any of the users of the Apex machine?" or "You know, just the other day a man walked into the office and purchased our machine without even so much as a demonstration. He explained that he had bought an Apex a few months before and wanted to trade it in. Naturally we tried to give him as much as possible, but you know how it goes with used equipment of this type." There are many similar statements which, in varying degrees, plant seeds of doubt in the prospect's mind concerning a competitor's wares. Great care must be taken lest the prospect be offended by an exaggeration or adverse comment that reflects on his judgment.

POSITIVE AND NEGATIVE SUGGESTION   A positive suggestion suggests that the hearer *do* something (buy the product) or *say* something (I like the product).

The positive suggestion implies that the prospect is moving toward a favorable decision on buying. The negative suggestion implies that he is moving in the opposite direction.

Positive: This certainly is a wonderful value, isn't it?

Neutral: What do you think of this proposition?

Negative: You couldn't use this, could you?

These are all stated as questions, because the salesman is always trying to induce a reaction of some kind to his presentation. A salesman might say, "You won't find a better value anywhere." That is a positive *statement,* but it suggests no *action* on the part of the prospect, not even an affirmative nod of his head. The prospect is supposed to agree with a positive suggestion and indicate his agreement in some way. [1]

In short, we are thinking about the reaction of the prospect. Is it positive (favorable) or negative (unfavorable)? Any statement or question or

---

[1] Another interpretation of "positive" and "negative" suggestion applies to situations outside the field of salesmanship. Here the negative suggests "Do *not* do or say something." The mother says, "Do not step off the curb into the street." That is negative. If she says, "Stay out of the street," that is said to be positive. The word "not" is absent. Child psychologists tell us that a "do not" suggestion is likely to cause a child to *do* that very thing. Another argument against the negative suggestions. In this discussion we are interested in whether the suggestion implies that the prospect *is* going to buy or is *not* going to buy. This may be applied to buying from competitors, but this is discussed elsewhere.

action that invites a favorable response is positive. The retail clerk's "Will that be all?" is negative. One should be a bit more positive and ask, "What else?"

Often the negative suggestion is *concealed.* "The chances are only one in four that you will lose" is negative. It suggests *losing.* If the same thought were put "Your chances of *winning* are three to one," the suggestion would be that of *winning* and therefore positive.

The salesman who says, "This roof won't leak during the next five years: we guarantee that," is suggesting a leak and all the attendant damage it brings. If he had said, "This roof is guaranteed to stay tight for at least five years," the suggestion would have been positive.

The automobile salesman might say, "This car will give you mighty little trouble." But why suggest *trouble?* The prospect may start worrying about the trouble and postpone his purchase, perhaps permanently. The positive and negative aspects of suggestion can be illustrated by analogy. The young man who asks the maiden of his choice, "You wouldn't want to marry me, would you?" virtually compels the girl to do the proposing, which she may consider a bit out of place even today.

Throughout the entire sales process the salesman implies, wherever possible, that he *expects* his prospect to purchase. He says, "*After* you have had this car a year" and not "*If* you should decide to get this car you would find. . . ." He says, "You *will* take a lot of comfort in this chair, I'm sure, on the long winter evenings," or "You *will* find that these goods will move off your shelves almost as fast as you can unpack them." Care must obviously be exercised to avoid making these suggestions too early, as some prospects would resent the implication that they had reached a decision when, as a matter of fact, they had not.

And the real salesman should never permit himself to use the word "regret." It is easy to say, "You will never regret this purchase," but why suggest regret? It would be better to suggest the positive satisfaction to be derived from possession, "I know you'll love it!"

COUNTERSUGGESTION   A countersuggestion is a suggestion, either positive or negative, used finally in the hope of eliciting an opposite response or reaction. It is used most often on a prospect who has shown himself to be somewhat contrary. One automobile salesman sold an expensive car to a wealthy, cantankerous old man by suggesting, "Let's look at those cars over in that corner. The one in the window is pretty expensive." A Pitney-Bowles salesman opened a successful interview with, "It appears to me as if your firm is not yet big enough to profit from using automatic mailing equipment; or is there something I don't see here?" The company president spent the next 20 minutes explaining that his company *was* big enough. The salesman had been tipped off that the president took a fierce pride in the volume his apparently small firm did and was sensitive to the inferior impression his plant made on outsiders.

Pleasant vs. unpleasant suggestion

The familiar story of the boy with the pony hitched to his little cart is a good illustration of the problem faced by salesmen in the presentation. The boy wanted the pony to run, but the pony did not choose to do so. First the boy used a whip. Soon the pony became so accustomed to whipping that he refused to go faster than a walk. Then the boy dangled a carrot on a long pole in front of the pony's nose, and this motivated the pony to run because *he wanted to get that carrot.* Some salesmen know of nothing more effective than the whip to make prospects move as desired. Hence they threaten them with dire prophecies of what may happen if they do not buy. Other salesmen, wiser and more experienced in the vagaries of human nature, utilize the other technique and have less difficulty in luring their prospects to run after the desired object. In the presentation *a judicious combination* of whip and carrot, determined somewhat by the kind of prospect in each case, usually proves effective in obtaining the desired result.

Examples of the use of the whip:

A. "That tire is getting pretty thin. Might have a bad blowout any day now. You know what that means, don't you? Don't gamble with the lives of your loved ones. Buy now."

B. "Mrs. Wilson is working at Woolworth's now. Her husband carried only a thousand. Too bad she has to leave those three children to look after themselves all day. Would you want your wife to have to do that?"

All these *unpleasant* talking points call attention to happenings that people naturally avoid or try to get away from, just as the pony wanted to avoid the blows of the boy's whip. On the other hand, *pleasant* talking points motivate people because they desire to gain the things that are held out before them.

Examples of the use of the "carrot" technique follow:

A. "That tire of yours may last another 1,000 miles, but think of the peace of mind driving on a blowout-proof tire! No worry, no fear, no expense. That is what you want, I know."

B. "Probably nothing is going to happen to you, Mr. Prospect. Of course, if it does, you know that your wife and three children are really provided for. But think of the thrill you and your wife will get from the retirement pension that contract will pay you when you are sixty-five. That is really something to look forward to, isn't it? To be able to quit work and let my company pay your salary from then on. That makes those years the best part of life."

Obviously, the salesman will use more unpleasant suggestions in the early stages of the presentation than he will later, because his first job is to make the prospect dissatisfied with things as they are. When a life insurance salesman was gloomily painting a sad picture of what might happen if the prospect should die without more insurance, the latter broke in, "Stop it! You're making me miserable!" To which the salesman happily replied, "That's fine! If you're miserable *enough,* you'll *do something about it.*" Sometimes, therefore, the salesman must use unpleasant suggestions to create dissatisfaction. But, the minute he has accomplished this, he should switch to the pleasant suggestions. The old revivalist's technique was based on this principle—first take the sinners on a tour of hell, after which heaven would appear more inviting.

Some words have pleasant or unpleasant connotations, and the smart salesman constantly searches his vocabulary for those that evoke pleasant responses and combs his presentation to eliminate those that may conjure up unpleasant memories or emotions. *Freedom* is pleasant; *slavery* is not. *Integration* may be a dangerous word to use in the South even though the salesman may be talking about accounting systems. This whole subject of semantics is fascinating and, to the salesman, of vastly greater importance than many of them seem to realize.

Using emotional words to stimulate prospects

Many times a salesman will use deliberately chosen words which he knows will stimulate certain desired emotional reactions in the prospect. One must remember that when he is calling upon a prospect he is not calling on an individual who is a dull, neutral machine devoid of any memory and emotions. To the contrary, the prospect has had a rich background of experiences, all of which have shaped his attitudes, opinions, and feelings about various subjects. He is not a neutral pawn to be manipulated. What he is and thinks today are largely a result of his previous experiences. During those experiences various values have been implanted in him by the culture from which he descends. For example, in our culture the word "mother" is full of favorable emotional connotations. In most instances when a salesman of cooking utensils says to a young woman, "I am certain your mother would have just loved to have owned a set of cooking ware such as this when she was married," a favorable response is likely to be forthcoming. Another example: suppose a salesman says, "Our machines are used by more successful executives than all other equipment combined." The word "successful" stimulates favorable responses in most business executives, since success is a goal they are striving to reach. The statement couples the salesman's product with the pleasant concept of success.

Some oil companies have discovered that the word "power" touches off a favorable emotional response in their customers. The same word used by an automobile salesman stimulates strong, favorable reactions. Hence, the salesman of a hydraulic press might stimulate a favorable response in his prospect by making a statement such as, "Just look at the massive power of that machine at work." Or the salesman of an automatic machine might be able to stir up an emotional response in an executive by: "This machine will remain *loyal* to you 24 hours a day, 365 days a year. It will never go on strike or slow down. Can you say the same of all your human employees?" The words "loyalty," "strike," and "slow down" are the fuses that ignite emotional bursts—to the advantage of the salesman.

There is an old saying in selling that the salesman should aim at the heart instead of the head, because it is 12 inches closer to the pocketbook. Emotional words are aimed at the heart instead of the head in line with the principle (developed in a previous chapter) that emotional appeals are more forceful in most instances than rational ones. Emotionally laden words make emotional appeals far more effective.

Briefly, verbs and adjectives should be studied and challenged by the salesman. Adverbs are often not needed if the best verb is chosen. For example, one might say, "He moved *very* slowly." But how about one of these: crept, crawled, lagged, loitered, sauntered, dragged, dawdled, shuffled, tottered, plodded? No adverb is needed.

Adjectives put color and depth into verbal pictures that may be merely sketched by the noun. The overworked "very" will be supplanted in many instances by stronger, more descriptive words. For example, many salesmen refer to the experience of some users of their product as being "very satisfactory." Perhaps he could find a better choice among "highly, charmingly, wholly, genuinely, gratifyingly, acceptably, vastly, profoundly, particularly, absolutely, universally, generally, utterly, entirely, happily."

Which is the more powerful statement? "This car handles with ease," or "This car handles with *fingertip* ease." "This machine will lower your costs," or "This machine will significantly lower your costs."

Words are the tools with which the salesman works to fashion a sale. He should equip his kit with the most efficient tools he can select.

LOGICAL REASONING

When the salesman uses logical argument in selling, he expects his prospect to reason, to think, to compare. This type of selling implies the formulation of a logical syllogism in the mind of the buyer.

Perhaps we should pause a moment and review this thing called a "logical syllogism." It is merely an argument consisting of three parts: a major premise, a minor premise, and a conclusion.

1. Major premise: All men are mortal.
2. Minor premise: I am a man.
3. Conclusion: Therefore, I am mortal.

In selling typewriters to an office manager, such logic might be:

1. Every able office manager wants to maximize the productivity of his office staff.
2. My typewriter will result in higher productivity.
3. Therefore, you must buy my typewriter.

Putting an argument[2] in this logical form may make it unanswerable, but it does not always make sales. It savors too strongly of the debating attitude; it is likely to place the prospect on the defensive. No man likes to be convinced against his will; in fact, he seldom can be so convinced. Prospects have been known to agree with everything the salesman says and the inescapable conclusions of his logic but still stubbornly say, "I don't want your blasted product." Most men prefer to do their own thinking or at least to be treated as if they are capable of doing it. Most salesmen avoid the syllogistic form of reasoning with their prospects, using instead either suggestion or an abbreviated syllogism which permits the prospect to draw his own conclusion. For example:

1. Every driver likes a car that is economical on gas.
2. You are a driver.
3. Therefore, you want a car that is economical on gas—this car delivers 22 miles to the gallon.

But the salesman skips part of the syllogism and simply says: "This car will give you 22 miles to the gallon." The prospect can fill in the omitted steps.

Logic used in selling implies an act of deliberation on the part of the prospect. The prospect must have the points at issue clearly in mind; he must catalogue and weigh the arguments pro and con; and he must reach a decision. This all takes time, and the salesman should not attempt to hurry the process. Indeed, quick selling is seldom accomplished by logic. Suggestion is a faster method, as already stated.

---

[2] The authors dislike the word "argument" in a book on salesmanship, but it is widely used. It smacks too much of debate and an acrimonious difference of opinion. The smart salesman never "argues" with a prospect.

Sometimes a salesman will attempt a sale by the use of suggestion, only to find that his prospect is growing thoughtful and reluctant to commit himself. Perhaps the prospect is merely trying to think the proposition out along logical lines. Where this seems to be the situation, it is wise for the salesman to slow down and resort to logic, permitting the prospect to deliberate carefully each point.

Or a prospect may want to buy; his emotions impel him to want the proposition. *But* his reason whispers "No!" The salesman's task here is to provide the prospect with reasons for buying—to appeal to logic. He must help the prospect to rationalize his urge to buy.

One of the best ways to accomplish this is to present the alternatives to buying. When a person reasons his way to a conclusion he must weigh various alternatives and ultimately choose one of them. In making many purchases he does not do this, merely buying on impulse. But in buying something involving a substantial amount of money, he is more likely to consider the alternatives open to him.

Let's say he is looking at a new model car. He is eager to have it. But his old car is still running well and he knows that he does not *need* the new one very badly. So the salesman tries to present alternatives. Obviously, there are only two: to keep the old car or to buy the new one. So he concentrates on the first, pointing out that, if he keeps the old car, he will have to get new tires shortly or risk an accident; that he will have to take less for it when he trades it in next year; that he will have to pay for various minor repairs during the next year; that he will have to forego such features as air conditioning and the new brakes; that, if he waits a year, he will have to put out larger monthly payments on account of the lower trade-in value on his old car. Thus he provides his prospect with logical arguments to support his desire to get the new model. Of course, he may, rather incidentally, try to heat up the prospect's desire for the new car. But his main purpose and objective is to help him to rationalize spending his money now.

Now, when should logic be used? There are a few general rules:

- In selling professional purchasing agents or buyers. These buyers are too experienced to be moved by suggestion alone; they want sound reasons. Besides, they are not buying for themselves.
- In selling buyers with trained minds, especially those trained in engineering or the sciences. These buyers think logically by habit.
- In selling complicated articles or propositions. It may not be used exclusively even here, as suggestion may help in the sales process, but few complex propositions can be sold without the use of facts and logic.
- In selling propositions involving a large expenditure. Any buyer deliberates longer over a large outlay than over spending a dime.

In selling something that is new to the prospect. Anything that involves a radical change in habit, thought, or style requires argument to support its introduction.

Sometimes it is hard to draw the line between logic and suggestion. The real distinction lies in the completeness of the syllogism.

When the filling station attendant says, "Shall I fill it up?" we see clearly that it is suggestion. He might have said:

All men wish to save time, as time is valuable.

You, being a man, wish to save time.

You will, therefore, be glad to save time by having your gas tank filled, to save the time of making another stop shortly.

We recognize this as a logical argument. It might be necessary to use it on some customers, but with most the suggestion is sufficient.

If—then

The "if—then" technique simply states an assumed premise and then reasons from that. An apparel salesman might say to a wavering dealer who had been carrying the line, "*If* you drop our line, *then* I hope you realize that we will have to find other distribution in your trading area and you will then be selling against our advertising and merchandising campaign." Or "*If* you wait another six months before buying this item, I hope you realize that the price could go up in the meantime and *then* you will end up by paying more."

Arguments such as these are logical if one accepts the assumed premise. Therefore, the salesman should be careful not to exaggerate this premise, thereby losing the confidence of his prospect.

Alternatives

Persuasion by alternatives involves appeals to reason rather than emotion. The salesman limits the possibilities to a small number, usually two, and then helps the prospect to determine the choice of one of those alternatives. The shirt salesman could approach his problem by saying, "Now let's examine each of these two alternatives you propose. First, let's examine what will happen if you change over to our competitor's line, and then let's see what will happen if you stay with us." Through this technique the shirt salesman hopes to show the prospect how the advantages of staying with the present line far outweigh those to be gained by switching and that he will encounter fewer disadvantages. The equipment salesman attempting to keep the executive from procrastinating in his purchase of an article might say, "Now let's examine what you have to gain and lose by waiting six months and then compare it with what you will gain and lose by buying now."

Comparison of similarities

This involves examining two situations and noting the similarities. The salesman endeavors to establish that what was true in one of the cases will be true in the other also. Suppose a men's wear salesman is faced with the problem of convincing a retail buyer that he should not switch over from the salesman's line to that of a competitor. He might say: "You know Sam Jones over in Smithville who runs the haberdashery, don't you? Three months ago he did exactly the same thing you are thinking about doing now; he changed lines. As you know, his store is about the same size as yours and caters to about the same type of customers. Well, I was over to see him yesterday, and he's switching back to us because his customers just haven't accepted the new line. They don't like the styling, and the fit isn't right for them."

Through the use of comparison the salesman attempts to get the customer to identify himself with another situation and conclude that if he behaves the same as the person in the other case the same results will happen to him. Of course, there may be a bit of fallacy in such reasoning if the two cases are not identical. However, the argument does carry much weight with many prospects if the parallel between the prospect's situation and the other is close.

NEED FOR RATIONALIZATION

Even though the prospect's behavior is caused basically by emotional forces, he will still feel a need for rational motives for his behavior, in case he is ever called upon for an explanation, and to satisfy himself that he is rational. Throughout the whole persuasion process the salesman must be conscious of this fact and must stand ready to provide reasons which the prospect may seize upon to justify his actions. The Cadillac salesman may have to show his prospect how small the percentage of depreciation is in comparison with low-priced cars, thus enabling the prospect to rationalize his behavior in terms of cost.

Many apparently illogical arguments presenting allegedly logical reasons are never seriously questioned by the prospect. He does not want them questioned, since they provide him with the reasons he needs to justify the emotional behavior he has in mind. The Cadillac owner wants to believe, no matter how illogically, that the Cadillac is his best low-cost purchase, all things considered. He wants to believe this so strongly that he makes no serious effort to discover discrepancies in the argument. Many faulty persuasion techniques succeed because the prospect wants them to succeed; he is eager to believe the things the salesman tells him. Hence, when the salesman sees that the prospect is in this category, he may use rather lame or leaky arguments to help the prospect to rationalize his act of buying.

Generalization

Probably the technique most widely used by salesmen, unfortunately, is that of generalization. The salesman flatly offers a broad, sweeping generalization without anything of a factual nature to support it. The apparel salesman who is having difficulty with his customer might generalize: "All experience shows that our line outsells the other two to one in every store where they are sold side by side." Nothing is given to back up the statement, and a smart buyer would either demand facts to support it or would ignore it as unworthy of consideration. The fact that a generalization is not challenged does not prove that the prospect has accepted it. He may merely have tossed it into his mental wastebasket.

Most good salesmen use generalizations only when their truth is so obvious that they will not be questioned.

DISCUSSION QUESTIONS

1. Devise a logical argument for selling an income tax service to a small businessman, and then illustrate how each point could be made either by suggestion or by other emotional persuasive means.
2. List various words which are usually loaded with favorable responses within the prospect.
3. Rephrase each of the following statements which you think is negative into positive terms:
   a. Our widget is not complex to install.
   b. This grass seed does not take long to germinate.
   c. This fabric won't wear out soon.
   d. Your wife won't have to work as hard with this machine.
   e. Your in-store theft losses will drop when we install our protection system.
4. As a service station attendant, you notice that a customer's tires are bald. Develop selling sentences using direct, indirect, positive, and negative suggestion.
5. How would you go about helping a housewife rationalize her desire to purchase an expensive ice-dispensing refrigerator rather than a more moderately priced model that would be more appropriate, considering her family's income?

6. Suppose you have developed the following logical argument:
   - You want the lowest-cost product.
   - My product is the lowest-cost one.
   - Therefore, you want to buy it.

   But the prospect tells you to get lost. What might have gone wrong with your logic?
7. By what means can you indirectly suggest to the prospect that your product is of the highest quality?
8. As a salesman for Hertz, you are trying to sign up a large firm that is now buying its own cars for salesmen and executives. Devise a logical argument to support your contention that the firm should be renting its cars from you.
9. In the car-rental situation above, devise various suggestions to accomplish the same objective.
10. You wish to impress upon your prospect the fact that the company you represent is a reputable concern with a record for quality and performance. How would you suggest this indirectly?

THE PRESENTATION: I

The Art of Salesmanship can be stated in five
words: believing something and convincing
others.
William Wrigley, Jr.

Despite all the important planning factors that have been discussed previously, the salesman's success still depends in most instances upon how well he makes his presentation. If he messes it up, the chain may be broken.

In this discussion the area of presentation is limited to the part of the interview between the approach and the time when the prospect has heard the story and begins to ask questions and raise objections. Of course, in many instances the prospect may raise objections during the early part of the presentation, but for the sake of clarity and order the techniques of handling objections and closing the sale are discussed in subsequent chapters.

OBJECTIVES OF THE PRESENTATION

Your task as a salesman in the presentation is to arouse the prospect's *desire* to have the product or service you are offering. After he has begun to want it, you can convince him that the proposition is sound, that the merchandise is good, and that any fears or mental reservations entertained by him are groundless. But there is no use doing this until the prospect has reached the stage of wanting it.

Much as the approach gained the prospect's decisions—(1) *I will see this salesman,* and (2) *I will hear his story*—the presentation also has its goals: (3) *I realize the disadvantages of my present situation,* (4) *I realize how I will benefit from this proposition,* (5) *I like this salesman's firm,* and (6) *I like the salesman.* The close aims at the decision: *I approve of this proposition.* And so the objectives of the presentation are to make the prospect aware that he has a problem, to show him how your product will solve this problem, and to sell him on your firm and yourself.

THE PRESENTATION IS REALLY A DUAL TASK

The sales interview is a *dual task*—to arouse a feeling of need in the prospect's mind and then to show how the salesman's proposition fills that need.

To illustrate these two goals of the presentation, let's look at the sale of an accounting service to a small businessman who is currently doing the work himself. First, the accountant (the salesman, in this case) must stimulate within the prospect a desire to divest himself of the work. This may not be as easy as it might appear to be, for the businessman may firmly believe that he should keep the books in order to understand better what is going on in his business. The very fact that the man is keeping his own books indicates some desire to do so, for a businessman who did not want to keep them would have sought out the services of a public accountant previously. So, early in the presentation, the accountant will have to probe deeply to discover the man's present feelings toward keeping his own records—the time it takes, the work, and the worry. The accountant will probably suggest that the enterprise will make more money if its owner spends his time managing the business rather than accounting for it. Naturally, the owner's desire for keeping close track of operations will have to be satisfied.

Until the prospect wants to stop keeping his own books, it is pointless to extoll the virtues of the accounting service. When the prospect indicates that he is dissatisfied with his present setup, then the accountant can begin to relate the excellence of his service.

This building of the presentation around the theme of *wants* is well illustrated by the following sales talk used by life insurance salesmen:[1]

"Mr. Prospect, the reason I called on you today is because I think I have an idea that will help you make sure of the things you want most out of life. I don't know that I can, but if I can, you will be glad I called; if I can't, I am sure you will be glad to have the idea for future reference anyway. It will take us only a few minutes to find out if my idea is of any value to you, Mr. Prospect, and I am sure you will feel that they are minutes well spent.

[1] The Rough Notes Co., Inc., Indianapolis. Used by permission.

"What do you want most out of life?" (Wait a few seconds and nine chances out of ten the prospect can't tell you. If he does mention anything, it will be on a broad scale, such as money, happiness, friends, health, etc. Whatever he says, you can deal with it briefly and then proceed as follows.)

"Mr. Prospect, the fact that you cannot easily state what you want most out of life does not surprise me and should not surprise you. Not one man in a hundred can. We discovered this fact by asking the question of many people. When sick or disabled, most persons want the assurance that there will be money to pay doctor bills and buy food for the family until they can get back to work. Isn't that one of the things that is hanging over us at all times to bring worry and fear—isn't that one of the things you want most in life—security from such misfortune?" (Wait for answer.)

"They want to pay their way out of life . . . to pay the bills created by death, and other outstanding bills. Also they want to leave some extra money for emergencies that always arise.

"This they want to make sure of! *Do you?* Most men tell us that they want to leave a clean slate—leave money to pay all bills and obligations, plus a little extra cash for emergencies, to help loved ones through crises that are sure to come when they are no longer here to take care of them. Is paying your way out of life one of the things you want?

"They want to leave enough income . . . at least enough for a few years, so their family can buy food, clothing and shelter while they prepare themselves to get along without the income that death has taken from them. This they want to make sure of! *Do you?* Is there anything that would mean more to you than to know, when you go to bed at night, that if you should not wake up, your family would have a living income, at least until the children are grown, and can take care of themselves—and their mother, if she needs it? Isn't that one of the most important things you want out of life, Mr. Prospect?"

If the prospect says "Yes" to all of these questions, you are well along towards developing the problem for which you can offer a solution. If he says "No" to any of them, you might say, "All right, since that isn't of interest to you, let's forget it and go on to the other things people tell us they want most out of life.

"These, then, are the things you want most out of life:

"We found that most of them are like you and me; that is, they just haven't had time to give the matter much thought, even though the answer means a lot to them.

"They have to really think and study before they know what they want most out of life. Yet, unless we do know what we want, we don't stand much chance of getting it, do we?

"One of the things we all want, I guess, is money, isn't it? But why do we work so hard for money? It's not just for the money, is it, Mr. Prospect? Money isn't everything, but it has a lot to do with most everything in your life—your Home, your Peace of Mind, your Fun, even your Love and Laughter. I think we want money most of all because it means security—freedom from want and freedom from fear, for yourself and for those you love. And that means happiness.

"Your future happiness very much depends on what you do now. You take your choice. Will it be Planned Happiness, or Chance Luck? It's too important, isn't it, to leave to a toss of a coin? But you can decide now what things you want most out of life. Lifetime happiness usually comes only to those who plan for it.

"Here are some things that hundreds of people have told us they want most out of life, and have included in their plans for happiness:

"They want ready cash . . . enough so they are prepared to grasp opportunities when they come . . . enough to meet Emergency Demands . . . enough to give them a feeling of Security and Stability. This they want to make sure of! *Do you?*

"They want [additional] income [to supplement their social security] for their later years . . . not a lot, but at least enough so their later years will be Happy Years . . . enough so they won't be dependent on anyone . . . enough so they won't have to work unless they choose to. Security for the distant future, so you never fear old age; enough income so that when you want to take it easy you can be independent of children or charity, with an income that will last as long as you do. This they want to make sure of! *Do you?"* (Let him answer this question.)

"They want an emergency income . . . to replace income lost due to Sickness or Accident, so they may have good Medical Care and their usual standard of living without going in debt. This they want to make sure of!

"You want to have ready cash, whenever you may need it, for opportunities or emergencies.

"You want to be sure that, when the time comes to quit work, you will have an income that will last as long as you will—so that you won't have to be dependent on charity or your children.

"You want to be able to pay your way out of life, and leave enough money so that all your bills can be paid.

"Then you want to be sure that your family will have some income, if your income is taken away from them—at the very least, enough to give them a few years in which to readjust themselves.

"And, in case of sickness or accident, you want to be sure there will be enough money to see you through.

"You can make sure of all these things that mean security, peace of mind, happiness, if you plan for them.

"Do you have a plan that will guarantee these things you want most out of life?"

The answer to this last question might very well be, "Well, I own some life insurance," or "Yes, we have done a little saving." Tactful questioning will bring out the amount of each.

Or it might be, "Well, no; I'm afraid I haven't done much about the future thus far." So of course you would ask, "Of course, you do own some life insurance, don't you?" And go on to find out just what he does have in the way of protection and savings.

In this suggested sales talk, we have tried to show only the use of the Sales Book in the interview. We have not attempted to set down the many developments that might take place in the interview. Above all, try to get your prospect to talk. You want an interview, not just a speech delivered to an audience of one. Ask questions—more questions than we have suggested here. Try to get his reaction to each "want."

Wants are not static—they are ever changing. As the psychologist might put it: "They are in constant process of elaboration, definition, integration, realization, fluctuation." The salesman's task is often as much to help the prospect identify a vaguely felt want as it is to create a new one.

The task of awakening or creating a want may be extremely brief and simple. A salesman for a reducing salon hands the prospect a 20-pound weight, asking, "How would you like to carry that around with you all day?" Most prospects get the message.

FOUR ESSENTIALS OF A GOOD PRESENTATION

An effective presentation has four characteristics: (1) It should be *complete,* covering every needed fact contributing either to the discontent of the prospect with present conditions or to his determination to improve them by accepting the proposition being presented. (2) It should eliminate *competition* from the picture, establishing the salesman's proposition as the one best way to solve the prospect's problems. (3) It should be *clear,* leaving no haze of misunderstanding in the prospect's mind. (4) It should win the prospect's *confidence* that the statements made by the salesman are true and that the salesman is thinking honestly of the prospect's interests.

Confidence is critical. Indeed, many sales are made solely because the prospect has such confidence in the salesman that little actual selling needs to be done. The prospect does what the salesman suggests. Of course, such confidence is not developed easily, but must be earned over a period of time. Since there is little point in giving a presentation unless confidence has been developed, this chapter will be devoted to it and to some other basic strategies of making a sale.

We have discussed the use of suggestion and the reasoned appeal, but nothing the salesman may say or do will move the prospect to buy unless he *believes* and is *convinced* of the truth of what the salesman has told him. Perhaps a skilled purchasing agent will buy in spite of some disbelief in the salesman's statements, but he would have bought anyway because he was able to evaluate the offer minus the exaggerations of the salesman. Even here the salesman has hurt his future chances of selling this buyer, for the latter will always swallow that salesman's claims with a generous grain of salt and perhaps discount claims which may be 100 percent true. One purchasing agent for a large Illinois manufacturing concern told the authors that fully 90 percent of the salesmen who called on him failed to gain his confidence in them or their propositions.

This confidence may be reposed in the goods or product being sold, in the maker, or in the salesman or dealer selling them.

It has been said that one statement in a sales talk which the prospect does not believe is like one drop of ink in a glass of water—it colors the entire contents.

The winning of the prospect's confidence is often listed as one distinct step in the sales process. It is so difficult to determine just where this step should be taken that it seems preferable to consider the gaining of the buyer's confidence as a factor that must permeate the entire presentation. This is why we discuss it first in this book.

An editorial in *Sales Management* says it this way:

Confidence is a plant of slow growth. It does not spring full-blown from a seed scattered at random. It requires hard work and tender care, just as good gardening does. When a salesman has confidence in the firm he represents, confidence in the line it makes and markets he can transmit that confidence to prospects and customers. More than mere merchandise, confidence is what he has for sale, first to last. For confidence is the catalyst . . . the priceless ingredient . . . of sales.

Any way you look at it, believability is the essence of persuasion.

This believability is obtained by two major factors: (1) the behavior and personality of the salesman and (2) the sales techniques he employs. Each factor will be examined in this chapter.

SALESMAN'S PERSONAL BEHAVIOR

The salesman by his behavior can either enhance or detract from the believability of his presentation. Seldom does a person separate a man from the statements he makes: he judges the entire situation from all the evidence he has at his disposal, which includes both the salesman's statements and his personal behavior.

Perhaps no one thing does more to build confidence than a display of genuine unselfishness on the part of the salesman. The salesman who really has the buyer's interest at heart can gain his confidence as he proves by deeds.

The necktie salesman says to the dealer: "Now here's a number that didn't sell so well in the test markets. Men just didn't like it. Guess their wives didn't either. Here's another that did a little better but not too well. I wouldn't urge you to stock either one. But here's one that the customers really went for. I figure you could handle two dozen. That about right?"

And he should be telling the truth! Hang the dealer with bad goods and all he will think about every time he sees them gathering dust on his shelves is "that no-good peddler who stuck me with those dogs!" Salesmen who call regularly upon retailers know that their long-run success depends upon gaining the dealer's confidence. This is not likely to happen if the salesman fails to deal fairly and truthfully.

One electrical equipment salesman said, "In all my dealings with purchasing agents and engineers I have one overriding thought in my mind at all times. If our positions were reversed, how would I want them to treat me?" He believed that his prospects realized that he had their interests at heart and that they consequently trusted him.

"Would you want someone trying to squeeze you into a suit two sizes too small or hang a tent from your shoulders, then try to tell you that it fits fine? Of course not! Well, neither do our customers, so don't you dare lie to them. If you can't fit them, tell them so," orders the owner of a successful men's wear store.

CONFIDENCE-BUILDING TECHNIQUES
Besides the salesman's overall behavior, there are some definite things he can do to instill confidence in the prospect.

Early claims should be conservative
Strong claims should not be made early in the interview for they are likely to be discounted by the buyer. However, if early claims are conservative and creditable, the subsequent ones may be bolder yet.

Some professional buyers deliberately lie in wait to pounce upon the first exaggerated statement made by a salesman by demanding proof of it then and there. They seize the offensive and never let the poor salesman recover his poise, keeping him off balance until he would hesitate to swear to his own name or age.

Indeed, it does not pay, in the long run, to exaggerate at *any* stage of the interview, especially if you are trying to build up a reputation and a clientele. Don't promise more than you can deliver, but deliver what you have promised. If "a satisfied customer is the best advertisement," then a dissatisfied customer is a firm's or salesman's *worst* advertisement and he is more likely to talk than is the satisfied one because he wants to get even.

Don't knock the "boss"
At times the salesman is tempted to take the side of his customer against his employer in the mistaken belief that by doing so he gains the favor of the customer. But it doesn't work out that way in most instances. It can destroy the buyer's confidence in the salesman's firm. Let an experienced purchasing agent state this attitude.

Do not appear to be disloyal to your company in your effort to be accommodating to your customers. I like to meet the man who "pats himself on the back" because he is with some particular concern, who is glad he is working for the "old man," whoever the old man may be. That man does more than printed advertising can ever do. His loyalty inspires the buyer's confidence in the firm which he represents. He sells not only the manufactured goods but also the reputation of the company.

In our plants we use a good many scales for weighing our products. These scales must be accurate at all times and require the care which all well-constructed mechanisms should have. Sometimes they get out of order—that is to be expected. It happened that we were using a new type for the first time, and, of course, we had some trouble with it. We sent for a representative of the selling company. No sooner did he arrive than he began to apologize to me that we would not have had any trouble with the scales if the men at the factory had known their business. Their design on this particular type was not what it ought to be, and they might have known that the mechanism would give trouble. In fact, he attempted to console me with the statement that Smith and Jones were having the same difficulty with the new scales.

There was nothing radically wrong with those scales, and that salesman did not believe what he was telling me, I am sure. He was so afraid of antagonizing me that he took pains to agree with me at every turn and even went one step further by adopting a conciliatory attitude of self-condemnation. That was an error, and a bad one, for it made him appear disloyal to his firm. The reaction on me was a loss of confidence in the company and its product. I stopped buying its scales as a consequence.

This statement of the proposition leaves little need for comment. Criticizing the company results only in a loss of business through loss of confidence.

A young representative for a large textbook publisher developed a habit of dropping in on one of the authors to pass the time of day. No doubt this habit was encouraged because the salesman thought he had found a sympathetic shoulder upon which to cry. He would go on at length about the injustices being heaped upon him by a hard-hearted, unreasonable management. He would complain about the company's stingy expense account, its policy of working its men right through the summer, and its "unenlightened" publishing program. Small wonder that the man was fired shortly, but the main point is that the prospect was left with an unfavorable image of the company. No doubt the representative wondered why he could never sell his "friend" any books. Why should anyone want to buy from such a company?

Salesmen tend to criticize their firms in the misguided hope that by so doing they are placing themselves on the prospect's side of the fence and gaining his goodwill. Only it does not work out that way. The buyer is apt to think, "What kind of fool do you think I am to buy from such an outfit? And what kind of fool are you to work for such an employer?"

However, this does not mean that the salesman should not represent his customer's interests to top management when the customer has been mistreated. If the customer has a legitimate claim, the salesman should help him press it.

Tests as confidence winners

Another method of winning the buyer's confidence is through tests of various sorts. "Just taste that. Did you ever taste anything so good?" the enthusiastic salesman for grape juice exclaims as he gives his prospect a taste of his product, kept cold in a thermos bottle. The clothing or textile salesman submits his product to the well-known tests. The paper salesman has his customer tear his product, hold it to the light at certain angles, and test it in other ways.

The headline on an article in *Sales Management* proclaims: "If you sell to the industrial market, get 'em to test it . . . and it's nine-tenths sold."

The willingness with which the salesman submits his product to these tests is a factor in gaining the prospect's confidence. If he is willing and even eager to have his product thoroughly tested, the prospect is impressed by his attitude.

Some tests, although impressive to the unskilled prospect, are unconvincing to the expert buyer. The salesman will do well to develop his preapproach in such a way as to avoid the mistake of using such a "grandstand" type of test on a buyer who appreciates its lack of value. With an experienced buyer it may be best to permit him to conduct his own tests.

In case the product has been tested by the U.S. Bureau of Standards or by some store that, like Macy's, maintains its own testing laboratory, the results of such a test inspire confidence. With some buyers reports from commercial testing firms, employed by the manufacturer on a fee basis, carry little weight.

The guarantee

This is a powerful sales aid, particularly in selling a new product or to a new prospect. Of course, the guarantee is of value only in so far as the company issuing it is reliable, but even with this qualification it makes it easier for salesmen to win the confidence of buyers.

Guarantees are of varying strength, some being absolute, like those used by the big mail-order houses, while others cover only certain matters such as material and workmanship. New products will often sell more readily if they are warranted, but established products of good quality find less need for such support. If a product is approved by the American Medical Association or the Good Housekeeping Institute, such approval almost equals a guarantee in the minds of many buyers. Guarantees should be in writing, for many prospects have had unfortunate experience with oral guarantees. Guarantees offering "double your money back if not satisfied" are usually confined to low-priced products. If applied to more expensive articles some unscrupulous buyers would take advantage of the offers. If the warranty appears to favor the buyer too strongly, it may backfire and raise the suspicion in the buyer's mind that the product must be of rather poor quality or it would sell without such a generous guarantee.

The use of testimonials

True, the testimonial has been grossly abused and overworked, but this is only because it can be so effective. It is still sound in principle, being based on the old saying, "A satisfied customer is the best advertisement."

S. H. White, President of Acetogen Gas Company, insists that one 200-word report from the chief engineer of a user-company is worth 10,000 words of explanation and persuasion by anyone representing the seller. The company's salesmen carry a list of big-company users and point out the names of those whose problems are similar to those of the prospect.

The testimonial is often used in *advertising* to gain *attention* rather than confidence. We like to read about well-known personalities, even if we do not always believe everything we read about them.

In *personal selling,* the testimonial is used for the purpose of inspiring *confidence* instead of attracting attention, inasmuch as the salesman has already won the prospect's attention.

The salesman must know how to use the testimonial. First, it should be from someone whose problems are similar to those of the prospect. To tell the proprietor of the crossroads general store that Marshall Field's and Wanamaker's use his system of accounting or window lighting would mean little, because he knows that he is not a Marshall Field or a Wanamaker. It may be different with consumption goods, for Bob Hope may wear a hat that any man in moderate circumstances could buy, but for production goods too great a discrepancy is likely to be apparent. It would be more effective if the salesman for a retail accounting system said, "You know George Anderson over in Lincoln. His store is about the size of yours, and he says that his profits have increased 12 percent since he installed this system."

A testimonial will also carry more weight when its author is known to the prospect—and known to be reliable. The experience of a local woman with a new type of clothes dryer may be more convincing than a testimonial from a famous actress who obviously does not do her own washing. Sometimes the source of the testimonial is a group or a society, as a trade association or regulatory authority. The seals of approval placed on certain products by the Good Housekeeping Institute and the Underwriters Laboratories are examples.

The salesman will be careful, in most instances, about quoting a competitor of his prospect, for many a buyer would refuse flatly to copy the practices of his competitor. "If that buzzard uses it, that's enough for me! I wouldn't have it around the place." This may not be an invariable rule, but the salesman should be on the alert to avoid thus "waving the red flag" in front of a buyer.

Testimonials may best be used in selling to a relatively inexperienced buyer. He, like the man buying his first automobile, relies heavily on the experience of others. The skilled buyer, learned in methods of judging values, scorns the testimonial and feels competent to make his own choice, except in cases involving very new products.

The way in which the testimonial is introduced into the presentation is also important. With the experienced buyer this must be done casually and not as though it were a vital talking point. It should be done in a "by-the-way" manner, and the salesman should not seem to stress the point. Perhaps he has a group of letters from satisfied users. These should not be gone over in detail with a purchasing agent who is presumed to know his business but should be referred to briefly and somewhat casually. The inexperienced buyer, unable to form his own judgments, may wish to read some of these letters in full. It may be mentioned in passing that photographic reproductions of letters are more convincing than printed or mimeograph copies. Grammatical errors may be found in such letters, but this very fact helps to convince the reader that they are genuine.

One company made up a little portfolio of testimonials for its salesmen and included in it some that registered slight complaints as well as praise for the product. This proved to be sound salesmanship, as the prospects believed the testimonials utterly. To increase still further the confidence of the prospects in the reliability of the testimonials, photographs were shown of the homes of all those who had given testimonials.

Some automobile dealers maintain on the wall of the salesroom a list of local owners of the car sold by that agency. Especially when it is a high-priced car, this list may be helpful in showing the prospect that others in his income bracket drive this make of car. Also, he may find the names of men in whose judgment he has confidence.

Experiences of others

These may take the form of case histories which the salesman has accumulated, a case history being simply the story of the experience of someone else whose situation was similar to that of the prospect. The aim is to induce the prospect to believe that, if he follows the same course, the results (naturally these are pleasant) will be the same.

It is necessary that the prospect believe the story even in the absence of convincing proof. The salesman uses several tactics to insure this.

First, he inserts numerous minor details to show that he is intimately familiar with the facts. Generalities are not convincing; specific statements are.

Second, whenever possible the salesman mentions the names of people, places, companies, and products so that the case history seems authentic. The prospect assumes that if the salesman mentions names and places the event really happened.

Third, if possible, the story should be about someone the prospect knows or can contact for verification.

Fourth, the possession of letters, pictures, or newspaper clippings about some part of the story will help validate the entire tale in the prospect's mind. Once one part of the story is proven true, the person has more reason to believe other parts of it.

Finally, the method of delivery is quite important to the history's acceptance. The salesman must relate it in a sincere and knowing manner. When he claims that he did his best to keep Bill Jones from making that mistake, his voice must communicate the emotion and frustration which he felt.

Inspection of previous sales

A contractor wished to convince the president of an electronics company that he was the best contractor to build a new factory. He had previously built a plant for another research firm in the same area, so he merely took the prospect on a detailed inspection tour of the previous job.

In industrial selling it is common for salesmen to take prospects on trips to inspect previous work or the operation of some new equipment. Seeing the equipment in actual use on the job is likely to be convincing if the prospect's problems and operations are similar.

Show records

A women's ready-to-wear salesman was trying to prove to a small-town merchant that his line was really moving. He convinced the prospect by showing bona fide reorders placed by merchants known to the buyer.

An industrial machine salesman wanted to convince the prospect that his turret lathe required a minimum of repair. He produced records for a sample of installations showing each repair call the firm had received from the customers.

Plant tours

An electronics firm was attempting to convince a large prime contractor that its quality-control system would insure the maintenance of output quality so that it could be placed on the approved list of suppliers. Several executives of the prime contractor were flown out to the plant to inspect firsthand the facilities and quality-control methods in operation. They were convinced.

Many food manufacturers have always encouraged tours of their plants to convince the public of the cleanliness of their operations. Such tours can communicate many messages to the public and prospects. Meeting and talking with the seller's personnel may increase the confidence the buyer has in the firm.

Talking with customers

This is akin to reading testimonials, yet it may be more effective. Many a salesman has saved a sale by suggesting to a prospect, "Just pick up your phone and call So-an-So and ask him about it. I'll pay the toll charge." At conventions of businessmen, salesmen are constantly trying to arrange meetings of prospects with satisfied customers.

Sometimes a salesman is at a loss as to precisely which method to use in gaining the prospect's complete confidence. To save time he may say: "I know that I make a good many statements about my proposition that may sound almost too good to be true. If you have any doubt about something I have said, what would convince you of its truth?" Perhaps the prospect is thinking of a free trial or some particular test or demonstration and will tell the salesman. If the latter can go along with the suggestion, he may make the sale right there.

OTHER BASIC STRATEGIES OF THE PRESENTATION

Although each salesman must devise many specific strategies and tactics for selling his particular line of products, there are some general strategies which are applicable to all interviews.

Selling should not be a battle

Terms suggesting battle, such as ammunition, attack, armor, defense, barrage, and retreat, are often used in speaking of selling. It is admitted that certain types of specialty selling are similar in some respects to small skirmishes, with the salesman and prospect opposing each other. The salesman will do well, however, to keep this conception of his work as much as possible in the background, for it is not conducive to the right viewpoint—that of helpfulness to the buyer.

Certainly in retail salesmanship the analogy of the battle is not nearly so applicable as it once was. When the salesman's chief asset was the ability to lie fluently and the price was arrived at by a process of hardfisted haggling, selling was much more of a combat; but the retail salesperson who thinks of his work as a continual fight with customers is bound to lose out today. There are several reasons for this.

- It is too easy for the customer to return goods purchased under undue pressure.
- If the salesperson thinks of himself as a belligerent, it probably results in a sullen greeting to the customer, the frown supplants the smile, and the entire atmosphere is charged with hostility.
- This type of salesperson is very likely to start arguments with his customers, thereby provoking them and perhaps insulting them.

This does not mean that the zest has been taken out of selling at retail. There is perhaps more room than ever for the display of talent, originality, and quick intelligence. The object of the game today is to discover what the prospect needs, make him feel the need, and then supply it. The ideal is to satisfy, not to "sting" him.

"Keep arguments out of the selling talk" is one of the best pieces of advice given out to young salesmen by their chiefs. One famous salesman, Rube Wardell, used to say, "Sure, you can prove to the buyer and to anybody that's around him that he doesn't know what he is talking about. But what does that get you? There's no nourishment in showing the buyer up. He isn't going to thank you for it. More often than not he'll remember the incident, and sooner or later it will cost you business."

Some salesmen seem to go out of their way to arouse the antagonism of the buyer. One of the commonest forms of this reverse technique is to make a remark to this effect: "Well, sooner or later you are going to buy from me. I'll be seeing you." An illustration brings out the psychology of such situations.

In a Western city a life insurance salesman is wondering why a man upon whom he had called for over ten years recently placed a $100,000 policy with another insurance salesman—a newcomer in that city. The inside story is this: Some eight or nine years ago, after he had made various calls on his prospect, the salesman remarked one day, "I'll get you yet, old boy!"

It was, no doubt, a sentiment showing admirable determination, but it should not have been uttered, because the "old boy" snapped back, "No, you won't—not a chance!" And from that day he stuck to his position. He had announced that decision impulsively, it is true; nevertheless, he announced it and he made up his mind not to back down.

Keep the interview friendly

No buyer is a computer-like mechanism who arrives at a decision by feeding facts into his brain and turning out the right answer. He is a human being and, as such, prefers to do business with people he likes. If he likes a certain salesman, he will give him a longer interview, will listen more sympathetically to his story, is more likely to give him repeat business. While it is not good business to buy from a salesman just because he is a friend, if other factors are equal the friend will usually get the business—and he should.

The salesman will do well to bear in mind that the buyer is often glad to stop a few minutes and talk with a friendly soul. He may have been having one of those days when everything goes wrong, when he is forced to make unpleasant decisions, when he is having arguments with too many people. His nerves are on edge, his blood pressure is up, and he wishes he could quit and raise chickens. Then a smiling salesman is ushered in, bringing a new idea that promises to help solve some problem confronting the harassed buyer. He brings a breath of the outside world, together with some trade gossip and *always* helpful ideas. The buyer may act tense and scowl fiercely at first, but this may be a holdover from hectic hours just preceding. If he feels the salesman is really friendly, he relaxes for a few minutes and is glad of the chance.

We have said many times that a sales interview should never be an argument. Rather, it should take on the aspect of a friendly conversation on a topic of mutual interest. With a friend we do not quibble over some minor point; we feel an urge to agree with him. The interview moves smoothly.

If the buyer is already a customer, the salesman must work hard at the job of *retaining* his friendship. He must always watch out for that customer's interests in every way, such as pushing for prompt deliveries, careful packing, or selling helps that have been promised. He must be dependable—absolutely.

A buyer related to the authors an incident which had stuck in his memory for twenty years. He had placed an initial order with a certain salesman and had been promised delivery on January 15, as the stuff was needed January 16. At 4 o'clock in the afternoon of January 15, the buyer's phone rang. It was the salesman who had promised to make delivery that day. "I'm at Jonesville only 120 miles away. I'm driving a company truck with your stuff in it and I'll get to your place by 8 o'clock tonight. We ran into a lot of unavoidable delays, and the roads are slippery, but we'll beat that deadline. Will someone be there to take the stuff inside at 8 o'clock?" That buyer, after twenty years, feelingly commented, "That salesman kept my business as long as he called on me. And *he never let me down* in any way."

Buying decision 6 is, *"I like this salesman's firm."* We must keep in mind that, to the average buyer, the salesman is pretty nearly the "firm." He is the firm's representative, its ambassador. It is he who sees to it that the firm gives good service, so far as he can make his influence felt. True, the "firm" has many contacts with the buyer, and these should all be friendly. If the Old Man wants it that way, it will probably be that way. The salesman must try to make the prospect feel that he will be dealing with friendly folks all up the line.

Controlling the interview

Just another word on this matter of dominating or controlling the interview. Some salesmen overdo it, striving hard to keep the conversation from straying to subjects other than the business in hand. But this may not always be the smart thing to do. It may easily happen that the sale is dragging, that failure is imminent, when the prospect suddenly thinks of something that interests him and starts to talk about it. The only hope for the salesman is to listen sympathetically and search for a means to connect up the prospect's interests, as expressed, with the proposition to be sold. Even when this cannot be accomplished, he must listen interestedly, and often the customer will return to the subject of the sale voluntarily and with a feeling that he owes the salesman the courtesy of listening to *him* for a while.

There are, of course, buyers who purposely break the thread of the interview and then turn the proposition down before the conversation can be resumed. Such persons must be held more strictly to the track. Other buyers are prone to let their thoughts wander afield from any subject under discussion and must be reined in and guided back to the highway.

As with other problems arising in the sales presentation, salesmen have developed techniques for solving this one. Many rely on questions, believing that he who asks the questions controls the interview. This is often similar to taking the pulse of the interview, although at times it may differ from this. For example, the salesman might ask, "Did you ever see a valve that operates on this principle? It's really revolutionary."

Occasionally, the salesman may have failed to make his presentation clear on some point, thereby prompting the prospect to ask about it. This may be just what the salesman wants; but again it may embarrass him if the question is a deliberately nasty one. The prospect asks: "Have you people ever solved all your quality-control problems?" It is like the oldie, "Have you stopped beating your wife?" The salesman hesitates to answer either yes or no, so he regains control of the situation with something like, "I wonder if perhaps you aren't thinking about some other company. If we ever had any quality-control problems, it was before I joined the outfit."

If the prospect's questions reveal a genuine interest in the proposition, they are, of course, welcome and do not jeopardize the salesman's control of the interview. Generally speaking, the salesman prefers to ask the prospect if he has any questions he would like to ask about the point just covered. In this way he can elicit questions and still retain control of the situation.

The salesman himself may be responsible for losing control of the interview through statements that are open to challenge. It matters not whether such statements are made as deliberate lies or through ignorance. An inexperienced salesman for a small plane, designed for use of executives who travel quite a bit, called on a prospect, unaware that the man was an old flier. The latter asked, "How many feet per minute will it climb on one engine?" The salesman chose to guess, and he guessed wrong, thereby losing control of that interview completely.

Timing

There are wrong times to try to make a sale. Prospects can be so busy or preoccupied with other problems that there is no room for the salesman in their thinking. A businessman whose plant has just burned down is in no mental state to listen to any salesman unless he is selling something that will directly alleviate his immediate problems.

Prospects can be in unfavorable mental or emotional states during which it is difficult to communicate with them in any rational manner. A man who has just had a death in the family is not in the mood to listen to a salesman extolling the virtues of a turret lathe.

The financial abilities of prospects vary with the times. The businessman who has just heard his accountant report a large increase in profits is a different buyer than one who has been told that he suffered a loss last quarter.

Obviously, the salesman must take the timing factor into consideration if some significant event is discovered during the preapproach, and he must be prepared to bow out quickly and gracefully upon encountering some unexpected event which places the prospect in an unfavorable frame of mind.

A good listener may sell too

Many salesmen seem to feel that it is necessary to keep up a constant flow of talk, that the enemy must be pinned down by a ceaseless chatter of oral machine guns.

More experienced salesmen have learned that it is wise to let the prospect do quite a bit of talking, especially if he appears favorably inclined toward the proposition. If the prospect wishes to elaborate on some advantage of the salesman's product, it is good strategy to keep silent and let him sell himself.

Indeed, many skilled salesmen make a practice of presenting their claims in a rather sketchy style, allowing the prospect to fill in the gaps and arrive at his own conclusions. Under such circumstances the prospect is likely to exclaim, "Then this would be true, too, wouldn't it?" This is precisely what the salesman is striving for—to help the buyer reach his own conclusions. When these tactics are employed, the buyer feels smugly pleased with himself because he has been able to figure the thing out more or less independently and forthwith embraces and champions the new idea as his own. Thus, he sells himself the proposition.

Obviously, the salesman can use these methods only when the prospect is not too firm in his opposition and when he has sufficient mental agility to leap the gaps in the presentation and reach the desired conclusions without being led step by step.

In selling the opinionated buyer, the salesman may perhaps fare better if he does not talk much. Also, when two people are shopping together, they may wish to discuss the articles without interference from the salesman and are likely to appreciate being allowed to make their own decisions. As long as they are interested in the article and are talking it over, the salesman can afford to await the time when it may be necessary to put in a word to save the sale. If this does not prove necessary, all is well. Many buyers prefer to be allowed to consider a proposition carefully without being pushed.

If the salesman insists on doing too much of the talking, several things are likely to happen.

The prospect loses interest. He can keep his mind moving better if he is moving physically. It is always the students in the lecture who go to sleep—never the prof. If a prospect is allowed to talk his share of the time, he will be more likely to grasp quickly what is said.

The prospect is mulling over in his mind the things that he would like to say, instead of giving attention to the things that the salesman is saying. This is fatal to successful selling.

The longer the prospect is forced to bottle up his questions and objections, the more inflated they become. Permitting the prospect to do his share of the talking often discloses the obstacles to his buying; it brings out objections; it airs his opinions on the proposition. With this knowledge the salesman can more intelligently plan his sale.

Another advantage of letting the prospect talk is that it makes him feel that he is not being high-pressured. It gives him the impression that the salesman is trying to learn all about his problem so that he can render him a real service. It builds confidence. It relaxes tensions.

There is a good deal more to listening than merely keeping your

mouth shut. You must make it plain to the prospect that you *are listening.*
Wife: "John, you aren't listening to a word I'm saying!"

What's the matter here? John isn't saying a word. Why does wifey feel so sure he isn't listening? Well, he may be

· *Doing* something such as glancing at the paper he is trying to read
· Letting his gaze wander to activities or objects other than his spouse
· Appearing to be thinking about something else

How can we give the impression that we are *really* listening?

We should *listen with our eyes;* we should look directly at the speaker.

We should permit or even encourage our facial expression to respond to the statements of the speaker. Smile, compress lips, raise eyebrows, nod head, or appear to reflect a moment on some point.

We may occasionally comment on a statement made by the speaker, as, "So that's why they use aluminum in that part." "Yours is a larger outfit than I realized." Anything like this will show that we *are* listening. We may even use a rising inflection, showing a bit of question as to some point.

We should be careful not to interrupt with some "off-beat" comment or remark, thereby revealing that we are not in step.

In thus listening—really listening—we are accomplishing several desirable objectives:

· We are complimenting the prospect and building up his ego.
· We are impressing him with our intelligence and interest.
· We are learning something. It has been truly said that nobody learns much while he is talking. But while our prospect is talking, we are learning things about him.
· We are making him like us and are putting him in a mood to be helpful to us.

This discussion should not be interpreted as meaning that the salesman need do little talking at the opening of the interview. It is usually necessary to talk long enough to get the interview well under way and to insure against being turned down before having a chance to present the proposition. After the interview is assured, then it is time to let the prospect take his part in it.

Later, when the presentation has been concluded and the salesman is ready to make his effort to close the sale, he will gradually do more of the talking.

Notice that the salesman does not lose control over the situation by allowing the prospect to talk; the sale is going as planned. One can maintain dominance even while listening.

THE SETTING FOR THE PRESENTATION

Sometimes the smallest details can influence the outcome of a sale. Certainly the immediate environment in which the presentation is to take place can most definitely affect the sale. For that reason, some forethought should be given to where the salesman wants to make the presentation. Many times it is wise to avoid making sales presentations in a prospect's place of business—confusion and interruptions can be ruinous to the train of thought required for the transaction. Pick a place where both you and the prospect can meet in comfort and in privacy. Frequently a prospect's behavior becomes more sociable when he is not in his business setting.

As the salesman enters the presence of the buyer, he tries to size up the situation and to plan quickly how he can arrange things to his advantage.

For example, some buyers try to make the salesman tell his story while they are standing in the outer office or in the doorway. The salesman should request a better chance to make his presentation, perhaps basing this on the need for a place to show samples, set up a projection machine, etc. He should be prepared with some sentence designed to accomplish this. "I've got a miniature model of our machine with me that you'll enjoy operating. It has three features that are really new and fascinating. You can work it right on your desk."

Once inside the buyer's office, the salesman quickly appraises certain factors. Lighting is one of these, as he wishes to show his samples or photographs in the most favorable light. He may move a table or a lamp, he may lower a shade or adjust Venetian blinds, he may turn out one light or turn on another. This can be done quietly and quickly, without much comment, and the result will be to give him a certain degree of command over the interview right from the start.

Noise is likely to interfere with the interview, unless it is noise to which the buyer has become so accustomed that he scarcely notices it. If it can be eliminated by closing a door or window, perhaps this should be done. Regular noises of a factory, for instance, cannot be entirely excluded although they may be minimized somewhat. Sometimes it is necessary to shift the scene of the interview to a hotel room or other quieter spot, but this possibility should be anticipated rather than left to the last minute.

The very fact that a salesman is forced to raise his voice to make himself heard above some distracting noise reduces his effectiveness. The interview loses its relaxed conversational tone, which is bad. Too, the voice usually becomes more strident and unpleasant under these conditions, which fact may jar on the sensibilities of the prospect and cause him to cut short the interview. Noise can ruin a sales presentation.

If, as is usually the case, the salesman is to seat himself, the question is "Where?" Many buyers have chairs for salesmen placed just where they want them—often where the salesman faces the light and the buyer's face is in a shadow. Some have even had the chair fastened to the floor! But ordinarily a chair can be shifted to an advantageous position, perhaps so that the salesman is facing more nearly in the same direction as the prospect. Thus they can both view various items which the salesman will exhibit; and the salesman is in a position to point to specific features which he wishes to emphasize.

He may have a choice between chairs on either side of the prospect's desk, in which event he will quickly appraise such factors as light, height of the chair (he will avoid one that is too low), room on the desk free from pictures, telephones, or letter trays. He will try to avoid a position that forces him to look around desk items such as statuettes, lamps, etc. And he will try to gain a position close enough to the buyer for unity of action, while avoiding sitting too close, as many buyers have a violent distaste for being crowded or made victims of halitosis or B.O. At the same time, the salesman wants to be close enough to talk in an easy conversational tone without shouting and to remain in actual physical control over easel, sample, or model which may form part of the presentation procedure.

If the space on the desk is too small, there is usually a larger table in the office or in some other room. It is unwise to make the selling effort under cramped conditions.

The salesman avoids the chair that is too low, because it places his eye level below that of the prospect and forces him to look *up,* while the prospect can look *down* at him. This is a very real psychological factor in their relationship.

Some sales managers instruct their men never to sit in the presence of the prospect because this places the sellers in a position where they cannot dominate the interview as they could if they were standing. Then, too, it is argued that the man on his feet is better able to gesture and emphasize his talk in various ways. A public speaker cannot address an audience so effectively seated as he can standing.

It is agreed that in retail selling the salesman should seldom be seated unless it is at a place like the glove counter. In open departments, also, it would seem best for the salesman to stand, but this is because it indicates a willingness to show goods. Here, also, we often find a practice of seating the customer, but this is not to enable the salesman to dominate the interview but rather to make the customer sufficiently comfortable so that he will remain until the salesman has an adequate opportunity to display and discuss his merchandise.

In house-to-house selling, most salesmen sit down, because they find it difficult to persuade prospects to seat themselves while they remain standing. And besides, the salesman wishes to assure himself that the interview will not be terminated too soon as it might be if he were to remain on his feet. Salesmen feel that to remain standing appears as though they did not expect to stay. The neighbor who runs in to borrow a cup of sugar says, "Can't stay a minute. No, I can't sit down." The salesman wishes to avoid giving this impression.

The salesman calling on a buyer in his office usually finds a chair placed for him and is likely to receive an invitation to be seated. It is a bit difficult for him to refuse the invitation unless there is an obvious reason for so doing. Here, as in the case of the house-to-house canvasser, to remain standing gives the call an air of brevity which may be unfortunate. It is easier for such a buyer to rise and end the interview when the salesman is already standing than when he also is seated.

Some salesmen, when they feel that the prospect is pretty well sold and not likely to dismiss them, remain seated during the sale until they are prepared to close. They then rise and make the final appeal standing, feeling that in this way it is more forceful.

A contrast in settings

A men's wear buyer, in New York for his semiannual buying trip, called at his appointed time of 9 A.M. at the offices of the manufacturers of Cricketeer, a line of medium-priced suits and sport coats. He had been carrying the line for several years and consequently was well-acquainted with the firm's personnel; he was greeted warmly and ushered into a showroom. The showroom was divided from the other showrooms by plastic folding room dividers; noise filtered through them. It developed that no showroom had the complete line of models for the season; salesmen kept running in and out asking for such-and-such model. The salesman attending to the buyer also had to leave the room frequently to locate something that was not in the room. There were constant interruptions. The sale dragged on hour after hour; the buyer had planned to spend the morning with Cricketeer, have lunch, then "work another line in the afternoon." The noon hour passed and a new problem arose; another buyer was scheduled into the room at 1 P.M. After much ado, other arrangements were made for the afternoon shift.

Now the real victim of this situation was a young salesman who was trying to introduce Cricketeer's new line of slacks to the buyer. He was brought into the showroom and introduced to the buyer at 11 A.M. Amid the confusion, the time pressures on the buyer's mind, and the interruptions, it is no wonder that he was unable to write an order for his slacks. Afterward the buyer confessed that he would probably have bought the slacks under better conditions, but he did not want to take time to make fabric selections and size the order. It was 2:30 P.M. when he went to lunch.

The same buyer proceeded to the offices of a high-quality suit and

sport coat manufacturer. He was ushered into a private, beautifully decorated showroom. Orders were given by the "salesman," who also happened
to own the company, that under no circumstances was he to be disturbed
nor were phone calls to be forwarded into the room. The room was completely equipped; he made the entire sale without leaving it and was finished in a little over an hour.

Witnessing the above scenes truly impressed the author with the importance of controlling the environment of the presentation.

DISCUSSION QUESTIONS

1. The advantages of getting the prospect to talk are well recognized, but
   how does a salesman manage to get a man to talk who seems to prefer to
   keep silent?
2. Why do people have difficulty listening?
3. What kinds of incidents cause the prospect or customer to lose confidence in the salesman?
4. Give your reasons for not being convinced by some tests of products as
   presented on television commercials. If you were not convinced of their
   honesty, did this have any effect on your confidence in the product?
5. What are the various factors which can cause the salesman to lose control of the interview?
6. If a prospect continues to disbelieve what you say after you have done
   everything possible to prove your claims, what do you then do?
7. A salesman of cement has tried for years to get a large ready-mix operator to switch a portion of his purchases to his firm instead of pooling them
   all with another large competitor. Both firms offer the same price, have
   identical products, and give the same services. He has been working on
   the idea that the buyer should not be completely dependent on one supplier, but the prospect fails to see the disadvantages of his policy in contrast to some of the intangible benefits of being a very large account to
   one supplier. How would you go about making this prospect believe your
   contention?
8. You are an executive vice-president of a large advertising agency in New
   York. You are making a presentation to a large food account to solicit its
   business, which amounts to $7,500,000 in billings a year. The competition
   for this account is fierce. You are trying to get across to the prospect that
   your agency will render his account more service and furnish more imaginative ideas than any other agency. Naturally, the competitors are trying
   to say something along the same lines. How would you go about proving
   your ability to make money for this prospect?
9. You are a junior executive with a large firm, and you desire increased
   responsibilities (a promotion) and more money. You are faced with the

problem of making your superiors believe you are not only worth it but that, if it is not forthcoming, they may face the problem of doing without your services. How would you get them to believe these claims?

10. It was claimed that the salesman should avoid making the sale appear as if it is a battle. What do salesmen do that give the presentation a battle flavor?

CASES

Here are five situations in which salesmen found themselves embarrassed. Analyze each, and tell where each man made his mistakes.[2]

CASE 10-1   THE ABSENT ORDER

Visiting a large corporation, Jack decided on the spur of the moment to drop in on one of the customer's four buyers. The buyer, normally a rather gruff man, obviously was swamped with work; there was a mountain of papers on his desk. Jack had no real reason for visiting, except to remind the buyer of his existence. But, as he sat down, Jack thought of a subject he could talk about.

"A couple of weeks ago," he said, "you put through an inquiry on our price for a half-dozen units. We quoted you a figure, and I wondered if you've decided to take any action on it."

"Did *I* put the inquiry through?" asked the buyer. "I don't remember."

"Yes. I'm pretty sure it was you."

"It might have been So-and-so, the buyer down the hall."

"No, I think it came from your office," Jack insisted.

"Have you a record of it?"

"I'll see," said Jack. He opened his brief case, which was on the floor, and leafed through a stack of papers while the buyer impatiently tapped his fingers on the desk. Unable to find the record, Jack pulled the brief case onto his lap, took out three envelopes stuffed with more papers and emptied each of them.

"I can't seem to find it," he said. "Perhaps the inquiry came in by phone."

"I still don't remember it," said the buyer.

Jack stood up and said, lamely, "When I get back to the office, I'll see if I can find a record of it."

[2] These were taken from Lassor Blumenthal, "A Portfolio of Six Serious Mistakes," *The American Salesman*, July, 1960, pp. 66–71.

By this time, the buyer had turned away to talk to an assistant who'd just walked in. He barely heard Jack say good-by, and probably didn't notice that he left with a look of pained embarrassment on his face.

CASE 10-2   THE MISSING ORDER

Henry knew he was in trouble the minute he walked into the p.a.'s office. The office, located in Chicago, was buying headquarters for six plants in the South and Middlewest.

"Henry," snapped the purchasing agent, "you promised that 40-barrel delivery to the Indiana plant a week ago, and they haven't gotten it yet. Are you people tired of our business?"

"You haven't gotten it yet? That's strange. You know we've always made a point of rush deliveries to your plants."

"I don't know anything about that," said the p.a. "The point is, we didn't get the order."

"I'll check with them as soon as I get back to the office and find out why," Henry promised.

"Never mind," answered the p.a. "I can't wait any longer. I'll phone the plant and tell them to order it from a local distributor."

CASE 10-3   SOME GOSSIP

It was 9 A.M. when Pete dropped into the office of a buyer who invited him to have a cup of coffee. While they drank, the buyer remarked, "I see where your company's really making a name for itself in this morning's headlines."

"Oh?" said Pete. "I haven't seen the paper this morning. What happened?"

"Nothing much; your president's son seems to have been too attentive to a neighbor's wife, and he got in a brawl with the husband. The cops arrested both of them."

"Good Lord," said Pete, "that's awful."

"Do all your executives lead such complicated lives?" asked the buyer.

"Well, I guess he must have got involved in a triangle," said Pete unhappily.

"Does he make a habit of getting that sort of publicity?"

"Not as far as I know. Of course, he's the boss's only son, and perhaps he was a little spoiled when he was a kid. I guess it's just that he hasn't really settled down yet."

"I wonder if this will hurt his chances to succeed his old man as president," said the buyer.

"Well, it could have happened to anyone," Pete replied. "Remember a couple of years ago when So-and-so (he named an officer of a competitor's company) ran away with his maid?"

"Yes, I remember. I guess that the men at the top of both your companies are a bunch of cutups."

CASE 10-4 THE TOUCHY TECHNICIAN

"Bill, I've had a complaint from downstairs," said the purchasing agent. "Those new gears of yours have burned out after only two weeks. You told me they were guaranteed to last for at least six months; that's the only reason I was willing to pay your premium price."

"That's odd," said the salesman. "Suppose we go down to the shop and take a look at them."

Bill and the p.a. descended a flight of narrow concrete steps to the shop and walked over to a machine that stood idle. As Bill opened a panel and examined the gears, Harry, the shop foreman, ambled over.

Poking a finger at the gears, Bill said, "They're burned out, all right. It looks to me as if you've been running them much faster than you should."

The shop foreman frowned. "We've been running them at the same speed as always," he said. "Yours just don't seem to be able to stand up any better than the ones we've been using."

"I just don't understand it," Bill replied. "But we'll send down an engineer to put in a new set."

"Why not hold off on that for a while?" suggested the buyer. "We still have some of the old gears in inventory and we'll use those for the time being. . . ."

CASE 10-5 THE PERFECT PRESENTATION

Fred's firm had created a beautiful flip-chart presentation, which showed in step-by-step fashion how its product was assembled and how it outperformed everything else on the market. Fred had rehearsed the talk that went with the presentation until he knew exactly when to speed up his delivery, when to slow down, and when to ask questions that were bound to get affirmative answers. He had already made half a dozen successful calls when he went in to see one of his toughest accounts.

"I don't have much time, Fred," warned the p.a.

"This will take about ten minutes," said Fred.

"OK, but make it fast."

Fred began his talk, carefully pointing out the main feature on each page of the presentation. After he'd gone through about five pages, the p.a. interrupted.

"You don't have to go through all that with me, Fred. I'm very pressed for time and I know your stuff is good. What I want to know is how you hook it into the machinery we're already using."

"If you'll bear with me until I get through this section," Fred replied, "I'll get to that point. But there are a couple of facts you ought to know first."

"Look," said the buyer, "I'm going away on vacation at the end of the week and I really don't have time to hear the whole thing now. Why don't you wait until I get back? . . ."

CASE 10-6 TOM SCOTT:
Developing a Convincing Demonstration

Tom Scott had been a salesman for a window-glass retailer for less than a year when his supervisor called him into the office for a conference. After the usual pleasantries were exchanged, he said, "Tom, you seem to be having some trouble selling shatterproof plate. You're far below quota on that line. What do you think the trouble is?"

Tom knew what the manager had said was true. He seemed to have a great deal of trouble convincing people who needed shatterproof plate for patio doors to buy it. He replied, "I just can't seem to make them believe that the benefits are worth the extra money. Sometimes I feel that they just don't believe that safety glass really works."

"Do you believe it's a good product?"

Tom was somewhat startled by the question, but recovered to answer, "Certainly!"

"Why?"

"What do you mean why?" Tom asked.

"I mean why do you think it's a good product?"

Tom wondered about the line of questioning, but said, "Because you said it was."

"Suppose I lied? Then what?"

Not knowing what to say, Tom said nothing. But it was to no avail. The manager pressed Tom to make his point, "Why don't you take this morning off and find out whether or not I lied to you."

"How can I do that?" Tom asked.

"That's your problem. Now haul it out of here and be back for lunch."

Tom left to ponder his plight.

At 12:02 an apprehensive Tom returned to his manager's office.

"Well, did I lie?"

"No, sir. It's a marvelous product," Tom replied.

"What makes you think so?"

"I tested it."

"How?"

"I broke some regular glass and then broke the safety plate. The safety plate can't cut you up," Tom explained.

"And that proved it to you?"

"Yes!"

"Then let's have lunch."

"But what's all this got to do with convincing customers?" Tom asked.

"Son, if you can't figure that out don't bother coming in tomorrow— you'll starve to death in sales. Go pump gas somewhere."

1. How can Tom use his experience to make people believe what he says about safety plate?

THE PRESENTATION: II

Plan your work, work your plan.
Anon.

Only salesmen who have had to develop a sales presentation appreciate the difficulty of doing so. Presentations don't just happen. Only rank amateurs walk unprepared into a sale with the intention of "winging" it extemporaneously. While it might appear to the casual observer that the professional salesman is not following a plan, his years of preparation, training, and experience combined with his talent give his performance a natural appearance that can be deceiving.

Effective sales presentations are developed over time using techniques that have been proven to work. All presentations should be planned; only the extent and rigidity of the plans are in question. Some sales presentations should be planned minutely to fit a particular situation, while other sales are not worthy of special planning but may be approached with a standard or "canned" or prepared presentation. Some interviews can be held to a fairly rigid pattern, while others must be conducted with great flexibility.

SHOULD THE SALES TALK BE MEMORIZED?

The memorized, standardized, or "canned" presentation is used by many salesmen selling a variety of products, because it enables them to make the demonstration clearer and more complete, to win the buyer's confidence and more effectively eliminate competition. But many other salesmen scorn the standardized talk and rely instead on the inspiration of the moment to guide their presentations. Why this variation in methods? Why the arguments that have continued vigorously for decades on this point? Regarding the violence of the discussion, the editor of *Printers' Ink* says:

If you wish to get yourself into a fistic controversy, just drop in casually where half a dozen sales managers are assembled and dogmatically declare that you believe every salesman should be obliged to use a memorized sales talk. It is a safe bet that you will spend a lively few minutes.

Prior to about 1890 the attitude prevailed that a salesman must possess a fluent tongue, a "gift of gab," in order to succeed. Extemporaneous eloquence was a *sine qua non* of successful salesmanship. But President John Patterson of the National Cash Register Company insisted in 1894 that his representatives memorize the contents of a little book which he rather tactlessly called a "primer,"[1] and which contained the sales arguments for his product. A vast improvement in salesmanship resulted in greatly increased sales, which led other manufacturers to insist that their salesmen should also memorize their presentations. The theory was that there must be one best way to sell a thing, just as there is one best way to handle a piece of work on a lathe, and that if this were true no other way could be so good. The "scientific management" movement in production had an influence on the vogue for selling in the one best way.

It was strenuously contended that few speakers could make as effective an appeal extemporaneously as after careful preparation. The actor feels the necessity for preparation and rehearsal; the lecturer memorizes his lecture and constantly aims to improve his diction; the debater gathers arguments and commits them to memory; and even the preacher appreciates that "the Lord helps those who help themselves" in preparing a message for his flock.

The point is made by advocates of the prepared sales talk that the salesman is able to deliver his talk more spontaneously and with more fire if he is free to devote his attention to the *method of delivery* rather than to a *search for words*. He can "size up" the prospect as the sale proceeds and plan his campaign as he talks. Without a prepared sales talk he could not do this.

---

[1] Patterson had not been happy with the overall sales performance of his men; however, there had been one man with an outstanding record. He called that man into his office and directed him to write down his sales presentation. After looking it over, he directed the rest of the sales force to use the same presentation.

Additional points in favor of the standardized presentation are:

- It covers all the ground, leaving no gaps. It does not leave a salesman wishing he had remembered to bring up certain points which might have clinched the sale. It is complete.
- It insures a logical order in the sales talk. The prospect is led from one point to another easily, the whole presentation building itself up into an effective pattern.
- It saves time for the salesman and for the prospect.
- It enables the beginner to sell effectively, whereas he would fail if left to his own devices.
- It gives the salesman more confidence when he knows that he is prepared for a complete presentation.

DEVELOPING A PREPARED PRESENTATION

Progress in standardizing the sales talk has been rapid in recent years. There are numerous sales consultants who help sales managers standardize their salesmen's presentations. These men operate something like this:

They accompany the salesmen in the field, watching their every word and move. For example, in working with the salesmen for a food company the consultant broke down the salesmen's operations into 354 different elements—different things that the salesmen did and said.

After this list was compiled, the next step was to reduce it to a code, for the company did not want the men to know that their performance was being checked. Trained, experienced observers then memorized this code. When they had mastered it, they went into the field. An observer would ride a day with a salesman, recording in code at each stop everything that the salesman did and said and what sales he made.

Next, the facts revealed by these records were tabulated—for each salesman—that is, the frequency with which he did each of these 354 things. This disclosed what the average frequency was on each point.

Then a comparison was made—in dollars and cents—of the volume of the men who did that thing more often than average with the volume of the men who did it less than the average.

Step by step in this analysis the 354 different things were measured in their relation to volume—in dollars and cents. And 95 percent of them turned out to have no direct relation to the size of the order.

But when this study was finished, the company got a brief, simple list of 16 selling methods that were important—the key methods that, beyond any question, really controlled the volume of their salesmen.

As an illustration of what may be meant by one of the key methods mentioned, it was found that a force of salesmen for a food jobber would do better if they suggested to the dealer the quantity that he ought to buy instead of leaving the decision up to him. Only 15 percent of the men made a practice of offering this suggestion, but the average order of these men was 300 percent larger than the average order of the salesmen who failed to employ this method.

Other standardized presentations have been worked out by having some of a firm's best salesmen dictate their sales talks to tape recorders, then picking out the best features of the various efforts and combining them into one strong presentation. Others have merely adopted the sales talk of their best salesman. This is not recommended, as it will probably reflect too strongly the personal traits of the salesman. Also, he may have the best sales record because he has the best territory or gives the best service, and not because he uses the best sales techniques.

On the other hand

Arguments *against* the standardized presentation are advanced by many successful salesmen who contend that the committal of a sales talk to memory is suicidal, that it makes a phonograph of a man, that it destroys initiative and places a premium upon mediocrity. They insist that a memorized, recited sales talk lacks punch, that it is likely to be delivered in a mechanical, "singsong" manner which robs it of vitality. Further, they point out that the salesman who is dependent upon a memorized presentation will lack the ability to meet interruptions, that he will be thrown off stride by the buyer who insists on asking questions and raising objections. But their chief criticism is that selling can never be standardized, because conditions are seldom the same. They claim that it is necessary to vary each interview considerably to meet differing conditions, that no two buyers can be handled alike.

No doubt elements of truth underlie these attitudes although most salesmen exaggerate the variations that they introduce into their presentations under different circumstances. An interesting experiment was performed by a Pittsburgh sales manager upon one of these objecting salesmen—a man who refused to memorize his sales talk and who boasted that he used entirely different tactics with different prospects. Arrangements were made with a number of prospects on whom the salesman was to call, the plans including the concealment of an expert shorthand operator in each office, where every word of salesman and prospect could be taken down. The prospects selected for the test were purposely chosen for their differences, with the idea of determining whether the salesman really did vary his techniques appreciably.

The results of the experiment were typed and handed to the salesman, the method by which the interviews had been reported being at the same time explained to him. He was left to follow his own judgment as to whether or not he would change his methods after looking over the "evidence." Following a careful perusal of the reports this salesman frankly confessed that he had no idea that his presentation was so similar on all occasions and, further, that it was so poor. He had sincerely believed that his methods varied widely and was chagrined to discover that they did not. He confessed that his presentation would be greatly improved by preparing it in advance.

A compromise
There is a middle ground for those people who rebel at the complete regimentation required by a "canned" presentation.

A salesman is less likely to allow his sales talk to wear itself into a rut if he organizes his arguments under the various buying motives, keeping in mind that he must be alert to discover which buying motives should be appealed to, and marshaling his talking points to support this appeal. In this way he is practically certain to avoid using the same presentation over and over—much more likely, in fact, to avoid a stereotyped effect and to achieve spontaneity than if he were to present his arguments with no thought of logical sequence or applicability to the task at hand.

Each talking point may be carefully worked out, rendered more effective by the use of analogy, metaphor, and other devices of the orator or debater; it may be reconstructed and polished as to diction; the delivery may be studied and the effort strengthened greatly as compared with an impromptu presentation. Then, if it seems desirable, the section may be committed to memory.

If a salesman attempts to work out his own standardized presentation he should do two things:

He should write it out in complete detail and then edit it carefully.

He should, when he thinks it is in final shape, speak it into a tape recorder and then play it back over and over. He will probably do some radical revision on his written copy, after which he can again make a recording of his new effort.

The presentation is not an occasion for an oration: it should be delivered not as though learned by rote and recited, but with all the earmarks of spontaneity and of being purely extemporaneous. The cast-iron sales talk is likely to be too rigid, too inflexible for many situations.

But for important points, power phrases, and probably the various closing efforts, most salesmen will do well to rely on word-for-word presentations. As has been said, "If you're playing the guitar just for fun, you can play by ear in your own way; but if you're playing for money, you'd better learn to play by note."

The salesman should organize his presentation more on the lines of a debate than an oration.[2] The debater has his material organized on cards, filed under the proper headings, and has each argument committed to memory. He does not expect to be compelled to use every argument in any debate, but he has a reservoir of arguments into which he can dip whenever the need arises. In this way he presents his constructive argument and his rebuttal in telling fashion, meeting the objections of the opposition and appealing to the various judges and the audience as seems wise. His talk flows on smoothly, however, for he has thoroughly mastered each point in advance.

Delivery

We have just used the terms "debate" and "oration." The effective sales talk is neither; it is far more like a friendly conversation between two people desirous of finding a solution to the problem confronting the prospect—a problem which the salesman has made his own and for which he believes he has a solution.

It cannot be too strongly emphasized that when a standardized sales talk is used, the salesmen should be carefully coached in the technique of its delivery. It is silly to think that because an actor or a salesman has learned his lines, he is ready to play his part. The concerns that have been most successful with standardized talks have taken great pains to insure the *effective delivery* of those talks. Merely memorizing the *words* is not enough. This coaching in delivery does two things: it prevents the talk from sounding like a memorized "piece" being recited by the salesman, and it places emphasis where it belongs. Tricks of dropping the voice, meeting the eye of the prospect squarely at certain points, slowing the tempo, and many other little devices of the skilled speaker can be incorporated in the talk, adding greatly to its effectiveness. Also, various items of "stage business" may be included, such as the use of sketches to illustrate certain points, the demonstration of the article, display of the firm's advertising, the showing of letters from happy customers. All these should be as carefully worked out in advance as is the verbal portion of the presentation.

Too few concerns have recognized the importance of this; they have stopped halfway in their training program. They have told their salesmen *what* to say without telling them *how* to say it. This partial training has given rise to much of the opposition to the standardized presentation, many salesmen and buyers receiving the impression that a letter or phonograph

---

[2] It should not, however, be inferred that a sales interview is to be considered a debate between prospect and salesman. This discussion is merely designed to indicate the principles underlying the preparation of the talking points and their organization.

record would do as well as a salesman who was reciting his piece in a singsong fashion.

To what extent should the presentation be memorized?

First, there is the salesman himself. Some people are gifted with the power of rapid thought and well-nigh faultless expression, but most salesmen may safely assume that preparation will improve their presentations. The experienced salesman, however, may take liberties with the standardized talk; after he has thoroughly mastered it in its original form, he may alter it to suit his own personality. There is a real possibility that a standardized presentation may "cramp his style" and that by departing somewhat from it he may increase its effectiveness. He may even develop a sales talk good enough to be adopted as a "standard" presentation by other salesmen.

For the inexperienced salesman, however, the standardized presentation is a boon. Without it he would find it difficult to get started and would become discouraged and quit. Firms using green salesmen as house-to-house canvassers find it necessary to provide them with sales talks in complete form or the majority will not stick to their jobs beyond the first week.

Second, the type of article being sold or the character of the proposition will play a role in deciding the amount of memorization advisable. A complicated commodity like an adding machine or an automobile will require more elaborate preparation on the part of the salesman than will a simple product, such as flour. Likewise, a salesman handling a variety of goods, as the jobber's salesman, will find it difficult to memorize a talk for each item. In this connection it should be mentioned, however, that many staple salesmen selling a large line of goods work up little sales talks for particular products that they wish to push on that trip. With these in mind they more effectively get their orders started than by merely inquiring, "What do you need today?"

A commodity made up according to buyer's specifications cannot, of course, be sold by the use of rigid presentations, as conditions here vary widely with the desired end use of the product.

A *third* variable factor in the matter of a memorized sales talk is the character of the buyer. As a general proposition, the experienced buyer, the hardened purchasing agent, will not "fall for" the memorized lines as surely as the buyer who is less experienced in dealing with highly trained salesmen. The professional buyer is familiar with the ways and wiles of the salesman. He sees through the devices easily; he is less influenced by methods and more by the actual merits of the proposition as he analyzes it for himself.

It must also be confessed that some buyers take delight in trying to trip the salesman and, when they see that his talk is learned by rote, make every effort to entangle and upset him. The average amateur buyer allows

courtesy to prevent such behavior even though he suspects that the salesman is merely speaking a piece.

A *fourth* factor is the frequency with which the salesman must call on
the same customer. Obviously, the salesman for a wholesale grocery house,
calling every two weeks on the same retailers, could not recite the same
speech each time. But he could perhaps work up little selling talks for
certain items, as already suggested.

With these points all in mind, it will be easy to settle upon the degree
or extent to which any salesman should be required to memorize his presentation. In the majority of cases the most satisfactory procedure will be to
prepare carefully arguments to appeal to each buying motive, answers to
every possible objection, ways of opening and closing the sale, and then
memorize these. The result is a happy compromise—a presentation at the
same time polished and flexible. The salesman is able to reach into his
mind and select just the arguments needed to meet the situation, finding
each one like a fine tool, sharpened and adjusted to the work at hand. His
presentation is not stiff or stilted, but at the same time it presents his
proposition in the strongest manner yet developed.

THE PERFECT-PRODUCT COMPARISON

One method which aids not only in completeness but also in the clarity of
a sales demonstration is the "perfect-product comparison" technique.

A buyer for a baby equipment store was approached by the salesman
for a baby walker manufacturer with the following appeal:

From your experience, you realize that the ideal baby walker must, above all,
be safe. Yet it should be inexpensive and easy for the baby to get around in,
easy to clean, lightweight, and easy to store. Finally, it should be adjustable to
fit children of different sizes and durable enough to take the beating that such
products are inevitably given. Now let's see how my product stacks up against
these specifications.

The salesman would then proceed to show the buyer how his product
compared with those standards. Obviously, a salesman would be unwise if
his claims for the product in comparison to the perfect product were too
sweeping. No prospect would be likely to place confidence in a salesman
who claimed that his article was absolutely without flaw or drawback of
any kind.

APPRAISAL OF THE SITUATION

While some sales interviews may run smoothly with the salesman following his memorized or organized presentation, quite often he finds that he
must depart from his routine. Sometimes he can forecast this, if his preap-

proach has been carefully done; but frequently he must change his prede-
termined strategy and tactics to meet some sudden and unexpected development. Perhaps the salesman had planned to conclude the sale after
several interviews only to find upon calling that the prospect is on the verge
of buying a competitor's product. An immediate change of strategy is called
for under those circumstances. Perhaps the salesman was anticipating a
very tough time with some prospect who on the surface appeared to be
highly sales resistant. However, midway in the presentation the salesman
senses that the prospect is ready to buy. This calls for an immediate change
in plans. The salesman must never allow himself to become so chained to
his presentation plans that he ignores all signals warning him to change
them. Flexibility is a *must* in selling.

The term applied to this philosophy is *situational selling*. It means that
the salesman must be prepared to meet any situation he encounters and
cannot become so attached to a certain pattern of action that some devi-
ations in the prospect's reaction will throw him off stride. This concept of
situational selling is in sharp contrast to *canned selling* in which the salesman follows a certain preset course of action and tries to force the prospect
to go along with him.

The element of *timing* may force the salesman to change his strategy.
That is, his call may not be well timed; the prospect may be in a violently
unreceptive frame of mind. A steel salesman told of the occasion when he
nearly lost an old account because he was unfortunate enough to be calling
upon the purchasing agent after he had been severely reprimanded by his
superior. The purchasing agent began berating the salesman for not giving
him a better deal; he was attempting to transfer the blame for his troubles
to someone else. The salesman began to defend himself, but quickly realized that the man merely wanted a scapegoat and that it accomplished
nothing for the salesman to defend the company's policies. Instead, he
wisely withdrew as gracefully as possible, carefully avoiding any argument.

People may buy readily before Christmas, but may be toughly resistant when they are making out their income tax returns. When a business
is doing well, the buyer will give salesmen a better hearing than when the
business is in a slump.

Industrial salesmen find this factor of timing particularly important, as
many industries are seasonal, and buying is done only at certain times.

SITUATIONAL STRATEGIES
Certain out-of-the-ordinary situations may arise often enough to prompt
the wise salesman to plan in advance his strategies for handling them.
There are eight basic strategies with which to handle such situations, and
the salesman should be master of them all because prospects differ widely.

Given identical situations with different customers, the salesman should vary his way of handling them because of personality differences, the salesman's rapport with the customer, and the particular circumstances of the customer. Suppose that an order is two weeks overdue and the customer calls the salesman to complain about it. In one case the salesman might be safe if he simply gave the reasons for the delay, while in another instance he would be wise if he immediately took action to expedite the order. The customer's need for the goods might explain the difference in actions taken.

In another situation involving late shipments, but in this case with the same customer at different times, the salesman might break his back expediting a critical shipment of toys for the Christmas season, while doing much less on a shipment during a less critical time of the year.

Ignore the static

There are situations in which the salesman should ignore outside static and go right ahead with his presentation. Many times this is the proper course to follow with people who are not serious about what they say or whose statements have no relevance to the presentation.

A tough old construction superintendent might growl, "If I bought any dozer that looked that pretty, the boys would think I'm gettin' soft and senile." Knowing the personality of the buyer and the way in which the statement was made, the salesman might feel perfectly safe in ignoring it. Or he might acknowledge that he is listening by remarking, "You getting soft and senile? Everybody knows that'll be the same day hell freezes over!" and then he would go right on with the presentation.

A cosmetic salesman walked into a buyer's office only to be greeted with a blast, "You have your nerve even showing up here again after what you did to me last time." Lesser men might quake and run under such fire, but this man knows better; he waits for what comes next. "You know that new lipstick you sold me? Well, its no good! I can't keep it in stock. Fool customers keep buying the junk for some weird reason. What are you trying to do? Work me to death?" Yes, some customers do have peculiar senses of humor. Many just like to give the salesman a lot of static and the salesman must learn to go along with it.

Agree and act

There are many times when the salesman should agree with the prospect and do something about it. Suppose the cosmetic buyer followed up her opening blast with, "You know that new lipstick you sold me? Well, it melts! Here, look at this!"

The situation calls for action. The representative should say, "You're absolutely right. Lipstick should not melt like that. Send it back and I'll have a credit memo made out to you. Or would you prefer that I take it with me? I'm eager to find out exactly what happened with this shipment because I know for a fact that the company thoroughly tests it for just such environmental factors as heat, cold, and dampness. I really appreciate your bringing it to our attention."

This strategy should be used whenever possible, for it makes the customer a hero; people like to be told they are right and have others take strong positive actions on their complaints.

The challenge

Sometimes it is best not to let the prospect get away with irresponsible statements or complete untruths; the salesman should challenge such claims. While great care must be exercised in using this strategy, there are times when it is needed.

A loud-mouth prospect shouts, "I heard you guys give rotten service." The salesman knows that this is not at all true, and so he might ask, "I would appreciate it if you would tell me from whom you heard such an outlandish statement. I am not worried about your now holding that view because I know I can prove to you beyond any doubt that we have excellent service, but I want to find and rectify whatever misunderstandings someone else has about our service." Usually the prospect will fold his cards in face of such a statement because he was bluffing, trying to throw the salesman onto the defensive and shake him up a bit.

Care must be taken not to criticize the prospect himself; never call him a liar no matter how clear-cut a case of prevarication it might be. Once a man has had his integrity challenged he is not likely to buy under any circumstances: Let the man save face by always blaming a third party for planting "misstatements" in his mind.

There are times when an account or prospect will persist with a lie. "I tell you these things were damaged when they came in! We didn't touch them." If the salesman wishes to keep this account he will have to give the customer credit despite the fact that the goods had obviously been tampered with. It is not good salesmanship to go around proving your customers are liars.

Mitigating circumstances

Many times what the customer or prospect says is true as far as it goes, but there are other aspects to the situation. "I heard that your firm gives lousy service." The salesman might have the reply, "Yes, I suppose that is one way to look at it. But we do it with your interests in mind. You know service costs money: takes lots of people with lots of parts waiting for something to go wrong. Well, things don't seem to go wrong that often with our product. We've found that we can service from headquarters the relatively few repair requests we have and save you a lot of money doing it. You know X company's price is higher and they have an annual service fee after the guarantee runs out. Let me show you the dollars you will save by doing it our way."

There almost always are mitigating circumstances involved in any situation, and if the salesman is sufficiently adroit he should be able to show a reasonable man the reasons for anything without making them sound like weak alibis.

An actual example: The salesman for Wall Streeter men's shoes was calling on one of his dealers. During the sale the merchant complained, "You know delivery of our special orders have really been bad these past two months."

The salesman calmly explained, "Yes, I know they have and I think I can assure you that the situation will be cleared up shortly. As you know, we are but a small shoe maker so when the boss saw business was slowing up a few months back and he had $90,000 in inventory, he shut down the plant. If your orders were not in stock, they couldn't be shipped until the plant reopened and the shoes were made. But on top of that, he found out that his shutdown cost him some good men who went to work elsewhere. So he has been having troubles getting the plant going again when business picked up. He now knows he was wrong to push the panic button so soon, but I guess it wasn't our money sitting in inventory."

The merchant smiled and said, "I want to thank you for the first straight, honest answer I have heard all week. The boys can tell you we've been involved in negotiating some leases in a shopping center all week and are tired of lies. Thanks for the fresh air." Needless to say, this salesman's rapport with the account was greatly strengthened by his honest answer stating the mitigating circumstances of a situation.

Withdrawal

Sometimes a strategic withdrawal is called for when a situation looks particularly explosive. It may be wise to let a man cool off before trying to deal with him. Perhaps the buyer has just had a battle with his superior which has left him looking for a scapegoat, and you are next in line. He may transfer the blame for his failure upon you and your products. There would be no arguing with him in such situations; better run for cover. Get out before you say something unfortunate that you will later regret.

This is not an invitation to run if the problem involves your products or your firm. The salesman had best be on the scene to defend himself and his wares when they are at issue.

Talk and play for time

The salesman frequently is wise if he asks for more details and encourages the buyer to relieve his mind. This is the best strategy for handling serious statements made by responsible people. It helps focus the discussion on the actual facts and gives the salesman time to think. Also, it lets the buyer unwind a bit and almost forces him to re-examine the whole picture. Frequently, after blowing off a lot of steam, the buyer will calm down and not demand any action; "I just wanted to let you know how I felt about it."

The strength of this strategy lies in its protection to the salesman; it helps to keep him from attempting an answer without complete information. Many times the buyer misstates his true feelings or thoughts, leaving the salesman to answer a phantom problem while the real one still blocks the buyer's mind. The more the buyer talks, the more likely it is the salesman can weather the storm.

Change the subject

Possibly the salesman can joke a bit or get the buyer to talk about something else. This is usually unwise when a serious topic is under discussion, but there are times for it. A buyer may ask, "Say, is it true that you guys are being bought out by the Apex Company?" If this is confidential information, the salesman might reply, jokingly, "I don't think they have enough money to buy us," or, "Naw, that's General Motors they are trying to buy out." Or he might change the subject by saying, "Say, before I forget it. Do you know of any old Apex machine around? I have a good customer who has one but can't get parts for it. He wants to buy a used one to cannibalize it."

Above all, the salesman should avoid appearing as if he is patronizing the buyer; for this reason, this strategy is dangerous to use. The truth, or what seems like it, usually is a better answer. The above salesman might be wiser to admit, "I really don't know. There's been no talk among our people about it and I fail to see why we would sell except for a frightful price."

Be a whipping boy

Your buyer errs; he ordered too much and now is on the hook with his superior for an overstocked condition. A salesman, able to place that overstock elsewhere, might offer, "I'm sorry. It's my fault. I should have caught that for you. How much do you need to get rid of? I'll try to place it for you." How can a buyer fail to like such a salesman? Don't be afraid to take the blame for something whether or not it is your responsibility, if the matter is relatively insignificant or can be remedied with ease.

Choosing the strategy

The successful use of strategy depends upon the wisdom with which the salesman chooses one for each situation. Many of the strategies mentioned above would be completely inappropriate under certain circumstances. If a prospect is serious about his statement, joking or laughing it off will prove disastrous. If the prospect is a chronic pessimist, many of his statements may be discounted. If a man is known to be a baiter of salesmen, many of his complaints may be ignored or laughed off. Key to the selection of the strategy is a correct appraisal of the prospect's personality. Naturally, the more a salesman calls on a man, the better he learns just how to handle him. He knows with whom he can joke and with whom he must be "all business." He knows the grouches and the playboys. As a general rule, it is best to treat all prospects' statements seriously until evidence indicates otherwise.

The interrupted interview

In spite of the salesman's efforts to stage the interview favorably, frequently the prospect will be interrupted in the midst of it. The telephone will ring, a subordinate will ask for instructions or make a report, a customer will enter the store, thereby breaking the continuity of the interview. Many a salesman has learned that this break may be disastrous for him, as it pulls the attention of the prospect elsewhere and halts the journey from decision to decision upon which the salesman is endeavoring to guide him.

Picture the prospect at his desk listening to the salesman. The telephone rings. A 5-minute conversation, evidently of considerable importance, ensues. At its conclusion the prospect swings back to face the salesman, but it is apparent that he is still pondering the matter discussed over the telephone. He cannot immediately transfer his attention to the salesman's message, even though he is willing to do so. The salesman must recognize this mental condition and make allowances for it or try to alter it. If the salesman does not handle this situation intelligently, his presentation will not be complete, because a gap will occur while the prospect's mind is mulling over the problem which caused the interruption. This gap must be filled.

One method of handling the problem is for the salesman to start the presentation again at once but, instead of continuing from the point at which the interruption occurred, to *review briefly the points last made.* This brings the prospect back gradually to the subject without leaving a gap in the presentation. Care must be taken to phrase the repeated points in new language so that the statements will not sound like a repetition. When it is evident to the salesman that the prospect's mind is again on the right track and traveling at the proper speed, he may proceed.

If the salesman can pick up a sample or an exhibit or a chart and hand it to the prospect, it may serve to pull his attention back to the matter in hand. An *action* may be better here than *words.*

When it appears that the interruption will offer the prospect an excuse for ending the interview, the salesman should have ready some forceful statement to use at this point to be sure that the interview is resumed. Indeed, the interruption is likely to prove permanent unless the salesman takes command of the situation *immediately* in a decided fashion, for the prospect is apt to feel that the break has given him an advantage, of which he is often quick to avail himself. If the salesman permits him to take the offensive after the recess, he is allowing himself to be put on the defensive—not a strategic position.

A question may be used at this point. It operates in the same way as a question put by a teacher to a student whose attention has been distracted. It serves to bring back that wandering attention to the subject as effectually as any device known in pedagogy and may be applied with equal success by the salesman, who, too, is fundamentally an educator.

Perhaps the salesman may start a discussion on a topic of mutual interest but foreign to his proposition, if he feels that there is scant chance of resuming the presentation favorably at once.

There will be times when the interruption has so distracted the prospect that it is hopeless to proceed. Under such conditions it is wise to stop trying to sell and to make an appointment to see him later, perhaps at his home or at lunch—some place where interruptions are less likely to occur.

In which stage is prospect's mind?
Early selling theorists recognized five stages the prospect's mind must traverse before he makes a buying decision: attention, interest, desire, conviction, and action. These stages were sometimes phrased as separate decisions which the prospect had to make.

Attention: I will hear this salesman.
Interest: I may be interested in this salesman's proposition.
Desire: I would like to have what the salesman is selling.
Conviction: I am confident this is a good deal for me.
Action: I will buy.

The prospect does not go through all five stages during every sale. He may have already passed through one or two or even four of them. For example, the woman who reads in a newspaper advertisement that a sale of fall coats is to start the next day enters the store having passed through the stages of attention and interest; the salesman's task now is to awaken her desire for a particular garment. Similarly the stage of confidence may have been passed before the salesman and prospect meet. The salesman for an automobile or a typewriter may not be compelled to develop confidence in his proposition, for the prospect may previously have owned one of the machines or have had a friend who vouched for its reliability. The customer in the drugstore who asks for a package of cigarettes by name has taken every step of the mental journey except the final one of action and enters the store prepared to take that.

But the real sale—the meeting of minds of salesman and prospect on a new proposition—requires the passage of the prospect's mind through each of these five stages. These steps need not, however, always be taken in the order given. If the salesman feels that both he and his proposition are unknown to his prospect, he may at the outset attempt to build a solid foundation of confidence before he tries to awaken desire or perhaps even to interest his prospect in the details of his proposition.

The skilled salesman will study to discover just how far his prospect has progressed on his journey, for it is unwise to begin the presentation at a point too far back. If the prospect already has complete confidence in the proposition, the salesman is injuring his chances by spending too much time in explaining his firm's reliability. Too much stress on these points arouses a suspicion that the salesman expected to be called upon to defend his house and its product. The prospect might feel that perhaps he ought to investigate more fully if the salesman so evidently feels the need for strengthening his case.

A salesman was sent to call on a man who had expressed interest in buying some law books by writing to the publisher. The salesman called; the prospect welcomed him; and the sale could have been concluded in 10 minutes had the salesman known where to start talking. But he started with his memorized presentation including a lengthy dissertation on the dignity of the legal profession and its opportunities for service and financial rewards. The prospect was an executive and director in a large manufacturing corporation and merely wanted to read up a little in the law that concerned his business; consequently he was not in the least interested in the salesman's picture of a lawyer's career. In 5 minutes he dismissed the stupid salesman with a curt, "I guess your books aren't what I want, after all. Good day."

HANDLING COMPETITION

Few sales are made without encountering competition of some sort. The salesman must be prepared to handle it, for if he isn't, he will give the prospect the idea that he can't. Certainly the prospect is aware of some competitive offers in most instances, but it is surprising the number of times a salesman will encounter a prospect who is unaware of some of the leading competitors in the field. Hence, the wise salesmen are reluctant to bring up the matter of competition for fear that they will be telling the prospect something he does not know.

A business executive was shopping for an inexpensive car for his son as a high school graduation present. He had been attracted to Saab by some advertising, so he dropped by a Saab dealership for a demonstration. Throughout the presentation the Saab salesman was preoccupied with relating how his product was superior to the Fiat and VW. It seemed to the prospect that in this salesman's mind the other two cars were serious competition; so the prospect decided that he had better check them out for himself even though he had been unaware of them previously. Let sleeping dogs . . . ! Hence:

Praise and pass on

Of the three views on the handling of competition, the *first* holds that salesmen should not mention their competitors except in praise. When and if the prospect brings up the matter of competition, praise it and pass on. "Yes, that is a good product. But ours is better! . . ." By ignoring competition entirely, the prospect is not led to consider the other fellow's proposition. The motto of the group seems to be, "Sell your own goods, and let the other guy sell his."

Unfortunately, this may not always be the best strategy. A competitive brand may loom large in the prospect's mind and ignoring it will do little to dislodge its place in the picture. In fact, some prospects will not bring up another product that is their favorite for fear that the salesman will show them the folly of their thinking. *There is security in silence.* If the salesman is to handle that competition, he will first have to get the prospect to bring it out and talk about it. Smart car salesmen determine the competitive setting early in a sale. They ask what other cars the prospects have seen and which they like best. "Of all the cars you have seen so far, which one do you like best?" The answer to this question provides a great deal of information to the perceptive salesman. If the prospect answers, "The Dodge Charger!" then it would be folly to try to push a four-door sedate sedan at him. Most car salesmen dread attempting a sale to prospects who have only begun to shop for cars because they know that no matter how good a deal is offered such prospects, they will still feel it necessary to look around. The wise car salesman prefers to get prospects after they have seen the other brands; then there is hope of closing a sale.

Meet it head on

The *second* viewpoint is that competition must be recognized and combated, that it cannot gracefully be ignored. Indeed, some advocates of the theory want a return to the day when competitors were not afraid to point out the weaknesses of the other's product. These stern old warriors feel that business has perhaps become too effete.

Some automobile manufacturers provide their dealers with confidential data showing in detail the points at which their car is superior to a certain competing car. Figures show comparative head room, horse power, etc. Nonstatistical facts are presented comparatively, so that the salesman can cover such details as door handles, rear bumper, windshield moldings, seat fabrics. Most prospects do not ask about these matters, but when one does, the salesman can be thoroughly prepared. Only when the prospect invites this comparison does the salesman indulge in it, but when this situation does arise, his ability to make such detailed comparisons may save a sale.

A salesman of men's work clothes is trying to sell to a dealer. The salesman's line has a new serged seam instead of the felled type. The dealer brings out from his stock a garment with felled seam and demands, "What's the matter with this seam?"

Salesman: "There's nothing the matter with it. The Army uses it. It wears as well as any seam you can put on a garment. But I can give you two reasons why *we* have quit using the felled seam. It doesn't lie as neatly as our serged seam, and it can't be repaired on an ordinary sewing machine. Our serged seam can be. Now, since this new seam wears just as well as the felled seam, looks better, and is more easily repaired, we feel sure it's going to sell more work clothes for you."

This is a far cry from the bitter, ranting knocking of competition indulged in by some salesmen. "You'd be nuts to buy that junk. Won't stand up. Repair bills every month. Hard to get quick service on it, too."

When it seems necessary to make a comparison between your product and a competitor's, such comparison should not be too detailed and try to cover every point. Rather, it is better to cover only those features which have seemed to interest your prospect the most. Four or five of these are usually sufficient. If your car prospect has dwelt on rear-end drag (he has a steep driveway) give him the figures on this point. If he tours a good deal, go into details on trunk room, air conditioning, gasoline consumption, reasons for easy riding. To cover *every* comparative advantage is to confuse him and kill his interest.

This involves knowing where your product is strong and your competitor's is weak. Better stick to these, if you can.

Some salesmen believe that it is shrewd to implant in the mind of a prospect a seed of doubt concerning a competing product. They may do this adroitly by telling something they have heard about it; or they may come out more frankly with their own opinion. If the salesman and prospect are well acquainted with each other, the salesman may be more frank than when they are strangers. But a seed of doubt, thus planted, may grow into a big doubt—big enough to prevent the purchase of the competing product.

However, this adverse comment by the salesman must have a basis in fact. Frequently the prospect may ask the competitor about this point and may receive such a convincing reply that his faith in the first salesman is shattered. But, if the reply is *not* convincing, the first salesman may gain the prospect's confidence and make the sale.

Recognize but handle with care

A *third* view lies somewhere between the extremes. It is doubtless wise to avoid vigorous "knocking" of competitors, and yet it seems impossible to ignore them completely. Knocking competitors creates the impression that the salesman is finding competition pretty keen, is feeling it strongly. The inference is that he feels so antagonistic toward the other fellow largely because he has suffered much at his hands. The next step in the prospect's reasoning is, "If this fellow loses so much business to his competitor, probably this competitor has a good proposition. I ought to look into it."

Another result of too vigorous criticism of competitors is to destroy confidence in the proposition in general. Back in the days when life insurance was newer, two rival solicitors in a small Illinois town agreed to a debate in the local "opera house." They had been so bitter in their denunciations of each other that the debate attracted a large crowd. The debaters devoted almost their entire time to pointing out the weaknesses, crookedness, and general evils of the opposing insurance companies. They provided much entertainment for the citizenry; but when the debate was over, nobody in town dared to buy insurance from either company.

The principle also applies to retail selling when salesmen attack the reliability of their competitors. A young man lived in a small town that supported but two jewelry stores. He wanted to buy a diamond ring—*the* diamond ring. The demand was actively present. Each dealer cast so many aspersions upon the integrity of his competitor that the young man concluded that, inasmuch as he knew so little about diamonds and there was so large a chance to be deceived as to the stone's real value, he would do better to patronize neither local dealer but go to a jeweler in a neighboring city.

A purchasing agent relates an incident of a salesman's knocking a competitor which illustrates the disastrous result (to the salesman):

> I was in the market for a supply of shipping cases. Bids were received, including one from a firm with which I had done considerable business and one from another company with which I had not so good an acquaintance but which bore a fine reputation. A salesman from the first firm put in his appearance and asked me what concerns were bidding. I told him, although I refrained from mentioning prices. Immediately he started in, "Well, of course, you know Jim is a good fellow, but can he deliver the goods as you want them? His factory is small, and I am not too sure of his methods. Can he give you what you want? You know he has not had much experience with your product." And so on.
>
> Good-natured knocking in a way, but knocking nevertheless. What was the result? I was filled with curiosity to see the inside of Jim's factory and to talk it over with him, so I made an inspection tour. He got the order and, incidentally, did a good job. There was a simple case of a man selling his competitor's goods, for it was really his discouraging comments that created in me a curiosity to go and see for myself, with an outcome extremely disappointing to the knocker.

The deadly comparison

Some manufacturers of mechanical products train their salesmen to make a point-by-point comparison between their product and the one competing product which stands highest in the prospect's opinion. They do this on paper, too, putting down each point and checking, in one of the two columns, which of the two products is superior on that point. When the process is finished, it is expected that the salesman's product will have more check marks in its column than the competing product does. This is bare-fisted selling but it is sometimes necessary and effective, especially if the comparisons are made in a fair and objective manner.

A variation of this method is to take a sheet of paper and draw a line down the middle, making two columns. Put the name of the competing product at the top of one column and your product at the top of the other. Then put the price of each—as, $2.20 and $2.50—in the proper column. The competing product is the cheaper, so the salesman's task is to justify the higher price. He therefore mentions one *exclusive* feature of his product and says: "Would you say that this feature would be worth $1 a year to you? That's a very conservative estimate, isn't it? All right, this will last much longer than 10 years, but let's be conservative again and say it will last 10 years. That's $10 benefit you get from this feature." Thus the salesman proceeds feature by feature until he has built up value exceeding the $30 difference in price.

In cases where the prospect has already bought from a competitor, the salesman must exercise care in making his comments on his competitor's proposition, for to criticize it is to question the taste or judgment of the prospect who purchased. Tact must be used, as the salesman for office filing equipment realized when he tried to persuade a prospect to change his system completely and install a new one costing nearly $2,000. He did not make the prospect feel that he had shown a lack of acumen in installing the first system; rather he complimented him on it but showed tactfully how enlarged business, changed conditions, and new inventions in the way of equipment now made a change desirable.

Transfer blame

Perhaps the blame for a previous poor purchase may be placed on the competitor or his salesman, thus making it appear that the former did not have the true interests of the buyer at heart. The shoe salesman, finding a customer wearing a shoe a size too short and a width too wide, might win the confidence of that customer by commenting, "The man who sold you these shoes must have been short of time or of shoes. You have an aristocratic foot; narrow and with a high arch. Let me show you the difference between this shoe and the one your foot requires."

Backhanded compliment

When comparisons are called for, the salesman should assume an air of fairness to his competitors, perhaps admitting something good about them that is undeniably true. For instance, the automobile salesman might say, "The Subsonic Eight is good in many ways. It certainly is handsome, and the local dealer tries hard. But did you ever consider the problem of touring? The man who drives around the country a bit wants to be near reliable service at all times, for with any car he can encounter trouble. You want to drive a car that is well represented throughout the country, so that you won't have to lay up in some town a week waiting for a part to come from the factory. We have 7,000 dealers as compared with only 3,000 for the Subsonic Eight. This gives the drivers of our car a tremendous advantage."

Testimonials

Testimonials may perhaps be used in combating the claims of competitors or in proving that the salesman's product is superior to a competing one. Office appliance salesmen are compelled to meet inquiries about competing devices. The sales manager equips each salesman with a loose-leaf binder filled with facsimile letters from satisfied users. When a prospect asks, "But will this stand up under hard use like the Blank machine?" the salesman merely has to open to the testimonial letter from a shoe manufacturer who wrote that, "After using both machines for several years, we have standardized on (the salesman's machine) because of its relative freedom from trouble." It is better to let some qualified outsider claim superiority for a product than for the salesman himself to do so. Tests by universities, the U.S. Bureau of Standards, and similar institutions are effective when used in this connection.

Tests

Sometimes, if competition grows keen, it is necessary to resort to a frank competitive test of merit between the competing products, as is done in selling agricultural implements, paint, calculating machines, etc.

Nothing is as effective in selling as a side-by-side test of products provided your product's performance is such that its superiority can be perceived by the prospect as worthy of his purchase. It would be rather pointless to prove that one car was faster than another if the prospect had a dislike of speed.

Competitive intelligence

Another reason for paying attention to competitors is pointed out by a manufacturer, who says:

I don't believe in competitive salesmanship with the trade, but I am convinced that it is the greatest mistake in the world to dodge discussing competition with my own salesmen. I used to "tend to my own knitting" so hard that I didn't know half that was going on in the field. Now I ask all my salesmen to send as quickly as possible any new competitive products which appear in their territories.

This mere willingness to look into the other fellow's goods has a tonic effect on our men. It shows at least that I don't propose to be caught napping; and if there's anything that discourages salesmen, it's having competing articles constantly discussed by the trade while "the house goes on sleeping."

We believe thoroughly in letting all the facts come out. A salesman on the road is constantly hearing about the other fellow's good points and his own weak ones. That is why a salesman should be brought back to the home office at frequent intervals and resold from top to bottom on his line. Then he will not be tempted to use defensive, competitive salesmanship.

Some general observations

With a bit of experience the new salesman quickly learns which competitive products pose the most potent threat and he is made aware of his ware's competitive strengths and weaknesses. Thus he can anticipate and forestall competitive arguments during his presentation. If he knows that his product is relatively high priced, then he will continually be building up the product's value—higher quality, additional features, etc.—during the interview. He can meet the claims he knows will be made—meet them with talking points showing the superiority of his product in those very particulars or in offsetting advantages. In this way he can shrink those competitive advantages or claims in the mind of the prospect before they are brought out into the open. This can be done without mentioning the competitor by name, thereby avoiding an argument or engaging in a rough knocking session.

It goes without saying that a thorough knowledge of competing propositions must underlie any such effort to eliminate them. This knowledge should include such matters as: trend of sales, how current models are catching on, service given, delivery performance, value of their dealer helps, advertising and sales promotion program, various trade practices, their *real* price. It is helpful to know just where your competition is most vulnerable. Talk with owners of competing products.

Be familiar with the claims made by your competitors. Watch their advertising; get hold of their sales literature; visit their sales- or showrooms if they have any. Ask your good customers what they hear about competitors.

Learn what your competitors are saying about *your* product. Get a competitor to try to sell you, if possible. Make a list of his claims against your product, line, or company.

Finally, it will help if you can identify just where your chief competition lies in each particular sale. Then you can slant your demonstration accordingly.

It is hard to remain silent in the face of unfair competition. Indeed, it may be a sound idea to fight back vigorously at a competitor who is trying by unethical means to ruin you. This is just about the only time it is wise to mention a competitor by name, and even here it is usually better to wait until the prospect has brought him into the conversation.

If your prospect has a good friend who is in competition with you for his business, it does not pay to criticize that friend. Rather, it is wise to present your own proposition so effectively that the prospect's self-interest overcomes his desire to buy from his friend. If he raises the question, you can point out briefly and simply that, if the competitor is actually a true friend of the prospect, he would want the prospect to buy the product which would best serve his purposes. Sometimes the alleged friendship may not be so warm as you imagine it to be; perhaps the prospect is really eager to end the arrangement, as the "friend" may be selling on friendship alone and not providing the best service or the best product. It is by no means a hopeless situation to be selling against a friend of the prospect.

The salesman must recollect that mere negative salesmanship usually avails nothing. Suppose a salesman for a fruit commission house should walk into the prospect's place of business, hand him a wormy, gnarled apple with the remark that this was the kind of apples his competitor was selling, and then turn around and walk out. Such a salesman would be adjudged mentally incompetent. The negative idea regarding competitors' goods should be merely supplementary to the positive idea concerning the salesman's product if a sale is to result.

An attitude of absolute fairness toward competitors, even when it is necessary to speak disparagingly of their goods, should be preserved by the salesman. He should say nothing derogatory that cannot be substantiated at once, and he should be very careful about saying even that if it does not seem necessary.

One reason for keeping on as friendly terms as possible with competitors is that the mean things said about them always get back to them and cause them to be even more vigorous and active in their efforts to win business. If your adverse comments are not true, they may adopt retaliatory measures.

Salesmen will, therefore, do well to avoid mentioning their competitors as far as possible; if they must make comparisons, these should be made in a spirit of fairness; and no statements should be made that cannot at once be substantiated. The ethics of business are improving, and the salesman must help to lead the way.

Unethical competitive tactics

Unfortunately, there are still far too many instances of unethical competitive behavior for it to go unmentioned. If the new salesman does not learn how to handle such tactics, he may be severely damaged while not knowing the real reason for it.

One salesman for a baby-food processor confessed that he planned his route so that he would be in each store the day after his major competitor serviced it. While the store manager was not present, he managed to "steal" a few baskets from the competition by combining their contents, and he would place them in a disadvantageous position on the shelves. He was rather clever at sabotaging the other fellow's efforts.

A beer salesman trying to get his brew into a tavern admitted to several interesting tricks. He spoke of "sandbagging" an owner by having several phone calls made to the owner requesting his brand of beer and emotionally refusing any substitution. The salesman would manage to be in the tavern during the last phone call so he could take the order. On one difficult owner who would not put in the salesman's brand of beer, he sabotaged the brew that was in by slipping a little grease into the nozzle of the spigot, thereby causing the beer flowing through it to become excessively foamy. He would do anything to make the buyer dissatisfied with his present supplier.

While eventually these tactics catch up with most salesmen using them, still in the short run they can cause the innocent salesman for the competition much grief—and money. He must learn the "tricks of the trade" in order to recognize when they are being used against him.

The best protection against such tactics is a smart, alert customer. Once the prospect or customer discovers such tactics, that salesman is through in that account. Help the customer discover them! But be sly about it or it may appear to the buyer that it is merely a case of "sour grapes."

DISCUSSION QUESTIONS
1. Suppose you are selling office copying machines. Devise a perfect-product comparison against which you can compare your machine.
2. Why can you accept the blame for something, yet not be made to suffer for it by the customer?
3. Describe some of the actions the salesman can take to keep the sale from appearing to be a battle or argument.
4. Under what circumstances is the use of a "canned" sales presentation most advisable?
5. What are some of the actions that can be taken to avoid interruptions?
6. How can the salesman determine which stage the buyer's mind is in?
7. In your opinion, what is the key to handling competition successfully?
8. One manufacturer of electronic equipment allows prospect to select from stock any item and conduct whatever tests he wishes on it. However, a competitor does not do this: he instructs his sales force to select the gear and conduct the tests themselves. What problems might arise for a salesman of the first manufacturer facing such competitive tests?
9. Selling folklore contains many stories of unethical competition: Salesmen throwing sand or dirt into competitors' machines or otherwise making them malfunction, or bread salesmen puncturing the packages of competing bakers. If you were a salesman being hit with such tactics, how would you go about handling the matter?
10. If you were assigned the task of developing a prepared sales presentation for the sales force of your company, how would you go about doing it?

THE PRESENTATION: III

It is a bad plan that admits of no modification.
Syrus

Chapters 10 and 11 dealt with three of the four requisites of a strong presentation—the winning of confidence, completeness, and the elimination of competition. This chapter discusses clarity and conviction.

The sales demonstration must be *clear*—so plain and understandable to the prospect that not one vestige of doubt remains about either the disadvantages of being without the proposition or the advantages to be gained from accepting it.

Clarity means not merely clear enough to be understood, but also so crystal clear as not to be *misunderstood.* Often there is a distinct difference.

Moreover, the prospect must be *convinced* by the presentation, convinced that he must have the product or service.

How can we make our presentation clear and convincing? Five suggestions are offered.

- Use showmanship! Dramatize! Visualize!
- Take the pulse of the interview often; make sure that the prospect comprehends what you have said.
- Use effective figures of speech!
- Talk the prospect's language!
- Demonstrate.

SHOWMANSHIP; DRAMATIZATION

Of the hundreds of ways in which showmanship can be introduced into the demonstration, it is possible to mention only a few, of which dramatization is perhaps the most important.[1]

It is often necessary to emphasize certain points in the demonstration by the use of the dramatic. Some illustrations will provide insight into the area of dramatizing your statements, which is limited only by your imagination.

An average tire salesman might say, "These tires are built to take it; they're tough!"

A more imaginative salesman might try to be dramatic by saying, "You're driving 70 miles per hour down the road with your wife and children in the car. Suddenly some jerk swerves over into your lane, forcing you onto the shoulder. You hit a big chuck hole . . . jars every bone in your body and every bolt in the car! But you only have to worry about your steering, not your tires. These tires can take all you can give!"

Now let's examine what such dramatization tries to accomplish. First, it tries to project the prospect into an emotional setting—relate the tires to the safety of his family and himself. We have previously discussed how people are more apt to buy because of emotional forces than rational reasons. Thus dramatization tries to cast rational talking points into an emotional framework.

Second, people like stories, so we create a plot with characters and make our product the hero of the action. It's entertaining.

Finally, people will more likely remember the point if it is dramatized than if it is simply stated. Any talking point can be dramatized with the assistance of a bit of imagination.

Showmanship can take bizarre forms. One space salesman for a large magazine dramatized and visualized to a prospective advertiser his claim that the magazine's readers represented a $3,000,000 potential market for the company by arranging to have $3,000,000 in currency brought to the prospect's office as he made the call. That's showmanship!

Visualizing the proposition

The old-style "barehanded" selling is virtually obsolete. Salesmen are now equipped with sales aids designed to tell the story quickly through the eye.

---

[1] The reader is referred to such books as Zenn Kaufman and Kenneth Goode, *Showmanship in Business* (Harper & Row, Publishers, Incorporated, New York, 1947); and Zenn Kaufman, *Profitable Showmanship* (Prentice-Hall, Inc., Englewood Cliffs, N.J., 1939). Starting in the December, 1966 issue of *The American Salesman* and continuing at least through the November, 1967 issue, Elmer Leterman has a series "How Showmanship Sells," which is based on his book of the same title published in 1965 by Harper & Row.

When the salesman utilizes any method of visualization, he does less talking than when he depends solely on appealing to the sense of hearing. The distinction is the same as that between a television announcer at a baseball game and a radio sportscaster at the same game. The latter knows that his hearers cannot see anything happening in the park, while the television fans can see a good deal and do not need or want the announcer to keep up a constant flow of chatter.

THE PRODUCT   The product itself is one of the best visuals the salesman can use, so use it. Whenever possible, show the product. But there are times when that is not possible, so other techniques are needed.

A salesman for the Clary militarized printer was perplexed when the engineers to whom he had been lecturing about the product's ruggedness showed no response. Their reaction seemed to be, "Ho Hum, so it prints. Big deal, when it's sitting on a nice quiet table." He got mad. He started pounding on his box full of electronic equipment while it was running; he picked it up and let it fall a foot; he took off his shoe and whaled away; it was jumping all over the table, all $12,000 worth of it. The audience crowded around the table to see what the madman was going to do next. One man growled, "Let me see that tape. . . . Well, look at that! It didn't miss a digit." It took a dramatic visualization of the ruggedness claim to make the audience perceive and believe what he was saying. Thereafter, the salesman developed a shock test kit containing a rubber mallet.[2]

PICTURES   Pictures of the product are much utilized by salesmen for products too bulky to carry. Furniture, machinery, and many other products can be shown fairly well in this way. The old method used to be to turn the pages of the catalogue or to toss out pictures from the brief case. Today, it is the custom to have these pictures arranged in the best order and frequently displayed on an easel built for the purpose. This makes them easier to look at and also helps to hold the salesman to the standardized presentation.

MODELS   Miniature models of the entire product may be used when they can be carried without too much trouble. The mechanical stoker may weigh tons but the model can be carried in a sample case. Miniature trucks prove interesting as toys for the buyer. The president of one company that uses miniature models of its product says:

[2] Charles McIntosh, "Make It Visual and Make Your Sale," *The American Salesman*, December, 1966, pp. 5–8.

No man who has played with toy trains in his boyhood ever gets over the trait of liking to monkey with mechanical things. I have seen a man take a model of our valve-reseating tool and twist it by the hour, just for the pleasure of watching the wheels go around. This is one of the biggest points of selling by model. You can never really finish the demonstration, for the prospect takes the model away from you and finishes it himself, thus adding a dash of personal accomplishment to the fascination which he has been showing.

To help its salesmen introduce a new "Oil-Mist" lubrication system, the Alemite Division of the Stewart-Warner Corporation built portable models which could be set up on a table top and placed in operation. Showmanship was brought into the demonstration through two original devices. A lucite tube, inside of which a brass cylinder revolves to simulate a bearing in operation, permits a see-through effect. The use of black light causes the oil mist, blown onto the surface of the cylinder in atomized form, to fluoresce. This gives a picture of lubrication-in-action which holds observers' interest.

This demonstrating device cut the sales story from 2 hours down to 10 minutes, making it possible for each salesman to talk to many more prospects each day. The manager of industrial sales for the company said:

Alemite executives always have believed in the value of demonstration. We have used demonstrations ever since we introduced pressure lubrication in 1918. Demonstration, if properly staged, grips the prospect, stirs his imagination, and convinces him as no mere sales argument based on words only ever can. Demonstration invites questioning, gives the salesman the floor, helps him to command the interview, and is a mighty factor in clinching the sale.

A company manufacturing heating equipment provides each salesman with a miniature model of one of its furnaces, complete with working parts. The salesmen assert that this is far more effective than pictures. The Rex-aire vacuum cleaner organization developed a clear plastic bottom for their demonstrator to visualize how the water it contained was filtering dust from the air which was being forced through it.

FILMS Many firms equip their representatives with projectors and film showing, for example, their products in use. It requires only a moment to plug in the projector and stage a show. Such a demonstration usually holds the interest of the prospect, for it is something in motion, and it also prevents the prospect from otherwise occupying himself. There are concerns that make a business of planning and producing these films, either with or without sound.

The Elba Corp. of Denver, Colo., produces complete sales presentations for clients such as insurance companies, mutual funds, and various door-to-door organizations. Armed with the Elba film presentation, the salesman merely obtains the prospect's consent to view it, sits back and lets the film do the selling. The film ends with a strong close that opens the door for the salesman to begin writing the order and meeting objections.

The slide film has met the needs of many salesmen, enabling them to show pictures more dramatically than by merely handing the prospect pieces of printed matter. These may or may not be accompanied by sound apparatus. Some salesmen prefer to do their own talking while showing the film, as this gives the prospect a chance to ask questions. It also lets the salesman dwell as long as he wishes on any picture which interests the prospect.

Another device for visualizing the product is the "viewer," a modern version of the old-fashioned stereoscope. Belding-Corticelli, Inc., manufacturer of lingerie, fabrics, thread, and sewing kits, uses this extensively, the transparencies being Kodachromes that show, in true color and with three-dimensional effect, the fit and style of garments, the texture of fabrics, etc. These kits are cheap and easy to carry, each slide costing less than 50 cents and the whole carrying case weighing less than 5 pounds. Salesmen hate to carry heavy and bulky sample cases, knowing that they frighten the prospect and make him feel that he is in for a long ordeal of examining every sample. Under such conditions he is tempted to send the salesman on his way without giving him an audience. But this small box is not alarming and, after the prospect has viewed a few transparencies showing lingerie photographed on live and lovely models, it is not hard to hold his attention while the entire line is shown.

Once again, we find that this visualizing device saves time, especially in equipping the salesmen for their seasonal trips. Instead of waiting until a set of samples has been prepared for the entire sales force, the first sample made up can be photographed and the slides put into the hands of the salesmen within a week. The salesmen are enthusiastic over the results they have achieved with this visualization kit.

A real estate broker photographs (with stereo camera and in 3-D color) interior and exterior details of property he has for sale. A prospect can thus view various properties in detail without driving miles. It's good visualization, and it saves time and gasoline.

How about visualizing a cooling fluid—a nonconductor—guaranteed not to cause short circuits if it leaks into electronic equipment? Its maker took the cabinet off a television set and placed the set inside a large glass tank filled with the fluid. Prospects saw the set working in it. Heat from the set's components boiled the coolant in places, causing bubbles to rise, but the set continued to operate perfectly. [3]

THE SALES PORTFOLIO   This is usually a collection of illustrations, graphs, letters from satisfied users, records of tests, and other material which the company believes will help the salesman to make an effective presentation. The pictures may be of the production processes leading to the completion of the product being sold, these scenes showing size of plant, special machinery used, careful inspection, cleanliness of factory, packaging processes, assembling techniques, etc. Or it may show the product in use, as is done by the Caterpillar Tractor Co. For bulky products, this portfolio shows the prospect, right in his office, all pertinent facts about the product—facts which would be difficult to bring before him in any other way. [4]

One type of portfolio deserves mention. This is the book which has a number of pages printed on transparent cellophane so that they can be laid one on top of the other, letting the reader see the various parts of an automobile engine or a gas stove added to the product as it is assembled. Thus, even though a part or all of one section may be later covered by another, the prospect can see each clearly as it is put in place. There is something fascinating about such a portfolio. However, its chief function is to make clear the features about the product which are ordinarily hidden from view, even in the product itself.

The salesman may sketch his own illustrative material. National Cash Register Company salesmen are taught to use a crayon on large pads of paper. Other salesmen draw visualizing aids on small sheets of paper in full view of the prospect. The moving pencil holds his attention as words alone cannot do. The drawings need not be expertly executed—a crude sketch will suffice.

Salesmen for the best-managed companies are usually provided with carefully prepared "visuals." All the salesman has to do is to learn to use them effectively. But sometimes it may be necessary for a salesman to devise and make his own visual. It may not be quite as professional appearing as one gotten out by the company and its advertising agency, but it may work just as well.

[3] Ibid.

[4] It is obviously impossible to show here samples of sales portfolios or even to describe them vividly. If this book is being used as a textbook in a salesmanship course the instructor may show the class some effective sales portfolios. If the reader is not taking such a course and is not familiar with these portfolios, he may learn about them by calling on the local representatives of firms using them. These will be largely in the specialty field, as automobiles, tires, air-conditioning equipment, office machines, factory machinery, etc.

Let's say the salesman is trying to sell a college professor an electric typewriter. He says to himself, I want to make this man dissatisfied with his old machine by showing him the advantages of my electric one. The points I want to make are: it will save his time; it will be easier to operate; it will turn out better-looking letters, lecture notes, and manuscripts.

Under point 1, I can draw a clock face and show savings of time in an hour. Then I can multiply that number of minutes by 10, assuming that he types 10 hours a week. That will run up to a good many minutes in a year.

On the ease of operation, I can get some pictures of tired secretaries, all worn out by pounding an old machine. I can get figures on the units of energy used in an hour on each type of machine and compare them in a bar chart.

On the third point, I can get samples of work on an old machine and some done on an electric, and have them photographed twice as large as the originals so he can see the difference clearly.

I'll think of other ideas later, but these will do for a start.

Now, how about the physical make-up of my visual? How big shall I make the pages? I don't need a lot of space, so I'll keep it down to about the size of a letterhead. How much shall I put on a page? Not very much, and I'll make it big enough to be easily read or seen, even without glasses.

Shall I use color? Mostly for emphasis I can use some red ink in my printing; I can show my machine in various colors.

As to the lettering, I'm not so good, so I'll get a kit at an office supply store.

Maybe I should visualize benefits a little. Take that first point—the time my prospect will save. What would he like to do with that time? Golf, bird watching, television, gardening? I'll clip a few attractive pictures showing those activities and emphasize the one he likes best. If I could show him that he could save 4 hours a week for a round of golf, that might do it.

The foregoing is only suggestive, but it does indicate how any salesman can build a visual for his own use.

VISUALIZING INTANGIBLES　　Intangible products or services such as insurance, investment bonds, and various services need effective visualization even more than tangible products possessing physical bodies which may be shown and tested. The old Chinese proverb, "One picture is worth a thousand words," is put into practical application by most successful salesmen of intangibles.

One life insurance salesman had an effective method of visualizing what the years are likely to do to a man. Whenever he saw a picture in the papers of a young man who had changed jobs, he clipped it. Then he had an expert artist retouch this photograph, whitening and thinning the hair, inserting wrinkles and sagging flesh; in short, making it look as nearly as possible like the man this young chap would be when he reached seventy. He called at the young man's office and sent in this retouched photo with this note: "What are you going to do for this old man?" The visualization was so shocking that it nearly always obtained an interview, and the salesman claimed he signed up one out of every three such prospects for an annuity contract.

In addition to such means of *showing* the prospect rather than *telling* him, salesmen in the intangible field realize the value of frequent use of pencil or pen during the presentation. Many times a simple chart or graph, completed as the interview progresses, aids clarity and maintains interest to the end. The casual jotting down of a figure or a fact upon a pad also utilizes the eye appeal successfully. Many salesmen write down the key word of each talking point given, entirely for purposes of emphasis and to help the prospect retain it both by hearing it and by *seeing* it. If certain psychologists are correct in saying that 87 percent of all impressions are gained through the eye and only 13 percent through the other four senses, then it becomes immediately plain how essential it is to utilize this eye appeal as much as possible in selling.

Tests as means of dramatizing the presentation

Tests are the second method of dramatizing the presentation. They should relate closely to the use of the product. The test should be a performance of the product at some stage of its legitimate use. Many tests are dramatic, but prove nothing about the actual performance of the product. Showing that a ball point pen writes under water is a dramatic test, but it is a non sequitur for that is not the way such pens are commonly used.

Also, the best tests are simple. The prospect may easily become skeptical of a test that appears to him too complex. If the prospect himself is supposed to make the test, there is a possibility of his making an error if the test is not simple, thereby ruining the chance of a sale.

Wherever possible, the test should be performed by the prospect himself rather than by the salesman. It not only interests him more but inspires greater confidence. When the prospect is allowed to conduct the test, it is wise for the salesman to tell him in advance just what results he is to look for. In this way the prospect's attention is focused on the right features of the test.

DRAMATIZATION THROUGH TESTS   The salesman for a plastic covering material used for upholstering furniture carries a swatch of his product mounted on a stiff card. He hands the prospect a nail file and challenges him to scratch the material.

A salesman for Corning Glass carried a hammer with which to hit the glass, thus proving it unbreakable. That worked pretty well, but he had a better idea—he let the prospect swing the hammer. That really convinced the most skeptical buyers and sales shot up.

A salesman for a new adhesive snips a shoelace in two and applies his adhesive to the ends, holding them together while he delivers his sales talk. Then he hands the shoelace to the prospect and invites him to pull it apart.

Several tire manufacturers let prospects drive an ice pick into a tire and pull it out; then they let the prospect test the pressure with the gauge.

Revere Copper & Brass, Inc., wants to prove that the copper-clad stainless steel they use in their cooking utensils transfers heat more quickly than ordinary steel does. They give each salesman a "heat stick," which is merely a rod, one-half of which is ordinary steel and the other half their Copperclad. The prospect is asked to take hold of it, one hand holding each end. The salesman holds a lighted match or a cigarette lighter under the middle and waits for the prospect to let go the hotter end of the "heat stick." This is always the Copperclad end, and the prospect is convinced by the evidence of his own senses.

The president of Eberhard Faber, Inc., manufacturers of pencils, says:[5]

Neither sales literature nor plain statements have the selling force of a dramatic demonstration. We can tell people that our Diamond Star lead is the strongest there is, but it won't mean as much as when a salesman puts an overcoat on a hanger, picks up a competitor's pencil from the prospect's desk and tries to suspend the hanger and coat on the point of the pencil. The point breaks. Then when he lets the customer himself hang the thing on our sharpened pencil, it holds the coat up.

The salesman for a roofing cement takes an ordinary handkerchief, coats it with his cement, and then uses it as a dish to hold water. When the handkerchief proves watertight, he has scored his point more emphatically than if he had quoted any number of statements from scientists or testing laboratories.

Owens-Corning Fiberglas Corp. stages a dramatic demonstration for its product as an insulation material. At the beginning of a typical show the master of ceremonies asks a member of the audience to come up on the stage and light the oven of a kitchen range. After the regulator is set for the desired temperature the M.C. displays a roll of Fiberglas, the same as that used to insulate the range. Next, he wraps a quart of ice cream in it, pops the ice cream into the oven. Beside it he places a cherry pie ready for baking.

Then a pot of hot coffee is wrapped in a blanket of Fiberglas and

[5] *The American Salesman*, June, 1961, pp. 46–52.

placed in a refrigerator on the stage. The show proceeds, the pie, ice cream, and coffee apparently forgotten. When it is time to take out the freshly baked pie, out comes the ice cream, too. The member of the audience, joined by many others eager to assure themselves that the demonstration is honest, unwraps the quart of ice cream and finds it frozen as firmly as when it was inserted in the oven. The pot of coffee is taken from the refrigerator and sampled by the amazed spectators, who find it still hot. Other equally dramatic tests are carried out, at the conclusion of which not the faintest doubt of the product's insulating qualities remains in the mind of any witness. Splendid dramatization and showmanship—and it sells.

A portable typewriter prospect complained that the machine looked flimsy. The salesman laid the typewriter down on the pavement, drove one wheel of his car on it, and stopped the car. Presently he drove on, then picked up his typewriter and wrote a letter with it. That dramatic test convinced his prospect.

A manufacturer of gas ranges teaches salesmen to dramatize the size of the oven by removing from it, one at a time, 48 pint jars.

Some companies making products used in industry provide samples to be used by the prospect in his own factory. In other words, the prospect makes the tests himself without the presence of salesmen. It is wise to give the prospect a clear idea as to the product's limitations, if any, and its strong points, too, before thus turning it over. These products to be tested may be offered free, or they may be loaned, as in the case of machines. Just the old "free trial" selling device.

TESTS IN RETAIL SELLING   Tests are just as valuable in retail selling as in other sales situations. A salesman is demonstrating a table lamp. Taking the light cord, he whips the plug against the wall and then drops it on the floor and steps on it to prove how many hard knocks and how much abuse it will stand.

The salesman for fine china takes a fragile looking teacup, places it on the floor, and then stands on it. Or he drops a plastic cup to show that it is truly unbreakable.

The Shell Oil Company at one time used in its advertising a test between two identical cars, one filled with its gasoline containing a certain additive and the other filled with the same brand of gasoline without the additive to see which went the farthest on the tank. The car with the additive won hands down, of course, thereby visualizing a claim difficult to make believable. Many so-called tests shown on television are unconvincing and insulting to the viewers' intelligence, but the advertisers seem to believe that they help to sell. The power of tests, even though they are questionable, is great.

CARE MUST BE TAKEN   Considerable care must be taken that the tests do not fail or backfire on the salesman. One salesman demonstrating a new dictating machine took pains to bang it around with great gusto, but when he began its demonstration, the machine would not work properly.

The salesman should always check out his demonstrator to make certain that it is in operating order before attempting a demonstration, as a faulty demonstration or test is worse than nothing at all.

It is usually unwise to subject the actual product which the salesman hopes to deliver to tests that are very rough, for it will upset the prospect if he is already thinking of himself as the owner. He wants a new, perfect product.

In planning to use showmanship, two facts should be remembered: Some prospects don't like it, and some salesmen can't use it effectively. Sales managers say that buyers in large cities rather expect it, but in smaller places they react unfavorably to it. Individual buyers are different in their reactions, also.

If a salesman is not much of an actor and finds it difficult to use showmanship, perhaps he will do better if he simply says, "Now I'm supposed to be very dramatic here and to use a lot of showmanship, but I just don't feel comfortable doing it." Then he can go into a sincere, quieter demonstration, and perhaps the prospect will accept his statements with even more confidence than if he had tried to be dramatic.

"Stage business" in showmanship

Showmanship has one characteristic in common with the stage—it requires rehearsal of "stage business." It is not enough to tell a young salesman, "At this point you show the prospect a photo of the Nashville installation of our machine." It is necessary to tell that young salesman just *how* to show that picture. For instance, will he hand it to the prospect? Lay it on his desk? Mount it so it can be stood up on the desk? Mount it in his portfolio? Make a slide of it and throw it on a screen? Use a viewer? Just hold it in his own hand?

This is only a hint of the many ways in which *acts* involving showmanship in the demonstration must be carefully planned and then practiced. A salesman for an electric refrigerator wishes to show the customer how easy it is to remove the shelves for cleaning. He had better practice taking them out and putting them back until he really has the hang of it; otherwise he may get a shelf stuck and ruin his demonstration.

Most salesmen can learn much from watching the commercials on TV. Those salesmen look at the prospect, as they should. They gear their words to their actions, as they should. They tell the prospect what to watch for before they do something, as they should if they want to make sure the prospect sees what is done. "Now watch how this opens up here when I press the button."

The big point here is that the salesman must plan and practice his *act* or actions until he has them down to perfection. This is fully as important as it is to plan and practice what he *says.*

THE DISPLAY OF GOODS   To insure a good impression on the prospect, it is vital that the goods be displayed under the most favorable conditions.

One principle concerning the display of the product always holds good. The salesman should handle the product with respect, as though he appreciated fully its value. If he is selling shoes, he wipes them off carefully before letting the customer handle them; he does not *toss* them carelessly on the floor but *lays* them down. If he sells textiles, he must manifest a genuine pleasure in feeling their fine texture, and should not toss a coat down on a pile carelessly without straightening out the sleeves. A bearing toward the goods should be maintained that will inspire in the prospect a similar feeling. Unless the salesman appears to like the product, he cannot generate this feeling in his prospect. It is not implied that every article must be handled as though it were delicate or fragile. The farmer who buys overalls may want to see the salesman try in vain to tear them in two; the vacuum bottle salesman hurls his sample to the floor to prove its nonbreakable feature. These rough methods of handling, however, only emphasize the salesman's respect for his merchandise. The salesman for the filing cabinet who jumps on the opened drawer to prove its sturdiness can be just as enthusiastic over the results of the test and treat the product with even more regard because it stood up under the severe strain. In this way, the salesman creates his own favorable conditions.

When showing an article to a prospect, it is often a good idea to move it a little. Movement catches and holds attention. A rabbit "freezes" to escape detection. Also, in comparing two items, a salesman often holds the larger or better one *over* or in front of the other, thereby making it look somewhat larger and bringing it more prominently to the buyer's attention.

Where possible, it is wise to show the goods as they will appear when actually in use. The salesman for shoes or clothing tries the article on the prospect, of course, but some products do not lend themselves so readily to this purpose. In selling piece goods to be made up into a dress, it is often necessary to drape the material on the customer in the fashion in which it is to be made up. In selling housefurnishings, some enterprising firms arrange complete outfits for a room, working out for the customer a harmonious combination of floor covering, drapes, and furniture.

Most people are deficient in imagination and need help from the salesman to visualize how the product will appear in use.

APPEAL TO SEVERAL SENSES   The salesman in his demonstration will do well to appeal to as many of the senses as possible. Educational psychologists tell us that children learn chiefly in three ways: by seeing, by hearing, and by feeling. For example, the child learns to spell by seeing the word written and printed; an image is formed in his memory. If he hears it spelled, the auditory sense is enlisted in the memorizing process, supplementing the effect of the appeal through the eye. But if the child also writes the word many times, he receives impressions from his sense of touch; the nerves of the hand and arm register their impression likewise, with the result that the child has learned to spell the word more certainly than if he had learned through an appeal to the one sense only.

The house-to-house salesman selling hand lotion hands the prospect a bottle of his product when she comes to the door. Then he takes his demonstrator bottle, opens it, and holds it for her to smell. "Delicate, isn't it?" Then he pours a few drops on her hands as he takes back the bottle he had given her. "Not sticky at all, is it?" He has appealed to the senses of smell, hearing, sight, and touch.

Bakeries sell products that appeal to the sense of taste; an exhaust fan is often placed in an aperture in front of the salesroom so that passers-by will catch the aroma of fresh cookies and pies. A department store found that sales of women's hose were stimulated by faintly scenting them with various perfumes.

LET THE PROSPECT HELP WITH THE DEMONSTRATING   As with testing, it is wise to let the prospect play an active role. Picture a salesman selling a shotgun or a golf club to a sportsman. The salesman would stand a very slight chance of selling the prospect unless the latter were allowed to handle the product. These illustrations are purposely extreme in order to bring out the principle, but there are hundreds of products whose appeal would be greatly strengthened if made through the sense of touch as well as the senses of sight and hearing.

There are probably two main reasons why salesmen dislike to hand over the product to the prospect. The first one undoubtedly is that the salesman himself likes to play with the article. It is interesting to watch the father fix his small son's electric train or help him fly his kite. The chances are excellent that Dad will have to be importuned several times before he relinquishes control of train or kite. The salesman should recognize the power of this same tendency and enlist its aid rather than permitting it to militate against his success.

Why merely *tell* a woman how easily a vacuum cleaner rolls when she can prove the point for herself by operating it a few seconds? Many retailers have discovered the necessity for permitting customers to handle certain goods if sales are to be made. The variety chains in particular have learned that it is often desirable to take a loss from theft or breakage rather than to place the goods out of reach. An outstanding example of this principle was the experience of one of the great chains in selling cheap flashlights. If they were left out on the counter, people would handle them and try them. They could not seem to keep their hands off, and the result was broken bulbs and exhausted batteries. So the flashlights were placed under glass. The breakage ceased, but so did sales, and the flashlights were once more placed within reach of the shoppers.

The second reason is that some salesmen feel that to hand over the article puts the control of the presentation in the hands of the prospect. Imagine the predicament of the book salesman who hands his prospectus over to his prospect, instead of keeping it in his own hand while he points out the features of chief interest! The prospect might turn the pages idly, stopping to look at parts of scant interest or concerning which the salesman had not been coached; he might ask questions that would be hard to answer; his comments and queries would certainly throw the salesman off his stride and render his prepared canvass less effective.

It may be, therefore, that in some cases it is advisable to retain possession of the product in order to keep control of the interview. The salesman may do well, however, to let the prospect handle the product until he interferes with the effective procedure of the sale, at which time the salesman may reach over and reclaim it on the pretext of pointing out some feature as yet unnoticed.

To avoid losing control of the interview, many salesmen, when they hand the product to the prospect, make a point of indicating just what features he should especially observe. For example, the shotgun salesman may tell his prospect to notice particularly the ease with which shells may be ejected; the golf club salesman emphasizes the balance and feel of the club; the automobile salesman, when he lets the prospect take the wheel, from time to time points out certain features such as ease of steering, responsiveness to the accelerator, and the manner in which the car took a bad bump in the road. Thus he may keep the interview under control while at the same time permitting the proposition to appeal to as many of the prospect's senses as possible.

In selling some propositions it is necessary to make certain computations—to do some "figgering." To be sure that the prospect is following and comprehending, he may be asked to do them himself. The salesman may start the computation, contrive to break the point of his pencil, and pass the paper to the prospect with the suggestion that he add up the column or multiply the figures while the salesman is fixing his pencil.

Plan each demonstration

It is easy to fall into a rut when one goes through the same routine time after time, but this is the lazy man's method of operation. The shrewd salesman deliberately tries to alter his demonstration to fit the particular circumstances of that sale. A high fidelity phonograph salesman should not play the same record for a musician in his forties that he would play for a teenager interested basically in beat. Similarly, the electric typewriter salesman will have to alter his demonstration when selling a private individual, in contrast with the secretary or purchasing agent of a corporation.

When the salesman fails to tailor his demonstration to fit the situation, he loses one of his major advantages over advertising as a selling medium. The salesman can shape his sales appeals to fit individual needs, while advertising cannot.

Sequence of points

As just pointed out, people are interested in different things about a product. One man may be most interested in its performance, while another is more concerned with safety. One prospect may be price-conscious, while another wants quality merchandise. If the salesman does not quickly focus his presentation on the points that are most important to the prospect, he may *never* get to talk about them. Once the prospect loses interest, it may be difficult to reattract him. By leading off with the strongest features, the salesman may get the prospect so excited that the sale can be closed before the weaker points arise. One car salesman almost lost a sale because he waited to the last to take the prospect on a drive into the country to test the car on the open road. The prospect was sold the instant he took a particularly bad curve at a rather high speed without any effort.

What should be demonstrated

Not all features should be demonstrated: the salesman should stress those most favorable to his wares and not dwell on those possessed by all competitors. Demonstrating features in which the competition betters you is dangerous, especially if the prospect is shopping around and likely to look at the competitor's product. Also some features may be of interest to the prospect. It would be a mistake to demonstrate the high speed of an automobile to a man who never exceeded 50 miles an hour.

It is easy for the prospect to become bored by the demonstration of minute details. A refrigerator salesman lost a sale when he insisted on demonstrating every little feature to the complete boredom of the prospect. He even went so far as to demonstrate the quality of the compressor by taking off the back and showing some of the details on it.

Pace

Some salesmen make the mistake of rushing through the demonstration too fast. Because they thoroughly understand the proposition, they assume others must understand it. No matter how alert the buyer may be, if the proposition is a new one he will need to be shown point by point just what it should mean to him. A trained chemist can remember a new formula much more easily than can the poor freshman to whom the whole thing is unfamiliar. The housewife can remember all the ingredients of a cake recipe, as told by a neighbor, but her husband, listening to the conversation, would not be able to remember a third of them. When the concept is *new* to the prospect's mind, he must be led *slowly* along until he has assimilated thoroughly each idea.

However, if the prospect is familiar with the product, the demonstration may move faster. A man is buying an electric razor as a gift. If he uses one himself, little demonstration is necessary; if he has never used one, a thorough demonstration may be in order.

If there is no hurry about closing the sale and if it is an important one, the salesman may pace himself with deliberation as did the one thus described by a retailer:

There is only one salesman who ever called on me and got over seven separate selling arguments. His method had nothing of the mass attack in it. He had plenty of time to work in, as we bought his kind of merchandise only twice a year.

On his first trip he took up the standing of his house. He was sparing of my time and talked very directly and clearly on that one point alone. He made no direct reference to my next purchase of his class of goods. As he went, his closing remark was something like this, "All I ask, Mr. Murchison, is that you remember the standing of my house in its field. We are not the largest, but we are specializing more directly in our line than other companies, and we believe for that reason alone that we are turning out better garments."

On his next call he talked to me about a single factor in design; and when he got up to leave, he delivered another friendly little closer on remembering the difference in design and what it would mean to me. As the talks went on, I felt certain that he had laid them all out very carefully and joshed him one day about his method of salesmanship. He took me quite seriously and agreed that my comments were correct. He said that he realized that I was very busy; and so long as there was plenty of time, he thought it best to deal with one factor at a sitting and get it clearly in my mind, so I wouldn't feel as though he had wasted time. . . . Then he took up deliveries with his customary thoroughness.

Well, by the time I got to thinking definitely about my next season's requirements he had me sold up and down and cross-lots, and all of his points are anchored as deeply in my consciousness today as they were when I gave him my first order.

REPEAT THE TALKING POINTS   It is usually helpful to *repeat* the out-standing talking points about the proposition. The prospect may not grasp the point when he hears it the first time; or he may be thinking about some other feature of the proposition. It may be wise to state the talking point in different words the second or third time, but all educators know that repetition is one of the indispensable teaching devices. No youngster ever learned the multiplication table the first time he read it through. Repeat and repeat your best points.

TAKING THE PULSE OF THE PRESENTATION

To learn just how clearly he has been putting across his selling points, the salesman will find it helpful to ask questions of his prospect as he goes along. There is a technique in the asking of these questions that will repay study.

They might be phrased in such a way as to disguise them slightly, as "This proposition certainly gives a man good value for his money, doesn't it?" Inasmuch as the salesman has not mentioned the price, if the prospect replies either in the affirmative or the negative, it is clear that he has not been attending carefully to what has been said. Or the salesman might drop the innocent query, "What do you think of that last point, sir? I'd like to know how it appeals to you."

Some salesmen make a practice of injecting a "See what I mean?" or "Do you understand?" into the presentation at various places. Although the purpose is good—to keep the prospect nodding his head in agreement and presumably listening to the arguments—the query can be more happily phrased. Nobody likes to be asked if he has sufficient intelligence to com-prehend a thing. The tactful salesman shoulders the burden of making his proposition clear and inquires, "I wonder if I made that point clear. I'm afraid I stated it awkwardly." This not only makes the prospect feel more comfortable but also opens the door to a fuller discussion on any points that may remain somewhat unsettled in the prospect's mind.

These pulse-taking questions serve more than one purpose. First, they can reveal which features or arguments are most effective with that pros-pect. When the salesman asks, "If you owned this machine, would you find this feature useful?" he should watch keenly the *way* the prospect replies. If he says, "Oh, yes," the salesman knows that this point should perhaps be stressed again, if necessary. If the reply is "Not very," then the salesman should hurry on and not bring that point up again.

Second, by getting an affirmative commitment on each point as he goes along, the salesman is blocking the prospect from raising objections on these points later in the interview. This makes the task of closing the sale much easier, as the salesman can say, "You have said that you liked this feature, etc."

COMPARISONS—SIMILE, METAPHOR, AND ANALOGY
While this book makes little effort to go into the rhetorical aspects of salesmanship, it is important that the salesman know how to put clarity and meaning into his presentation. The comparison is one of the most valuable tools in the salesman's verbal kit, so important that many sales manuals devote considerable attention to it. This is especially noticeable in the manual instructions for meeting objections, frequently more than half of the suggested answers taking the forms of comparisons—either simile, metaphor, or analogy.

For example, "This electric hot-water heater is so well insulated that it is just like a big thermos bottle. And it's as safe as an electric light." Here are two effective *similes,* in which a comparison is made between the familiar qualities of the thermos bottle and of the electric light—good insulation and perfect safety—and the same qualities of the product. In a similar fashion the salesman of electric appliances might say, still employing the simile, "it is as silent as a burning match," "as cheerful as a log fire," "as warm as summer sunshine at midday."

Notice how, in each of these similes, something familiar to the prospect has been mentioned in a *comparative* way, using the "like" or "as" to emphasize that same desirable quality in the salesman's product.

The *metaphor* is like the simile except that the comparative word *as* or *like* is omitted. Listen to the comments of the crowd at any football game. "Who's that big moose at right tackle?" "Isn't that left halfback a flash?" "Our fullback is a regular tank in plowing through that line, isn't he?" "Our quarterback is an important cog in our machine." So the comments go in the use of the metaphor, another valuable tool of rhetoric in clarifying the sales story.

The *analogy* is psychologically sound, for it leads the mind of the prospect from the known to the unknown. The analogy should be selected with this thought in mind, for unless it is so chosen the prospect is as much in the dark as ever. An analogy taken from seafaring experiences might be very effective with a prospect who had lived in a seaport all his life but would mean little to the young man reared on the plains of western Kansas. The analogy from farm life would be effective only with a prospect familiar with rural existence.

This means that the salesman must have many analogies on file in his mind, so that he can select the one that will best fit his particular prospect's experiences.

Abraham Lincoln often won his argument through the use of a homely "story" which illustrated his point so clearly that his hearers at once grasped it. His stories, for which he is so famed, were usually carefully selected, or invented, analogies.

The insurance salesman employs analogy when he tells you about the custom, now required by law, of a passenger vessel having adequate lifebelt and lifeboat facilities for the passengers. On a very few voyages are they needed, but they are available *if* a need arises. "It is the same way with many types of insurance protection, Mr. Businessman; you may not need it, but if you did, you would want to have the protection provided."

The car salesman, in explaining to a lady driver how simply his car operates, in spite of the confusing controls and gadgets, uses a simple analogy when he says, "Madam, have you ever stopped to think how difficult it is for a child to learn to tie his shoes, but how soon this process becomes routine and easy? It is the same way about driving this car. You become so accustomed to doing the little essentials of operating it that they become habitual and are performed unconsciously."

In selling the service of a direct-mail advertising agency, the salesman says, "You would not have your salesman try to sell 500 prospects at once in a large room. No, you have him see each one individually, as our mailing pieces do."

When the prospect tells the Dictaphone salesman that his machine is too mechanical, the salesman reasons from analogy and inquires, "If so, why do you continue to use the telephone? You understand, of course, that dictating to the Dictaphone is exactly the same as talking into the telephone?" To illustrate the waste of time when stenographers sit idle while the dictator answers the telephone or attends to other business, the same salesman says, "Suppose, because of a certain system in your factory, the workmen sat around the foreman for two or three hours a day doing nothing—how long would you stand for it?" The prospect visualizes the picture of idle workmen in his plant and takes the necessary step from the known to the unknown, or at least the unappreciated, situation existing in his office.

TALKING THE LANGUAGE OF THE PROSPECT

It seems so obvious to state that a salesman should talk the language of his prospect that the reader might well remark, "Why bring that up?" The plain fact of the matter is, however, that many salesmen do not do it. The importance of using short, simple words that convey meaning and weight cannot be emphasized too greatly.

Examine Lincoln's Gettysburg Address, and you will find that it con-

tains 268 words. Examine it more closely, and you will learn that 196 of
those words are of one syllable, 52 are of only two syllables, and only 20
have three or more. Lincoln used short, simple words to construct one of
the finest speeches ever delivered.

This does not mean to imply that for some prospects words of more
than two syllables are ineffective. It does suggest a careful selection of
language appropriate to the prospect in every different interview. A good
illustration of the use of language fitted to the prospect is obtained in the
account of a life insurance salesman's effort to sell a policy to a young man
and his father who were trying to build up a dairy farm. The son managed
the farm while the father worked as a finish carpenter putting all surplus
funds into building up the herd on which they both hoped to retire some
day. The prospects admitted that if something should happen to the father
in the next 10 years the family would not be able to reach its goals because
the dairy now needed the extra funds provided by him; it was not yet self-
sustaining. However, when the salesman mentioned the annual premium
which would be necessary to buy sufficient life insurance on the father to
provide the funds needed to bring the herd up to a profitable operating
level should something happen to him, the family threw up their hands and
claimed that it was impossible. The salesman then made his appeal in other
terms. "In order to make certain that you reach your stated goals should
something unfortunate happen to your breadwinner, would you be willing
to give me the milk from those two cows? Just pretend that you don't have
those two cows; their milk will insure that you will have your profitably
operating dairy no matter what happens." He made the sale.

A real estate salesman went to a prospect and said:

"Mr. Prospect, I've been wondering why you don't buy that property
on Elm Street that I showed you. You told me that it suited your needs and
that the price was right. I felt that you wanted it, and I still do. Yet you
don't buy. The only answer is that I've fluffed the presentation somewhere
and failed to make some point clear. Maybe you have some question in
your mind that I didn't answer. Would you just forget that I have been
trying to sell you this property and tell me frankly where the obstacle lies?
Maybe we can straighten things out."

So the prospect accepted the invitation:

"You're right; I do like the property and want it. But I don't understand your financing plan. I'm hazy about that junior mortgage you mentioned. Until I know where I stand on that, I'm not getting my feet wet."

A purchasing agent with a sense of humor relates his experiences with
a young salesman who had not learned to speak the language of the prospect:

Having had occasion the past three months to purchase a great variety of office building supplies, this hitherto unsuspected condition has been effectually demonstrated in my own case.

The first disillusion came with the salesman who represented letter-filing cases. Having heard our requirements, in terms of approximate number of letters daily, the young man looked wise, considered a minute, and decided what we needed was their CS1.

"What is CS1?" I inquired.

"Why," came in a somewhat grieved and condescending tone, "that's our letter file you want."

"Is it made of paper, metal, or wood?" I ventured.

"Oh, in case you are considering metal you want our FDX, and probably two NCOs for each FDX."

"Some of our manuscripts are pretty long," I confessed.

"In that event you will need FDX with two NCOs for transfer for ordinary correspondence, and PL1, with RIP transfer for manuscripts."

By this time I recovered a little of my lost nerve and remarked, "Young man, what you say strikes me as ROT. What I am trying to buy is office furniture, not alphabets. If you will only talk Greek, Armenian, or Western Chinese, our translator can probably get a little intelligence out of it, as to the material, size, operation, capacity, color, and price of your goods."

"But," quoth he, "those are our catalogue numbers."

After a questioning that would have done credit to a lawyer on cross-examination, I managed to worm out of him the size, capacity, material, color, and cost of his various file cases, but it was like pulling back teeth with tweezers, and he seemed to think he had grossly betrayed secrets belonging exclusively to his firm.

If he had been the last and only one, these lines would never have been written. But unfortunately, he merely opened the ball. They came in droves: fine, clean, bright-faced, earnest young fellows; every one good to look at, and all talking the same catalogue lingo, which, of course, was unintelligible to me. Even when I got down to scrubbing brushes, one tried to sell me FHB, which turned out to be "fiber and hog's bristles"; and when the stuff came, C18 turned out to be some kind of a mop.

With scarcely an exception they all reeled off yards of (to me) utterly meaningless trade letters and numbers with a confident air of profundity which at first was amusing but quickly became exasperating. My conclusion was that if these young salesmen were selling my goods, I would get some friend to send for one of them, and I would sit concealed where I could hear their puzzle talk and then go home, call the boys all in, and give a few first easy lessons in salesmanship or buy a course in some correspondence school for each of them, or both.

Indeed, companies whose sales forces cover a wide area make an effort to choose their salesmen partly on account of their ability to talk the languages of the various territories. Likewise, occupational backgrounds of the salesmen are considered. Thus men with a farm background would be chosen to sell in agricultural sections, men with retail shoe experience would be picked to sell to shoe retailers, etc.

DISCUSSION QUESTIONS

1. Why is showmanship effective?
2. Select some product and develop a presentation for it.
3. What are some of the dangers involved in trying to talk the language of the prospect?
4. As a car salesman, what are some of the questions you might devise to take the pulse of the sale?
5. If you were selling landscaping, what would you want to include in a sales portfolio?
6. Describe the various visuals you would want in selling water softeners to homeowners.
7. In what ways could a skiing equipment salesman be dramatic in his demonstration of a set of skis and bindings?
8. As a salesman for electronic printed circuits, what visuals would you develop? What features would you build your presentation around?
9. As a salesman for a mutual fund, what visuals would you try to develop?
10. Devise some tests that will prove a certain top-quality golf ball is superior to all others.

CASE 12-1   MOUNTAIN GLASS COMPANY

Tom Scott, a salesman for the Mountain Glass Company, had just received a sudden special assignment from his boss—to sell a new line of safety plate glass patio doors and windows to people whose homes had suffered glass breakage during a particularly heavy windstorm the previous night.

The Mountain Glass Company was located in a Western city of 85,000 people, which was usually buffeted several times each winter by extremely high winds. Glass breakage during such windstorms was always extensive. Homes in the area almost without exception had both large patio doors and large picture windows because of the spectacular views that were available to most homeowners.

During such windstorms, which usually hit at night with velocities in excess of 130 miles per hour, families would abandon all rooms with windows facing the west—the direction from which the wind would come but also the direction of the view. The windows were usually shattered not so much because of the force of the wind directly but rather by some object— rock or wood—picked up by the wind.

Once shattered, the flying glass, carried by the sudden explosion of wind into the room, would shred over everything in the room. If the door to the room was not closed, the sudden increase in pressure inside the house combined with the low pressure on the sides of the house where the wind was at high velocity frequently blew out the windows on the sides of the house.

Inasmuch as such windstorms could last for 6 to 12 hours, they were fearsome affairs, particularly to those homeowners whose houses were in certain locations that were exposed to the full force.

The glass damage had been especially heavy the previous night; the firm's telephones had been busy from dawn. The company had a policy of going to work the minute the wind subsided sufficiently for work to begin.

Tom's boss had called to say, "This time let's sell these guys some safety plate glass to replace that junk that keeps blowing out. Develop a short, hard-hitting pitch that'll do the job. Then go see everybody who was hit hard last night."

Tom realized that the main barrier to selling the safety glass was that the insurance companies would only pay damages based on the cost of the cheapest glass available. The excess cost had to be borne by the home-owner.

Tom wondered just what he should put into the presentation.

1.   Develop a step-by-step outline of a presentation that Tom could use.
2.   Develop a few key selling sentences for him to use.
3.   Develop an approach for Tom to use.

HANDLING OBJECTIONS: I

Difficulties are things that show what men are.
Epictetus

Up to this point a person with a bit of training can proceed through the sales process somewhat as a mechanic fixes a car—do this and then do that. While a good "mechanic" can make a lot of sales, and the mechanics of selling are very important, as we have seen, still many professional salesmen maintain that real selling does not begin until objections are encountered. When the prospect says "No," salesmanship begins.

Unfortunately, too many salesmen are unable to cope with even the simplest of objections. Should the prospect say, "I'll think about it," some salesmen may not know what to do. You cannot consider yourself to be a proficient professional salesman until an objection triggers a competitive reaction in you that results in your digging into it with vigor, with the confidence that you know how to handle it. So let's get on with studying objections.

ATTITUDE TOWARD OBJECTIONS
Objections are an integral part of the sales process. Once you accept the idea that objections are to be expected and are a normal result of the sales process, you will have a much sounder philosophical attitude with which to approach them.

Bear in mind that when you try to sell something you frequently ask the prospect to change his behavior: he has been driving a Ford, you are asking him to drive another make of car; a businessman has a traditional accounting system and you are asking him to change over to your computerized system. People seldom change behavior without resistance. Most of us are opposed to change. The old way is the easiest, the old brand a trusted friend. We fear the new, the untried.

Almost instinctively the prospect assumes a defensive attitude. The more often he has to meet the "attacks" of salesmen, the more pronounced becomes his defensive attitude until it often develops into an antagonism toward anyone trying to sell him anything. In fact, the much-tried buyer may actually take the offensive with the intention of forcing the salesman to assume the defensive and thus placing him at a disadvantage.

How should the salesman regard objections? If he is a beginner, he may feel disheartened when an objection is raised. To him it may appear as a refusal to buy—an insuperable obstacle to making the sale. Sometimes it is, although usually it need not be.

But *the veteran salesman welcomes the expressed objection,* for he knows that it is a sales aid rather than a hindrance. One of the most difficult types of prospects to sell is the "clam" who does not show any interest in the proposition, who does not comment upon it at all, who merely sits in stony silence while the salesman strives to pierce his armor of indifference. The salesman who is trying to sell to such "clams" cannot tell whether he is making a favorable or an unfavorable impression and wishes fervently that the prospect would give him some clue to how the sale is progressing and what the prospect is thinking about.

Objections are guideposts to prospect's reactions

The prospect who voices his honest objections is assisting the salesman by telling him how far away he is from a sale. He is also providing more valuable information about what it will take to make the sale than all the preapproach data the salesman has assembled. Proper *interpretation* of objections should tell the wise salesman a great deal.

During the sale the pulse of the prospect should be taken frequently to determine just what his thoughts are upon the points being presented. The salesman should ask such questions as, "That makes sense, doesn't it?" "You'd like that, wouldn't you?" "Am I making myself clear?" "That's what you want, isn't it?" "Would that feature be useful?"

But, no matter how careful the salesman may be to gain these assents and agreements, as the prospect begins to get more familiar with the proposition, he is likely to interpose objections. These, however, may serve as effective guides to the alert salesman.

Sometimes the prospect remains unconvinced simply because the salesman has failed to meet one objection or to answer one question in his mind. When that point is raised and cleared up, the prospect may be ready to buy. A prospect being shown a fork-lift truck fears that it may be too small to handle the loads in his warehouse, although otherwise he likes it. A demonstration or proof that the truck can handle the job may get the order right there.

A veteran salesman commented that he always looked upon an objection as a request for information. "Objections arise," he declared, "for one of two reasons. Either the prospect does not understand what I have told him, or he does not have enough information to grasp the significance of my point. So I consider objections as requests for more facts and respond by giving the information desired." "I'm glad you brought that up, Mr. Prospect, because I was going to explain it anyway," is an excellent way for a salesman to make the prospect feel that his objections are welcomed. "That is a good question,[1] Mr. Prospect, and I am glad to give you full information upon it," is the way many salesmen take hold of important objections. Thus the prospect is assured that the salesman has no fear of any objection raised, and he accepts the answer in the same spirit that he would any other reply to a request for information. It should be pointed out that if a salesman replies in the same way to *every objection* the prospect makes, it soon becomes monotonous and somewhat phony. However, with slight variations in language, these methods may be employed successfully in most instances.

OVERALL STRATEGY FOR HANDLING OBJECTIONS
The successful handling of objections requires the salesman to incorporate into his pattern of behavior certain attitudes and methods. It should be observed that many of these can be applied to advantage in numerous human relationships quite outside the selling of products.

Avoid arguments in handling objections
This is not the first time that the importance of avoiding arguments has been mentioned. However, there is probably a greater tendency on the part of salesmen to indulge in arguments when answering questions or objections than in other parts of the interview. It is so easy to do and so disastrous. A salesman can suddenly realize he has slipped into an argument

---

[1] Observe that the salesman does not refer to an objection by that name. Rather he calls it a "question" or a "point." In fact, many objections are offered in the form of questions and it is usually good practice to treat as many actual objections as possible as if they had been merely questions and not firmly held objections. Some salesmen try to restate many objections in the form of questions.

with the prospect, yet not know how he got there. **No matter how violently your prospect disagrees—or how directly he contradicts—or how persistently he tries to argue—***don't argue with him.*

The salesman should conceive of his position as being in *cooperation* with the prospect and *not in conflict* with him. This attitude helps him to keep his good humor and aids him in maintaining friendly relations with the prospect. If he thinks of himself as an ally and not an enemy, it gives the prospect a similar feeling. As long as the salesman stays out of the fight, both prospect and salesman will avoid injury. The salesman lets the prospect fight the battle out within himself, so that, when it is over, the prospect will not feel that he has been forced by the salesman to make a decision but rather that he has arrived at his conclusion independently. If he is allowed freedom, he will be more likely to stay sold and not regret his decision when the salesman has gone. Few men are really convinced by argument. The members of college debating teams are always of the same conviction following the debate as they were previously. The members of the losing team did not have their opinions changed by the superior arguments of their opponents. Frank Crane, the essayist, believed that argument is poor sales strategy. He presented the point in his inimitable way thus:

Don't argue. Suggest. An ounce of suggestion is worth a ton of argument. When you suggest, it means that you get me to arrive at my own conclusion. When you argue, it means that you force me to arrive at yours. And what you want to do is to make your conclusion mine and lead me to it.

Guide me deftly to the decision you wish me to make. Don't shove. Let my mind amble along at its own gait.

I have known few men to be convinced by argument. And no women.

When you argue with me and beat me down by your facts and figures and logic, I may say you are right. But I go home and think it over; and unless I can arrive at the same conviction myself, by my own processes of thought, I don't stick. I come loose the next day. But when you are skilled enough to suggest and induce me to persuade myself, then when you put your blank before me and hand me your fountain pen and say, "Sign here"—I sign.

All argument arouses antagonism. I am stubborn and vain, you know; and if you don't want to get this mule to balking, handle me gently.

The oft-quoted experience of Benjamin Franklin on this subject serves to stress the value of the proper attitude:

A Quaker friend informed me I was not content with being in the right when discussing any point but had to be overbearing and insolent about it—of which he convinced me by mentioning several instances.

Endeavoring to cure myself of this fault, which I now realized had lost me many an argument, I made the following rule: to forbear all direct contradictions of the sentiments of others and all overpositive assertions of my own.

Thereafter, when another asserted something I thought an error, I denied myself the pleasure of contradicting him abruptly and of showing immediately some absurdity in his proposition. Instead, I began by observing that . . . in certain cases or circumstances his opinion would be right . . . but in the present case there *appeared* or seemed to me some difference, etc.

I soon found the advantage of this change in my manner. The conversations I engaged in went on more pleasantly. The modest way in which I proposed my opinions procured them a readier reception and less contradiction. I had less mortification when I was found to be in the wrong, and I more easily prevailed upon others to give up their mistakes and join with me when I happened to be right.

This Franklin philosophy is echoed by a present-day paint manufacturer which advises its salesmen to "use anti-argument phrases" in handling questions and objections. Example: "Don't say, 'This paint has the best reputation in town.' Do say, 'From what others tell me, I'm led to believe that this paint has the best reputation in town.'" When the prospect objects, "Your price is too high," the salesman is instructed to reply, "I don't blame you. Many others have thought the price was too high until they found out what this paint would do for them." Instead of flatly stating, "This paint will save you a lot of money" these salesmen are taught to say, "I don't blame you if you doubt what I am going to say, but this will save you a lot of money." These are sample "anti-argument phrases."

Many salesmen listen intently to a prospect's objection and try to find some point in it with which they can agree. They *restate* this point of agreement and then proceed from there.

Avoidance of irrelevant objections

Too often a salesman permits himself to be led into a controversy on a point unrelated to the proposition that he is selling. If the buyer is prejudiced, if he holds odd ideas, it is not the salesman's business to convert him on those irrelevant points. The salesman is interested solely in the buyer's opinion of the proposition and should not concern himself with his views on anything else.

Of particular importance are the matters of politics, religion, local issues, controversial persons in the news, and other "hot" topics. Usually little can be gained and everything can be lost if the salesman allows himself to be drawn into such discussions. Even if the two individuals are of the same party, they can easily fall into disagreement on minor issues and each leave the interview wondering about the other's basic intelligence and intellectual integrity. Unless the objection directly deals with the proposition at hand, the salesman is wise not to take issue with the prospect's statement. If he says that the world is flat, agree that a good deal of it surely looks like it and go on with your presentation. One office machines sales-man lost a sale by getting into a discussion with the prospect over the appearance of the seller's new quarters. The prospect stated that he did not like the looks of the firm's new building. The salesman flew to his firm's defense, and the fat was in the fire.

Removing objections inoffensively

The essence of the Franklin theory is that the salesman must learn to remove the objection or the "objectionable idea" from the mind of the prospect without giving offense. That is not always an easy thing to accom-plish, depending upon the tenacity with which the person clings to the objection raised. However, a number of ways to do this without jeopardiz-ing the sale are open to the salesman.

EXONERATION FROM BLAME It is within the salesman's power to ex-onerate the prospect from blame for expressing an objectionable idea. He can give such excuses as "I see that I did not clearly explain that feature." Or "I'm sorry that I misled you into thinking that. . . ." Or "It is quite easy to get the wrong idea because of the complexity of factors." The strategy behind this tactic is to allow the prospect to save face and to minimize the chances for ego involvement when the salesman tells him, in essence, that he is wrong.

CONCESSIONS The salesman can take the sting from a rebuttal by making some concessions before giving his answer. He might allow, "There is a great deal of truth in what you say, however, . . ." Or "You know, I think you have a good thought there. That's a new point! I wonder if. . . ." People like to be told that their thoughts are great and they are not apt to be as resentful when the salesman subsequently points out how their thoughts just aren't quite appropriate in this instance.

DELIBERATE ATTITUDE Few people like their thoughts dealt with lightly; they want their ideas taken seriously and not passed off without due consideration. So the wise salesman will say at such times, "You know, I'd like to mull that over a minute." Or "That's worth thinking about!"

OTHERS WHO AGREE Somewhat in the same vein, sometimes the salesman is able to point out that there are many other people who agree

with him; he is not alone in his misconception. "You know, a great number
of people believe that, however, . . ." Or "Under similar circumstances,
many men take your view, however, . . ." are statements typical of handling
objections by this means.

PAYING TRIBUTE   At times the salesman can pay tribute to the prospect
in several ways, thereby erecting a buffer to protect the prospect's ego
when the rebuttal is made. The salesman may note that the prospect's
motives are worthy by saying, "I admire your idealism and know that you
are sincere, but. . . ." Or "I know that you are honest and fair-minded, so
allow me to show you just where our discussion went astray." Other times
the salesman can tell him that he is generally right by saying, "I know that
you are an authority on this and are seldom wrong, however, . . ." Or "I
seldom hesitate in taking your advice, but. . . ."

When should an objection be answered?

Most authorities agree that an objection should usually be met the moment
it is raised. Several logical reasons support this policy.

Assume that the prospect raises an objection which the salesman promises to
answer. Not wishing to forget the objection and thinking that the salesman
may neglect to come back to it, the prospect concentrates upon the point and
is so preoccupied with it that he does not hear what the salesman tells him in
the meantime.

The prospect may get the impression that the salesman does not have a valid
answer and hopes the prospect may forget the objection if it is passed by for
the moment. Confidence is shaken if the salesman replies, "I'm glad you
brought that up. I will come to it in just a few minutes."

The deferment of the answer also makes the prospect feel that the salesman
is just speaking his piece and that he is unable to reply to an objection without
throwing himself off stride. The desired impression of spontaneity is de-
stroyed; also it is likely to draw the prospect's attention to the salesman's
technique rather than to the points he makes.

When an objection has been met effectively, it may turn out to have been the
only obstacle to the order. Many salesmen seize upon a well-met objection as
a good closing time. They ask the prospect whether that is the only matter
about which he wants information. They make it a focal point and try to set it
up as the one deciding factor that, if answered, will lead the prospect to buy.

It may be concluded, therefore, that in most instances it is better to
answer objections the moment they are raised by the prospect.

When should an objection not be answered?

However, certain specific situations may be mentioned which seem to justify postponing the answer. These are as follows:

When the price objection arises early in the interview.

When the objection raised will be answered more effectively later in the salesman's orderly presentation of his proposition.

When the objections raised are so frequent or so petty that the salesman becomes convinced that they are simply an effort to disconcert him and slow up the sale.

Each of these three situations deserves brief consideration.

THE EARLY PRICE QUESTION The first situation—the price objection—frequently comes up in an interview before the salesman has awakened a desire for the product or shown its value. It is often used by prospects as a stall to avoid listening to the proposition at all. When this objection is raised early in the interview, it may be postponed until the prospect has enough information about the proposition to be able to decide intelligently.

The salesman of air-conditioning equipment for the private house defers the premature question about price in this manner: "I can't give you the price until I've made a detailed study of how best to make your home comfortable in hot, muggy weather. There are many ways we can do it, but they vary greatly in price, so it takes some work to figure out how to do it for you for the lowest cost." Note how the salesman has turned the question into an opportunity to make a sales point. Also note how the salesman uses the words "home," "comfortable," "lowest cost," "hot," and "muggy" to stimulate the emotional reactions he wants in the prospect's mind.

PREMATURE QUESTION The second situation permitting postponement of the reply is where the objection is concerned with a different subject from the one then being discussed by the salesman, but one to which he is coming soon.

Admittedly, from a purely psychological point of view, it would be advantageous to answer the prospect's question immediately, thus removing it from his mind. However, to do so many times disrupts the point that the salesman is trying to make and perhaps sidetracks the presentation into fruitless channels thus bogging matters down in confusion.

Suppose a men's apparel representative is in the midst of presenting his fall line of sport coats when the dealer asks, "When am I going to get delivery on that last fill-in order I sent you last month?" Yes, prospects do throw in such non sequiturs, much to the salesman's dismay, but it can be handled. "I'll go get my invoice book to see after we finish working this line." It is important that the delaying answer be logical and reasonable, lest the prospect be irritated by nonsensical replies.

TRIVIA   The last situation calling for postponement of the answer to an objection is where the question or comment is so trivial that the salesman is certain that the prospect is trying to delay the interview. When such is the case, the salesman may use the following strategy to justify his refusal to answer: "Mr. Prospect, I appreciate your interest in this proposition, and I certainly want to answer all your questions before I leave; but it has been my experience that about all these questions on details will have been covered when we are through with the presentation. I am sure we could save time (and I know you are a busy man) if you will just wait a few minutes and then ask your questions about anything that I have not covered." Most prospects are fair-minded enough to go along with such a suggestion if it is offered with a smile.

A situation demanding postponement of some answers arises when the prospect rattles off several objections without waiting for a reply. The answers to some of them must obviously wait until the salesman has answered the others; so he smiles and says, "You're going too fast for me. Now tell me which one of these points you would like to discuss first."

Forestalling objections

It is not possible, therefore, to lay down an inviolable rule on the matter of meeting objections promptly or postponing them; the decision will depend on the circumstances. One general proposition may be laid down, however: *many objections can be forestalled.* The principle previously stated (that it is wise to keep a prospect from placing himself on record as opposed to the proposition) is well proved. The salesman can, by watching his interviews carefully, observe the stages at which certain objections are usually raised. He will note that the same objections are raised in most cases at about the same time. A knowledge of the prospect's type and nature will help greatly in anticipating when certain common objections will be brought up. The preapproach should aid the salesman in thus answering *in advance* those stock objections. When this policy is pursued, it is not uncommon to have the prospect say, "I was just wondering about that."

Just what is meant by "forestalling" objections? It does not mean first stating the objection and then answering it. *No mention of the objection is made,* but the counterargument is presented in such a manner as to forestall the raising of the objection.

Salesmen for a machine costing several hundred dollars are taught to forestall the price objection. They know that most prospects will insist that they cannot afford it, so early in the interview the salesmen say, "Mr. Prospect, I've talked with a number of people who apparently know you pretty well, and they all tell me that you are a first-class businessman—a real money-maker. I can see plenty of signs that you are doing well. I wouldn't have called on you unless I had assured myself of this. You aren't exactly facing bankruptcy, are you?" (With a broad smile.) In many cases the buyer will grin in return and admit that he is managing to stay in business. This forestalls the objection, "I can't afford it."

Other objections may be similarly forestalled. For example, many buyers want to "think it over."

The hard-selling salesman may forestall this by saying:

"I know you are a busy man, and I'm not going to waste your time. I'm busy myself. If I explain how my proposition will make you real money and if I prove every point to your satisfaction, will you tell me today how it strikes you and not ask me to come back next week? That's a fair proposal, isn't it?" After this it is difficult for the buyer to say he wants to think it over.

When the salesman for a small car wishes to forestall the objection that the size of the tires is too small, he points out early in the interview that the light weight of the car makes it possible to use smaller and less expensive tires, although these tires are as large as stipulated by the Tire Manufacturers' Association for cars of this weight.

The anticipated price objection is often forestalled like this: "You are thinking that a product with all these new features will cost you at least $300; so you'll be happy to know that we're selling so many that production costs have been driven way down and we can let you have it for only $197.50."

One securities salesman constantly encountered the two objections, *I haven't got any money* and *I've got to talk it over with my wife.* He whipped these obstacles by opening the interview with the question, "I am interested in talking with a businessman who has at least $3,000 to put into a business venture which he is convinced is sound and who makes his own decisions without having to consult his wife. Are you such a man?" Once the prospect admitted that he qualified, he could hardly use those excuses as objections later.

When the salesman has a particularly forceful answer to some common objection, it may be good strategy not to try to forestall it and to let the prospect raise it, so it can be used as the basis for a "trap close" in which the salesman responds in effect to the prospect's objection, "If I answer your objection, will you buy?" Naturally, few salesmen would use those words, but they would try to get the prospect committed to buying upon meeting the objections. More is said about the trap close later.

Before answering an objection

No matter how a salesman plans to handle an objection, he will be wise to do these things first:

Listen carefully before answering! Let the prospect state his objection fully, even though it is one which the salesman has heard a thousand times. Do not interrupt! This courtesy of interested attention places the prospect under the obligation to accord the salesman similar attention when he answers the objection. It also helps to keep the interview on a friendly basis thus avoiding tension.

Act interested in the objection, don't attempt to belittle it. Pay the prospect the compliment of receiving his opinion with respect. Appear to regard it as one worth voicing.

Don't hurry the answer too quickly. Pause long enough to appear to be weighing it carefully, even though that objection may be old stuff and the answer memorized. This pause flatters the prospect and, at the same time, prevents him from feeling that he is being high-pressured.

Sometimes it is good salesmanship to restate an objection before answering it, because:

The salesman can sometimes restate the objection a *trifle* more favorably to his own case. This can often be done by putting it in the form of a question rather than a declarative statement. But the restatement should be honest and not twisted out of its original meaning.

The prospect is assured that the salesman understands clearly the exact nature of the objection.

It gives the salesman a moment in which to consider the best method of answering the objection.

If the prospect has offered the objection in an effort to break up the continuity of the presentation, the restatement of it enables the salesman to retain control of the interview.

In opposition to these reasons, however, there is the danger that restating an objection may tend to give it greater importance in the prospect's mind than it really deserves. The prospect may feel that he has hit upon something that puzzles or surprises the salesman and may be less apt to forget his objection than if it had not been thus emphasized. In general, restating objections may be good policy in cases where the objection is somewhat vague or may be restated so that it can be met more easily.

It slows down the progress of the presentation and may waste time. And it becomes monotonous if done too often.

Never magnify an objection

Too much should not be made of any particular objection; it should not be exaggerated in the eyes of the prospect. It is just as fatal to make this mistake as it is to ridicule an objection or pass over it too lightly.

The salesman should answer each sincere objection clearly, emphatically, and in a straightforward manner, making sure that the answer is intelligible to the prospect and that he agrees entirely with the way of meeting it. It may be wise to comment upon every answer by saying, "Isn't that the right way to look at that point, Mr. Prospect?" or "Have I answered that question to your complete satisfaction, Mr. Prospect?" If you have, then forget about that one, and get on to something else.

"When the baby goes to sleep, you had better quit singing," counsels the experienced father. "You might wake him up again."

Or, to change the figure of speech, objections have been likened to steppingstones through a bog. If you just keep going, you're all right; but if you stop and stand on one of them, you'll sink down into the mud.

For the salesman to linger too long over an objection is like holding a magnifying glass over it. The more it is discussed, the more important it becomes in the prospect's mind until finally it may seem much bigger to him that it did at the start.

DETERMINING HIDDEN OBJECTIONS

Up to this point we have assumed that the prospect, if he has an objection in mind, overtly states it, whereupon the salesman answers it. But it is not that simple. The prospect is often reluctant to bring his objections out into the open, forcing the salesman to ferret them out before he can deal with them.

To make the problem even more baffling, a prospect may offer a false objection, thereby wasting the salesman's time while not advancing the sale at all. Why do people behave this way?

A common example is found in the person who cannot afford to pay the price asked. He is embarrassed to confess his poverty, so offers some other reason for not buying. Other prospects are afraid of being influenced by the salesman, so they pose as tough, hard-nosed buyers who challenge almost everything the salesman says. This pose is a cover-up for a soft or weak character.

Sometimes a prospect is too kind to come right out and say he thinks the product is junk. Or the prospect may simply say nothing at all, thus effectively concealing all his reactions. Another defense is to appear to be going along with the salesman, nodding his head in agreement and appearing to be about ready to buy. These prospects usually resort to a stall. Just what is a *stall?*

The stall

In this case the prospect offers some objection which is not the real objection and serves only to obscure the real one. Such an objection may be raised early in the interview or at any time right down to the closing effort. Let us first examine the stalling objection that is raised even *before* the salesman has had a chance to present his proposition.

Suppose that a life insurance salesman calls on Mr. Prospect to explain a new type of annuity policy. He is given a cordial welcome. For several minutes the two men engage in a friendly discussion of a mutually interesting topic. However, the moment that the nature of the salesman's business is divulged, Mr. Prospect goes on the defensive. Why? Because he fears that the salesman may take too much of his time; may perhaps talk him into buying more insurance, which means more premiums to pay; or because he just does not want to listen to any proposition involving insurance. He does not know enough about the salesman's offer to raise any objections to it; hence by use of the stalling objection he *objects to giving the interview.* Any one of the following might serve the purpose.

"Sorry, but I have to meet my wife in 20 minutes."

"Leave one of your circulars. I will look it over and call you in a few days."

"I just rang for my secretary. I must get my dictation off in the next half hour."

"I'm not interested now. See me in the fall. I'll be in the market for more life insurance at that time."

What should the salesman do to avoid this *early dismissal?* First, he must make certain that it *really is a stall* rather than a sincere objection. He may quickly ascertain whether, for example, the first objection given above is sincere or just a stall by asking the prospect, "Oh, I'm sorry to have called at such an inconvenient time. When may I see you for 30 minutes this afternoon (or tomorrow morning)?" If the prospect is just stalling, he will immediately invent an excuse for not seeing the salesman at another time. In that case the salesman is fully justified in ignoring the stall and trying to secure the interview immediately. If the prospect readily agrees to meeting the salesman at a definite hour later, the assumption is warranted that he did have a date with his wife, and the salesman should thank him for the appointment and leave. Should the prospect fail to keep the definite appointment, then perhaps he is employing that device to stall off the interview.

Many of the specific objections discussed later might be stalling or shielding objections; or they might be honest ones. It is not always easy to determine in which category an objection falls. If there is a doubt about this, it is usually wise to treat it as if it were an honest objection, always reserving the right to change your opinion. Some salesmen, when they are sure or strongly suspect that an objection is a stall, just ignore it and go ahead.

Others, confronted with the old stall, "I'll have to talk it over with my partner," come back with, "I have an idea that your partner would trust you to make the decision on a deal like this." Then they proceed to sell.

Sometimes the best way to handle a weak objection is to encourage the prospect to state it fully. He may thus reveal how silly it sounds. Besides, he is often chiefly interested in getting it off his chest. In either case, the interview can proceed better after he has voiced his objection.

Caution should be exercised not to treat an *honest* refusal to act immediately as a stalling objection. Suppose that Mr. Prospect tries to conclude the interview by saying, "Mr. Salesman, I like your proposition. I will talk it over with my wife and call you in the next few days." It sounds like a stall; yet it may be a sincere explanation of the customary procedure of this prospect. The salesman will need to use tact in handling such objections, since an erroneous conclusion about its true character might antagonize the prospect sufficiently to prevent the salesman from ever making the sale. Ordinarily a question or two will test the sincerity of any objection that might be either a stall or a real objection.

Whatever the reason for concealing the real objection or obstacle to buying, the salesman must school himself to recognize false objections and stalls and then to uncover the real ones. Several techniques are used.

Asking questions

Questions encourage the prospect to talk and, sooner or later, he is likely to reveal what is really holding him back.

Sometimes the salesman may ask frankly: "Mr. Prospect, I feel that we aren't getting anywhere in our conference, and I'm afraid it is my fault.

There must be something that I have failed to bring out clearly. If you would just tell me what it is, it might save us both quite a bit of time."

If the prospect is inexperienced or unwary, or if he feels the urge to level with the salesman, he may state his objection. If the salesman can meet this objection, the prospect is almost committed to buy.

Some salesmen carry the practice still further. When the buyer says that he does not want the proposition, the salesman queries, "Just what is your reason?" The prospect will offer an objection, in reply to which the salesman asks, "Is that your only reason?" If the prospect says, "Yes," he has eliminated all others and virtually promised to buy if the obstacle to buying can be removed.

A difference of opinion exists on the desirability of asking outright for the inhibiting objections. In favor of asking for the information there is the argument already cited—that if the prospect can be induced to put himself on record as being deterred from buying by a specific objection, he has practically said that he will buy if the objection is removed. Another argument in favor of asking for the objection is that it speeds up the interview by making it unnecessary to present many talking points which may be utterly beside the point and therefore of such scant interest to the prospect that he may dismiss the salesman summarily. If the salesman could talk right to the big point, he could perhaps close the sale.

The argument against asking for a statement of objections is based on the thought that it is an admission of defeat, is saying, in effect, "You have whipped me, and I admit it; how did you do it?" Such a confession robs the salesman of the initiative; it places him on the defensive and may be bad for his morale. If the objection can be discovered without forcing the prospect to state it, the salesman's work may be easier. When a prospect has once stated an objection, he clings to it more tenaciously than if he has not.

If the salesman is reluctant to ask the nature of the prospect's objection, how can he discover it? Perhaps he can use slightly indirect questions, hinting at the probable objection and watching closely to see what effect his question has upon the prospect. He might say, "The other day I was talking over my proposition with Mr. Jones, and we couldn't reach any conclusion until I had made clear to him our guarantee. Maybe you, too, would like to have me go a little further into that?" Then he could see if his remarks were well directed, for the prospect would be likely to give some sign that would enable the salesman to know whether or not he had hit upon the right objection.

The salesman may even more forcefully pry into certain touchy areas in which he has learned objections frequently lurk, thereby encouraging prospects to talk about what is bothering them.

One common technique is asking for the *additional* objections. After the prospect has voiced his objections, the salesman then says, "Now then, Mr. Jones, what *else* is really bothering you? Isn't there something else you don't like or want to know about my proposition?" The prospect is encouraged to reply with his real objection, once he sees that he has not fooled the salesman.

"Honest John" technique or the appeal for fair play

One insurance salesman has developed a unique and effective method for handling the hidden objection. He calls it his "Honest John" method. When he suspects that some hidden objection is blocking progress toward an order, he says, "Mr. Jones, if I am ever invited to your office again, it will be for only one reason—you believe that I am an honest man. That is the way it should be. If you feel that I am dishonest, you should throw me out quickly and never see me again. After all, you have every reason to expect to do business with an honest man. Isn't that right? . . . Well, Mr. Jones, in return haven't I the same right? The right to sell to an honest man? Now I have a feeling that you are not being completely frank with me. There is something bothering you about this deal that you are not telling me. Be honest with me, and tell me what is really on your mind." He claims this appeal to honesty and fair play works almost every time. This basic tactic is not limited to the insurance field. Most people respond to an appeal for fair play.

Habeas corpus technique

One industrial equipment salesman has developed a special method for ascertaining a prospect's hidden objections which he calls his "habeas corpus" technique. When he sees that some hidden objection is preventing a sale, he relaxes the prospect by certain movements to indicate that he is leaving. Then he says, "Suppose two policemen walked into your office right now and hauled you off to jail without so much as a word about what charges are against you. You would be fuming mad at the injustice, and your lawyer would without doubt obtain a habeas corpus to force them to produce you in court and charge you with *something*. Well, Mr. Jones, our legal system makes certain that you know what you are charged with, and it allows you to retain the ablest defense lawyer you can get. Unfortunately, I am not being given the same rights. You have some charges against my product which you are not bringing out into the open so my product's best defender (smilingly tapping himself on his chest) can cope with them. Go ahead and prosecute this product all you want, but please let me be here to defend it against the charges so we can reach a decision as to whether it is guilty or innocent."

The four noes technique

An industrial supplies salesman claims that there are four noes which a salesman encounters in selling: no need, no want, no money, and no hurry. He uses these to help him dig out the hidden objection by saying to the prospect, "It has been my experience that there are only four basic reasons why people don't buy my supplies. They think they don't need them; they don't want them; they don't have the money; or they are not in any hurry."

As he is saying this he writes down each item.

NO NEED _____
NO WANT _____
NO MONEY _____
NO HURRY _____

He then says, "I would deeply appreciate it if you would place a check mark after the real reason you are not buying."

He claims that people will frequently be willing to do this when they are reluctant to state it orally. Once the prospect has indicated the area in which his hidden objection lies, then the salesman can begin probing to determine its precise nature.

Perception-insight

Many hidden objections are uncovered mainly through the insights or perception of the salesman. A run-down office, store, or factory would suggest a lack of working capital. Sometimes it is just the salesman's shrewdness that turns the trick. One paint salesman selling to a large corporation was at a loss to understand why he was not getting at least his share of that firm's business. His company was the largest local manufacturer. He knew that his price was right and that there was nothing wrong with the paint, particularly in comparison with the paint they were buying. He knew that his firm had given good service and had a fine reputation in the industry. He felt that he had done a good job selling to the purchasing agent who had the authority to buy. He concluded that someone was being paid off under the table. He slyly made a few remarks one day to the p.a., indicating in a noncommittal way that the company might be willing to contribute a little extra to the p.a.'s personal welfare fund. The p.a. responded with unwise candor, and "the cat was out of the bag."

It may be that from the prospect's actions in handling the samples or the merchandise the salesman could tell easily that price or quality was not satisfactory. If, for example, a customer in a retail shoe store appears interested in a pair of shoes until the price is mentioned, whereupon he transfers his interest to other, lower-priced shoes, the salesman does not need to be told that the objection is "too high price." But it is better to learn this without having allowed the customer to take a definite stand on the matter, for it will be much easier to show him the superior value of the higher-priced shoes and finally to sell them to him if he has not declared himself as wanting something cheaper.

In case the salesman has had one interview with the prospect that was almost satisfactory but did not result in a sale because the buyer seemed to cool off inexplicably during the presentation, the salesman should mentally retrace the interview to discover just where he made a statement or asked a question that showed a lack of tact. It may be that a critical reference was made to competing goods already purchased by the prospect; perhaps it was a lack of knowledge concerning the prospect or his business. The chances are excellent that by some unfortunate remark an antagonism has been created that acts as a hidden objection or obstacle to the sale.

It may be advisable to face such a prospect frankly a second time and apologize for what must have been said. It will often thaw him to the extent of talking business on a new and friendly basis.

CONCLUSION

One mark of the professional salesman is his ability to recognize the presence of a hidden objection and then to ferret it out. As one top producer put it, "If I'm not getting anywhere in the interview or the objections don't make sense, I know the prospect hasn't told me his real objection; so I start digging for it."

One cynical salesman claimed that prospects seldom state their real objections; he always looks for the real reason for not buying—the hidden one.

BASIC METHODS FOR HANDLING OBJECTIONS

In most interviews the prospect will raise some objections which cannot be anticipated or forestalled by the salesman. In fact, these objections constitute *reasons for not buying,* and they are brought up to justify the prospect's unwillingness to buy.

The next step is to examine some of the ways by which the salesman can handle important objections that are neither concealed nor too trivial to merit consideration and not common enough to be forestalled.

There are half a dozen distinct methods of handling the honest objection, *after* it has been raised. Obviously these do not include the method of forestalling, which must be employed *before* the objection is raised.

The six ways to handle objections are:

The *direct-denial* method, also called the head-on method, or the contradiction method.

The *indirect-denial* method, also referred to as the "Yes . . . but . . ." method, or the side-stepping method.

The *boomerang* method, called the reverse English method, translation method, or capitalization method. It capitalizes on the objection, translates it into a reason for buying, and returns the objection, boomerang-fashion, at the prospect as a talking point *for* the proposition.

The *compensation* method, called by some the superior-point method, the offset method, or outweighing the objection with advantages that more than compensate for it.

The *question* or interrogation method.

The *pass-up* method, used only where the objection is flimsy or unimportant.

The direct denial

Many trainers of salesmen contend that the salesman should never contradict the buyer in any circumstance. They point out that a contradiction stirs up antagonism and makes of the interview an acrimonious debate, thereby rendering more difficult the salesman's task of obtaining the prospect's complete agreement to his proposition. The view is generally correct, but there *may* be times when the direct method is effective, although such occasions are rare.

The realtor is showing a house to a prospect who objects, "I hear the taxes on this property are over $1,000. That's too high." The salesman might reply, "The taxes are $724.50. We can verify it by asking the county treasurer."

Under conditions such as those outlined, what is the effect upon the prospect of the direct denial? When handled properly, it may well impress him with the salesman's absolute sincerity and belief in what he is selling. It is possible for a salesman to be too much of a yes man, with the result that his prospect gets the feeling that he is insincere.

It is probably wise for the salesman to soften the impact of a direct denial a bit. This may be done by a smile as he utters it or by a brief follow-up similar to that used by the salesmen just quoted.

However, five warnings are needed.

First, a word of caution concerning the *manner* in which the salesman states his denial. He must be earnest but not offensive—smile and not frown. He must not appear to lose his temper, or he weakens his cause. Only a skilled salesman should attempt to use the method, for in the hands of a bungler it is suicidal.

Second, It is not wise for the average retail clerk to attempt the direct denial. The clerk is seldom in a position to meet the customer on such an equal plane as use of the method demands. Besides, most clerks would not use the right technique in handling the situation.

A *third* point concerns the class of prospects with which the method is most likely to work successfully. If the prospect is extremely sensitive and fond of his own opinion, such a method might give serious offense. If the prospect is too small to give another person credit for his convictions, the method should not be used. But if he is fair-minded he may admire the salesman for his courage.

In the *fourth* place, the direct denial is better in reply to an objection put in the form of a question than to one phrased as a declaration of opinion or a statement of fact.

"Won't that color fade in the sun?" asks the anxious prospect. The salesman replies, "No, definitely not. Tests prove it and we guarantee it."

Fifth, a direct denial should never be used if the objection has any ego involvement in it. The salesman should never place the prospect in a position of having to defend some erroneous opinion. The prospect objects, "Your motor looks too little for that car." He has stated an opinion and to deny it directly questions his intelligence and will only serve to make him hold his opinion more firmly. This is especially true when the point at issue is important. The direct denial should usually be confined to answering minor objections.

The direct, or "head on," method of meeting objections, therefore, should be regarded as a "desperate remedy for a desperate disease," not to be attempted except by an expert salesman under circumstances where he is sure it would be likely to succeed.

A careful study of scores of sales manuals and instruction courses for salesmen reveals very few cases where the direct-denial method of meeting objections is recommended. There is a tendency for the salesman to use this method too often, to use it without thinking. Hence, the warnings and the small number of illustrations of its use.

The indirect denial

The second, or indirect-denial, method of meeting objections is unquestionably the most widely used. It fits more situations and can be used with more types of prospects than any other.

It recognizes the fact that most people resent being flatly contradicted. They prefer to have the salesman bend a bit to avoid being broken. Analogies are not difficult to find. The baseball player permits his hand to give way slightly before the ball as he catches it, rather than to allow the ball to inflict a painful bruise, as it might if he held his hand in a tense position. The boxer tries to roll with his opponent's blow to lessen its impact. The salesman does not usually meet the prospect's objections head on but gives ground a trifle before he replies. He says, "You are quite right, Mr. Prospect, in saying that this is often true, but in this particular case . . ." etc. Or,

"There is a lot of truth in what you say, but don't you think also that . . . ?"
Or, "I'm not surprised that you feel that way about it at first; I did myself,
but when I had time to go into the matter a little more I found that. . . ."
How much more comfortable the prospect feels than if the salesman had
said, "No, I can't see your point at all," or "It may seem that way to you,
but as a matter of fact . . ." or "You are wrong there," or "That's not so."

Often the use of the indirect-denial method may be exaggerated in
dealing with a buyer who holds an unusually good opinion of himself.
With this type of prospect the salesman must give him credit for having
given birth to a real idea. Here the salesman may pause a bit when the
objection is raised, may perhaps appear puzzled over it. The plan is to
convey to the prospect the impression that he has thought up a reason that
is not commonly raised, that requires consideration to answer. He is subtly
flattered by the thought that he has rather "stumped" the salesman; he
feels that the salesman is properly giving him credit for possessing a keener
insight than is enjoyed by the average man. After the salesman has thus
given due weight to the objection, he can answer it with a reasonable
assurance that the prospect will in turn give *him* credit for *his* ideas and will
be more likely to view the matter fairly than he would have done had the
salesman belittled his objection. When the prospect states his objection
flatly as a declaration of belief, the indirect denial is more tactful than the
direct denial.

In selling gas furnaces, the objection is often encountered, "I can get a
furnace for less money that is as good as yours."

The salesman replies, "That is a logical statement, in view of the wide
range in price of many articles, such as automobiles. You can get anything
from a used Volks to a new Rolls-Royce, and you'll get your money's worth
at any price. But gas furnaces are different. All the better ones are now
about the same price. Of course, you get a few more features in the ones
that cost a little more."

Sometimes the indirect denial is less obviously tactful. That is, the
salesman does not noticeably yield ground to the objection, and yet he does
not directly deny it. A few illustrations:

The prospect for a lot in a new subdivision may object, "Your lots are
too far out." The salesman is taught to answer, "That is what some people
thought of every subdivision we ever put on the market. Many of the
sections that we opened up years ago are all built up and would be considered close in now, but they were called too far out by people then. It pays
to look ahead a few years when making investments."

The prospect for an oil burner objects that it would make an oily
smudge on the walls of his home. The salesman says, "I'm inclined to think
that your statement is based on the experience of someone who had an old
burner of the natural-draft type. Those early burners did smudge the walls

because the supply of air was not measured to fit the oil supply. Our new burner measures the oil and air so exactly that there is no carbon, smoke, soot, or even odor." The salesman has denied the statement but has done it indirectly without contradicting the prospect.

This method is, as has been said, sometimes referred to as the "Yes, but . . ." method. Some prefer "Recognize, but. . . ." However, the word "but" is avoided whenever possible. The word is filled with negative connotations; it arouses antagonism. Frequently the word "and" can be substituted. Try this and note how it softens your answer.

While we are on the subject of semantics, the word "unless" is a good one.

Prospect: I don't like to pay so much.
Salesman: Neither do I . . . *unless* I know I'm getting full value for every penny of it, as you are here.

We should keep in mind that both this method and the previous one are *denials* of the objection's validity.

The boomerang, or translation, method

The third method of handling objections is frequently called the "boomerang," because the objection hurled by the prospect comes back at him as a reason why he *should* buy. It is also sometimes referred to as the "translation" method because it translates an objection into a reason for purchasing. To illustrate in a general way: The prospect raises an objection, and the salesman immediately replies, "Why, that's the strongest reason I can think of why you need it!"

To illustrate more specifically: The Dictaphone salesman, when his prospect objects, "But my business is different," replies, "The Dictaphone is particularly adapted to the man who believes that his business is different. The more important it is for a business to have its dictation understood and its letters correctly written, the greater the value of the Dictaphone system in that business."

The well-drilled salesman for the book that is sold to mothers of grade school children, when the prospect objects, "My boy takes no interest in his schoolbooks; I doubt if he would read it if I bought it," replies promptly, "Right there, Mrs. Blank, you have voiced the strongest argument in favor of this work that I can think of. Why doesn't Johnny like his schoolwork? Because he has not been encouraged to understand thoroughly the studies that he is required to take. He has a good mind: help him to see and learn."

Or when the salesman for a well-advertised line of men's clothing meets a retailer who objects, "Your firm spends too much in advertising. If you would cut out some of that expense and give us retailers a wider margin of profit, I might handle your line," the salesman uses the boomerang method. He says, "Mr. Retailer, it is the advertising that makes it easy for you to sell this brand. Your customers are already sold on its quality before they come into the store, and it is our advertising that brings them in." He continues to talk quick turnover, small selling cost per garment and total profits, until this objection is thoroughly laid to rest.

The prospect for a fire extinguisher may object, "I can't afford it." The salesman may reply, "I'd rather hear you say that than anything else that you could say, because if you can't afford to invest a few dollars in positive fire prevention, you surely couldn't afford to have a fire."

The prospect for an office appliance may object, "I'm a busy man; can't take time to talk to you." The salesman turns the objection into a reason for buying with "If you are a busy man, then I am just the man you want to see, because busy men know the value of time and are eager to discover new ways to save time. I have a real time-saver."

The boomerang method is effective only in the hands of the skilled salesman. Particularly it is useful in meeting excuses that are not strongly backed by facts. The excuse is thus disposed of before facts or reasons can be marshaled to support it. Care should be exercised to avoid giving the prospect the impression that his objection is of no consequence. The manner of the salesman is important in this connection; for if he allows the least hint of a sneer to creep in or appears to be enjoying a triumph over the luckless prospect, he will ruin his chances. His manner must be friendly and sincere; a smile must dull any edge that the words might in themselves seem to possess.

Above all, it is necessary to avoid giving the prospect the impression that he has "laid himself wide open" or "led with his chin." Unless used with discretion, this method may cause the interview to assume the aspect of a sparring match or contest.

The compensation method

The fourth way of handling objections—the compensation method—admits the validity of the objection but points out some advantage that is supposed to compensate for it. The prospect for a pair of shoes might object that the leather did not seem to be of the best quality. The clerk would probably admit the fact that the leather was not the highest grade but tactfully point out that, if it were, the price would probably be several dollars higher. The low price compensates for the lower quality. This method of meeting objections is based on the broad principle of compensation, made famous by Emerson and other philosophers and epitomized in "You can't have everything." If the wheel base of the car is too short for easy riding, the compensating feature is that it handles and parks more easily.

One should remember that there is no perfect product. All of them have limitations and features to which some prospect can legitimately object. The compensation method is used in handling such valid product objections. The only possible defense against a valid objection made in good faith is to point out the compensating features which outweigh the mentioned deficiency. The salesman must simply make the prospect desire the product's advantages more than he dislikes its disadvantages. It does actual harm to try to beat down a legitimate objection, for the prospect may lose all confidence in the salesman if he refuses to acknowledge valid objections.

Usually there are good reasons why a product is designed as it is. One salesman for baby equipment often encountered product objections from department store buyers such as: "Why don't you put a handle on it so it can be used as a stroller?" or "Why don't you put some beads on the front of it?" or "Why don't you put rubber bumpers on it?" The answer always was: "That does sound like a good idea, and we did give it careful consideration. How much more do you think your customers would pay for it with these features? . . . Well, that's just what we found out; they wouldn't pay any more. So we just could not do it and keep the price down to where it sells in good volume."

A product's compensating advantages and relative disadvantages can be visualized by listing each point with possibly a picture or diagram explaining it.

Fundamentally, what the salesman tries to convey is that his product will give the prospect what he really needs and what it does not give is not really important after all.

The question method

The question affords an excellent means of answering objections. When a prospect has raised an objection, an answer is just about necessary, yet a statement of fact is likely to open the way for further objections. The question form of answering the objection not only does not invite other objections, but it makes the prospect answer his own objections.

Suppose a prospect says to an electric typewriter salesman, "You have a marvelous machine and I would love to own it, but I just can't see putting $500 into a typewriter."

A great many questions can be asked to attack this objection ranging from a simple, "Why do you feel that way?" to such queries as, "Are you willing to invest $500 in an asset whose rate of return exceeds 100 percent a year?"

One of the most exasperating excuses a salesman has to answer is the statement that "All our buying is done through the home office at——." To most salesmen it is finis, and many buyers use the excuse even where it is not true.

One salesman has developed an effective method of handling the situation. When he finds that he is talking with a prospect who thinks that he is not a prospect because someone else will have to OK the requisition, he says, "Would the home office (or the boss) allow you to consider a plan for improving any detail of the work at your branch (or in your department)? Can you look into any plan that *might* help you, provided the home office (or boss) doesn't have to buy anything in advance?

"Wouldn't it be possible to consider my plan, and if it pleases you, then you can recommend its adoption for all branch offices (or departments)? If we can work out a plan that is really good, we'll present it to the home office (or the boss) as *your* plan and help you sell it to them. Or would you rather have some other branch manager (or department head) sell *his* plan to the home office (or the boss) for *you* to use?"

One of the most valuable words in the salesman's vocabulary is the little word "why." It's true for a number of reasons, such as:

It forces the prospect to talk. This gives the salesman information, especially about why the prospect is not buying yet.

It forces the salesman to listen.

It takes the salesman off the hook, and gives him time to think.

It pushes the prospect to examine his reasons.

Many common objections can be met with this little word: Why?

I'm not buying now. . . . I think prices are coming down. . . . Sales are falling off. . . . I don't like your price. . . . I want to think it over. . . . I want to look into some other deals. . . . I've always bought from the ABC company. . . . I'm not interested in having you make a survey. . . . My business is different. . . . I want to talk this over with a friend first. Why? Why? Why?

You can take any one of these and build an imaginary but probable little conversation growing out of the powerful "why." Such a conversation can be channeled to an agreement on the point.

If a woman says to the vacuum cleaner salesman, "Your machine is too heavy," the salesman asks, "Too heavy for what, Mrs. Jones?" That forces the prospect to say something and gives the salesman a chance to demonstrate that his cleaner is really not too heavy.

If she says, "Your cleaner wears out the carpet," the salesman meets the objection with a question, "What makes you think so?" Usually the woman has no sound reasons for her statement; she has heard rumors. The salesman can then more effectively meet the objection, for he has disclosed its weakness.

When the prospect objects that the seller's company is too small—that he wants to buy from a bigger concern—the salesman replies, "What is it, Mr. Prospect, that insures the permanency of an organization? Is it size or sound management?"

The question engages the attention and thought of the prospect. It is specific. It ties the prospect down to brass tacks. No matter when it is used—whether in the approach, during the opening argument, in the presentation, or in the closing arguments—the question can be a strong form of delivering a selling talk.

In many circumstances the asking of a question will cause the objection to evaporate. The baby-equipment buyer would want more colors in the line; the salesman would ask, "Why do you want to complicate your inventory with a multitude of colors?" The buyer would then admit that the thought did not appeal to her; the objection would evaporate.

Frequently it is wise to combine this method with others in answering particularly difficult objections. The salesman should first ask questions to focus the prospect's thoughts and clarify the exact nature of the objection. Then he can proceed to use some other technique for answering it if it still exists after the questioning.

The pass-up method
Some salesmen attempt to smile and pass off many objections. When the housewife objects, "I'll have to ask my husband," the salesman for vacuum cleaners smiles and replies, "He would say, 'Ask my wife.'"

Other salesmen affect not to have heard the objection, passing on rapidly to the next point. Dodging the issue may be effective now and then but it is not recommended for use when the objection is a valid one. When the prospect has offered an obviously flimsy excuse, the method may be justified.

The five main methods of handling objections may be combined in various ways. The question and boomerang methods are frequently combined, as may be the compensation and question forms.

Conclusions concerning use of six methods
Although it is impossible to state definitely that one method should be used in one situation, and some other for another, certain general conclusions may be drawn concerning the use of the various ways.

Direct denial may occasionally be employed when the objection raised is a *false* one.

Indirect denial is the chief weapon of good salesmen in meeting most important objections. It removes the idea from the prospect's mind *inoffensively* and courteously. It is used in all cases where the objection may be shown to be *inapplicable* to the product or proposition offered by the salesman.

Compensation should always be used where the objection is perfectly *valid* and *true* and must be admitted by the salesman.

The boomerang method should be used carefully, since few prospects relish having their objection thrown back at them as a reason for buying. However, in some situations it offers an effective reply to objections that actually constitute reasons for buying when properly presented.

The question method is used in three situations. (1) When the objection is so vague and general that the salesman is not sure just what is in the prospect's mind, it may be employed to force the prospect to qualify the objection further. (2) It is used frequently to show the folly or lack of logic in the objection raised. (3) It can be used to have the prospect answer his own objections.

The pass-up method is used only when the objection is too trivial or flimsy to deserve a careful answer. It does not actually *meet* or *answer* the objection.

DISCUSSION QUESTIONS

1. Why do most salesmen find it difficult to answer objections?
2. Can procrastinations be forestalled?
3. What objections cannot be met?
4. How does the salesman know there is some hidden objection blocking the sale?
5. As a salesman of electric typewriters you are constantly encountering an objection to their high price ($600). How would you forestall this objection?
6. How do arguments occur in a sale when the salesman has made up his mind in advance not to get into one?
7. A salesman for a small machine tool company was constantly meeting the objection that his firm was unknown. How could he forestall this objection?
8. As a salesman of office equipment you suspect that a prospect is keeping hidden a price objection. What questions could you ask to determine if price was the real barrier to the sale?

9. You are an account executive with an advertising agency that is making a presentation to a large national food account. The president states that he likes your work but that he thinks your agency is really too small to service the account properly. What method would you employ to meet this objection? Give an example of what you would say if you used each of the different methods.

10. A large food processor tells you, a container salesman, that he has been doing business with his present supplier for a long time and that he is perfectly happy with him. He is not about to change suppliers. What method would you use to meet this objection?

11. Why are a prospect's real objections likely to be kept hidden?

HANDLING OBJECTIONS: II

There is no excellence without difficulty.
Ovid

The previous chapter was devoted to an overall look at the nature of objections and various basic strategies for handling them. It took the broad view. This chapter will be focused on the details of meeting specific types of objections.

TYPES OF OBJECTIONS

Objections can be classified in various ways. There are stated and hidden objections. These were discussed previously. Then there are valid and invalid ones. Objections may also be classified according to the phase of the sale to which they apply (which buying decision the prospect is not ready to make). There are objections to the product, to its price, to the terms of sale, to its source, to the salesman, and to the time when the purchase should be made.

Each of these types of objections will be discussed here in detail.

Valid vs. invalid objections

Many objections are perfectly valid; the prospect is speaking the truth. Some of these valid objections are answerable, while others are not. The *unanswerable* objections generally take one of two forms: (1) no money or (2) no need for the proposition.[1] Unfortunately for the salesman, these are often used as excuses to cover some hidden objections; hence, the salesman must immediately determine whether they are valid or are merely excuses.

Of course, there are limits beyond which a prospect is truly unable to go in obligating himself to pay. It would be useless to try to sell a new Rolls-Royce or a million-dollar life insurance policy to some poor fellow trying to eke out a living on $100 a week. He cannot pay for them, and the salesman would be unethical, as well as foolish, if he forced such a sale.

Lack of buying power and of need are problems that are practically hopeless for the average salesman, although even here the resourceful man will sometimes find a way out. If he is selling a production good—something that will make or save money for the purchaser—he may yet sell him and let him pay for it as he is able. However, where the article is not capable of producing anything for its owner, there may be no sensible means of selling such a person. Anyway, the salesman should not make such a sale, even if he could.

Even where the salesman finds the need for his product apparently well satisfied, he may sometimes persuade the owner to make a change. The fact that a man already owns a certain make of automobile or typewriter or carries in stock a certain brand of canned goods or cutlery does not necessarily deter the enterprising salesman from making an effort to persuade him to change. It should perhaps be pointed out that sales can usually be made with less effort to other prospects, but perhaps the prestige derived from inducing these users of other products to change may make the effort worthwhile. An indictment frequently directed against salesmanship is that there is too much competitive, and hence unproductive, effort.

There are situations in which the buyer has no *apparent* need for a proposition even though he may have the means to buy. The blind man may not feel the need for a television set, but he may perhaps be led to want one as an article of furniture or to give pleasure to other members of his family or as an inducement to friends to visit him.

The professional salesman will, however, avoid selling where there is no need, since this only creates dissatisfaction, which will hurt the salesman's future chances in selling to this person or to his friends.

There are, in short, real and valid reasons for refusing to purchase. These are often unanswerable and need not be discussed further.

Valid objections on other phases of the proposition will be discussed in detail later. However, a word of caution is needed at this point. There is a

---

[1] Speaking accurately, the person without money or without need is not a true *prospect*. The work done by the salesman in prospecting and in his preapproach will eliminate many of these, but it is impossible to screen out all of them.

tendency among salesmen to treat all objections as invalid. This is unfortunate, for it frequently injects into the interview an antagonism as the prospect realizes that his perfectly valid objection is being treated lightly by the salesman.

An executive objects, "I've heard too many bad reports on the service your company renders after the sale. I am afraid that I just can't see giving my business to your organization." Many salesmen would treat this as being an untruth, but the fact may be that he has *heard* some bad reports on the firm. Notice that he says he has *heard* bad reports, not that the alleged poor service is a fact. The salesman may be convinced that his firm gives excellent service, so he immediately labels the objection as invalid. This is a mistake, for the prospect believes it to be valid, and it must be treated as such if it is to be successfully met.

OBJECTIONS ON SPECIFIC BUYING DECISIONS

This final group embraces the objections which are most important in selling the prospect. When these are removed from the prospect's mind, he should be ready to buy. Their number is limitless, but we shall try to arrange a few of them in a sort of pattern.

When a prospect raises an honest objection, it informs the salesman that the prospect has not yet made one or more of the buying decisions which he must make before he is ready to accept the proposition. *Every objection can thus be related to some buying decision* and the salesman's task is to go back and gain that decision before he can make the sale.

The buying decisions involved are 3, 4, 5, 6, 7, 8. Numbers 1 and 2 have already been gained when the prospect agrees to see and hear the salesman. These six decisions, in review, are

3. I realize the disadvantages of my present position; I am dissatisfied with things as they are.
4. I see where this product would improve my position and make me more satisfied.
5. I approve this proposition, including price, terms, service, etc.
6. I like the firm that this salesman represents.
7. I like this salesman and would like to do business with him.
8. I want to buy now.

Now let us examine some of the more common objections and see where they fit into this classification. We shall also discuss some suggestions for handling these objections—suggestions collected from the experience of thousands of salesmen over many years.

Objections blocking buying decision 3—no need

The prospect raising an objection in this category does not yet feel a *need* for the proposition; the salesman has failed to arouse in him a *desire* to own it. He is cold to the whole matter.

The objections in this group frequently require careful study for their answers, because no salesman can say with certainty that a prospect *does* need his goods unless he has given some thought to the needs of that prospect. As discussed earlier, the salesman may be able to show the prospect that he needs the proposition, even though no need has been *felt* before.

A few typical objections under this head as offered by retailers will be discussed.

WE ARE ALL STOCKED UP, AND UNTIL THIS STUFF MOVES I'M NOT GOING TO LOAD UP ANY MORE   (A retailer is speaking.) This may be a difficult objection to meet satisfactorily, for it may indicate that the salesman has done his work poorly on the previous trip, either by overstocking his customer or by failing to show him how he could best sell the goods he bought.

In this situation the salesman may offer suggestions for moving the goods or may reply, "Of course, you aren't entirely cleaned out yet. You don't plan your buying that way; you want to have some on hand constantly to supply your customers. But your stock won't last more than three weeks, and you will want new stuff coming in to replace it."

If the buyer's excuse is a bluff, the salesman can "call" it by taking a hurried inventory and ascertaining just what the situation is. If the stock on hand is not large, he may point this out and obtain an order.

The ways in which the salesmen for one firm are instructed to meet this objection may throw added light on the subject.

The Sealy Mattress Co. recognizes the importance of arming its salesmen so that they will be prepared to meet this objection. The Sealy road force is told that "I'm loaded up" is just as common as "How will you have your eggs?" or "Do you want cream in your coffee?" The men are advised to enter a store quite convinced beforehand that the merchant is all stocked up. In fact they are warned to be suspicious of eager buyers.

With this in mind, the suggestion is made that the salesman knock the props from under the merchant's barricade of "I'm all stocked up" before he has an opportunity to voice this objection. After the usual greeting and compliments of the day, during which the salesman can scan the stock of mattresses, a sales talk somewhat as follows is suggested:

"Mr. Poindexter, I see you carry quite a large stock of mattresses, don't

you? Notice you carry some high-grade ones, too. Say, this is a fine mattress—you bought it from So-and-So, didn't you? They are good people—
clean competition—make good stuff.

"Don't you find it much easier to sell high-grade mattresses now than you
did several years ago? Now you don't think anything of it when you sell one for
$60, or even more, do you?

"These days it is absolutely necessary for a live merchant to carry high-
grade goods. People are buying them; and if you haven't them, they go to
some other town where they can buy them—isn't that so?

"You ship a lot of goods to neighboring towns, don't you? I noticed Mr.
So-and-So (name some town close by where you made a sale shortly before
you came to this town) does not carry so large a stock as you do, but he is
waking up. I sold him a nice bunch of mattresses yesterday."

Generally, the merchant wants to know what the other dealer bought. If
not, the Sealy salesman volunteers the information. Then he proceeds to
show his line, immediately mentioning the price. Promptly the dealer objects,
for the Sealy price is high as compared with the price of most ordinary mattresses. The salesman immediately hammers away at the price objection, giving the dealer information concerning mattress fillings which he probably
never received before.

If this part of the selling talk is convincing, the company's experience
shows that the dealer generally says he would buy if he did not have such a
large stock of other makes. However, the preliminary talk has lessened the
effect of this objection, and the salesman proceeds to dispose of it entirely by
saying:

"Of course, Mr. Poindexter, you have a large stock on hand—naturally
so—every large merchant has a large stock on hand. If you didn't have it you
would not be a live merchant, but you are selling it, aren't you? You will not
always have this stock on hand and will have to replenish your stock from time
to time. It will take some little time for us to ship these mattresses, say about
two weeks, and if you think that is too soon, suppose you give me an order for
shipment 30 days later? You will need something about that time."

In any sales talk designed to get around the "I'm all stocked up" objection, it should be recognized that excessive stocks constitute an important
cause of retail failures. Salesmen must be educated to realize that no advantage is gained by forcing an order when it is obvious that the dealer already is
carrying too much merchandise, unless the sale is accompanied by a determined effort to assist the merchant to dispose of his overstock.

I HAVE NO CALL FOR YOUR GOODS   This is a common objection
encountered by salesmen selling to dealers. The representative for Kendall
motor oil answers this in a manner that can be adapted to any product. He
says, "I'm not at all surprised by your statement. Do you ever have any call
for a haircut or a shave? Of course not! But you would have if you displayed the red-and-white barber's pole. It is the same with Kendall. All you

have to do is to display the well-known Kendall sign in a conspicuous place. The motorist is not in the habit of stopping to ask for a particular brand of motor oil, unless he is reasonably sure that he can get what he wants. He drives on, keeping a look-out for the brand he seeks; and when he sees the sign, he stops."

Another way of meeting the objection is to say, "Mr. Prospect, if all merchants took that stand, very little business would be done. If you get a call for our goods before stocking them, would your customer wait until you could fill the order? No, sir, you would be sending a customer to your competitor. The goods will sell just as soon as people see you carry them in stock. If they didn't, we couldn't have stayed in business so long, could we? Display our line, and I will be taking your order for more on my next trip."

NO ROOM FOR A NEW LINE   This objection is usually an excuse, for any dealer has room for a line or product that will make him money. When he offers this objection, it simply indicates that he is not thoroughly convinced that he needs another line.

Inasmuch as this objection is merely an excuse for not buying, it cannot be answered directly; you cannot answer an excuse because the prospect will simply think up another excuse. It is like boxing shadows. The salesman must get at the root of the problem—the hidden real objection. This was covered fully in the previous chapter.

WE LIKE OUR PRESENT SUPPLIER AND SEE NO REASON TO CHANGE   This objection may be offered either by a retailer or by a manufacturer and is a tough one to get around, for the buyer sees no need for taking up your line. The salesman's strategy must be aimed at persuading him that it is good business to have alternate sources of supply for an item just in case something happens to the present source. He might say, "There is no question that they are a good company. In fact, most of our customers also buy from them. For example, just last week I was talking to Mr. Diamond, the buyer over at Acme Steel, about pooling all his business with us instead of splitting it. He shot me down real fast when he reminded me of the time that Acme couldn't ship because of a strike. He declared that it was the policy of his firm to maintain multiple sources of supply so they can minimize their chances of having their supply cut off should anything happen to one firm. Don't you think that makes sense?"

Or the salesman might try to show how the two lines complement each other—they are not really competitors. This is particularly relevant when selling to retailers. In many instances two similar products, which on the surface seem to be directly competitive, are not; they appeal to two separate market segments. The salesman might say something along these lines: "Yes, I noticed you carry the Qualtimo line and we both know that it's a good one. In almost every store carrying our line, Qualtimo is selling alongside it. All these dealers tell us the same story; the two lines are bought by different markets, they don't compete with each other. You are now missing some sales volume by not having our particular segment of the market covered."

In other situations, the salesman's strategy is to obtain a small trial order, get his product in on a limited basis, and then slowly expand his beachhead by giving excellent service and waiting for his competition to make a mistake. This can be a slow waiting game, but well worth it for a large account because it is surprising how many times the competition will make some mistake that changes the balance of trade between suppliers.

MY OLD ONE WILL LAST FOR A WHILE LONGER   Many prospects are reluctant to abandon their old possessions in favor of the new. "Sure it will. You can make about anything last as long as you want to, but at what cost?" That is the point of attack for the salesman—the cost. The cost in dollars for repairs of increasing frequency. The cost in inconvenience of equipment that may lie idle while repairs are being made. The cost of not enjoying the many modern features now available. Usually prospects voicing this objection are somewhat small-visioned and penny conscious. Therefore, appeals to savings and sometimes profits are likely to be effective.

Sometimes social pressure or an appeal to pride can be used to advantage. The salesman might reply, "Certainly it will! Your old coal furnace would still heat your house, but you installed gas. And your old suit is now being worn by some beggar! And your old car is now driven by someone less fortunate than you. But you got rid of those old items for better ones. So it is with this product."

I DON'T NEED IT   This may be voiced by almost any type of prospect and shows that you have failed to create the necessary desire with your presentation and must return to the start of the interview and retrace your steps in order to locate just where you lost your prospect. Ask him, "Why?" That may provide some idea of where the trouble lies. Does he really need it? Verify your *qualification* information again! Did he agree with your need-proof statements? Just where does he disagree with your presentation? Go back and dig to prove the particular points in dispute.

Objections based on buying decision 4—product

When an objection in this group is raised the salesman may assume that the prospect has been awakened to his need—that he feels dissatisfied with things as they are. But he is not yet sure that the product being presented will be the best one to satisfy his need.

These objections, if *valid,* may most frequently be met by use of the compensation method, or by the indirect denial if they are *not valid.* If the goods are not of the best quality, the salesman usually has a lower price to offer as a compensating inducement. It may be that the compensation method can be used in another way here. Sometimes the prospect compares one aspect or characteristic of the goods with the same aspect or characteristic of a competitor's product—a point-for-point comparison. Few products can win all of the points in such matches, but the salesman can be prepared to minimize the significance of those in which his product compares unfavorably. If the salesman has reason to fear that his goods will not stand the closest scrutiny as to quality, he must avoid making extravagant claims early in the interview, for these will be thrown back at him later. The presentation should rather be devoted to pointing out what other advantages the product possesses.

If the product actually is a second or an irregular, this should be admitted at the outset before the prospect calls attention to it, thus disposing of the objection that it is not up to standard.

The use of analogy is sometimes resorted to in meeting the quality objection. "You can't buy a Lincoln for the price of a Ford, you know, although the same company makes them both. And more Fords are sold than Lincolns."

In other instances the salesman may be able to show the prospect that the several features or qualities he prizes in other products are, in reality, superfluous for his applications—he does not need them. "Certainly, another product has a much heavier-duty motor, but it is not needed in your situation. Why pay for something you don't need?" Here the *concept of useless quality* can be brought forth: All parts of a product should be designed to give the same length of life. It makes little sense to design a motor to last 10 years if the gear mechanisms are designed to last only 5: the customer pays for 5-years' quality that he won't get. A paint salesman claims that his paint will last for 10 years. But if the customer is going to repaint in 5 years because of soot and dirt, he needs only a 5-year paint. How many "lifetime" guaranteed pens are still in use? Few people have any desire to use something a lifetime; this is one of the bases for the success of Timex watches. These are some of the arguments that can be put forth by the salesman who is trying to meet a quality objection.

**I HAVE A FRIEND WHO BOUGHT YOUR PRODUCT AND WAS UN-
HAPPY WITH IT**   The salesman cannot deny this statement; so he tries to
learn more of the facts. He urges the prospect to tell him all about it. Often
this will reveal that the complaint is trivial and sounds silly when brought
out into the open. If it is not thus disposed of, the salesman may say: "This
is the first I have heard about this and I'll take it right up with my company
and with this friend of yours. Could I use your phone to ask him what he
thinks we ought to do about it?" This may serve to screen out the false
from the honest objection and certainly will impress the prospect with the
salesman's eagerness to do the right thing. Then the salesman might say:
"Now that this is taken care of (and I assure you it will be) I hope you will
give my proposition the same consideration that you would have given it if
you had never heard of your friend's experience."

Complaints are similar to some objections and should be handled similarly.

Don't deny them; don't contradict; and don't ignore or ridicule them.
Hear them.

If true, *agree* that prospect has grounds for grievance.

Don't blame your company's credit or shipping department. Accept
the responsibility yourself.

Explain how it happened, making it clear that it was most unusual and
that steps have been taken to insure that it could never happen again.

Then turn attention to the best way to correct or settle the trouble.

If the complaint is justified, make generous adjustment *at once.*

It may be smart to ask: "What do you feel would be a fair adjustment?" or "What do *you* think we ought to do about this?"

Stay cheerful; don't be grudging in your attitude. Don't dicker with
prospect if he seems to be a straight shooter. Act *glad* to square things with
him.

The embarrassed salesman might be able to take some of the sting
from the customer's barbs by saying, "Obviously, it is disturbing to learn of
such occurrences, but you will have to admit that such things happen in all
companies and with all products. They can happen to you no matter from
whom you buy and you know it. The important things to know, however,
are: How often do such mistakes happen and, when they do occur, what
kind of service and factory support will be forthcoming? So let's go right
into our total performance record." With that statement the salesman tries
to convince the prospect that his firm gives excellent service to back up its
relatively few mistakes. Guarantees, case histories, testimonials, personal
telephone calls to satisfied users, repair records, and visits to facilities are all
techniques that can be used.

I'VE USED THE AJAX MACHINE FOR A LONG TIME, AND I SIMPLY LIKE IT BETTER THAN YOURS Many times product objections are broad-based attitudes solidly backed with strong prejudice. This situation frequently is based on sheer unfamiliarity. People are comfortable with the familiar; the new and unknown frightens them. A secretary learned to type on an IBM machine in high school; she is familiar with its workings and used to its touch. She will have product objections to changing machines. The best strategy for overcoming this type of broad product objection is to get the prospect to agree to a trial usage. Leave the machine, and let her get used to it.

A man has been wearing H. Freeman suits for several years and is thoroughly satisfied. Changing his buying habits will be difficult. You can't offer him a free trial! So you may ask questions such as, "I am interested in knowing exactly what it is you like about these suits." By getting the prospect to outline the features he likes about the competitor's product, the salesman learns what he must stress in his product. Also such questions will aid in determining if the preference for the other product is based on some solid reasons or is only prejudice or habit.

About the only workable strategy available to the enterprising salesman in such cases is an appeal for open-mindedness and fair play in giving the product a fair trial. If the salesman is confident that his product will sell itself if used by the prospect, then he should focus all efforts upon getting the prospect to try it, with no obligation. Since most men believe that they are open-minded, they should respond when the salesman says, "Yes, I heard that the Ajax machine gives good results, but I would like to know more about it. As you are an open-minded, objective individual I would really appreciate it if you would give my machine a fair trial and then tell me just how it stacks up against Ajax. This would help me considerably because right now I am not as well acquainted with the Ajax as I would like to be."

I LIKE YOUR HOUSE, BUT I NEED A DOUBLE GARAGE INSTEAD OF THE SINGLE ONES YOU PUT ON ALL THESE MODELS Frequently a product objection can be answered most simply by giving the prospect what he wants. Many builders are in a position to answer, "Fine, let's get everything down on paper to see for just how little I can get you your double garage. I personally agree with you; a double is a good investment and a real improvement over these models."

A customer of a men's apparel store complained that a certain sport shirt was not tapered sufficiently around the waist to suit his tastes. The owner said, "We can have our alterations shop take it in to suit you for a

slight alteration charge." As money was not important to that particular
customer, the sale was made. Normally, that owner gives free alterations on
all major items of apparel as a means for meeting objections as to the fit of
the suits and coats. Other times he meets objections about the design,
color, or fabric of his garments by offering to order from the factory exactly
what the customer wants. Sometimes they take him up on it; other times
the objection evaporates.

It is in this field of objections that a salesman's imagination can save
many lost causes. A woman motorist wanted a peculiar shade of pink paint
on a new car she was trying to buy. She had been to several dealers, and
none of them had the color in his line. Our hero took the color swatch from
the young lady and asked her to pick out the *model* she wanted. He merely
figured into the deal the cost of a repaint job and made the sale.

The salesman should always examine his position carefully to see if he
can actually give the customer the exact product wanted. Can the product
be altered in some way to meet the objection? A clerk in a woman's ready-
to-wear department claims that she frequently has to rearrange the dress to
conform to the customer's desires. She snips off unwanted flowers or buttons, adds a different belt, or perhaps puts some costume jewelry on it.

The salesman who is willing to go out of his way to give the prospect
what he wants will find closing the sale to be easier and the customer
appreciative. People like to be catered to.

Objections based on buying decision 5—price

These objections cover those aimed at such matters as price, terms, delivery, advertising allowances, services, and many other factors that directly
bear on the out-of-pocket costs of the product.

When the prospect says, "Your price is too high," he may mean any
one of several things. First, he may mean that in his opinion your product
is not worth the price you are asking; it is not a good value. Or, he may be
saying in effect, "I haven't enough money to meet your price." This, of
course, is a different matter, for it assumes that if he did have sufficient
money he would buy. Naturally, the approach used in handling this type of
price objection is entirely different from that required to answer the first. In
the latter case, the salesman would attempt to work out some plan of
payment that would meet the prospect's financial requirements. In the former case, he would use one or several of the various techniques, discussed
later in this section, for building up the value of the product in the prospect's mind.

In other instances, the prospect may be saying, "I think I can buy your
product elsewhere for less money." He's sold on your product and would
buy it at your price if it weren't for these other opportunities he has in

mind. The techniques used to handle this type of objection naturally vary still further from those previously used.

In conclusion, before the salesman can hope to answer a price objection, he must first ascertain exactly what the prospect is objecting to. He must determine whether the price objection is one of value, lack of money, or competition.

Now it is time to discuss several methods of meeting these different types of price objections.

HIDDEN QUALITY OR MERITS

The classic answer to price objections has usually been to focus efforts on increasing the value of the product in the eyes of the prospect. Many times the reasons for an item's higher price are not obvious but must be specifically pointed out to the prospect. After all, if a product carries a legitimately higher price, there must be some reason for it; the salesman should, therefore, stand ready to prove these reasons.

Salesmen for a check writer, designed to prevent checks from being raised, use this method effectively: "I have a watch here. What would you estimate it is worth? You say you don't know because you have not examined the works. That is true—you cannot tell whether it is worth $10 or $100 merely by looking at the outside. What is true of this watch is even more true of our machine. Inside this machine are seven segments, each with 10 individual dies of a hard composition, besides an oscillating and two stationary dies, making 73 in all. Every character must be true to the thousandth of an inch. This means the finest kind of workmanship." From here the salesman goes on to explain the other hidden parts of the machine, stressing quality all the way.

The salesman for a manufacturer may be trying to sell the purchasing agent of another manufacturer and may find it effective to say, "No doubt your own salesmen have to meet the same objection every day and they answer it in the same way I'm going to answer you. You believe that your product is good—that it is worth what you ask for it. You could probably cheapen it in places, but you don't want to sacrifice quality to do it. We are in exactly the same boat and I know you understand."

John Ruskin, nearly 100 years ago, wrote, "There is hardly anything in the world that some man cannot make a little worse and sell a little cheaper, and the people who consider price only are this man's lawful prey."

Another approach to this problem is to make quality and benefits stand out so emphatically that price seems relatively unimportant. The familiar story of the sale of potatoes illustrates this method.

Two farm wagons stood in a public market. Both were loaded with potatoes in bags. A customer stopped before the first wagon.

"How much are potatoes today?" she asked the farmer's wife who was selling them.

"A dollar and a quarter a bag," replied the farmer's wife.

"Oh, my," protested the woman, "that is pretty high, isn't it? I gave one dollar for the last bag I bought."

" 'Taters has gone up," was the only information the farmer's wife gave.

The housewife went to the next wagon and asked the same question. But Ma McGuire "knew her potatoes," as the saying goes. Instead of treating her customer with indifference, she replied:

"These are specially fine white potatoes, madam. They are the best potatoes grown. In the first place, you see, we only raise the kind with small eyes so that there will be no waste in peeling. Then we sort them by sizes. In each bag you will find a large size for boiling and cutting up and a medium size for baking. The baking size cook quickly and are all done at the same time, which means a big saving in gas. Then we wash all our potatoes clean before sacking them, as you see. You can put one of these bags in your parlor without soiling your carpet—you don't pay for a lot of dirt. I'm getting $1.50 a bag for them—shall I have them put in your car or deliver them?"

Ma McGuire sold two bags, at a higher price than her competitor asked, in spite of the fact that the customer had refused to buy because she thought the first price was too high!

All of which proves that a customer's idea of price depends entirely upon the ideas in his or her mind. The more you know about what you are selling—regardless of whether it is a highly technical product or just potatoes—the better able you will be to overcome price objections. Customers should not be allowed to feel that a price is too high. They won't feel prices are high if you know the fine points of your quality merchandise as well as the farmer's wife knew her potatoes.

A salesman for Head skis justified the higher price asked for them over those of a competitor, whose skis are quite similar in appearance, by showing the prospect a cutaway cross section of the two skis. He pointed out certain details of construction which obviously were superior to and more costly than the competitor's wares.

Sometimes the idea that the product is truly of high quality can be established if the salesman focuses the prospect's attention upon one key part or component and proceeds to prove its quality beyond doubt, thus suggesting that the rest of the product is similarly constructed.

SAVINGS OR PROFITS   Many times, particularly in selling to industrial concerns or middlemen, the qualities or merits of the product may be completely beside the point. The important factor businessmen frequently look for is the product's ability to save them money or make them a profit. Suppose a certain product cost but $100 to make and was of obviously cheap construction; however, it would save the prospect $6,000 during the first year. Would the buyer refuse to pay $1,000 for it? In pricing theory, *costs* do not determine prices; the *market* does. Costs determine profits and, therefore, who stays in business. A salesman should not get into the habit of thinking that the price of his product must be justified on a cost basis, for too often he will be unable to do this. After all, it is often impossible to ascertain the costs of a certain product. Do forequarters of beef cost more than hindquarters? No, but they have to be priced differently in order to clear the market in equal amounts.

The best justification for a high price is that the product will save or make the buyer more than its price. If the salesman can prove that fact, the prospect will buy.

A men's apparel store owner was objecting to a sweater salesman that his prices were too high. The sweaters were a highly advertised line which sold for around $25. The salesman replied, "Would you rather sell a $25 sweater or a $15 one? You get about 40 percent on each, so why not be making $10 on each sweater sale rather than $6? Besides, it is actually easier to sell our $25 line that is being pushed vigorously than it is to persuade a customer to accept your present unknown $15 line." The merchant bought and was pleased to find that the salesman was right; his sweater sales doubled that year, with the $25 line leading the parade.

Most industrial sales are built around the profit or savings which will accrue to the buyer. Once this has been convincingly demonstrated, price is seldom a barrier. IBM's electric typewriters are the highest-priced line in the industry, but they are the leading seller. The Hughes Tool Company was able to obtain a handsome price for its rotary diamond drilling bit because it saved the oil well drilling contractor considerable money as compared with the old cable drilling method.

In conclusion, one of the best methods for overcoming a price objection is to show that the product would not cost the buyer a cent; he would be actually making money. If such is the case, the salesman can reply to the objection "I can't afford to buy it," with "You can't afford *not* to buy it."

BREAKDOWN INTO SMALL UNITS Sometimes the high unit price of the item may scare the prospect into a price objection without really giving thought to exactly how much is being asked for it.

An adding machine salesman says, "Mr. Prospect, I have already shown you how you can save money by the purchase of one of our machines, but I see that I have not made myself clear in comparing the cost of this machine and the saving that it will give you. You have already told me that your loss through incorrect additions, etc., totals up to several cents per day. All right. Let's bring the cost of this machine down to cost per day.

Let's assume that you will wish to renew the machine every five years, by turning in the old machine on a new one and paying the balance in cash. The price of the machine is $350, and at the end of five years it can be turned in for about $100. That leaves you a cost of $250 over a period of five years, or $50 for one year. Dividing that by 300, the number of working days in a year, we have a cost of $16\frac{2}{3}$ cents per day. Your present system is certainly costing you more than that, isn't it?"

Door-to-door salesmen have long used this technique to show the prospect how little is really being asked. One vacuum cleaner salesman in New York developed what he called his "Fifth Avenue bus" technique in which he dramatized the fact that the cost per week for his product was less than the cost of a bus ride to downtown Manhattan. One book salesman equated the cost of his set of encyclopedias to a quart of milk. He would say, "Mrs. Jones, if your doctor told you that your son needed an extra quart of milk each day for his physical development, you would find the money to buy it, wouldn't you? Well, that is all I am asking. Billy needs these books for his mental development, and all they cost is that quart of milk each day. His mental development is just as important to you as his physical well-being, isn't it, Mrs. Jones?"

The basic idea behind this breakdown technique is to quote the price on some other basis than the product itself. The price can be related to some short unit of time or to some unit of productivity. A paper salesman made a sale of quality letterheads to a purchasing agent by saying, "Isn't it worth one-tenth of a cent to you to know that your firm is being represented on the best letterhead paper available? That's all it will cost to give you the best instead of what you are now buying."

Of course, one way to meet the price objection is to offer easy terms of payment, reducing the statement of the price to fractions of the original amounts.

An executive complains about the high price of a check writer to which the salesman replies, "Our $250 machine will last for fifty years, but let's figure it on the Internal Revenue Service ten-year basis. The other forty years are for free, okay? That's $25 a year or a bit more than eight cents a day. Eight cents for the time you save and the protection you gain is a bargain!"

More recently salesmen offer leasing plans to overcome price objections. "Okay, $250 is more than you want to pay right now. I'll lease it to you for $5 a month."

PRESTIGE APPEAL   Usually people who are buying a product for its prestige know its price and do not object. J. P. Morgan is reputed to have told a young man who had asked him how much a yacht costs, "Young man, if you must ask the price of a yacht, you have no business owning one." The regular customer entering the Steuben Room of an exclusive department store fully expects to pay the high prices asked for that brand of artware. However, many times certain products are on the borderline of prestige, or the prospects are not fully aware of the product's reputation. The salesman must develop some tactful ways of informing these people of the situation without offending them.

This problem of communicating a prestige price is quite touchy and if bungled can lose the firm a potential customer. People resent being talked down to or insulted by some statement implying that they can't pay the price. Perhaps they can't afford the product at hand, but that is still no reason to alienate them as future customers, for many poor people acquire money later in life and retain memories of slights from certain salespeople.

One dress saleswoman frequently used the following reply to objections that a certain dress seemed to be high priced for its quality, "When you buy a dress from us, you are not buying merely fabric and stitching. You are buying assurance that you will be dressed in the best of taste and that no other woman in this city will have a dress similar to yours. You will be unique. The price for high fashion can never be measured by fabrics and workmanship, only by what it does for you. If the dress is not for you, any price would be too high. If it makes you elegant and brings out the real you, the price is low."

A design engineer for an electronics firm planning on making a high fidelity phonograph objected to the relatively high price of a certain well-known brand of record changer which was to be used as a component. The salesman said, "You will admit that of all the changers on the market we have the best-known name and the reputation for being the most reliable unit made, won't you? . . . With our changer in your box your customer's salesmen won't have to explain to their customers the quality of the changer. Our name speaks for itself. The changer is one of the visible components in your unit, and it naturally is one to which most questions will be directed. Why compromise here? Compromise, if you must, on some hidden component that doesn't affect sales appeal so much."

In conclusion, if a product truly possesses prestige, a clever salesman can find the proper words to convey that thought to the prospect without offending him.

COMPARISON   Many times the prospect unfavorably reacts to price only because he has not carefully compared it with other products selling for similar prices. A father objected strenuously to the seemingly high price of a bicycle for his son until the salesman asked, "How much did you pay for those golf clubs I see in your car? . . . Which do you think it takes more time and effort to make, golf clubs or bicycles?" Since the man had just laid out $300 for his clubs, he had no alternative but to buy the bicycle.

When the price difficulty seems to be based on a comparison between the salesman's product and a competing product, it may be good strategy to get the exact difference between the two and then show clearly just what this product offers for the extra amount asked. In this way, by stressing *exclusive* advantages, the difference in price may be made to appear small.

A potential buyer of filing cabinets complained that he could buy another brand for $10 less than was being asked for a particularly well-known brand. The salesman replied, "Let's see, you say that $10 is the difference between my brand and the one you have in mind. Let me show you what you are getting for your $10. First, our cabinets are 2 inches deeper, giving you about 8 percent more filing space. On a $50 investment that alone is worth $4. Next, if you will inspect the ball-bearing rollers on which our drawers are mounted, you will find them much superior to the friction roller used in the other brand. Next, look at the way the movable support in each drawer is operated. Ours works much easier. Feel the way our drawers lock shut. It is obvious that this is quality hardware. So you see, you are getting a lot of quality and superior performance for your $10."

The salesman attempting to sell a complete outfit of aluminum cooking utensils, costing perhaps $100, minimizes the price by comparison. "How often do you use your piano, Mrs. Haring? It must have cost around $1,000. You use it almost every day for a few minutes? Good! Few people use a piano much, but they appreciate it when they do use it and feel that it is well worth the investment. As you say, we are here only a few years at most and ought to make them as genuinely pleasant as possible. Now take this aluminum outfit. You will certainly use it many more hours a week than you use the piano, and it costs only a fraction as much. Besides, you *must* have dishes to cook with; it is only a question of getting the best. Proper cooking is the very foundation of good health in the family. I have shown you that, owing to their long life, these utensils cost less per year than others; but even if they did cost more, good health is pretty cheap at the price, isn't it? And think of the compliments you will get on your cooking!"

Sometimes the retail shopper objects, "I saw the same thing for sale at a lower price at Blank's." When this objection is raised, it does little good to deny it flatly. It may be true; if it is not, a contradiction accomplishes nothing. It boils down to a matter of the customer's word against the salesman's. The clever salesman, therefore, will not deny the statement but will ask questions with the aim of finding out the facts. "You can doubtless find something at a lower price, but did you notice carefully the material used in the other coat? Are you sure it was as heavy as this, and was it made of virgin wool instead of wool that had been used once before? There are no imperfections in the weave of this one, and the color is very fashionable."

Perhaps the other article was a duplicate design in a cheaper material, often found in leather goods, such as purses, or upholstered furniture. The salesman who suspects this should set about to educate the customer on materials, so that the latter can tell the difference. The salesman may compare the article under discussion with cheaper articles carried in stock and point out the differences. "This looks almost identical at first glance, but a closer examination shows that the lining is not so durable and the color is a more ordinary shade of brown."

The customer may, indeed, be wrong, for the goods may be handled only by the one store in the city. In this case the salesperson can point out that his store has the exclusive agency for the city and that it is unlikely that the other store is selling the same article. It occasionally happens that a store will obtain, through devious channels, a small quantity of an article sold by another store that has been given the exclusive agency. The first store then makes much ado about the article, using it perhaps as a loss leader while the stock lasts. This is often done with trade-marked clothing or shoes, the practice being to have in stock unusual sizes or styles so that they will not readily sell. If the salesperson suspects that his customer is referring to such a situation, he might ask, "Were you able to find what you wanted there?"

Sometimes the customer's statement is true. In this case the salesman has two alternatives. The first is to show that although the price of this particular article may be a trifle higher at his store, the price of other articles might easily be less. He can explain that in marking new goods the estimates of two merchants as to a fair selling price might differ slightly. The other method is to point out that his store perhaps offers other advantages that may compensate for the slightly higher price.

This last point is illustrated by the experience of a man who went to a certain store to buy a pair of shoes. He found a satisfactory style at $15 but could not get his size. Going to another store he found the same shoe, but it was priced at $15.50. He asked the salesman why this store charged more than the other for the same shoe. The salesman smiled and replied, "Here's the way I figure it. In the first place, for that extra 50 cents you get the shoe." Here he paused. "That means that we keep a larger stock and are more likely to have some left over at the end of the season, on which we either are compelled to take a loss or carry until the next season. Maintaining a complete stock costs money, as you know. In the second place, you can have these shoes charged, which you could not do at the other store. We have the most liberal exchange policy of any store in the city. If the goods are not satisfactory in every way or if you don't want them, you may return them without trouble or embarrassment. In addition this store tries to educate its salespeople to an appreciation of their duty toward the customer. They give service that you don't get in some stores. We have a delivery system that reaches every part of the city twice a day. The other store does not. These advantages you receive for the extra 50 cents. And don't overlook the important fact that you get the shoe," he concluded with a smile. This man proved himself worthy of the name of salesman, and the customer was satisfied.

The way in which the customer offers the objection will help the salesperson to know how to meet it. If it is offered seriously, the matter is worth discussing. If it is mentioned in a casual manner, it is probably a flimsy excuse made by a shopper who has little intention of buying.

QUESTIONING   The question technique can prove quite effective in handling certain types of price objections. Many times a person believes a price to be high only because of ignorance or lack of thought about it. The right questions can encourage such prospects to realize that the price is in line, after all. The salesman may ask such questions as, "Why do you think the price is out of line?" or "What price do you have in mind?" or "I wonder what you have in mind when you say our price is too high. High compared to what?"

After getting the prospect to bring out his thoughts on the matter of price, the salesman can swing into one of the other methods for answering the price objection, his choice depending on the particular situation uncovered by his questions.

ADJUSTING THE PRICE   Although most salesmen do not have control over the prices charged for their goods, some are authorized to meet competitive prices under some circumstances. Some firms have a policy of meeting any legally quoted price lower than theirs if the salesman can show some tangible proof of that lower quotation. In such cases, the salesman should ask the prospect to give him positive evidence of the lower price to which he referred, and it will be immediately taken up with the home office. However, a word of caution. A salesman should never intimate to a prospect that he can meet such lower prices unless he is certain of it, for to hold out the hope of a lower price only to refuse it later will antagonize the prospect and chase him right into the competitor's camp.

In a later chapter many of the ethical problems connected with price negotiations will be discussed in detail. It must be acknowledged that in many industries there is considerable price flexibility, with each salesman trying to get everything he can and each prospect trying to get the price down. However, this is business—negotiating. To be successful in such sparring or duels, the salesman must learn never to give away his limits and to determine quickly those of his prospect.

He must be able to judge what the market will bear without letting the other party know how eager he is to sell. Above all, he must learn how to be firm when he quotes a price, for the slightest evidence of any weakness will automatically force the prospect to demand the lower price. He must learn to close with any adjustment in price so that the prospect is not free to bargain for another price decrease after he has obtained the first concession. Real estate salesmen must become particularly adept at this type of bargaining in order to bring buyer and seller together.

HANDLING THE TRADE-IN   In selling many products, such as automobiles, television sets, vacuum cleaners, refrigerators, furniture, and typewriters, the salesman is likely to encounter a prospect who has a used article that he wishes to turn in as part payment for the new one. Even in selling industrial equipment the salesman must be prepared to deal in two markets—the new and the used. He must know how and where his prospective customer can sell his old equipment if its existence is blocking the sale of the new equipment. In nearly every case the prospect places upon his old car or stove a much higher value than it actually possesses on the market. The salesman is faced with the problem of making two sales—that of the new article and at the same time depreciating the value of the used article. Because so many sales are ruined at this point, it seems desirable to discuss briefly some of the methods that have proved helpful.

- It is better not to place a valuation on the used article until after all the value in the new one has been fully explained. The prospect should be brought to desire ardently the new car before anything is said about how much will be allowed on the old one. This principle holds especially true when the salesman is not in a position to allow very much on the old article. Of course, if he has a liberal trading allowance and can appraise the old article at a high price, he may use this fact as a talking point and bring it out early in the interview.
- When the appraised value will be low, have the appraising of the old article done by a third party rather than by the salesman. Thereby, any antagonism aroused by a low appraisal will not be aimed so directly at the salesman.
- The appraising should *not* be done in the presence of the owner. When it is so done, every point leads to an argument and makes the sale that much harder.
- Have a formalized appraisal program in which the prospect sees that his possession is getting a complete examination rather than an offhand,

eyeball evaluation. He will gain confidence in the firm's integrity and thoroughness.

- Have some outside, independent authority upon which to base the trade-in price. Automobile dealers use their red and blue books to give an independent look to their pricing. Many appliance and office equipment manufacturers are furnishing their dealers with such trade-in information in order to support their valuations. The salesman might print up his own trade-in valuation tables to fall back upon in case of emergency. Blame the low trade-in valuation on someone else.
- Encourage the prospect to sell the equipment himself by showing him how to do it and giving him case histories of others who have done so.

Now, how can the salesman handle the prospect who insists that his car is worth more than the appraisal? Indirect-denial method of handling objections is probably most widely used here, the salesman agreeing that the old "bus" has doubtless rendered splendid service, but—. In selling cars, for example, the salesman may turn to the classified section of the daily paper, showing the prospect the prices at which such cars are offered. He may visit one or two used-car markets with him. He may show him the used-car market report. He may show a duplicate bill of sale for a car of the same make and model. He may show actual cars of the same make and model for sale in his used-car department. He may explain how expensive it will be to recondition the old car for the market, how the selling expense on it will be fully as great as on a new car, how rent and other overhead must be charged against the car.

One salesman developed the following analogy for handling situations in which the prospect's trade-in apparently should be worth more than can be offered. "I know how you feel. I owned some stock in a real good firm, good growth, good earnings. Anyway one wanted to look at it, it was worth at least $60 a share. But the market said it was worth only $42. You know, I've never met a man yet that won an argument with the market!"

When the prospect insists that he has been offered more for his old car by a rival dealer, what should the salesman do? There is just one thing to do here, and that is to tell the facts about the larger trading allowances that some dealers are given by the manufacturers. The prospect should be shown that he will lose all this when he trades in the competing car, should he buy it; that the larger allowance must come out of the quality of the new car, since few manufacturers are willing to sacrifice profits. And, all the while, the salesman must sell his own car hard, pointing out its exclusive advantages and superior features.

Many salesmen claim that it is wise to praise the prospect who has a trade-in for the care he has taken of it. Some statement such as, "I see that you have taken exceptional care of your present machine. That's good, for it will allow us to give you top dollar for it." Of course, this tactic should not be used if it is obviously untrue.

Most salesmen prefer to get the prospect to commit himself on what he thinks he should have for his trade-in before they commit themselves on its trade-in value. Sometimes the prospect is quite reasonable, and the figure he gives is one the salesman can close on. For example, the salesman might say, "Then if I can get you $500 for your trade-in you will go ahead with this deal. Is that right? . . . OK, let's write up the deal for the boss's approval and see what happens."

On the other hand, the prospect may give the salesman a figure so far out of line that there is little hope of a sale until the market has pounded some of the inflation out of the prospect's system—until he has shopped around and been educated as to the value of his property. Other times the salesman sees that there is a good chance for a deal if he can but get around the trade-in smoothly. This phenomenon gave rise in the automobile business to the practice of giving the prospect what he wanted for his trade-in but upping the price of the new product commensurately. In some instances the salesman is wise in putting into his original price ample room for granting generous trade-in allowances.

Objections based on buying decision 6—source

These objections are leveled against the firm which the salesman represents. Often they are not so much objections as questions and can be met with a straightforward statement of facts covering such matters as age of firm, its size, its financial standing, affiliation with well-known firms, important customers, rate of growth, patents held, other products manufactured, efficiency of operation, sound labor relations, etc.

Sometimes, however, the prospect has had unpleasant dealings with the firm and is personally unfriendly. For example, he may have had a dispute with the credit department over some claim. In this case the salesman may be tempted to join with the prospect in giving his firm a thorough "bawling out."

Such tactics, however, are bad, for no buyer respects a disloyal representative of any concern. If a mistake has been made, the salesman can promise a careful investigation and proper adjustment of the difficulty. The use of analogy may also help. "You wouldn't refuse to patronize a barber shop just because one barber in it gave you a poor haircut, once, would you? The other barbers are all good, and even the one would probably try extra hard to do a good job on you next time." The salesman must remember that he is the representative of his house and must not be led into taking sides against his employer.

Often, when the buyer has suffered annoying experiences with the salesman's firm, the only way to correct the situation is to keep calling until the prospect is convinced that the salesman is a fine chap and not in any way to blame for the misunderstanding. These tactics, pursued persistently, have won back thousands of former customers.

The two most common causes of source objections are past experiences with poor quality and late delivery. The salesman is posed with the problem of proving to the prospect that the causes of those past experiences no longer exist. The buyer must be given reason to believe that things have changed for the better. It is not an easy task in many cases.

Some buyers permit personalities to influence them to an extent that seems ridiculous. The position of an executive of the salesman's firm on a political issue may prevent some narrow-minded prospect from patronizing that concern. One answer could be: "Do you refuse to *sell* to everyone who does not agree with you on this question?"

Perhaps the best way to meet this objection is to side-step it: "You may be right, and our president wrong. There seems to be a lot on both sides, and I can't take time to figure the thing out. But I *am* sure that you would profit a whole lot from handling our line."

Possibly the president of the corporation has been mixed up in an unsavory divorce case or otherwise conducted himself in an undignified manner. The use of analogy is probably as effective as any method here. The salesman might say, "You remind me a little bit of the old deacon who refused to read the Psalms of David because David got mixed up in a little scandal once. The minister pointed out that the Psalms were just as helpful as if David hadn't slipped, but the deacon didn't like to patronize him by reading his writings."

The problem of prejudice is not easy to handle. You can't just smash it with argument. It is often based on emotion or on some experience unique with the prospect. The prejudices on general topics such as politics, personalities, sports, and educational methods had better be avoided with little comment by the salesman. A prejudice based on unpleasant experience must be treated with sympathetic respect and a promise to set things right, if this is possible.

Objections to the source are most frequently encountered in selling to large industry where the ability of the firm to deliver the needed goods in proper quantities, of specified quality, and on time is vital. Many large concerns will not take a chance on a smaller, unproven firm no matter how good its story on price may be. Thus such firms often find it difficult to break into big accounts except after a long period of selling efforts. These larger firms usually maintain lists of approved vendors or sources of supply, and firms are placed on these lists only after a team of the buyer's personnel has visited the seller's plant and investigated its ability to perform as claimed. One small electronics firm selling exotic hardware to defense contractors has a policy of automatically bringing the top executives of buyers' companies to its plant for firsthand exposure to its capabilities.

Sincere testimonials from executives of similar firms can go a long way toward assuring a doubting purchasing agent. Nothing sells such a prospect better than a record of good performance. The fact that the firm is on the list of approved suppliers to certain well-known and respected companies is reassuring to skeptical buyers.

Objections based on buying decision 7—the salesman

Here the prospect does not like the salesman. This is often an objection that is hard to discover. As a matter of fact, the salesman seldom knows whether or not the customer is refusing to buy for this reason. Most buyers do not tell the salesman that they do not like the way he spoke of his competitors or the manner in which he "kidded" the switchboard girl or the indelicate stories that he has told. So the salesman usually is compelled to guess at this objection and should always be on the alert to discover any personal weaknesses or unfortunate mannerisms that result in an unfriendly feeling on the part of his prospects. As a rule, the preapproach will disclose facts about the prospect that should help the salesman to avoid running counter to a pet hobby or prejudice.

Some salesmen, after being turned down, have asked prospects if the refusal to purchase was based on any personal peculiarity that might be overcome. If the salesman is sincere in his request, the buyer may enlighten him and help him to become more efficient.

Obviously, if the salesman has not played square with the buyer, the objection is valid. For example, if he promised advertising aids that were not forthcoming or if he overloaded his customer on a previous visit or if he exaggerated the merits of his proposition, there is nothing left for him to do but acknowledge his error and promise to reform.

Some buyers are cautious on account of experiences with unscrupulous salesmen. *I've been stung too many times on propositions that sounded good.* A reply, involving a judicious use of compliment and an analogy, may meet the objection. "I suppose, Mr. Prospect, that every man who has done much business has made some poor investments at times or at least feels that he has. However, if someone had passed counterfeit money on you a couple of times, you wouldn't refuse thereafter to accept any and all money offered you, would you? You would examine it more carefully before you accepted it, which is precisely what I should like to have you do with this proposition."

Personality conflicts do arise occasionally in which a salesman just can't get along with a certain buyer. In such cases he may arrange to swap accounts with another of his firm's salesmen, perhaps thereby benefiting both salesmen and customers. But this should not be a common situation; if it is, there is something wrong with the salesman. Good salesmen are able to get along with almost anyone, especially when they know something about the person in advance.

Objections based on buying decision 8—procrastinations

The motto of many men is never to do anything today that can be put off until tomorrow. So it is in buying; prospects frequently want to delay making a decision if they can. It would seem that making a decision to buy is a most painful experience.

The salesman continually hears, "I want to sleep on it." "I want to talk it over with my wife." "See me next month, and I'll be ready to buy." "I want to think about it for a while." "I want to look around a bit more." There is no end to the variations of the stall: the prospects just want to avoid making a decision *now*.

Admittedly, some procrastinations are legitimate. The prospect has to consult with some higher executive or has to wait for some event to happen, but most of them are just excuses.

The salesman who is unable to cope with procrastinations will never be highly successful, for he will lose too many sales to more aggressive competitors. The following is told by a Seattle real estate salesman.

I am sitting in the office one Saturday afternoon taking my turn at floor duty when this couple walks in and asks if we will build a house on their lot in the South end. I check and find out that we do go that far south, so I ask some questions to find out what they need in the way of a house. It turns out that they need a four-bedroom house of modest price. We had one about completed for show purposes so I took them over to the site, and they fell in love with it. The price was right, and we could deliver on time, so it looked like another sale. However, as usual, they wanted a few minor changes made, which required a visit to our architect for cost estimates before we could sign a firm contract. I called and found that the earliest time we could get together was on Tuesday morning, so an appointment was made for then. The couple was extremely happy; they even took me to dinner and spent the hour telling me what a good outfit we were because we would quote firm prices and delivery dates instead of giving them the runaround they had been given elsewhere. Well, on Monday I called to remind these prospects of the appointment and to confirm it. I was greeted enthusiastically with a big "Hello, there, Mr. Salesman. Gee, I'm sure glad you called. Guess what happened to us over the week end—we bought a house!" Some other salesman had gotten hold of them on Sunday and sold them a used house, taking their lot in payment. Which all goes to show you that when people are ready to buy they will find someone who will sell them if you are stupid enough to turn them loose un-signed. I made my mistake by not getting them signed to *something* right at the time and then amending it *after* the architects had given the additional cost figures. As a matter of fact, they really got stung, for the old house they bought did not fit their needs at all.

Every salesman can match that story with some of his own about how excellent prospects got away when allowed to delay. The salesman must be prepared to cope with procrastination forcefully, for these prospects are, in essence, agreeing to buy your merchandise but are just arguing over the timing of the sale. If they are that well sold on it, then the present is the best time to close the sale, for the love affair may wane if another salesman gets into the act in the meantime.

Fortunately, there are several good ways of handling procrastinations. First, the salesman learns to "put a hook in his close." He provides a reason for buying *today*. Second, he can outline the advantages and disadvantages of waiting. Third, he may be able to use the "Standing Room Only" close to discourage waiting. Finally, he may be able to use impending events as a good reason for acting now.

PUT A HOOK IN THE CLOSE   Door-to-door salesmen continually face this problem of getting people to make up their minds on the first call. Hence, they have included in their proposition various premiums which are "given" to the prospect for acting promptly.

The automobile salesman claims that he is in the best position *today* to give you top dollar for your old car because there happened to come into the office that morning a man who was looking for a used car just like the one you are driving. "If we can get together today, I can give you more for your old car because we won't have to fix it up for this man, and we won't have it sitting out on the lot."

Many firms selling to middlemen always have a special deal for the salesman to offer, this being "good only on this call." There is ample cost justification for such inducements, for it costs money to have a salesman make two or three calls to get an order when he might have gotten it on the first call.

One book salesman would say to the trade-book buyer for a book-store, "If you give me your order now, I'll send you a couple of extra books for yourself." A bribe? Yes! Effective? Definitely!

WHAT DO YOU GAIN BY WAITING?   Many times the prospect will see the light by simply comparing what he gains by waiting with what he loses. Usually he gains little or nothing, while he loses the use of the product for a period of time, plus possible risks of price increases, etc. The salesman may ask the prospect to write down on paper exactly what he thinks he will gain by waiting, while the salesman writes down what may be lost.

A salesman for an industrial janitorial service told a procrastinating prospect, "You're a very busy man. It's obvious you have many things to do with your time. Well, I'm a busy man, too, so let's be nice to each other and get this business over with so we can both get on with our other affairs. Sign the order. You're not going to get a better deal if you spend another 100 hours searching for it."

"STANDING ROOM ONLY" CLOSE   In the next chapter a more detailed discussion of this closing method is found, but right here it will suffice to point out that it can effectively prevent procrastination if properly used. In many situations the salesman can truthfully say, "I am sorry, but I can't promise that I will be able to make you this same offer later."

Supplies may be short, prices may be increased, models may change, or delivery dates may be altered. There are many reasons why a salesman cannot always promise that his offer will be the same at a later date. Some vacillating buyers have to be educated to the realities of the market. In selling real estate one of the big problems is to get a prospect to act promptly on a hot property—one which will move off the market quickly. Experience may indicate that if the prospects don't act now, the property will be sold by the time their decision is made, but many prospects do not believe such assertions. However, once a couple has lost a few desired properties to others who were more decisive, it becomes easier to deal with them. Sometimes the salesman can help this process along by relating some real case histories of people who lost their "dream house" because they vacillated. One salesman would say, "You really love this house, don't you? It's priced right and is attractive in every way, isn't it? Well, I guarantee you that there are 100 couples right at this instant in this city who are looking for a house just like this. They will agree with you, for you are right. Among these couples in the market now are some that know a bargain when they see it and will grab it. In fact, I cannot guarantee you that if you made me an offer this instant the owner has not already accepted another offer. If you want this house, then you had better make up your mind right now, for I feel sure that this property will be off the market soon."

Few things will make a prospect want to buy quicker than the thought that he might not be able to buy later. One southern California builder of luxury homes deliberately creates a "standing room only" environment around his projects by only placing them on the market in small batches at a time and then arranging it so that most of the homes in that batch have been previously spoken for. When a prospect walks into his "trap" (southern California slang for the model-home sales complex a builder erects from which to sell the homes in his tract), he manages to convey the impression that the houses are almost all gone and the prospect is lucky that one or two are left for him to buy.

IMPENDING EVENTS Sometimes impending events such as price increases, strikes, upturns in business activity, model changes, etc., will create a situation on which the salesman can capitalize to forestall the procrastinator. He can calmly mention these events during the presentation, thereby priming the prospect to buy promptly when he is convinced that the proposition is what he wants.

Not every procrastinating objection is a stall or insincere. In many industries no buyer would think of giving an order on the salesman's first call. This is true in most industrial selling, where the salesman knows that he must make several calls before he can expect even a token order. One firm reports that its salesmen make an average of eight calls before receiving their first order. There are many situations in which the prospect legitimately requires a little time to think and perhaps to discuss the matter with others before he places an order. To pressure such a prospect too hard would lose the sale.

DISCUSSION QUESTIONS

1. It was suggested that one excellent way the salesman can avoid procrastinating objections is to put a hook in his close. If you were the sales manager for a manufacturer of office supplies, what kind of bait would you furnish your men for their hooks? How can management assist the salesman in closing such sales?
2. Suppose a prospect simply will not believe what you say regarding his objections. What should you do?
3. Many insurance prospects claim they have no need for insurance when in fact they are saying that they simply do not care about protecting their family—they are irresponsible. What kind of objection is irresponsibility? How can the salesman meet it?
4. What are some of the methods by which the salesman can meet a buyer's objection to the newness of his company?
5. A customer refuses to do business with you again because of an unfortunate experience with his last purchase. What should you do?
6. There is an old saying in selling, "Be your own casting director!" It refers to the strategy of placing your prospect in the role you want him to play. If you want him to be fair-minded, you tell him he is. Why does this frequently work?

7. Many car salesmen have been known to use a selling technique known as *high balling* in which they quote the car shopper an unrealistically high trade-in price in order to get him back into the showroom after he has completed shopping all the dealers in the area. Then by some fast figuring the *high ball* price evaporates and the prospect is left facing the dealer's price. Why does this frequently work? What is the basis of its success?

8. When meeting a lower price quoted by a competitor, why does a good salesman get the prospect's signature on an order with the lower price before going to his superiors for approval?

9. Under what circumstances does the salesman accept a prospect's objections to buying and quit?

10. If a prospect still stalls after you've exhausted all your methods for handling stalls, what should you do?

CASE 14-1 NATIONAL CAN COMPANY

Don Bowen was the sales representative for the National Can Company in a territory in northwestern Washington. Located in a small town in his territory was the Pacific Coast Canning Company (Pacco), which was the largest single potential customer in his area. Unfortunately, they had been steady customers of the United Can Company for many years. Don was determined to eventually obtain this account for his firm.

For several years he dutifully called on all executives who were in any way connected with letting the can contract until he was now on familiar social terms with them. He had given them whatever little help he could whenever the occasion arose.

Pacco had always had a certain difficulty using United Cans for certain fruits. Until now Don could not exploit this weakness since he knew his own cans would do the same as United's. However, quite recently National had solved this problem through research on a new type of lining.

Don decided he would use this product improvement as the wedge to get the Pacco contract from United. He made a sales presentation of the new item to the interested executives of Pacco and received an enthusiastic approval with some definite commitments that a contract would be forthcoming upon expiration of the present one.

Two weeks later Mr. Owens, the vice president of canning operations, called Don and asked him to stop by and see him sometime. Don made an appointment for two days later.

Mr. Owens opened the conversation by saying "Some unfortunate hitches have developed in our negotiations. You know Sam Bruce, United's salesman. Well, his daughter recently died of polio. As you know, Sam has lived in town for a long time and has his roots down here. We go to the same church and are members of Rotary. When I told him that we were going to change can suppliers, he was visibly shaken, but he took it fairly well at the time. However, he was in to see me just before I called you. He said that when he informed his boss of the development he was told that if he lost that account the company would have to move him to another district since the territory's potential would be insufficient to permit keeping him here. He asked me to go with him to Chicago to explain the whole affair to top management to get him off the hook. They think he botched the account and won't buy the idea that their product is no good. So I am going to Chicago tomorrow morning. We can sign our contracts when I return."

Don said that would be fine and made a definite appointment for three days later for signing the contracts.

Upon his return from Chicago Mr. Owens called Don and said, "Some very unfortunate developments took place in Chicago. They said outright that they would move Sam from this town if we signed with you because they just would not have enough volume around here to justify his costs otherwise. Sam pleaded with me to stay with them and said they were working on the lining problem and would have it solved soon. I became all confused and felt so sorry for Sam with his daughter buried here so recently and his moving out at his age, and everything, well, I signed for another year. I am sorry for you, but you're young and can wait another year. Next year I sign with you."

1. What can Don do to save the situation?
2. Where did he lose this sale?
3. How could it have been avoided?

CASE 14-2   THE KING PAINT COMPANY:
The Hidden Objection

Jim Ellis, salesman for the King Paint Company, was extremely disheartened when he learned that he had not gotten the paint contract for the coming year for the McCoy Company, a large defense contractor located in the King Company's hometown. This was the sixth straight year in which the contract, a very large one, was awarded to another firm.

The King Company was a well-established manufacturer of a full line of quality paints. It was well-known throughout the area and was the largest paint company in the region. It maintained a policy of being completely competitive in price for the grade of paint being specified. Relationships between King and McCoy had always been good; there was nothing in the background that would indicate any source of objection.

Jim had been unable to ascertain the price at which the contracts were let because it was not the buyer's policy to play one supplier against another. All Jim knew was that the XL Paint Company had gotten the bid for the last 6 years. This made little sense to Jim. In no other account was XL serious competition; its prices seemed to be relatively high for the quality of paint produced. XL was a small firm and the McCoy contract accounted for a large portion of its output.

On several occasions Jim had asked the purchasing agent at McCoy for an explanation but had been rebuffed by the statement, "They simply underbid you. There's nothing else I can say."

1.   What do you think is the objection?
2.   What should Jim do about it?

CASE 14-3   AMERICAN CASH REGISTER

Early in 1966, Mr. Ben Bowles, owner of Danelle's, a high fashion women's specialty shop, opened a new store in a large shopping center located in a Chicago suburb. At that time he seriously considered coverting his accounting and control system over to some computerized system. His banker recommended that he tie into the bank's IBM system and after some contact with IBM nothing developed. He also looked at a control system based around a cash register, but he was against having costly registers in his stores because of their "department storish" image. He used hidden cash drawers with each sale written up on a sales check.

Early in 1968, Ben was again expanding and had been wondering if he should again investigate computer control systems. He knew that many apparel stores had installed the American system, but he was still strongly opposed to cash registers. One day a good friend of Ben's, who was an expert on American's computer system, told him that he could have the entire system without any cash registers. American also produced for its system a device that was usually employed as an auxiliary to the cash registers for the purpose of putting into the system much nonsales (nonregister) information such as purchases, markdowns, accounts payables, expenses, etc. However, the Encoder could create the same information as the registers but, admittedly, it did not have a great number of convenient features offered by the register. But the friend emphasized that there were stores on the system that were using only the Encoder quite successfully. One big advantage, according to his friend, was that the Encoder cost only $1,400, while the cash register cost $4,900.

Encouraged by this news, Ben immediately called his American sales-man and told him that he wanted to see the Encoder system demonstrated. An appointment was made for the next day at 9:30 A.M. for the salesman to demonstrate the system to Ben, his bookkeeper, and his financial advisor.

Later that day the salesman called back to ask the bookkeeper if it would be all right if he postponed the demonstration for 6 weeks until after the company's sales convention. He said, "A lot of new things are happen-ing and I'll be able to show you the latest at that time."

The bookkeeper replied, "No, it won't be all right. We need it now."

And so the salesman agreed.

The next morning at 9:30 the salesman came in the store and asked a clerk to assist him in lifting some equipment from a car. The two rolled a large cash register into the office.

"Where's the Encoder?" asked Ben.

"We don't have one," was the reply. "But I can show you how the whole system works through this register which you can keep here in the office. You can go ahead and use your cash drawers and then punch every-thing into the system through the register."

The salesman then proceeded through the demonstration, at the con-clusion of which he gave Ben an estimate of the monthly charges for the computer print-out of desired information. It came to about $300 per month.

Ben repeated, "How about the Encoder?"

The salesman said, "To tell you the truth I wouldn't sell you the En-coder. You would throw it out of here within a month and be mad at me. It costs $2,200 alone and it doesn't even start to do the job you need done."

"Well, thanks. We'll discuss it at the next board meeting and let you know," replied Ben.

1.   Evaluate this sale.
2.   What would you have done?

THE CLOSE

A salesman who cannot close sales is not a
salesman; he is merely a conversationalist.
Charles B. Roth

A good salesman is always a good closer, and a poor closer is always a poor
salesman, for the close is the "one far-off divine event to which the whole
creation moves." Everything that has gone before—prospecting, preapproach, approach, presentation, handling objections—all the preparation
and effort have been focused on this objective. The salesman who cannot
close is like the runner who trains faithfully all season, leads the field in the
big race until he is 10 yards from the tape, and then falls flat on his face.

Young or unsuccessful salesmen are often heard to say, "I go all right
up to the time I start to close. Then I just don't seem able to put it over, like
a football team that can make its first downs in the middle of the field but
lacks the punch to go the last 10 yards for a touchdown. I'm a good salesman but a poor closer." There may be *some* truth in this analysis of the
difficulty, but more often than not the trouble lies farther back in the sale.
The salesman who is a really good salesman all the way through the interview will not experience *chronic* difficulty in completing the sale.[1]

This should not be interpreted as meaning that the prospective salesman need give no special study to this phase of selling. Indeed, there is
reason to feel that is has perhaps been somewhat neglected of recent years.

[1] This calls to mind the cub salesman who reported to his sales manager, "I could lead 'em right up
to the watering trough, but I couldn't make 'em drink." His boss bellowed: "Whoever said you had to
make 'em *drink*? It's your job to make 'em *thirsty.*"

It should not be inferred that every presentation should result in a sale. No salesman ever made such a record. The best salesmen can sell only a fraction of the prospects called upon. But there is a tremendous difference between a baseball player who hits .250 and one who hits .350. The same is true of salesmen.

Reverting once more to our golf analogy, the salesman's closing effort is like the golfer's effort to hole out. All that has gone before, no matter how brilliantly executed, avails nothing if that final putt refuses to drop. The golfing adage, "If you can't putt, you can't win," can be matched by the selling slogan, "If you can't close, you can't sell."

The man who is uncertain of his closing abilities is handicapping himself throughout the presentation, for he cannot help being worried about the impending obstacle with which he has so much difficulty. Some men actually develop a fear of closing which eventually drives them out of selling. This has usually come about through a combination of ignorance of closing techniques and outright bashfulness about asking for the order. Many sales have been made simply because the salesman had the fortitude to ask for the order.

REASONS FOR FAILURE TO CLOSE

The difficulty many salesmen seem to have with closing has fascinated and perplexed sales managers for years. Only recently have we begun to understand the barriers in the salesman's mind that block his closing efforts.

Fear of failure

First, and probably foremost, is the fear of failure. Most of us are so psychologically programmed toward success as being the only worthy goal that the mere thought of failure frightens us into a semiparalytic state in which we are afraid to *ask* for the order or final decision for fear of being refused. We seem to think that so long as the prospect is not asked for the order we have avoided failure even though no sale transpires. We just do not like to hear such awful words as, "No!" "Not interested!" "Sorry, I don't want it!" These terms bruise our egos and that hurts us. This is much the same fear that keeps the young man from asking that certain girl for a date even though he is fairly sure she is interested; he is afraid that she just might say "no." But no ask—no date. So why *not* take the chance? Nothing ventured, nothing gained! Suppose the prospect does say "no." Really that doesn't hurt one little bit. The salesman can even learn to ignore it. He can develop a deafness for the word. If he cannot learn to take "no" for an answer and bounce right back without allowing it to affect his confidence, then he had better look somewhere else for a job. He will never make it in selling.

Guilt

Some men fail to close because of guilt feelings. They are ashamed of their profession. After much research the Life Insurance Institute determined the biggest single cause for failure of new life insurance salesmen is that they feel guilty about their work. They feel as if they are intruders begging for a living instead of men helping other men solve serious problems. This guilt feeling usually exists in salesmen who do not yet fully understand the proposition they are selling and what benefits it can bring the prospect. A life insurance salesman who has delivered many fat checks to beneficiaries entertains no feeling of guilt as he sees how much good in time of need is accomplished by the insurance policies he sold. Such a salesman sincerely believes that he may be doing the prospect a real favor in being pretty insistent. To him a "no" is a challenge, not a red light to stop him.

If you aren't proud of what you are doing, then you would be better off if you didn't do it. There is no room in selling for those who are ashamed of it. Unfortunately, some of this guilt stems from a lack of understanding by the man of his purpose in the scheme of things, the importance of his role in our socioeconomic system.

Imperception of need

Some men fail to close because they feel little need to do so; they think the prospect will automatically buy at the end of the presentation. Of course, some prospects do buy at the end of the presentation. But it has been proved that a larger percentage of prospects will buy if a good close is used than if it isn't, because many of them need a push to get them to act. Natural inertia stifles many purchases; it is easier to do nothing than to take action. Such prospects need a push to overcome their inertia.

Ineptness

Fourth, some inept salesmen just get so bogged down meeting objections that the thought of trying to close never enters their minds. They are fighting for their lives; they are confused; they have lost control of the sale. The close must be so natural to the salesman that he swings into it at every opportunity automatically. An analogy to a golf swing seems appropriate: the pro golfer gives little thought to his swing—he has "grooved" it previously by years of practice. It is automatic!

Cultural taboos

Everyone is raised in an environment that inculcates in him a host of cultural attitudes and behavior patterns. A great many people are raised in the tradition that there is something a bit impolite, improper, about asking another person for money or to do something for you. Closing means asking for the order, thus it can run afoul of cultural taboos in some circles.

BASIC CLOSING TACTICS

Aside from the actual closing techniques discussed in detail later in the chapter, there are certain overall tactics which are helpful in closing a sale. These apply to all sales, whereas a given closing technique has application to certain situations.

Avoid the interrupting third party

It is usually difficult to close a sale when a third party has intruded himself near the closing point. The salesman has succeeded in presenting his proposition so that the prospect is really sold, only the formalities of closing being left, when a third party drops in. He is not familiar with the proposition, has no appreciation of its merits, and tends to "throw cold water" on the whole scheme if the prospect asks him for his opinion. For this reason the salesman should try to close without allowing interruptions to occur. One salesman tells of a sale that he lost because he forgot to bring a blank contract with him; so, as the buyer was going that way, he suggested that they drop in together at the salesman's office and close the deal. On the way over a friend joined them and so chilled the atmosphere that the prospective buyer decided not to sign the contract at all. It may be argued that this smacks of so-called "high-pressure" salesmanship, and that if a man is thoroughly sold he will not so easily be led to change his mind. But it must be remembered that in buying something new the balance in the buyer's mind is very delicate and has perhaps been turned so slightly in favor of the proposition that it requires little to tip the scales the other way. This may be true, even though the proposition is a meritorious one, for it may require actual trial by the buyer to throw the balance heavily in its favor.

For this reason, when ready to close the sale, many salesmen endeavor to get the prospect isolated in some special office or in a location where they will not be bothered by outsiders. Ever notice the closing booths in automobile dealerships? Many sales are closed at private dinners or clubs where the salesman has arranged for privacy.

Simplify the contract

If the seller uses his own contract blank, it should usually be simple and short. The buyer has no time to puzzle out a complicated legal document and search for the "joker" that he suspects is concealed in the small print. The long order blank, which is in effect a contract, tends to frighten the average buyer unless he has had dealings with the selling firm.

Although it is undoubtedly wise to simplify the contract, this should not be construed as meaning that it should be ignored. Indeed, many salesmen have far less trouble with returned goods, with failure on the buyer's part to live up to his agreement, if they go over the provisions of the contract with him and make certain that he understands them fully. The seriousness of the contract is thus impressed on the buyer, with the happy result that the goods stay sold. If the buyer is made to feel that he is *expected* to live up to the contract, he is more likely to do so.

If the buyer hesitates at the actual act of signing, the salesman should point out where the contract is as binding on the seller as on the buyer. He can show where the seller agrees to deliver, on or before a certain date, goods of stipulated quality and amount, etc. Sometimes a guarantee is included on the order blank, thus providing a talking point and at the same time furnishing an excuse to bring out the order book or blank.

And, speaking of the order book, it is a good idea to bring it to view early in the interview, to accustom the prospect to seeing it, to convey by suggestion the idea that it is going to be used soon. Various devices are tried to make this act of bringing out the order book less noticeable, but experienced salesmen scorn these and bring it out with no comment or excuse.

The contract or order form may be designed so that one or two specifications are left blank, and the prospect may be asked to fill them in himself. The salesman for an air conditioner discusses rather briefly the down payment and monthly installments, at which point he hands the prospect the order blank and pen, saying, "Just fill in whatever figures would be most convenient to you. You know better than I do what you can do." In this fashion he gets the order blank and pen into his prospect's hands. The well-known dotted line is located just below the line that the prospect is asked to fill in.

When calling on a new prospect the salesman likes to use an order book in which many orders have been written. The act of thumbing through the carbons of these orders while turning to the right page reassures the buyer; he sees that many are buying, so it must be a good proposition. It appeals to his imitative tendency, also. With an old customer it is safe to break in a new book, for he knows that it is doubtless due to good business and not poor business that the new book is used.

Attitude of salesman in closing
As the sale approaches its close, the salesman is likely to feel an increase in the nervous tension under which he is working. He is keyed up, as a coach

would say. This is natural, yet the salesman should be careful not to reveal this feeling. In most cases, and especially when selling an experienced buyer, it is better to maintain a calm and casual attitude, for the appearance of excitement betrays the novice, and the buyer thinks, "Evidently the lad doesn't make many sales, he's so excited over the prospect of making this one. If he doesn't make many sales there must be a reason. Probably I have overlooked something and had better hold off a bit and check up."

The experienced salesman approaches the close without trepidation and maintains an attitude that conveys the impression that getting the order is all in the day's work, a bit of routine which must be gone through. The calm assurance in his bearing leads the buyer to conclude that taking orders is quite the usual thing with this salesman, that there is nothing to fear. He says, "If you will just OK it here," handing the order to the buyer, rather than, "Sign on the dotted line." He avoids the use of the word "sign," preferring to say "write" or some more casual-sounding word.

He may say: "I think I have everything here just as you want it, Mr. Prospect, but you'd better check it over yourself. Then put your name right there. (Indicating.) You may have to press a little hard to make a good carbon copy, but my pen can take it."

The salesman should shift into his closing efforts as smoothly as the automatic transmission on a good car slips into high gear.

And don't wisecrack when you start to close, as "Now we're coming into the home stretch. Hope I don't have to go to the whip." Spending money is too serious a matter to be treated lightly.

This matter of maintaining one's poise may be stated negatively by suggesting that the salesman should avoid such acts as getting out his pen with a big flourish, mopping brow, wetting lips, taking a deep breath before the plunge, suddenly whipping out order blank or contract, putting away his visual aids, clearing throat, or nervously lighting a cigarette. These things all call the prospect's attention to the fact that the salesman is about to deliver the lethal wallop. He should avoid appearing as if he thinks he is a victor and the buyer is the vanquished.

This poise comes only with experience, but its growth can be stimulated by a conscious effort on the salesman's part to induce a feeling of confidence within himself. This is accomplished by reminding himself: "I know this prospect needs my proposition because my preapproach and the interview indicate it clearly. I know that my proposition will satisfy that need and make him happier. I have made my presentation complete, clear, and have taken care of competition. I think he has confidence in my proposition and in me. He has made all seven decisions except the final one. It is logical and natural that he should be ready to make that one by now."

As in the case of the orator, the actor, the musician, or the athlete, the highest evidence of art is the ability to conceal it. That is, the spectator sees only the *result* without being conscious of the *means* by which the result is accomplished. The amateur pianist or violinist indulges in contortions and "agony," thereby calling attention to his efforts; the real artist plays the same difficult passages with ease, concealing his art. The big league fielder makes an almost impossible play look easy.

The attitude of the salesman in the closing phase of the interview has a profound effect on the prospect. If the salesman entertains doubts as to the outcome, the prospect shares these doubts. A calm confidence, between nonchalance and nervousness, should flow from salesman to prospect, creating a relaxed atmosphere that should carry over into the departure of the salesman after the sale is completed.

The right time to close

Much has been written about the "psychological moment," when the minds of prospect and salesman are in perfect accord. It is often assumed that at some moment the two minds are attuned to the same wave length and that if the salesman does not close the sale at this particular moment, his chance of doing so is forever lost. It is apparent, however, in most sales that there is more than one time at which the sale can be closed and, furthermore, that this time may be of longer duration than is implied in the word "moment." A salesman may bring his prospect to the buying stage and, not realizing that he has done so, continue the talk too long while the prospect "cools off" and loses interest. But even under these conditions the sale may not be lost, for the salesman may warm up his prospect once more and sell him.

In the average sale, however, there is a "rising tide of interest" which can be detected by the salesman who is alert and trained to feel the attitude of others. Any experienced salesman can tell the signs by which to judge, although some say that they do not know precisely how they tell—they just *feel* it through a kind of sixth sense.

Closing signals

Some closing signs are voluntary and some are involuntary. If the prospect asks, "How soon could you ship it?" this is a *voluntary* sign of real interest. It signals the salesman that it is time to close without going into more detail, even though he may not be finished with his presentation.

Other comments or questions by the prospect help the salesman to know when to close. It has been said that, when the prospect asks the price, he is keenly interested; and that, when he inquires about terms, he is practically sold. These are voluntary signs. But it is the *involuntary* sign which the salesman must learn to read.

The attention given by the prospect is one indication. As his meager interest is fanned to a flame of desire by the salesman's presentation, his air of indifference drops away and his whole attitude betrays his interest. He leans forward in his chair; his eye indicates a less skeptical or hostile frame of mind. Some salesmen say that they always watch the prospect's hands, for they open and close with his mind. So long as he is unconvinced and unwilling to buy, he keeps his mind and hands closed; but when his mind opens and his mental tension relaxes, his hands relax likewise. The muscles around the corners of the mouth and eyes may also betray the same change in mental attitude. Hunched shoulders may be lowered as the buyer relaxes.

One manual of instructions for house-to-house salesmen advises them to watch for these indications:

An act of hesitation. When your prospect hesitates just for a moment over one article in the line, that is the time for you to step in and close.

Tone of voice. Listen to the prospect's voice very carefully. With the slightest inflection or a raise or lowering of tone, it may give you the tip that you want in closing.

A negative remark. It comes easily, sometimes like this, "Now really that's good but I—I ought not to buy it." Watch for that.

A twinkle of the eye. Watch your prospect's eyes. They tell you far more than words do.

A nod of the head. When the prospect nods half to herself, it is a sign to get busy with the order book.

Perhaps the prospect rubs his chin or pulls at his ear or scratches his head; he may re-examine the product or sample or contract. Any one of these gestures may reveal an "almost persuaded" attitude.

Possibly the best way to learn the prospect's frame of mind is to ask certain questions designed to bring out this point. For example, the washing machine salesman might exclaim with enthusiasm, "Do you wonder that Mrs. Jones thought the price must be about $300?" If the prospect says, "I don't wonder at it at all; it certainly is a nice machine," then the salesman knows that it is time to close. Or the salesman might say, "Do you suppose you could keep house without it again after you've had it six months?" The reply will probably reveal the state of the prospect's mind. Similar questions may be formulated to meet any situation and are recommended for use by salesmen seeking to avoid the embarrassment which follows an attempt to close too early.

One young salesman selling refrigerators was so imbued with knowledge of his product and his various presentation techniques that he lost a sale to a young man who had entered the store with two friends for the purpose of buying his wife a refrigerator as an anniversary present (a highly questionable strategy). After the salesman had talked a few minutes, one of the friends said, "Kenny, that box is just right for you." The other agreed and Kenny nodded. And our villain went right on talking. Several other very forceful closing signs were given, and still the salesman (?) talked on. He was still talking as the trio departed to buy elsewhere.

Prospect's "no" does not end the interview

Many salesmen fear that if they attempt to close too soon, they will ruin their chances for making the sale. This trying to close before the prospect is ready may not be so serious a blunder as it seems, however. It is not difficult for the salesman to attempt to close and, discovering that his prospect is unprepared, to swing back into his sales talk again.

The suggestion does show, however, that a salesman must be fortified with more than one "close." Where the presentation is carefully prepared, several methods of closing should be arranged, so that, if the first attempt is unsuccessful, a subsequent effort may produce better results.

One of the most successful salesmen on the Pacific Coast makes the statement that only in about one sale out of ten has he been able to close on his first attempt. He expects to be turned down once, twice, five, seven, or eight times before he finally makes the sale. He builds his sales talk around the expectation of being turned down; merely adds more value and tries again to close.

He does not stop to argue the decision; he tries to *figure out which buying decision the prospect has not yet made* and proceeds, "By the way, I should have made another point clear to you," starting off on another selling point.

A certain amount of this imperviousness to rebuffs is beyond doubt an asset to nearly any salesman. He finds it helpful to be hard of hearing when the prospect says "no." One such salesman was trying to sell his valves to a Chicago candy manufacturer who had used another brand for 25 years. This salesman intercepted the master mechanic at lunch and informed him that he would see him at 2 o'clock that afternoon.

Shortly after 2, the master mechanic stormed into the lobby, glowering fiercely. "Let's sit down here," said Carlson, the salesman. "Do you have any leaky valves?"

"I can't buy valves," shouted the M.M. "The chief engineer buys them."

Carlson's hearing failed him. "Where do you have the most trouble with leaky valves?"

"On our caramel steam kettles," the M.M. reluctantly admitted. "But *I* can't buy any valves."

By this time Carlson was demonstrating how his valve's superhard seat and disc were unblemished after smashing a steel paper clip between them. "What size valves do you use on those caramel steam kettles?" he queried.

"Three-quarter inch," answered the M.M. "But's it's like I told you—I can't buy any."

At this point Carlson went stone deaf and issued this command to the baffled M.M. "You write out a requisition for *one* ¾ inch Hardhearted valve and go in and get an order from your purchasing agent. Then you'll see how to get rid of leaky valves. Go ahead!"

The master mechanic went in and got the order for that single trial valve. Carlson had done in a few minutes what the distributor and his salesmen had been unable to accomplish in 25 years. His ears just automatically tuned out the word *no.*

Eventually a prospect grows weary of saying a thing over and over when it makes no impression. He concludes that the easiest way out is to buy.

Last-ditch efforts

A sale may yet be made after the interview is apparently at an end. The buyer is relaxed; he is feeling a bit sympathetic for the poor salesman and may yield to a renewed effort. Many a sale has been revived and brought to a successful culmination after the salesman has begun to repack his samples and is apparently taking his leave. He might pause in the act of putting away some sample or perhaps discover an undisplayed sample in his case and hand it casually to the prospect while he continues his packing. This opens the way for a new attempt which may yield an order.

Sometimes a one-call salesman will issue a mild insult to the prospect as he is leaving in the hope that it will provoke him into further debate over the proposition. The barb is usually phrased to shock the prospect into reconsidering some emotional objection he has been harboring.

One encyclopedia saleswoman said to a stubborn prospect as she was leaving, "I came here tonight expecting to meet a family that really cared for their children. I am sorry to see I was wrong." If the prospect rises to the bait, the sale is live again but on a different emotional basis. Now there will be no holds barred.

In general, it may be said that the salesman is justified in trying an experimental close whenever he feels that he has succeeded in arousing the prospect's desire. And he should keep right on trying to close until he takes his leave.

It has been stated that the rule for closing a sale is as simple as ABC— *Always Be Closing.* It isn't quite that simple, but the idea is sound.

Hold a touchdown play in reserve

One common difficulty encountered in closing the sale is to reach the important point only to discover that all the best talking points have been used; there is no reserve "punch." The careful salesman guards against this predicament by saving a few strong points for the closing effort, so that he will not find himself exhausted just at the time when he needs all the strength that he can muster.

When the salesman sees that the prospect has almost reached a decision but is still hesitating, it may close the sale if he can say, "By the way, I don't believe I called your attention to our special packing methods which absolutely protect you against losses through damage and yet save you 3 cents a hundred in freight. This saving, on the quantity that you will buy in a year, will amount to over $50, at a conservative estimate. That is worth saving, isn't it?"

"It just occurred to me, I don't believe I mentioned that, on an order of this size, we pay all transportation charges."

CLOSING METHODS

There are nine tactics for facilitating the prospect's final buying decision. The salesman may use them in combinations. He may use them as trial closes. He may work out variations of them. But he can't sell without them. While these nine closing methods will be discussed one at a time, here is a list of them that may help give an overall impression of the closing tools with which the salesman works:

Continued affirmation
Erection of barriers
Assumptive behavior
Closing on minor point
Reduction of options
"Standing room only" close
Inducement
Asking for the order
Closing on objection

The first three methods are used throughout the interview; they are basic sales tactics and fundamental to the other six techniques which are used mainly as closes.

Continued affirmation

The prospect should never be asked any question to which he can make a negative reply easily. Every question should be so framed that it will be answered favorably or affirmatively. The theory underlying this practice holds that by so doing the prospect is encouraged to think positively, to give favorable answers, and that from this force of habit he will more likely answer affirmatively at the time of the close. It is also based on the belief that if the prospect has been encouraged to realize that he is favorable toward the various segments of the offer, he more likely will be favorable to the whole proposition when the time comes for accepting it.

A man and wife walk into a carpet shop looking for a floor covering for their new house. The salesman is trying to sell them on buying an acrylic carpet rather than the wool one they had in mind. Some of the questions that he might be heard asking during the sale could be, "I would suspect that you are looking for a carpet that will take hard wear yet keep its fine appearance. Is that right? . . . Do you want a carpet that can be easily cleaned, even the tough Coke stains that won't come out of wool? . . . Would you like to have a carpet that would not mat down permanently in spots where furniture has been set? . . . Which of these colors do you feel is best for your decor? . . . How much carpet will you need? . . . When will you need it? . . . Which of these two patterns appeals to you most? . . . Which of these two weights do you feel would be most appropriate for you?" Notice that it would not be natural for the prospect to give a negative answer to any of these questions. The good salesman would never ask the woman, "Do you like this color?" A "no" answer is highly probable, so rephrase it. Ask, "Which of these colors appeals to you most?" Keep the entire presentation positive!

The purpose of this closing method should be plain by now. It attempts to *make the closing decision only another favorable decision out of many* made during the interview. By pursuing the method here outlined, the salesman gently leads the buyer to the desired point without a struggle and has gained his assent to many statements that make it difficult to take a stand against the proposition. This *builds up* gradually to a much stronger claim than would have been admitted to at first.

Erection of barriers

The erection of barriers throughout the presentation is closely allied with the previous technique of asking questions, except in this instance the purpose is to block the prospect from using certain reasons or factors as excuses for not buying at the close. The security salesman who approached his prospects with the question, "I am interested in talking with a businessman who has $25,000 to invest in what he considers an excellent business opportunity and who makes his own decisions without asking his wife. Are you such a man?" was erecting a barrier right at the start of the sale. To hear the proposition the man had to admit he had money and did not have to talk it over with his wife. To lean on those lame excuses at the close could be embarrassing to him.

The auto salesman tries to block the procrastinator by asking him early in the sale, "If I can get you the right deal, are you prepared to act today?" The looker hedges, paws the ground, and plays with his keys, thus telling the salesman what he wanted to know.

The men's wear representative asks the dealer, "Are you open to buy if you see a new style that appeals to you?" thus blocking the old stall, "I'm not open to buy."

Most insincere objections can be blocked early in the sale if the salesman is sufficiently clever to perceive them soon enough. A real objection cannot be blocked so easily.

The good salesman tries to erect a barrier for every major objection he usually encounters. Perhaps he commonly meets a price objection because he is selling a premium product, so he will endeavor to get the prospect to acknowledge during the presentation that the product's features are well worth the price and that he can use those premium features. "Now, our new design has an automatic feed that gives you a constant control over input quantity and quality. You would find that profitable, wouldn't you? . . . And the surprising thing about it is that we were able to do it at an amazingly small cost considering what it does for you."

Sometimes when a consumer benefit is priced well below what the buyer would expect to pay for it, the salesman will ask the buyer what he thinks the feature would sell for. Then when the salesman quotes a lower price, the buyer is even more eager to buy it. At other times the salesman must structure the buyer's scale of values toward a feature by pointing out costs, or competitor's prices, or some bit of seeming logic so that the product's true value is perceived by the prospect.

Suppose the salesman senses that his prospect is a procrastinator. He might say, "I have been told that you are a man of action, a man who makes decisions and gets into gear." Has a barrier been erected that may make it more difficult for him to procrastinate?

The assumptive close

The assumptive close is basic to every sale and should underlie all actions throughout the presentation, as well as at the time of closing. "The prospect is going to buy. He is going to buy. There is no doubt about it! He is going to buy. I know he is a prospect: he has money and the need. I have done an excellent job selling him. My product is the best and my company the finest. There is no reason in the world why he will not jump at this opportunity. He is going to buy." These thoughts should be reflected in the salesman's attitude and demeanor. Not that he should seem cocky or overly confident, but that there should be no trace of doubt in his speech or actions that would indicate to the prospect that the salesman even feels there is a reason for not buying.

This is nothing more than the principle of positive suggestion applied to the closing of the sale. The salesman assumes by word and act that the prospect has made up his mind to buy. If the prospect does not stop him, the sale is made. It might go like this:

By an industrial adhesive salesman to a purchasing agent: "Let's see, you need 1,000 gallons of No. 153 epoxy on the 15th of each month for the next year at 15 percent off our list price. Look over my write-up and if I have it right, initial it at the bottom."

By a box salesman to a toy manufacturer: "When can we get your artwork for the box?"

Some other assumptive closes:
    "Where are deliveries to be made?"
    "To whom do we send the invoice?"
    "Can we deliver the order Monday?"

Any fact that must be determined to make the deal can be used as the basis of an assumptive close.

Many times *action* without words serves the same purpose, such as clearing a space on the desk to fill out the order blank, getting the pen ready, or merely pulling a chair up closer to the desk.

Perhaps the salesman can do something which the prospect must stop him from doing if he is not going to buy. "May I use your phone to see if we have the quantity you want for immediate shipment?" Unless the prospect stops him, the sale has been virtually closed.

Sometimes such actions are called the "physical action close"—the salesman by some physical action communicates to the prospect that he believes the proposition is acceptable to the prospect and all that remains is to complete the details. The carpet salesman might stand up, take out a tape measure, and proceed to draw up a schematic. The retail clerk might start wrapping up the merchandise or writing out the sales check. The car salesman might hand the keys to the buyer. The industrial salesman might start drawing up the contract or specifications demanded by the buyer. The essence of this tack is action: get into action to indicate to the buyer that the matter is seemingly settled. The buyer has to make a special effort to stop the process, and many buyers will fail to overcome their natural inertia, so the sale is consummated.

It will be recalled that this matter of assuming the prospect is going to buy was discussed earlier. Now we understand why. If the salesman has used this assumptive technique throughout the interview, it does not shock the prospect when he meets it in the closing phase. If the salesman has said, "You *will* find yourself enjoying many more hours of great music with this stereo machine than you ever have with your older model," or "When you pull into a motel at the end of a 500-mile drive you won't feel tired with this car." In every interview the salesman should be assuming that the prospect will buy. He says "when" and not "if." He says "will" and not "would."

Of course, no salesman starts out too obviously with this assumptive technique; this might offend the prospect. But gradually these little assumptive words are slipped in and, if not resented, are introduced more frequently. Then the final assumption seems to come naturally.

It should be noticed that this technique is closely connected with several others; it is the basic assumptive close underlying many of the other techniques. For example, if the salesman has erected barriers he would normally move right into an assumptive close.

Many salesmen use this close by simply starting to fill out the order blank, asking such questions as, "Where do you want this order delivered?" "When will you need this merchandise?" "Do you think three dozen will be enough, or should I send your four?" "What is this address?"

There is really no reason for the salesman to be bashful in using this assumptive close, for in many types of selling the buyer fully expects to give an order. In some instances in which the salesman calls regularly upon some retailers the entire presentation is built around the filling out of an order blank. One men's toiletries firm has devised a rather large order blank on which each item it makes is printed. The salesman merely goes right down the order blank asking the merchant how much of this or that he thinks he will need, with the salesman making suggestions occasionally.

Closing on a minor point

It is easier to make a minor decision than a major one, so make it easier for the prospect by avoiding the *major* decision, "Yes, I will buy," and substituting a *minor* decision.

The industrial equipment representative might ask, "Are you interested in our lease plan or are you thinking of outright ownership?" thereby focusing the buyer's attention on this relatively minor point rather than the major issue of the acquisition itself.

Usually there are many minor issues to be decided by the prospect in a purchase: delivery dates, payment plans, colors, optional features, and quantities required. Any of these factors can be used as a basis for closing.

The salesmen for a subscription book house are instructed to close in this manner: "A great majority of the people like our two-payment plan, by which the first two volumes are sent out at once and the second two volumes three or four weeks later. In this style (showing bindings) it comes in the three-quarter fiber-skin binding at just $— each mailing. In this form (showing buckram binding) it can be had for $1 a volume less. Now, would you want it in the fiber-skin or the buckram?"

The brush salesman says, "Would you like the extension handle on your wall brush, or will the regular handle be long enough?"

The salesman seldom asks *if,* he asks *which.*

This device is widely used by all types of salesmen on all types of prospects except those who insist on making their own decisions without any pressure from the salesman.

Narrowing the choice

This technique is useful in situations where the prospect is offered quite a range of products from which to choose and as a consequence may find it hard to reach a decision. The woman surrounded by 20 pairs of shoes—all of which she has probably tried on—cannot make up her mind as surely as she could if there were fewer shoes from which to choose.

The smart salesman somehow shoves out of sight the shoes in which the customer has shown least interest, gradually focusing her attention on the two or three pairs that seem most suitable and favored.

The industrial machine salesman would not show his entire line of equipment to the prospect for fear of confusing him. Instead, he would narrow the items down to those that would be best for the application at hand. A prospect's natural curiosity sometimes encourages him to ask the salesman about products for which he has no need, if he just happens to see them in the portfolio. This tends to confuse the sale and get the salesman off track.

Sometimes the prospect can be overwhelmed by a multitude of products to the point that he becomes apprehensive, afraid of making a mistake by picking one product from the many, and will flee the scene even though he wants to buy one of the products. A good salesman will assist the buyer by helping him eliminate the products that are not appropriate for him.

The wise real estate salesman learns early in the game not to show a prospective couple every house in town, but carefully to select only those that seem to meet their stated requirements.

The foregoing illustrations cover situations where the product is tangible and present. But the method of narrowing the choice can be utilized where the product is intangible and not present. The security salesman could narrow the choice to two or three issues merely by talking about them. And he could still further narrow the choice to one by the same procedure. Often the salesman's task is to narrow the choice from two to one, as in the case of the prospect who can't decide whether he prefers a typewriter with pica-size type or with elite type.

Sometimes it is necessary to narrow the choice to the *amount* which is best for the prospect to purchase.

The salesman for securities, who has presented a plan for investing a fixed sum each month, says, "Do you figure that $50 a month is about right, or could you perhaps spare $60?"

This device helps the prospect make a wise decision by eliminating conflicting and confusing concepts until his attention is focused on his final choice. It may render a real service as well as close a sale.

The "standing room only" close

Frequently the hesitating buyer may be closed by what salesmen call "hanging out the SRO sign," the initials signifying, of course, "Standing Room Only." People want what others want. It is an inborn trait; let the mother remove a plaything from the reach of her year-old infant, and immediately a protest arises, although the child might not have touched that particular toy for an hour. "Blessings brighten as they take their flight."

It is contrary to human nature to let an opportunity slip. If a salesman wishes to make a strong appeal to this buying motive, let him say, "I'm sorry you can't have that; it's sold." Nine times out of ten, that particular article will be the one desired, and no other will do. Isn't there a mistake? Has the deal been actually closed? Is he sure the purchaser will take it? Can't the *manager* do something?

The appeal to this trait takes many forms. The jobber's salesman tells the retailer, "I would prefer to give you the agency; but if you can't see your way clear to add the line right now, I suppose I'll have to put it in with Jones." Rather than see the dealership go to his nearest rival, the dealer may sign the order.

"This is the last pair of blankets that we have at this special price. Tomorrow we shall be compelled to sell them at the regular price, which is $2.50 a pair higher." It is not only the motive of gain being appealed to, it is the instinct that impels us to seize the things that we are sure will be demanded by someone else.

To be sure, the experienced buyer may react unfavorably to this suggestion, especially if it is presented in a crude manner. The salesman will do well first to earn a reputation for integrity before he attempts to urge the buyer to come to a decision through the use of such tactics. In other words, the threat that "another party was looking at this house yesterday and said that he would make up his mind in a day or two" is too often a transparent bluff.

Ideally this closing method should be used in complete truth. Many times a seller does have only one of the item left and that fact can be used to sell it. Shortages of goods do occur and price deals are limited in time, so events like these can be used to close sales.

More than any of the other closing methods, the SRO plan attempts to scare the prospect because of a loss to be suffered if action is not taken immediately.

Many a wealthy man has said that he would not sit up a single night to make another $1,000 but that he would sit up every night in the week to save $1,000 that he already had. Prospects are like that; they are not nearly so much concerned about the acquisition of more dollars or comforts as they are about the protection and continuation of those which they now possess. Effective bribes in the closing moments of the sale have to do with protecting the property and the comforts already enjoyed or desired by the prospect because his friends have them.

Examples of these are familiar. "That color is so popular that we cannot get another like it after that car is gone. It's the last one we have." "Next week the price on this goes up 10 percent." "Mrs. Smith has looked at that rug twice. I think she wants it. It is the only one of its kind in stock. I hope you will not be disappointed, if you really want it." All these are samples of the way in which salesmen threaten prospects into acting immediately through the fear of loss if they delay.

Industrial salesmen can make frequent use of this technique and with complete honesty. At the same time they are furnishing information which the prospect needs to make an intelligent decision. There may be some impending event such as a strike, either in the seller's plant or in that of one of his suppliers or transport agents; or inventories may be running short in that particular model; or the special deal will be discontinued after this week; or some other event may occur that will prevent the prospect from exercising free choice at a later time.

Offering special inducements to buy now

This technique was referred to in the previous chapter as putting a hook in your close. It is used widely to encourage prospects to buy now. A gypsum salesman for a new concern trying to expand its market share offered with each boxcar of "rock" 25 sacks of plaster. The Minnesota Mining and Manufacturing salesmen usually have a special inducement to offer the dealer if he will buy some package deal today: on one trip they were giving the dealer a billfold.

It is important not to use this technique as a trick. The same inducement should not be used twice on the same prospect, or he will quickly see that he could have had the premium whether or not he had bought at that time. But, judiciously employed, this is a highly effective way to prod some prospects into prompt action.

Asking for the order

In discussing methods for closing the sale, we are likely to overlook the
perfectly obvious—ask the prospect to buy. Professional buyers declare
that it is amazing how many salesmen seem unable to bring themselves to
ask for the order. Perhaps they are afraid of being turned down; maybe
they forget to do it.

When the sale has been conducted on rather a matter-of-fact basis, it
is natural for the salesman to say, "Can I get your purchase order number
right now for my order form?"

Naturally, there are many variations in the way a salesman can ask for
an order, but few of them ask bluntly, "Do you want to buy?" Instead,
most prefer to word the question along the lines of the assumptive close,
using such questions as: "When do you think you can get your purchase
order on this shipment?" or "How much of your business will you give us
at this time?" or "It would help our production planners if you could let me
know your buying plans as they affect us."

But one salesman, who knew his prospect well, closed a large sale by
saying: "I want you to buy this now so both of us can get a good night's
rest. If you don't, we will both be nervous wrecks." The sale was important
to both parties and had been causing worry to both of them.

Under the right conditions, a flat statement declaring that the prospect
ought to buy may be effective, as "That seems to cover everything. You can
OK the order right there." (Pointing to right place.)

Asking for the order can salvage sales that are apparently hopeless.
One book salesman had been having little luck trying to get a professor
whom he had known for some time to adopt a certain book. The professor
had thrown all sorts of trivial objections into the picture, thus thoroughly
muddying the water. Finally the salesman yelled, "For crying out loud,
Harry! Stop giving me all this flak and buy my blankety-blank book!"

Harry broke out laughing and said, "Okay, okay, it's yours."

Naturally the salesman must know his prospect, but it is surprising the
results one can get by forceful requests for the order.

Closing on an objection or the trap close

The trap close, sometimes known as closing on an objection, can be effectively used when the prospect voices but one significant objection and the
salesman knows that he can answer it to the prospect's complete satisfaction. Suppose a typewriter prospect offers a product objection such as, "But
I would like to have a wide carriage machine with special mathematical
symbols on it." Since the salesman knows that he can have the standard
typewriter altered to meet this requirement, he says, "Then, as I understand it, if I can get you a wide carriage typewriter with the symbols that

you want, you will give me the order today?" If the prospect goes along with the question, and if he has indicated that this is the only thing bothering him, there is nothing left for him to do except to buy.

Trap closes are used frequently in handling price objections. It is a serious error to give way on price without getting the prospect committed to buy if the price is met, as the prospect may continue to press for even larger concessions if his first demand is met. So the salesman says, "Let's write up the proposition with the price you mentioned and just see what the office will do with it. You've nothing to lose that way, and, who knows, maybe we can really get you a deal today. Never know how the boss feels; he might accept this contract." Once the prospect has signed for the lower price, if the seller agrees to it, the deal is binding. Real estate salesmen find this technique very useful.

The trial order as a sop

A temptation that comes to every salesman selling to retailers arises when the buyer says, "Well, you can send me a small trial order, and we'll see if the stuff is as good as you claim." The danger here lies in the fact that the trial order seldom gets a fair chance with the other lines on the dealer's shelves. It is small and cannot make much of a display. Furthermore, the dealer is not fully convinced of the proposition's merits and does not get behind the goods and try to sell them. He is inclined to feel somewhat antagonistic toward them and secretly hopes that when the salesman next appears, the trial order will be practically intact. He believes that he can eventually unload, and it may be the easiest way to get rid of the salesman permanently. When a trial order is sold, it should be large enough to make a good display, and the salesman should take pains to assure himself that the dealer and his clerks will make a serious effort to sell the goods.

The fate of the trial order is not always oblivion and dust. A small stock of a well-advertised brand of underwear was bought by the proprietor of a general store in a small town. When the order arrived, there seemed to be no good place on the shelves for the boxes, so they were thrown on the counter, where the goods promptly sold themselves. This getting a trial order on display is important. If it is well displayed, perhaps by means of a special rack or case, it may sell very well.

Staple goods, for which there is a steady consumer demand regardless of the dealer's efforts, may be sold in small quantities without danger, although there is still the disadvantage of higher unit selling costs unless reorders by mail are reasonably certain. Usually, however, it is wiser for the salesman to try for a fair-sized representative order. A merchant can scarcely become seriously interested in a line of merchandise, or really enthusiastic about it, until he has a representative stock and learns that it can be sold. This, however, is no brief for the salesman who would load up a merchant with a new line and then forget about him; for he, like the man who is content to sell "sample" orders to merchants who would profit by purchasing representative stocks, is thinking only of his own immediate interests and is not giving serious consideration to the merchandising problems of either his house or his customer.

In selling *to industry* a trial order may prove strategic, as in the case of the valve salesman narrated earlier in this chapter. If this valve performed better in comparison with competing makes on the other kettles this fact very likely would lead to the adoption of these valves throughout the factory. The problem here is quite different from that presented in selling a small trial order to a retailer.

But even in selling to industry the salesman should not sell a smaller machine than is really required, or a grade that is cheaper but will not give satisfaction. Such sales do not lead to future business.

Underselling may be as bad as overselling

Still another reason for insisting on an ample order is that the salesman who is satisfied with small orders unconsciously carries an atmosphere of pessimism around with him. He is not sure of the merits of his own proposition; how can he imbue the dealer with any confidence in its salability?

Still another evil of underselling is that it encourages substitution. When the dealer is forced to say, "I'm sorry, but we are just out of that," he naturally tries to sell something else in its stead. In this he is so often successful that he is likely to conclude that it is not necessary to stock the original article at all. If the product is advertised widely, this danger is even greater; for consumer demand is being created, and dealers are likely to substitute freely when their meager stocks are exhausted.

There are many reasons for the tendency to undersell, such as lack of room, lack of information as to the quantity that should be purchased, lack of appreciation of the evils following a policy of underselling, and just plain timidity. The last is probably the most common.

A few random hints

A good word to use in the closing effort is "let's." "Let's start with . . ." "Let's say you want this by the 15th." "Let's just run over some of the points you want to consider the most carefully." That "us" identifies the interests of prospect and salesman; the two of them are trying to work things out *together;* they are not *opposing* each other.

The salesman for a collection agency says, "Let's start collecting some of your overdue accounts right away. You can use the money now, can't you?"

The little word "when" is also helpful, especially when attempting a trial close. "When will you be wanting the initial shipment of this order?" "When would it be most convenient for me to take the measurements for the new awnings?" "I can get this heater installed in time for you to enjoy it over the weekend. When would it be better for you—Thursday or Friday?"

Sometimes it is necessary to ask for payment when the sale is made. Here it is essential to appear casual about it. The salesman can continue to write up the order and remark, "If you'll give me your check now, I'll send it right in with this order." Or, "You can be making out your check while I'm finishing up the order. The amount is . . ."

And while we are talking about dollars, salesmen try to make the amount sound less formidable by omitting the word "dollars." Thus "$23,500" becomes "twenty-three five." "Twenty-three thousand and five hundred dollars" sounds like much, much more!

Get it in writing

The spoken word is a mischievous culprit of misunderstanding. Never trust your ear or your memory. Always, repeat, *always* put the order in writing at the time it is obtained and have the buyer sign it after checking it for accuracy.

There are salesmen who are reluctant to go into a great many details with the buyer at the close for fear that something will come up that will cause the buyer to change his mind. The answer to this dilemma lies in the nature of the sale. It is foolish for a salesman not to make clear certain details that are important in the transaction. Similarly, it is foolish to bring up matters that are of minor consequence. It is a matter of judgment, but bear in mind that just getting the order is not the same as getting a customer. A great deal can happen between the close of a sale and the creation of a satisfied customer. Misunderstandings created at the time of closing can result in order cancellations and, worse, unhappy customers. When in doubt, clarify.

Silence

There is a time for silence during a close. A salesman for industrial properties related, "I had made all my points, laid out the whole situation, answered the man's questions. I saw he was thinking, thinking hard, so I shut up and just sat there. Seconds stretched into minutes. We just sat there. Pretty soon I sensed that the first man to speak was lost, so I let it ride. We sat there for fifteen minutes, not saying a thing. Suddenly he said, 'Let's do it!' and I had a sale."

The chatterbox who raves on and on long after he has exhausted his story will be discounted as a fool by the wise buyer. People don't like to deal with fools.

DISCUSSION QUESTIONS

1. In what way does the assumptive close underlie all other closing techniques?
2. You are an audio consultant (you sell hi-fis) who has been working with the owner of a substantial new home about a complete stereo system in his home. You think it is time to close the deal. What are some of the ways that you could close the prospect that day?
3. You are the manager of a retreading firm that is seeking the business of a large trucking company. You have called on the owner-manager many times but without success. While he has encouraged you on each visit, you still have been unable to get the business; he claims that your prices are a bit higher than those granted him by the other concern. Now your top management has given you the authority to meet whatever price is necessary to get that business. What are some of the closing statements you would prepare for this interview with the trucker?
4. You are a salesman for an electronics firm seeking a subcontract for printed circuit boards from a large prime contractor. Bids have been made, and it is now up to the purchasing agent as to which of two low bidders, you and another firm, will get the $150,000 contract. What are some of the closing techniques you might use in an interview with this p.a.? Give your exact words.
5. As a salesman for a large chemical company you are attempting to close a deal with a small plastic-injecting molding company for a boxcar of a certain plastic. What are some of the closes you could use? Give exact words.
6. You are a CPA who has been contacted by the president of a small manufacturing concern about the possibility of your auditing their books on a continual basis. He has told you that he is looking over all potential accountants for his job. How would you close the deal that day? Give all the possible closes you could use with complete ethical observance.
7. What are the forces at work to make the "standing room only" close effective?
8. In using the trap close on a price objection, what precautions should be taken?
9. Some salesmen try to close during their approach. Under what circumstances is this wise? Give an example of how you would do it.
10. A new salesman confides to you that he has a fear of closing: he is always reluctant to go into a close. What would you advise him to do about it?

SERVICING ACCOUNTS

Neglected customers never buy,
they just fade away.
Elmer Leterman

"And there I stood with the order in my hand muttering something about being grateful while the buyer just sat there giving me a pained look. Finally he said, 'All you have to do, son, is turn around and walk out the door. It's as easy as that!' I was so embarrassed. Nobody ever told me what to do after I got the order," painfully related a new representative for an abrasives manufacturer. It had not occurred to him that a graceful departure might be an important part of the selling process. But think one moment! Doesn't a good departure lay the foundation or set the stage for the next approach to that buyer or prospect? The wise salesman leaves with his fences mended and bridges intact.

THE DEPARTURE AFTER A SUCCESSFUL SALE
When the salesman is ready to leave, one of two things has happened—either the sale has been made or it has not.

Assume first, that the sale has been made. In this case the salesman must guard against certain dangerous faults.

An inexperienced salesman may suffer a reaction from the nervous tension under which he has been working. In this reaction his prime feeling is one of thankfulness that the interview is over and the order obtained.

Under the impulse of gratitude and relief it is easy to grow effusive in thanking the customer for his order; there is a tendency to release the pent-up emotion in a flood of talk, which may border on the semihysterical with the young and high-strung salesman. Here is the place to keep a tight rein on one's feelings and a close watch on one's actions. Remember that the sale is a mutually profitable transaction, that the buyer has neither done a favor nor received one, and that he will have less respect for the salesman and less confidence in his proposition if the salesman reveals by his attitude that getting an order is a rare event. The salesman should thank the buyer for the order, but not overeffusively, and then turn the conversation into other channels, perhaps regarding the new advertising campaign, successful methods practiced by some other buyer of the goods, or any matter of interest to the buyer. While the prospect is signing, the salesman does not stage a dramatic silence but *maintains a conversation*—unhurried and friendly—as if the act of getting an order were a commonplace affair.

As he gathers up his possessions and is taking his leave, the salesman may remark, "Thank you for your courtesy and for the order. I'll be on my way to get things moving on it promptly." Or "You have made a wise choice, Mrs. Prospect. Good-by and thank you."

This raises the question as to whether a salesman should take his departure at once or should linger a time. This depends on certain factors, but it is safe to say that *the salesman should always be the first to rise.*

The most important factor is whether or not the buyer wants the salesman to stay. The merchant, particularly in smaller places, usually appreciates having the salesman display an active interest in him and his problems and rather resents having him rush off as soon as he has the order. The professional purchasing agent, on the other hand, works faster and will appreciate having the salesman show his understanding of this fact. Here a prompt getaway is advisable.

If the buyer wants to chat a bit, the time may be right for a friendly smoke together. Most salesmen prefer not to smoke while selling, but when the deal is consummated the situation is altered.

Some salesmen advocate a quick departure to avoid having the buyer change his mind and cancel the order, in part at least. If the sale has been thoroughly made, however, there is little danger of the buyer's changing his mind at the last minute. If he is fully convinced of the *value to him* of the proposition, he will not consider losing its benefits. If he is not so convinced, he can usually cancel the order after the salesman has left. It is ordinarily an indication of weak salesmanship if the salesman has reason to fear such sudden cancellation. It shows that the salesman imagines he has *oversold* the buyer, pushing him into purchasing without really convincing him that it is to his interest to buy. The proposition has been *sold,* not *bought.*

A second blunder that the salesman may commit after he has successfully consummated the sale is to assume a superior attitude, as though feeling that he had won a victory. There is an air of condescension about such a salesman which is maddening to his "victim" and may result in cancellation and certainly in little future business. Any tendency to patronize the buyer will be resented. The sale should not be thought of as a battle, which the salesman has won, but as a mutual agreement on a business matter.

The third danger, and one to which the retail salesman is peculiarly liable, is that of indifference. How often has the reader made a retail purchase only to have the clerk hand him his package and change without a "Thank you, sir," without a smile, without even a glance, while he turned to greet the next customer? The fact that a man has bought does not remove him from the list of prospective purchasers for the future. Here is the time to start the next sale, to leave with him a feeling of satisfaction that will bring him back again. This is really the approach to the next sale.

A successful securities salesman in New York insists that a sale is not ended when the prospect buys. And it is the salesman's job to tell the buyer that he will not be forgotten by that salesman.

An insurance salesman, when he has sold a policy, says: "This isn't the end of this transaction; it's just the beginning. You see, my job is *servicing* life insurance, not merely selling it. I'll be seeing you from time to time, but please call me *any time* if you ever have a question about this policy or any others you have. I'll do my best to help you answer your question or solve your problem."

The departure is, in truth, merely the beginning of the follow-up, to be discussed in a later section.

THE DEPARTURE WHEN NO SALE IS MADE

First, it may be laid down as a general rule that the attitude of the salesman who has lost the sale should be no different from that of the successful salesman. This is easier to preach than to practice, for it takes a good sportsman to smile and act friendly when he has tried in vain to make an obdurate prospect see the light. But it must be done.

After one unsuccessful call on a prospect, a salesman called a second time. After putting his signature on a liberal order the buyer burst out, "Say, young fellow, do you know you are the first salesman who ever went away without an order who actually thanked me for the time I gave him? You sold me these goods when you were here before."

A well-known sales manager says:

It isn't the bounding, tearing, hammering type of salesman who develops the
best and surest business for a house. On the contrary, the man who can
develop business, the man who can take a turndown and another and another
but still profit by each turndown and let it lead to the next interview and make
the next interview just a little closer to the order—that is the type of man who
is a real source of satisfaction to his sales manager.

When the interview has resulted in no sale, the salesman must avoid
all of three attitudes: scorn, anger, and inferiority. The salesman who has
failed to sell a car may "register scorn" of the prospect who had too little
taste or means to buy. Or he may be angry and show it. Or, lastly, he may
feel so defeated that he assumes an apologetic air which is almost equally
bad. It is hard to remain pleasant in the face of a turndown, but it must be
done, for right there a new sale may be started.

When the turndown is received in the outer office, it is hard to take it
without wincing, but this, too, must be done. It does not pay to let subordinates see that one has been humiliated in any way. The salesman must
keep his cheerful self-confidence and poise unshaken. A good final impression on the subordinates will be valuable later.

He may say, in effect: "Mr. Prospect, you're a busy man and it's been
very kind of you to give me so much time. I understand why you don't feel
quite ready to take on my proposition yet. But when you *are* ready, I'm
sure it will be to your advantage to do so, just as it has for many, many
others. So I'll be seeing you before too long. Thanks again!"

If the salesman is a real artist, he will be able to sense the *certain*
turndown before it arrives and will contrive to make his getaway very
unostentatiously. He will guide the conversation into new channels, deftly
and without a break, finally rising and perhaps remarking, "Well, I've got
to be getting on. I've enjoyed our visit a lot and will look in again some day
soon. Good-by." The purpose of making some such getaway is to *leave the
way open for a return.* He has prevented the prospect from turning him
down flatly and finally; the prospect has not gone definitely on record.
There is a better chance to reopen the sale, than if he had been permitted
to do so.

A danger connected with this method should be mentioned. If a salesman uses it too often, he may acquire the "call-back" habit. Many sales
managers try to instill in their men's minds the idea that they should try
hard to sell at the first interview. Some have gone further and ruled that a
call-back should *never* be made. These managers feel that if the salesman
thus burns his bridges behind him, he will be more likely to fight vigorously for an immediate sale.

But where the interview is being conducted under serious difficulties, it may be suicidal to attempt to close, the next best thing being to effect a graceful exit, leaving the door open for another interview.

THE FOLLOW-UP

The purpose of the follow-up is to make certain that the buyer is as completely satisfied with his purchase as it is possible for him to be. This applies to all buyers, whether they are expected to become regular customers, or whether they will never buy again from that salesman.

Before we proceed with this discussion, it may be wise to pause and point out some qualifying factors which may govern the scope, intensity, and duration of the follow-up.

The importance of the sale is perhaps the chief factor. Obviously, a salesman who has just sold a magazine subscription to a housewife cannot afford to call back several times to educate her in the ways she and her family can get the most pleasure and profit from his magazine. He may be one of a crew that moves from city to city. Anyway, his profit on the sale is too small to permit any follow-up, and the publisher can take care of repeat business (renewals) by mail.

But when the sale is a big one, it may be vitally important that the buyer be motivated and educated to extract the utmost in satisfaction from his purchase. The price he paid probably includes a margin for this service, and he is entitled to it.

A second factor is the likelihood of repeat business from the buyer. If a long-time relationship is hoped for, with frequent and profitable orders from him, he should receive a follow-up that will develop the desired permanent relationship.

A third factor may be termed "educational." That is, how much does the buyer need to know about his new purchase before he can get the most out of it? It may be a complicated machine or a new system of keeping office records based on unfamiliar forms and equipment. It could be raw material requiring careful and unfamiliar processing. Perhaps it is merely a new line to be sold through retail outlets. Whatever the item, if it needs special knowledge and definite performance techniques on the part of operators or sales clerks, it is the salesman's job to follow up that sale until he is sure that his product is being handled *right*. Ignorant or slipshod personnel may ruin the success of the installation and create a most unhappy customer who will go out of his way to knock the product and kill chances of making other sales.

It is this last point that makes it important for the salesman to follow up fully even on buyers who may never buy anything from him again. They can still hurt him badly with other prospects.

With the foregoing thoughts in mind, the salesman must strike a balance between active selling effort and follow-up activities. The test of whether he should devote a given hour to selling or to follow-up is simply which way of spending that hour will result in more sales in the long run, because the basic purpose of any follow-up is to increase sales. He is not being altruistic; he is not *giving away* that time. Rather, he is *investing* it in the manner he hopes will bring him greater sales.

Now let's see what he may be getting in return for an investment of his time in follow-up.

Checking on the order

First, he can gain the goodwill of the buyer by checking up to make sure that the order was filled and delivered properly. This is especially necessary when the sale is the first one made to that buyer. Occasionally a salesman is in a position where he can personally check the order out of the factory or warehouse or store. A furniture salesman for a large department store in Kansas City, Mo., makes a practice of personally selecting the pieces from the warehouse when the customer, who is perhaps furnishing a new home, has chosen certain items from the retail stock. These are treated as samples, and the salesman tries to select pieces constructed of fine woods and flawless upholstery from the many duplicate items in the warehouse. He has cultivated the friendship of the delivery truck drivers, who take pride in careful handling of the merchandise when they deliver it.

The salesman for a color television set will usually try to be on hand when the set is delivered so he can instruct the new owner just how to operate the controls to insure the best reception. He also makes certain that the set is in perfect working condition.

Even a professional man can utilize this follow-up idea. A physician in Seattle makes a practice of calling up a patient who is under new medication and inquiring about how things are going. He may be able to suggest a slight change in the prescribed procedure, and he often can exhort his patient to follow orders. He is simply checking to see that his "customers" get what they wanted—well.

Adjusting size of order

A retailer is often not sure just how much he ought to order; he cannot accurately forecast demand, especially for a new product or line. The salesman can, when he follows up his sale, help the dealer adjust his order, adding some here and perhaps taking back a little somewhere; but more often than not he finds it possible to add to the original order. The furniture salesman just mentioned finds that he can usually sell one or two additional pieces when he follows up with a visit to the home of his customers after the new furniture is in place. They are happy with the new things but are conscious of a gap or two that they wish to fill.

In industrial selling conditions can change quickly as new orders come in or new contracts are signed, so the salesman who is on the job can often add to the original order he sold.

Proper installation or use

This has already been touched on. Obviously a buyer who does not know how to operate or use his new purchase will be unhappy and may even return it.

Here the problem frequently lies in the salesman's thorough familiarity with the equipment. He knows it so well that he tends to think everyone else will quickly grasp it with but one explanation. Unfortunately, people are reluctant to admit that they did not fully comprehend the first explanation or do not understand some aspect—ego involvement. It takes a wise man to admit he does not understand something. The wise salesman will understand this and take care to test covertly the buyer's comprehension of the equipment: e.g., make sure he can operate it by himself!

Getting new prospects

In the chapter on Prospecting it was stated that present customers are a good source of leads for new business. The suburbanite who has just bought a new power mower and is riding it triumphantly around his yard is likely to be visited by neighbors who want to see the new contraption and find out how (and if) it works. The salesman who is on hand when the mower is delivered and is showing himself to be helpful to the new owner is in a prime position to pick up new prospects.

There is a vast amount of word-of-mouth advertising going on in this land where every home has a telephone. Employees discuss such matters over lunch and coffee breaks. Employers meet frequently and exchange experiences. The salesman who follows up promptly on a sale can often catch his customer at the time when he can recall easily the names of several friends with whom he had been discussing his recent purchase.

A later check on satisfaction

This is made some time after the first type of follow-up, and it has for its purpose the creation of goodwill and perhaps getting names of prospects. After a buyer has lived a while with his new purchase, he may have questions or even complaints about it. It is wise to get these answered and straightened out before they grow into big ones. Perhaps an adjustment is in order, which may be far preferable to losing a customer.

Cementing friendships

Some critics of business may doubt this, but many salesmen are close friends of their customers. They are seeking the same objectives; they find themselves congenial in personality; they help each other in many ways. Most of us like to do business with friends when it is possible. Time invested in such follow-ups is like investing money in an annuity—it continues to pay off for many years.

Indeed, one important gain from a good follow-up is the holding of customers in line or keeping them from shifting to another source of supply.

Sometimes a salesman is tempted to overdo this business of making friends; he finds it easy to step over the line into the area of commercial bribery or buying of business. This is especially true when he is selling to employees of a large corporation rather than to the proprietor of a business. Entertainment of prospects and clients has always been a part of business, and some of this is legitimate as an expression of appreciation to the persons who have thrown business to the company or salesman who does the entertaining. The income tax people view a certain amount of this as legitimate, but even they are scrutinizing expense accounts more skeptically than they once did. The forms of entertainment or near-bribery are varied and some are crude, going beyond the common night clubbing, football games, and Christmas gifts.

The smart salesman strives to make friends by more sincere and subtle means. He passes along tips on possible new business to his clients. He brings them fresh ideas for making greater profit. He helps them obtain efficient personnel for key posts in their organizations. He remembers certain occasions such as birthdays, graduation of offspring from high school and college, various anniversaries, etc. In short, he manifests a genuine interest in the customer or perhaps the prospect, trying to find ways to establish their relationship on a basis of true personal friendship as well as merely profitable business.

Such a salesman will go far out of his way when the occasion demands in order to help his customer in some way. He may find a job for someone in his customer's organization who is forced to leave.

One office machine salesman in a big city has only one customer—a very large bank. He regards himself as a part of that bank's organization and often jumps in and helps out with a rush load of work in any department that uses his machines. When he delivers a new machine, he sets up a course of instruction for the employees who will use it, making sure that they all know how to utilize it efficiently and without damage. He sometimes smilingly says: "I think of myself as this bank's vice-president in charge of bookkeeping or accounting machines. The other day I recommended that the bank buy a competitor's machine for a certain job because it was better than ours. It was the natural thing to do, and my employer understood." This man constantly studies the bank's systems for keeping its records and can frequently offer suggestions for improving them.

Another example of efficient follow-up methods is provided by an electrical contractor who calls on every family a week after they have been in a new house (which he wired) to find out how the system is working out. He sometimes suggests changes, like a new outlet or two, which would make the system more convenient. His purpose is not to get additional business but to insure satisfaction, as he knows much of his business comes through the recommendations of old customers.

Then, one year after the house was first occupied, he calls again, just before the expiration of the warranties, to see whether anything should be replaced under warranty and to learn whether anything needs adjusting or minor repair. Of course, he is always ready to respond to calls for emergency service, but he insists that the program outlined above reduces total costs because he catches many little things before they develop into real trouble.

The salesman for ready-to-wear garments takes his orders months ahead of delivery, but after the goods are in the store he follows up carefully. He wants to know how each item is selling, where the stock is spotty, how the advertising is taking hold, how well the salesmen in the store know the talking points of his merchandise, and a score of little details. He says that these follow-up calls make him a lot of business.

Indeed, this is the purpose of the follow-up—to lead into the next sale to that same buyer. This next sale may come at once or years later, but the smart salesman is starting it the minute he follows up on any sale. And he never forgets that, even though he may not sell this same buyer for a long time, it is important to win his goodwill. Truly, a satisfied customer is a firm's best advertisement; and every top-flight salesman knows that he can trace much new business to the kind words uttered by some customer who appreciated the efforts of the salesman to make certain that this customer was completely satisfied in his dealings with both salesman and his firm.

In a survey of 400 purchasing agents, they were asked: "Do salesmen follow up adequately on orders?" Some 38 percent answered "Yes," but 62 percent replied "No." Obviously, there is ample room for improvement in this area.

DISCUSSION QUESTIONS
1. What signals might indicate that the salesman has stayed too long?
2. How can the salesman use the telephone to save time on follow-up? In what instances would the telephone be inappropriate?
3. What techniques can the salesman use to systematize his follow-up procedure to insure its excellence?
4. You are a salesman for a large aluminum company. Outline the follow-up system you would employ after having sold a manufacturer on using a special alloy in place of the steel he is now using in a certain part.
5. In which instance would a good follow-up system be more profitable, in selling women's shoes to retailers or a stereo phonograph to an ultimate consumer?
6. One auto salesman complained that he just did not have enough time to use follow-ups. If you were his manager, what would you tell him?
7. You are a pro at a large country club. Devise a follow-up system after you have sold a set of golf clubs.
8. As a salesman for a large soft drink bottling company you have just gotten your line into a big supermarket chain that features its own private brands. What follow-up efforts would you make?
9. As a salesman for a feed company you have made a large sale to a noted hog raiser who has previously been using a grain mixture of his own. What follow-up would you use?
10. As a salesman for newspaper space you contact a regular route of retailers in a small city. What follow-up system would you use?
11. An automobile dealer, unsuccessful in his attempt to sell a new car to a university teacher of salesmanship, lost his temper and said some very intemperate things to the prospect. Of course, he lost the sale, but in what other ways may he have hurt himself and his business?
12. Viewing the problem of turndowns from the other side, what future benefits may accrue to the salesman who takes a turndown like a good sport and a gentleman?
13. Bobby Layne, the great pro quarterback, once said, "I never lost a game. Time just ran out on me." What did he mean by this? Do you see in this attitude how it might apply to a salesman who had just lost a sale?

RETAIL SALESMANSHIP

*Discretion of speech is more than eloquence;
and to speak agreeably to him with whom we
deal is more than to speak in good words or in
good order.*
Bacon

Throughout this book, where a selling principle was applicable both to industrial or outside selling and to retail selling, both aspects have been considered. In this chapter, however, attention will be confined to problems encountered in retail selling.

WHAT IS WRONG WITH RETAIL SALESMANSHIP?

The distinction between retail selling and other types is not always sharp, and a wide area exists where the distinction is almost nonexistent. A lazy specialty salesman can wait for business to come to him, while an alert retail salesman can go out after business. Salesmen for such items as electrical appliances, automobiles, etc., usually work part time on the floor as store salesmen and part time outside as specialty salesmen. There are good salesmen and poor salesmen in both groups.

In the late fifties and early sixties a rash of articles appeared in the trade press deploring the low estate to which retail selling had fallen. In recent years this complaint has been tempered with the realization that the distributive system at the retail level has undergone a fundamental change toward presold merchandising and mass distribution. The basic marketing strategy for a large number of common goods is to move them quickly and cheaply through the retail stage using low-skilled help who are little more than stock boys, checkers, and wrappers. For many goods, the demand-creation function has shifted from the salesman to the advertising man.

Despite these changes, much true salesmanship survives in many small specialty shops not participating in the mass distributive system. In fact, it may be doubted the salesmanship in the good old days was as good as it is pictured in nostalgic memories. What the critics remember were probably not so much good salesmen as hungry ones—salesmen who had to exert themselves because of a scarcity of customers and other jobs to which they could flee. It was not a time of plenty.

Destructive criticism is easy to find and easy to offer, but it does not go far toward solving the problem. An effort to discover the reasons for the situation would be more helpful.

Some store managers insist that the public does not want good service—at least not strongly enough to be willing to pay for it. Customers are now so used to self-service stores with virtually no service from sales clerks that they expect very little from them in any store.

It has also been pointed out that many customers are responsible for the poor treatment they receive. They are unreasonable and unkind in their attitudes, thereby arousing feelings of resentment and dislike on the part of the sales personnel. "If customers would treat us with some degree of courtesy and consideration, we would try much harder to please them" seems to be the reaction of many salespeople. There is undoubtedly some basis for this position.

Another reason often assigned is that stores simply cannot afford to pay enough to their sales personnel to attract top-notch people. The managers of the stores study their "cost to sell" figures and see them steadily rising. It costs more to sell a dollar's worth of goods today than it did some years ago. The natural reaction is to cut selling expense wherever possible—and one place is wages of salespeople.

Our retail executives see the marketing process growing more automatic year by year; robots dispense coffee, cigarettes, gum, cold drinks, entire meals, and scores of other items. Self-service stores are taking over one field after another, while department stores are transforming various departments into self-service units. Advertising sells the customer in advance, especially now that television has entered the lists. It is only natural that a retail executive, harried by rising costs of operation, should trim expenses by cutting down on sums spent for salespeople.

This means that he hires many young women who do not regard the job as permanent and who, therefore, are not greatly concerned with trying to climb or advance in it. They therefore put forth a minimum of effort.

Just what would happen if all the retail executives decided to raise the pay of their salespeople and thereby attempt to attract and encourage more efficient personnel is anybody's guess. But a few stores have done precisely this and have discovered that their sales increased and the cost of selling each dollar's worth of goods dropped. These stores are chiefly those selling "shopping lines" and catering to the higher-income patrons. If all stores tried to follow their example, there might not be enough good salespeople to go around. So most stores continue to pay a weekly wage appreciably lower than that paid to workers in other lines.

But the problem of poor salesmanship would not be solved by merely offering higher wages to salespeople. Of equal importance is sound training of all sales personnel in the store. Hundreds of stores have found that the volume of sales per salesperson has risen sharply after a program of training has been put into effect. If the salespeople sell more, they should be paid more; and this could often be done without increasing the cost of selling each dollar's worth of goods. It might actually decrease it.

It is clear that management is by no means free from blame in this matter of inefficient retail selling. The new clerk has too often been permitted to struggle along, picking up what ideas he could from colleagues, and many of these ideas were not calculated to improve his technique. He deserves better treatment.

Finally, few retail salespeople today perceive themselves as career professional salespeople. Too frequently it is just a job to hold "until something better comes along." With little pride in their work, it is small wonder that their skills at it lie uncultivated.

THE APPROACH

Instead of being obliged to search for customers, retail salespeople rely upon the advertising, attractive display windows and counters, and numerous services in the store to bring in buyers. For this reason *the retail salesperson is in the position of a host receiving a guest*. It devolves upon him to extend every courtesy and consideration to make the visitor feel welcome and at ease. A further difference between specialty and retail selling lies in the fact that the prospect for the specialty salesman is frequently not even interested in the sales offer until he has been educated about its advantages, but the buyer in the retail establishment usually comes into the store with some idea of what he wants.

Service approach
"Have you been attended to?"
"Have you been waited on?"
"Do you wish attention?"
"Do you wish to be served?"

"May I wait on you please?" (This last one is used by a large variety chain and is good for that type of store.)

These service approaches are so similar that they may be considered together. They surely indicate a desire to be of service, if asked in the proper tone of voice and with the proper expression and attitude. They would, however, be manifestly out of place in a small specialty store where the customer could be plainly seen as he entered the store. It would be evident that he had not received attention, and he might resent such an inquiry as pointless and inane. In the large department store it would be more excusable; but even here, where it is possible that the customer has already made a purchase in another department, there is in it a suggestion that could frighten away the "looker" who might otherwise be induced to linger, look, and perhaps buy. In other words it is too easy for the customer to reply "Yes" to the first two questions or "No" to the latter three, then move on without becoming interested.

The objection may be made that the assumption is that the customer does not *wish* to buy, that only the customer who is not a good prospect is considered. This is true. It requires no salesmanship to sell a person who knows and states exactly what he wants. But it does require salesmanship to sell the person who has little intention of buying. Therefore students of salesmanship are justified in devoting major attention to this type of prospect, as the others are easily cared for.

"Something?"

"Something for you?"

"Something special I could show you?"

"Was there something in particular?"

These questions are typical. The consensus seems to be against them. The reason these greetings are not more popular is because of their weakness. A petulant customer naturally replies (mentally at least), "Of course there's something, or I wouldn't have come in here!" If the customer is not certain just what he does want, such a salutation places him on the defensive and causes him to hurry on to some other part of the store. The inclusion of the word "special" or "particular" is bad, as it implies a lack of willingness to display goods unless the customer is able to state precisely what he wants.

"What will it be for you?"

"What can I do for you?"

"What for you?"

"What did you want?"

"What was it you wanted?"

In this group there is an obvious attempt to utilize the principle of the positive suggestion—that the customer wants *something,* in which respect they are perhaps better than the previous group. This type of salutation is applicable in a store dealing in convenience goods, as a drugstore. Here it may more safely be assumed that the customer intends to purchase something than in a store handling shopping lines, as millinery or shoes.

These questions are dangerous ones to be put in the mouths of uninterested clerks, however, as they may so easily be made to sound brusque and abrupt. There is no suggestion of service in any of them except the second, and this has been so frequently inverted to "What can I do you for?" that there is danger in its use.

"Yes, sir," or "Yes, madam."

This greeting is used in some stores as the salesperson steps up to the customer after having been otherwise occupied for a moment. It is best in the type of store where the counter does not separate the salesman and customer, although it may be used over the counter. Much depends on the manner and tone used by the salesman, but properly handled, it is good. Obviously, it could not be used on the casual shopper roaming through the aisles of a department store.

"May I serve you?"

"May I assist you?"

"May I be of any service, madam?"

"May I help you?" (Widely used. Best of the four.)

These are typical greetings that stress the idea of service. They are adapted to use in a high-class store by salespeople possessing more than the average amount of culture. Many salespeople could not utter such a salutation easily and naturally, and to many classes of customers it would sound forced, almost laughable. In smaller communities where acquaintance exists between customer and clerk such a salutation would appear little short of ridiculous.

When addressed to the casual shopper, such a salutation may cause the latter to say, "No, thank you," and move on. Much depends on the way the question is asked.

Salutation approach

"Good morning, sir," or "Good afternoon, madam."

In case of doubt, this greeting is perhaps the safest to use. Almost any clerk can use it without making it sound brusque, as all of us have been accustomed from childhood to smile or at least register good humor as we voice such a salutation. It should not be shouted at the customer. On the contrary, many salespeople murmur it almost inaudibly so that it will not appear to call for an answering "Good morning." One objection to this salutation is that a few customers feel that it assumes a social equality between salesperson and customer which is unwarranted. This objection applies chiefly in the cities, where the gulf between society matron and salesgirl is wider than in the smaller towns. The class of trade to which the particular store caters is an important factor here also.

When coupled with the customer's name, as "Good afternoon, Mrs. Bennett," or "Good morning, Mr. McIntyre," it is good. In communities where customers are well-known to the salespeople and no social chasm lies between them, the salutation may be familiarized by "Hello, Jim!" or "How are you, Bertha?" without giving offense.

When this "Good morning" salutation is used, it is important to give it a *rising* inflection. Used with a falling inflection, it starts the sale off wrong. It does not sound friendly—and the big objective in the approach and salutation is to start the sale in an atmosphere of friendliness. Whether the customer seems friendly or not, the salesperson *must* be. Smile!

And this is important—*speak the first word yourself* and don't wait for the customer to set the tone of the interview. If you offer a greeting that is genuinely friendly, accompanying it with a smile and a meeting of the eyes, the customer will usually take his cue from you.

Merchandise approach

Many times it is best not to greet the customer with a salutation or a service approach but rather to use a modification of the product approach discussed in Chapter 10, which is referred to in retail circles as a merchandise approach.

The merchandise approach is used largely with two types of customers. It is the best way to approach rather uninterested "lookers" and also to handle someone who is ardently looking at some goods with obvious interest.

Retail clerks quickly learn to detect the person who is "just looking." To approach these people with, "May I serve you?" always prompts the answer, "No, thank you, I am just looking." After this turndown the clerk will find it embarrassing to reapproach the customer it if appears that the "looker" now wants service. It is best not to approach these lookers too quickly or eagerly.

How does one identify "lookers"? They usually are wandering with an obvious aimlessness. They avoid the eyes of the clerks. They try to keep at some distance from clerks, for they do not want to be waited upon.

A clerk should wait until a looker settles down to look at one item before moving in with the merchandise approach. Suppose a "looker" stops and examines some sport shirts. One of the following merchandise approaches could be used: "What size are you interested in?" "Is there a particular color you have in mind?" "We have some additional stock if you don't find what you like here." "We just received these new Dacron shirts today. We think they are the best buy we have seen for a long time."

"These have a new tapered body that gives a better fit for the man who has kept himself trim."

The salesperson walks up and starts talking about the merchandise without asking the customer whether he wants to be waited upon. The comment used in the merchandise approach should be the most appropriate to the situation and should give the "looker" some information that is not apparent to his eye. More will be said about handling "lookers" in a following section.

In other cases a customer may speed directly for a certain section obviously bent on buying something. He picks it up and eagerly examines it when the salesman walks up. A merchandise approach is indicated in such an instance also. In fact, some clerks approach with a trial close in such cases. Some question as "Which color do you like?" or "What size are you?" may reveal that the man is ready to buy.

A word about asking for the customer's size. The skilled salesman can judge the prospect's size by observation; thus he is able to demonstrate his experience by saying, "The XLs are all on the top shelf," or "The 46-regulars begin here." If the salesman is in error, no harm is usually done as the prospect will quickly provide the correct information. Admittedly there are instances where tact requires that the size of the prospect be minimized and not brought out so overtly that it might embarrass the customer. Extremely obese people may be sensitive to their size and not appreciate the salesman who makes an issue of it.

The merchandise approach is particularly adapted to the "looker," so let's examine it a bit further.

For example, to the customer who pauses before some blouses the saleswoman might say, "Those are splendid values at $5.98, don't you think so?"

Or, "That cologne bottle has a nonslip grip."

The shirt salesman might easily offer the comment, "Solid colors seem to be going out this season, don't they? Stripes are good now, though." Such a comment would be more likely to induce the customer to linger and look than a query, "May I show you some shirts today?"

Let's see how one outstanding retailer handles the looking problem.

'JUST LOOKING' by Jim Lavenson [1]

There's a men's and boys' store in lower Manhattan whose advertising and promotional zing have established it as a successful paradox in retailing. The

[1] Reprinted by permission of *Sales Management*, Oct. 2, 1972, p. 3.

advertising is funny, and yet hard sell. Price is emphasized but designer clothes are featured. Service is touted and fit is revered, but you can walk in and out of the store the same hour in a suit off the rack that's been shaped to you.

When you walk into Barney's a hostess greets you at the door and directs you to one, or all, of the many departments. The place is a block long, but city planners could take a lesson from Barney's store designers. And then there's the name, Barney's. It's not something dignified like Alphonse or Carlton, or even something obvious like ManTown.

It's Barney's, and the hero in its TV commercials is a fat little bespectacled kid straight out of Our Gang. And the next voice you hear is the cultured tones of Miller Harris, president of Pierre Cardin shirts telling you how impressed *he* is with Barney's Wall of Shirts, the biggest collection in the world.

I spent two years in New York before I succumbed to Barney's invitation to "come on down to Seventh Avenue and 17th Street" to enter the competition for Best Dressed Man On My Block. So last week I went and, in the process, learned more about salesmanship in two hours than I've learned in 30 years of shopping in every kind of store from Sears to Neiman-Marcus. What's more surprising, I'm now broke.

"Hello, there," said the bright girl in a tight slack suit as I walked in Barney's main entrance. "May I escort you through our many departments? Or do you know your way?" It was broad daylight; despite the lecherous thoughts that popped into my dirty old mind, I decided this was neither the time nor place, so I said I was just looking.

"Mr. Fred," she yelled over her shoulder, "this gentleman is 'just looking.'" I thought maybe I was going to be arrested for what she must have known I was thinking.

"Just looking, sir?" said Mr. Fred, a dapper young man in Bill Blass blazer with flare-bottom knit grey slacks. "Then you probably would prefer to amble about the store without our super-enthusiastic sales people following you around. Let me put this badge on you and no one will bother you."

Then he pinned a big round button on my lapel with the words "Just Looking" in large block letters. For the next hour I had the time of my life, wandering from one department of goodies to another. Each time a salesman would spot me approaching a rack of clothes, he'd start sprinting toward me, spot the badge and wheel away like he'd been blinded by an Yves Saint Laurent tie.

When I finally wanted a salesman to help me try on a suit, I had to hold my hand over the badge to hide it. Then, I bought like mad.

"Don't you lose a lot of business with these badges?" I asked the salesman while three tailors were, all at the same time, fitting the pants and coat for immediate alterations.

"No sir," he said. "We understand the steps in the selling process here at Barney's. When a man says he's 'just looking' he's really 'looking to buy.'"

This attitude on the part of the retail salesman is worth cultivating, as it aids him to sell many idly curious shoppers who would otherwise pass on without purchasing. A shopper was standing in a bookstore one day looking over a book with the idea of learning if the vocabulary was too difficult for his children to understand, when a clerk bustled up with, "Did you want to buy that book?" The immediate impulse was to deny any such intention, to lay the book down, and leave. The clerk's attitude and words produced an effect similar to that produced upon a loitering vagabond by a blue-coated officer who prods him in the ribs with his club and exhorts him to "Move on, you!" In striking contrast was the skill displayed by another salesperson in the same store, who, under identical circumstances, casually strolled near, rearranging books as he came, and finally remarked, "That's a splendid book you have there for children around ten years of age. Did you happen to hear the talk by Mrs. Whittier, of the Detroit Public Library's juvenile department, before the Parent-Teacher Association last week? She specifically mentioned it as one of the very best books for children of this age because. . . ." This salesman did not frighten his customer away; he sold the book.

This casual attitude, devoid of all signs of *selling,* has a large part in enabling a salesman to gain the attention and interest of the undecided shopper. One man, who has made a success of a men's department in a large department store, never goes behind the counter but sells "out front," following the method illustrated by the previous examples.

Sometimes the store has advertised a special offering for the day or week. In this case the salesman may ask a question, as "Have you seen the new line of sport shirts we advertised this morning for $4.95?" The prospect, although he may not have any definite intention of buying, usually replies, "No, I haven't," perhaps adding, "What are they like?" This question, which carries scant suggestion of either buying or selling, is more effective than one which makes the prospect feel that he is being importuned to spend his money.

A Florida furniture store, when a shopper says, "I'm just looking around," promptly pins a tag on her. On it is one word—"browser." She is told that the salespeople won't pester her, although they will be glad to answer questions or discuss any item. The clerks smile and nod pleasantly at these browsers, making it clear that they are welcome there and also indicating that the salespeople are ready to help if they are wanted.

It is evident that the retail salesman has many options as to an opening salutation. He may even greet the customer silently, waiting for the latter to open the conversation. In this case it is necessary for the salesman to be very careful in his attitude and facial expression, indicating clearly that he is willing to be of service.

Proper attitude

The salesman's verbal greeting is important but not so important as his attitude.

One of the first points in a good approach is promptness. The salesman must drop his conversation with fellow salesmen, must stop his work with the stock—in short, must show instant willingness to wait on the customer. This point appears self-evident, yet there is a peculiar trait in most of us that makes us like to seem busy. It crops out in the purchasing agent who enjoys keeping salesmen waiting while he fusses with papers on his desk; the clerk exhibits the identical characteristic when he keeps on diligently rearranging his stock after the customer has entered. It is partly mental inertia and partly a desire to appear important. Whichever it may be, no customer likes to wait while the salesman continues an occupation which could easily be suspended.

Promptness is essential in approaching a customer but this should not be interpreted as meaning *haste.* The speed of the salesman's approach will be governed largely by that of the customer. If the latter is hurrying, the salesman will exhibit more alacrity in an effort to accommodate himself to his customer's mental state. In an open department it is safe to time the approach so that the customer will be met about halfway. At a counter the salesman must walk toward that part of the counter before which the customer has paused.

The importance of promptness is not fully appreciated by many salespeople. One authority ventures the opinion that the prompt salesman gains 25 to 50 percent more trade than a slow salesman who may in other ways be equally efficient. This does not mean that salesmen should engage in a scramble to wait on a customer, but merely that the prompt salesman will be given the preference in the long run by customers who feel that they like to deal with him.

Some salespeople seem to forget that their main duty is to sell goods. They become so engrossed in other details, such as arranging or dusting stock, that they lose sight of the fundamental fact that they are there to serve the customers. Others are timid about approaching a customer and need to have their courage strengthened.

The salesman should be alert for the customer's first words, as it places a damper on a sale to ask, "What did you say?" or "I beg your pardon?" The customer likes to have the salesman alert enough to understand his wants at once.

Expectancy should be conveyed to the customer by the salesman's facial expression—not the expectancy of a terrier waiting for a rat to be shaken out of a trap but the expectancy that hopes to be able to serve. A real smile helps here.

The eagerness with which the salesman approaches his customer depends largely upon the goods that he is selling. If he is in a department like men's furnishings, where many men pass and perhaps pause momentarily, he will conduct himself differently than he would in the overcoat department where it may safely be assumed that every caller has an interest in overcoats. At the furnishings counter he must be careful not to appear overeager to sell; he must open the sale more impersonally and conservatively, as discussed in the next section.

It is unnecessary for a store to standardize approaches. Some sales trainers have suggested to the various departments the openings that would be appropriate, recognizing that conditions in different departments are not the same. Some go further and do not attempt standardization, even by departments, contenting themselves with a general discussion of them and leaving it to the salesman to select the proper one for any occasion. With an intelligent sales force this last method may prove entirely satisfactory, but with low-salaried clerks it is probably well to standardize to some extent.

MAKING THE SALE

Those all-important first words

Top-notch retail salespeople try to develop short sentences that will open the sale favorably. These selling sentences state or imply a customer benefit or gain from buying the item. They are not mere statements of product facts; they interpret such facts in terms of customer benefits.

The late Elmer Wheeler made this technique famous and was called upon to work out what he called "tested sentences that sell" for many products, often with spectacular results.

A few of these tested sentences made famous by Wheeler are:

It won't rub off. For white shoe dressing.

How would you like to cut your shaving time in half? For Barbasol. This sentence was followed with "Use Barbasol—just spread it on—shave it off—nothing else required." Sales in one store increased 300 percent.

They won't roll. For square clothespins. These three words reminded housewives of experiences with round clothespins—stepping on them and falling, fishing them out from under tubs and tables where they had rolled.

A sporting goods salesman sold a ski outfit to a reluctant customer who had entered the store for the sole purpose of buying a parka. He opened his sales presentation on a package deal the store was featuring with the words, "These skis and bindings are for the man who can't afford a broken leg." He had read the prospect correctly.

What goods to show first

In his effort to determine the customer's needs, the retail salesman is often puzzled as to what grade of merchandise to show him first. If he shows too cheap a grade, the customer may be offended, whereas if he shows too high a grade, it may mean the loss of the sale.

This last point is not understood by all salespeople, many of whom reason that showing high-grade goods to a customer will flatter him and induce him to purchase a better grade than he otherwise might have done. Frequently, however, the customer, knowing that he cannot afford to pay such a price and disliking to admit his poverty, decides to play the role which the salesman has assigned him, haughtily looking over the best goods in stock but finding nothing that exactly suits him. He then leaves without buying.

It may be argued that the customer, if he does not see the better grade of goods, will never buy them, so they should be exhibited. This may be granted, but they need not always be shown *first*. The practice in most stores is to lay before the customer a good medium grade, if his desire is not evident from his appearance or inquiry. From this point it is easy to work up or down the price scale, as the situation demands. The customer can more easily say, "Have you something a little lower in price?" than he could if he were compelled to make the descent from the peak price level. Similarly, if he wants something better, he can ask for it without feeling as offended as he might have felt had the salesman first shown him a cheap article.

If the customer *asks for* a $5.00 item, bring it out. If he does not indicate that the sale is already made, try bringing out a $6.50 item and see whether he is interested. If he takes time to look at it or ask about it, you might show him an $8.00 item. Confronted with these better-quality products, he may choose the $6.50 one, or even the best one.

Of course, the quality that will be shown depends partly upon the bearing and appearance of the customer, although either may be deceptive and cannot be relied upon implicitly.

One caution: it is a mistake to show a customer too many items at once; it will only confuse him. When a customer indicates that he is not happy with one item, then that one should be put out of sight and not be allowed to lie around to confuse the issue.

Not too many questions at first

In its place the question is a powerful tool, but it should not be dulled by hard usage. It is easy to overdo questioning in opening a sale. For example, if a man walks in and asks for a hat, the following dialogue may take place:

"What size please?" "Seven and one-eighth." "Did you have in mind a

particular color?" "I guess I want a dark one that won't show soil easily."
"Did you want a high crown like the one you have on?" "I suppose so."
"Did you want a narrow brim, too?" "Maybe; I guess so." "About what
price did you have in mind?" "About $10 ought to buy a decent hat,
oughtn't it?"

This opening is poor, because too many questions are asked.

First, it conveys an impression of laziness on the part of the salesman.
The customer may feel that the salesman is unwilling to show goods. He as
much as says, "If you know just what you want, I'll get it for you, but don't
expect me to haul out a lot of stuff for you to look over while making up
your mind." Many customers expect help in making up their minds on
matters of style or design and hence may resent this appearance of reluctance to be of service.

Second, this is poor selling because it commits the prospect too definitely. In the foregoing case, after the clerk had asked the questions about
the hat, if a search of the stock revealed no hat that met the specifications,
it would be easy for the prospect to walk out without buying. He had
defined the hat he wished, the store did not have it, so what else was to be
done?

Third, if the salesman produced a $10 hat of the required size, color,
and style, he had lost his opportunity to sell a better hat. Once a customer
commits himself to a price, it is hard indeed to induce him to purchase a
better article. He has confessed his poverty; he has "rated" himself as one
of the lower classes; he has nothing to lose by sticking to his original
decision. Particularly in a period of rising prices it is poor salesmanship to
ask just what price the prospect wishes to pay, as the buyer may not have
kept pace in his mind with the trend.

Often the higher-priced article may be the wiser purchase in the long
run, giving the buyer more value per dollar than the cheaper one. Similarly,
the prospect may see something on display later that he would rather have
and would have purchased if his decision had not been forced too early.

There are cases where it may be legitimate to ask a series of questions,
as where the customer is obviously in a hurry. Even here it is well to bring
out several articles *while the questions are being asked,* to make it clear
that the salesman is willing to render service.

In a kitchenware department a customer asks for a saucepan. The clerk
should inquire, "What kind of a stove have you?" or "Do you like fast
heat?" This type of question shows that the salesman is interested in helping the customer to get just *the* saucepan best suited to her needs. It also
indicates that he knows his business.

Some questions are always legitimate, because they allow the salesman
to give helpful suggestions. It would be proper to ask a man what size he
wanted in a shirt or socks, because these are standardized and no possible

reason could be advanced for refusing to tell. No opportunity is given to try on the articles, either. In the case of a hat or cap, many salesmen ask the size; but if a man's head is small, he may be sensitive about mentioning the size. If it is fairly large, he is likely to be a bit proud of it. Not so with his feet or hands, so here we find that the custom has arisen of measuring the foot or the hand rather than asking the size. This is especially true with women customers. Then, too, the object is to fit the hand or the foot and not the customer's idea of what size he should have. In this way the customer is usually given a more satisfactory article than when the attempt is made merely to sell the size mentioned.

With other kinds of apparel the customer may not know what size is wanted—in pajamas, for example—or the goods may be so poorly standardized that little is gained by giving the size, except in the same brand of merchandise.

"Do you wish the rug for the dining room, bedroom, or living room?" would be a legitimate question, as would be such a query as "Are these drapes for a north or a south room?" The book salesman who asks about the age or occupation of the prospective recipient of a gift book is obtaining information that will enable him to help his customer in making a judicious selection. The furniture salesman should inquire concerning other furniture in the room with which the table or chair would be expected to harmonize.

Another factor that may govern the salesman in the number of questions that he will ask is the condition of his stock. If it is near the beginning of the season and stocks are fairly complete, it is safer to ask questions than when stocks are depleted at the close of the season. In the small store, therefore, that handles a shopping line such as furniture, millinery, or shoes, it is wisest to ask few questions.

The more extensive the line, the more necessary it may be to ask questions to obtain an idea of what is wanted.

It may be concluded, therefore, that it is usually best not to ask many questions at the opening of a retail sale but rather to rely on showing the goods and discovering from the customer's reaction which ones offer the strongest appeal. In any event the questions should be asked somewhat casually and not too many at a time but, rather, introduced while showing goods. Care must be exercised against appearing to be either unwilling to show goods or too curious about the customer's personal affairs.

Using questions and suggestions to define customer's needs

There is a right way and a wrong way to ask questions. For example, a customer enters a store to buy paint for his new garage doors. If the salesman bluntly asks, "What are you going to do with it?" the customer may think him impertinent. But if the salesman smilingly remarks that he could better help choose the right paint if he knew what sort of a job it was for, following up quickly with, "Is it for an inside or outside job?" the customer will see that the salesman is trying to help. Other questions can be used, as, "What kind of surface is it—wood, metal, or plastic?" "In what condition is the surface now—painted or unpainted?" "Do you have in mind a dull, gloss, semi-gloss, or flat finish?" Between questions, the salesman could suggest, "You see, there are several ways you can do this job and I'd like to help you pick the paint that would give you the most economical, longest wearing, and best looking results."

The manufacturers of Arrow shirts try to teach retail salesmen to help the customer solve his shirt problems. They do this by using a clever combination of questions and suggestions.

By solving the customer's problems, the salesperson benefits . . . through greater satisfaction for the customer with his purchase. . . .

But . . . a salesperson cannot "solve" a customer's problem . . . unless

1. The customer is "aware" of the problem.
2. The customer is "concerned" with the problem.
3. The customer regards it as an "important" problem.

This therefore becomes the salesman's most important selling task . . . to "reveal" the problem . . . and its importance . . . to the customer . . . so that the customer may become "concerned" with solving that problem.

How does the salesman do this?

One of the most practical ways is to "point" to the customer's problem . . . in this way:

1. Ask a "revealing" question.

One of the salesmen at the Cluett, Peabody "Round Tables" volunteered this experience. . . .

I had a customer who wanted a dress shirt.

He had just purchased a full-dress suit and a Tuxedo and wanted a full-dress shirt . . . to wear to a full-dress party. I showed him one, and he asked: "Could this be worn with the Tuxedo, too?" I knew if a man could afford a full dress as well as a Tuxedo, he could afford another $5 for a special shirt to go with the Tuxedo. I explained to him that while it is true that the shirt could be worn with both suits, a special shirt for the Tuxedo is considered to be much better. I put it up to him by a question: "Would you be satisfied to wear the Tuxedo to your full-dress party?" He said, "Naturally not." He reflected a minute and decided to buy both kinds of shirts.

And there it is . . . the salesman asked a "revealing" question. . . . Let's look at a few other examples . . . which were volunteered at the Cluett "Round Tables." . . .

A customer's sleeves were obviously too long.

He asked for some shirts, mentioning the size sleeve he wanted. I asked him: "Do you have trouble with your cuffs wearing out?" He looked down at his sleeves and said: "Why, yes . . . do you think I could get shorter sleeves?" He just hadn't been aware that his sleeves were too long.

The customer's collar seemed too small. . . .

I asked him: "Is that collar comfortable enough for you?" Of course, I could see it wasn't. He pulled at his collar a moment and said: "Not very." I then asked him: "Did it feel all right before you had it laundered?" He answered . . . "It seemed all right when I bought it . . . must have shrunk down in laundering." I suggested a Sanforized shirt which wouldn't shrink out of fit. . . . He readily followed my advice.

And that's the first way to point to the customer's problem . . . ask revealing questions . . . like these:

"Would you be satisfied with . . . ?"

"Do you have trouble with . . . ?"

"Is it comfortable enough . . . ?"

"Did it feel all right before . . . ?"

"Ever notice how . . . ?"

"Do your shirts always do that . . . ?"

A revealing question enables a customer really to consider the problem he had never thought about before. . . .

And in that way . . . makes him "aware" of it.

And here is another way to point to a customer problem.

2. Present contrasting problems.

In order to make a customer realize that he *has* a problem . . . the salesman can present to him a simple choice of "alternatives" . . . "opposites" . . . in other words . . . a "contrast" in problems.

In that way . . . being invited to consider alternatives . . . the customer immediately "forms an opinion" . . . and realizes that he has a problem.

Let us see how one salesman did this as told to us at a recent "Round Table" conference.

The customer's collar appeared too tight.

I wasn't sure whether the customer preferred it that way . . . or just didn't realize it . . . so I asked: "How do you like your collar . . . do you like it *snug and close* . . . like you are now wearing it . . . or would you like a collar to fit *more comfortably?*" He replied: "It is a little too tight." . . . He wore Sanforized shirts, so I knew that shrinkage was not the reason. I measured him for size and saw that he really needed a half-size larger shirt.

A contrast in problems gives the customer a chance to see clearly which of two problems is more important to him. . . .

Present "contrasting problems" . . . like these. . . .

"Snug and close" . . . or "more comfortable?"

"Bright colors" . . . or "simpler and more conservative?"

"Practical" . . . or "showy . . . ?"

"You" . . . or "your wife . . . ?"

"Snug before laundering" . . . or "comfortable after?"

"Worn a lot this year" . . . or "like the appearance better?"

The answers to many customer problems are often quite simple . . . it is the "problem" itself of which the customer is unaware. . . .

The salesman often can take a "short cut" . . . he points to the "answer" . . . and in that way the customer immediately becomes aware of the problem. . . .

Here is a third way to "point" to the customer's problem:

3. Point by "suggestion."

One such "suggestion pointer" is the familiar question which begins with . . . "Did you ever try . . . ?"

Here is how one salesman used it:

The customer wore a collar which was too high for him. . . .

Resulting in crushing down at the front. I asked him: "Did you ever try our Arrow Hull shirt . . . it has a much lower collar . . . and will prevent that crushing down in front with the chin which spoils the appearance of your shirt so much." He said: "Well, I've never tried it . . . but let's see what it looks like." And very soon he was completely sold on that particular shirt, and very much appreciative of the suggestion.

And there it is . . . the salesman pointed to a problem . . . by suggestion . . . and the customer immediately became aware of his problem.

Here is another example of the "Have you ever tried . . . ?" suggestion. . . .

A customer's sleeves were too long . . . to be attractive. When he mentioned the sleeve length which he wanted, I asked: "Have you ever tried wearing your sleeves a little shorter? I think a shorter sleeve would *look much better* on you."

That salesman pointed to the problem of "looks" . . . by making a suggestion. . . .

But here is another salesman who pointed to the same "answer" . . . but a different "problem" . . . in this way. . . .

The cuffs of a customer's shirt extended almost all the way beyond the sleeves. They had a rumpled and soiled appearance. I asked: "Have you ever tried a size 32? Your cuffs *will stay clean longer* . . . and *won't wear* so quickly. . . ."

Both these customers accepted the suggestions of these salesmen . . . because the salesmen had pointed to their problem . . . pointing by suggestion. . . .

Another useful question that points to a customer problem by suggestion . . . is the familiar question which begins with . . . "Don't you think . . . ?"

And here is the fourth way to "point" to the customer's problem:

4. "Demonstrate" the problem. . . .

To "demonstrate" means to show physical, tangible evidence . . . "proof" . . . things that the customer can see . . . touch . . . feel . . . and hear.

For example . . . here is an experience contributed by one of the salesmen at a recent "Round Table." . . .

"*The customer just would not believe that he required* a size 15½. I called one of the other salesmen over, and I measured the man and asked the other salesman to read the tape measure, and then I asked the customer if he, also, would like to read it. The customer was very much amused, and I not only won his friendship and confidence but also completely demonstrated to him that he really needed a size 15½."

The same demonstration of course can be made with less dramatics but equally effective by simply using the tape measure . . . for instance. . . .

A man insisted he knew the sleeve size he wore.

But after having sold shirts for twelve years, I knew he was mistaken. I said to him: "Do you mind very much if I measure you for your correct sleeve length, as sometimes shirts vary?" Few customers will refuse this request when you give them a reason like this. After that, I merely measured him and showed him the size as shown by the tape. He made no further objections.

And that is how salesmen point to a problem by demonstrating. . . .

To demonstrate a problem means to reveal to a customer that the problem exists. . . .

Reveal the customer's problem with physical, tangible "proofs" . . . like these. . . .

Show in the mirror.

Measure with a tape measure.

Demonstrate by actual fitting.

Demonstrate by trial at home.

Show evidence in magazines and advertisements.

This discussion of suggestion in selling shirts emphasizes again the necessity of making the customer aware of his *problem* and then by one of four effective methods showing how the product solves the problem. To make the buyer aware of his problem

- Ask revealing questions.
- Present a contrasting problem.
- Point out the problem by suggestion.
- Demonstrate the problem.

PROBLEMS IN RETAIL SELLING

Knowledge of stock

One of the most common failings of the typical clerk is that he is not well-informed about the goods in stock. One clerk in the dinnerware department of a large department store, when asked for a certain item, said, "We don't carry that line." The customer replied, "But you advertised it last month." The reply, "Oh! Well, I'll call the buyer and see." The parting words: "Don't bother."

A manager of a Western Auto store complained: "Every time I go to Denver for buying my sales drop 50 percent. I see why every day. A customer comes in and asks for a widget. The clerk says that we don't have it. I have to butt in and say, 'Yes, we do. Right over here.' The clerks just will not take the trouble to learn the stock. If something is in the back room or in the warehouse, they will deny its existence to save themselves the trouble of going after it."

Good retail salesmanship starts with a knowledge of the stock and product knowledge of the items carried.

The customer who does not buy

The retail salesman is frequently confronted with the problem of the shopper who is looking around at goods in several stores before buying. This is particularly true in shopping lines—as furniture or jewelry—where the customer frankly proclaims that he is looking around at various places to compare styles and values before making his decision.

Of course the salesman under such circumstances cannot restrain his customer from leaving and usually proves himself a good sport, telling the customer, "Certainly you should look over the goods in other stores before buying. We feel that our goods and prices will compare favorably with any and are glad to have our customers investigate fully, because we are sure they will then be better satisfied." But often the customer does not come back, when, with good salesmanship, he would have done so.

Probably the greatest weakness in dealing with this type of customer is allowing him to leave the store with no clear-cut, indelible impressions of just what that store has to offer. He has looked around at many articles, and he is more or less confused by the many items and prices. Therefore when he leaves the store he has nothing specific in mind with which to compare the values offered elsewhere.

The remedy for this is to concentrate his attention on one or two articles that seem best suited to his needs and to point out strongly their advantages, so that when the customer leaves he will carry with him definite mental pictures of them. At another furniture store he might say to himself, "I don't see anything here as good as the davenport at Thompson's. Why not look at it again?"

The salesman who allows a shopper to wander idly about, pricing this and that article, is overlooking a real opportunity, for he might so center his interest on one or two items that he would be practically certain to return before buying. Just because the customer is not going to buy at that visit is no reason why an effort should not be made to sell to him.

One jewelry salesman sketches on a pad the various patterns in which the customer has appeared particularly interested, putting opposite each one the price and perhaps one or two other facts of interest regarding it. It is sound selling tactics to point out advantages possessed *exclusively* by these goods, so that when the customer looks at goods in other stores he finds that they do not have these particular features.

If descriptive printed matter concerning the item is available, the sales-man may give it to the departing prospect.

The question of turnover

In retail salesmanship the term "turnover" has a meaning different from that attached to it by the accountant. In many retail stores it is the policy to turn a customer over to another salesman when it appears clear that the first salesman has exhausted all his efforts to make the sale. Where this is done, the second salesman is usually introduced to the customer as "the buyer" or "the manager of this department" in an effort to give him added prestige with the customer. Another reason behind thus introducing him is the fact that his ostensible position of authority makes it easier for him to offer any concessions that may be needed to clinch the sale.

From the customer's point of view the policy has advantages, too. He may be served by a more efficient salesman, one whose tact or knowledge of his stock enables him to find something that will prove satisfactory. There is always a chance that, in a large store, any one salesman may overlook an item that may be known to another. The second salesman may make a stronger effort to render service, also, inasmuch as he has been placed on his mettle by being called in to handle a task too difficult for his colleague.

The most legitimate use of this technique occurs in instances where the first salesman is technically incompetent to render good service in sell-ing certain more complex goods yet is perfectly able to handle 80 percent of the transactions normally encountered. Men's apparel stores frequently must restrict the selling of suits to those experienced men who know how to fit a customer properly and mark the suit for alterations. This is not a skill that comes quickly to the new clerk, so he is instructed to call an experienced man should his customer ask to look at suits. It is not an ideal situation, but the reality of the times makes it the only pragmatic course of action.

More than one customer at same time

One of the most difficult situations a retail salesperson is called upon to face is that presented when he is compelled to serve more than one cus-tomer at a time. This situation may arise in more than one way.

He may be waiting on one customer when a second enters. Of course, if it is practicable, he should call another salesman; but if not, he may do one of two things. *First,* he may continue to serve the first customer, ac-knowledging, however, the presence of the new arrival by a nod or a low-spoken word of greeting. Care must be exercised to avoid giving the first customer the impression that he is in the way. This unfortunate result is sometimes unwittingly accomplished by the salesman's saying to the second, "Good morning, sir. I'll be with you in just a minute." If the first customer has not decided on his purchase, this is likely to cause him to leave without buying. However, if the sale is quite obviously near completion, such tactics may be proper. Usually, the greeting of this character should be offered somewhat out of the first customer's hearing, as the salesman moves about in search of stock or for other purposes. A better greeting is: "Good morning, sir. *Someone* will wait on you soon."

Before leaving a customer with prior claim on his attention the salesman should excuse himself and make it clear that he expects to return very soon. If he finds it impossible to complete the sale to the second customer quickly, the salesman faces the dreaded second possibility, that of handling two or more customers at once. This is done in many stores selling shoes or clothing. As one customer examines and deliberates over a pair of shoes or tries on a suit the salesman approaches another customer. On a busy day a shoe salesman has been known to keep six customers occupied at once, making more sales than he would have made if he had waited on one at a time.

Many times customers can be quickly handled by answering a question or taking their money or directing them to the goods in which they are interested.

A deliberate, careful-thinking customer may be served first and left to examine the merchandise, while the salesman approaches the other quickly with "I'm sorry to have kept you waiting." He should then try hard to please her. If he sees that the first customer has stopped examining the goods, she wants him again, and he should try to return to her. Perhaps some question to her will reveal where the transaction stands and point the way to the next move. Any way he handles it, he has a problem that challenges his ingenuity and ability to maintain his poise.

The group shopper

Most retail salespersons dread to see people shopping in pairs or threes, as it usually means that the sale will be about twice or three times as difficult as if the customer had come alone. The friend has perhaps been brought along to act as expert advisor and interprets this as a mandate to criticize freely. In any event it is harder to find something that will suit two persons, for tastes differ widely.

The salesperson will usually do well under these circumstances to maintain a discreet silence until he has discovered something more of the situation. It is probable that one of the shoppers really has a greater voice in making the selection than has the other, and it is an advantage to find out which one is the dominating personality before making many statements to either. Then, too, the salesman wishes to learn something more of the tastes of his two or three patrons before he ventures to turn their choice in a particular direction.

It may prove that the friend is the one who must be sold, the real buyer relying implicitly upon his friend's judgment. Even under these circumstances it is not wise to neglect the customer. The person who pays for the goods is entitled to attention and will resent being ignored. Sometimes the friend's cooperation can be enlisted by the salesman, who adopts an attitude of consideration for the friend's opinion but meanwhile keeps control of the interview by means of positive suggestions.

Occasionally the second person may prove a decided hindrance to the sale, in which event it is wise to eliminate him. The aid of another salesman may be enlisted by means of distress signals. This salesman saunters up and gains the attention of the friend, engaging him in conversation and perhaps interesting him in other merchandise. In a clothing store the friend was thus led to one side and sold a sport coat while the original customer was buying a suit, which he never would have bought had his friend been allowed to continue his criticism.

In the retail store this situation is one demanding all the diplomacy the salesman can muster. He may regard as an interesting game this effort to analyze a more than commonly complex situation and to master the problems presented. Thus much of the usual irritation will be avoided.

But all is not gloom for the salesman upon whom a group descends, for if he is skillful, he can use them to advantage. Once one member of a group buys something there is internal pressure on the others to buy something also, so as not to be outdone by the others. Many times people buy things just to impress those who accompany them. They want to play the role of the big-time spender, show their affluence. Hence each member of a group may be a prospect.

The technique of substitution

Every salesman finds that situations inevitably arise that make it necessary for him to try to sell something other than the article asked for. This problem of substitution is encountered more in retail selling than in other selling situations.

There are two conditions under which substitution may be attempted: (1) where the salesman *has* in stock the article asked for and can, therefore, meet the demand and (2) where he *does not have it* in stock and is, therefore, compelled to substitute if he would make a sale.

SUBSTITUTION FOR GOODS CARRIED IN STOCK The chief point to keep in mind is that the salesman should show himself willing to sell the article asked for before he tries to sell the other. For example, a customer asks for a pair of "Swish" oxfords. The salesman should first bring out a pair in the correct size and style before attempting a selling talk on the "Pheet" brand, which he would like to push. If the customer is in a hurry, no sales talk should be attempted; but if the customer appears relaxed and in no hurry, he might be glad to listen.

The substitute brand should usually be introduced somewhat casually, as, "Here is a shoe that you might like *because* it has a shorter vamp than the 'Swish.' Your toes are short, and you don't need a long vamp, so you can wear a size shorter in this shoe than in the other." The student of salesmanship will note that "because" in the last sentence. The prospect who sees that the salesman is trying to substitute immediately suspects that a selfish motive is behind the effort; hence he is on his guard at once. His mind should be led from his suspicions to a consideration of the *reason* why the salesman is pushing an article other than the one requested. A prompt statement of a plausible *reason* for preferring the "Pheet" brand saves the situation. To be able to handle this situation effectively, the salesman must have a fund of information about his goods. The customer is likely to ask questions, too; and if the salesman is unprepared with convincing replies, he is almost sure to lose the sale.

"This is just as good." The salesperson who uses this weak comment in attempting to substitute, when he *has* the article asked for, is inviting defeat. It is a poor expression at best, and meaningless here; for unless the article offered is not just as good as, but *better* than, the one asked for, the salesman is only making trouble for himself by giving the customer something to confuse him and hinder his immediate action.

This problem of judicious substitution is unusually troublesome when the customer wants something *apparently* unsuited to his needs. It seems evident that he will regret the selection and harbor a distrust of the salesman in the future as a result of the unfortunate purchase. Under these circumstances it is wise for the salesman to ascertain, first, just what the customer's *real* needs are, and second, whether or not he will accept suggestions made in his interests.

The ascertainment of the customer's needs requires tact on the part of the salesman, for there is danger of giving serious offense by a seeming inquisitiveness. The customer may be buying for someone else, as is frequently the case, and would resent any prying questions. He may be buying a hat or a suit for use in another part of the country.

Regarding the second point—the customer's willingness to heed suggestions—the salesman must judge by watching his reactions to minor suggestions. If the customer combats the salesman's ideas, it is safe to avoid an argument and give him what he wants.

SUBSTITUTION FOR ITEMS NOT CARRIED   When the salesman *cannot* supply the article asked for, his task is more difficult. His first impulse is to say, "I'm sorry we don't have it. Was there something else today?" If he is a bit more of a fighter, he probably says, "No, we don't have it, but we have something just as good." This expression has been so grossly overworked that it is best to avoid it.

Another pitfall to be avoided is, "No, we don't carry that any more. We had so few calls for it that we dropped it." This makes the buyer feel that he has asked for something that is badly out of style or that he has revealed extremely poor taste. He is uncomfortable and in no mood to accept suggestions as to alternatives.

A better way to handle this:

A customer may ask, "Have you any silk shoe laces?" (Not in stock.) So the salesman promptly replies, "No, we haven't, but we have these rayon laces which look almost exactly like silk and wear much longer. They are less expensive, too. Just feel how soft and silky they are!" As soon as possible the salesman has handed a pair of these laces to the customer, pointing out the feature he wants the customer to examine.

Some tactless salesmen even deny that there is any such article made as that asked for. "They don't make that size platter," asserted the salesman to the housewife, who retorted, "I had one of that size and broke it this morning." Many clerks, ignorant of their line, attempt to conceal their ignorance in this way.

In making substitutes for goods demanded when they are not in stock, the salesman has to act quickly, although he should avoid the appearance of haste. If he is selling a tangible article, it is advisable to place it in the hands of the prospect at once, thus delaying his departure long enough to make it possible to present a few of its advantages. When he is ready to leave, merely *telling* him about these advantages will avail little in comparison with *showing* them.

Frequently the salesman need not say that the article is not in stock but may show something very nearly like it in the hope that the prospect will become interested and buy. This may happen if the prospect does not have too definite an idea as to what he wants.

In showing a substitute, it is sound psychology to point out first those features in which it *resembles* the article asked for. This makes the transition in the customer's mind easier than if the substitute were represented as something entirely different. After the points of similarity have been explained, the salesman may focus the prospect's attention on certain points of superiority or on exclusive advantages.

Lest the salesman feel guilty about substituting when a customer requests a specific brand of goods, he should be aware that in most instances customers use brand names as symbols to communicate their thoughts about goods to others. Hence, the housewife who wants to know where the Jello is stocked is, in reality, asking for the location of the desserts. Most experienced retail salespeople claim that there are few truly strong brand preferences. Even though the customer requests a specific brand, substitution is usually easy if the right goods are in stock. In instances where substitution is difficult, the smart retailer sees to it that he carries that brand so no substitution is needed. The critical factor in substituting is the protection of the customer's ego. The salesman must be sufficiently adroit to get his goods into the customer's hands without communicating in some manner, "No, you don't want your brand; you want my brand."

Increasing the sale by suggestion

Most salesmen have at one time or another had their attention called to the desirability of increasing the size of the purchase through the use of suggestion. The girl at the cigar stand achieves this crudely, but often effectively, when she hands out two packages of gum to the customer who asked merely for Juicy Fruit. She can "get away with it" because the amount involved is so insignificant.

Selling the customer more than he asked for is sometimes a real kindness to him and not merely a selfish effort on the part of the salesman to increase his total for the day. For example, most men do not buy a pair of shoe laces until they have broken one and are compelled to replace it. If the salesman were smilingly to point out this general practice and ask whether the customer would not like to have an extra pair or two in reserve against the next time he breaks a string, it is probable that he could double or treble the sale. The same is true of shaving cream, tooth paste, and other items purchased frequently.

Some ways of suggesting buying more at a time are

* "There's a saving in buying three for a dollar."
* "Shall I send you the larger one? It's really more economical."

The last suggestion does not increase the size of the purchase, but it is more diplomatically phrased and therefore more likely to be accepted.

The makers of Cooper underwear and hosiery teach retail salespeople:

Don't Say	Say
1. Will one be enough?	1. Will six be enough?
2. You'll need a couple pairs.	2. You'll need six, so you can have a fresh pair every day.
3. Why not buy half a dozen?	3. Why not take home six, and save yourself future buying trips?

With higher-priced goods, these tactics cannot be employed, obviously, but perhaps something may be accomplished along this line. When the salesman has sold a suit, he should make some slight effort to interest his prospect in ties, handkerchiefs, hose, or whatnot. Indeed, this principle has been recognized by most retail merchants in the planning of their stores and the arrangement of the various departments in relation with each other. Thus related items are grouped together, to allow them to exercise their silent salesmanship on the customer and to facilitate the salesman's efforts in that direction.

The salesman should try for an associate sale *before* the goods are wrapped and change made, for the customer often does not wish to start an entire new transaction. He may put off the purchase on this account, when he might have bought if his attention had been called to the matter at the right moment.

Some stores, especially the drug chains, have compiled lists of goods which suggest each other, and their salesmen are taught to suggest these items, or some of them, while the article purchased is being wrapped but before change has been made. Care must be taken not to give offense in this matter, for some buyers resent any effort to sell them more than the original purchase. The buyer's reply to the first suggestion will give the clue to his reaction, and the salesman must govern his actions accordingly. He should adopt the attitude that he is making the suggestion, not to pile up his sales total but to help the customer get everything he needs. As a matter of fact, such suggestions are of real value to the shopper who has not made out a list of items needed.

Salesmen in hardware stores are exhorted to suggest "tie-ins" whenever they sell nearly anything.

A dish drainer needs a drain tray. One floor mat can sell three. A pair of sink mats is incomplete without a sink divider mat. Shelf cushioning leads to plate and cup holders. A 39-cent plate scraper is pretty useless without a sink strainer. When you make a sale of interior paint, always ask if it is for remodeling a bathroom. If the shopper admits it is, turn your sales talk to bathroom accessories which will follow the color scheme of the paint you have sold. A customer for a rug cleaner can usually be sold an applicator brush. A customer for a glass cleaner can usually be sold a chamois, sponge, or cheese-cloth. When a customer comes in for grass seed, does he need fertilizer, a spreader, lawn seeder, new hose, nozzle, sprinkler, hose reel, lawn roller or mower? Never throw a whole list of suggested items at the customer. He will instinctively answer No. When you do suggest something, *how* you suggest it can either close off the sale immediately or leave the door open for more suggestions. If a customer is buying flower seeds, you might suggest a pair of canvas work gloves. But don't ask the customer if he *has* a pair of gloves. He may answer Yes and that would end it. Instead, ask if his work gloves are in good condition. Point out that you are featuring a good buy in work gloves.

These ideas appear axiomatic and self-evident. But do salesmen follow this course? They do not.

The Willmark Service reported a test of this point in which 100 women were each given a $5 bill and instructed to go to their favorite drugstore and purchase a 49-cent tube of tooth paste, after which they were to spend as much of the remaining $4.51 as the salesman *suggested.* An overwhelming majority of the women left the stores with the tooth paste and $4.51 in change, emphasizing once more the fact that an untold volume of benefit-giving sales is lost daily by lazy salespeople.

Some of these excuse themselves by pleading that such tactics would constitute high-pressure salesmanship. The chief distinction between high-pressure salesmanship and proper selling methods is found in the effect on the customer. If the customer will truly benefit from buying, the salesman is trying to help him much as a dentist may try to help a patient by urging him to have a tooth fixed before it is too late to save it.

We see that most efforts to suggest to the customer that he buy more than he had planned to buy fall into one of four classes. Each of these should be mentally checked by the salesman whenever he makes a sale.

1. The purchase of more than one unit. This may effect a saving to the customer or it may be merely a matter of convenience to him to have a spare on hand when badly needed.
2. The purchase of a larger size, which often saves money to the buyer. It also saves time in shopping and makes less likely the embarrassment of running short of the product.
3. The purchase of a tie-in product, already discussed in detail.
4. The purchase of something distinct from the item asked for or bought. This may be a special offering at a special price, or it may be something new, just received.

Adjusting complaints

Here is a situation calling for real salesmanship! The customer is unhappy, dissatisfied, and perhaps angry. Unless treated properly he is apt to be lost as a customer.

Even in stores that have complaint or adjustment departments, the salesperson is apt to be drawn into the affair, as the typical customer heads straight for the salesperson from whom the article was purchased. Even though the fault may lie with the wrapping or delivery or accounting or advertising, the salesperson is appealed to first.

The chief rule to bear in mind is that "a soft answer turneth away wrath." No matter how insulting the irate customer may be, the salesperson must maintain a calm and sympathetic attitude, showing a willingness to see the problem from the customer's viewpoint. From there the selling job starts; but first it is necessary to find out the reason for the patron's dissatisfaction.

A word of warning! When the fault lies with some other department of the store, such as delivery, the salesperson is tempted to join the customer in roundly condemning this department. This temptation should be resisted, as it merely reflects on the store and injures its reputation. Nothing is gained by commenting, "We're always having trouble with those delivery truck drivers. They can't seem to get anything straight." And much may be lost. All through the conversation with the complaining customer the salesperson should seek to convey the impression that such incidents are decidedly rare. The idea is to send the customer away pleased and convinced that the store and the salesperson were very nice—so nice that the customer is friendlier than ever.

It must be confessed that too often the trouble can be traced to a poor job of selling in the first place. Perhaps the goods were not right for that customer. Or the salesman did not instruct the customer as to how to use the product. The purchaser of a car roared into the dealer's salesroom: "You told me that the air conditioning in this car would start cooling it within two minutes. Yesterday, after Rotary meeting, I took four of my friends to the country club. The car had been sitting in the sun and was hotter than a Dutch oven when we got in. And did it cool off at all while I drove those three miles? Not that we could notice! Here I pay you $6,000 for a car and it's a lemon!"

The dealer replied calmly: "Did you open the windows when you started the air conditioning? You must do this in order to let the hot air out as the cool air pours in."

"Well, why in blazes didn't your salesman tell me this when I bought the car?"

Many a sale goes sour because the buyer fails to read instructions on the package or tag. He mixes the paint with turpentine instead of benzene. She insists on washing a fabric when the tag says "For Dry Cleaning Only." Not the salesman's fault? But it may have been! He should have called attention to these things or at least have stressed the fact that the instructions should be read and followed.

If the product is mechanical and the customer claims it won't work, it may be necessary to test it right there. If it does work when properly operated, the sale is nicely saved. If it does not work, it should be put in working order or a new machine given the buyer. Whatever is done should be done promptly and not grudgingly.

Sometimes the salesman can calm an angry customer by the use of a question. The customer shouts his complaint and then yells, "Well, what are you going to do about it?" To which the salesman may reply smilingly, "What do *you* feel would be the fair thing for us to do?"

Strictly speaking, *exchanges* are complaints, inasmuch as the customer is not satisfied. Here, too, a similar reselling job must be done.

The handling of a complaint is not something distinct from selling; it is primarily and definitely a selling problem.

This point is illustrated by the following incident. A businessman entered an exclusive men's shop in the financial district of the city. He carried a suit which he complained had not given good service. It had been purchased two years previously and looked as if it had seen hard wear. The customer figured that some adjustment should be made. The salesman agreed without argument and suggested that the man pick out another suit in place of the one he had brought in. This sounds incredible and as if the salesman had lost sight of his employer's interests and was intent only upon keeping a customer for himself. But the suit had cost $300; and that customer spent at least $3,000 a year in that store and had never before complained. He probably would be even more loyal after such a generous adjustment. Was this too great a price to pay for his continued patronage and the word-of-mouth advertising he would give the store? The store proprietor took the matter up with the manufacturer and received an adjustment on the grounds that the particular fabric in that suit was inferior. The handling of this complaint by the salesman was a piece of fine, long-range salesmanship.

DISCUSSION QUESTIONS

1. A lady cannot make up her mind between two dresses she likes. She has been vacillating between them for more than 30 minutes. What are some of the tactics you could use in assisting her?
2. What do you think is the most important facet of retail salesmanship that should be taught new clerks?
3. Should a clerk ever recommend that a customer go to a competitor's store? If so, under what circumstances?

4. A furniture salesman is doubtful that his prospects will be able to qualify for credit. He has perceived many danger signals. What course of action should he take?

5. Late Saturday afternoon a couple walks into an appliance store and after briefly looking at a washing machine, dryer, refrigerator, stove, and color television set, give the salesman an order for each of them. They explain that they have just moved to town and have just gotten possession of their new house; they need immediate delivery of the goods. They are buying on installment credit, but the late hour makes it impossible to check with the bank or credit bureau. What should the salesman do?

6. Should an automobile salesman accompany his prospects on a test ride or should he allow them to take the car alone?

7. A young man walks into your apparel store and asks to see some Jantzen swim wear. It happens you do not handle this brand but instead carry a line you believe to be its equal at a more attractive price. What are some of the statements you could make to substitute your brand for his request?

8. It is Christmas time in your women's apparel store when a man in his early twenties enters. When you approach him, he tells you that he is just looking. What are some of the tactics you could use in this situation?

9. A young couple of apparently modest means enters your fur shop and asks to see a low-priced mink stole you have been featuring as a leader. You bring it out and have it modeled for them. From the expression on their faces you can see that they are disappointed in its appearance; they expected the sheen and obvious quality available in furs of about twice the price. Would you try to trade them up? What would you say?

10. Shoplifting has in recent years become a major problem in most retail stores. Many articles have been written about it and merchants have instituted training programs for enlisting the aid of their salespeople in combating shoplifting. What rules should the clerk follow in protecting against theft?

FOUR

THE SALESMAN AS A PERSON

ETHICAL PROBLEMS
IN SELLING

When you do it, it's unethical;
when I do it, it's competition.
Anon.

People in every calling face ethical problems daily which not only have no answers but also are severe tests of character. Discussions about ethics are usually rather fruitless affairs bogged down in platitudes about right and wrong, good and bad, and moral and immoral. Unfortunately, such platitudes are of little use to the man who finds himself in the midst of a situation that contains ethical considerations. Indeed, by their very nature, ethics defy answers. Therefore we will try only to point out the areas in selling which seem to contain ethical problems. We have few, if any, answers.

From early days the ethical behavior of salesmen has been roundly condemned by honest folk who considered them little more than swindlers and thieves. Even today their conduct is subject to steady criticism by the trade press, by government agencies, by buyers, and by each other. Beyond question, this is a live and troublesome problem.

The philosophers distinguish between absolute ethics and relative ethics, the former being inflexible and always applicable, while the latter are somewhat flexible and adaptable to differing situations. The salesman usually operates under a system of relative ethics, for it is virtually impossible to develop a single code that would cover a significant segment of the situations that arise and still take into account the problems peculiar to each industry and type of selling activity. Practices condemned in one industry are considered permissible in another. Different companies lay down widely varying rulings for their salesmen's guidance.

Therefore, the purpose of this chapter is not to provide an absolute code of selling ethics, but rather to introduce the reader to some of the ethical problems that salesmen meet and to suggest some of the consequences of dealing with them unwisely.

There seems to be no one simple test or rule that can be applied to all acts of salesmen to determine which is right and which is wrong. Experience indicates, however, that some standards are more widely applicable than others. For example, a salesman may evaluate the ethical status of an act by answering the question, "Is this sound from a long-run viewpoint?" Other standards are set by the way a man answers such questions as: "Would I do this to a friend?" "Is society harmed or benefited by this practice?" "Who will be injured if I do this?" "Am I willing to have this done to me?" (Golden Rule) "If other people learn of this act, what will be their reactions?" "Will I be ashamed to tell about this?"

The man who is guilty of some unethical act usually knows it; he has inner qualms about it because he is not comfortable with some of the answers he must make to such questions as those above.

But sometimes the pressure on a salesman is almost irresistible; he feels that his personal interests or those of his firm are at stake. He may revert to the code of the jungle, which decrees that survival may be purchased at any price; ethical considerations are forgotten. It is easy to be ethical when it involves no hardship, and most salesmen prefer to play it that way as long as they can. The real problems arise when it costs something to stick to what one believes is right.

ETHICAL PROBLEMS INVOLVED IN CUSTOMER RELATIONS
These constitute a large portion of the salesman's ethical problems. In the long run it usually pays to deal ethically with one's customers, as most salesmen find it profitable to build up a large and loyal clientele.

Keeping confidences
Industrial salesmen, as well as many selling to retail outlets, call on accounts that are competing with each other. The salesman naturally learns much vital, confidential information which could be of great value to a competitor, such as plans for new products, volume of sales in various lines and territories, marketing campaigns in preparation, contemplated changes in personnel, and other facts which the executives would dislike to have broadcast.

Naturally, should the salesman violate such confidences, he will never receive any more and might not even be welcome to call on that account in future. It would seem that only the worst and weakest of gossips would succumb to the temptation to tell one customer any facts about a competitor which had been given him under seal of secrecy, but the problem is not that simple. Sometimes the poor salesman is subjected to severe pressure to divulge critical information as the price he must pay for a firm's patronage.

The sales manager of a chemical company was keenly interested in learning the sales volume of a certain chemical compound sold by a competitor, the only other seller of that product. He was haunted by the suspicion that the other firm was outselling him, so he figured out what he thought was a clever scheme to get this information. One of the ingredients in the compound was purchased by both firms from the same source, a refiner of corn syrup. So he pressured the corn syrup salesman to find out how many carloads of the ingredient his competitor bought each year. He hinted that, if the salesman failed to come across with this information, he would buy from another corn products refiner. Naturally, no salesman wants to lose a large-volume account, so these threats were taken seriously. The salesman promised to see what he could do, but he stated clearly that such information was not available to the sales force and he might find it hard to obtain. Later he reported back that the other account was handled by a different salesman, who flatly refused to tell him what he wanted to know, and that the office sharply informed him that it was none of his business and that, if he valued his job, he had better keep things that way. Thus he avoided offending his customer and losing the account, but not all salesmen can evade the issue so smoothly, for the customer may know that they do have the facts that are wanted.

Some salesmen prefer to meet such requests firmly with, "If your competitor asked me to give him the same information about you, what would you want me to do? If I told you what you just asked for, you should throw me out of this plant, for you could no longer trust me. If I would tell *you*, how could you ever feel sure that I wouldn't tell your competitors your secrets? One thing you can be sure of in dealing with me is that your secrets stay secret. I tell *no one*, not my boss or my colleagues or my family. That's one rule of the game I'll never break."

This ethical attitude is not always maintained. In fact, in certain industries it is not expected, and executives are careful not to reveal to salesmen anything they do not want repeated.

Bribes

An unpleasant fact of selling life is the existence of bribery. Not that bribery does not thrive in other areas of activity, for it does. It is sometimes

TABLE 18-1 WHAT FORM DOES "CHISELING" USUALLY TAKE?

	PERCENT
Fictitious price bids to lower your price	47
Suggestions that you give special price or handling (in violation of Robinson-Patman Act)	38
Misrepresenting your competitors' products	31
Suggestions for elaborate gifts or entertainment	18
Requests for kickbacks	15
Blackmail	2
Other (extra free goods, reciprocity, threats to cancel orders, play one quote against another)	11

Source: The American Salesman, November, 1961, p. 56.

called by nicer names, such as "reward" or "in appreciation for services rendered," and is regarded as standard procedure in some circles. But in selling it is not standard.

However, some firms and some salesmen have found that it is effective, at least in the short run. A small businessman selling an item to oil well drillers took an active part in private meetings where field prices were established, all firms selling this standard product at identical list prices. He said, "Everything is billed out at the agreed price, but I manage to get a fair hunk of it back to them under the table to the right men who won't spill the beans."

In other cases buyers request bribes of some sort. The sales manager for a regional paint manufacturer related that he had this problem with a large aircraft company. He said, "They had a purchasing agent who was on the take. He was rather open about it and made it clear that if we wanted any of their business, he had to be paid off. We just won't do business that way, so we pulled out of bidding and stopped calling on them. One day the big brass in the east stumbled onto the fact that the region's largest paint manufacturer was not bidding for their business. I got a call from their Executive VP who asked me why we hadn't submitted bids lately. I told him exactly the reason. Now we do business with a new purchasing agent. But I know there are still some buyers out there who are on the take."

One survey of salesmen made on the subject of "chiseling purchasing agents" concluded, "Ninety-eight percent of those responding are confronted with a minority of buyers who sometimes try to 'chisel.'"[1] "The proportion . . . who try to 'chisel' in some way varies all the way from ½ of 1 percent to 50 percent." Table 18-1 presents the frequency of replies to the question "What form does 'chiseling' usually take?"

[1] "Sales Panel Reports on Buyers' Ethics," *The American Salesman*, November, 1961, pp. 56–58.

TABLE 18-2 HOW DO YOU HANDLE REQUESTS FROM P.A.S WHICH YOU CON-
SIDER OUT OF LINE?

	PERCENT
Refuse point-blank	51
Ignore	36
Pass off as a joke	29
Go along with them	9
Other (demand proof of competitor's price, pass on to home office, explain company policy and law)	27

Source: The American Salesman, November, 1961, p. 56.

Table 18-2 records what the salesmen say they reply to these requests.

Few purchasing agents are so clumsy as to ask for outright bribes. Instead, some drop veiled hints that they are in need of something or other. The salesman for one electronics firm recalls the time an executive of a potential account mentioned that his family had been pressuring him for a new stereo set, a product which one division of the salesman's firm "just happened" to make.

However, far more clever are the purchasing agents who say nothing of their larcenous inclinations but manage to patronize the perceptive salesman who senses their bent. These buyers, while not openly soliciting bribes and preferential treatment, nevertheless bestow their business on the firms that are most generous.

One sales manager admonishes his salesmen to start looking for a bribe or personal friendship somewhere in the background if they cannot understand why some other firm is getting an account's business. He says, "In our industry buyers have good reasons for buying from the sources they do. If none of the usual business reasons are present in a certain situation, then I immediately start looking for the existence of personal friendships, family ties, or bribes. It makes no sense for one of our salesmen to beat his head against a stone wall trying to sell a purchasing agent who is in the control of one of our competitors. Once we find this to be the situation, we simply stop calling on him."

It would be nice if there were some easy answers to this problem, but unfortunately there are none. A salesman will encounter buyers who want to be bribed and competitors who are willing to do so. How he handles the situation depends to such a large extent upon the conditions peculiar to the industry and the situation that it is impossible to provide any meaningful rule for action. There are many salesmen and many firms that refuse under any circumstances to be parties to commercial bribery not only on legal grounds, but also on moral ones. Likewise, there are some firms and some salesmen who will not hesitate if they feel that a bribe will gain them what they want.

Gifts

Closely akin to bribes is the practice of giving gifts, particularly at Christmas time. The practice has become so widespread in industry that outcries are being heard from many sectors of the business community complaining of their general ineffectiveness and meaninglessness. Clearly, the dividing line between a gift and a bribe is rather arbitrary at best. Some firms have declared that their executives may not accept gifts over a certain nominal value, thus in effect saying that articles under that amount are gifts while items over it constitute bribes. Salesmen, as frequent bearers of gifts, are caught in the middle of this confusion of top management over the role of the gift in business. One psychologist is quoted[2] as saying. "We train children from infancy to be generous, to share, to show appreciation. It's part of the way people reach each other. What we need in business is to reduce gift-giving again to the level of generosity, where a gift is a nice gesture, an extension of self."

Fortunately, there are a few guideposts which have been erected to keep the salesman from making too many serious errors in his gift-giving. One purchasing agent for a large oil company warned, "Never give us a gift *before* we have done business with you. Use sales ability, not thirty pieces of silver."

A psychologist claims that the way in which a man gives is probably tied in with his personality. He says,[3] "The best salesmen do it with finesse. They give unobtrusively; they never talk about it, and they never show signs of expecting a return. If a salesman feels queasy about a gift, it's probably a sign that he doesn't have the right motive and ought to be careful."

According to one buyer, only 5 percent of business gift-giving is done deftly enough to benefit salesmen. What are the mistakes that reduce the effectiveness of gifts? The experts list the following common mistakes made in gift-giving.[4]

(1) Any gift that puts the recipient at a disadvantage is in bad taste and a mistake. When it appears to be given from a selfish and monetary point of view, a gift may make a man feel threatened. But if it is clearly symbolic of appreciation, no strings attached, the gift has a good effect. (2) If it is so extravagant as to approach bribery or if it is blatant advertising, it is in bad taste. (3) If an item can be misinterpreted, a wrong connotation put on it, it's dangerous. For example, one man never gives another grooming aids. (4) Another mistake is to overestimate the effect of barroom humor. Just because you think nude figures on the inside of beer glasses are amusing doesn't

[2] Velma A. Adams, "What's Hidden in Your Christmas Gifts?" *The American Salesman*, November, 1961, p. 43.
[3] Ibid., p. 44.
[4] Ibid., p. 45.

mean your best customer will. You have to know the man. (5) In most cases good taste prohibits the giving of gifts to the purchasing agent's wife, but gifts to his children are fine and may be especially effective.

The timing of a gift may be particularly critical to its effectiveness. Another box of candy at Christmas time gets lost in the deluge, but the same gift at another time of year—say, the purchasing agent's wedding anniversary—may be deeply appreciated. Many of the most effective gift programs in business are not routinized to the point of boredom, but instead are administered by salesmen who attempt to send only appropriate gifts to the right people at the right time. A pair of tickets to a football game may be far more effective in creating goodwill than an expensive portable television set.

Probably the best guidepost yet available has been furnished by the Internal Revenue Service which allows the firm to deduct only up to $25 for gifts to any one individual in a year. This ruling has had the effect of placing a realistic ceiling on gift-giving which was getting out of hand.

Entertainment

The problem of entertainment is in much the same category as bribes and gift-giving. It can be an attempt by the salesman to influence the buyer on a basis other than the merits of his proposition. Nonetheless, it is a widespread practice, and most salesmen must decide who should be entertained and to what extent.

Naturally, there are problems connected with entertainment. A large portion of the salesman's expense money is devoted to it. If he does not spend it wisely, if he wastes it on prospects with little potential, his productivity will be seriously impaired and his costs of selling out of line. Indeed, in many industries one of the key factors in a salesman's success is his ability to know who is the right person to entertain and what the nature of the entertainment should be. It is a mistake to assume that all entertainment takes the form of eating and drinking. In many circumstances unusual forms of entertainment are far more effective. One book representative was particularly effective in his entertainment by inviting prospects to go skiing with him—he would pay for the tow tickets, a modest amount in comparison with a night of wining and dining. His philosophy of entertaining was to do something a little different. He tried to determine what the prospect best liked to do and then treated him to it. An invitation to play golf at some swank country club is highly appreciated by the avid golfer.

One psychologist[5] who carefully investigated the phenomena of busi-

[5] Daniel Brower, "A Psychologist Looks at Business Entertainment," *The American Salesman*, July, 1960, pp. 90–96.

ness entertainment put forth a few suggestions for making it psychologically sounder and thus more effective. He said:

Salesmen shouldn't be in too big a hurry to entertain. Invitations extended on
impulse may be taken lightly. As a general rule, it is far better to withhold the
more lavish entertainment until after the first order, when it becomes a psychological "reward," and may help build a permanent relationship. On his
early calls, the salesman may make it a point not to invite the prospect to
lunch just when it seems he is going to do so. Then when the invitation
comes, it may mean something. Of course, there are exceptions. If a buyer
hints broadly that he wants to be taken to lunch to get away from the office for
an hour or so, then the thing to do is to invite him on the spur of the moment.
But to retain the upper hand, the salesman should assure him that no business will be discussed—and stick to it.
    It's a mistake to take away from the prospect's dearly protected freedom
of choice. A salesman shouldn't assume the buyer or purchasing agent wants
to go to a most expensive restaurant, or even that he wants a drink. It's better
to ask, and a good salesman should have the social skill necessary to determine whether the answer is sincere or not.
    Salesmen should be careful about doing actual selling during entertain-
ment, especially at meals. Whenever feasible, it's better to talk about subjects
other than business, giving the prospect the confidence that he is an enjoyable person.
    Salesmen ought to try to understand their own reasons for entertaining.
They should ask themselves such searching questions as: Was it necessary to
impress this particular customer? Was I afraid I wouldn't make the sale otherwise? What would have happened on this if I had not taken the prospect to
dinner?

    One survey of salesmen disclosed that they entertain not to earn a
specific order but for long-term awards. Various quotes from the salesmen
were:
    "A friend is always more useful than a cold business contact in getting
hold of some business."
    "I like to get better acquainted with customers so that negotiations can
be conducted on a warmer, personal basis."
    "Selling would be a lonesome life without entertainment."
    "It's a courtesy that is expected and a natural way to do business."
    "Away from the prospect's office, the salesman can add color to what is
sometimes a concise presentation. At the same time, he can learn more
about the customer's problems."
    "To get the buyer out from behind his desk and find out what he likes
to talk about."
    These surveyed salesmen pointed out that too great a dependence on
entertainment works against the salesman. "If it's done to buy business,
someone can always bid higher."

"It's like price-cutting. Anyone influenced by me can be wined away by another."

"It's no substitute for product and service."

"Some salesmen entertain because they want to be big operators. They get carried away."

Seventy-four percent of the men said they streamline their entertaining to fit the type of customer and the potential volume of the account. In their own words here's how they make up their minds:

"If a potential is not there, I cannot spend the time."

"I don't entertain customers without social inclinations."

"Some buyers don't expect or don't want to be entertained; others wouldn't respond to entertainment."

"Company policies may prohibit buyers from being entertained."

"Depends on the personality of the customer and how big the account is—from buying a coat to a trip to the Kentucky Derby."

In conclusion, business entertainment is definitely a part of the work of most salesmen. And if he is to use it effectively, the salesman must learn the niceties of the art. He must know who should be entertained and what diversions should be offered. He should allocate his entertainment budget properly among accounts according to their potential and the anticipated effectiveness of the expenditures. It might be unwise for a salesman to spend large sums of money on the purchasing agent of a prospective account that is firmly locked to another firm on the basis of reciprocity. Finally, he must learn how to behave during entertainment to avoid offending the sensibilities of the prospect, for there is a right and wrong time to talk business. This does not mean to imply that a salesman can never discuss business matters during social respites, for many men like to talk business while relaxing socially.

Reciprocity

Some firms maintain a policy of reciprocity; they give preference in buying to firms that buy from them. Similarly, some sales departments attempt to use the reciprocity appeal in selling to companies from which they are buying. It is not unknown for a salesman, with the approval of his manager, to hint that unless an order is forthcoming, the prospect's sales to his firm may suffer.

Obviously, this is a form of commercial blackmail. In theory a purchasing agent should buy the right product without regard to the seller's purchasing policies, but in many competitive situations there is little difference between the products offered by competing concerns. Hence, competition comes down to various differentiating factors, among which reciprocity may be one. In some industries, such as oil, reciprocity is widely practiced. The drilling contractor automatically uses lubricants from the company for which he is drilling. Where reciprocity is a matter of standard practice, purchasing agents may attempt to split their business among all competitors, thereby making it easier for their sales forces to sell to all concerns.

However, great care must be exercised in using a reciprocity appeal even if it is ethically permissible in the existing competitive environment. Should the salesman lean too heavily on reciprocity and fail to do a good job of selling and servicing, he will lose the account, reciprocity or no. When reciprocity is not considered ethical, the salesman who relies upon it is walking on rather thin ice. Many executives will rebel strongly at any hint of such blackmail and will regard it not only as an affront to their integrity but also as a sign that the salesman and his proposition have little merit. A good salesman with a worthy proposition does not need to rely heavily on reciprocity.

Reciprocity is now being challenged by the Federal Trade Commission as an unfair business practice, so there are legal constraints on the practice.

Conflicts of interest

In some cases a salesman may be faced with a conflict of interests in handling an account. One salesman selling to an electronics firm proved to all parties his high ethical standards by withdrawing from the account on the grounds that his brother-in-law was the president of a competing firm. He preferred to avoid a position in which he might be suspected of passing along to his brother-in-law information gained from servicing a competitor's account.

A salesman may have interests in firms in conflict with those of customers or his employer. The ethical, professional salesman will take great pains to make his exact position clear to all parties concerned, lest his interests be misinterpreted at some later date when they are discovered—as they usually will be.

Favoritism

Salesmen have favorite accounts, people with whom they like to do business. The cynic would reply, "Yes, they certainly do—the large accounts!" But that is not always the case, for many times the large accounts push the salesman around so much that often he hates to call on them.

A salesman for a popular line of casual pants was fond of calling upon a certain small but prospering merchant, for the people in the store were most congenial and he enjoyed visiting with them. One season a certain item was in extremely short supply because of an unusually large demand for it. Quotas had been set on the item in ratio to each account's total sales volume, so the small merchant's allotment was rather slim. But no matter, for friend salesman "robbed" the item from the order of a large department store whose buyer he hated. The salesman actually chuckled as he was arranging the scheme.

People, being people, like and hate other people. And salesmen, after all, are people so they tend to play favorites.

ETHICAL PROBLEMS CONNECTED WITH EMPLOYERS

A salesman's relationships with his employer are even closer than those with his customers and give rise to just as many, if not more, ethical problems.

Changing jobs

There usually comes a time when a salesman considers changing jobs and must weigh certain ethical considerations.

In some industries the ethical code is so strict that it precludes the salesman from going to work for a direct competitor lest that firm benefit by information and knowledge obtained by the man from his first employer. However, this is the exception.

More commonly, it is considered unethical for a competitor to initiate negotiations with the salesman in trying to lure him away from his present employer. However, usually a dissatisfied salesman may ethically initiate contacts with competitors. Needless to say, in some industries open piracy of men is considered perfectly ethical and is practiced by all.

The salesman is faced with the ethical problem of how much notice he should give his employer, because it may be difficult to replace him immediately. It may take several months to train the replacement, and in the meantime the company may be severely damaged should it not have a representative in that territory. Clearly, the ethical man would not want to place his employer in such a position by leaving without notice. He would try to reach an amicable agreement as to the date of severance.

In severance situations there arises the problem of the salesman's present accounts. Should he attempt to take them with him to the new employer? Accounts have been known to follow the salesman rather than stay with the house; however, that usually happens in competitive environments in which there is little difference between products, and the accounts have been buying the salesman's services rather than the firm's wares. One survey of appliance dealers made by Philco directly asked dealers if they would switch lines if their favorite salesman changed houses. The dealers unanimously claimed they would not follow any salesman to another distributor but would stick with the lines they were selling. Many salesmen have been deluded into thinking they had a clientele loyal to them only to be rudely shocked when they discovered that their previous customers had been buying products, not personalities.

Sometimes a firm will lure away key salesmen of successful competitors for the knowledge they may have of important operational details. Naturally, it is difficult to control the information a salesman gives his new employer, but there are limits beyond which a salesman's behavior is clearly unethical. One man resigned as a salesman to accept the sales managership of a smaller competitor. He managed to get into the files before leaving and take with him important marketing research information and data on the firm's customers. Needless to say, the president of the firm was quite disturbed at this unethical behavior, but there was little he could do about it. Some employers take precautions to protect themselves against this risk.

Expense accounts

The salesman's handling of his expense account naturally encompasses many ethical considerations. For the moment, let's ignore the situation in which the company encourages fictional expense accounts and assume that accurate statements of legitimate sales expenses are desired.

The ethical problems connected with expense accounts are not concerned with whether or not the salesman should abide by his employer's wishes, for that is rather clear-cut ethically. But many little problems arise which are seemingly quite innocent. Suppose the employer has set limits on what can be spent for certain activities. For example, he will pay only 10 cents a mile for automobile expenses. Yet the salesman, in all honesty, has computed his operating costs at 15 cents a mile. Now he may be tempted to pad his mileage to make up for the difference between the 10 and 15 cents. In his own mind he may try to justify his actions on the basis that the money was actually spent for business purposes and that the spirit of the expense account was not being violated. The salesman faces the ethical problem: Should he manipulate the expense account in order to protect himself from the niggardly policies of his management, thereby recovering money honestly spent on the solicitation of business for his firm? Or should the salesman strenuously attempt to get the policies changed, and failing that, change employers rather than commit what he believes to be unethical acts? What are the dangers of such manipulation? Quite simple! Once a salesman finds he can manipulate figures with ease for honest amounts, does this not encourage him to manipulate a bit more and increase his earnings? Just where can he draw the line at manipulation?

There is an old story about a salesman who lost his Stetson while making a sales call. He thought the company should compensate him for the loss of his hat since it was in the pursuit of business. He put at the bottom of his next expense account, "New Stetson hat to replace one damaged while calling on customer: $20." The auditor disallowed his claim. The next week he put it in again and, once again, it was disallowed. The third week at the bottom of his expense account was the notation, "OK, Wise Guy. It's in there. Just try to find it."

Suppose a company allows $10 a night for lodging. Should the salesman average out one night which cost $12 with another which cost only $8 by recording both as $10 nights? Should he put overages on one account into others? For example, suppose it cost him $3 more for lodging than is allowable, should he take his $3 from the entertainment fund?

It is a mistake to assume that all salesmen cheat on their expense accounts. One outstanding book salesman and a customer took a long trip in the salesman's car to a football game in which they both were interested. It would have been easy for the salesman to charge a good portion of the expenses of both himself and the customer to the employer, but he did not. Because of the customer's interest in the subject of expense accounts, the two got into a rather long discussion concerning them. The salesman said, "I made up my mind a long time ago that I was not going to cheat my boss out of a dime. I like this job, and he's been very good to me. There's nobody in this world I'd rather work for, and I decided that I would be a fool to cheat him and jeopardize our relationship. It's not so much that he would ever find out or even suspect. But I would know that I was cheating him, and this would affect my relationship with him. As it is, I honestly feel that I am the best employee he has, and when it comes time for promotion, I will have nothing on my conscience." Incidentally, the same salesman frequently entertained certain customers and prospects at poker parties. While he was kidded about not charging his losses to the expense account, he replied, "I don't expect my boss to pay for my poor judgment of cards, just as I wouldn't expect him to benefit by any streak of luck which I might have." This man has since become the president of a new subsidiary that his boss set up for him.

Most unethical expense account practices evolve when the salesman can rationalize them because of some niggardly policies of his employer. If a salesman is able to justify his actions to himself by thinking that the amounts he steals on the expense account are justly due him, stealing becomes much easier. It is quite similar to the situation in which the underpaid bank clerk embezzles, rationalizing that it was due him.

So far, we have been discussing situations in which the employer does not condone the manipulation of expense accounts. Unfortunately, there are many cases in which the salesman is directly encouraged by his superiors to file inflated expense claims. Many such policies have been forced upon the sales management organization by some unwise accounting policies. The district managers for one large industrial equipment manufacturer openly instruct their salesmen on how to fill out expense accounts in order to avoid conflict with the auditors. An autonomous accounting department has imposed upon them certain limits on the money they can spend for entertainment in any one day or on any one account. The salesmen are told that if they go over those limits to spread the amounts into other categories or to report that they worked days they didn't and file expense accounts for them.

The managers justify this practice as simply being an internal convenience to keep peace within the family. In this manner the sales department gets what it wants and is able to spend money as it deems necessary, and the accountants are happy because they are deluded into thinking the sales force is abiding by their rules. But is such conduct ethical, even assuming that it is legal?

When these deceptions violate the Internal Revenue laws, other ethical considerations come into the picture. For example, the Internal Revenue Service takes a dim view of expenditures for bribes or large gifts. Should a salesman, at the direction of his manager, hide such gifts in other categories? Obviously, the action might be illegal, but so might be other things a salesman does. He never knows when some action of his might be declared an unfair business practice or a violation of some other law. Clearly, the salesman has an ethical problem which may become more serious as the Internal Revenue Service continues to clamp down on certain practices.

Moonlighting

In some situations a salesman can quite easily carry additional lines of merchandise other than those furnished by his principal employer. One representative for a manufacturer of women's high-priced dresses without the approval of his employer carried lines of underwear, lingerie, and sportswear. His employer had clearly disapproved of such moonlighting activities when he had fired a salesman in Texas for exactly the same practice. The employer's reasoning was that the men were making good money, about $30,000 a year, selling his line and that they should devote their entire attention to it. The dress salesman justified his moonlighting by saying, "It's true that my principal line is making me sufficient money presently. But in this business it is 'here today and gone tomorrow.' While the market is buying our styles in large quantities today, I've got to look ahead because I never know when this line will go sour. So I take on these other lines of merchandise to keep in with my accounts. I don't want to become too identified with one line, so that when it goes bad, the buyers won't look at anything else from me. In this industry you have to take care of yourself. I don't know who they (the management) think they're kidding, for they pay us on a straight commission basis, and we pay all of our own expenses. We have no fringe benefits; really I don't see how we are employees of the company, for they certainly don't treat us that way. We even have to pay our own way back to pick up our samples in New York City. I'm really in business for myself."

Thus, the ethical dilemma is neatly posed. To what extent is a man entitled to go in order to protect his own interests at the expense of his employer?

Fellow salesmen

One's relationships with his fellow salesmen are fraught with ethical problems. Although most companies endeavor to minimize conflicts between their men by assigning specific territories and accounts, ample room still exists for misunderstandings. What about the account that is a personal friend of the salesman, and is located in another salesman's territory? What about the prospect a fellow salesman fails to sell? When is it ethical for another to call upon him? Should permission be asked of the first salesman? Does a salesman owe a split commission for leads furnished by others? Firms do set policies to handle a few of such problems, but naturally they cannot cover all contingencies.

When salesmen are turned loose in an area without territorial assignments, conflicts arise. Suppose a prospect contacts a realty firm in January about a house, and Salesman Jones shows him around but fails to close a deal. In September the prospect contacts Salesman Smith, who closes a deal on a house first shown him by Salesman Jones. Obviously, troubles will arise when Jones learns of this. It is for this reason that real estate men have established boards to judge these matters and have set forth fairly clear-cut rules governing such situations. However, in other fields this type of regulation is not available.

Personal use of company assets

One of the unique attributes of the salesman's position is that corporate assets are entrusted to him. Frequently cars, expensive samples, or equipment are furnished. Most managers establish policies governing the use of the company cars. A few firms allow the salesman to use the company car just as if it were his own, with the company paying the costs, but this is the exception. More commonly, the salesman may use the car for his personal needs, but he must pay so much a mile to cover direct costs. Some concerns severely limit personal use. Some insist that he not take *long* personal trips, while a few restrict *all* personal usage. Whatever the company's policies on these matters, the salesman has ample opportunity to violate them.

On the other hand, a slightly different problem arises in the case of samples and equipment. There have been numerous cases in which salesmen have sold samples for personal gain, claiming that they lost them or that they had been given to some customer in furtherance of a sale. Some firms instruct salesmen to sell their samples when they become shopworn or damaged. The result—opportunity for questionable practices. Minnesota Mining and Manufacturing salesmen are sometimes faced with an ethical problem in picking up old stock on dealers' hands and writing it off. Top management does not want outdated stock shipped back to the factory; the quicker it is junked, the less expense is involved with it. Hence, authority is vested at very low levels for writing the stock off as a complete loss. Some salesmen have been known to take such stock home and sell it later for personal gain. This is particularly true with Christmas tapes the company uniformly picks up after each Yuletide. This behavior is not only unethical but also illegal, but it is mentioned to illustrate that these problems do exist.

Contests

Contests, and other managerial tools, frequently pose ethical problems for the salesman because the opportunistic operator can take advantage of loopholes in the rules. For example, one man was able to win a large monthly contest by withholding orders during the last 10 days of the previous month and filing them with those taken during the contest month, thereby significantly enlarging his sales volume. While this is clearly unethical, a salesman might defend it because management established the situation which fostered it.

And what of the contest that is designed to promote tremendous volume production? Does it not tempt the salesman to overload his customers or dealers to a degree that is unethical? What about the contest that offers great rewards for selling a certain product? Does it not encourage some salesmen to sell it to prospects despite the fact that it might not be the best product for them? These are problems that the salesman must work out for himself.

Adherence to company policies

The typical salesman operates within a rather formidable framework of policies that attempt to regulate his behavior along the lines desired by management. But these policies do not always make economic sense nor are they always conducive to selling more goods. Hence, the salesman is frequently tempted to deal outside of policy for the sake of either profit or expediency. One office machine manufacturer has a firm policy on handling trade-ins: the price allowed on the trade-in is set forth in a small booklet, at a rather disgustingly low figure, and the salesman is not allowed to buy or sell them on the side for himself. But one of the firm's biggest producers has aligned himself with an independent office machines dealer who buys at a higher price than the salesman can allow from the trade-in and then sells it so the salesman can be more competitive in selling the new equipment. "The company's policy stinks. They trim the customer on the trade-in, but I won't deal that way. If I can't give a square deal, then they can have my job. And if they learn of my wheeling and dealing they'll can me, but to heck with them. I'm making a lot of money for them and myself now and know where I can earn more any time," explained the salesman involved.

Should a salesman work for a firm whose policies he cannot follow in all good conscience?

Management tells the salesman to push a certain new product line, yet he knows that it is a "dog"; the trade will scream at him next time around if he shoves these goods on them. To whom does he owe his first allegiance? Is he not acting in the best interests of the company by ignoring such orders? These are some of the problems that are encountered frequently in applying company policy to actual field conditions. The problem arises many times because the policy maker may not have a realistic view of actual field conditions or he may be strongly prejudiced by his own emotions on a matter. Many policy makers have never had to face an irate customer cheated by some company policy. It can be a traumatic experience.

ETHICAL PROBLEMS CONNECTED WITH COMPETITORS

When a salesman is accused of unethical behavior, the chances are that those accusations are being made by a competitor. If any particular tactics or tricks were used to gain the victory, the loser is tempted to yell "Foul." However, this does not automatically make it unethical, for the very essence of competition involves certain sharp practices. All too often the price-cutter is called unethical. Yet genuine competition usually involves price variation. The industrial salesman who persuades a customer's engineering department to establish certain specifications which favor his firm may be accused by a competitor of being unethical, but others would merely consider him an excellent salesman. A competitor may claim that it is unethical for one to sell direct to a certain account at a lower price. Yet, is not this just a matter of business policy under our competitive system?

There are some competitive practices, however, that *are* clearly unethical. At one time a business machines manufacturer had his salesmen drop sand in competing machines whenever they could. The practice became so

bad that finally the Federal Trade Commission issued a cease-and-desist
order against this firm, which is in effect today. The order specifically for-
bids the company's salesmen to drop sand in competitors' equipment.

Many salesmen admit that if they are forced to make a demonstration
against the leading competitor's equipment, they can always make it look
bad in comparison to their own. One favorite tactic of a vacuum cleaner
salesman is to clean a rug with the owner's present machine first and then
reclean it with his own to show the superiority of his cleaner. Just how far
can a salesman go in adroitly disparaging the competition? Should he even
agree to such tests?

Naturally, these are questions that cannot be answered categorically,
for they depend upon the circumstances. In many situations the salesman
must agree to a test demonstration against all the competitive equipment if
the prospect demands it. In some instances the competitive equipment may
have disadvantages which should be pointed out to the prospect, but the
salesman must remember that if he goes too far, the word will get back to
the competition. A victory gained by an unethical tactic may cost the salesman dearly in the future as competitors retaliate.

There is one area in selling where competition is particularly vicious
and unethical practices are common. The merchandisers calling upon supermarkets have gotten into dog fights over the shelf space allotted to
them. This is understandable because sales volume in a supermarket is
almost directly proportional to shelf space. Hence, a salesman's productivity is directly correlated with the amount and quality of display space he
can obtain. One baby-food salesman told of his success in stealing baskets
away from a competitor. He explained that when he took over the territory
the major competitor had about 90 percent of the market. Where his firm
would be granted only about 4 or 5 baskets for its baby food, the competitor would have 20 to 25. In the larger, more significant supermarkets he
would manage to call at a time when he knew that the baskets would be
empty; he had observed the restocking schedules of his customers. He
would combine the contents of two or three of the competitor's almost
empty baskets into one and fill the now free baskets with his own brand.
Supermarket managers can become angry with quarreling salesmen and
may throw both of them out, for they do not like to spend their time
refereeing such disputes between squabbling salesmen.

Bread salesmen may steal space from competitors, burying some of
their merchandise at the same time. Salesmen have ruined the goods of
competitors deliberately, hoping to make the accounts unhappy with that
source of supply. Naturally, all of this behavior can backfire very badly on
a salesman, should he be too aggressive; but he must take care of himself
against competing salesmen eager to steal his space, if that is the nature of
the business.

CONCLUSION

This chapter can best be concluded by quoting Reverend Raymond C. Baumhart of the Harvard Graduate School of Business Administration who writes of a study of 1,800 businessmen. He found:[6]

The typical businessman is more ethical than generally believed, but not quite as upright and unselfish as the speeches and articles of some business leaders indicate. . . . Two thirds of the respondents agreed that some unethical practices were prevalent in their respective industries. They disagreed to some degree on gift-giving and personnel pirating. What almost all said they would like eliminated are unfair pricing tactics, bribery, customer cheating and dishonesty in advertising and fulfilling commitments. . . .

Workers in occupations that don't bring them into contact with the cash register find it easier to be ethical than those who do, because of the absence of temptation. A scientist or engineer whose work appears in blueprints stands a better chance of staying on the straight and narrow than a bookkeeper—not that there aren't crooked engineers and honest bookkeepers.

Another of our findings was that unethical practices increase with competition. Wherever poor ethics are prevalent, say, in the garment industry, they stem from the cut-throat competition that characterizes the industry.

This seems to be the nub of ethics in selling. It comes down to how competitive the market is. The more competitive the industry, the more temptations the salesman will face, and the more ethical problems he will encounter. It's easy for a salesman selling for a monopoly to be ethical. Clearly the classical economist's concept of competition makes no allowances for ethics, for in their theoretical framework the firm must do everything legally possible to get the better of its competition if maximum efficiency and productivity are to be achieved.

DISCUSSION QUESTIONS

1. Just how much time and effort do you owe your employer ethically? Some firms demand one's complete dedication to the job day or night.
2. Under what circumstances would it be ethical for a salesman to carry additional lines of goods?
3. What are management's ethical duties to its salesmen?
4. What are some of the unethical acts by management that have given rise to unionism in some areas of selling?
5. What are some of the ways a salesman can handle the buyer with the outstretched hand?

[6] Reverend Raymond C. Baumhart, "Business Ethics Is an Elephant," *Printers' Ink*, June 8, 1962, p. 60.

6. As a salesman for used cars, draw up a code of ethics to be presented for adoption at the next meeting of the retail car dealers in your city.
7. You believe that a competitor's salesman is being unethical in certain remarks he makes about your equipment. What courses of action are open to you?
8. You discover that you have significantly overcharged a customer on one item he has ordered. The situation is such that it is unlikely that the overcharge will be discovered. What, if anything, would you do about it?
9. You have been a salesman for a manufacturer of electronic components for the past decade and are presently earning $18,000 a year. A competitive firm offers you $25,000 but you *must* start immediately. The territory would be the same. You feel that you owe your employer at least one month's notice, but the competitor is adamant—it's now or never. What would you do?

ATTITUDES, PHILOSOPHIES, AND WORK HABITS

You are what you think you are.
Anon.

Time and again we are approached by eager young men with such questions as, "What does it take to be a successful salesman?" "What techniques will make me successful?" "What must I do to be successful?" They want to be given a "magic" bag of tricks with which they can go forth and conquer the world.

We are sorry to report that success is not to be found in a "bag of tricks." Rather, it lies in one's philosophies of life: such things as your attitude toward your work and how to do it best, your attitude toward people, and toward yourself. The key to success lies in your mind.

While the cynic rejects such statements as being meaningless platitudes, nevertheless many personal experiences with successful people in all endeavors—sports, war, business, government—continually reaffirm our observation that the most important factor in winning (and that is another way of looking at success) is mental attitude, the label placed upon the complex batch of intangibles manifest in one's behavior.

IMPORTANCE OF RIGHT ATTITUDES

One of the observable phenomena of sales life is that the mere knowledge of sound selling methods does not insure success. Indeed, salesmen using almost identical selling methods vary widely in their production. On the other hand, two men using widely divergent methods can both be highly productive. Clearly, knowledge alone is inadequate preparation for a successful selling career. Some of the missing ingredients are the salesman's philosophies and attitudes.

Any prospect senses at once the fact that a salesman is not in the right frame of mind. No salesman is a good enough actor to conceal anger, discouragement, boredom, a hangover, or other disturbing factors. Besides, a wrong attitude adversely affects a salesman's work methods so that he may make fewer calls, show little enthusiasm, plan his work poorly, etc.

Years ago the senior author of this book used to chat with Dr. Walter Dill Scott,[1] president of Northwestern University, over a lunch or a game of billiards at the faculty club. One statement of this great man made a lasting impression. It was: "Most great salesmen owe their success more to their mental *attitude* than to their mental capacity or ability."

"Red" Grange, in his capacity of play-by-play reporter and commentator of a nationally televised football game, recently proclaimed his belief that the greatest factor contributing to a team's success was "mental attitude." He estimated its value at about 75 percent. In using the word "mental" he included the emotional element, of course. "Red" was right; and he might have expanded his shrewd observation to include a good deal larger area than a football field. Football is a keenly competitive activity in which the participants must be prepared to go at top speed all the way. So is selling; and this fact explains why the salesman's attitude toward his work is so tremendously important.

Knowing and *doing* are two quite different things. As Shakespeare said: "If to do were as easy as to know what were good to do, chapels had been churches, and poor men's cottages princes' palaces."

The salesman may *know* "what were good to do," but if he is not disposed to *do* it, the knowledge avails him little. This problem has baffled sales managers from the beginning. They all wail: "We train our men thoroughly in the technique of selling; we give them the results of years of experience and experiment. We *know* that they would succeed if they would follow the prescribed methods. *But they won't!* How can we persuade them to do it?"

Attention is called to another book in which the author presents the backgrounds of several men to whom he applies the term "supersalesmen."[2] All possessed certain attitudes, as a drive toward perfectionism in their jobs, a willingness to work harder than most men over some extended

[1] Dr. Scott was the first theoretical psychologist of high standing to apply the principles of psychology to the problems of advertising and selling.
[2] Edwin P. Hoyt, *The Supersalesmen* (The World Publishing Company, New York, 1962).

period of their lives, perseverance in the face of obstacles, and a degree of flexibility that permitted them to change their plans when a change seemed necessary. Every one was able to discipline himself and never lost faith in himself.

It boils down to a problem of *attitudes*. The football coach tries to get his players "up" for the next game. The sales manager is confronted with the identical problem—getting his salesmen "up" for *their* competitive effort. And he has to do it *every day!*

We sometimes hear a football coach assert: "I didn't have to key the boys up for this game; they did it themselves." This is the ideal situation for the coach and for the sales manager. If the player or salesman can learn to generate his own head of steam and keep the fire going under his emotional boiler, he is independent of outside and more or less artificial influences directed at this end.

It is, obviously, even more important for the salesman to be able to do this than it is for the football player, because the latter can always draw inspiration from his coach and his teammates. The salesman, in contrast, may be out of personal touch with his sales manager and fellow salesmen for days and weeks at a time. In fact, he may not even have a sales manager at all. The problem is strictly and solely up to him.

Reading for inspiration

If a salesman can't draw inspiration from his boss, where can he get it? The commonest and easiest way is by reading. Some salesmen recharge their batteries by reading books and magazine articles that are informational and inspirational. But too many salesmen are allergic to this type of literature, insisting that the only way to learn how to sell is to get out and sell. Some will concede that they pick up pointers from other salesmen, seeming to believe that the best source of help is not *books,* but *people.*

But books *are* people! People have written every book ever printed. And if these people have proved themselves outstanding successes as salesmen, and have written books telling how they accomplished their success, why is not the salesman who reads these books learning from *people?*

Some of the most successful salesmen in America assert that they *always* are reading a book about selling. That is, they keep one handy and pick it up often. It may be a book which they have already read, but they can always discover something helpful in it.

This mention of books as a source of attitudes is offered thus early in the discussion because a person can find in books a stimulus to any attitude he may wish to make dominant for a given situation. If he needs more fighting spirit, he can find it; if he is too tense, he can find calming, soothing reading matter; if he is feeling out of sorts and at odds with life, he can

easily counteract this attitude by reading something cheering and optimis-
tic. Salesmen expend much nervous energy in their work and are, as a
consequence, likely to be moody at times. Some men take a drink as the
means of relaxing tensions; others resort to soothing music; still others read
poems or passages from the Bible which have served the same purpose in
the past.

To every attitude there is an opposite attitude, which can be induced
by factors controllable by the individual. This matter of attitudes is so
important to the ambitious and intelligent salesman that he studies it and
then does something about it.

In recent years many phonograph records have been made recording
inspirational speeches directed at salesmen. One concern, Sales Motivational Institute, specializes in selling motivational and inspirational programs to concerns that feel their sales forces are in need of some spiritual
tonic.

ACQUIRING AND MAINTAINING THE RIGHT ATTITUDES
FOR SELLING SUCCESSFULLY

Worry and depression

Periods of depression and worry are natural to all of us. Perhaps salesmen
are even more susceptible to these emotional ups and downs than are
persons whose activities place less of an emotional drain on them. A salesman can *soar* emotionally; therefore he can *sink*. And when he is in a
selling slump he feels depressed and he worries.

We humans may be, as some psychologists claim, subject to emotional
cycles, as are so many other things in this world. But this does not mean
that we are to surrender limply and use our emotional cycle as an excuse
for not trying to sell. We are not entirely creatures or puppets of this or of
other forces; we can do many things to counteract them.

There are definite times at which a salesman can be pretty sure he will
be feeling low. The smart thing is to anticipate these and counteract them.
Take Monday morning, for instance. We have all heard preachers speak of
"Blue Monday," when they were emotionally exhausted from their labors
of the Sabbath. Most salesmen do not preach a couple of sermons on
Sunday, but it may be hard for them to get back into the swing of selling
on Monday morning. So they take certain measures to help them get "up"
for the new day and week.

Some utilize autosuggestion and read or recite something inspirational
to sort of get their motors warmed up. Not a few give themselves an extra-
vigorous pep talk while showering and shaving. Silly? Not a bit of it! Thousands of successful salesmen have done this to their great benefit. Men who

like music may play some stirring military numbers on the phonograph. Sousa's marches are favorites. Others, with a religious bent, pray for strength to meet the day's problems—and receive it.

One of the authors of this book roomed in college with a young man who was wont to quote, as he started for his first class every day, the stirring poem by William E. Henley, declaiming as he crossed the campus,

It matters not how strait the gate,
    How charged with punishments the scroll,
I am the master of my fate,
    I am the captain of my soul.

We used to laugh at him, but he had accumulated his first million dollars long before his death and had enjoyed a life filled with satisfactions and service.

Wives of lucky salesmen make a point of starting their husbands off on the new week with encouraging words and expressions of confidence that their men will return as victors.

Of course, it helps if our salesman has had a healthful, restful week-end and is *physically* fit on Monday morning. Fatigue and hangovers are powerful depression promoters! Even a teetotaler can come up tired after too strenuous a Saturday-Sunday auto trip or 72 holes of golf.

The last hours of the week can also be expected to bring a let-down due to weariness. About the only remedy for this is a sort of emotional "second wind." Distance runners count on this, as do many salesmen. An extra hour of sleep about Wednesday or Thursday night helps, too.

There are, in most lines of selling, *seasonal* factors contributing to a feeling of futility, which leads to worry. If these are unavoidable, we simply have to ride them out and refrain from worrying. If there are things we can do to counteract the seasonal trend, it is smart to do them. Then, if sales hold up fairly well, we don't have to worry. Either way we win.

All of this discussion about worry is not intended to convey the idea that worry is basically silly or wrong. It isn't. Actually, worry is a form of wholesome fear, and fear is implanted in us to protect us from doing harmful and even suicidal things. It's part of our survival mechanism. Worry is bad only if we let it become a *habit* and ride us constantly.

We *ought* to worry about some things! We *should* worry just enough to make us find out *why* the unwanted condition exists—then we should *do* something about it. Worry as a stimulus to remedial action is good. But when we have taken this action, it's stupid to keep on worrying.

Some worry is closely akin to looking ahead and planning for the future. Perhaps "concern" is a better word than "worry" and this attitude is to be commended, of course.

When we use the word "worry" we do not mean a *proper* concern for what may happen. It is *proper* for a salesman to preview, with his imagination turned way up, what is likely to happen during the next interview. He tries to anticipate every factor that might militate against his making the sale. This is quite a different matter from worry that involves stewing and biting fingernails and fretting and lying awake nights and chain smoking and losing his appetite.

It has been sagely stated that most (perhaps 70 or 80 percent) of our worries are about two groups of problems: those which we can do nothing about and those which never come to pass anyhow. If we can just eliminate these from our thoughts, we shall have taken a long step toward emotional maturity and a sound selling attitude.

When we find ourselves worrying because we are fatigued, we would be intelligent to rest up a bit. But we ought to be sure that our fatigue is not principally from a lack of interest or boredom in our work. Many a lad finds himself dead tired after a session with the lawn mower or battling weeds in the garden, but his weariness falls away when he steps out for five strenuous sets of tennis. A girl whose feet are killing her as she stands behind a store counter can dance blithely for hours that night. Fatigue is often more nervous or mental than physical. The salesman who finds too much nervous fatigue in his job should change either his job or his attitude toward the one he has.

If the fatigue is normal to his selling work, a sharp change of activity after hours is often more helpful than sitting in his favorite chair doing nothing. This is where a hobby may prove better than idleness.

The late Vince Lombardi maintained that fatigue makes us cowards, makes us lazy. The tired man just won't make the effort that is needed to win.

Enthusiasm

But the best remedy of all is a genuine enthusiasm for one's work. Can a salesman do anything about generating such enthusiasm? *Yes!*

As has been mentioned in an earlier chapter, the first step is to learn a lot about what he is selling. One of the authors of this book was asked to give a pep talk to the solicitors in a community fund drive. He thought about this talk and tried to get some good points down on paper; but the points would not come. He knew his remarks would fall flat and accomplish nothing. So he went to the man in charge of this particular project and asked him: "Are you doing anything *worthwhile* with the money raised for your organization? What *do* you do with it?" For an instant the man looked stunned, then his face began to light up and he said: "Come on; let's go and see." We went and we saw. And we came home so filled with enthusiasm for what this organization was doing that we didn't even need to make any notes or to write any speech. We simply told those solicitors what we had learned; and when they, too, *knew,* they went out and got 23 percent more money than the goal which had been set. It was just *knowing* what they were selling.

Some salesmen insist that they are simply not the enthusiastic type. They can't fake an attitude they don't feel. It may as well be admitted right here that most salesmen need to "put on an act" now and then. If they don't have a slice of "ham" in their make-up, they don't do so well in selling. This touch of histrionic skill can be acquired without much trouble. If a salesman finds this truly impossible, he should get into a different kind of selling job where enthusiasm is not so vital. This may be in calling on a regular trade where the selling is strictly low pressure. Or maybe he should get out of selling.

Some companies, in testing applicants for selling positions, scan closely the scores on this factor of Enthusiasm. If the score is high, the applicant is accorded careful consideration.

Incidentally, in applying for a selling job, it is a good idea to insert a sentence in your letter suggesting that you feel you could really be enthusiastic in serving as a salesman for that proposition.

Enthusiasm needs to be kindled and stoked before it gets hot. One device is to warm up, like a baseball pitcher or basketball player, before starting your presentation. You can do this in front of a mirror, or while driving to the interview, or by using someone else as a stand-in prospect. Some wives of salesmen learn to perform creditably as such "prospects" and to force their husbands to put forth their best efforts in these warm-ups. Many public speakers and performers on radio and television thus work up their enthusiasm in advance of the actual performance.

Another way to fire up your enthusiasm is to expose yourself to the enthusiasm of someone else. This involves a wise choice of friends and the cultivation of those who radiate enthusiasm. It can also be accomplished by reading the right things. A cold splinter of wood, held near enough to an open flame, will itself catch fire and ignite other cold objects.

An interesting sidelight on this subject of enthusiasm is the fact that action kindles it and inaction kills it. Too many salesmen, finding themselves so lacking in this quality that they can't seem to get going that day, drop into a movie or cocktail lounge to rest. They try to convince themselves that this rest will restore their energy; but it actually operates in the opposite fashion. The way to get warmed up is to keep throwing, not to go back to the bench and relax, as any baseball player will attest.

The whole secret, as thousands of salesmen have learned, is to *act* enthusiastic or excited, and shortly you will really be *feeling* that way. This is sound psychology and is exemplified before our eyes constantly in the work of good actors. They *live* their parts so completely that it often requires them several hours to get back to normal after a show.

After all, this business of enthusiasm is nothing more than a practical application of the old principle of suggestion, used by every good salesman. If we suggest by our actions and attitude that we are enthusiastic about our proposition, our prospect will follow the suggestion and get excited about it, too. Suggestion detours around reason and hits the emotion—and emotions prompt most decisions to buy.

The name of Frank Bettger is known to salesmen the world over.[3] He relates the story of how enthusiasm changed the course of his whole life. He was a failure as a professional baseball player many years ago, playing for peanuts in the deep minors. Then he decided, upon advice, to put on an act of enthusiasm as a player. He shortly discovered that he was enthusiastic and full of pep, an important factor in his climb to a position with the St. Louis Cardinals. Then he hurt his throwing arm and had to quit baseball. Entering selling, he forgot the lesson of enthusiasm and flopped flatly in several jobs. Then he remembered and decided to discover whether a display of enthusiasm would work in selling as it had in baseball. It did—promptly and emphatically.

In his book he asserts unequivocally: "During my thirty-two years of selling I have seen enthusiasm double and treble the income of dozens of salesmen, and I have seen the lack of it cause hundreds of salesmen to fail. I firmly believe enthusiasm is by far the biggest single factor in successful selling."

Strong words, those! But few can argue with success, and Mr. Bettger certainly had enjoyed a full measure of success. So we respect his words. We conclude this section with Mr. Bettger's own statement:

It [enthusiasm] will help you overcome fear, become more successful in business, make more money, enjoy a healthier, richer and happier life.

When can you begin? Right now. Just say to yourself, "This is one thing I can do."

How can you begin? There is just one rule:

To become enthusiastic—act enthusiastic.

Self-confidence

It is not necessary to convince anyone that self-confidence is an asset to most salesmen. We all know that a salesman who does not *expect* to make a sale seldom does. And the converse is true—if he expects to make it, he usually *does*.

[3] Mr. Bettger is the author of one of the most widely read and inspiring books on salesmanship, *How I Raised Myself from Failure to Success in Selling* (Prentice-Hall, Inc., Englewood Cliffs, N.J., 1949).

The problem confronting most salesmen is, "How can I acquire this self-confidence without waiting until I have earned the right to it?"

Successful salesmen, psychologists, and many others have offered their solutions to this problem. Some of their suggestions seem sound, and from these many bits of advice we present a few.

Obviously, an attitude of self-confidence is the antithesis of a feeling of inferiority or inadequacy. Now we are suddenly on familiar ground, for we have been briefed on inferiority complexes, their causes and cures.

Few of us suffer from such severe cases of inferiority complex that we need to visit a psychiatrist, but this treatment has effected a good many cures. The skilled psychiatrist does more than diagnose the cause of the trouble—he prescribes a new program of behavior, aimed at building new attitudes toward life by substituting the positive for the negative. He does not dismiss his patient to a life of failure, a failure founded on the newly discovered excuse that he got a poor start through some quirk of his early environment and is therefore not responsible for his present warped outlook.

Self-pity is the great enemy of self-confidence. The victim of a feeling of inadequacy must, first of all, make up his mind that *he* is not a flabby blob of protoplasm floating around in his environment without any means of self-propulsion. He must assert and believe that he *is* the master of his fate and the captain of his soul. Those who seek to prepare our young people for a life of supine subservience to an all-powerful state or central government strive first to convince them that environment is everything and that we are entirely its product, without power to do anything of our own will. The individual who is convinced that he does possess a free will is a danger to the rulers of such a state; he must be taught differently, and at the earliest possible age.

But most of us do not need the services of a psychiatrist. We are clever enough to figure out for ourselves where some of the troubles lie. Maybe it is timidity, cultivated by an overly solicitous mother who really wanted a girl and got a boy instead, or vice versa.

We knew a young chap who got into high school still laboring under his handicap. He took a few psychological tests and his counselor gave him a hint that he was lacking in physical courage. So the gritty youngster went out for football, not with the thought of making the team, but merely determined to rid himself of this timidity and fear of bodily contact. He did both.

Another chap we knew in college was panicky whenever he had to stand up before a group of people and speak. He actually became physically ill at the prospect. But he wanted to be a preacher; so he started standing up and declaiming at his roommate. Later, he would bribe two or three other fraternity brothers to serve as an audience (cookies from home were his bait). Then he joined a literary society and practiced on the members, many of whom harbored similar inhibitions and ambitions. In the evenings he would hie himself to the athletic field and orate at the top of his lungs to gain vocal power. That boy, in his senior year, won the state intercollegiate oratorical contest and went on to become a prominent preacher. How could he have done otherwise? He believed in himself and in his own powers to remake himself despite his handicap.

Unless we have this belief in our own power to accomplish our objectives, we might as well reconcile ourselves to an existence as a piece of inert protoplasm, helpless in the eddies of our environment.

So—let's analyze ourselves and identify the trouble. Then let's get rid of it!

One of the best cures for a feeling of inadequacy as a salesman is to discover that you are *adequate*. That is, to make some sales. This involves starting small and gradually building up, as a baseball player does when he starts in the lower minors and works up. He gets a feeling of confidence as he finds he can hit successively better pitching. If he started trying to hit against the best pitchers in the world, he would develop a ruinous inferiority complex. So the young salesman starts by picking smaller and not too tough prospects. As one young fellow says, "I don't know very much about my proposition yet, so I try to call on prospects who know less about it than I do." If he continues to study his proposition, he will soon know more about it than most of his prospects, and this source of his inferiority feeling will be eliminated.

What are some other causes of an inferiority complex?

LACK OF EDUCATION   Many people exaggerate the values derived from advanced formal education. They exaggerate them because they are not familiar with them. They do not realize that a man *can* acquire for himself most of the knowledge and culture he would get in college. A guided program of reading will compensate for much of this lack of education.

LOW IQ   Most school pupils take intelligence tests from time to time and many of them find out about where they stand relatively. If they learn that they are only average or perhaps a trifle below average, they may give up. But they needn't. Many a successful salesman would not score above average on such tests, because these tests do not measure many of the qualities or traits that make for success in selling. Besides, it is possible to raise one's IQ.

POOR SOCIAL OR ECONOMIC ORIGIN   This is actually not much of a handicap and can be overcome by any determined individual. For ambitious young folk to climb, to cross to the better side of the tracks, is so common and so typically American that being born on the wrong side merits no serious consideration as an excuse for remaining mediocre. Of course, the agitators and promoters of protest marches, demonstrations, and riots magnify the importance of environment and play down the triumphs enjoyed by thousands of individuals who have achieved successful lives despite a slow start. If a person *wants* to climb, he *will* climb.

LACK OF BREEZINESS AND SKILL AS A RACONTEUR Some people still think that a salesman must be a jovial character, always ready with the latest story, quick with a clever *bon mot*. This is simply not true. If he is sincerely interested in helping his prospect, eager to render service, able to offer helpful advice, dependable, and friendly, he can discard his worries about being serious-minded. Buying or spending money is rather generally a serious matter anyway, and few people buy anything of importance merely because the salesman makes them laugh.

PHYSICAL APPEARANCE This has been adequately dealt with in previous pages. Cleanliness, neatness, gestures, and a measure of bodily grace can be acquired. Beauty of features or figure is far from indispensable.

Concerning these and other causes of a sense of inadequacy two suggestions are offered:

1. Do all you can to counteract and overcome them.
2. Then forget about them. Focus your attention on your prospect and how you can help him solve his problems. Think about the product or service you are selling and not about yourself.

First, *form habits*—good habits—of presenting yourself and your proposition. Then concentrate on understanding just what your prospect wants to accomplish and how you can help him do this. The incorrigibly egocentric salesman cannot achieve this disinterest in himself, the ability to forget himself and immerse himself in the interests and wants of his prospect. The baseball pitcher works on the technique of his delivery until he can forget about it and concentrate on the batter.

Did you ever see a little dog yelping in terror as it fled from a bigger dog? Then when the frightened pup reached the sanctuary of its master's legs it turned on its pursuer and yapped a ferocious challenge to come on and fight! We are all like that in so far as we draw confidence from a faith in something stronger than we are. Many a prodigy of valor has been committed because the hero was sustained by his religion or his patriotism. Faith in something bigger than ourselves undoubtedly helps, and no sensible person denies this.

J. P. Morgan was wont to admonish investors, "Never sell America short." Faith in the future of his country was the foundation of his financial promotions. The salesman who believes that the country is going to the dogs will never sell up to his capacity.

A man never grows much bigger than his dreams about himself. If he is satisfied with a $10,000 income, the chances are that he will never make $20,000. But his dreams must be of the right kind. They may be idle, fluffy, vaporous wisps of wishing, or they may take the form of plans, specifications, and blueprints of substantial structures to be erected on solid foundations of effort. Dreams of this latter variety are likely to come true.

This brings us to a final point.

Let's Keep Growing.

When we stop growing we start shrinking.

In managing our nonselling time we should reserve a few minutes each day for growth-promoting activity. Mostly, we learn from the experiences of others, as well as from our own. There are helpful books and periodicals on salesmanship, but this is only a start. From here we can go on and on, the next step probably being general biography. We glean information and inspiration from the lives of outstanding men in all walks of life. Most successful men will admit that they are constant readers of biographies and that they draw strength and ideas from them.

Emerson said it: "There is properly no history, only biography."

It is here suggested that the reader enlist the cooperation of two individuals in this search for invigorating mental fare—a cooperative librarian in a good public library and an intelligent salesman in a bookstore. Between them you can keep yourself supplied with the best of biography and other helpful books, so that you need never grow stale or stagnant in your thinking and your selling. Your thoughts and speech will flow fresh and refreshing; your friends will be glad to see you; you will generate and radiate a joy in living and you will reap the rewards of success in tangible ways, as well.

One vital but practicable phase of continuing growth is your vocabulary.

The surgeon, the dentist, the plumber, the machinist, and the electrician have one thing in common—they all use tools and they all tend to accumulate special tools for special tasks as they progress in their professions. The tools of the salesman are words and he will be wise to emulate these other artisans and keep his kit filled with the most modern, the most efficient, the sharpest tools he can find. His assortment should grow, until he finds he can lay his tongue to the precise tool he needs for a particular job. In this way he can grow constantly more expert, able to do a neater job in shorter time.

THE SALESMAN'S WORK METHODS

When a person has trained himself to approach life and its problems with certain definite attitudes, he has gone only part way toward his goal. The next step is *action*—action based on these attitudes and on the general philosophy these attitudes add up to.

Theory must usually precede action, but theory without action is fruitless and sterile. Let's see how the salesman puts his theories into practice.

MANAGEMENT OF SELLING TIME

Salesmen in the higher brackets work without much close supervision. They can do pretty much as they please with their time.

This fact removes one potent incentive to effort—the presence of a boss or foreman or supervisor whose watchful eye is ever on us and whose tongue is ever ready to remind us that we are taking things too easily. In many lines of industry, it requires one supervisor to about every ten employees to keep those ten from loafing on the job. True, a supervisor has other functions, but this one is primary. The race horse without a rider or driver will not win the race, although he should do so because he is "traveling light." The average young person in school *could* acquire much of his education by himself, but he doesn't. He needs a teacher to see that he studies the assignments. For the most part, human beings are very, very human; they need supervision to do their best.

But the experience of mankind is that the need for such supervision decreases as the individual *matures.* The youngster in the first grade does all his schoolwork under the eye of his teacher. Later he is given some homework to do and "study hours" at school are fewer. In college he has no "study hours" and all his studying is done outside the classroom. As a graduate student, 80 or 90 percent of his work is done "on his own" without supervision.

In short, only the truly *mature* person can be depended on to act as his own boss and work effectively without some superior watching him.

Sales managers are unanimous in asserting that the commonest reason for failure of salesmen—*outside* salesmen, that is—is their lack of this essential maturity, the ability to work without supervision, the *power to manage themselves.* Without this, they remain mediocre.

This power to manage oneself can be *acquired.* All that is needed is what athletic coaches call "desire." And this desire can be acquired! That's why this chapter has been written.

How to make more calls

One of the country's most successful football coaches figures that if his teams average 4½ yards per play on offense, the way to make more yardage is to run off more plays. So his boys hastily unscramble themselves from each pile-up, race back into their huddle, and launch another play almost before their opponents have picked themselves up. This system pays off in increased yardage and higher scores.

There is a lesson here for any salesman. If he will just run more plays he will roll up higher scores.

How can he run more plays—that is, see more prospects every day?

There is only one way and that is to plan, a day or so before, just what he will try to be doing every minute of each selling day. It isn't enough to formulate a rough plan for the day as he rides to work or eats breakfast. Too many things can happen to break up such a plan. Each day must be planned well ahead because this planning involves telephoning for appointments and fitting these appointments into a pattern that requires a minimum of traveling between prospects. Only thus can a salesman make certain that he is seeing his quota of prospects.

In passing, it may be mentioned that this advance planning saves not only time but heart and legs. Some salesmen learn this *after* suffering a heart attack; others learn it earlier and avoid the attack.

Planning also saves worry and futile "post mortems." One is reminded of the young minister who told his bishop about how he lay awake Sunday nights worrying about the sermon he had preached that morning. The wise old bishop suggested that it might be better to lie awake *Saturday* night thinking about and planning the sermon *in advance.*

This careful preparation also begets a confidence impossible of attainment by a salesman who feels himself inadequately prepared. The surgeon who has spent hours reading up on the latest techniques in a rare operation approaches his task with a confidence he could never feel if he had not prepared himself for it.

Let's take a longer look at this problem of making more calls and getting more interviews. It is the latter that really count. Making calls is merely a means of getting more interviews. This matter should have been taken care of in prospecting. That is, the salesman should be calling on his *best* prospects rather than on china eggs. Also, it should have been considered in making the preapproach, so that the salesman will gain the interview and get it off to a propitious start and insure that it will not be ended prematurely. We have assumed that these factors have been recognized and utilized.

SHORTEN YOUR PRESENTATION   The chances are that it has worn itself into a fairly standardized effort. Dictate it to a recording device and then play it back. Write it out in full and edit it thoroughly. You ought to be able to trim away 10 to 20 percent of the "fat" without weakening it at all. Use sentences that are clearer and pack more punch. Make full use of visual aids that might convey the idea more quickly than words.

Many salesmen have found they can save time by sending the prospect something in advance of the call, thereby partially selling him.

Try to close earlier and oftener. You may find that your prospect is sold before you realize it. If not, you can always pile on more value and then try to close again.

Minimize *needless* chatter; your prospect has to listen to plenty of this from other salesmen.

If your presentation is not rigidly standardized, *plan* it to include the points most likely to interest *the particular prospect.* Try to learn *his* problems *before* you call, and then shape your presentation to offer solutions to these problems.

Of course, some prospects like to buy more leisurely and resent any appearance of haste on the part of the salesman. These must be humored. Even here, it often helps to start the presentation with something like: "I realize that you're a busy man and your time is worth money; so I'll try to tell my story as briefly as possible. But please stop me and ask any question at any time. I'll be glad to discuss it. I'm simply trying to avoid wasting *your* time."

STRETCH THE WORKING WEEK This is contrary to the trend in modern business where hours of work have been shortened sharply. This trend affects salesmen differently. If they must make their calls at prospects' places of business, they may find their own working day shortened. But if they can sell to people in their homes, they find them there *more* hours a week than formerly. Many salesmen can sell at both places.

To stretch the working week a salesman must utilize days like Saturday and some holidays. There are salesmen who do some productive selling on Sunday. The days just before and immediately following holidays are often slighted by salesmen seeking an excuse to take it easy on those days. But the man who works those days finds that it is easier to get interviews because he has less competition. The same reasoning applies to days when the weather is unpleasant. Bad weather eliminates many competitors; it makes it easier to schedule interviews with live prospects.

The author knows a great many successful men from all walks of life and, without exception, all of them work far in excess of 40 hours a week; 60 to 80 hours a week are not uncommon. Indeed, the presidents with whom we are acquainted work at their affairs every waking moment. Their jobs are their lives.

Winners don't work 40-hour weeks. If you are of the bent to put in your 40 hours and go home, then wonder not why you remain among the mass of the mediocre. Such is the price demanded by success, but the mature individual has realized that everything has a price and that if one wants something he must be willing to pay the price for getting it.

STRETCH THE WORKING DAY   This is one of the best and easiest ways to see more prospects. But it involves *planning.*

Most salesmen believe that they cannot make calls outside the traditional 9 to 12 and 2 to 4:30 or 5 pattern. But there are still many business and professional men who are accessible earlier than 9 A.M. and later than 5 P.M. This is especially true in the smaller cities where commuting time is eliminated. Even in the cities many an executive prides himself on being at his desk before his employees appear, and he may still be there when they leave. This is where the planning comes in, based on a sound preapproach and some advance telephoning for appointments.

Salesmen calling on the retail trade have long ago learned which of their customers are on the job early and which stay late. Calling on these "early and late" buyers can add hours to the working day.

Then there is the lunch hour. This permits friendly social interviews, less hurried than those conducted in the prospect's place of business. These appointments should be arranged with those prospects whose reaction would be favorable. It may be that no selling should be attempted at such a time, but even here the occasion should advance the time when a selling effort can wisely be made.

Another way to stretch the selling day is to cut down on time used in traveling between prospects. This traveling time, even under favorable circumstances, amounts to about one-third of the selling day. With city salesmen it may run less and with country salesmen it will usually amount to more than one-third; but this figure can be taken as a rough average. By planning calls in advance and "bunching" prospects, these nonproductive hours can be lessened appreciably.

Finally, we have our evenings. This possibility is rejected by many salesmen who feel that they should spend these hours with their families. Here we are merely pointing out that many ambitious salesmen do sell a wide variety of products and services after dinner or supper. These are usually items which affect both the husband and wife and their children, if any. As examples we can mention various types of insurance, home heating or air conditioning or insulation, automobiles, electrical appliances for the home, investment programs, sterling silver, landscaping services, real estate, tours and cruises, and the services of interior decorators.

You may not wish to devote every evening to selling, but perhaps you may compromise and employ quite profitably two or three evenings a week from 7 to 9.

Don't concentrate on congenial prospects

The young salesman tends to concentrate on prospects with whom he is most comfortable, with whom he has much in common. He will tend to spend his time calling upon people of his own age group and socioeconomic class.[4] He will spend far more time than is wise with people who may represent but a small segment of his market potential while in theory he should apportion his time in ratio to the prospect's market potential. But big buyers tend to be brief and curt while the little boys may be willing to talk all day; the salesman feels more at home in the pleasant environment. This natural tendency must be fought. The salesman must go where the action is, where the volume is to be had.

One fine salesman confided that one night he and his wife suddenly realized on the way home from a regular party of friends with whom they had been associating for 5 years that they had been utterly bored by listening to the same stories and nonsense week after week from these friends. He had realized for some time that these people did not really give him much business; they couldn't afford his product. So he set forth on a program to broaden his range of friends and stop leaning completely upon his old cronies for social contacts. He spotted successful young men and then went out of his way to meet them. The program was successful and he not only gained much new business, but he is enjoying a much richer social life.

The amazing value of a minute

It has been calculated that the average salesman has about 1,000 hours a year actually face to face with prospects. Holidays, vacations, absence because of illness, weekends, traveling, waiting, desk work, etc., account for the rest of his time.

Another study (see Table 19-1) verifies that the industrial salesman has only about 1,000 selling hours per year in which to do his job.

If a salesman makes $15,000 a year, every hour of his *selling* time is worth $15, which is pretty good pay. Viewing it in this light, he will appreciate more keenly the value of his time. It has been observed that we cannot save time wholesale. We can save it only by saving minutes. Just one minute is worth 25 cents, and almost any man would feel well rewarded if he could pick up a quarter every minute from the sidewalk.

Thus each minute is precious and we focus our brain power on ways to utilize it instead of wasting it. We salesmen do waste a good many minutes every day in some of these ways:

Writing overlengthy reports to headquarters, much of them explaining why we failed to sell more.

[4] M. S. Gadel, "Concentration by Salesmen on Congenial Prospects," *Journal of Marketing*, April, 1964, pp. 64–66.

TABLE 19-1 HOW INDUSTRIAL SALESMEN SPEND THEIR TIME

INDUSTRY	NUMBER OF SALESMEN	AVERAGE LENGTH OF DAY, HOURS	FACE-TO-FACE SELLING, %	TRAVELING AND WAITING FOR INTERVIEWS, %	PAPER WORK AND MEETINGS, %	SERVICE CALLS, %
Furniture and fixtures	47	9:01	41	36	16	7
Industrial organic and inorganic chemicals	105	9:34	36	43	18	3
Other chemical industries	87	9:47	39	37	19	5
Primary smelting of nonferrous metals	94	8:59	42	32	21	5
Other primary metal industries	28	9:20	44	34	18	4
Fabricated metal products	40	9:17	43	37	13	7
Metalworking machinery	120	9:14	40	37	15	8
General industrial machinery	118	9:24	43	32	22	3
Other machinery except electrical	109	9:29	42	36	18	4
Electrical industrial apparatus	105	9:13	41	28	28	3
Other electrical machinery	128	9:22	46	30	20	4
Instruments	42	10:10	41	28	22	9
Other industries	66	8:56	41	29	24	6
Total	1,089	9:22	41	34	20	5

Additional Notes: Average no. of calls: 8.4; average length of sales calls: 28 minutes; average total face-to-face selling per day: 3 hours 52 minutes.
Source: McGraw-Hill Publishing Company. Each man was asked to keep an actual one-day diary of his activities and then send it in to McGraw-Hill.

Dawdling too long over lunch or coffee break.

Doing things during working hours which we could do just as well after hours when we can't see prospects.

Fretting in waiting rooms to see prospects when we could have made definite appointments in advance and saved this waiting time.

Spending too much time at our desk when we should be selling.

Calling on poor prospects who will never buy.

Poor travel planning. For example, it is smart to schedule a call farthest from headquarters as the first or the last call of the day, thereby using nonselling time for traveling to or from this prospect.

Some salesmen have taken to the air to reduce traveling time between calls, while others have scheduled calls more carefully so that time between them is minimized. Numerous other tactics have been employed to give the salesman more productive selling time each day. Many apparel salesmen have the buyers from small towns come to a showroom in some nearby large city to "work the line," a most significant saving of time and money.

The salesman's own time study of his job

In this chapter we talk a good deal about planning. True, planning is vital—the heart and soul of time-saving.

But before you can plan intelligently you must have some *facts*. If a college student should say, "*I* will make 25 calls a day when I start *my* selling career," this would mean little. He does not know how many calls he ought to make, and he never will know until he does some honest experimenting. In other words, he must keep some careful records of what he *is doing* before he can intelligently calculate what he *might do*.

It might be helpful if we went a little more into detail on this matter of keeping tabs on yourself.

Some salesmen use a pocket notebook with blank pages and rule them into columns to suit their own convenience. These can show in the first column the periods of time spent on each activity, as 10:15-10:40.

In other columns the salesman may make check marks to show whether the time was consumed in traveling from call to call, in waiting to see prospects, in carrying on an interview, in planning the next day's work, in making out reports of the day's work just completed, whether the interview resulted in a sale, etc.

One thing is important—to *make the entries at once* instead of waiting until the end of the day. This can be done in a few seconds *immediately* after leaving each prospect. Delay distorts the record and destroys its value.

If the salesman keeps a record of what he does every waking minute of even one day, that would help; but a week or two would be better.

Setting quotas

When he has these records spread out on his desk he can analyze them. He can compute just what percent of his average selling day is spent face to face with prospects, how much in waiting rooms, how much in making appointments, how much in prospecting, how much in call-backs, how much in getting from one prospect to another, etc.

Confronted with the results of his calculations, he can devise ways to improve his performance where he is weak.

Having spotted the places where he can do better, he is in a position to set for himself a goal or quota at which to aim over the next week or month. This quota may take several forms.

THE CALL QUOTA   As a result of his computations, a salesman may learn that he gets one interview out of every three calls he makes. The other two prospects are not interested. Let's assume that this salesman is able to sell half the prospects with whom he has interviews. He then knows that he must make six calls and get two interviews to make each sale. Now he can set his quota on the basis of the number of calls he is able to make in a working day. If he can make a dozen calls, he will average two sales per day. If each sale nets him $20, he will be making $40 per day. If he wants to make more, he will have to find some way to make more calls, assuming that his presentation is effective.

One life insurance salesman has worked out some stimulating conclusions on this subject. He calls it his "Ten, Three, and One Ratio." Interpreted, this means that ten calls produce three solid interviews and these three interviews produce one sale. So, for each sale, he must make ten calls. On a weekly basis, he tries to make fifty calls which yield fifteen interviews and five sales.

One of the results of establishing a ratio like this one is that it puts greater emphasis on the *quality* of prospects. The salesman learns to stop wasting his time on the small fry and concentrate on those who are able to use and pay for larger quantities of the product, whatever this may be. When a salesman has learned to utilize every minute of his day, this is about the only way he can keep on increasing his sales and income.

In setting quotas of various types, it is, therefore, necessary to distinguish between the *end* and the *means* used to attain this end. That is, we must be careful not to be satisfied with reaching our quota of "means."

To be specific, if we have set a quota of calls which we think will bring to fruition the desired number of sales, we must be vigilant to insure making those *sales* and not permit ourselves to be content with making the quota of *calls*. Going through the motions is not enough; we must keep our eyes fixed on the *results* of going through the motions.[5] This point is important and often overlooked, even by the conscientious salesman. *The ultimate objective is sales,* not calls or even interviews. If the calls and interviews are not producing the sales, we must review the situation and correct it, either by improving our presentation or by making our calls on better prospects or by making more calls.

Any quota we may establish has only one purpose—the making of sales. Never let the *means* come between your eye and the *real goal,* which is *sales.*

DISCUSSION QUESTIONS
1. How would you go about widening your circle of friends?
2. After reading the material on not wasting time, a salesman protests, "That's no fun. I like coffee breaks. If I have to hustle every minute of the day, then forget it. I'll get another job." What would you tell this salesman?
3. Interview some successful salesman and find out:
    a. What his employer or manager does to help him cultivate sound attitudes and methods.
    b. How he plans his own schedule.
4. With perhaps some help from the librarian, mention several books or periodicals you could recommend for a salesman's reading in his effort to acquire better attitudes and methods of work.

CASE 19-1   CHARLES DAVID:
A Week on the Road[6]
This is the record of a week's selling by a jewelry salesman with a large territory who normally covers several hundred miles from the time he

5 We are here reminded of the oft-repeated story about the young salesman who had been thoroughly indoctrinated with the necessity of making as many calls as possible each day. When his boss complimented him on making 46 calls his first day, the youngster replied: "I'm not satisfied with that figure. I'd have made it an even 50 if a couple of prospects hadn't stopped me and asked me what I was selling."
6 This case is based on an article by Edward Fales, Jr., "Hour by Hour through a Salesman's Week," *The American Salesman,* June, 1960, pp. 50–61.

leaves home Sunday evening or Monday morning until his return the following weekend. The man's name is Charles David. His territory is the
whole Northeastern United States, as far south as Washington, D.C., as far
west as Pittsburgh and Buffalo, but omitting New York City. The week
covered began on Monday, April 4, when David took off by car from his
Long Island home for New England.

Like most men with large territories, one of David's chief problems is
the conservation of time. Having to stop sometimes in two or three towns
and cities in a day, he's found it impractical to call ahead for appointments
or even to check to see if a given buyer will be in the store on the day he's
coming. It's more costly, he's found, to zigzag around and back-track than
occasionally to miss some buyers. And when a buyer is out, David tries to
make his visit worthwhile by talking to other persons in the store or by
looking around to learn more about the store's operation.

David sells to many different kinds of stores; big ones like Filene's in
Boston, Woodward & Lothrop in Washington, Strawbridge & Clothier in
Philadelphia; and also to small department, specialty, and variety stores.
His line, which for business reasons he prefers to leave unidentified, in-
cludes earrings, necklaces, bracelets, and other costume jewelry.

At the end of this particular week of selling, David reviewed what had
happened, and his comments and criticisms on what he did are given here.

Monday's schedule: David planned to leave home (in North Woodmere,
L.I.) around 8 A.M. and drive 50 miles to Mt. Vernon, N.Y., where he had
recently acquired a good new account. At 9:14 an associate was to meet him
at the store, which is buying headquarters for a fast-growing chain of six
department stores. Following their joint call on the chain buyer, David
intended to push on along to Greenwich, Conn., to see a woman buyer
before lunch, then to Stamford to call on a department store and drop in
more or less informally on a couple of other outlets.

Monday's log:

8:05:   Left home.

9:15:   Lost his way, since it was his first visit to Mt. Vernon. Stopped twice
to ask directions.

9:30:   Arrived at the store. No sign of associate. He waited on the street
for three minutes; then, seeing other salesmen going in, he rushed upstairs
alone.

"That dash saved the day," he repeated. "I got there just ahead of the
first competitor. I told the buyer I wanted her to meet my friend and that I
would look outside for him. She said: 'You'd better not! There's a line
forming to see me.' I took her advice and opened my sample case. When I

came out an hour later I had two orders and there were 10 salesmen waiting in the reception room!"

David's associate joined the conference at 10. He'd been lost, too.

10:40: Second breakfast. "I get all wound up when I'm selling," David explained. "The only thing that can calm me down after closing a deal is something to eat." (Despite this habit, he has a trim figure.)

11:20–11:50: Lost time getting gas for associate's car and waiting at toll gates on Connecticut Turnpike. There were exact-change gates through which he could have whisked if he had not needed receipts for income tax purposes.

12:00: Arrived Greenwich. The buyer was on her way to lunch, but David caught her at the door. She went back to her office with him.

This buyer was overstocked, so David sold nothing. During the lunch hour, he decided to look over the fast-growing main business street. "It pays to look around constantly in each town," he said. "I usually do this at lunch time or when I'm waiting for buyers." He strolled downtown to a big, attractive new store.

12:10: Found the buyer for the new store, a man, in his office. Within 15 minutes had shown his sample panels and written a small order. "It was just a pilot," he said, "a couple of hundred dollars. But accounts like that can amount to thousands before the year is over if you keep working at them."

12:40: Lunch. "I was all wound up again," he said.

1:30: Left Greenwich for Stamford.

1:55: David strolled into a large store on a missionary visit without his sample cases. He didn't expect a sale because he had received a $2,000 order by mail after his last call. The buyer was at lunch, and David decided to wait.

2:00: The buyer came in, chatted with David for 15 minutes. "They're expanding," he said. "As soon as they get settled, I'll have another order there."

2:25: Carrying his samples, he called on a department store. "Is Miss S. around?" he asked a salesgirl. She was, but no one knew where. David said, "I'll be back."

2:35: He stopped at a store he had sold formerly, studied the show windows, didn't go in. "I might land a small order here," he said, "but the place shows no promise."

2:45: Back to the first store. Buyer still not in. She is a woman who usually has exceptional trouble making up her mind and sometimes changes it after ordering, so David decided not to wait. He drove a few blocks to one of the East's biggest and newest suburban stores.

3:00: Parked near the store. Couldn't find the buyer immediately.

3:20: The buyer appeared and David showed her some earrings, urging her to check her stock. "No sale," David said, "but I got in some good spade work." (When David returned to his New York office 10 days later he found a mail order.)

4:00: David ended his calls early.

5:00: Checked in at a motel near Stamford, sat down to write up the day's orders for immediate mailing. "If I can get the orders in early next day it may save the buyer as much as a week or two," he explained. "If my orders don't go out until next morning, they might arrive just after orders from other salesmen for 100 gross leave the company temporarily out of stock."

7:00: Supper. An hour and a quarter later, David was back at his room telephoning his wife and children as he does every night.

8:30: He turned on the television set; nothing appealed to him, so he read a book.

10:30: Snapped out the light.

Monday's score: David had hoped to see six buyers in three cities during the day, two of them for missionary purposes only. He actually did see five buyers and made two sales.

Tuesday's schedule: David planned an early call on a buyer in Bridgeport, Conn. He wanted to make two other sales calls in Bridgeport and then head for a large New Haven department store, making quick calls on as many smaller outlets as possible before driving to Providence that evening to be ready for an early start on Wednesday.

Tuesday's log:

7:30: Woke up; weather stormy.

8:30: Breakfast at roadside restaurant; 15 minutes. Storm getting worse.

8:50: Ran into 40-minute traffic jam caused by flooded roads.

10:20: More than an hour late at first Bridgeport call, David found the buyer had just gone out. "I wanted especially to hit that buyer, who owns his own busy store and buys for two more that are even larger."

10:30:　Rain pouring down. Deciding to get some coffee before tackling the other stores, David ducked into a coffee shop, saw the buyer he'd missed and joined him. At first, David considered the 15 minutes he spent with the buyer lost time but later changed his mind. The buyer did most of the talking, getting some complaints off his chest. "This is an important man who knows the business, so I listened and learned," David explained.

10:45:　Scooted back through the rain with the buyer to his store, showed him samples. Undecided on colors and styles, the buyer called his wife who picked out the best items. The buyer approved, wrote the order and then talked again about business conditions for half an hour more.

11:45:　Now began a spell of jack-rabbiting in the rain between two stores, waiting for their buyers to appear.

12:10:　Finally found one buyer in. A pleasant young woman, she chatted briefly but needed no goods. David asked her to lunch but she pleaded too bad a cold. He started for his own lunch, but decided at the last moment to shoot over to another store a few blocks away. Its pretty buyer at first turned down what David showed her: "Weather's been too bad; things aren't moving."

"One thing in my type of selling," David explained later, "is to keep bringing in new things, letting buyers catch a glimpse, teasing their curiosity, making them learn to like you."

With this buyer, David listened to her weather troubles until she noticed an unopened sample panel at his elbow. A few glittering beads were dangling out. "What have you got in there?" she asked.

David showed her. Lifting one item, the buyer weighed it approvingly in her hand.

1:15:　David left the store with the promise of an order within two weeks. "That girl keeps her word and her orders stick," he said happily. "If your samples are made up properly, good buyers can't keep hands off them! They can't resist these beads and sometimes I just let them discover them for themselves."

1:20:　David tramped back to the hotel coffee shop through the rain for lunch. The buyer with a cold who had turned down a lunch date with him was there. "May I join you?" David asked. "I'll take a chance on your cold."

He didn't talk business. Afterward, he explained: "Although they're not buying much here now, by my trip next month, she'll be buying again. You have to keep up that friendly relationship." After eating lunch, he left for New Haven.

2:25:　David's Plymouth turned off the Connecticut Turnpike at New Haven. Hoping to park in the center of town, he passed up one lot, tried another that was full, got caught in a traffic jam, and had to back-track to the first lot.

3:00: He tackled a large department store, steered the buyer into a $200 order, then upped it to $300 and finally $400. "Where's your order book?" the buyer asked. David had left it in his car. On some calls he tries to have the order written up on the buyer's own book so he can make sure while he's still there that it has started through the company's administrative machinery. "If I write the order in my own book," he explained, "the buyer has to transcribe it to the company's forms before it's approved, and it might never get transcribed and approved."

When the buyer had written out his orders, he said, "Now double them for our other stores!"

4:00–5:30: David packed in five calls on small stores, and wrote two orders.

5:40: Left for Providence.

8:25: Arrived Colonial Motel, 10 miles out of Providence.

8:30: Telephoned home and got two business messages.

8:40–9:10: Wrote and mailed orders; then read for a couple of hours.

Tuesday's score: In Bridgeport and New Haven, David saw a total of nine buyers, missed only one. He made four sales, two of them big, and had a definite promise of a fifth order.

Wednesday's schedule: David planned to spend most of the day making a series of fast calls in Providence, then to head for Boston, where, because Wednesday is a late closing day, he could make evening calls.

Wednesday's log:

8:45: Left for downtown Providence.

9:30: First call. Buyer was ill and not expected in until noon. David spent 40 minutes talking to an assistant.

10:15: Second call. Lost 30 minutes waiting to see a buyer who didn't buy.

10:45: Third call. Buyer in New York. David spent 30 minutes checking goods in the department and talking to salesgirls.

11:15: Hoping the first buyer might have come in earlier than expected, David rechecked the store, for this was a must call. Buyer wasn't there, so he began jack-rabbiting between other stores.

11:25:   Wrote a fast order at one store.

11:45:   Another store. Buyer had gone to early lunch, was due back at 2:30.

12:00:   Third check on the must buyer. No luck. Spent 15 minutes chatting with assistant. "Got to rely on her help to get me to him when he arrives."

12:30:   Lunch alone.

1:30:   Fourth call at must store. No buyer yet!

1:45:   Stopped at hotel to get morning's order in the mail.

2:20:   Called at a small store. Buyer in New York.

2:30:   Returned to the store whose buyer was due back at 2:30. He did come back at 2:45 with two salesmen who had previous appointments. Decided to wait, spending the time exploring the store.

3:30:   Finally got to see the buyer.

4:00:   Landed a good order.

4:30:   Fifth call in search of the must buyer, who still hadn't come in. David now had a third talk with the assistant, and got her promise to discuss with the buyer a reorder that David felt was needed.

5:00:   Mailed in his afternoon order and left for Boston, stopping for 15 minutes to telephone for hotel reservations. When he came out of the phone booth, traffic was tied up worse than before. David had hoped to cover the 40 miles to Boston by 6:30, but it was 7:15 before he reached Jordan Marsh. This was a missionary call. When the buyer turned out to be in Europe, David showed an assistant a new group of necklaces.

7:30:   Filene's—the buyer was in New York, returning Thursday.

7:40:   Called at another department store. Buyer also in New York.

7:50:   Called at Gilchrist's. Buyer's evening off.

8:00:   Called on a smaller account. Found owner and worked with him for an hour. Wrote two nice orders.

9:00:   Back to hotel for supper.

10:00–1:00 A.M.:   Wrote orders and letters, read, dozed, and watched TV.

Wednesday's score: David saw four buyers and one assistant, and missed six. Total sales: three.

Thursday's schedule: David planned a quick trip in the morning to Quincy, Mass., to meet a new buyer for five active stores and drop in on a couple of other outlets. In the afternoon, he intended to return to Boston for calls on the buyers who'd been out of town Wednesday night.

Thursday's log:

9:00: "Overslept."

9:40: Left for Quincy.

10:15: Arrived in Quincy. First buyer in New York.

10:25: Second call. Buyer out of town.

10:30: Called on a new buyer and got two orders.

11:30–12:00: Post-sale discussion of business and styles. Invited buyer to lunch, but she couldn't make it.

12:00: Lunching alone gave David time to look over Quincy. "Scouted around for sleepers and found a beautiful, brand-new store. Buyer out of town, so will try next trip."

1:00: Left for Boston.

2:05: Called on a Boston specialty store. Buyer still in New York.

2:20: Called on a department store. Buyer seeing other salesmen.

2:30: Called on a large jewelry store. Buyer in, but no sale.

2:45: Went to a large store to keep a 3 P.M. appointment made the day before. Call produced a sizable order.

3:45: Called on another store; buyer out.

4:00: Called on another store. Showed goods to buyer, but no sale.

4:30: Called again at one of the larger stores. Buyer tied up, but suggested David return after 5. He made another brief call, sold nothing, then returned as promised.

5:30: Landed third order of the day.

6:00: Returned to hotel, wrote up orders and mailed them.

7:30: Supper.

10:00: Went to bed, but read for a couple of hours.

Thursday's score: David saw six buyers, missed six. Three sales.

Friday's schedule: On the last day of the trip, David hoped to wrap up his Boston business with calls on Filene's, one other department store, and two specialty stores and then stop briefly in Worcester in the afternoon.

Friday's log:

8:30:   Got up.

9:30:   First call produced an immediate turndown from a well-stocked buyer. But she chatted for a half hour, a good omen for a future order.

10:15:   Filene's buyer was in but hurrying to a Friday meeting. Asked if David could come back in the afternoon. This knocked out Worcester but Filene's is too important to be skipped.

10:45:   Called on a big specialty house. Buyer suggested an appointment at 4:00, but David managed to switch it to noon.

11:20:   Called at a department store to find that the buyer's day off had been switched to Friday.

11:40:   Made a quick call on another store visited the previous evening. The buyer was new. David introduced himself, showed two lines and chatted briefly. No order this time, but promising atmosphere created.

12:15:   Back to specialty house to keep appointment. Worked two lines with buyer for a full hour and got an order.

1:30:   Raining. Still without lunch, David rushed back to Filene's and found the buyer with some free time. Worked two lines, spending extra time on one in which she showed a special interest. Also went through samples with an assistant who came into the office. Even though it produced no sale, David felt it was a good call which might result in orders on his next trip, by mail or on the buyer's next trip to New York.

2:15:   Quick, late lunch.

2:40:   Called on a large apparel store which had been a customer for years. "Here," he explained, "your order may never come through. It gets hung up on a spike after you leave, or the buyer loses her confidence, or some other salesman comes in and sells her something else." So once again, David left his own order book behind. The buyer was interested in some colorful new beads that had been selling so well the manufacturer was having trouble keeping up with the demand. "I told her they might be hard to get," he said.

3:10:   David had the order, signed by the buyer on the store's own order book. Then he said: "Just to make *sure* that the factory gets your order quickly, may I phone it in right now?" When the buyer hesitated, David added, "That will insure your receiving the beads within a day or two instead of, maybe, three weeks."

"All right," she agreed, finally telling him to give the factory the store's own order number. "That way," David said, "she knows she's got to pass it through her own company for final okay."

3:40:   It was too late to think about going to Worcester, so David mailed his orders, checked out of his hotel and, at 4:30 started driving home.

9:00:   Arrived North Woodmere.

Friday's score: David didn't get to see the Jordan Marsh buyer, usually one of his main targets in Boston, because of her European trip. But he did come away from Filene's with a definite feeling that he had done some good spade work, making up for the missed side trip to Worcester. He'd seen five buyers, missed one, and made two sales.

Final score: In his one-week swing from Mt. Vernon, N.Y., to Boston and back, salesman Charles David made 45 calls and wrote 14 orders, not counting several additional which could be expected later from buyers who took notes during his calls.

His trip totaled about 500 miles on the map, but in-city driving and doubling back and forth to find parking areas ran the total up to more than 600 miles. The following figures were compiled from David's log for the week:

Towns and cities visited	8
Total working time	44 hours, 45 minutes
Actual selling time, including time spent in missionary work	18 hours, 50 minutes
Total city-to-city travel time	15 hours, 15 minutes

The salesman's second thoughts: "This record just emphasizes something I had already been impressed by: how little time a salesman spends actually selling. My real selling time for the week seems to have totaled less than three hours a day. I'll have to work hard to increase it.

"I spent over nine hours on missionary work, but that will bring in profits. I don't consider a single minute of it lost.

"Absent buyers are a serious problem, but it is an inevitable one in my business. I don't like to call or write for appointments. For other fellows, especially those with huge accounts, they may be important, but it's much better for me just to drop in and rely on my goods, my personality and my luck to get attention.

"On some days I've seen as many as 15 buyers by noon, and it would be impossible for me to arrange appointments like that. During this week I missed 20 buyers. I made up for this by saturation effort; it's that jack-rabbiting back and forth between stores that saves me.

"Lost time which did hurt came from traffic jams and similar delays, and time lost in buyers' offices.

"I can see how vital it is to save minutes at critical times, such as store opening or lunch. A few minutes delay here can cost you half a day or make you miss a buyer entirely.

"On Monday, since I'd never been to Mt. Vernon before, I should have checked the road map before starting out. Later on I lost six minutes getting gas for my associate's car and four minutes chasing down change for a parking meter in Greenwich. It's best to have cars serviced at night and carry change for meters and phones.

"Late starts plagued me. Also, I should have checked the weather forecast Monday and pushed on to the next town that night when I learned that driving conditions would be bad Tuesday. In New Haven, I lost time trying to save it. When traffic is heavy, it pays to park a bit farther out and walk or take a taxi.

"Avoiding traffic delays is becoming, increasingly, a fine art. I should have phoned Boston for hotel reservations when I had some free time at noon Wednesday. The few minutes I took to call landed me right in that traffic jam.

"Another reminder: the time I spent listening to that buyer in Bridgeport was well invested, but I try to remember it could have been wasted with some buyers who talk to avoid making a buying decision. You have to know your buyers.

"I ran into quite a bit of good luck. For example, after finding several buyers away in Boston, I went to Quincy and found the buyer for that chain at her store. There were other bits of good luck. Henceforth, when something goes wrong, I'll tell myself: 'Don't let it get you down, Charlie! Your luck always turns for the better.'

"When I go back to New England after visiting the rest of my territory, I'll have an advantage over this last trip—I'll have the log of what happened to review. I'll remember to beat that 9:30 A.M. rush of salesmen in Mt. Vernon; I'll know that some buyers in Boston take Fridays off; and I'll remember to get to Bridgeport before that buyer goes out for his 10:15 A.M. coffee!"

1. Evaluate Charlie's work habits.
2. Evaluate Charlie's review of his trip.

THE MANAGERIAL ENVIRONMENT

And the boss is the boss!
A successful salesman

Thus far the discussion has concerned itself with the relation of the sales-man to the *prospect* and with competitors. But he has another contact of great importance—that with his *firm*. Although the salesman is admittedly more independent than most workers in other lines, he is under supervi-sion and owes to "the house" certain obligations that he cannot wisely ignore. He must realize that he has joined a team; and this involves team-work. The typical salesman is likely to be somewhat of an individualist, but he must work under a boss. Whether selling in a store or on the road, he is part of an organization and subject to its rules.

A couple of generations ago the traveling salesman was more indepen-dent. Communication between him and the home office was slower and more difficult; he did pretty much as he pleased. He regarded his customers as his personal property; and he went from one employer to another and from product to product as the inclination or the reward prompted him. Today, salesmen are far more closely knit into a smooth-functioning ma-chine, each man feeling a greater dependence upon management in prepar-ing and equipping him for his job. Customers belong to the firm; the sales-man is only the connecting link, the serviceman maintaining the contact. Adequate compensation, encouragement, and control develop loyalty to the firm and the sales manager. Each man has or should have a feeling of permanence and importance with his company.

PURPOSE OF THE CHAPTER

The major purpose of this discussion is not to instruct the reader on how to become a sales manager but rather to provide him with some insights into the managerial framework within which he will be working. Sales managers have some specially developed managerial tools with which the salesman should be familiar in order that he may comprehend completely the managerial environment which governs his selling activities.

When he does comprehend this, it will help the prospective salesman to get the kind of job in which he will be most successful and happy, and to approach it more intelligently. It is also hoped that some things in this chapter may facilitate the adjustment process for the young salesman just embarked on his "shake-down cruise." The more quickly this adjustment process can be accomplished, the more contented and efficient he will be.

GETTING THE JOB

It has been said by some sales managers that the firm should always select the salesman and never the reverse. Of course, the sales manager must do the hiring, but this does not mean that the aspiring salesman may not exercise his choice as to the type of firm he asks for a job. He should not sit back and await a summons to appear for an interview.

The student of salesmanship who has reached this chapter should have formulated some rather definite opinions as to his own fitness for selling. He should know whether he is best qualified to sell staples or specialties, in large cities or in smaller places, one-time sellers or repeaters, tangibles or intangibles, to consumers or to industrial firms.

His next step in seeking a connection will be to study various firms with which he might find congenial employment. He may consider their history, policies, products, and personnel in an effort to determine which of them might offer him the opportunities he seeks.

Then he may look into the question of sales managers. He would prefer, if possible, to work for a strong sales manager, because he has heard it said that a great sales manager will build a great organization. Most ambitious young salesmen aspire to be sales managers or heads of their own businesses, and they want to learn how to be good administrators from a boss who is a master of the art. Of course, there may be a number of intermediate steps between a salesman's first job and the big one at which he is aiming, such as head of a department in a store, field manager over a group of salesmen, assistant branch manager and later branch manager. All are steppingstones.

But it is important to choose one's boss carefully. It has been demonstrated repeatedly that a good administrator will always build a strong organization, while a weak administrator never can build one or even maintain one that was strong when he assumed charge.

The young man seeking his first selling job will, of course, realize that although he may not be so fortunate as to connect immediately with the precise firm and sales manager that he may have chosen, he may be successful in doing so later.

The reader who has battled his way thus far will or should realize that *obtaining a job is often a selling task* in which he can utilize everything he has learned about salesmanship. He will make a careful preapproach; he will plan his approach and generally bring into play every bit of selling skill at his command.

The one matter most requiring emphasis here is that he should have something to sell. If he presents himself with an *idea of value* to his prospective employer, he is *in*.

Take the young fellow who wanted a job on a newspaper. His first step was to study the paper and compare it with other papers. Presently he noted that it had no department devoted to a discussion of new phonograph records, a subject of interest to many readers. So he haunted a record store, read up on the subject, spotted similar departments in other papers (the local library subscribed to these). When he felt he was ready he wrote up several sample articles and took them to the editor. He also pointed out the possibility of stimulating new advertising from stores selling records. He had promises of such advertising if his articles were run regularly.

About one applicant in a hundred bothers to present an idea of value to his prospective employer. This one lands the job.

This matter of obtaining a job is only one side of the question. The other side is obtaining a salesman. That is, it is a mutual problem, of equal interest to applicant and employer. It costs the employer several hundred dollars[1] to train a salesman, and he tries to avoid spending this money on a poor prospect. Many firms go to great lengths to tell prospective salesmen all about the company and the work of its salesmen, often stressing the unpleasant aspects of the job. They figure that this eliminates some applicants who feel that they would not fit into the job or fear they would find it too hard.

Where does one find out about the qualities of these potential employers? One good source of information is from the firm's own salesmen. The word gets around rapidly in selling circles as to which firms are "good places to work." If a salesman has a good boss, he usually lets everyone know it. Conversely, the reputation of poor managers is usually broadcast widely in an industry. By all means the job seeker should talk with the salesmen of a firm for which he is considering working.

Jobs vary greatly in their attractiveness. Unfortunately, it is the "bad" jobs that are most readily available, particularly to the beginning salesman.

---

[1] Firms like IBM and Armstrong Cork spend from $6,000 up on each college graduate trained.

After all, men do not quit good jobs often and when they do, the employer has a long list of proven, top-notch men who are eager to go to work for him. Good jobs do not go looking for the man; the man must go after the job. And that requires salesmanship.

RECRUITING[2]

When a sales manager first perceives that he needs more men, there are certain procedures that he usually goes through in seeking them. First, he usually looks within his own company in the nonselling ranks to see if there is someone who would like to get into sales and has the requisite talents to do so. This is the cheapest and easiest action he can take and it is good for company morale because many men in the plant look upon being transferred into sales as a promotion. So if there is a particular firm for which the individual wishes to sell but finds there is presently no opening on the sales force, he might well accept employment in another capacity making his ultimate desire for sales work known at the time.

Second, most good firms have a file of applicants from men seeking employment with them. True, the quality of men represented by these applications may not be as high as management would prefer, but many times they will still go through them because of the low cost of doing so. However, the wise applicant will periodically follow up on such applications to let the firm know he is still interested.

Third, many managers ask their salesmen for leads to good recruits on the theory that good men know and recognize other good men. Again this is inexpensive and relatively easy recruiting. The job seeker can take advantage of this practice by letting the sales representatives of target employers know of his interest in their firm.

Fourth, personal contact with the sales manager can be highly effective. Many salesmen owe their jobs to some chance meeting with the sales manager during which he became impressed with the man's abilities. Perhaps he saw the man in action selling something. No matter what the circumstances, no man was ever damaged by impressing favorably a potential employer.

Many firms, after exhausting the previously discussed sources for recruits, contact employment agencies, but numerous sales managers avow that a real salesman should not rely on someone else to "sell" him. Really good selling jobs seldom come through employment agencies, but there are, no doubt, exceptions.

Advertising for salesmen is usually the last resort reserved for employers who need a large number of applicants to process. Some fairly decent

2 Much of the following material is taken from William Stanton and Richard H. Buskirk, *Management of the Sales Force* (Richard D. Irwin, Inc., Homewood, Ill., 1974), 4th ed.

jobs can be found, particularly in the nonclassified advertising in the financial or sports sections of the newspaper or in trade journals, so the job hunter should not automatically ignore this source, but he must discriminate between the advertisements that promise to make him rich overnight and those that offer bona fide possibilities with reputable concerns.

The best advice that can be given the job hunter is simply this: Choose a firm that you would like to sell for and then directly approach its sales manager for a job. Then sell yourself!

But remember that sales managers who have developed situations that are really attractive seldom have to recruit, for they are usually deluged with voluntary applicants.

THE SELECTION PROCESS

Four or possibly five steps are usually followed in the selection of applicants for sales jobs. Each one of these steps should be looked upon by applicants as a separate attempt to weed out the undesirable and to employ only the most qualified persons. This is advantageous from the standpoint of the individual salesman, since it is an honest effort on the part of management to make salesmanship more selective, to hire only those persons who can put it upon a higher plane, and to protect those engaged in it from the encroachment of others who are poorly prepared to work in a professional manner. The steps in this selective or eliminative program are (1) the application blank; (2) the careful checking of references given by the applicant; (3) the personal interview, usually more than one; and (4) tests of various sorts to measure qualities desired in applicants, such as mentality, initiative, good health, persistence, poise, and aptitude for the particular job in mind. (5) A fifth step is the requirement that the applicant give bond to his employer, guaranteeing honest dealings during the period of employment.

Bear in mind that in sales management theory nothing is more important to the building of a successful organization than the hiring of the right men. With the right men, the sales manager's tasks are greatly simplified. With the wrong men, he will know nothing but grief. The more important the salesman is to the success of the firm the more careful management will be in selecting him.

The application blank

The qualified applicant should welcome the opportunity to put his record down on paper for the inspection of the employer. Every question should be answered accurately and completely. The manner in which an application blank is filled out is in itself an indication of the character of the applicant. Careless, untidy, and poorly written blanks indicate the same qualities in the work of the individual; neat, thoughtful, painstaking completion of the blank is some assurance of those standards being maintained in future tasks that might be assigned. A hesitant, grudging compliance with the request to fill out the blank may indicate that the applicant will have the same attitude toward routine tasks and reports that must be filled out. On the other hand, a cheerful and cooperative attitude is apt to indicate a similar handling of unpleasant and tedious duties that must be performed later. The application blank furnishes a valuable record of the applicant for future reference in case he is employed. It also supplies an effective means of eliminating a number of applicants before the time of the sales manager has been wasted in personal interviews.

Some application blanks are awesome in their proportions and in the minuteness of the information requested. They pry into the applicant's personal history with a thoroughness that may be irritating if he has anything he prefers to conceal. But he will be wise to fill it in fully, with no gaps unaccounted for and no discrepancies or contradictions.

When these application blanks are evaluated after they are filled out, some of the questions are given greater weight than are others. Since the applicant may not know which ones are thus weighted, it behooves him to answer each question as carefully as possible.

References

Experienced sales managers say, "The man who needs a lot of references will usually have them." If former friends and business acquaintances of the applicant are given as references, they will normally give the person a good send-off just to be helpful. In many instances they will not know enough about the applicant to furnish any valuable facts to the employer. When former employers of the applicant are given as references, two difficulties arise. In some cases the applicant may have been dismissed by the person, and a recommendation will be given out of sympathy. In other cases where the applicant has left the former employer voluntarily, there may be some feeling of resentment or unfriendliness toward the applicant. The most effective use of references is to secure enough of them so that a cross section of opinion is obtained. By this method the practice of "whitewashing" by former friends or employers as well as the tendency to "run down" an applicant usually can be detected. Some reference blanks come out baldly with the request for statements about weaknesses and shortcomings of the applicant so that the new employer, knowing them in advance, can attempt to prevent their recurrence in the future.

Most smart sales managers rely more on telephone conversations with references whose opinions they respect. A reference is more likely to disclose pertinent facts about an applicant if he is not forced to put them on paper, as he never knows who may read what he has written. Also, the sales manager can learn much about a potential recruit by the *way* his references talk about him. There are many ways of saying the same sentence; little overtones, nuances, inflection, emphasis on certain words, and general attitude reveal much when *spoken.*

The applicant should try to provide references who mean something. The name of a leading sales executive will carry more weight than that of a neighbor or fraternity chum. Careful thought should be given to the choice of references for still another reason. Many people cannot write effective letters of recommendation, thereby injuring the applicant's chances. The potential employer wishes to hear about a man's work habits, his dependability, his productivity, his loyalty, and his ability to work with others, rather than about his religion, family connections, how sweet he was as a small boy, or what a fine father he has.

The personal interview

Few salesmen are hired without a series of personal interviews, which are far more important to the sales manager making a hiring decision than are application blanks or references. In the personal interview the sales manager forms his opinion of the applicant's appearance, voice, bearing, poise, resourcefulness, and general philosophy of selling. He likes a man who is well groomed and who looks as though he made it a regular practice to be that way. He likes a man who can look him squarely in the eye without embarrassment. He likes a man who has a firm handshake. He likes a man whose voice is pleasant and who knows how to use it to advantage. He likes a man who cannot be thrown into a display of temper; who does not laugh immoderately at the sales manager's jokes; who, in short, has poise.

Many sales managers make it a practice to draw the applicant out, to encourage him to tell his life story, to state his hobbies and favorite forms of recreation or reading. They claim that more can be learned in this way about a man's real character than by all the application blanks in existence. Somewhere in this interview most reputable concerns insert a topic of conversation designed to test an applicant's code of business ethics. They usually prefer honest men.

The applicant for a sales position will do well to make a preapproach before submitting to this interview. He should learn as much as possible about the company, its policies, and its products, so that he can intelligently answer the sales manager when he suddenly inquires, "What makes you think you want to work for *us*?" Most of the principles of the preapproach may profitably be applied by the applicant for a selling job. The very fact that he has made such an investigation proves to the prospective employer that he believes in its value and would probably continue the practice in actual selling.

Usually an applicant is interviewed several times by the same man or in succession by several men. This is done to get a better line on the applicant and to check up on him. For example, a young chap might bear up well under the ordeal of the first interview, but begin to "crack" at the second or third. Also, if he has been careless with the truth, he is likely to contradict himself at some point in the various interviews.

The young man aspiring to a sales position should take very seriously the experience of applying for a job. The impression that he makes may stand him in good stead later, even though he does not at once get the job. Also, it helps him to get a position that suits his talents and in which he can succeed.

This interviewing process may even carry over after a salesman is on the job. He should not resent such attempts to learn these facts about him, but should cooperate with the questioners, who are only trying to discover where he will best fit into the sales organization.

Dr. McMurry[3] describes the interview system used by a large national advertiser to uncover personality traits or facts which contribute to a salesman's *promotability.* Many of these same questions may also be asked of an applicant *before* he is employed. The essential personality facts which Dr. McMurry endeavored to discover in this interview program were (1) a high development of industry, ambition, loyalty, self-reliance, willingness to accept responsibility, and capability of dealing with and handling people; (2) a capacity for meeting emergencies and handling situations demanding courage, initiative, and moral stamina. He was also interested in the influence of the man's domestic life. These do not lend themselves to measurement so simply and exactly as intelligence or product knowledge which may be ascertained from tests; there are no written psychological tests which provide complete insight into one's personality complex or which determine what a man will do under pressure or the influence of his domestic relationships. Because of this, interview and observation techniques must be employed that use clinical rather than statistical methodology. Personality is a combination of many traits, which may be present in different patterns and configurations in different individuals. A single index that adequately expresses these complicated relationships is, therefore, impossible. The *dominant* traits of a person's personality must be determined accurately because it is these that govern his actions and responses and make possible the prediction of his behavior under any given situation.

Therefore, Dr. McMurry concludes that the best way to gain an insight

[3] Robert N. McMurry, head of the consulting firm bearing his name, is a psychologist specializing in sales personnel problems.

into these dominant traits which make up a man's personality is, first, to let him tell the story of his own life from boyhood to maturity, stressing his social, domestic, and business relationships. Secondly, observe carefully his behavior on the job or while among his friends or in his home. In the third place, assign him a hard or unpleasant task to perform, and then watch his response to it, that is, whether he does it cheerfully and efficiently or tries to shift the responsibility to someone else or evades it entirely. It is claimed that such a series of tests will invariably provide sufficient material to allow a thorough "personalysis," because it is practically impossible for the man to conceal or change certain personality traits or behavior trends that always assert themselves under certain conditions. Dr. McMurry describes the detailed working of this plan and comments as follows upon its chief aim or purpose:

A program of this type has been in use now for nearly three years with considerable success by a national sales organization. It consists of three parts:

1. *The field interview:* A specially trained representative of the company spends from one to two days in the field with each candidate who is regarded as promising on the basis of production and service records and a rating by at least four men. In order to conceal the true purpose of the interview, the home-office representative explains that he is studying sales methods and he is interested in obtaining any constructive suggestions the men may care to offer.

The interview is conducted with the man as he works on the job and with complete informality. This is done partly because many of the men are busy and would be reluctant to spare the time; partly because much can be learned by observing the man in action among his prospects and associates (even if the man himself suspects the true purpose of the call and attempts to put on an act for the interviewer, he cannot alter the attitudes of others toward him); and partly because an interview in an office is necessarily somewhat artificial and tends to put the man on the defensive.

In the course of these informal talks, information is obtained specifically upon the following points:

a. His early upbringing, with particular reference to his formation of habits of industry and self-reliance and his ability to get along with other persons.

b. His schooling, with special attention to his social adjustment and evidences of leadership.

c. His work history, with emphasis on his attitudes toward his work, his associates, his superiors; the extent to which he has shown initiative, ambition, and creative imagination; and the progress which he has made in gaining increases in compensation and responsibility.

d. His social adjustment as an adult, with reference to his friendships, hobbies, and modes of recreation; his social, religious, and political beliefs; and the extent to which he is respected and a leader in his community.

e. His domestic adjustments, with special attention to his family relationships; whether he has established a home of his own; whether he is dependent upon his wife or others for a portion of his support; the extent to which his wife may be expected to be a help or a hindrance to him in his work.

2. *Difficult assignments and frustration:* The second step in the program is to subject the man to pressure. Here, for example, he may be required to make an effort to sell unusually difficult prospects. Or he may be asked to handle particularly unpleasant customer complaints. In the course of carrying out these assignments an opportunity is provided not only to observe his response to the assignments themselves but also, in those cases where he is unable to carry them through, to see how he responds to disappointment, failure, and frustration.

3. *The home interview:* The third step (the program is not necessarily carried out in any regular order) is the conduct of a very informal interview— ostensibly a friendly call—with the man's wife and other family members in the home, preferably at the man's own invitation. Here, however, unless extreme care and tact are used by the interviewer, little of value will be obtained. If it is necessary to apply pressure or use artificial pretexts, not only will little information be obtained but actual ill will may be created.

In these interviews the answers to two principal questions are sought: First, who is the dominant member of the household—the husband or some other family member? Second, are there undercurrents of hostility between the husband and other family members which might interfere with the man's work?

The man who is quite eager to obtain a position with a particular organization is well advised to locate someone who has been through the firm's selection process recently. He may be able to prepare himself for certain rather tricky situations that some managers like to create for the recruit. One sales manager startles applicants by asking them first off, "So you think you are a salesman? Well, sell me a new car!" Applicants who are prepared for such tactics naturally have a better chance of successfully handling them and still maintaining their poise than those who are caught by surprise.

The use of tests

The application blank, in spite of its detail, may fail to disclose weaknesses in the applicant. In some cases the careful checking of references and even the personal interview may not divulge serious shortcomings. For this reason tests of many kinds are increasingly used to further the job of selection. Belief in the saying "Poor selection means rapid turnover in salesmen" influences the sales manager to employ every possible device to reduce the number of mistakes in selection that have been all too common in the past.

Space does not permit a lengthy discussion of these tests, but the college student of today is fairly familiar with some of them. While such tests are far from infallible and are usually supplemented by other means of appraising a candidate's fitness, nevertheless they are used by many firms and are being improved steadily. They measure such things as:

MENTAL ABILITY OR CAPACITY TO LEARN

If the product to be sold is complicated and the training course long and difficult, the salesman lacking the capacity to learn cannot master the material. It is a kindness to him to eliminate him before he wastes his time and the company's money. In the case of simple propositions the selling of which demands little mental ability, this test may serve the purpose of eliminating the candidates who are too smart and would soon quit the job because it is below their capacities.

INFORMATION ACQUIRED IN SCHOOL AND BY HOME STUDY

The prospective salesman for office machines should know his accountancy and business practices, while the salesman for road-building machinery should remember what he learned in his engineering courses. Some firms especially favor the applicant who has taken correspondence or night school courses while employed regularly on a job. Such information can be determined by tests or oral questioning.

PERSONALITY CHARACTERISTICS

In recent years much discussion has taken place as to the value of personality testing in the selection of salesmen. Many employers swear by such tests while others swear at them.[4] For the purposes of this discussion it need only be said that a great number of the larger concerns in this country use such tests. How much they really believe in them is another matter. An executive of one of the nation's largest employers of highly skilled salesmen confessed to the author recently that for all the time and money the corporation had put behind the development and standardization of their highly regarded testing program, a recent internal study of its validity had disclosed the disheartening fact that the tests had not distinguished between their successful and unsuccessful men. But the company continues to use these tests. So the job seeker had best prepare himself for the ordeal by pencil.

Firms have reported success using personal history ratings such as those shown in Table 20-1. These are developed by each firm through an

4 See Martin L. Gross, *The Brain Watchers* (Random House, Inc., New York, 1962) for an engrossing popular account concerning the use of testing by the nation's business firms. For a more technical treatment of the subject, see Anne Anastasi, *Psychological Testing* (The Macmillan Company, New York, 1968), 3d ed.

analysis of the personal characteristics of its own men. Each of the traits is weighted by its apparent correlation to the success of the men. For example, in the illustration used men over fifty years old with less than one year of high school and who have been in the community less than three months evidently have not been very successful with the company. The applicant needed 16 points to command further consideration.

Requiring a bond

The fifth step may be the requirement that the applicant, if he is selected for the job, be bonded, protecting the company against any defalcations or other dishonest acts. Many salesmen handle cash and others are supplied with expensive items of equipment such as sales kits, motion-picture projectors, cars, portfolios, and samples. A bond serves two important purposes. First, the bonding company makes a far more exhaustive examination of the applicant's past financial record than the company itself can make, thus promoting better selection. Second, a bond has a salutary effect upon the salesman after he is on the job. The knowledge that he will be prosecuted by the bonding company for misuse of property keeps a man in line when other measures might fail. Such matters as the return of equipment when a salesman leaves a company indicate how a bond protects the employer. Many companies have learned from experience that the cost of a bond is cheap insurance against the losses to which they would be subjected without it. So not only from the standpoint of better selection but also of effective supervision, the bond has come into common usage by firms employing salesmen.

THE CONTRACT

Many firms follow the policy of putting in writing the conditions of a salesman's employment, thereby reducing misunderstandings and friction at a later date. Whether the contract is a formal document or merely a series of letters, it accomplishes the same purpose. And it is up to the salesman to know just what is covered by it.

Commonly, an agreement will cover such matters as the following:

- Obligations of salesman and employer
- Statement of territory assigned to salesman
- Compensation arrangements
- When contract begins and how it can be terminated
- The handling of expenses
- Salesman's samples, or other property of employer

The contract protects both parties. The employer knows what is covered by it; the salesman should make it a point to learn this.

TABLE 20-1   PERSONAL RATING CHART: QUALIFICATIONS FOR LIFE INSURANCE
SELLING

RATING SCALE 1		2	3	4	5
Factors		Qualifications for standard rating	Maxi-mum points	Penal-ties	Net points
Age		25 to 40 years, inclusive	3		
Education		College graduate	3		
Marital status		Married Single, if under age 25	3		
Previous experience		1 year or more outside selling (see penalty table for exceptions) Retail store proprietors Executives Insurance clerks Sales promotion or management	4		
Financial status	Life ins. owned	Under age 25—$1,000 or more Ages 25 to 29—$3,000 or more Ages 30 and over—$5,000 or more	1		
	Savings (including life ins. cash value)	Under age 25—$250 or more Ages 25 to 29—$500 or more Ages 30 and over—$1,000 or more	1		
Years in community		2 years or more	3		
Employed		Employed	2		
		Total	20		

TRAINING

Some training of new men is required in all concerns even if it is no more
than a brief introduction to the product line and some information on the
firm's policies. But today most large concerns have found it necessary to
institute formal sales training programs for their new salesmen, particularly
where young, inexperienced men are being hired. However, these vary
widely in excellence: some are good and some not so good.

In fact, a young man planning upon a sales career may be wise if he
accepts his first employment with an eye to the firm's sales training pro-

TABLE 20-1   PERSONAL RATING CHART: QUALIFICATIONS FOR LIFE INSURANCE
SELLING (Continued)

PENALTY POINT TABLE 6		7	PENALTY POINTS 8
Age		Under age 25	2
		Ages 41 to 50 inclusive	2
		Over 50 years	3
Education		Less than college graduate, but at least high school graduate	1
		Less than high school graduate, but at least 1 year high school	2
		Less than 1 year high school	3
Marital status		Single (ages 25 to 40)	1
		Single (ages 41 and over)	2
		Separated, divorced, widower	1
Previous experience		General insurance selling	1
		Two years or more financial selling	2
		Less than 1 year outside selling (less than 6 months—take prior occupation)	1
		Inside (store) selling	2
		Student, teacher, clergy, social service	1
		Clerical workers (other than insurance)	2
		Bankers, doctors, lawyers, scientists	3
		Nonselling occupations not mentioned	3
Financial status	Life ins. owned	Under age 25—less than $1,000 Ages 25 to 29—less than $3,000 Ages 30 and over—less than $5,000	1
	Savings (including life ins. cash value)	Under age 25—less than $250 Ages 25 to 29—less than $500 Ages 30 and over—less than $1,000	1
Years in community		Less than 2 years but more than 1 year	1
		Less than 1 year but more than 3 months	2
		Less than 3 months	3
Employed		Unemployed 3 to 6 months	1
		Unemployed 6 months or more	2

gram even though he may harbor other thoughts for his eventual career. It is usually not too difficult to determine the amount and nature of training offered the applicant; it is certainly fair to ask about such things during the interviews.

Wise management usually spreads the recruit's training over considerable time initially giving only what is needed to get him into the field with an adequate degree of proficiency. Then additional training is forthcoming as he gains experience and proves his dedication to selling and the firm.

A word of warning: Although it may not appear so, management is carefully appraising the trainees while they are in training and their performance bears heavily in the type of assignment they will be given upon graduation. The best trainee usually gets the best assignment.

While sales training begins by using the conventional educational tools such as lectures, movies, and discussion, it is difficult to hone one's selling skills through exposure to those methods alone. To learn selling one must sell. And that means role playing.

ROLE PLAYING

Role playing consists of placing the trainee in a realistic situation and allowing him to sell a simulated prospect. If the method is to work effectively, care must be taken to make the prospect realistic in his reactions and to place him in a realistic environment. The trainee must be given the preapproach information an actual salesman would have before calling on the individual.

This type of learning-by-doing education can be highly effective in the teaching of selling techniques, particularly in initial training programs. The trainee is placed in a situation that subjects him to the many unforeseen developments that always arise in selling. Besides the training the student obtains in handling selling techniques, role playing also allows the instructor to work with the man on such things as voice, poise, bearing, mannerisms, speech, and movements, which are all highly important factors bearing on the ultimate success of a salesman.

Many things brought to light by role-playing situations would otherwise remain unknown. Ordinarily calm and collected students have broken down in an actual sale from nervousness or lack of confidence. There is no question that role playing is the best method yet developed for convincing the student of the validity of certain principles. The instructor can emphatically stress the necessity for product information, but let a trainee come before the class in a role-playing situation not adequately knowing his product, and the ridiculousness of his position is brought to the class's attention in an unforgettable manner. In one instance, a student was to sell Pyrex glass cooking ware to a hardware store owner. Thinking that the "unbreakable" feature of the product meant that it was literally unbreakable, the student's approach consisted of coming in the door and deliberately dropping a set of Pyrex onto the floor. He had hoped to demonstrate forcibly to the merchant his product's major selling point. This could have been an excellent approach. Unfortunately, as he swept up the broken glass he succeeded only in convincing everyone that he did not know his product—that the "unbreakable" feature he had been told about referred only to application of heat. This demonstration was indelibly etched into the memory of the students; to this day when members of the class see the teacher they laugh about the incident, and many have related just how it taught them an unforgettable lesson. They said they resolved right then and there never to be caught in the same position as that man standing there, embarrassed, sweeping up a pile of broken glass.

Role playing also shows the student in a most convincing fashion that *knowing* what to do is one thing, but *doing* it is another. One of the major weaknesses of most salesmanship courses is that they only teach the student *about* selling, not *how* to sell. Many students can recite all the various methods of approaching prospects, answering objections, and closing the sale. However, many are shocked to learn how much of this knowledge they can forget under the emotional involvement in a sales situation.

In a sales training program designed for teaching new recruits selling techniques, extensive use should be made of role playing. It takes practice to perfect a sales presentation; one or two attempts are inadequate to accomplish the task. Although it would be impossible to definitely establish any given minimum number of times each trainee should be placed into a role-playing situation, the trainer should be thinking in terms of four or five times as the absolute minimum.

Observers

Many trainers prefer to have each sales presentation performed before the entire class in order that all students can benefit from it. While this obviously reduces the number of presentations that can be made in a given length of time, it does have much to recommend it. First, many times the students can see in the sale things that escape the teacher and can recommend actions that may go unmentioned by him. Second, the teacher can escape some possible resentment by the salesman if he allows the class rather than himself to do the major criticizing. Further, if the class uniformly says the same thing the man is more likely to accept it as the truth. Third, while the salesman is learning through role playing, the class learns by watching and often is deeply impressed. They see things that they resolve never to do. For this reason, each presentation invariably gets better as the teacher progresses through the class, even though for each student it is the first sale. The first few presentations are usually very poor; the teacher must take great care to inform the class and the salesman chosen to lead off the series that many mistakes will be made and things will not go so smoothly as might have been expected. However, he should point out to the students that basically they will learn best through making mistakes. Sometimes, the instructor is wise if he picks for the first few presentations men who apparently have some skill in verbal activities and selling. This can get the sessions off to a good start and give the completely inexperienced trainees some idea about the entire process.

It is usually wise to prepare some form of a rating sheet for each observer to complete on each sale. Otherwise, during the sale the observer can forget the point he wants to bring out. He should write down immediately any comments he wants to make on any phase of the sale. The rating form also serves as a record for the salesman to study in his attempt to improve his performance. In connection with this rating sheet, it is usually wise for the instructor to make clear that no grades are given on any sale; that it is merely a learning device. Grading is usually unfair, since the first salesmen are penalized and the later performers are rewarded because of the learning that takes place during each sale. The last man should have learned much about selling by the time his turn occurs.

In handling the role-playing sessions, the trainer must go to extreme lengths to convince the students of the importance of taking criticisms in the right way. He must convince the men that he is there only to help them earn more money and that absolutely nothing is meant personally by any criticism. He must point out that there is no such thing as a perfect sale— that all salesmen make mistakes in every sale. He must convince them that for many situations there are no cut and dried answers to the problem, and that criticisms on those points are only designed to give them some ideas about other ways of handling the problems.

Role playing without criticism is of limited value, since the man has no way of determining what he is doing wrong. Although practice without observers may aid the man in polishing his delivery and mastery of the presentation, much more is accomplished when observers are present to give him their reactions to his performance.

An important fact frequently overlooked by many teachers of salesmanship is that the man should be commended on the good features of his sale, and that these can provide a learning experience as valuable to him and the class as are mistakes. In one sale when the prospect was a blustering, loud individual who had strong opinions about the product being sold, the salesman spoke in a soft, calm voice and allowed the prospect to talk freely about his feelings. Certainly, the interview took more time than usual, but after the prospect had expressed his feelings the salesman was able to shape his presentation to fit the man's stated desires and dislikes. Also, the class observed how the prospect quieted down as the salesman got calmer, in direct contrast to a previous sales presentation when the salesman made the mistake of getting loud right along with the prospect until they were yelling at each other.

Frequently, the trainer is tempted to concentrate too much on the small details at the expense of ignoring the larger factors involved. One of the first questions the instructor should put to the class is: "Just why did the salesman fail to make the sale?" or "Just why did the salesman get the order?" It is important for the students to acquire an ability to see just where a sale was made or lost. Frequently, one major reason or event decided the affair. For instance, one trainee did a rather poor job in making his presentation and in attempting to close, but he got the order anyway. It was easy to point out the many mistakes that occurred, but much more was learned by indicating the basic reason why the order was obtained. In this case, it was because the salesman had taken the trouble to locate an excellent prospect and had allowed him to do all the talking. He just let the man talk himself into the sale, which is good selling in many circumstances. This one factor overrode all the small errors the man had made.

Importance of the buyer

In role-playing situations, the buyers should be given specific identities, such as the owner of a certain store actually in existence or the purchasing agent of a real company. Then, the buyer should have information about the company he is representing so that he can make the proper reactions to the salesman's proposition. Without a definite company situation, the buyer is unable to answer questions intelligently; he must fabricate his answers, and this prevents the salesman from preparing answers to them. If the trainee is selling Friden calculators to business executives, then the buyer should be told that he is Mr. Jones, who is controller of a given local concern. The buyer then should project himself into the role and try to act just as he would if he were really the controller of that firm. If he fails to do this, the sale is unrealistic and little learning takes place. The trainer should go to some effort to locate individuals who can successfully fill the role of a realistic buyer. Many times, he may find it advisable to act as buyer if he feels he is best qualified for the role. One danger with this is that the trainees tend to think the instructor is being too hard on them when in reality he is only trying to give the trainee a maximum amount of sales resistance. The trainer must convince the men that they will never excel in selling by practicing only on easy buyers.

COMPENSATION PLANS

There are literally scores of different plans for paying salesmen, but they all break down into two types of payments: payment for a man's time and payment for his productivity. A salary is paid for a man's time; you put in the time as the employer tells you and receive your salary. A commission, however, is paid for selling something—productivity. A bonus, depending upon what it is paid for, can be either a time payment or a productivity payment. A Christmas bonus is a time payment while a bonus for sales over quota is a productivity payment.

There is no perfect system of compensation. Nearly every plan is a compromise, a combination of time and productivity payments. Each concern tries to construct a plan which will attract the type of salesman wanted, which will not be too complicated to compute and administer, which will be fair to *all* the salesmen, which will keep the salesmen contented, and which will pay the salesmen for doing the things that management wants them to do. This last point is very important. We have already observed that the salesman is usually expected to do many things besides sell. The plan of compensation should reward him for doing these things.

The salary or time wage

This is often preferred by the beginning salesman, as it pays him an assured income that may be more than he is worth at first. Even the older salesman may like to have a *part* of his pay in the form of straight salary so that he will not need to worry about certain regularly recurring obligations such as taxes, rent, insurance, etc.

From the firm's viewpoint, the straight time wage gives the management control over the salesman. They are paying him for his time and have the right to tell him what to do, thus making it possible to take care of many nonselling activities.

The main trouble with straight salary is that it does not provide much incentive to sell. And it does discriminate against the good salesman in favor of the poor one. The really outstanding man is seldom paid what he is truly worth because some of his productivity must be used to subsidize those salesmen whose productivity is insufficient to warrant their salaries.

Most plans now contain large elements of salary and if the salary program is carefully administered it can be made to reward the productive salesman. However, in situations requiring a high level of salesmanship in which truly professional salesmen are engaged, commission plans still dominate. Truly great salesmen opt for the commission, for they know they will make far more money by doing so. Almost without exception, the salesmen who make in excess of $20,000 a year are on a commission plan.

Commission on sales or piece rate

This is simple and it does offer a strong incentive to sell—no sales, no pay. But it does not give the employer much control over the salesman and does not pay the latter directly for doing nonselling duties. It is easy for the firm to finance, as it does not pay the salesman until after the sale has been made.

From the standpoint of the salesman it is uncertain—he never knows how much he is going to make. Young salesmen often dislike this method as they are not sure of their ability to make a living. They become nervous and worried and cannot sell so well. The incentive is perhaps *too* strong, defeating its own purpose by making the salesman too tense, too eager. To use a golf analogy, he begins to "press" and dubs his shots.

He is also tempted to concentrate on present sales and neglect the many duties that build for future sales.

As in the case of the salary factor, the commission is included as a part of a great many compensation plans. The salary is designed to give the house *control* over the salesman's activities and to offer him *security;* the commission provides *incentive* to make more sales.

There are circumstances in which management has good control despite paying a straight commission; the job is so good that the man wants to keep it and the price for keeping it is to do what management tells him to do.

Bonuses for special services

Offered by many firms, these are sometimes awarded on the basis of points compiled by the salesman for such things as making collections, opening new accounts, selling special items, setting up window displays, staging demonstrations in stores, cutting down expenses of selling, exceeding quotas, etc. Bonuses are widely used in paying retail store salespeople also.

If the plan can be kept simple, it may work admirably. The tendency is for it to grow complicated and difficult to understand and compute. Bonuses are sometimes added to a base salary and a commission on sales volume, thereby making a rather complicated system.

Profit sharing

This element has never attained a large place in the payment of salesmen. It places the salesman at the mercy of the employer's cost accountant. It may operate to cut down the salesman's earnings when he is not in any way responsible for decreased profits. Profit sharing works best where the workers can all watch and stimulate one another. Salesmen, scattered throughout the country, are as far as possible from meeting this requirement. The principle of profit sharing may be sound; but its application has proved difficult.

The expense account

The expense account has been the subject of many a jest, but it persists. From the standpoint of the salesmen there are two main questions: what items may properly be included in the expense account and whether or not the firm expects him to make a profit on it. A clear understanding of just which items will be passed by the sales manager and which items rejected should be had at the time the salesman accepts the position. For example, some firms pay for laundry and tips; others do not. Regarding the second point—whether or not the house expects the salesman to make any money on his expense account—it may be said that where the firm does not expect this, the salesman should not try it. He will probably make better progress if he does not pad his account. But if the house will stand for a padded account just so long as it does not exceed a certain percentage of sales, there seems to be no good reason for refusing it. Many firms consider this as a regular part of the salesman's compensation and expect their men to make a little from this source. This policy is not here recommended; it is merely stated.

SALESMEN'S QUOTAS

Reference has been made several times to the quota. Many concerns use the quota system of defining the task expected of the salesman. Thus quotas may be established for number of calls, volume of sales, or other factors, although the most common form is that on sales volume, expressed either in dollars or in units of product.

Some salesmen do not like a quota, but it is an established fact that most of them sell more when they are given a mark at which to shoot. To be sure, the quota is not always set equitably, but the usual practice is to set one that the salesman can reach with reasonable effort. Frequently the sales manager consults the salesman concerning a fair quota for his territory.

The quota may be set for the entire year or for a shorter period, the latter ordinarily being the plan. Salesmen are inclined to take it easy the first part of the year, expecting to start a belated drive that will carry them over the line; but where the quota is set for each month or quarter such postponement of effort cannot achieve the desired results.

The salesman's compensation is often based on attainment of his quota, a higher rate of commission or a bonus being offered on sales in excess of the quota.

All in all, the quota is something that the salesman should take seriously, for it is very likely that his chief takes it so.

SALES TERRITORIES

Most firms assign each salesman to a definite territory, which he can consider his own. It is felt that this policy offers a greater incentive to cultivate the territory with an eye for future business than the policy of permitting salesmen for the same firm to compete for business in the same territory. This is especially true in organizations selling a repeat product. Where the proposition is a one-time seller or a slow repeater, salesmen may be permitted to compete with one another on the theory that such competition keeps them all hustling for business. Examples of this are real estate, insurance, automobiles. Even here, the competition is largely for *prospects,* and once a salesman has a prospect on his list, his competing colleagues withdraw.

The chief factors governing the size of the territory are the number of customers and prospects, the frequency of the salesman's calls on old customers, and the number of calls that he can make in a day.

Regarding the first point—the number of prospects—it may be said that there are more prospects in most territories than either the salesman or his chief realizes. A careful analysis of the territory should be made to determine just how many prospects there are in it, before it is laid out. Most salesmen want a large territory and are deeply offended when they are forced to accept a smaller one. But experience has shown that more sales can often be made in the smaller territory than in the larger one, as less time is consumed in traveling from one prospect to the next. Intensive cultivation of a territory is the modern ideal.

The frequency of a salesman's calls obviously is a factor only when selling to old customers. With the emphasis being placed on quick turnover of stocks by retailers, it is now necessary for traveling salesmen to call more often than formerly. Of course, customers can be held in line and some orders secured by phone or by mail; but if personal selling is the main means of creating demand, the salesman must call often enough to hold the business and keep competition from breaking in.

The third factor—the number of calls that a salesman can make in a day—varies widely with the type of selling. It is estimated that many salesmen spend no more than two hours a day in the presence of prospects. Careful planning of the day's work will help in making more calls by saving needless crisscrossing of territory and poorly timed calls. Most sales managers attempt to set a quota of calls for their salesmen, knowing that without some such incentive not enough calls will be made.

The assignment of territory is sometimes made on the basis of customer classification, one salesman being assigned the banks, another the department stores, while still another sells the meat dealers, for example. Geographical lines are partially ignored.

Every effort is made by most sales managers to assign their salesmen to territories where they will fit, but the new salesman may be sent anywhere.

Some firms route their salesmen on a set schedule, laying out their trips in detail for them. Where this is the practice, the only thing to do is to stick to the schedule. If improvements can be devised in the routing, the salesman may offer suggestions, but he should be sure that the suggestions are of value.

Modern sales managers attempt to establish territories on the basis of economic trading areas rather than on political boundaries. It makes little sense to have one salesman responsible for Kansas City, Kans., and another for Kansas City, Mo., yet that sometimes happens when one man is assigned the state of Kansas and another the state of Missouri. Wise territorial layout can save the salesman considerable time in traveling and minimize his time away from home. Historically, many firms have failed to realize their full sales potential by assigning too much territory to each man in order to get full coverage with the limited number of men at their disposal.

From the salesman's point of view the particular territory assigned him may have a great bearing upon his eventual success. Because of the inadequacies of statistical information on various sections of the nation plus the ignorance of the impact of growth and stagnation upon consumption in a given area, salesmen assigned growth territories are given a tremendous advantage over their colleagues in static or declining areas. One miscellaneous group of salesmen were polled concerning contests being run by their employers. One fact uncovered by this study was that invariably the winners in the contests were in growth areas.

If a salesman cannot make up his mind about which concern to work for, then he would be wise to consider the probable territories each might give him. Also the nature of the territory can have great impact upon his morale. It is only natural to prefer one area over another. Such preferences should be given full consideration. However, the salesman who is too fussy about his location severely limits his attractiveness to employers who look upon their sales trainees as potential managerial talent. Mobility is usually one of the attributes expected of most corporate executives, because in their advancement it is usually necessary for them to move several times.

STIMULATION OF EFFORT

One of management's constant problems is that of stimulating the efforts of its sales force to do a better job. Such tactics as contests, conferences, pep letters, and honor awards are used for this purpose.

Contests

Many varieties of contests have been devised to keep salesmen on their toes. Baseball games, airplane races, golf games, cross-country runs, round-the-world trips, and just plain statements of each man's sales are all calculated to yield the same result—increased selling effort.

Some salesmen consider contests as juvenile, holding that no mature man would be inveigled by such childish devices into working harder than he otherwise would work. These blasé skeptics contend that the contest is too obviously a means of getting *all* the salesmen to increase their efforts, while rewarding only a *few* of them.

The best answer to this argument is that mature salesmen who have participated in contests for years *do* take part in them with gusto and grim determination. There is in most men, and perhaps especially in salesmen, a competitive spirit that responds to this stimulus.

The most potent arguments against sales contests are that they may be followed by a slump in sales and that they may lead the salesmen to over-sell in their eagerness to win. If the contest is well planned and managed, however, it need have neither of these evil results.

But the management of a contest is no easy matter. The weak sales-men, the ones who need the stimulation the most, must be handicapped in such a way that they have a good chance of winning something if they do a good job.

Prizes are sometimes cash and sometimes merchandise. Frequently the salesman who wins is given the choice between a prize for himself or one for his wife. This is to enlist the backing of the wives, who can often be of considerable help in encouraging their husbands to sell more.

Conventions and conferences

Most sales organizations of any size hold conventions or conferences of some kind at more or less regular intervals. These have one or more of three general purposes: education, inspiration, or reward for effort.

The national convention, to which all the salesmen or the quota mak-ers are brought, is not so common as formerly. It is expensive; it takes the men out of their territories for long periods; it encourages dissipation; and it may be too big to handle efficiently.

For these reasons many concerns have turned largely to the regional or district conference. Here the group is small enough so that the sales man-ager, who usually conducts it, can learn to know each of his men; discus-sion is free and more to the point; the sales manager comes to know the territories better; the time consumed is less; and it is cheaper.

For purposes of education, the district conference is undoubtedly supe-rior to the national convention. But for inspiration and reward the national meeting may be better. Another advantage of the national convention held at the factory is that the salesmen learn many things that will be of value to them in selling.

The convention held in the hotel of a large city is probably about the poorest variety, likely to have all the evils and few of the virtues of conven-tions. For this reason conventions are sometimes held in small towns, on islands, in summer camps, or even on shipboard while cruising. Under these conditions the men are under better control and the wrong kinds of extracurricular activity are not so prevalent.

Much progress has been made in building convention programs so that they are interesting and helpful. Frequently they contain a good deal of showmanship and much of the dramatic.

After the convention is over, the company usually attempts to follow it up and cash in on it. Bulletins, letters, the house organ, sales supervisors, and every other medium of communication are used to emphasize and press home the teachings of the convention.

Many salesmen insist that they learn more at conventions through the informal exchange of experiences with fellow salesmen than they do in the formal sessions. But many other places provide this opportunity. The real benefit of the convention is derived from the programs, when they are efficiently planned and staged.

Communications from the house

The salesman is an isolated worker, subject to many disheartening influences. The sales manager would like to be able to meet him face to face every week, to inspire him by the sound of his voice, the friendly smile, the warm handclasp, the word of advice. But he cannot do this, so he does the next best thing: he keeps the lines of communication open with letters, bulletins, perhaps a house organ, telephone calls, etc.

These communications are of two main types, the purely "pep" or "ginger" type and the kind that is written with a sympathetic understanding of the salesman's needs.

Too much of the purely "pep" kind has gone out from sales managers. A little of this element is good, but too much disgusts the salesman and causes him to regard his chief as a lazy, swivel-chair hypocrite who dictates a scorching bulletin exhorting his salesmen to quit offering alibis and put in an extra hour each day, and then picks up his bag of golf clubs for a quick eighteen.

The kind of communication welcomed by the salesman is the kind that helps him to sell more. This type contains specific, practical suggestions rather than inspirational "fluff." As one watches salesmen toss sales-promotion literature from their firms into wastebaskets, it becomes apparent that not all this literature accomplishes its aim. The young salesman, however, should find something of value in nearly everything sent out from headquarters.

SALESMEN'S REPORTS AND LETTERS

In a small organization it may not be necessary to have a system of reports from salesmen; but as the number of salesmen increases, it becomes more and more necessary to ask them for a variety of facts and opinions. Some salesmen are antagonistic toward this policy, insisting that they are paid to sell goods and not to make out reports.

But it is undoubtedly desirable that the salesman should make out these reports, for two reasons:

1. The making of such reports is of value to the salesman himself and might be worth doing even though he never mailed them in to headquarters. They force him to analyze his territory, to study his own work, to check back over each failure to sell, to observe details about his prospects' businesses, etc. The new salesman will do well to make out the required reports with conscientious care and completeness.
2. The second reason why reports are worthwhile is that the information thus obtained is usually used by the sales-promotion department to help the salesman make more sales. Fortified with facts about a prospect, the sales-promotion manager can write him and send him literature that may prepare the way for a sale the next time the salesman calls.

Most companies ask their salesmen to send in daily reports or letters. These usually contain such items as the number of calls made, the names of prospects sold, and names of those whom he was unable to sell, together with reasons for such failures, business conditions in the community, total sales for the day, and expenses incurred. A few firms ask their salesmen to fill out reports that are virtually work tickets, accounting for every minute of every day.

There is a tendency for the report forms to increase in size and number as more facts are wanted from time to time by officials at headquarters. They may become a burden to the salesman, who may be justified in raising the question whether or not all the facts requested are put to any good use and if some of the computations could not be done more cheaply by the staff in the office.

One thing more about reports. The salesman who will not make them satisfactorily is killing his chances for promotion. He is showing that he does not grasp the problems of management; he cannot view his work from the top. An appreciation of the viewpoint of the sales manager on the part of the salesman is an indication that he himself has the qualifications for that post.

EVALUATION OF PERFORMANCE

Many salesmen seem to be unaware that their selling performances are constantly being evaluated by management. Data gleaned from call reports, invoices, expense accounts, and personal evaluations all help the astute manager to evaluate the abilities and weaknesses of each of his men. The purpose is twofold. First, such evaluations assist considerably in training. It is difficult to know on what aspects of selling a man needs additional training without some clue as to his weaknesses. It is insufficient just to scream at a man whose performance is unsatisfactory; he may have little idea of what he should do or just where he is going wrong. A good evaluation of his performance should pinpoint his difficulties so that training can be focused on them.

Second, evaluation efforts are used as a basis for promotions, transfers, pay raises, and terminations. Fundamentally, each man is compared with a company norm, the performance of the average salesman. This comparison strongly prejudices management for or against the man so the ambitious man will strive to compare favorably with the other men.

Management usually develops figures on such factors as calls per day, cost per call, orders per call, average order, cost per order, cost per dollar sales, percentage sales, percentage of market potential realized, sales by product line, profitability of sales by product line, effectiveness by class of customer called upon, and any other index that seems to make sense for that management. These indices usually are the bases around which periodic review sessions between the salesman and his boss are built. So the man will learn what is important to management and what is not important.

DISCUSSION QUESTIONS
1. You have decided that you would like to sell women's ready-to-wear to retailers. How would you go about getting a selling job in this industry?
2. What are the earmarks of a good sales training program?
3. If you were being interviewed for a sales job at the present time, what weaknesses would an astute sales manager spot in your record or background or you?
4. How would you overcome them in his mind?
5. You have decided that you would like to work for X company. Its sales manager asks, "Why do you want to work for us?" Along what lines should your answer be constructed?

CASE 20-1 JOHN BRYANT AND ASSOCIATES:
Recruiting Sales Personnel
"Would you happen to know of a sharp young man who would like to learn the traditional clothing business?" Johnny Bryant asked one of his large retailers.

Johnny Bryant, a personable young man, had in the span of six years built a substantial business serving as a manufacturers' agent for several manufacturers of traditional men's clothing. His product line included Sero shirts, Jefferson slacks, Briar ties, Thane sport shirts and sweaters, Canterbury belts and accessories, and a few other minor lines. He sold to highly selected traditional men's stores in the four-state region of Utah, Colorado, Arizona, and New Mexico. "Traditional" men's stores, in contrast to "fashion" and "conventional" outlets, feature natural shoulder (Ivy League) styles.

He had built his total sales volume to about $800,000 a year. In his role as a manufacturers' representative, Johnny in effect served as the sales force for several producers of related, but noncompeting, lines. Manufacturers paid him a straight commission on his sales volume of their products. On the sale of men's shirts, for example, he earned a commission of 6 percent, while on neckwear and accessories his commission was 10 percent. He had to pay all of his own expenses including that of maintaining a sales office in the Denver Merchandise Mart although he lived and worked out of Salt Lake City.

The Denver Merchandise Mart had only recently been opened, but it was already an obvious success because the retailers showed a great preference for going to one place to contact a large number of suppliers and "work the lines" in the organized atmosphere of the showrooms.

Johnny bragged, "I've already sold far more merchandise to dealers who were just walking by the salesroom than is needed to pay its costs. It's been a great thing and I think it can be even greater if I can just get it properly manned. That's my problem. I need somebody, some young man, who will operate the Denver showroom and handle that end of the business while I'm on the road. I'll also give him a few accounts on which he can call in the Colorado area, and break him into that end of the business once he's learned the product lines."

One of the problems encountered by manufacturers' representatives who maintained showrooms or offices was that of staffing them. The representative had to spend so much time on the road, frequently leaving his office locked, that he missed a considerable amount of business waiting to walk through the door. Some men tried to solve this problem by having female receptionists, but this did not completely fill the bill. Usually such girls were unable to do anything other than smile and take orders for some specific item the customer knew he wanted. These girls were order takers, not salespeople.

Johnny continued, "I'm looking for some young man, preferably just out of college, but not necessarily so, who is a sharp dresser and makes an excellent impression. He needs to be able to wear clothes well, and he probably shouldn't be married because I can't really afford to pay a lot of money. I'm thinking of starting him at $600 a month plus expenses, but you know what he can soon make in this business." It was not at all unusual for representatives of men's apparel manufacturers to make between $30,000–50,000 a year, depending upon the lines they carried and the territories in which they worked.

1. What recruiting sources and methods should Johnny use to find the man he wants?
2. Should Johnny hire and train a young woman to do the sales job in his Merchandise Mart office?

THE LEGAL ASPECTS
OF SELLING

Ignorance of the law excuses no man.
John Selden

Not only is the salesman an important economic cog in the organization, but he also plays a significant role in the organization's legal affairs. A great many things he can do have serious legal ramifications. It would seem prudent, therefore, to spend some time discussing the legal problems the salesman encounters.

IMPORTANCE OF LEGAL ASPECTS

It seems to be a natural tendency of most people to minimize the importance of the legal aspects of business operations, but that propensity is usually terminated upon encountering costly legal difficulties caused by such a nonchalant, cavalier attitude toward the law.

The fact is that anyone engaged in business will be party to quite a few legal disputes in his lifetime. He must be prepared for them, for they are as inevitable as taxes and inflation. This is mentioned because there seems to be a certain mental attitude, philosophy, all too prevalent among people, that attendance to legal details is somehow ungentlemanly, not the thing to be observed among friends. Experience clearly indicates otherwise. As a matter of fact, one is more likely to maintain his friendships if he closely observes the legal niceties of doing business than if he allows misunderstandings to arise through careless attendance to such details.

Cost of errors

If for no other reason, the salesman must be cognizant of these legal aspects because one error can cost his company millions of dollars. Possibly an error can cost him his job, for legal carelessness or oversights are the stuff from which lawsuits are made.

A retail clothing salesman sold $600 worth of clothes to a nice young man on open-book credit. The customer's credit record was good and everything seemed in order. The bill became 30 days overdue, 60 days overdue, 90 days overdue, and no record of the customer's whereabouts could be discovered. Investigation revealed that he had moved from Denver to Kansas City, Mo. He was located there and the retailer's lawyer sent him a collection letter threatening suit unless the matter was settled. The customer's lawyer answered with a stiff letter, claiming that the individual did not make such a purchase. They demanded proof of purchase—a signed sales slip. A check through the sales slips quickly disclosed that the salesman had failed to get the customer's signature on the sales slip. The retailer's lawyer advised that he drop the matter, for there was no practical way of proving that the customer ever purchased the goods.

An electronics parts salesman received a very large purchase order from a small defense electronics manufacturer. The purchase order spelled out in great detail the items ordered, the prices to be paid for them, and the terms under which the sale was to be made. The salesman wrote up his sales order on the basis of the customer's purchase order, but changed the terms somewhat to coincide with company policy. He knew that this customer was always pushing him for a larger cash discount than his firm allowed, 2 percent-10 days, net 30 rather than the customary ½ of 1 percent-10 days, net 30. He wrote up the order and put it in the mill. The customer's contracts were suddenly cancelled by the Department of Defense, thus causing them to start scrambling to cancel out firm orders on the best basis possible, with the Department of Defense picking up the costs of such cancellations.

When the invoice for the shipment came in, the customer yelled, "Foul! We have no contract. You didn't accept our terms and we didn't agree to yours, so it's no deal!"

The supplier replied, "Oh yes, we do have a deal. We merely changed your terms to coincide with the discounts you know we offer. Your attempt to get a larger cash discount was just a cheap trick to squeeze a few more bucks out of us. Besides, it's an insignificant change."

The buyer's lawyers replied, "There is nothing insignificant about 1½ percent on a $78,000 order."

The judge was asked for his opinion in the matter, and he said, "No contract. The buyer's offer was not accepted by the firm. The counteroffer was not accepted by the customer."

A salesman simply cannot go around changing the terms of a customer's purchase order without the customer's approval. The employer was stuck with $78,000 worth of goods for which he had no other use.

As a general rule a salesman is an "order taker" and is not authorized to bind his employer to a contract. If the salesman changed the terms on a written order after the customer had signed it that would void the agreement and no contract would result.

A salesman for a line of luggage that was stringently fair-traded throughout the nation had a problem dealer in his territory. The man liked to sell under the table at discount prices to people he recognized. The discount trade was sufficiently significant that other dealers in the area continually complained to the salesman about it. They wanted the salesman to have the discounting dealer's supply cut off. So one day the salesman strolled into the discounter's store and after a brief talk about the weather and sports on a nice, friendly basis, he delicately opened up the subject of discount sales in a most friendly manner: "Now look, George, I want to go on selling you goods. You are a good dealer and we get along fine. We value your business. But the other dealers in the area are continually complaining to us about your discount sales and they've showed me a lot of evidence to support what they're saying. They want me to take the line away from you. Now, George, if you don't stop this under-the-table discounting of our line I'm going to have to stop selling you the merchandise. I don't want to do it, but the other dealers are just going to force the home office to make me do it."

These words were sufficiently unfortunate when spoken alone with the dealer, but more unfortunately the salesman said it within hearing range of a sales clerk and a customer who was lounging in the store— potential witnesses. This salesman has just made his employer vulnerable to a suit on conspiracy and restraint of trade. He has just admitted in public that he and his company have been conspiring with competing dealers to restrain the trade of this one discount dealer.

The law says that you can refuse to sell your goods to any dealer, but it also clearly says you can't do so when it is part of a conspiracy. You must make up your mind autotomously without the help of other companies. This salesman's attempt to be a nice guy and explain the real world to the dealer resulted in a Federal Trade Commission order against his employer.

Not only is there a possibility of governmental action against the offending company in such matters, but also the antitrust laws offer potential triple damages in a civil suit by the offended party. The salesman must continually be aware of exactly what he is saying and the legal significance of it. In this case, he made two classic blunders. First, he threatened the dealer and second, he did so in front of witnesses. It's one thing when it is the salesman's word against the dealer's, but quite another thing when there are other people to support the other person's contentions. Moreover, it is always bad policy to threaten anyone so overtly. There are ways of getting the point across without such an obvious threat.

For example, the salesman could have related a tale of what had happened to a similar dealer—an analogy—thus the discounting dealer might get the point without being told, "Look, continue discounting and we'll cut off your supply!"

This could go on at great length, for there is no shortage of legal cases. Rather, these three widely divergent samples have been shown to give you an idea of the difficulties that salesmen can easily get into if they are not aware of the legal complexities of their business.

Customer ill will

The most valuable asset of any business is its customers. This is a cliche of long standing, but nevertheless it is quite true. Businesses spend a great deal of money cultivating the goodwill of their customers. When a customer is lost through some unfortunate incident not related to the merits of the company's proposition, management usually becomes rather cross with the salesman.

In a great many situations, salesmen may do things that are illegal and the customer may know they are illegal but is in such a position that he is unable to do anything about it—at that time.

A salesman for a particularly popular line of blue jeans was making a call on a men's wear store that had not sold the line previously. The merchant had contacted the company to indicate his interest in taking on the line. The salesman had been told to respond because investigation by the home office had revealed that the store was a rapidly growing, aggressive operation. The sale was taking place rather late in the buying season, and the merchant had already purchased most of the requirements for other items. After giving the salesman a rather substantial order for all sorts of blue jeans—blue denims, wheat, faded denims, greens, etc.—the salesman then asked him for his order on casual slacks, a new line the company had just introduced.

The merchant replied, "Ed, I'm sorry, but this season I've already placed my order for casuals with Days and Haggars. I'm all bought up; I have no open-to-buy in casuals right now. We can talk about it next time around."

The salesman replied, "Harry, I don't think you understand. If you're not willing to take on our line of casual slacks, we're not willing to give you the blue jeans."

Whee! Illegal as all get-out! Tie-in sale in violation of the Clayton Act. The merchant sat there seething, for he knew this was illegal behavior on

the part of the salesman. More importantly, it was exceedingly stupid behavior. Nevertheless, the merchant was over a barrel because he needed the
blue jeans, so he threw a token order for casuals to him, just enough to get
by.

This incident did not end up in court. Rather, the merchant made a
point to let the top management of the blue jeans company know what had
happened. The salesman was fired. He was way outside company policy,
using the cheap tie-in trick only as a last resort to meet his quotas in selling
casual slacks. The fact was that the casual line had not been moving as well
as management had hoped and the salesman's boss had been placing a
great deal of pressure on him to sell the casual slacks so he opted for the
easy way out.

UNIFORM COMMERCIAL CODE

The basic law under which sales are made is called the Uniform Commercial Code, which has now been adopted by most of the legislatures of the
states. This code spells out the law of contracts and the law of sales.

Let's take a look at some of the salient details in each of these areas.
Bear in mind that the Uniform Commercial Code itself contains fairly brief
statements of the law in each area. These rules are amplified greatly by the
plethora of cases decided under them daily in the courts of the land.

But before we get into studying the law, let's clear the air with a few of
the realities of operating in this legal arena.

One of the lesser recognized factors of the law is the relative importance of knowing the rule of law and the importance of the facts involved
in the case. Realistically, court cases are not a matter of deciding on the
rules of law, for the rules of law are fairly easy to learn and are really quite
clear. For example, if an offer has been made and accepted and if there is
consideration and the matter is within public policy and in writing, it is
fairly clear that a contract exists. Courtroom battles are not over the rule of
law but rather over whether or not, in fact, an offer was made and whether
or not, in fact, an acceptance was made and if, in fact, the agreement was
supported by legal consideration. The disputes come not on the rule of law
but rather on what the facts of the matter were, and that is where the
courts come into play. When the parties cannot agree on the facts, this
disagreement becomes the stuff of which court suits are made. If both
parties are completely in agreement on the facts their lawyers can apply the
rule of the law and advise their clients on what they should do—what the
courts would tell them if they went to court.

The important thing from the salesman's point of view is that he is the
individual who is creating most of the facts and he must be cognizant of
how these facts appear at all times. Every letter he sends out, every order he

writes, everything he says become facts and they may come back to haunt him if he is careless in creating them.

The key to winning most court cases is to reconstruct the case so that the facts look favorable to one's self. In reality, a certain fact can be made to look many different ways. Facts can be twisted. They are not the cold, hard, immutable realities some people would like them to be.

SOME PRACTICAL ADVICE ON LEGAL BEHAVIOR

As most businessmen learn eventually, there is a great deal of difference between the technical aspects of the law and one's practical behavior in legal matters. The idea is that one wants to conduct his daily affairs in such a manner as to minimize his chances of ending up in court. The old adage, "The only people who win in court are the lawyers," is quite true. Only a masochist would relish going to court. No matter how strong your case might be, you can rest assured that the other fellow's attorney will do everything possible to make you miserable. The process will take a great deal of your time and money and severely tax your patience and rationality. Stay out of court if at all possible. However, that brings up counteradvice.

If you have an unreasonable fear of going to court and your adversary senses it, you will lose most of your bargaining power in transactions for your opponent will immediately recognize that all he has to do to make you fold your tent is to threaten to go to court. Thus you will be continually waltzed to the courthouse steps where you will fold your winning hand out of fear.

You must never fear going to court and must be completely willing to do so and let it be known. Such a stand will usually work to your advantage, for your adversary has little desire to go to court and will thus be more likely to settle disputes to your advantage. Indeed, this is one of the basic tactics lawyers use in writing letters for the purpose of precipitating some action from an adversary. The letter will usually be written in a rather stiff, demanding form and usually ends with the statement that the lawyer has been instructed to file suit if the matter is not settled by a certain date.

On making statements

Bear in mind that evidence in court cases usually consists of statements made in letters, sales orders, purchase orders, and memos; all can be forceful evidence substantiating various claims.

Putting things in writing

While it is true that oral contracts can be enforced in court as long as the statute of frauds is not applicable, from a practical standpoint it is a most difficult undertaking. Moreover, any documentary evidence is usually considered by the courts to supersede all testimony. Courts are well aware that people lie and twist things for their own benefit; thus they are reluctant to believe all testimony unless it is amply supported by competent, independent witnesses who have no interest in the case.

So from a pragmatic standpoint, oral contracts for the sale of goods in excess of $500 are unenforceable unless there is some memorandum signed by the party against whom enforcement is sought which indicates there has been an agreement between the parties. The memorandum does not have to be a complete document spelling out all terms. Moreover, oral agreements are honestly fraught with grave dangers arising from misunderstandings. You said one thing but your customer heard another. When the salesman suggests to the customer, "Let's put our agreement down on paper so there will be no misunderstanding between us," he is being astute in protecting himself, for inevitably customers have a way of expecting more from a deal than was agreed on.

Put it in writing, but be careful *what* you put in writing. Don't promise something or even suggest something that you are not prepared to do.

Who should do the writing

There are two schools of thought on the matter of who should write up an agreement. In many large corporations only the corporate legal staff is empowered to write contracts that bind the corporation so, in such instances, the question is moot. We are referring to the many day-to-day agreements that are made during the course of routine business. There are advantages accruing to the one who writes the contract. He is able to write it in a way that favors himself in many small, but highly important, respects. Many sellers have preprinted standard contracts to cover the situation. The real estate industry is particularly plagued with such "standard" forms. In many instances the salesman is forced by company policy to accept business only on the company's standard contract that has been prepared by the company's legal staff. He has no power whatsoever to change any of the terms in the contract. However, this may give rise to an impasse when encountering an equally astute purchasing agent who replies, "We have a standard contract, also, with which we do business, so which 'standard' contract is to be used?"

Well, the fact is that there is no such thing as a standard contract. Any time a salesman or a purchasing agent pulls that one on you, you know you're being treated as a naïve cluck. A buyer and a seller are free to make whatever contract they so desire. Standard contracts arise from the corporation lawyer's desire to create a document that protects his company to the maximum possible extent while giving the buyer as few rights as possible.

Such standard contracts may be so totally one-sided that they create an additional problem.

Many courts have thrown out such one-sided agreements on just that basis: they were so totally one-sided as to make the proposition "unconscionable." This means that the court believes that the person signing the contract simply could not have been aware of what he was agreeing to. Thus the court can throw out all or any part of the contract.

A rule of interpretation of written documents is that in the event ambiguous words or terms are used they will be interpreted against the person who selected the language and in favor of the other contracting party. The court will accept the interpretation of the person who did not write the contract if his interpretation is reasonable and logical.

The extremes to which some people will go in making up contracts is probably represented best by those in which the signer waives his right to legal recourse on the contract.[1] This, of course, can be a lot of legal nonsense, for many courts won't honor such clauses for one moment. You might wonder why lawyers include such outrageous clauses in contracts. Well, the answer is simply that most people believe that if they put their signatures to something, that makes it law. The fact is that it doesn't, but if a company shows the buyer that he has waived his right to sue, a great many naïve customers will believe it and drop the matter. These clauses are included in the so-called standard contracts simply for out-of-court bargaining with people who have no legal training and no legal counsel.

So there is considerable danger when a salesman writes a contract and makes it so much in favor of himself that he, in fact, nullifies the contract.

Don't play lawyer

The average salesman is not a lawyer, has had no legal training, and should not attempt to behave as one. It is sheer folly for him to attempt to draft a contract in legalese with all the whereases and whereofs. All he will do is manage to look silly and if the matter ever gets to court, judges react severely to amateur lawyers. Rather, when a salesman must create an agreement without legal advice, he is advised to write down the matters agreed upon in handwriting and using plain English, making certain that all of the things agreed upon, such as dates, places, amounts, prices, and quality, are clearly spelled out. The court won't try to guess what you meant to agree upon if you fail to be specific. Such a handwritten document in plain English signed by both parties is considered much stronger evidence in court than even the formally drafted contracts prepared by many lawyers.

---

[1] This is not to imply that contracts in which both parties agree to binding arbitration in the event of a dispute are not perfectly sound.

So don't think you have to be fancy and imitate the lawyers in your business negotiations. Simply learn how to nail down all the details of an agreement in clear, concise English. The salesman who thinks he is a lawyer is a dangerous animal. As the old adage relates, the man who acts as his own attorney has a fool for a client.

Relationships with the employer

The relationship between you and your boss contains a great many legal overtones which frequently erupt and cause great discomfort to both parties. A large number of legal misunderstandings arise at the time the salesman is hired.

It is not at all uncommon in the courting days when the employer is trying to lure the man to come to work for him to make promises and say a great many things in the hope of enticing the salesman into camp. This is particularly the case when the employer is going after a particularly able salesman. He will make him promises about high commission rates, protected territories, house accounts, overrides, guarantees of the job for a certain period of time, expense accounts, and other perquisites. In short, he will usually tell him whatever he has to in order to get the man to come to work for him. From the salesman's standpoint, he should get all that talk on paper, even if it is only a letter stating all of the conditions under which he is accepting employment. Time and again courts have ruled that a formal contract under such circumstances is not necessary. As a general principle, courts go out of their way to protect employees in such matters; if an employee has a letter in his possession signed by the employer and promising certain things, the employer will be made to honor those commitments.

So always get the terms of your employment down on paper, and if your employer will not give them to you on paper, you will have to be awfully naïve not to perceive what is going on.

From the employer's point of view, all of this means that he should be extremely careful about what he promises a new salesman when he comes on the job. The courts are filled with instances where, in the spirit of enthusiasm surrounding the hiring of a new salesman who has great promise, the employer makes a number of valuable concessions, only to have later developments prove those concessions to be economically unwise. When the employer tries to rectify the situation, the salesman brings forth the contract and demands that it be honored. A great deal of grief results.

The classic case usually evolves with new companies just starting into business. In their desire to procure the services of particularly adept salespeople who can build the trade, they usually agree to allow such salesmen a large protected territory and a substantial commission. Moreover, they may agree upon a commission for all sales made to customers within the salesman's territory.

The salesmen go out and perform admirably well, many times too admirably. The business grows fast and prospers. Then there comes a time when management wants to put more salesmen into the field in order to achieve a better coverage of the territory—they want to take some of the salesman's territory away from him. Or they may see the sales force making handsome earnings and the thought that commissions could be cut enters their mind. As they move to alter the compensation plan, the salesmen haul out the agreements. Clearly, unless there are some definite termination points placed in the salesman's contract with the company, an employer may be saddled with his initial promises for a very long time.

Naturally, any lawyer worth his salt will recommend to an employer that he make the contract good for only a stipulated period of time, such as a year or two. While this sounds wise and prudent and is very easy to say, the fact is that if the new firm were to offer such a contract initially to a top-notch salesman to lure him away from his present job, he simply would not go for the limitations. The reason he would leave his job would be for the outstanding deal he was being offered.

So there are no easy answers to this question, only the admonition that both parties should be very careful to insure that they get everything in writing and that they must be particularly careful about *what* they put in writing.

You might wonder what the salesman would have to fear in such arrangements. Well, there are ways he can be victimized. There is the agreement not to compete. Many times an employer will force the salesman to sign an agreement that he will not work for a competitor for a stipulated period of years should he quit his job. A great many salesmen blithely go along with such a noncompeting clause, not realizing the seriousness of it to their careers. The fact is that a salesman has the most value when selling his services to a competing firm in the same line of business. After all, if you have spent ten years selling IBM typewriters you are of more value to Underwood-Olivetti in selling their typewriters than you would be to the Glidden Paint Company. All your know-how, expertise, and contacts are in the typewriter business, but your employer may ask that you sign away your rights to work in that industry. Today many large corporations require all of their employees to sign such agreements as a matter of routine, but the employee should recognize that these documents can rise up and cause him a great deal of inconvenience.

Of course, such agreements can give rise to some useless nonsense. One salesman who was being ardently wooed by a competitor had to sign an agreement that if he were to quit his employer, he could not work for a competing firm for a period of five years. But the agreement stipulated that if he were laid off or discharged, he was free to work for whomever he pleased. So the salesman was forced to create a situation in which he was fired. He simply stopped going to work and laid down on the job, still turning in expense accounts and such. It didn't take long for the sales manager to fire him, thus freeing him to go to work for the competitor who had been apprised of what was going to take place.

The courts will protect the employee from unreasonable restraints on his right to make a living but that may be scant comfort to him if he is dragged into court by a former employer. Moreover, the reasonable restraints are the very ones that are usually most binding, for they are ones that usually offer the best opportunity to the man.

GREEN RIVER ORDINANCES

A great many cities have enacted so-called "Green River" ordinances which require that all nonresidents who try to sell goods or services directly to consumers (door-to-door salesmen) must register with city authorities and obtain a license to sell. The exact nature of each of these ordinances differs from city to city so the prudent door-to-door salesman always begins working a town by going to City Hall.

FEDERAL TRADE COMMISSION RULES

The recent agitation concerning the protection of the consumer from a wide variety of business practices has not overlooked door-to-door salesmen.

The Federal Trade Commission has been particularly aggressive in trying to stop salesmen from using various ruses to gain entry into the home. In the not too distant past door-to-door salesmen were never "selling" anything: they were "making a survey," "introducing a free program," "establishing demonstration homes for advertising purposes." But salesmen, never! It was only natural for salesmen to resort to such deceptions, for the big problem faced by the door-to-door salesman was getting into the house to make his presentation. Once he could make his pitch, his chances of making the sale were good. Experience had clearly shown that if the salesman made his true mission known to the housewife at the door, his chances of making a presentation were slim. But promise her something free. . . . And this is the crux of the enforcement problem—management claims it has little control over what the salesman actually says at the door. But be not deceived by this defense for in all candor most door-to-door selling organizations in the past have taught such deceptions to their men. They are incorporated into the prepared presentation.

Indeed, many such presentations were nothing but a pack of lies from beginning to end. One very large merchandising chain has a division that sells encyclopedias door to door; let's look at its pitch.

First, the salesman was instructed to gain entry by saying that he was visiting customers of the chain to get their opinion of a new educational program the company had just developed. Nowhere in the presentation was the word encyclopedia used—it was always a home educational program. And it was free. Oh, yes, free. All the recipient of the chain's generosity had to do was pay $17.95 a month for 12 months to cover "research costs."

This is the type of nonsense the Federal Trade Commission is seeking to eliminate. It is trying to institute a three-day-cooling-off-period rule which will allow the customer to change his mind about buying, thus nullifying the use of high-pressure sales tactics. However, 33 states and many cities have beaten the Federal Trade Commission to the punch by establishing a wide variety of laws regulating door-opening tactics and contract cancellation privileges.

CONFIDENCE GAMES

Some naïve individuals are entrapped each year in schemes which can result in their criminal prosecution. In some instances they are the victims of the confidence game; in other cases they are made accomplices in some scheme to bilk a third party.

Salesmen as victims

Any time a person is asked to invest a substantial amount of money as a condition for employment he had better investigate the proposition most carefully. Sometimes he is asked to pay rather handsomely for a sales kit. Most legitimate firms do not ask their salesmen to "buy" their jobs. When a potential employer asks you for money, you would be wise to walk on.

The few exceptions are those in which the salesman is asked to buy a reasonable amount of salable inventory.

Salesmen as accomplices

One of the "get rich quick" boy wonders built a complex of companies around a stock-selling "swindle." The mainspring of his venture was an investment sales company which hired hundreds of salesmen. These salesmen were conned into believing everything was "as advertised." But there were those who saw through the scheme; a man who had been hired as vice-president of sales resigned three days after beginning work. He told his family, "This whole operation is nothing but a swindle. I'm getting out quick." He was a very smart man, for many of the people who failed, or refused, to see through the scheme suffered great losses and legal prosecution.

There are also some real estate sales schemes which are resulting in legal difficulties for the people involved.

The real culprit, of course, is greed. The salesmen in such schemes are motivated by the promise of great return for their efforts.

MISREPRESENTATION

It is illegal to lie to the customer in such a manner that he is caused to buy when if the truth were told he would not have bought. This practice is called misrepresentation. It can be cited by the customer as the basis for nullifying the contract.

Moreover, silence is not always a safe course of action. Courts have held that the salesman who fails to disclose a critical factor which, if known, would have caused the prospect not to buy has misrepresented his goods. The contract can be declared void or financial adjustments may be ordered.

ANTITRUST ASPECTS

The so-called antitrust laws (Sherman Act, Clayton Act, Robinson-Patman, and Federal Trade Commission Act) are so complex and cover such a wide range of behavior that it is not within the scope of this book to cover them completely. Rather we will just point out a few of the areas in which salesmen may be involved.

Tie-in sales

The Clayton Act specifically outlaws tie-in sales, which means that the salesman cannot force the customer to buy some product or service in order to buy some other item. You can't tie two sales together, make one contingent upon the other.

The law feels most strongly that the customer should be free to buy exactly what he wants and not be forced to buy things he does not want.

Price discrimination

The law feels that two buyers of the same goods in the same quantities should be charged the same price.

The general principle is that all customers should be treated relatively the same—benefits should be bestowed in proportion to each customer's sales volume. Moreover, when the customer is given some allowance for doing something, then he must actually do it.

It may be of some comfort to the salesman to learn that the buyer who knowingly accepts an illegal price can be held as guilty as the firm offering it. At times this fact can be used to hold off the buyer who demands price concessions. "I would like nothing better, Mr. Prospect, than to give you a lower price, but if I did we would both be in violation of the law—it would be price discrimination."

Conspiracy in restraint of trade

It is illegal to conspire with others to damage in some way a third party's trade. A sport coat manufacturer had two dealers in one small town in the South; one was large, the other small. One day the manufacturer's salesman called upon the buyer of the larger store only to encounter the threat that if the company didn't stop selling coats to the other store the buyer would throw the line out of his store. The two talked about it for a while and came to an agreement that the salesman would stop selling to the other dealer. Had the other dealer found out about the conspiracy to keep him from buying that line of coats he would have had the basis for a suit against the company.

Collusion

The law winces when competitors become chummy. In some industries the executives scarcely dare to attend the same social functions lest the fact be later used against them in some antitrust litigation. The salesman should be aware of this situation. One oil company salesman wasn't and it resulted in a large antitrust case. One of his customers—the owner of a gas station—complained that he had to charge gas-war prices because another station across the street was charging them. In front of witnesses the salesman was able to get the price of gasoline raised in the other station. Competitors should not collude.

BRIBES

It is against the law to bribe people. The salesman who bribes a purchasing agent may well find himself in trouble. One salesman thought he detected a state government official on the take so he offered a bribe in return for a contract. Instead he was indicted and subsequently did time. Be warned that there are dangers other than refusal and rejection connected with offering bribes.

EXCLUSIVE DEALING

The courts have progressively moved toward the position that exclusive dealerships in which the dealer is given a monopoly to sell a product in a certain trading area are illegal. Moreover, a manufacturer cannot insist that the dealer not handle competing lines. An oil company found itself in a losing court case when it tried to force a dealer to sell only its products. An independent businessman is free to buy from whomever he so desires and the courts intend that he shall keep that freedom.

Thus the salesman must take care that he does nothing that smacks of coercion in trying to persuade the dealer to do business only with him.

DISCUSSION QUESTIONS

1. As a salesman for a manufacturer of fine men's sweaters you have been trying to get the line into one large men's specialty store for some time but with no success because the line is also being sold to a nearby large department store.

   "Stop selling to them and I'll buy!" the merchant has continually told you. The department store bought $22,000 of sweaters last year. The buyer for the specialty store will not be pinned down on what his volume would be. What would you do?

2. A purchasing agent for a large aerospace firm was to be laid off at the end of the project on which he was working. A salesman of a potential sub-contractor for a substantial electronic component costing $5,000 a unit—1,000 units were needed—took the p.a. to lunch. Over a few drinks the p.a. managed to convey the thought that if he were to get $50,000 the contract would be awarded to the salesman's firm. You are the salesman. What would you tell the p.a.? Then what would you do?

NAME INDEX

Acetogen Gas Company, 255
Adams, Velma, 452
Aero Commander, 71
Albert Pick Co., Inc., 32
American Chain & Cable, 152
American Lumberman, 166
American Marketing Association, 3, 37
American Salesman, 143, 151, 173, 199, 204, 220, 450, 487
American Telephone & Telegraph, 196
American Tobacco Company, 18
Anastasi, Anna, 508
Armstrong Cork, 16, 500
Arrow Shirts, 429

Baker, Richard M., Jr., 102
Ballantine Breweries, 32
Bauer, Raymond A., 9
Baumhart, Rev. Raymond C., 465
Beckman Instruments, Inc., 32
Beech Aircraft Corporation, 5
Belding-Corticelli, Inc., 303
Belknap, Inc., 89
Bench, Johnny, 233
Better Business by *Telephone,* 196
Bettger, Frank, 201, 474

Bigelow, Burton, 39
Blumenthal, Lassor, 269
Brower, Daniel, 453
Burroughs Corporation, 89
Buskirk, Richard H., 501

Cadillac, 5
Cain's, 24
Carson Pirie Scott & Co., 14, 75
Certified Grocers of California, 9
Chase Bag Company, 147
Clary, 301
Clay, Henry, 211
Cole, Robert H., 100
Commercial Credit, 17
Cooper, 440
Corning Glass, 307
Crane, Frank, 325
Cricketeer, 267
Curtis, Wayne, 71
Curtis Equipment Company, 71

Diamond Alkali, 17
Dictaphone, 317
Dowell, Dudley, 8

Eberhard Faber, Inc., 307
Elba Corporation, 303
Erlicher, Harry, 78

Fales, Edward, Jr., 487
Farmers Mutual Hail Insurance Company,
  196
Florsheim, 24
Franklin, Benjamin, 63, 325
Fuller Brush, 209

Gadel, M. S., 483
Gardner-Denver, 54, 70
General Electric, 78
General Foods, 6
General Motors, 5
Gillette Safety Razor Company, 6
Glidden Company, 154
Goode, Kenneth, 300
Gooding, Stewart, 151
Gordon, Bruce, 199
Grace, W. R., & Company, 17
Grange, "Red," 468
Gross, Martin L., 508

Hahn, A. R., 190
Hardware Age, 74
Harvard Graduate School of Business,
  465
Henley, William E., 471
Hotpoint, 229
Hoyt, Edwin P., 468
Hughes Tool Company, 363

IBM, 10, 28, 54, 89, 363, 500
Industrial Marketing, 81
Internal Revenue Service, 29
International Correspondence Schools,
  138
Irving Trust Company, 5

Johnson & Johnson, 17, 83
Journal of Marketing, 483

Kaufman, Zenn, 300

Lanz, 24
Larkin, Arthur E., Jr., 6
Lavenson, Jim, 421

Learjet, 101
Lester, Bernard, 43
Leterman, Elmer, 300
Lily-Tulip Cup Company, 143

McMurry, Dr. Robert N., 505
Macy's, 201
Marchant Calculator Company, 209
Massachusetts Mutual, 17
Maytag Company, 150
Metrecal, 37
Minnesota Mining & Manufacturing, 16
Mohawk Carpet Mills, Inc., 76
Moline Body Company, 198
Monsanto Chemical Company, 44
Morgan, Boyce, 196
Morgan, J. P., 99
Motley, Arthur "Red," 58, 190

National Cash Register, 16, 89, 147, 275
National Industrial Conference Board, 24
Norman Hilton Company, 71

Owens-Corning, 307

Patterson, John, 275
Pend, Rowe, 204
Penn Mutual Life Insurance Company,
  136
Phifer, Gregg, 102
Pitney-Bowles, 236
Procter & Gamble, 30
Purchasing Magazine, 79

Quaker Oats, 122

R & R Service, 197
Radiant Manufacturing Company, 76
Ralston Purina Company, 55, 88
Reader's Digest, 28
Remington Rand, 12, 151
Revere Copper & Brass, Inc., 307
Rich Plan, 153
Riggio, Vincent, 18
Roche, James M., 5
Rough Notes Company, Inc., 247
Runkle, Warren, 152
Ruskin, John, 361

Sales Management, 6, 190, 251, 422
Schreibweiss, Walter, 142
Schwab, Charles, 60
Scott, Dr. Walter Dill, 468
Sealy Mattress Company, 353
Sears, 148
Shell Oil Company, 308
Singer, 73, 140
Southern Railway, 17
Spenser, Edmund, 57
Stanton, William, 501
Stern, Charles M., 144
Stewart Warner Corporation, 89, 302
Stone, Norman, 136
Stone Container Corporation, 136
Swift, Jonathan, 210

Todd Chemical Company, 199
Toni, 77

U.S. Steel Corporation, 89

Velie, Lester, 28

Wanamaker, John, 13
Wardell, Rube, 259
Watson, Thomas J., 55
Webster, Daniel, 86
Weiss, E. B., 8
Western Auto, 432
Weyand, Louis F., 16
Weyerhaeuser, 71
Wheeler, Elmer, 425
White, S. H., 255
Wide Area Telephone Service (WATS),
    199
Willmark Service, 441
Wolf, Hans A., 100
Wood, William, 199
Wortzel, Lawrence H., 9

Xerox, 16, 42, 89

Ziegler, Vincent C., 6

SUBJECT INDEX

Accounts, servicing, 405
Adaptability, 154
Adjusting orders, 410
Analogy, 316
Antitrust, 539
Appearance, 54, 477
  deceptive, 178
Application of products, 70
Application blank, 502
Appointments, 211
Approach:
  importance of, 187
  merchandise, 420
  methods of, 200
  objectives of, 186
  planned, 215
  retail, 417
  salutation, 419
  service, 417
  strategy, 166
  summary of, 219
  timing, 212
Arguments, avoiding, 324
Assumptive close, 394
Attention, gaining, 186, 216
Attitude of salesman, 424, 467
Autosuggestion, 233

Barriers:
  to buying, 123
  erection of, 393
Behavior, legal, 532
Behavioral sciences, 93
Believability, 251
Benefit, statement of, 208
Bird Dogs, 145, 176
Bonding, 509
Bonuses, 517
Boomerang method, 343
Bribery, 449, 540
Business card, use of, 213
"Buy now" close, 399
Buyer:
  attention of, 216
  expert, 77
  importance of, 515
Buying:
  authority, 8
  barriers to, 123
  behavior, 124
  by committee, 8
  decision, 182, 199
    objections to, 352
    stages of, 288

Buying:
  impulse, 35
  motivation, 93
Buying motives, 73, 225
  acquisitiveness, 109
  avoidance of effort, 104
  creative urges, 112
  curiosity, 112
  ego striving, 106
  emotional, 103
  emulation, 107
  esthetic pleasure, 105
  fear, 113
  imitation, 107
  physical fitness, 111
  play, 104
  pleasure, 104
  power, 106
  profit, 108
  rational, 102
  romantic and sexual drives, 110
  self-esteem, 106
  status, 106
Buying process, 94

Call-back approach, 219
Call-back cards, 155
Calls, making more, 479
"Canned" presentation, 274
Canvass, call-back, 219
Careers in selling, 21
Case history, 256
Catalytic agent, 11
Center of influence, 140, 176
Challenge, 27
China eggs, 135
"Chiseling," 450
Clarity, 299
Class-of-customer organization, 70
Classified lists, 152
Clayton Act, 539
Closing, 375, 382
Closing methods, 392
Closing signals, 388
Closing tactics, 385
Clothing, 55
Cold canvassing, 135, 145
Collusion, 540
Commission plans, 24, 516
Committee, buying by, 8
Communications, 522
  problem of, 11
Company assets, use of, 461
Company policies, 80
Company training course, 87
Comparison, 316
  deadly, 293
Compatability factor, 154

Compensation:
  average by industry, 23
  average by type, 25
  method, 344
  plans, 515
  straight commission, 24
Competition, 7, 82
  handling, 290
Competitive intelligence, 295
  unethical tactics, 297
Competitors, ethical problems with, 463
Complaints, adjustment of, 441
Concessions, 327
Conferences, 521
Confidence, 167, 250
  building, 252
  games, 538
Confidences, 448
Conflict of interest, 456
Conformity, 118
Conspiracy, 540
Consumer-benefit approach, 202, 205
  theory of, 114
Consumer goods, selling, 41
Contacts, loss of, 153
Contests, 462, 520
Continued affirmation, 392
Contract:
  employment, 509
  simplifying, 385
  writing, 532
Controlling the interview, 261
Conventions, 521
Cost of errors, 528
Countersuggestion, 236
Courtesy, 58
Curiosity approach, 202
Customer:
  contact, 29
  density factor, 28
  file, 155
  ill-will, 530
  as information source, 176
  multiple, 434
  need definition, 428
  regular, 174
  relations, ethics of, 448
  satisfaction, 412

Deadly comparison, 293
Dealers, selling to, 33
Dealership, exclusive, 540
Decision:
  to buy, 182
  state of, 182
Decision maker, 199
Delivery, 83, 279
  method of, 275
Demand, 182

Demonstration, 311
Departure, 405
Dependability, 62
Detail men, 9, 36
Determination, 64
Direct-denial method, 339
Direct mail prospecting, 148
Direct suggestion, 234
Directories, 152, 177
Discrimination, price, 539
Display, 35
    of goods, 310
Distribution, 82
Distributors, selling to, 33
Dominance, 62
Door-to-door salesmen, 209
Dramatization, 300
Drive, 98

Early dismissal, 213
Earnings, 22
Education, lack of, 476
Employer:
    ethical problems of, 457
    legal relationship with, 535
Employment contract, 509
Emotional buying motives, 103
Emotional words, 238
Endless chain system, 138
Entertainment, 29, 453
Enthusiasm, 472
Environment, managerial, 498
Erection of barriers, 393
Errors, cost of, 528
Ethics, 15, 447
Evaluation of performance, 523
Exclusive dealing, 540
Expense accounts, 29, 458, 517
Expert buyers, 77
Exposure, 152

Failure, 383
Fair play, 337
Favoritism, 456
Federal Trade Commission, 456, 537
Field operators, 32
Follow-up, 405, 409
Forestalling objections, 330
Four noes technique, 338
Frame of reference, 95
    chart, 96

Generalization, 244
Getting the job, 499
Gifts, 452
Goals, 226
Golden silence, 61
Goods, display of, 310
Green River ordinances, 537

Group shopper, 435
Group theory, 118
Guarantee, use of, 254
Guilt, 124, 384

Habeas corpus technique, 337
Hidden objections, 333
Hidden quality, 361
History of firm, 80
Hook-in close, 375
House salesmen, 32
House-to-house selling, 41, 209
Human behavior, 93

Ideal other, 116
Ideal self, 116
Ideomotor suggestion, 233
Imagination, 64
Impulse purchases, 35
Indirect denial method, 341
Indirect suggestion, 234
Industrial selling, 42
Information, sources of, 175
Innovation, 9
Insight, 338
Inspiration, 469
Installation, 411
Instincts, 98
Intangibles, 305
Integrating interests, 226
Intelligence, 476
    agent, 11
    competitive, 295
    social, 59
Interview:
    controlling, 261
    gaining an, 188
    home, 507
    interrupted, 287
    personal, 504
    technique of, 197
Introductions, 194
Introductory approach, 200
Invalid objections, 350

Job:
    changing, ethics of, 457
    description, 44
    seeking, 499
Jobbers, 36
Junior salesmen, 145

Key-town plan, 198

Last-ditch effort, 391
Lead, 135
    qualifying, 135
    referred, 140

Leadership, 4
Legal aspects of selling, 527
Letter of introduction, 194
Life cycle, product, 9
Listening, 61, 262
   objectives of, 264
Logic, 240
Logical reasoning, 230, 239
Logical syllogism, 240

Management, sales, 498
Managerial environment, 498
Manners, 57
Manufacturer's salesman, 33
Memorization, 280
Merchandise approach, 420
Merchandising counselors, 36
Metaphor, 316
Methods:
   of closing, 392
   of delivery, 275
   for handling objections, 339
Middleman, 37
Minor point close, 396
Misrepresentation, 539
Missionary men, 36
Mobility, 26
Moonlighting, 460
Motivation, 93, 225
   research, 99
   theories of, 102
Motivational analysis, 125
Motives:
   buying (see Buying motives)
   complexity of, 101

Narrowing choice, 397
Need:
   defining, 428
   imperception of, 384
   objection, 353
Negative suggestion, 235
New accounts, 135
New products, 33
No-sale departure, 407

Objections:
   closing on, 400
   handling, 322
   hidden, 333
   removal of, 327
   types of, 350
   unanswerable, 351
Old customers, 151
One-call salesman, 32
Order:
   asking for, 400
   checking on, 410

Pace, demonstration, 314
Paperwork, 522
Pass-up method, 347
Perceived risk, 123
Perception, 338
Perfect-product comparison, 281
Performance, evaluation of, 523
Performance data, 84
Personal interview, 504
Personal observation, 143
Personal rating chart, 510
Personal use of company assets, 461
Personality, 508
   helpful elements of, 59
   importance of, 53
Persuasion, 4, 225
Philosophies, 467
Philosophy of life, 226
Planned approach, 215
Play therapy, 105
Poise, 387
Policy:
   adherence to, 462
   company, 80
Positive suggestion, 235
Preapproach, 164
   extent of, 168
   factors, 169
   objectives, 166
   sources, 175
Premium approach, 209
Presentation:
   "canned," 274
   development, 276
   essentials, 250
   objectives, 246
   organization, 126
   setting for, 265
   shortening, 480
Prestige appeal, 364
Prestige suggestion, 233
Price adjusting, 368
Price discrimination, 539
Price objections, 360
Price question, 329
Pricing policies, 82
Primary demand, 182
Principles:
   of integrating interests, 226
   of suggestion, 229
Problem-solving approach, 69, 114
Procrastination, 374
Product:
   life cycle of, 9
   objections to, 357
   technical details of, 84
Product approach, 201

Product knowledge, 69
  in retail selling, 71
  sources of, 86
  training, 75
Production methods, 81
Productivity, increasing, 481
Professional buyers, 78
Professional salesmen, 16
Profit motive, 108
Profit sharing, 517
Promptness, 424
Proposition, visualizing, 300
Prospect:
  congenial, 483
  definition of, 134
  file, 155
  gaining attention of, 186
  motivational analysis of, 125
  new, 411
  qualifying, 136
  sizing up, 178
  sources of, 150
Prospecting, 132
Prospecting systems, 137
  determination of, 153
Pulse-taking, 315
Purchasing agent, 77

Qualifying prospects, 135, 166
Quality, hidden, 361
Question approach, 205
Question method, 345
Questions, 426
Quotas, 486, 518

Rational buying motives, 102
Rationalization, 243
Reading programs, 469
Real other, 116
Real self, 116
Reasoning, logical, 239
Recency, 231
Receptionists, 189
Reciprocity, 455
Recruiting, 501
  college, 24
Reference groups, 118
References, 503
Referred lead, 140
Repetition, 231
Reports, 522
Restraint of trade, 540
Retail approach, 417
Retail product knowledge, 71
Retail salesman, 38, 415
Retail selling problems, 432
Rhetoric, 279
Risk, perceived, 123

Road salesmen, 32
Robinson-Patman Act, 539
Role playing, 512

Salary, 516
Sales:
  making, 425
  "tie-in," 440, 539
Sales associate, 146
Sales careers, 22
Sales engineer, 43
Sales management, 498
Sales manual, 87
Sales plan, 165
Sales portfolio, 87, 304
Sales talk, "canned," 274
Sales territories, 518
Sales timing element, 97
Sales training, 510
  schools, 16
Salesman:
  appearance of, 477
  average compensation, 23
  average earnings by plan, 25
  characteristics of professional, 16
  closing attitude of, 386
  dealer-servicing, 34
  door-to-door, 209
  ethical attitude of, 15
  as an expert, 70
  function of, 7
  job description, 44
  junior, 145
  manners of, 57
  manufacturer's, 33
  paperwork load of, 522
  personal behavior of, 251
  personal characteristics, 54
  quotas, 518
  retail, 38
  specialty, 40
  types of, 32
  unseen, 46
  wholesalers', 37
Salesmanship:
  professionalizing, 16
  retail, 415
  uses for, 4
Salutation approach, 419
Satisfaction, 411
Schools, sales training, 16
Seasonal factors, 471
Selection process, 501
Selective demand, 182
Self-concept theory, 102, 115
Self-confidence, 63, 474
Self-management, 65
Selling:
  art of, 15

Selling:
    careers, 21
    definition of, 3
    ethics, 447
    house-to-house, 41
    industrial, 42
    legal aspects of, 527
    problems, 29
        retail, 432
    process, 165
    sentences to aid, 425
    top-level, 6
    types of jobs, 30
    viewpoint, 86
Semantics, 238
Senses, appeal to, 311
Service, 82
Service approach, 417
Service attitude, 13
Service function, 8, 12
Service personnel, 151
Servicemen, 32
Servicing accounts, 405
Sherman Act, 539
Shock approach, 203
Shoppers, 433
    group, 435
Showmanship, 300
Showmanship approach, 204
Signals, closing, 388
Simile, 316
Skip-stop plan, 199
Social intelligence, 60, 476
Source objections, 371
Specialty salesman, 40
Specific statements, 79
Spontaneity, 232
Spotters, 145
Stalling, 334
Standing-room-only close, 375, 398
State of decision, 182
Status motive, 106
Status symbol, 101
Stimulation of effort, 520
Stock knowledge, 432
Straight commission, 24
Strategy:
    approach, 166
    for handling objections, 324
    selection, 287
    situational, 282
Substitution, 436
Success factors, 53, 467
Suggestion, 439
    principle of, 229
    types of, 232
Survey approach, 209
Suspect, 135
Syllogism, 240
Systems, prospecting, 137

Taboos, 384
Tact, 60
Tactics:
    basic closing, 385
    unethical, 297
Talking point, 125
Technical details, 84
Technical experts, 32
Techniques:
    confidence-building, 252
    substitution, 436
Telephone prospecting, 148
Telephone selling, 196
Tension, relieving, 218
Territories, 28, 518
Testimonials, 255, 294
Tests, 295, 507
    dramatization by, 306
Theory:
    consumer benefit, 114
    group behavior, 118
    motivation, 102
    self-concept, 102, 115
Tickler file, 155
"Tie-in" sale, 440, 539
Time, management of, 479
Time study, 485
Timing, 262
    approach, 212
    of close, 388
    element in sales, 97
Trade, restraint of, 540
Trade-ins, 369
Training, 76, 87, 510
Transition, 187
Trap close, 400
Traveling, 28
Trial order, 401
Tribute, 328
Turnover, 434

Underselling, 402
Unethical tactics, 297
Uniform Commercial Code, 531

Valid objections, 350
Value of minute, 483
Visualizing, 300
Vocabulary, 64
Voice, 56

Wholesalers, 37
    selling to, 33
Work habits, 467
Work methods, 479
Working conditions, 28